-kainga? What is the thing in thy
They are only fish hoo[ks] ... Hee
By whom were the[y] ...
Taka certainly. Question. E tangata pai
there (spoken of) Answer. Ae, na oki
Question Heihea kora tona kaing[a]
tona na oki At Rangitoua. Questio[n]
visited there? Answer. Kua tae na
[Questi]on. Inahea When was it? Answer
[R]au Ka i oki mai In the winter;
wahine oti ta Taka? Has Taka
have a wife. Question Tokohia ana
-les? Answer Toko ono, Six. Ques[tion]
Answer. Taire ana na oki rau.
tau? I am going or I do go.
may study. — Haere atu na

A BLIGHTED FAME

A BLIGHTED FAME

GEORGE S. EVANS 1802–1868
A LIFE

Helen Riddiford

VICTORIA UNIVERSITY PRESS

TE WHARE WĀNANGA O TE ŪPOKO O TE IKA A MĀUI
VICTORIA
UNIVERSITY OF WELLINGTON

Victoria University of Wellington
PO Box 600 Wellington
vup.victoria.ac.nz

First published 2014

National Library of New Zealand Cataloguing-in-Publication Data

Riddiford, Helen.
A blighted fame : George S. Evans 1802-1868, a life / Helen Riddiford.
Includes bibliographical references and index.
ISBN 978-0-86473-896-7
1. Evans, George S. (George Samuel), 1802-1868. 2. Colonists—New Zealand—Wellington—Biography. 3. Politicians—Australia—Victoria—Biography. I. Title.
993.6302092—dc 23

Printed by 1010 Printing International

For John Permezel.

For my children Dunbar and Christopher Sloane,
Julia Cargill and Olivia Doig.

And for Hugh.

Well, some may hate, and some may scorn,
And some may quite forget thy name;
But my sad heart must ever mourn
Thy ruined hopes, thy blighted fame!

Emily Brontë, xvii [105], *Stanzas to ---*, 1846

LIST OF CONTENTS

Acknowledgements		ix
Preface		xii
Prologue		xvii
Part One:	**England 1802–1839**	
Chapter 1	Student and Scholar	22
Chapter 2	Headmaster and Reformer	40
Chapter 3	The Hare and the Tortoise	61
Chapter 4	'A Damned Plucky Scheme!'	88
Chapter 5	Taking Leave	109
Chapter 6	The Voyage of the *Adelaide*	120
Part Two:	**Wellington 1840–1844**	
Chapter 7	The Schoolmaster Abroad	143
Chapter 8	'Umpire' No Longer	160
Chapter 9	A Glimmer of Hope	177
Chapter 10	Meetings Repaired	193
Chapter 11	Trials and Tribulations	211
Chapter 12	The Smiling Land	232
Chapter 13	'A Good and Pious Man'	245
Chapter 14	Wairau	269
Chapter 15	FitzRoy	291
Part Three:	**England and Wellington 1845–1852**	
Chapter 16	'A Proper Sphere'	311
Chapter 17	A Colonial in London	336
Chapter 18	Back to Wellington	347

Part Four **Melbourne and Wellington 1853–1868**

Chapter 19	Editor and Politician	293
Chapter 20	A Most Uncommon Man	308
Chapter 21	Fire, Steam and Ice	320
Chapter 22	Opposition	336
Chapter 23	Trojan Soul	349
Chapter 24	'The Scarf-Skin of the Frame'	366

Epilogue 375

Appendices

1. 'Song of the Colonists Departing for New Zealand', by Thomas Campbell 385
2. Regulations for the Emigrants of the New Zealand Company's First Colony 387
3. The New Zealand Company's Contract with Samuel Revans for Management and Editing of the *Gazette* 390
4. Ratification and Extension of the Provisional Constitution of the Settlers of the First Colony by the Sovereign Chiefs of Port Nicholson (drawn up by Dr George Samuel Evans and Richard Davies Hanson, with the approval of Colonel William Wakefield) 391
5. Extract from a Meeting of Burgesses held in Barrett's Hotel on 18 September 1842 393
6. Extract from the *Wellington Independent*, Saturday, 9 January 1864 399
7. Sample Pages of G. S. Evans, The Grammar of the New Zealand Language, 1839 405

Notes 410

Bibliography 473

Index 486

ILLUSTRATIONS

Between pp.40 and 41

1. Reverend George Evans. Engraving, London, 1829, from *Congregational Magazine*, Permezel Collection, Melbourne.
2. Brunswick Chapel, Mile End, London. Engraving, London, 1829, from *Congregational Magazine*, Permezel Collection, Melbourne.
3. Thomas Campbell. Engraving by C. H. Jeens, frontispiece of Rev. W. Alfred Hill (ed.), *The Poetical Works of Thomas Campbell: With a Sketch of his Life* by William Allingham, George Bell & Sons, London, 1875.
4. Protestant Dissenters Grammar School, Mill Hill, Hendon, Rock and Co., RC 18. With kind permission of the Mill Hill School Foundation.
5. Mill Hill School pond. From N. G. Brett-James, *The History of Mill Hill School 1807–1907*, Mill Hill School, London, 1909. With kind permission of the Mill Hill School Foundation.
6. Harriet Strother Riddiford Evans, 'The High Stepper'. With kind permission of Philippa Riddiford.
7. Daniel Riddiford. With kind permission of Mrs E. A. Riddiford.
8. Edward Gibbon Wakefield, by E. J. Collins (dogs by Richard Ansdell). By kind permission of Canterbury Museum.
9. North End House, Hampstead, London. Hampstead Illustrations Collection, 'LDB North End House'. By permission of the Camden Local Studies and Archives Centre, London.
10. Detail from the first page of the Prospectus of the New Zealand Colonization Company, September 1838. CO 209/4 Micro 352, p.521, Archives New Zealand.

Between pp.232 and 233

1. Edward Betts Hopper. 'Self portrait 1835–39', by Edward Betts Hopper, A-001-055, Alexander Turnbull Library.
2. Sir Richard Davies Hanson, Chief Justice of the Supreme Court, South Australia, from the *Illustrated London News*, July–December 1869, Vol. XV, p.117, National Library of New Zealand.
3. Dr Isaac Featherston. Photograph by kind permission of Mrs E. A. Riddiford.
4. Samuel Revans. A. H. & A. W. Reed, photographs, ca. 1860, 1/2-038720-F, Alexander Turnbull Library.
5. Left-hand section of Panorama of Wellington, Port Nicholson, taken upon Thorndon Flat [1847], by Samuel Charles Brees, from an engraving by Henry Melville. PUBL-0020-22-1, Alexander Turnbull Library.

6. Part two of 'City of Wellington New Zealand: Sketch of Thorndon Quay and Beach', 1841, by Luke Nattrass (W. Richardson, lithographer), C-029-004-2-3, Alexander Turnbull Library.
7. Part three of 'City of Wellington New Zealand: Sketch of Thorndon Quay and Beach', 1841, by Luke Nattrass (W. Richardson, lithographer), C-029-004-3-2, Alexander Turnbull Library.
8. Te Rauparaha. 'Te Raparaha, Chief of the Kawias', A-114-047, Alexander Turnbull Library.
9. Rangihaeata. 'Te Rauparaha's fighting general', by Isaac Coates [1843?], A-286-014, Alexander Turnbull Library.
10. 'Evans's Bay near Wellington, New Zealand, 1857', by Henry Stratton Bates, Private Collection, copy held in Alexander Turnbull Library, 052726 1/2, Alexander Turnbull Library.
11. Courts of Justice, Wellington, 1843, by Samuel Charles Brees, B-031-009, Alexander Turnbull Library.
12. Bird's-eye view of Wellington Harbour from the southern entrance, by Charles Heaphy, C-029-006b, Alexander Turnbull Library.

Between pp.360 and 361

1. G. S. Evans, circa 1858. Image by kind permission of Mrs E. A. Riddiford.
2. 'Brutus and Cassius', *Melbourne Punch*, Vol. IV, 9 July 1857, p.189. Courtesy of the State Library of New South Wales.
3. 'Bear Baiting', *Melbourne Punch*, Vol. VIII, 24 February 1859, p.37. Courtesy of the State Library of New South Wales.
4. 'The India Rubber Brothers', *Melbourne Punch*, Vol. VI, 1 April 1858, p.85. Courtesy of the State Library of New South Wales.
5. 'The Travelled Minister', *Melbourne Punch*, Vol. VII, 12 August 1858, p.19. Courtesy of the State Library of New South Wales.
6. Edward Joshua Riddiford. With kind permission of Mrs E. A. Riddiford.
7. 'Macaulay's New Zealander on London Bridge', *Melbourne Punch*, Vol. IX, 15 December 1859, p.167. Courtesy of the State Library of New South Wales.
8. 'The Original Sphynx', *Melbourne Punch*, Vol. IX, 1 December 1859, p.153. Courtesy of the State Library of New South Wales.
9. 'The Old Roman', *Melbourne Punch*, Vol. VIII, 7 April 1859, p.85. Courtesy of the State Library of New South Wales.
10. 'Coriolanus Relents', *Melbourne Punch*, Vol. XIII, 24 October 1861, p.261. Courtesy of the State Library of New South Wales.
11. 'The End of the Comedy', *Melbourne Punch*, Vol. XVIII, 26 May 1864, p.173. Courtesy of the State Library of New South Wales.
12. G. S. Evans, circa 1864–65. Wood engraving by C. H. H. accompanying article by David Blair, 'Three Melbourne Barristers', *Centennial Magazine*, Vol. 2, No. 9, April 1890, p.692. Courtesy of the State Library of Victoria.

ACKNOWLEDGEMENTS

This biography began as a modest attempt to draw up a Riddiford family tree and write a short history of the early generations.

Then two things happened. Firstly, having joined Christine Cole Catley's Wellington Writing School, she encouraged me to pursue my interest in George Samuel Evans, the stepfather of Daniel. At the beginning of my search, I came upon an article in the form of a letter written to the editor of the *Evening Post* on 16 July 1927. H. W. Fildes, an early Wellington historian, was objecting to the name of Golders Hill, Evans's home off Hill Street, being altered to Eccleston Hill to commemorate Prime Minister Seddon's birthplace. The article outlined Evans's career, including his key part in the settlement of Wellington and wider contributions to the country. It concluded by mentioning that Mr E. Hampden-Cook, MA, of Manchester, England, was writing a biography of Evans. It has never appeared.

After a bit of sleuthing I then contacted John Permezel in Melbourne, the great-great-nephew of Evans. He has been a treasure with his generous and unflagging assistance.

My research having spanned more than a decade, many of my contacts have either passed away or have been replaced in their positions. Early in my research, Paul Phillips from Auckland, through historian Angela Caughey, drew my attention to the Brett's Historical Series of Early New Zealand by R. A. A. Sheerin, which mentioned Evans several times as a leader and spokesperson for early Wellington's interests. In Wellington I received sound advice from my former English professor, the late Stuart Johnston, and historian Brad Patterson. Roberta McIntyre generously read a draft and offered advice. The late Dame Christine Cole Catley and members of her Wellington Writers' Course kept me going from the beginning – especially Rosemary Norman who read a draft and offered encouragement and advice. The late historian Ray Fargher from the same group followed up a letter I was given by Belinda Cranswick and found William Fox's observation on the pivotal role Evans played in colonising Wellington.

The late Dr Michael King read an early draft, gave me advice and promised to give me every assistance before his untimely death. Belinda Cranswick, daughter of the late Earle Riddiford, provided the family tree and much of her own prodigious research. The late Lionel Brown of Whangarei was able to offer me another unique perspective.

It is difficult to single out any one member of the staff who gave me their time and patience in the National and Turnbull Libraries, Wellington. Recently Jocelyn Chalmers and her team were superb in their assistance. Ann Reweti of the history section of the Wellington Central Library was of great help in the early stages and members of the Auckland Central

Library's Research Centre were very helpful. I must also acknowledge the assistance of Marian Minson and Mark Bagnall of the illustrations and map departments of the ATL. And Archives New Zealand provided a dizzying array of material, through which its staff managed to guide me over the years. In pursuing the details of Evans's will and the saga of his financial trials, I received assistance from Dan Stevenson and John Stevenson of Izard Weston in Wellington – the firm which handled Evans's estate.

In England I received information from J. G. (Geoffrey) Brown, the archivist of Merchant Taylors' School. My friend Anthony O'Connell connected me with the Mill Hill School historian Roderick Braithwaite, MA FRHists FIMgt, whose assistance was invaluable. Most recently another friend Dorothy Hudson connected me with the current Mill Hill School archivist Kate Thompson. Guy Holborn of the Lincoln's Inn Library provided me with information. Glasgow University's assistant archivist Simon Bennett supplied all the records of Evans's achievements, and more recently Claire Daniel assisted. The late Christopher Hurst, descendant of Harriot Stone's family, found Evans's link with the Reform Club, and Simon Blundell, the Reform Club librarian, sent me valuable material. Dr John H. Thompson of London, the Coward Trust's historian (of Dissenters), also gave me a great deal of valuable information. Richard Knight and Tudor Allen of the Camden Local Studies and Archives Centre found the illustration of North End House in Hampstead. Dick Weindling, also passed on information. David Small of the Chetham Strode family was of great assistance.

In Australia the staffs of the libraries of the States of Victoria and New South Wales and the Mitchell Library were generous with their help. Janice Ryan of the Melbourne Law Institute confirmed Evans's enrolment as a barrister. John Permezel, as already mentioned, gave me every assistance with the Evans family history. Len Dewes and John Riddiford of Sydney also contributed.

I am most grateful to my editor, Ginny Sullivan, ever warm and encouraging, who has guided me expertly and patiently through the process. Her patience and perception has been unflagging.

I am grateful to Fergus Barrowman of Victoria University Press who accepted the challenge of allowing Evans's voice to be heard after such a long silence. My thanks also go to Kyleigh Hodgson, editor of Victoria University Press.

My mother-in-law Joan Riddiford (Mrs E. A. Riddiford) was always interested and encouraging. And finally, I thank my husband Hugh, without whose support and practical help I could not have persevered.

Helen Riddiford
November 2013

PREFACE

> I held it truth, with him who sings
> To one clear harp in divers tones,
> That men may rise on stepping-stones
> Of their dead selves to higher things.
>
> But who shall so forecast the years
> And find in loss a gain to match?
> Or reach a hand thro' time to catch
> The far-off interest of tears?
>
> Alfred, Lord Tennyson (1809–1892), 'In Memoriam'

This biography of George Samuel Evans LLD (1802–68) began simply as the story of a man's life. It was not intended to be a history of early Wellington, nor an apology for the actions of the New Zealand Company, although Evans was prominently and intimately connected with both.

From late 1998, I have researched a variety of materials to present as clear a picture as possible of the background influences of the period. I have also endeavoured to portray events from the perspective of Evans, while at the same time giving an account of the alternate views of the groups or factions with which he interacted: Maori, missionaries, the Crown and the settlers.

The events – especially from 1837, when Evans became heavily involved with the New Zealand Association, which eventually became the New Zealand Company – show a man devoted to promoting Wakefield's scheme of colonisation who became dependent on the outcome of the Company's success or failure. For this reason, particularly in the Wellington section, 1840–44, I have consulted the *Gazette*, as it has become known, as its viewpoint in that period was almost exclusively that of the Company.

There are comparatively few personal letters extant to and from Evans. However, he wrote extensively for London papers in the reform period and helped Wakefield with Company propaganda. In Wellington he wrote several leaders for the *Gazette*, and later in 1852–53 for the *Wellington Independent*. He penned most of the 'memorials' or petitions from Wellington in the years of his residence

1840–44 and briefly in the year 1852–53 on his return. He was editor of the *Melbourne Herald* from 1855 to 1858, writing more than a thousand articles in that time. These provide a valuable insight into the views he held on a variety of topics, from political questions, to the Chinese, to the conduct of women, the freedom of the press, the Land Wars in New Zealand and many other issues.

Evans made scores of speeches in Wellington, most of which were recorded. He was a member of the Victorian Legislative Assembly 1856–64, so Victorian Hansard has been extensively researched. Many of his peers wrote of him: Richard Davies Hanson devoted an editorial to him, and the private letters of Hanson, William Fox, Thomas Partridge, Samuel Revans and others reflected their views of the man. The diaries of William Cotton, Edward Betts Hopper, Thomas McKenzie, Eleanor Petre, Jerningham Wakefield and Francis Yates, together with the 'Recollections' of David Blair and the *Reminiscences* of James John Taine, have offered more insights.

Evans was an ideal subject for *Melbourne Punch*, which devoted a remarkable amount of space to him: many full-length cartoons, articles, letters, skits and poems ranging from trenchant criticism to light-hearted mockery are scattered throughout its volumes. He was, as more than one observer noted, 'an uncommon man, rarely seen in the colonies'.

Although Evans was a brilliant scholar, writer, orator and debater, today many of his articles appear ponderous, his speeches declamatory, and his recollections and historical references pompous and boastful. But they gave heart to the settlers, and guidance to his peers in Parliament, especially on constitutional matters.

Later, in July 1927, Horace Fildes wrote to the *Evening Post* outlining the life of Evans, and it is this that has been the chief inspiration for my work. John Permezel of Melbourne, Evans's great-great-nephew, has generously shared his archive of material, and given me prompt and unflagging assistance.

The early nineteenth century in Britain was a time of prodigious energy. In a period of great upheaval it produced a remarkable number of gifted eccentric men – men who excelled and pushed through the boundaries in many fields: the arts, law, politics, science, philosophy, discovery, colonisation and exploration. It was a time when education occurred in a variety of private and sponsored schools, academies and colleges – well before the state took responsibility for it.

Those who made the leap to settle in New Zealand, a country at the other end of the earth, were not only courageous, but in many cases also desperate to find a better life and future for their families. After the Wairau episode in 1843, they lived in a climate of increasing fear and hostility, privation and uncertainty. The outrage against the Crown's early despotic leaders could barely be contained by the founders of the Wellington settlement. The internal squabbling and fiery debate became rancorous. In two cases there were notable duels. The first ended tragically when two lawyers fought over a case before the court – Hugh Ross fatally shot William Brewer. Later, Wakefield and Featherston faced each other in a duel in 1844 – but although, according to Taine, they fired at each other, neither was injured.[1]

Some words had subtle but different connotations then from their meanings today. In Britain, especially up to and beyond the era of the Great Reform Act of 1832, the terms 'Whigs' and 'Tories' were not as clear as we would understand them to be today. There were many conservative 'Whigs' who baulked at the idea of reform, and several progressive 'Tories' who welcomed it in some degree. And in the writing and speeches of the time, the Aborigines' Protection Society, the New Zealand Company and the Church Missionary Society used more than one word to describe indigenous peoples of the countries in which they were interested. Generic terms such as 'Natives', 'Aboriginals' and even 'savages' were common when referring to New Zealand, the last meaning merely 'uncivilised', that is, not yet influenced by western religion and civilisation. Conversely, the word 'philanthropist' was frequently used derisively to denote a meddler or armchair theorist – a 'do-gooder'. A poem called 'The Philanthropists', published in *Blackwood's Magazine* and reproduced in the *New Zealand Spectator and Cook's Straits Guardian* of 4 October 1845 is a scathing indictment of the hypocrisy of habitués of Exeter Hall – men who attended meetings, listened to stirring speeches and professed to care for the plight of 'the wearers of black skins beneath the equator', while ignoring the desperate needs of their own families and neighbours.

The English historian Paul Johnson once wrote, 'There is something repellent, as well as profoundly unhistorical, about judging the past by the standards or prejudices of another age. Let the dead bury the dead. Or at least let us not dig them up . . .'[2] There are many traps for the biographer excavating the life of a man who has been dead for over 140 years. It is a presumptuous act and one fraught with pitfalls. It is never safe to 'play with edge tools', as Evans himself said of Justice Stephen's reference to Horace. Equally, it is not appropriate to apply our twenty-first century views on character and temperament to the men of the early nineteenth century. And to paraphrase the advice Evans once gave (of a defence lawyer in a court case), an author must go 'through his part as gingerly, and with as much apparent dread of exploding his own case, as if he had been compelled to walk with hob-nails in his shoes and a pipe in his mouth, through a powder magazine'.[3] Or, as the late eminent New Zealand historian Michael King and his friend and publisher Christine Cole Catley urged, 'Tell the compassionate truth.'

Was Evans a visionary? In England his views on teaching and education were certainly enlightened and in some instances well ahead of his time. As the son of a dissenting clergyman who was also active in the reform movement, his views on reform, on the abolition of slavery, on the equitable expansion of the franchise – on civil and religious liberty – were in keeping with the most liberal views of the day. His ready acceptance and promotion of Edward Gibbon Wakefield's great scheme of systematic colonisation was shared by some of the most powerful forward-thinking minds of the time. His plan for the 'Administration of Justice in the absence of Government in Port Nicholson' in the earliest days of 1840, drawn up with Richard Davies Hanson and approved by Colonel Wakefield, was certainly enlightened.

I have referred to several of the early histories, for example, those of William Gisborne, J. H. Wallace and G. W. Rusden, the last of whom was decidedly anti-Wakefield but a contemporary of Evans. Jerningham Wakefield's *Adventure in New Zealand* is usually dismissed as being a one-sided but personal view from the perspective of a Company man. The accounts of J. S. Marais and A. H. McLintock more nearly reflect the tension felt by the members of the Association/Company, and their belief they were not being dealt with fairly by the Colonial Office. Guy H. Scholefield eloquently summarised the treatment meted to the Company and Hobson in his work *Captain William Hobson R.N. 1793–1842*. More recent historians – Alan Ward, Ian Wards and Peter Adams – provide excellent scholarly and balanced views of the question.

Evans made a significant contribution to parliamentary debates on constitutional issues when the vexed questions of ownership and distribution of lands in New Zealand and Victoria dogged him and his contemporaries.[4] Only an expert political historian can fully analyse his political career in Melbourne. It was a turbulent time in history: of transition from the old ways to the new; from the safety of certainty and hard-and-fast rules, to the modern age. Geoffrey Serle's account of the era has been a key source for this section.

George Samuel Evans was a man of his time. He was a zealous, driven, extremely hard-working advocate for the liberal causes of the day. He worked tirelessly for parliamentary reform, colonial reform, and religious and civil freedom. He was formidably well equipped, not merely to espouse these issues but actively to promote them. Throughout his public life he was respected and even admired – but not liked or 'loved' by many. His importunate conduct led to many professional problems, and not least of all to a series of actions, the aftershocks of which resonate to this day in New Zealand. There is a deep irony in that a man who was unreliable and invariably late for appointments and meetings, led the premature and precipitate expedition to colonise New Zealand. Yet Evans showed immense courage in his dogged persistence, in his standing up to authority and by remaining steadfast to his commitment to colonisation – especially to the success of Wellington.

Yet today, after five or more decades of revisionism, the New Zealand Company's servants of the Wellington settlement and beyond have been consigned to our history as two-dimensional demons. The Wakefields are seen as slippery and opportunistic criminals; Evans, their colleague, has been largely ignored or derisively dismissed as a pompous, peppery buffoon. But his legacy cannot easily be dismissed. In the historical archives of Australia, Evans is described as being 'a founder, prime mover and settler of the New Zealand Company'.[5]

In urging me to complete this work and offering his assistance, our most eminent modern historian, the late Dr Michael King, was astonished he had not heard of the man.

Helen Riddiford
October 2013

PROLOGUE

7 March 1840

Three gentlemen sat outside a large silk tent on 'Pitone Beach',[1] basking in the last of a glorious late summer's day. Their idle conversation came to an abrupt halt when they saw on the southern horizon three large ships appearing, with their sails plumped proudly in fanfare. Jumping to their feet, the men pulled out their spy-glasses to identify them, but were soon distracted by the brooding storm nipping at the ships' heels. On board the ships, as heavy black clouds skimmed the masts, the captains and crews struggled to negotiate the reefs and find anchorage, but their efforts were frustrated by torrential rain and nightfall. Amidst thunder and lightning, they were finally forced to anchor north of Somes Island, a mile or so off Pitone Beach, and opposite Waiwhetu pa.[2]

On the largest of the ships, the *Adelaide*, the Umpire of the New Zealand Company's First Colony insisted on being rowed ashore, but the captain refused, reluctant to risk his crew in the atrocious conditions. In spite of this, two other passengers joined the first, a voluntary crew was assembled, and into a darkness as 'black as Erebus', a small boat was quickly lowered into the churning sea.[3]

A little later the three gentlemen in the tent – Colonel William Wakefield, his nephew Edward Jerningham and Henry Moreing – heard a voice approaching. A flurry of movement outside, the flap was flung open, and Dr George Samuel Evans 'burst into the tent', his drenched oilskins clinging to his tall powerful frame and glistening in the lamplight. 'Wild with excitement and pleasure at having at length landed on the shores of the country in which he had so long been interested', he boomed a greeting as the men sat for an instant, speechless.[4]

That indelible moment, frozen in time, has captured the essence of one of Wellington's most remarkable pioneers.

In many ways George Samuel Evans was the embodiment of the early nineteenth-century thinking Englishman. He was born at the dawn of the century into an age of social upheaval and political unrest. The country was reeling from the aftermath of the American and French revolutions, and plunged in the midst of the Napoleonic Wars. King George III was suffering from a form of madness,[5] the industrial revolution was creating a tide of human dislocation and despair, and the time was ripe for reform.

Evans was born to battle. He was bred by an ambitious and zealous father to pursue the goals of civil and religious liberty at a time when men increasingly agitated for social and political reform. They looked outwards with a fervent desire to found new societies and colonies that would offer hope to people devastated by the changing face of their own country.

A brilliant scholar who acquired formidable skills in both oratory and journalism, Evans also gained the legal skills to contribute to the great reforming causes of the day. His life was a kaleidoscope of adventure. It took him from picturesque rural England to the squalor of London's slums, and on to the tranquillity of clean air and village life just north of the great city. But before he could really enjoy the security and comforts of the educated middle class, he was propelled from reform into the arena of colonisation, leaping from an old country – England – to New Zealand, a colony of ragged uncertainty, ambition, jealousy and deprivation.

When Edward Gibbon Wakefield, the architect of the systematic colonisation of New Zealand, virtually abandoned his project and accompanied Lord Durham to Canada, it was Evans who took up the reins. In the face of increasing hostility from the British government, he and a small band of others assured the scheme's continuation and, for better or worse, spurred a reluctant government into taking action to procure the country for the Crown.

By the time he arrived in Wellington, Evans had completed a Maori grammar[6] and spoke the language 'very well'. For Maori he became 'nui nui rangatira', 'a very important leader'.[7] But in those crucial first years of settlement he was the outspoken critic of successive governors at a time when government and missionaries appeared to combine forces to pit themselves against the undertaking of the New Zealand Company.[8] After nearly five years as Colonel Wakefield's legal advisor, and as representative of the settlers' interests, he returned to the old country to continue lobbying on their behalf and to promote the colony's desire for self-government.

Wellington drew him back for a brief time, where once again he took up the cudgels on behalf of the settlers. From there, ill health and better prospects took him to Victoria, Australia, where he used his political role to improve communication links with Wellington.

In the colonies, he was head and shoulders above many of his peers in education and ability. He operated within an influential network of men, but was always independent in his views, which isolated him from many of his contemporaries. He was viewed as a 'singular character', a gentleman almost unique in this setting. His many visionary ideas were handicapped by a volatile temperament and principles that were compromised by circumstances and frustrated ambition. He was a bundle of restless contradictions, an unpredictable man of reckless courage whose steadfast commitment to the creation and success of Wellington was fully acknowledged after his death. Amongst others, the *Independent* noted that he was 'one of the founders, if not the real founder of this colony . . . there is scarcely an official document of the period in which [his] name is not conspicuous'.[9]

But today, if a visitor to Wellington asked for the story behind the name of the large bay at the southern end of the harbour, few could provide it. Only by entering Easdale Street from Bolton Street in the city, descending the steps to the steep embankment above the motorway, and threading a way through the crumbling gravestones planted over empty ground, might the visitor find a forlorn marker of the man who was instrumental in having the site of Wellington moved from Petone to its present position.

More than a century and a half later, and after fifty years of our history's reassessment, Evans has become little more than a footnote. He is irrevocably and fatally linked to the New Zealand Company, which, with the benefit of hindsight and modern research, has come to be regarded by many historians with the same suspicion and loathing with which the Colonial Office tainted it from the first. If mentioned at all, Evans is scornfully dismissed or reviled as 'a most obnoxious man'.[10] Yet there were few at the time and for many years after who would have disagreed with New Zealand Premier William Fox's assessment of Evans as 'perhaps the most influential originator of New Zealand Colonization we ever had'.[11]

PART ONE:
ENGLAND 1802–1839

CHAPTER ONE. STUDENT AND SCHOLAR

> During the first thirty years of the nineteenth century, many changes [in England] in habits and life were due to the steady infiltration of evangelical religion into all classes of society. When [the 'enjoying classes'] saw their privileges and possessions threatened by Jacobin Doctrines from across the Channel, a sharp revulsion from French 'atheism and deism' prepared a favourable soil for greater 'seriousness' among the gentry. Indifferentism in religion now seemed seditious and unpatriotic, and a concurrent change in manners took place from licence or gaiety to hypocrisy or to virtue.
>
> G. M. Trevelyan, *English Social History*, Longmans, London, rev. edn, 1986, p.505

George Samuel Evans was born on 3 June 1802, in the cottage attached to the Congregational chapel of St Mary in Gloucester. A short time later, he was christened by his father, Reverend George Evans, in the Lady Huntingdon Chapel at Bath.[1]

Like his Christian name, the infant's dissenting background went back at least four generations. In 1744, the orphaned baby son of George Evans, a parish clerk from Cadbury, Somerset, had been reared by his maternal grandmother, Madam Furze, a puritanical businesswoman who ran 'The Cadbury Crop' – probably an inn.[2] Thirty-five years later, orphaned George's wife Mary Carpenter produced a son who inherited their combined religious zeal.[3] In 1796, at the age of seventeen, George preached for many weeks at Ilford – then a small village without any church – by conducting open-air services 'standing on a pile of logs'. Five years later he entered the Congregational ministry under the patronage of the late Countess of Huntingdon. In this way he joined an exclusive and more sophisticated branch, the members of which were generally regarded as 'genteel Methodists'.[4]

After his ordination, George Evans married Hannah Cotterell, the daughter of Richard Cotterell, a man of property and a lawyer in practice with his maternal grandfather, William Lewis. Hannah's mother, Mary Morrison, who had inherited some property in Wales, was the daughter of a colonel in the Artillery at Woolwich.

When Hannah gave birth to George Samuel in 1802, the political and religious climate into which he was born was anything but easy. The establishment regarded Jews, Catholics and dissenters with fierce antipathy, denying them the franchise and allowing them few rights. The Marriage Act of 1753 had refused to recognise marriages conducted outside the Church of England, and civil and military offices were disallowed to those outside the fold. In 1800 George III denounced placing 'Papists and Presbyterians in a state of equality with the Church of England'; and seven years later, the Canon of St Paul's and well-known wit Reverend Sydney Smith taunted:

> When a country squire hears of an ape, his first feeling is to give it nuts and apples; when he hears of a Dissenter his immediate impulse is to commit it to the County Jail, to shave its head, to alter its customary food, and to have it privately whipped.[5]

At the same time, Anglican ministries were marked by corruption and neglect. The Church of England 'owned a massive array of temporalities' and several pastors held two or more benefices at once. Dr Manners Sutton, Archbishop of Canterbury from 1808 to 1828, and the Bishop of Durham each collected £19,000 annually, and Dr Sutton 'distributed sixteen livings and other cathedral appointments to seven members of his family'.[6] Even more outrageously, the Reverend Earl of Bridgewater was gloriously absent from his Durham prebend and two benefices in Shropshire for forty-nine years; instead, he lived in Paris, 'surrounded by cats and dogs dressed as humans'.[7]

Such abuse allowed dissenting ministries such as that of Reverend Evans, and the influence of individuals like the writer and social reformer Hannah More, to grow steadily and fill the void. Through denying the rights and privileges held by the establishment, they developed great strength and independence, being free to explore new territories forged by earlier dissenters who had helped pave the way for the modern age.[8]

Reverend Evans preached all over England,[9] gratuitously from Sussex to Guernsey, from Worcester to Hereford and Bristol, and in his own parish of Goring, Oxfordshire. The church's administrators were so impressed by his energy and 'spirit of zeal and enterprise' that they asked him to take charge of a small but very old independent church in Red Lion Court, Spitalfields, the next year.

Evans accepted the challenge with alacrity, but in moving his family to the east end of London in 1807, the contrast with England's countryside could not have been more dramatic. The district of Stepney was fast gaining a reputation for 'the worst slums, the worst overcrowding, [and] the worst death rates'. Spitalfields' population of 15,000 was made up mostly of poor migrants, including Huguenot Protestants driven from France who were weavers of silks, satins, velvets and tapestries, boot-makers, and specialists in watch-making and engraving. There were Quakers too, many of whom were successful businessmen, and Jewish traders.[10] At its centre, Red Lion Court was a warren of filthy lanes leading off Red Lion Street, a crowded Jewish quarter of wooden shacks and run-down tenements. Brick-making flourished in the area, and a giant old brewery, the Black Eagle, belched its soot and sickly smells.[11]

By this time a second son had been born, Richard Cotterell (1806), and Reverend Evans found he had plunged his family into a world of crime, disease and the direst poverty. Daily living was squalid and difficult. Sewage filled large ditches, whose stench was aggravated by the prevailing wind carrying the city's pollution to mingle with the yellow fog and factory soot.[12] Clean water was as scarce as fresh air, and fevers – including typhus – were frequent visitors. Young George's naturally robust constitution was weakened, especially by respiratory illnesses that would recur throughout his life. And the noise was continuous – one learned to shout above the din of cart wheels on cobblestones.

But his world was also a feast of colour and magical change. In Spitalfields, old Roman tiles, coins and pottery dating from the time of Claudius and Nero had been discovered; and a Roman cemetery with thousands of urns containing bones and ashes had been excavated and was still yielding finds. When gas-lighting was introduced onto London's streets the year of the family's arrival,[13] the city was more exposed, which meant George could travel further afield with his father.He went to the large fruit and vegetable market nearby, and mingled with the cooks from the great homes of London. He saw bearded Jewish traders, their arms filled with old clothing and hats stacked like colourful chimney pots on their heads, setting up their stalls in the notorious thieves' quarter, Peticote (Petticoat) Lane, alongside the weavers' displays.[14]

The weavers' homes were of dark red brick, with wide latticed windows in the attics lighting their workrooms where they laboured fourteen to sixteen hours a day for meagre wages. In spite of this, they were 'wonderfully uncomplaining and self-reliant', and famous for singing day and night at their looms.[15] Through the next challenging decades when their craft was superseded by industrial looms, they supplemented their income by setting bird traps on their roofs to snare song-birds like linnets and chaffinches, selling them in the markets to the city's wealthy. Accompanying his father on his parish rounds, George would look up and see what another witness described in mid-century Bethnal Green:

> . . . dirty men in their sooty shirt-sleeves . . . on the house-tops, peeping out of little rough wooden structures built on the roofs to keep their pigeons in. They suck their short pipes, fly their fancy birds, whistle shrilly with their forefingers placed in their mouths, beat the sides of the wooden building with a long stick like a fishing rod, and use all their ingenuity to snare their neighbours' stray birds.[16]

George climbed the stairs with his father to visit weavers in their attics, and went to the almshouses in the area where he met grizzled old seamen, listening to their tales of adventure in exotic lands, and hearing of loss and hardship from lonely widows.

A little over a year after their arrival, the birth of a third son, James Cook Evans (1808) and the rapid growth of Reverend Evans's congregation meant a move further east to Church Street, which was located in Mile End, New Town. From west to east, Church Street (now Fournier Street) began not far from Red Lion Court, was bisected by Brick Lane and High Street and the small fields that divided them, and continued to its eastern end. Here, George's father became pastor of a much larger chapel.[17]

Some of the homes of the prosperous master weavers were located in Mile End. They grew mulberry trees for silkworms in their gardens, and nearly all had their own carriages.[18] The area appeared more salubrious, but there was a 'common open sewer running from west to east through Mile End New Town, and the proximity of lime kilns, brickfields, piggeries, stagnant ponds, and undrained marshes', together with the addition of more sweat shops and 'stink industries' spreading into the area over the ensuing years, meant there was little difference between the two ends of Church Street.[19]

At home the atmosphere was one of religious fervour, strict discipline and high expectations, fuelled by the urgent charge of Reverend Evans's nervous energy. Frivolity was frowned upon; in the Puritan tradition, the theatre, dancing and works of fiction were banned, but good clean wholesome fun was not. Reverend Evans had a lively sense of humour and was openly affectionate, as letters to his family attest.[20] He instilled a sense of family pride in his sons, schooling them in the social graces common amongst gentlemen so that they would be at ease in any company. He regarded his wife as an equal in whom he confided, sending her instructions to convey to his assistants during his frequent absences.

Outside the home, the dynamic pastor struck an impressive figure. Over six feet tall and solidly built, with large compelling eyes, he stood out from the crowd as he swept about his parish in sober garb. The highlight of the week was the sermon, delivered each Sunday night from the pulpit, when George thrilled to his father's dramatic display, which was perhaps as mesmeric as that of the famous dissenter Reverend W. J. Fox. Fox 'had eyes like burning coals and long white hair like a comet's tail':

> He would transfix his congregation. Their hearts would be in their mouths as he enacted in the pulpit some such scene from holy writ as Jacob wrestling with the angel. By his hypnotic arts Fox would make his auditors feel in their own muscles the agonies of that struggle of mortal flesh with supernatural powers. They would groan, they would writhe in their seats, sweat would spring out on their brows.[21]

George and his brothers were educated in the school next to the chapel, where familiarity with the Bible was as essential as the rudimentary subjects. The day at home started with at least fifteen minutes of prayer, then catechism. George would read a chapter from Homer's *Odyssey*, Pope's translation of the *Iliad* or the dramas of Hannah More, and be quizzed on the moral lessons he had learned. Sundays were traditional Sabbaths: there was no housework, but many prayers and Bible readings and three church services. History, geography and current affairs were discussed at length, while frugality and responsibility for personal finances were encouraged. George Samuel's military inheritance also resonated, as he declared decades later:

> . . . he was proud to have been educated in principles of Protestantism of the most rigid kind perhaps – he had been trained as a Puritan amongst the Puritans . . . the blood that flowed in his veins flowed in those of one who had held a commission in Cromwell's Ironsides . . . his ancestor fought at Naseby and Worcester.[22]

Reverend Evans was a fierce advocate for reform. With others, he founded the Home Missionary Society, and worked with the London Itinerant Society and similar organisations. As the years passed, he included George in his work, imbuing him with the righteous certainty of the 'good old cause' – civil and religious liberty. Their neighbourhood hummed with religious dissent and political radicalism, and groups of men often gathered in the evenings to discuss the burning issues of the day. The several breweries scattered through Stepney were mostly owned or managed by philanthropic Quakers, and the family became well acquainted with many of them. The prominent reformer and evangelical Thomas Fowell Buxton was not far away in Brick Lane, having become a part-owner of the Black Eagle brewery, and his group worked to educate the poor and to abolish slavery.[23]

The dissenters' methods were effective: the deputations, the magazines and tracts, the parish and public meetings, and the practical work in voluntary organisations taught George the power of the written word, of good oratory and of rousing passions within the humble man's breast without inciting him to violence. By the time George was ten, 'there were 256 dissenting places of worship in London, compared with just 186 Anglican churches'.[24]

The family had grown as well. William (1811) and Alfred (1813) took the total of sons to five. William was an invalid from birth, causing the family much anxiety and placing heavy demands on Hannah, who was often prostrate with illness. The two or three domestic staff helped her cope with her husband's absences – sometimes for weeks at a time – as she juggled her parish and family duties. George assumed more and more responsibility for his brothers: helping the older boys with their schoolwork, performing tasks and running errands. But the mean streets of his neighbourhood were the scenes of many skirmishes with roaming bullies, and George, who took his role seriously as head of the family in his father's absences, learned quickly to defend himself and his brothers.

Highlights were family visits, especially at Christmas. Decades later, George lamented the contrast between the Christmases of his boyhood and those celebrated in the southern hemisphere where he found:

> No snowballs, no sliding, no skating, no frosted ivy, no diamond bracelets hanging from the trees, no brilliants bespangling the pointed glass, no crystalline drop depending from Aunt Dorothea's purple nose, – no mufflers, no comforters, no genuine yule log – required to still the involuntary chattering of teeth, or to thaw the

> stupefaction brought on in pilgrims to the paternal fireside, by piercing winds or driving sleet. [The antipodean Christmas] is all 'a mockery, a delusion, and a snare'.[25]

At his father's school, George displayed more than common ability, so at the age of eleven he was sent to Merchant Taylors' School, one of the 'great' public schools of London, for his secondary education.[26] Although it was an establishment school, its headmaster Thomas Cherry had told the painter and diarist Joseph Farington it was 'open to all the world, the payments are very small'.[27] There, George was able to mingle with the sons of London's more privileged citizens and, although it was a baptism of fire for the son of a nonconformist minister from the poorest part of the city, Merchant Taylors' offered George opportunities for advancement.

That first long walk alone to school was a test of his courage. He ran the gamut of passers-by: hawkers, gangs of pickpockets and bullies, waifs and strays, and young girls forced into prostitution shouting their insults and ribald remarks. Although he was tall and sturdy for his age, he would have been an obvious prey in his distinctive striped trousers and starched high Eton collar, then – on becoming a prompter – a swallow-tailed or evening-dress coat, and later, a tall hat and black tie. Shortly after six in the morning he walked from Church Street down Brick Lane to Whitechapel Road, past butchers' shops and inns, dodging brewers' drays and coaches, and carts laden with fruit and vegetables.[28] He wended his way through Aldgate High and Fenchurch streets and turned left towards the river and to the heart of the old city. Here at Cheapside frequent savage fights took place between the pupils of the City of London School and the boys from Merchant Taylors'. Cannon Street was riddled with a maze of narrow lanes running off towards the Thames, with Thames Street leading to Suffolk Lane and Merchant Taylors' School. Close to the school the apprentices from a noisy printing works fought the boys nearly every day. George had learned to be quick with his fists, and had a handy weapon in the heavy blue book bag he carried over his shoulder with his ink-bottle looped into the buttonhole.

The school was in a 'long dingy brick building' that was jammed between a tall block of offices and towering warehouses.[29] Inside the Great Schoolroom, measuring eighty-five feet by thirty feet, four tiers of benches were arranged along each side, with writing tables on the top tier for monitors. The room was lit only by the six or seven leaded windows coated with generations of dirt, so every boy had to supply his own candle.

Most schools of the time were tough, and Merchant Taylors' was no exception. It was woefully understaffed – four masters and senior monitors controlled two hundred boys in six forms. Headmaster Mr Cherry in particular did not spare the birch.[30] The curriculum consisted almost entirely of the classics and their translation from Greek, Latin and Hebrew. The day was long, beginning at 7 a.m. and ending at 4 p.m., with only a short break for lunch, when the boys rushed to a bakery or a chophouse for a chop and a glass of stout.

Bullying was rife. There were many types of torture: dripping burning wax on hair and clothes, painful 'bumping', a vicious attack on the crowded stairs, or 'roasting' the victim on the iron cage that surrounded the open grate of burning coal. But in spite of his vulnerability, George had distinct advantages: his size and his exceptional ability in the classroom. He could hold his own in the schoolyard, but he preferred the sanctuary of the famed school library that housed some of the best works in English theology.[31]

There were highlights. In his first year, on 11 October, he was among the 'young gentlemen' of the school who breakfasted at the Lord Mayor's Mansion House. They were formally introduced to the Mayor and 'ushered into the Egyptian Hall, where they were greeted with tables spread with jellies, sweetmeats, and pastry, fowl, plum-cake, coffee, ale and glasses of warm negus'.[32]

During that winter of 1813, the Thames froze over, and wax and glue solidified in their pots. Londoners struggled through moats of mud and icy sleet. Darkness fell at midday, hands froze and shoes became sodden. But George skated with his brothers and friends on the Thames, and visited the 'greatest "frost fair" ever staged', with a grand mall running from Blackfriars Bridge.[33]

When the Duke of Wellington returned from defeating the enemy at the Peninsula, his father took twelve-year-old George to Westminster Hall. It was 1 July 1814, a day he cherished for the rest of his life. Everywhere, it seemed, were men of power strolling or strutting through the House. Although windows were firmly shut, nothing could lessen the stench of the Thames. But the whiff of British power was stronger, and all was forgotten as his hero approached.[34] George thrilled to the members of both Houses cheering the quintessential Englishman returning from war, to the Sergeant-at Arms carrying the gold mace and conducting the Duke of Wellington to a special chair at the central table, and to the entire Parliament rising 'as one man' and remaining standing throughout the Speaker's address. Sitting in the gallery of the Commons marked a turning point for him. From that day, he 'never withdrew [his] attention from public affairs'.[35]

At Merchant Taylors' it usually took four years for a clever pupil to win one of a number of scholarships to Oxford or Cambridge. But after two years, on St Barnabas day, 11 June 1815, George gave the Dean of St John's College, Oxford, such an impressive display of his ability in translating and reciting Latin and Greek prose and verse, of his mastery of Hebrew and his proficiency in geography, that he won a coveted place. He had just turned thirteen years old.[36]

But 'for family reasons' the scholarship was not taken up.[37]

Although a short time later a sixth child and first daughter, Hannah Cotterell Evans, was born, hardship was not the issue. The major handicap for the family involved religious intolerance and class. The two universities – Oxford and Cambridge – excluded Jews, Catholics and dissenters, as undergraduates had to swear by the thirty-nine articles of the Anglican faith. Oxford, then, was out of the question for George. Besides, his father disliked his son being exposed to the corrupting influences of the era. It was the Regency period (1811–20) when scandals and dissipation abounded, when bucks led racy lives of self-indulgence and vicious sport, and when the Prince Regent – who set the tone – was famously described by Leigh Hunt as a 'corpulent . . . violator of his word, a libertine . . . the Companion of gamblers and demi-reps'. The paragons of George's generation were mostly privileged gentlemen from the two universities who could easily adopt Adam Smith's theory that, 'for a man to push his own fortunes as actively as he could was actually the best way in which he could serve his fellow man'.[38]

George's character was built on tougher ground. For the next nine years he worked in apprenticeship for the ministry. For two years he tutored at his father's school and taught his brothers. In 1817, aged fifteen, he progressed to the dissenters' Hoxton Academy in London, one of the leading schools of its kind.[39] Here he spent four years studying the Greek and Hebrew testaments, poetry and natural science. He read Gibbon and the philosophies of David Hume, Voltaire, Thomas Reid and John Locke. He also followed events closely, joining the shockwave of protest that swept the country after the savage struggle at Peterloo in August 1819.

In the new year of 1822 George followed his younger brother Richard to Wymondley College in Hertfordshire, the famous theological college for dissenters, for two more years of study.[40] At twenty-two he was just a step away from the ministry. Then he became ill and was forced to resign.

For a long time George had wrestled inwardly with his father's expectations and his own ambitions. He was typical of the many young men of the time for whom the 'necessity to force [himself] into a rigid mould inevitably produced psychological conflicts, often kept underground'.[41] Two more daughters, Mary (b. 1817) and Claudia (b. 1822), had brought the family's total to eight children. Equally frustrated by the distractions of living in a clamorous household and the burden of responsibility that accompanied his position in the family, George escaped frequently to the Williams' Dissenting Library in Cripplegate to browse through some of its rare collection.[42] He was especially interested in studying 'the peculiarities of personal idiosyncrasy' – a kind of nascent psychology.[43]

And opportunities had been multiplying for people of George's background. The middle classes were securing their claims to social prestige and political power. The visiting French Magistrate Alexis de Tocqueville observed that, unlike in France, anyone enriched by mercantile interests in England could enter the ranks of the upper classes. He noted also the 'democratic spirit' that had 'made startling progress among them.'[44]

While recuperating from his illness, George preached for a while at the Zion Chapel in Birmingham. His fame spread and the pews filled rapidly. He fulfilled his obligations, but he finally summoned the courage to beg his father to send him to Glasgow University. Many English gentlemen were encouraging their sons to go to the Scottish universities, where the standards of teaching and achievement were impressive, and the subject range was broader.[45]

There may have been a formidable clash of wills between father and son, but Reverend Evans submitted with good grace, and nine long years after winning his scholarship to Oxford, George travelled to Glasgow. He moved into living quarters typical at the time, where students could read only by the light from a half-opened shutter, with little heat, a scarcity of water and plenty of dirt.[46] In a squalid city with a crude sewerage system, typhus, smallpox and measles were rife, and George again fell desperately ill. It is likely he succumbed to smallpox, as a photograph shows what look like the classic scars of the disease.[47]

Reverend Evans prayed endlessly for his son, but it was not until late November that he could tell his wife from Birmingham, 'the recovery of George's health is a very great blessing'. His paternal letters of instruction to Hannah, aged nine, also contained a note of wistful pride in her eldest brother:

> The people [in Birmingham] say that [George] is quite learned enough, and that if he would come and be their Minister, they should soon have the largest congregation in the Town, which I think would be the case . . . . When [the parishioners] had a good piece of roast beef for dinner here they used to tell George that the Scotchies at Glasgow would only give him oatmeal porridge, he said he thought he should be tired of them altogether very soon. Poor fellow I am afraid there [*sic*] cold mornings will not suit him.[48]

When his strength returned, George found a Glasgow simmering with discontent. Employer–employee relations were so dire that when Pitt's Combination Act of 1800 was repealed, legalising the right to strike, rioting became so frequent that armed cavalry patrolling the city's streets became a common sight. But his years at Glasgow (1824–27) were probably some of his happiest. After life at Mile End with such a large and busy family, Glasgow College in High Street was a haven of quiet peace, consisting of two courts separated by a tall steeple and embraced from behind by a huge garden. George studied alongside sons of local farmers and labourers and clever young men from throughout Britain. He sailed on the Clyde River in paddle steamers. And he threw himself into his studies, covering himself with glory.

In his first year he won First Prize in Logic after giving an impressive oral display while seated on 'The Black Stone' – an antique chair – in front of his two hundred fellow students. He was 'perfectly accurate' in ancient and Aristotelian logic; in modern logic, including the theory of evidence; in various Greek and Latin texts; in the philosophy of grammar, taste and criticism; and in the art of rhetoric.[49] The students' vote was unanimous, said Professor Reverend R. Buchanan, who paid tribute to George's 'remarkable powers of illustration, readiness of elocution, and . . . flow of nervous eloquence'.[50] His 'acute and vigorous intellect . . . and prompt and excursive imagination' helped him excel in moral and natural philosophy – the metaphysical, ethical and political doctrines of the great philosophers.[51]

It was in Latin that he achieved the highest distinction, in his study of Virgil's *Aeneid*, Livy, the plays of Plautus and the satires of Persius. And after devouring the entire works of Thucydides, Aristotle, Aeschylus, Euripides and Aristophanes, his Greek tutor Professor Sandford wrote, 'In genius, in love of ancient literature . . . [George] has few superiors. His exertions here were crowned with great honour and reputation.' Rector Thomas Campbell agreed, saying, 'I can say, as Professor Sandford said, after publicly examining you, "I never heard Greek better interpreted".'[52]

George was undoubtedly a brilliant scholar, but perhaps the most significant events for him at Glasgow were his meeting and being befriended by two famous men who would exert a profound influence on him for at least the next decade.

The first was Henry Brougham (1778–1868), the college's rector for 1825. Like George, Brougham had won a scholarship to university – in his case Edinburgh – at the age of thirteen. In 1802 he had been a co-founder of the *Edinburgh Review*, the ground-breaking quarterly that embraced literature, politics, philosophy, mathematics and science. Brougham was an outspoken politician, a great orator, a law reformer and a barrister of prodigious talents. Following the scandal of George IV's divorce suit against Queen Caroline in 1820, Brougham's brilliant defence of the Queen had cemented his reputation. A tall, erect man with an expressive angular face, he was a respected yet unpopular public figure: 'His temper was irritable, he was easily excited' and rash.[53] In his address to the students, Brougham reminded them that their education incurred a personal responsibility to better mankind. He spoke of James Watt, the Scot who proved that the working man's daily toil could lead to the highest intellectual achievement:

> Assuming the improvements of his own mind and the lot of his fellow-creatures to be the great end of every man's existence, who is removed above the care of providing for his sustenance, and to be the indispensable duty of every man, as far as his own immediate wants leave him any portion of time unemployed, our attention is naturally directed to the means by which so great and urgent a work may best be formed.[54]

In 1826, the popular Glaswegian poet, Thomas Campbell (1777–1844) succeeded Brougham as rector. The youngest of eleven children of a Virginian tobacco merchant, Campbell had won fame throughout the country with his poem, 'The Pleasures of Hope' (1799), which was a passionate plea for civil and religious freedom. His powerful passage on the sufferings of the oppressed Poles had struck a chord with thinking people everywhere.[55]

Several years before becoming rector, Campbell had announced his intention to found a university in London open to all classes and creeds, but it was Brougham who acted on the idea, consulting and including Campbell, and rallying support from influential and radical dissenters like the Quaker banker, Joseph Gurney, and the Jewish bullion broker, Sir Isaac Goldsmid. He introduced a Bill in the House of Commons for a charter in May 1825, but hearing it would be thrown out by Peel and the Lords he withdrew it and called a public meeting to offer shares to the public at £100 each. Land was soon purchased in Gower Street, and the University of London was formally founded and divided into two faculties: Arts and Law, and Medicine.[56] Its foundation was the birth of a new idea: it provided training for specific professions: medicine, law, engineering and teaching. As George observed these events unfold during his time at Glasgow, Brougham's actions in response to the hostile Lords left a deep impression on him.

After scarcely two and a half years at Glasgow, Evans graduated Master of Arts first class with the highest honours at the end of April 1827, with a special commendation by the principal, Dr Duncan Macfarlan.[57] He had already been ordained by his father, possibly during a visit home in June 1825, when the new chapel for the Reverend Evans's congregation, which had been built from benefactors' funds, was dedicated. Brunswick Chapel in Mile End Road was one of the more notable of the Congregational churches: an imposing stone building adorned by grand towers and turrets, with a parsonage, almshouses and schoolrooms attached.[58]

On his return to London in 1827, perhaps in fulfilment of a promise to his father, George agreed to become minister of the Congregational Church in White Row, Spitalfields, but, to his father's lasting disappointment, he did not take up his duties – or at least he did so for only a short time.[59]

He had been encouraged, probably by Brougham, Campbell and his professors – who 'looked forward' to his 'not only useful but brilliant' future as a classics tutor – to apply for London University's Chair in Greek for its inaugural academic year of 1828. He began to acquire testimonials from his professors and mentors.[60] In November the position of headmaster of Mill Hill School was advertised. George may have made a quick calculation – the Greek Chair was an infinitely more attractive prospect for his talents than the position of minister in the poorest part of London, and if he were selected, he could complete the academic year at Mill Hill in time to take up the post at London. His younger brother Richard had been ordained in 1826, so George might have felt less of an obligation to fulfil his father's wishes. He duly submitted an application to Mill Hill, was accepted and made preparations to begin duties after the Christmas break.

It may have been more than a coincidence that less than a month after Evans took up his position there, Brougham was proclaiming to the House:

> There have been periods when the country heard with dismay that the soldier was abroad in the land. That is not the case now. Let the soldier be ever so much abroad, in the present age he can do nothing. There is another person abroad . . . . The schoolmaster is abroad, and I trust to the schoolmaster armed with his primer more than I do to the soldier in full military array for upholding and extending the liberties of the country.[61]

CHAPTER TWO.

HEADMASTER AND REFORMER

> We are in an age . . . of flashing eyes and curling lips, more easily touched, more easily shocked, more ready to spurn, to flaunt, to admire, and, above all, to preach.
>
> G. M. Young (ed.), *Early Victorian England, 1830–1865*, Oxford University Press, London, 1934, Vol. 2, p.425

Located near Golders Green in the parish of Hendon, Mill Hill Grammar School was founded in 1807 for the sons of professional dissenters. For some time, it had struggled to attract pupils. The old Ridgeway House had been replaced with an impressive new building designed by Sir William Tite, but the school's inherent problem lay in its administration. No fewer than five sub-committees were answerable to a general committee. This led to continual problems of communication, access and delegation, and interfered with the day-to-day running of the school.[1]

When George Evans was appointed, the school had been managed for two years by Reverend Henry March, a well-meaning but insecure chaplain who had been recommended by the eminent Dr John Pye Smith, a committee member. March was ill-equipped for the role and felt keenly his lack of 'classical attainments'.[2] His diary is filled with entries complaining of the boys' 'levity', insolence and lack of respect.

The pupils were no happier. There was no organised sport and periods of play were brief. Exeats were few and the students were taken for walks outside the school boundaries only once or twice every half-term. Added to this, the endless prayers and pious sermonising had a depressing and unsettling effect on them.

Before the summer break of 1827, March had complained privately to both the house and education committees that the servants, most of the masters and the matron Mrs Harriet Riddiford were 'worldly minded'.[3] Mrs Riddiford received a written rebuke from the committee, 'acutely perceived' the part March had played and immediately tackled him after the break. An outraged staff shunned March, and the temporary headmaster, Dr Corrie, resigned. The committee retaliated by enlarging March's powers to include supervision of the domestic and moral tone of the school, and by confining the incoming headmaster's duties to the classical and school departments.

After Christmas break, a week went by before Reverend G. S. Evans, MA, burst into the school full of apologies. March's disapproval was strong: 'He has been beating about at sea in a vessel, when he ought to have been here teaching. An inauspicious beginning.'

Evans soon created a more favourable impression, although March was aghast at his youth. 'It is certain', he wrote, 'he is only twenty-four [although] his conversation showed him to be clever and ardent.'[4] March was determined to regard him 'simply as the first classical master', but to his chagrin Evans proved to be a gifted teacher who had no trouble earning his pupils' respect and admiration. He cut an impressive figure with his height, broad chest and strong build. And he had a voice to match – a powerful stentorian instrument that quickly captured the boys' attention. When Reverend Dr Mayo, a Fellow of St John's College, Oxford, paid an 'accidental visit' to the school, he observed Evans teaching the senior Greek class, and noted his 'enthusiastic attachment . . . calculated to excite a kindred feeling in the minds of his pupils'.[5] With March's approval, Evans revived the monitorial system that had been abolished earlier,[6] but, unlike the newly appointed headmaster of Rugby Public School, Thomas Arnold, Evans was unable to introduce his own ideas for the curriculum or school because of the committee's constant interference. His circumscribed role was an insult.

Despite the fact that the school now had an able headmaster who fulfilled his duties quickly and efficiently, every Sunday in chapel March's nightmare played on, with the boys 'covering their faces and showing other signs of indifference', and the masters on duty unable to keep order. March offered to resign, but the committee begged him to stay.

Dr Pye Smith, ever March's champion, visited Evans to complain about his frequent absences from his study, but with Evans's energies frustrated, he had to find stimulation elsewhere. It is likely he visited the slavery reformer William Wilberforce (1759–1833) on Highwood Hill, an active parishioner and school benefactor who entertained March and other staff regularly. Evans might have discussed with Wilberforce the issues of the day. The Test and Corporations Act of Charles II was repealed in February that year, 1828, and opened the door to protestant dissenters – who numbered two million out of a population of thirteen million – to hold public office in Britain.[7] Lord Chancellor Eldon summed up the establishment's hostility to the repeal, saying it was 'as bad, as mischievous and as revolutionary as the most captious Dissenter would wish it to be'. But it would not be until 1867 that dissenters had any real chance of holding office.[8]

Evans had also found another interest. He had barely raised his head from his books and ceased his religious duties when he realised he was drawn to the charms and companionship of the matron. The boys thrilled to the romantic attachment between their 'popular' headmaster and the kindly matron. To their delight, Evans displayed the usual courtesies of a 'newly-engaged gentleman, taking Matron on his arm into the hall at prayers, and tea-time'. Frederick, the younger brother of Tom Helmore, who was captain of Evans's senior class, recorded the ensuing events over fifty years later:

> Mischievous reports having been spread relating to these polite attentions, which in the minds of the head-master and the boys were perfectly harmless and innocent, resulted in a communication of an insulting character from the Secretary of Committee.
>
> This letter determined the head-master to instant resignation.[9]

Evans's reaction was impulsive as he felt his honour was being impugned, but he reassured the shocked Tom Helmore that he intended to vindicate his character on Public Day, the last day of the school year. In turn the fearless Helmore, sporting an impressive set of whiskers and at full height at the age of sixteen, secretly consulted his classmates, all of whom were bitterly angry at the forced resignation of their 'beloved' tutor, and planned an uprising in support.

Public Day fell on 26 June, when parents and friends arrived to watch their sons perform and receive reports from their masters. It was a fine, warm day but there were fewer visitors than usual. March, whose resignation had also reluctantly been accepted, believed there had been none of the usual preparation for the boys' recitations on the stage, and expected the exhibition to be 'a miserable one'. But he was pleasantly surprised to find that in a short time Evans's skills had been rewarded by the boys' finest work. The recitations were fewer and shorter, but were 'more calmly and simply spoken, and therefore more agreeable . . . than I have ever yet heard them'.

During dinner there were the usual toasts to March and the teachers, but no mention made of the headmaster or his resignation. Evans rose, acknowledged the toast on behalf of his colleagues, and referred to 'the testimonies . . . paid to his class by three fellows of colleges, and other vaunts; and then spoke of the distressing feelings with which he addressed them, being for the last time'.[10]

The parents' dismayed reaction caused an angry committee member, Mr Yockney, to rise and accuse Evans of announcing his resignation without first informing the committee. But Yockney was out of order as Evans's letter of resignation had been minuted by the committee two days earlier in Yockney's absence. Evans leaped to his feet to correct him, but at that moment, the door to the hall burst open, and forty boys of the senior class led by Thomas Helmore 'marched into the hall, up to the front of the platform, and gave three hearty cheers for the headmaster':

> An attempt was made by some of the Committee and one or two of the masters to turn them out. Upon which [the boys] mounted to the platform amidst the screams of the ladies, who fled precipitately, [the boys] pitched into the committee, some of whom they pommelled severely, and finally cleared the hall. Coachmen, footmen, and school-servants were summoned to turn the rebels out. This they did without coming to a fight, most of them admiring the pluck of the lads to whom they touched their hats as they retired from the battle-field.[11]

Amongst the noise and confusion, the shaken chairman declared, somewhat unnecessarily, the ceremony adjourned. But not content with the disruption of the official programme, the senior class had arranged for the boys of the second class to carry all the benches down to the pond and hurl them in. Word quickly spread to the younger boys, who rushed to the passage by the linen room and turned on the taps of thirty urns filled with boiling tea made by matron for the visitors. A full-scale riot had erupted at Mill Hill School.

The school's 'servants' stood aside in tacit support, while bewildered relatives pursued committee members for answers, and the matron and headmaster rushed after the boys, who finally heeded their frantic exhortations.

There is one surprising twist to this story. It may not have been known to the boys, or perhaps even when Frederick Helmore wrote of his brother's experience fifty years after the event, but it exonerates, to a certain degree, the committee's harsh conduct.

Mrs Riddiford was already married and her husband Daniel lived in the parish of St Michael Bassishaw, in the heart of the old city of London. He was a merchant who had been in partnership in Basinghall Street with Henry Hughes, who was married to his wife's sister Elizabeth. The partnership had dissolved and Daniel became bankrupt, probably causing his wife to take up her position as matron. The pair might have separated, and it seems that Mrs Riddiford was apparently not averse to attention from other men, as the committee's earlier rebuke and sudden resignation of Dr Corrie may suggest. Daniel Riddiford died the following year and was buried – not as a pauper – on 26 April 1829 at St Michael Bassishaw.

This experience at Mill Hill had a profound impact on Evans. It is inconceivable – although not impossible – that he did not know of Harriet's husband and it is unlikely the couple became engaged while Daniel was alive. His attentions to her were most probably no more than those of a gentleman, but one who was clearly interested.

Evans felt his honour had been impugned by his fellow dissenters. Already a highly sensitive man, the seed of bitterness sown here would grow over the ensuing years with each real or imagined slight. Along with the narrow self-righteousness of the dissenter, his mistrust of others and his removal of himself to loftier but lonelier ground would be misinterpreted by many of his contemporaries in later life as the conduct of a man who believed himself to be superior. It was not an uncommon trait but was quite probably his Achilles heel. After Mill Hill, he appears professionally never to have used his title, Reverend, again.

❧

There had been many applicants for the Chair in Greek at the new University of London, and when the choice finally came down to Evans and George Long, Professor of Ancient Languages at the University of Virginia, Evans was unsuccessful.[12] Brougham's persistence in his establishment of the new university in the face of government rejection was a gamble that paid off, and the university rose 'at once to the first rank' and flourishes to this day.[13]

After the summer break, and encouraged probably by several of the boys and their parents – and no doubt the matron – George Evans opened a school at Waterloo Cottage on the corner of Willesden Lane and the High Road, Kilburn, which was then a hamlet at the south-west end of Hampstead. Several of the boys from Mill Hill followed him, Tom Helmore went as an assistant and continued to receive tuition, and Harriet accompanied Evans as matron.

A year later his school's success forced Evans to seek larger premises. With his father's assistance he borrowed £400 from Mary Day of Bristol, a benefactor and dissenter. In July 1829, notices appeared in the *Morning Chronicle* and *The Times* informing 'the friends of his pupils' that he had 'removed his establishment from

Kilburn to North End House, Hampstead', and that the school would reopen on 27 July.[14]

Hampstead was then only five miles north of the city, but a whole world away with its clean air, famed mineral spring, small cottages with red-tiled roofs, and many quaint inns. North End House in North End Place, a substantial two-storeyed mansion with stables and grounds that had once belonged to Lord North, was perfect. The poet Coleridge was a neighbour, living in South Grove from 1816 to 1832.[15]

Finally, nine months after her husband's death, Harriet married Evans on 16 January 1830 at St John's, Hampstead. Helmore noted approvingly that Harriet 'madc an excellent wife and manager, contributing a great deal to the comfort and happiness of the household'. Not long after, Tom left Evans to teach at his own father's school.[16]

At the age of twenty-eight, Evans's marriage to thirty-eight-year-old Harriet made him a stepfather to her two children – Daniel born in 1814 and Amelia in 1817. A portrait of Harriet shows a handsome woman with large dark eyes, thick brunette hair topped by an elaborate confection of feathers, and a determined, strong jaw. Although not without some means, Harriet was relieved to have made the advantageous match in turbulent times. To this day, the Riddiford family refers to her as the High Stepper, in reference to her fortunate marriage as much as to her imperious manner. She was a strong, indomitable woman, well-matched by her husband. In marrying her, Evans found stability and irrevocably stepped away from his father's powerful influence.

In 1830, the prospectus of Evans's Academy offered a range of study and a form of discipline very advanced for its time – even revolutionary. More advanced even than that of Thomas Arnold at Rugby, it would not be for another thirty-odd years that a similar curriculum was attempted, at Clifton College, Bristol, under its headmaster, John Percival.[17] Evans believed that the system pursued at the grammar schools of England was 'fundamentally erroneous'; and that 'time may be redeemed from the exclusive pursuit of the dead languages . . . for the study of the mathematics, modern languages, arithmetic, writing, drawing and other accomplishments essential to the character of the gentleman and the man of business'.[18]

The usual Greek, Latin and Hebrew were offered with the addition of French, German and Italian. The physical sciences were not forgotten, as pupils could explore 'the peculiar botanical resources of Hampstead'. In an innovative move, Evans taught geography and history by incorporating the geography and history of ancient and modern times 'in one continuous chain of instruction on the history of the globe and its inhabitants'. Fencing was preferred to 'the more violent of the gymnastic exercises', and optional courses of dancing, pianoforte and the flute were offered at six guineas per year. Food would be of the best quality, 'unrestricted' in quantity. Most unusually, Evans eschewed corporal punishment, 'reserving' it only 'for occasions of moral delinquency' and replacing it with a system of fines taken from a weekly allowance of one shilling.[19]

Parents were invited to attend the examination of Evans's classes. The poet and former rector of Glasgow University, Thomas Campbell, paid a visit to test the senior and junior classes. The examinations produced a dazzling display of Greek and Latin, French and history. The senior class had also studied 'with diligence the first six books of Euclid, plane trigonometry, and algebra, as far as quadratic equations'.[20]

Campbell became a frequent visitor. His wife had died, leaving him a lonely widower with one child deceased and the other incurably insane. He was a fragile man, unable to fend for himself, but he found comfort amongst his friends. Soon, Golders Green and Hampstead Heath became favourite rambling haunts for Campbell and Evans. Both Campbell and Brougham were members of the exclusive Literary Club in London, and as Evans's friendships with these men grew, visits to the club became a regular feature of his walks about the city.[21]

It was probably here that Evans was introduced to Dr John Black (1783–1855), the editor of the intellectual liberal paper, the *Morning Chronicle*. The uncompromising Black, who numbered among his friends the reformers Jeremy Bentham and Henry Brougham, hired Evans to write articles and report events, and quickly became another mentor and friend. Interestingly, these men – Brougham, Black and Campbell – had excitable, proud temperaments and were of Evans's father's generation; and all, like his father, were his greatest influences. Black had issued a dozen challenges to duels before he turned thirty.[22] Brougham was temperamental and unpopular, in spite of being regarded as the 'ablest public man of his generation', and was perhaps the most significant leader for reform. Even Campbell was described by a close friend as having 'after his own wayward fashion, a great deal of ambition in him . . . too much pride and hauteur . . . ready to fire up at the remotest indication of a slight or affront'.[23]

Through Black, Evans met John Stuart Mill (whose father James was a particular friend of Black), reformer Henry Parkes, and eventually the courteous and clever Charles Buller.[24] Evans also met and would make a lifelong friend of the non-conformist solicitor Richard Davies Hanson (1805–76) through the *Morning Chronicle* and also through his writing for the *Globe*.[25] Evans was introduced by Brougham to Thomas Barnes, editor of *The Times*, an equally strong advocate for reform for whom Evans began to write ardently in its cause.[26]

The year 1830 was a benchmark for Evans. It was a time of significant radical restlessness, when cries for parliamentary reform, repeal of the Corn Laws and cheap bread were hard to ignore. Labourers demanded higher wages, attacked farmers, destroyed their threshing machines and burned hayricks. Coinciding neatly with the end of the school year, on 26 June 1830 George IV died, King William succeeded him and there was a general election a month later. The Congregationalists formed their own union, a revolution broke out in Paris and Louis Phillipe replaced Charles X in a virtually bloodless coup.[27]

The reformers wanted universal suffrage, shorter-term parliaments and a closer surveillance of members by their constituents.[28] The question of abolishing the rotten boroughs was the most urgent. For a handful of votes a man could enter Parliament and influence the decision-making process for the entire country. Evans was eager to see this sort of abuse of Parliament eliminated. Later in Parliament he recalled the issues at stake. He had observed:

> Hundreds of men who had stood on a platform at an election, but who ought to have been standing on a very different sort of scaffolding; hundreds also who merely went into the House of Commons for the purpose of escaping their creditors, and he had known these men anxiously watch for the close of Parliament, in order that before the forty days expired, which was allowed them by law, they might clear out of the jurisdiction of the Westminster Courts. They would then go to Boulogne, or some other place, where they could make their arrangements for again entering Parliament as soon as it was necessary for them to do so.[29]

Another of their goals was to redress inequalities in representation. In the county of Middlesex, for example, few of the population of between 800,000 and 900,000 had representation. Evans and most reformers could clearly see that, as things stood, the country was 'governed by a minority in the partial interests of the minority'.[30] But, as Evans said, nearly twenty-eight years later, he 'would rather see a powerful minority of gentlemen, if they represented the interests of the country in the House, than that they should be fretting out of doors because they had been shut out from the legislation of their country':

> Joseph Hume first entered into Parliament through a rotten borough. How, I would ask, did Wilberforce and other champions of reform find their way into Parliament? All of them went in by a rotten borough. How was it that they could reconcile to their consciences to enter by such means? It was because England at that time had not made any provision for the representation of minorities.[31]

In Parliament the Tories' ideal of a 'hierarchical and aristocratic society' was so deeply entrenched that any democratic idea or notion of reform was anathema to them.[32] Prime Minister the Duke of Wellington had exemplified this attitude in September 1830: when the Liverpool and Manchester railway was opened he protested that it might encourage 'the lower classes to travel about'. Although the Whigs – under aristocrats like Lord Grey and Lord John Russell, and backed by merchants, manufacturers and dissenters – shared many of the Tories' fears, they realised that the upheaval in Europe indicated that reform at home would be the only alternative to revolution.[33]

After Wellington's resignation on 15 November 1830, King William asked Lord Grey (1764–1845) to form a government. Ten days later, Brougham – who was mistrusted by both the King and Grey – was offered the Chancellorship and elevated to the peerage with the title of Baron Brougham and Vaux. But the honour was double-edged, as it all but gagged him and he was excluded from the committee chosen to work on the draft Reform Bill.

At the end of the year, Glasgow College's Senate unanimously agreed to grant Evans a Doctorate of Civil and Canon Law – LLD – a degree conferred by Royal 'Decree' or 'Commission'. This usually followed a published treatise or significant contribution of some kind by the recipient.[34]

The eighteen months leading up to the passing of the Reform Bill were charged with heady drama. Evans was in his element, attending Parliament, penning articles, bringing his proselytising zeal to the platform, and enjoying the cut and thrust of debate in the salons and clubs. In his writing for the newspapers and speeches, he had honed his skills in the 'language of menace' that stopped short of revolutionary incitement.[35] He joined men like Buller, Richard Ricardo Jr and Mill's friends and followers in a group that became known as the 'philosophic radicals'.[36] Roebuck said their style of writing in radical papers such as the *Morning Chronicle* and the *Globe* made all classes 'reason after a new fashion . . . according to principles wholly different from those to which they had been previously accustomed'.[37] Their papers regularly sold 40,000 copies, swamping the combined effort of the Tory papers the *Morning Post* and the *Standard*.

On 1 March 1831 when Lord John Russell introduced his first Reform Bill to the House of Commons, reporters and reformers jostled past people from all parts of the country to listen to him read the list of the rotten boroughs his Bill proposed to disenfranchise, and the seats he wished to create, including Manchester, Leeds and Birmingham. If his Bill succeeded, London would gain eight seats and the national electorate would be increased by about 500,000 men – including the 283,000 who lived in Reverend Evans's area, the Tower Hamlets.[38] But the attempt failed, William dissolved Parliament on St George's Day, 23 April, and the mob attacked anti-reformists, mostly peers.[39]

Evans travelled all over the city to address meetings, urging his audiences to throw their support behind the liberals (Whigs) rather than any of the government's traditional followers – the church and the breweries. At one parish meeting he recalled:

> . . . one burly Boniface [had been] remonstrated with for his apparent breach of faith with the Liberal Party, in supporting the clergyman, 'Why', said he, 'the licensed *wittlers* [victuallers] always goes with the regular clergy'. (Great laughter.) These were two public institutions supported by the State. He [Evans] was surprised that those who were interested in carrying through the length and breadth of the land the cause of the greatest demoralisation, should be so anxious to send in the same train the tithe-paid and State-supported clergy.[40]

At the general election the Whigs swept into power, giving the reformers an overwhelming majority. On 21 June, the King opened Parliament and Russell introduced his second attempt at reform. The *Morning Chronicle* predicted prolonged agitation and stagnating trade if it failed.[41] On its third reading in September, the Bill was carried by over a hundred votes and sent to the House of Lords who threw out the Bill by forty-one votes. There were huge demonstrations in London.[42]

Russell's third Bill looked as if it might succeed. Parliament reassembled in mid-January, but the Asiatic cholera, which had spread throughout the country, reached London in February, so it was not until 23 March that the Commons passed the third reading. On that same day, Evans's father, on behalf of a deputation from the Tower Hamlets and presented by Lord Melbourne, read a submission to King William in support of Lord Russell's measure for parliamentary reform at Court.[43]

The Lords' second reading squeaked through with a majority of nine votes on 13 April, but in May Lord Lyndhurst's motion stalled the process, Grey resigned and the country's constitutional future hung in the balance. The Tories couldn't form a government so the King was forced to ask again for Grey who, abetted by Brougham, shrewdly asked for the power to create enough new peers to guarantee the Bill. The King's Secretary, Sir Herbert Taylor, immediately sent a circular to the most trenchant Tory opponents urging them to approve the Bill, and it went through the Committee stage in six days.[44]

On 3 June, Evans celebrated his thirtieth birthday in his usual flurry of activity. End of term was looming, but there was a hasty visit to the city to await the third reading of the Bill the next day. Many of the peers were absent in protest, and the vote went 106 to 22 in favour. The King gave his royal assent on 7 June and there were banquets, fireworks, illuminations and the sound of church bells throughout London.

In extending the franchise, redistributing seats and creating forty-three new boroughs, the Reform Bill gave the middle classes of industry and business a significant share of representation in the House of Commons and opened the door for further reform. Certainly, the impetus for civil and religious reform was never allowed to falter in either of the Evans households. In July, Evans's father presented a petition to the King on behalf of his congregation, 'praying for the early and entire emancipation of all slaves throughout the British Empire'.[45]

Decades later Evans recalled that the reformers had been treated with 'scorn and derision'.[46] But they had persisted, and years after the Bill, Lord Russell was to say, 'I know the dissenters, they carried the Reform Bill; they carried the abolition of slavery; they carried Free Trade; and they'll carry the abolition of Church rates.'[47]

☙

By this time, according to their neighbour Edward Betts Hopper, Evans and his wife were a 'highly respected' team. Betts Hopper was a member of the Church of England Society, but by no means uncritical of his religion's organisation. He shared his neighbours' interest in reform, enjoyed their hospitality, and took many long walks with Evans and Campbell over the heath. He recorded scraps of their conversations in his diary. When Evans read aloud of the mob throwing 'dirt and filth' at the Duke of Wellington after the Bill, Campbell exclaimed, 'Dirt and filth! Indeed there is no dirt and filth in it till it touched him!'

Campbell also satisfied Harriet's curiosity with a story illustrating his belief that Lord Byron's daughter had 'a little of the devil in her', like her father. When he had called on her mother, the seven-year-old was 'nursing a beautifull [*sic*] Prussian cat'. He asked her, 'Well, Miss Byron, and does your cat mew in the Prussian language?' 'You fool', replied the child, 'do you think the cat could mew in Prussian?'[48]

On a fine Sunday not long after the passage of the Reform Bill, Evans and Betts Hopper walked to Westminster Abbey, on the way enjoying the panoramic view from Highgate Road on the heath. They crossed the fields to climb Primrose Hill and came upon a follower of Robert Owen (the so-called father of English socialism), who:

> . . . with all the pomp of an unwashed artificer, with his greasy coat buttoned to his chin to hide the deficiency of a shirt, was holding forth to a number of equally respectable smutted operatives . . . . This unwashed orator was endeavouring to persuade his audience that . . . [his] were the only true principles . . . . He exclaimed violently against the non-productive classes of society. All shopkeepers [were] useless . . . beings . . . and so on with all others who follow any occupation for profit.[49]

'Tired of listening to his sophistry', said Betts Hopper, they proceeded to the Abbey where they attended a 'farcical' service conducted by a young curate who received only three shillings and sixpence. 'Who receives the rest of the revenue?', they wondered, appalled at the uneven distribution of church funds. They called on Campbell at the Literary Club, who invited them to dine at wool-broker Mr Hughes's home in Finsbury Square. Hughes had been 'a great and active promoter of the progressive improvements of Van Diemen's Land, having an interest in the grant of land given to the Company of that Island'.[50] Evans's interest in the subject of colonisation may have been awakened that night, but by then he had been encouraged by his friends to study for the Bar.

Possibly having been sponsored by Brougham who was a distinguished member, he selected Lincoln's Inn for its Equity Counsel and Equity Courts.[51] He enrolled two months after the Reform Bill had been passed, in September 1832, and immersed himself in legal studies while juggling his school and other commitments.

But a career at the Bar would not be cheap. Rent for chambers could cost up to £60 per year. There would be a yearly round of assizes; two ten-week circuits cost £80 per circuit. Then there was accommodation and transport to consider; a horse was not a cheap item, nor was travel by coach.[52]

While studying for the Bar, Evans continued working for reform. In February 1832 Campbell had formed a new society supporting the struggle in Poland against Russian oppression. He asked Evans to act as honorary secretary and held the inaugural meeting of the Polish Society at his home in Duke Street, St James's Square. The society attracted several prominent people, including Lord Nugent, Adolphus Bach and Edward Duke Moore, and was officially launched after the Reform Bill's success with extensive advertising and publicity. Very soon it became one of the more notable and influential societies of the day.[53]

In August 1833, after the destitute Poles had fled France for Switzerland, about 1200 people crammed into the hall for a meeting of the Polish Society. Campbell, Evans and others presided on the stage. Accompanied by the radical MP Edward George Earle Bulwer-Lytton, the French magistrate Alexis de Tocqueville listened to speeches from Lord Morpeth and Joseph Hume. He also heard a 'Mr. Duffey' attack government members who had asked for alms, 'instead of protecting [Poland] effectively in Parliament'. For five minutes the crowd roared its approval of Duffey. De Tocqueville noted incredulously that the aristocrats had been 'put in the background without a word to say; or [were] being actually driven to flatter the passions of democracy, to buy its indulgence and to win its cheers'.[54]

From its opening in 1828, North End Academy had flourished.[55] But now Evans's fervent political interests meant that, while his commitment to education had not abated, there was less time for his role as headmaster and teacher. Consequently, he called on his brothers for help in running his school. Richard Evans had spent five years studying and tutoring at Wymondley Academy before being ordained as a minister. In 1830 he applied for the headmaster's post at Chatham and Rochester Classical and Mathematical School but apparently was not successful in his application. He continued tutoring in classics at Wymondley, leaving after the establishment of Coward College, and joined the staff at Evans's North End Academy some time at the beginning of the decade. It is probable he stayed on as acting head in Evans's absence; and also that Evans's younger brother James, aged twenty-two, taught at North End and acted as headmaster when neither George nor Richard was available.[56]

But in 1835 family tragedy struck. Richard Evans died, aged only twenty-nine, and his death was a grievous blow for the family.

Evans's formidable energy was matched by his intellectual curiosity. Being able to argue a question from every angle was a trait particularly common amongst educated men at the time, not just those training for the Bar. Especially in London, men were eager to exchange ideas and theories, to tailor a single view to serve every possible circumstance, and to probe ideas on every conceivable subject.[57] In the sciences great questions were being slowly answered, and Darwin had embarked on his five-year voyage of the *Beagle*. In religion the very existence of God was coming under the microscope; in politics, economic thought, socialism and democracy were being argued. Psychology was in its nascent stages.[58] Not for nothing had Thomas Macaulay called his generation in 1830, 'the most enlightened generation of the most enlightened people that ever existed'.[59]

In 1836 many of the key reformers, including Edward Ellice, Hume and Francis Place, founded the Reform Club, personally inviting a thousand men to become members. Evans was one of that number and was recorded as a Founding and Life Member at the club's launch on 24 May. Again he expanded his network, mingling with elder statesmen, noblemen, and captains of industry and commerce.[60]

While studying for the Bar, Evans must have weighed his chances of carving out for himself a successful legal career in England. The ranks of barristers were growing, and he knew at the age of thirty-four that he would be competing against younger men for briefs. As the eldest in his family, he had been imbued with familial responsibility from birth. It was a burden weighed down by what Thomas Carlyle called an Englishman's 'Hell': 'The terror of "not succeeding", of not making money, fame, or some other figure in the world, – chiefly of not making money! Is not that a somewhat singular Hell?'[61]

Evans shifted his focus to the colonies, with a vague idea of emigrating to India to practise at the Bar. To this end, in 1834, he had contacted George Long, the scholar who had pipped him for the Chair in Greek at London University, and studied Sanskrit under him for two years. As he excelled at languages, Evans had the capacity for this work and eventually gained a reputation for being a fine scholar of eastern languages.[62]

At the time the government viewed colonies with their governors and troops as 'expensive luxuries'.[63] The Colonial Office had pursued a flawed policy of Free Grant, where the Crown allowed the governor to set a 'fair price' on 'waste land' for would-be emigrants and absentee owners. But in North America particularly, which had attracted a wave of immigrants in the 1820s, large areas of waste lands had been left untouched by absentee landlords, while the Crown's lands were deemed insufficient for the needs of genuine emigrants.

Evans knew of Edward Gibbon Wakefield (1796–1862), a skilled writer and publicist with a charismatic personality and a criminal past. Wakefield's trial for the abduction of an under-age heiress had been widely publicised. Evans must have known of it, as Brougham had acted as Crown prosecutor during the trial.

During his three years' imprisonment, Wakefield had developed a plan for 'systematic colonization'. Two years after being released, he led an unsuccessful attempt to colonise South Australia, helped by promoters such as Richard Davies Hanson, Evans's colleague from the *Morning Chronicle*, and Betts Hopper, either of whom must have discussed the plan with Evans.[64] After its failure, Colonel Robert Torrens, Wakefield and others formed the South Australia Association with more success, the South Australian Bill being passed in August 1834. They had also 'won their first point when, in 1831–32 free grants of land were abolished in New South Wales, and sale by auction at a minimum price was substituted, the proceeds to be devoted to the transport of emigrants to the colony. The establishment in 1834 under Act of Parliament of the Colony of South Australia . . . [embodied Wakefield's] own leading principles.'[65]

Ever restless, in the summer break of 1836 Evans took his wife and stepdaughter to Paris to begin an exploration of Europe. It has been suggested by more than one biographer that Evans became involved from the start in the negotiations that formed the South Australia Company, but there is no evidence to support the theory.[66] By the time the family returned from Europe, Evans's attention had been diverted from affairs in England to those in South Australia, and he visited Downing Street to inquire about its land regulations. After waiting for ninety minutes in the anteroom, he was given only a lithographed Paper of Regulations, although he asked several times for more details. Frustrated, he moved on to the South Australian Board in the Adelphi where he was given all the information he needed.[67]

Probably directed there by the Board, Evans met Wakefield in early September on board the ship *Coromandel*, which was crammed with emigrants for Australia. Wakefield accepted his invitation to dine at North End House, where Evans told him of his ambition to practise law in Calcutta. Wakefield cautioned Evans against it, saying he had a better idea for him. The two men were standing in front of a globe, Wakefield carefully turning it. When New Zealand rose to the top, Wakefield said, 'Let us colonize New Zealand!' But he asked Evans to wait until they had received further information.[68]

Wakefield immediately approved of Evans. The younger man's zeal and energy, combined with his influential contacts and evident skills in writing boded well. Both were dissenters – though nominally Anglican, Wakefield came from a Quaker background – and both were eldest sons who had been raised to fight for reform and whose fathers had been absent for long periods.[69] The two men complemented each other – Wakefield understanding men, Evans understanding ideas. Where Wakefield thought of the grand plan and left it to others to fill in the details, Evans was a profound thinker for whom detail was necessary to sustain any argument.

But there were differences between them as well. Wakefield's formal education had been erratic and marked by brawls, resulting in moves to different institutions.[70] And where Evans was impetuous and outspoken, Wakefield 'was never simple and straightforward [but] . . . calculating and self-contained'.[71] He was 'regarded with unalterable suspicion by those out of range of his persuasive voice, and the fascination of his personality', but he had 'a genius for talking people into doing what he was deterred from doing himself'. He was 'a sort of intellectual confidence man'.[72] Brougham also believed Wakefield to be a 'swindler', and must have tried to deter Evans from associating with him.[73] But Evans's desire to emigrate had been influenced by his wife, who saw greater opportunity in a new country for her son to fulfil his ambition of acquiring land for a farm.

Wakefield became a frequent visitor to North End House, charming his hosts and introducing Mr Platt, a 'catechist' who had just returned from New Zealand and gave a glowing account of the country. As well, there were several newly published works on New Zealand to whet Evans's appetite.[74] He had finally found his focus, and began steeping himself in the intricacies of international law.

CHAPTER THREE.
THE HARE AND THE TORTOISE

> The patriotism of early Victorian England, not yet blooded by the Crimean war and the Indian Mutiny, irritated by Napoleon III, or exalted by the vision of Empire, was at heart a pride in human capacity, which time had led to fruition in England; and in the great humanist, who brought all history to glorify the age of which he was the most honoured child, it heard its own voice speaking.
>
> G. M. Young (ed.), *Early Victorian England 1830–1865*, Oxford University Press, London, 1934, Vol. 2, p.419

In early 1837, Wakefield finally switched his attention to New Zealand. After 'maturing' his plan with the Hon. Francis Baring, an MP experienced in the work of colonisation, and enlisting his brother Captain Arthur Wakefield, he contacted Evans.[1] Baring was appointed chairman of the New Zealand Association (the Association), and Evans its honorary secretary.

After Evans had read Wakefield's works, *Sketch of a Proposal for Colonizing Australia* and *A Letter From Sydney*, he viewed Wakefield as 'one of the few great men' of their age. He could see great merit in Wakefield's scheme – built upon and modified by others – which consisted of 'organised emigration, and social and economic development'.[2] For Evans, Wakefield's plans for the 'transfer of society and the transplantation of empire' were a 'great view of colonization' and a 'scientific truth'. Wakefield, he believed, had discovered 'a great law in political economy, for which science he has done what Dalton did for chemistry – the one pointing out the law of "definite proportions" and the other that of "necessary relations"':

> Adam Smith and all the older economists spoke of Labour and Capital (or the savings of labour), as the elements of wealth. To these Mr. Wakefield added the 'Field of Production'. In the art of colonization this is land, and the application of principle as

> shewn in 'the sufficient price', the object of which is to secure the due proportion among the three elements. Other secondary consequences flow from it, but the primary one is what we have stated.[3]

The colonisation of New Zealand appeared to be a viable solution to the problems of the time. The advent of the railway had compounded the country's social problems of overcrowding and disease; between 1825 and 1835 fifty-four railway Acts had been passed, and in the year 1836–37 another thirty-nine Bills had added over a thousand miles to the country's railroads.[4] Homelessness also ballooned when the London and Blackwall railway destroyed 2,850 houses, dispossessing thousands.

In 1825 there had been an early attempt to colonise the country by a company spearheaded by John George Lambton. This had been aborted at the very last leg, when the expedition pulled off the country's coast and returned, incurring severe financial loss. In 1831, thirteen Maori chiefs had petitioned the King for British protection against ex-convicts, brawling whalers and traders, but it took another two years before James Busby was sent from New South Wales as British Resident. Although the British government signed a declaration conferring national sovereignty on the United Tribes of New Zealand in 1835, it had little real authority and scarcely any military support in the country. Adding to the sense of urgency, the French were showing interest in expanding their trade into the area for flax for ships' ropes and timber for spars. In 1837 two hundred missionaries and settlers petitioned the King for protection, alarmed by the lawlessness in the country, the lack of effective official control and the inability of the missionaries to maintain order.[5]

But the government baulked at the expense of administering colonies and seemed determined to do as little as possible. Its Colonial Office had enormous problems with the colonies it administered – 'revolt in Canada, wars in South Africa, turmoil in the West Indies' – and Australia was little more than a convenient dumping ground for convicts.[6] The Office's policy of 'free grant' of land in its colonies was seriously flawed, even though the Crown occasionally charged an 'average price'. 'In the British North American colonies, where the system had had its longest trial, such large tracts of land had passed into the hands of individuals or associations, often absentee, that the Crown had hardly any land available for the settling of emigrants, though the waste lands of those huge territories were crying out for settlement.'[7] The Colonial Office had also considered involving private companies in its new colonies. In 1828 the Colonial Secretary had proposed that the Swan River colony in 'Western Australia might be founded by the East India Company'.[8]

The Church Missionary Society (CMS) jealously clung to its exclusive role in New Zealand, believing Christianity alone could civilise Maori. The New Zealand Association was a threat to missionary work, and when Dandeson Coates, the lay secretary of the CMS, heard of its plans, he immediately published a pamphlet condemning it. He had powerful colleagues in the Colonial Office: Lord Glenelg, the Colonial Secretary, was a vice-president of the CMS who 'enjoyed almost unfettered power', although he was generally viewed as being inept and apathetic; and James Stephen and Sir George Grey, Parliamentary Under-Secretaries for the Colonies, who were lay members on its committee – but it was the former who was perceived by the Association to be its real threat.[9] Stephen loathed Wakefield for his lack of 'truth and honour', eschewing any 'official acquaintance' with him and rejoicing in his 'unabated' 'hostility' towards Wakefield.[10] Unsurprisingly, it was not long before members of the Association such as Buller devised epithets like 'Mr. Mother Country' for him.

Against this background of tensions, Evans proved his worth with his customary zeal, attracting emigrants, promoting Wakefield's scheme and contributing to publicity generally. In May he received a letter from Wakefield who had responded to Coates's attack with a pamphlet 'by way of a goad to your Honor and the Admiral, for I cannot help fearing that our Dominions may be snatched from us'. But, he told Evans, he had 'another object in writing':

> The facts relating to:
> 1 the proportion of unoccupied land
> 2 the inclination of the natives to sell land and encourage English settlers
> 3 the evils which they suffer through the permanent or temporary residence of lawless foreigners, should be classed under separate heads; and it is most desirable that your labour should produce, not a mere map of facts, but a well-selected collection and digest upon each point. The physical geography of the country, I told my brother today, should be en suite . . . so that the reader may follow you, chart in hand. Any satisfactory proofs of conversion to Christianity, especially amongst the young, should appear under the head of capacity for civilization. I dare to say that other points will occur to you as you proceed. At your leisure, pray think of settlers – emigrant Founders. The first question asked by the great men, will be – Where are the colonists? Where are the funds? With

> a good body of intending settlers all will probably go well from the first. This is the lever with which every move is to be effected. As long as you are well employed, stay at Hampstead and write away. I shall not be idle. With best regards to Mrs. Evans.
> Your everything, E. G. Wakefield.[11]

Evans immediately began work and contributed at least a third (pages 13–21) of the twenty-seven pages of the pamphlet published a week or so later, *A Statement of the Objects of the New Zealand Association, with some Particulars concerning the Position, Extent, Soil and Climate, Natural Productions and Natives of New Zealand.* For his information, he relied on the material he, Arthur and Wakefield had accumulated from a number of sources: Augustus Earle, the draughtsman and artist; William Yate, the missionary; and John Savage, R. Cruise, L. Le Breton and J. L. Nicholas.

He wrote of the extraordinary capacity of Maori for civilisation, their ardent love for poetry, music and the fine arts, and their 'wit and eloquence, that remind us, in reading all the accounts of them, and in conversing with those who have resided among them, of the Greeks of Homer'. The Maori population was 'quite insignificant in proportion to the immense fertile territory they possess', and the chiefs were 'offended that we do not colonize their country; and with good reason, for they see the substantial benefits that would accrue to them from the establishment of our laws and the rest of our civilization'. He continued:

> . . . it is no longer a question whether Englishmen shall come into their country, but whether they shall do so, under the sanction and control of a proper authority, acting with strict impartiality between both parties, or whether they shall come with gunpowder, brandy and debauchery, to corrupt their wives and daughters, plunder their potatoe grounds, and set all the neighbouring tribes at variance; whilst the unhappy natives, if impelled by the irregular impulses of their nature to seek for justice in the form of revenge, are held up to the execration of mankind as murderers, and as proper objects of cruel retaliation.[12]

He addressed the lawlessness of the runaway convicts, sealers, traders and whalers; the evil wrought by land-jobbers and swindlers; the good that the missionaries had done for the Maori in civilising them; and the extent of unoccupied territory and the insignificant amount of cultivated land.

When the New Zealand Association met again in November, Wakefield presented *The British Colonization of New Zealand*, a book of 423 pages that included word for word the original pamphlet.

The ideals in both pamphlet and book were utopian, Evans predicting that because Maori had a 'remarkable' 'capacity for civilization', there was 'good reason to hope that under favourable circumstances, future generations of Europeans and natives may intermarry and become one people'. By intermarriage they might 'form the basis of a great nation'. Maori were adept at many forms of labour: 'in some places they save a capital, and buy and sell as traders, and in these places, where they have learned to value the institution of property, they anxiously desire the benefits of regular government'.[13]

> Captain Cook bears testimony to their modesty by which he says they are distinguished from all other inhabitants of the South Sea. They are as ardent in friendship and love as they are cruel in their jealousy, hatred and revenge . . . there is a natural politeness and grandeur in their deportment . . . . Large purchases of land have been made by the Missionaries, at various times, and have been held sacred by the natives. The price appears to have been a few axes, or other implements of industry, articles of dress etc. Mr. Cruise describes a chieftain as offering to sell a large and fertile island for a single hatchet . . .[14]

A Maori government was suggested, 'guided and upheld by a foreign authority; it would be really and truly a British government, though in a native garb'. In the past:

> . . . the rights of the natives would have been wholly disregarded . . . though it were ever so easy to pursue the old course of substituting might for right, this would defeat [our main object]. Wishing to civilize the New Zealanders by means of their amalgamation with our own race, it is indispensable that we should treat them with exact justice.

By living alongside Maori in the areas they were willing to sell, the British colonists with 'fostering care' would soon place them 'on terms of intellectual, moral and social equality'. A court of justice would be set up with a magistrate 'well-acquainted with the native language' presiding. A 'Protector of Natives would represent them in all respects'. The public would pay the expenses of all legal action involving Maori, and slavery amongst the race would be abolished. In exchange, the chiefs would be encouraged to 'engage in military and civil employments under the government'.[15]

At the time, these ideas were those of 'enlightened humanity'. They were the New Zealand Association's basic premises and expressed the ideals upon which these plans for colonising the country were based.

Wakefield is now generally credited with the authorship of this pamphlet and the more detailed book that followed in November, although he was, according to historian Douglas Pike, an 'unblushing' plagiarist, 'and the greatest care had to be taken before making any attribution of authorship, still less, originality, to him'.[16] Young Thomas Wilmor McKenzie, who intended emigrating with his widowed mother, testified to Evans's input, saying that while Wakefield 'triumphantly' answered his 'deadly opponent' Coates (referring to Wakefield's pamphlet, *Mr. Dandeson Coates and the New Zealand Association*), 'Dr. Evans and Dr. Hinds [Archbishop Whately's chaplain] also wrote on the subject and successfully combatted [*sic*] [Coates's] arguments.'[17]

Evans introduced his friends Thomas Campbell and William Cook to the Association's directors at its inaugural public meeting on 22 May in rooms at Adams Street, Adelphi, WC2. The Adelphi, as it was collectively known, comprised 'a riverside development of 24 terraced houses, designed and built' by the Adam brothers in the late eighteenth century.[18] The directors included John George Lambton, the first Earl of Durham, a Whig MP who had helped draft the great Reform Bill of 1832 as Lord Privy Seal and was known popularly as 'Radical Jack'; the reformer William Molesworth; the Catholic aristocrat Hon. Henry Petre; and Sir George Sinclair, William Hutt and Henry George Ward MP, who would join forces with Baring to lobby Lord Howick, the Secretary at War and former Parliamentary Under-Secretary of the Colonial Office. Members included Robert Stephen Rintoul, editor of the *Spectator*; Captain Arthur Wakefield; and Henry Chapman, the able journalist and political reformer, who, like Evans, was studying for the Bar. Evans and other intending emigrants attended meetings, and paid all the Association's expenses. As one historian has observed, 'the committee [of the Association] was thus predominantly whig with a strong admixture of radicalism'.[19]

From the start, Evans found his chief ally in director William Hutt. Despite his Anglicanism, Hutt fully supported the new colony, in which the usual Anglican rights and privileges would be excluded. Hutt was a wealthy man who had been well educated at private schools before matriculating from Oxford and gaining an MA at

Cambridge. Like Evans, he was 'a friend of civil and religious liberty' who believed systematic colonisation to be a cure for pauperism. He had taken an active role from the start, having advanced £500 towards the South Australian Act of 1834. As MP for Hull, he was highly regarded as a level-headed politician.[20]

As well as recording the minutes meticulously, which he did for the next two years, Evans advertised the pamphlet in several newspapers: *The Times*, the *Morning Chronicle*, the *Globe*, the *Spectator* and Molesworth's *Examiner*.

At the second meeting a week later, Evans brought along Daniel Riddiford as his assistant, and introduced him to John Wright, the Catholic banker; John Hutt, William's brother; journalist John Ward; lawyer Richard Davies Hanson; and Captain Hon. W. Wellesley and others. The 'sovereignty and independence of the Maori' and their rights as landowners were discussed. It was explained that there were several tribes with no central authority. The meeting concluded that, as 'it was impossible for [Maori] to cede the whole territory immediately to the Crown', it should be 'a gradual process'. They agreed Parliament was the proper channel for approval before a treaty could be signed with Maori.[21]

At some point the men pored over maps of the country to find the best place for the first settlement. No one knew of a 'harbour in the southern part of the north island'. They asked Arthur Wakefield to advise them, and using his nautical instruments he measured the distances between New South Wales in Australia and possible harbours in New Zealand that would make trade feasible. 'Adopting the circle sailing principle, he put his finger finally on [the site of] Port Nicholson and said, "There, if there is a port".'[22]

On 6 June, accompanied by Arthur Wakefield and Captain Wellesley, Evans visited the Church Missionary Society to outline the Association's plan, but their overture met with hostility. Coates was obdurate, telling Evans that 'he had no doubt of [their] respectability or of the purity of their intentions, but that he was opposed to the colonization of New Zealand upon *any* plan, and *would thwart them by all the means in his power*'.[23]

Coates had already persuaded Grey on 31 May to agree that the CMS could submit their objections as soon as the New Zealand Association detailed its plans to the government.[24] From the start the CMS stated that 'gain was the mainspring'[25] and 'ultimate end of the whole [Wakefield] scheme', a view held firmly by James Stephen.[26] This was a deliberate ploy to derail the scheme and one that would be used to great effect for a very long time. It was patently untrue as historians point out. The government agreed with the CMS that an influx of Europeans might be detrimental to the welfare of Maori. This stance was supported by public opinion that tended to resist any new ideas about colonisation – particularly given the government's sorry record in that area.

Shocked at Coates's hostility, the trio sought approval from the recently formed Aborigines' Protection Society (APS), which had evolved from six years' work towards colonial reform and the abolition of slavery 'to watch over and protect the natives'.[27] Evans had many friends and acquaintances amongst the Aborigines' Protection Society's leading members, including Standish Motte; Benjamin Hawes, MP for Lambeth;[28] and Charles Lushington and his older brother Stephen, who had been MP for Tower Hamlets in December 1832.After this meeting, the APS gave the Association its qualified support, as they agreed that the two concepts – colonisation and protection – were not irreconcilable.[29] In contrast to the missionaries' stance, the APS believed in colonisation as a means of relieving distress at home. As long as Wakefield's scheme was tempered with humanity, the Association had the APS's support.

A committee of directors drew up a draft of a Bill that was aired at a meeting on 9 June, and three days later a deputation met the Prime Minister. Lord Howick was present, examined their Bill for a charter and later wrote detailed suggestions to be included in the Bill, assuring the deputation their enterprise would be backed by the government.[30] Lord Melbourne promised to 'decide on it without delay', recorded Evans in the minutes book.[31] All of Howick's suggestions were added to the draft, and the Association felt confident of its success, having been assured, the committee reported, of Howick's 'powerful influence and support'.[32] Before Betts Hopper was introduced to the Association by Evans, he had watched Evans give a lesson at North End. Evans compared the morality of Samson with that of Maori. Samson's life appeared to be 'one continued series of . . . blood-thirsty revenge. How similar is the New Zealander who seeks revenge until satisfied in his own mind that his wrongs have been atoned for by the shedding of blood, without discriminating the innocent from the guilty. See Chapters 15 and 16, Judges', Betts Hopper duly noted in his diary. At the rooms in the Adelphi, Betts Hopper's first impressions were telling. He was particularly struck by the 'deference' everyone 'paid to Wakefield's opinions'.[33]

The period between King William's death in June and Queen Victoria's accession put a temporary stop to the Association's communication with government. During that year, London was also swept by an epidemic of influenza.[34] People moved about the city with caution and many organisations curtailed their activities. But nobody in the Association was idle. Wakefield turned to Evans for help in another matter. He had heard that two young Maori men, Ngaiti (Nahiti or Nayti) and Hiakai (Tiaki or 'Jackey'),[35] who had been passengers on the French ship *Mississippi*, were stranded in Le Havre. As it was rumoured that companies were being formed in the ports of France to colonise New Zealand, the Association acted swiftly and brought the young men across the channel in July.[36] Wakefield and Evans scooped them up, outfitted them in the highest fashion, and while Wakefield took Ngaiti to his home in Hans Square, Chelsea, Evans bore Tiaki off to North End House. Very soon the two young men were mingling with London society.

Evans described Ngaiti in the *British Colonization of New Zealand* as being 'about twenty-six years, five feet eight inches in height, stout, brawny and athletic – slightly tattooed, more on one side of the face than the other'. Hiakai was

> a native of Port Otago, one of the tribe almost exterminated in 1830 by the Kapiti tribe, the chief of which is [Te Rauparaha] who brutally massacred the chiefs of a hostile tribe. He is not much more than eighteen or nineteen years old, was unwell when he reached Havre, and has remained so ever since. He is very intelligent, has made great progress in learning English, and in helping an English gentleman to learn the New Zealand language, and is much liked by two families with whom he has resided since his arrival in England.[37]

From June to November, Evans was in a frenzy of activity, preparing for the Bar, dealing with correspondence and meeting with his contacts. The whole family was involved: Daniel wanted to farm and Harriet was determined he should be given every opportunity. Daniel checked and copied the Association's minutes, Harriet dealt with household arrangements, and Amelia painted Hiakai's portrait and helped him with his English.

Evans quickly picked up much of the Maori language from Hiakai. As he hoped for a judicial role in the colony, it was vital he learned something of the customs and culture of the Maori. Hiakai, the brother of Iwikau, a chief from Banks Peninsula, impressed Evans by having 'a disposition of the most amiable kind, and a capacity of the very first order'. Evans believed that had he been taught any of the abstract sciences, Hiakai would have mastered them 'with distinction'.[38] Contrary to the assertion that 'neither Maori was taught English seriously', Evans and his family taught Hiakai English orally and in written form.[39]

Evans began to compile a grammar of the Maori language, probably using the earlier dictionary of Thomas Kendall as a model. Completed in 1839, his *Grammar* describes elements of Maori pronunciation and all parts of grammar, including tenses and moods. It also includes church services from baptism to funeral, a lamentation of the widow of the chief Hinaki slain in battle in 1821, examples of dialogue, a waiata with translation, a funeral ode, a baptismal service for native children, the Maori version of the history of humankind, and addresses to the deceased and spectators. The Ten Commandments, the Apostles' Creed and the Lord's Prayer are faithfully translated. There is also a copy of a letter written by Hiakai to Tommy Woon (perhaps a missionary) in 1837, written in both Maori and English:

> Amelia [Miss Riddiford] has made a portrait of Hiakai. It is very much like him. Would you like Tommy Woon to have your portrait taken. Yesterday Mr. — went to see Captain W.'s ship. On Sunday he will come to see his female friends and to see his male friends to bid them goodbye when he goes to his ship. Captain Wakefield is a good man, in three years he will come back. Tommy Woon all the white men that see you say you are a good man.[40]

At the back of John Ward's book, *Information Relative to New Zealand for the Use of Colonists*, published two years later, an advertisement proclaims that Evans's *Grammar* was 'in the Press'. But it was never published. Archdeacon Herbert W. Williams suggested the contents were used instead by Dr Dieffenbach in the second volume of his work *Travels in New Zealand*, published in 1843.[41] Evans's unpublished 'Grammar of the New Zealand Language' later found its way into the hands of Professor G. B. Kerferd of the University of Swansea in Wales, who donated it to the Alexander Turnbull Library in 1963.

ꕤ

By the end of 1837, the Association was a formidable influence in social and political ranks as 'men of wealth and culture' were drawn to the enterprise. It took an extraordinary amount of energy to maintain the impetus. The Association appeared to be the only group with 'constructive proposals' – the only men at the time 'less interested in the West Indies and Emancipation', and more interested in the new countries.[42]

Top left: Famed poet, mentor and friend of George S. Evans, Thomas Campbell took a keen interest in the New Zealand Company's colonisation scheme, and celebrated the emigrants' departure with a poem. Engraving by C. H. Jeens, frontispiece of Rev. W. Alfred Hill (ed.), *The Poetical Works of Thomas Campbell: With a Sketch of his Life* by William Allingham, George Bell & Sons, London, 1875.
Top right: A noted Congregational minister, and pastor of Mile End parish for thirty-eight years, Reverend George Evans lived with his wife amongst the poor, and preached gratuitously at hundreds of churches in 26 counties of England and Wales. Engraving, London, 1829, from *Congregational Magazine*, Permezel Collection, Melbourne.
Right: Built with donations from Reverend Evans's parishioners in 1825, Brunswick Chapel, Mile End, London, was destroyed during the Blitz on London in the Second World War. Engraving, London, 1829, from *Congregational Magazine*, Permezel Collection, Melbourne.

G. S. Evans was headmaster of Mill Hill School for six months in 1828. His resignation triggered a riot. Protestant Dissenters Grammar School, Mill Hill, Hendon, Rock and Co., RC 18. With kind permission of the Mill Hill School Foundation.

The school's pond, into which were thrown the classroom benches during the riot. Illustration facing page 88 of N. G. Brett-James, *The History of Mill Hill School 1807–1907*, Mill Hill School, London, 1909. With kind permission of the Mill Hill School Foundation.

Top left: Daniel Riddiford was Evans's assistant Honorary Secretary from 1837 to 1839, and was rewarded with the position of Emigration Agent at Port Nicholson. With kind permission of Mrs E. A. Riddiford.
Top right: Harriet Strother Riddiford Evans, 'The High Stepper'. Revans said of her, 'Mrs Evans would really make the mischievous woman of a book to great advantage.' With kind permission of Philippa Riddiford.
Left: Evans believed in Edward Gibbon Wakefield's scheme of systematic colonisation, sacrificing a great deal to further its aims. Edward Gibbon Wakefield, by E. J. Collins; dogs, by Richard Ansdell. By kind permission of Canterbury Museum.

NORTH-END HOUSE.

(From a Photograph taken expressly for this work.)

North End House, Hampstead, London, Lord North's former home. Here Evans kept his Private Grammar School for eight years. Hampstead Illustrations Collection, 'LDB North End House'. By permission of the Camden Local Studies and Archives Centre, London.

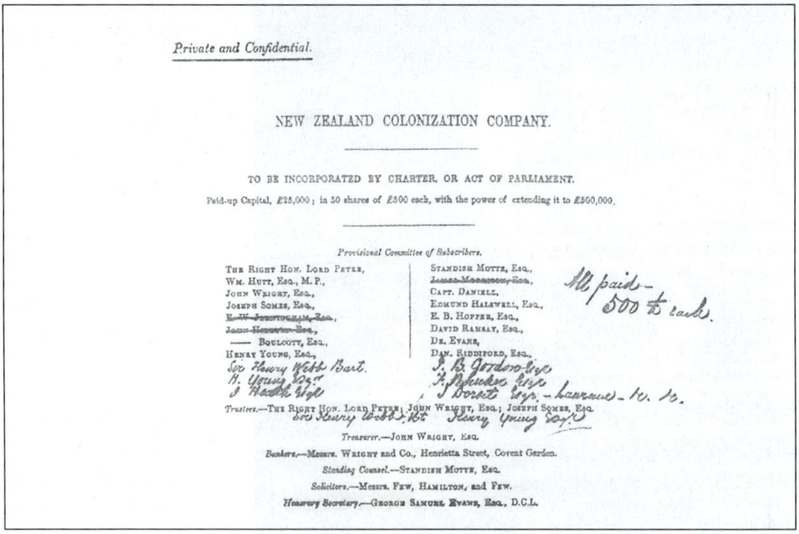

Private and Confidential.

NEW ZEALAND COLONIZATION COMPANY.

TO BE INCORPORATED BY CHARTER, OR ACT OF PARLIAMENT.

Paid-up Capital, £25,000; in 50 shares of £500 each, with the power of extending it to £500,000.

Provisional Committee of Subscribers.

The Right Hon. Lord Petre,
Wm. Hutt, Esq., M.P.,
John Wright, Esq.,
Joseph Somes, Esq.,
[illegible], Esq.,
[illegible], Esq.,
—— Boulcott, Esq.,
Henry Young, Esq.,
Sir Henry Webb Bart.
H. Young Esqr
J. [illegible] Esqr

Standish Motte, Esq.,
[illegible], Esq.,
Capt. Daniell,
Edmund Halswell, Esq.,
E. B. Hopper, Esq.,
David Ramsay, Esq.,
Dr. Evans,
Dan. Riddiford, Esq.,
J. B. Gordon Esqr
[illegible] Esqr
J. Dorset Esqr. – [illegible]

All paid – 500 £ each.

Trustees.—The Right Hon. Lord Petre; John Wright, Esq.; Joseph Somes, Esq. Sir Henry Webb Bt Henry Young Esqr

Treasurer.—John Wright, Esq.

Bankers.—Messrs. Wright and Co., Henrietta Street, Covent Garden.

Standing Counsel.—Standish Motte, Esq.

Solicitors.—Messrs. Few, Hamilton, and Few.

Honorary Secretary.—George Samuel Evans, Esq., D.C.L.

Detail from the first page of a three-page draft of the Prospectus of the New Zealand Colonization Company, September 1838, with the names of the Provisional Committee of Subscribers added or amended by Evans's hand. Drawn up by Evans and submitted to the Colonial Office by Standish Motte. CO 209/4 Micro 352, p.521, Archives New Zealand.

On the Association's behalf, Evans was fielding queries with confidence, writing to one hopeful immigrant Mr W. I. Beattie that its founders would bear the same 'relation to New Zealand that the Directors of the East India Company sustain to our Indian Empire'. His promises were lavish, saying professional men would be paid at more generous rates than those in 'the mother country', and that the regulations for land represented a 'great discovery in Political Economy'.[43] On 21 November 1837, Evans was called to the Bar at Lincoln's Inn, officially now a barrister. But given their confidence in the success of their enterprise, Evans and his family had decided to sell up and devote their energies to colonising and emigrating. It had already been resolved that all the Association's expenses were to be met by 'those members who contemplated settling in New Zealand'.[44] Wakefield had also urged Evans to move closer to the Adelphi, the hub of the Association, perhaps promising him a judicial role in the new settlement. Wakefield was not above threatening members who were reluctant to move closer to his rooms, hinting that they might not receive any favours from him. In November he wrote to Betts Hopper in Dover about information for prospective emigrants, idly adding:

> The book tells well, and is making a most favourable impression . . . . Our friend Evans is now a barrister and attends here daily. He is intending to live in Town at Christmas. You will naturally suppose that there are many applications for offices, and need not be told, as respects yourself, that it is disadvantageous to be long absent from headquarters.[45]

Evans now wound up his private grammar school, North End Academy, and wrapped up his financial arrangements. He moved his family and the ailing Hiakai to a rented house at 3 Pelham Road, Brompton, West Kensington. It was a great leap of faith in Wakefield and his scheme, and a huge personal risk.

The Association wished to merge with the members of the earlier 1825 Company that had been set up to colonise New Zealand. Evans was asked by Colonel Torrens of that organisation to negotiate the merger. The fifteen members of this Company – who had collectively lost their investment of £20,000 – included Lord Durham, J. W. Buckle, Edward Ellice, Edward Littleton, George Lyall, Stewart Marjoribanks and George Palmer. They all agitated for full reimbursement but some suggested that because the money had been spent on the acquisition of one million acres of land in New Zealand, they should cut their losses.

Evans's solution was based on 'the cession of all [the 1825 Company members'] rights to the Crown in return for colonial revenue bonds, bearing 5% interest to the amount of their actual outlay in acquiring such rights'. He also suggested including in the Association's Bill a clause providing for a committee of three members to settle the compensation due to the 1825 group.[46] After a lengthy debate it was resolved that Baring would negotiate according to Evans's terms. Lord Durham, a key member of the New Zealand Company of 1825, finally succumbed to Wakefield's pleas and joined the Association in September, so all were optimistic about its success.[47] A grateful Torrens later wrote to Evans:

> The zeal, ability, integrity, and success with which you conducted the important and difficult business which I entrusted to your sole and exclusive guidance, entitle me . . . to bear testimony to your possessing the character of mind peculiarly suited to the position [of Judge of the Tower Hamlets Court of Requests].[48]

Evans had been giving some thought to the financial aspect of Wakefield's scheme and wrote to the London banker John Wright on 11 December on behalf of several others seeking a loan for £100,000. A New Zealand Act would authorise interest of not more than 10 per cent, but a payment of 5 per cent would be more likely, he surmised. The principal would be used for emigration costs and to fund colonial government. The security for the loan would be 'firstly the future sales of lands, and secondly the colonial revenue, and this security would be fully established by the Act of Parliament'. A guarantee fund would be set up for interest payments before sales of public land and colonial taxation had accumulated funds. Evans believed this scheme was superior to the provisions of the South Australia Act.[49]

At about the same time, Lord Melbourne, who had just called together the new Parliament, found himself being pressed for an urgent meeting to discuss the amended draft of a Bill for a charter with members of the New Zealand Association. He was an aristocrat of the eighteenth-century mould, who not only viewed Durham as a third-rate man,[50] but also regarded colonial affairs as being of minor importance. At the time he was also being distracted by the demands of the young Queen, who relied heavily on him for advice. Nevertheless, he agreed to the meeting for 4 p.m. on 13 December. Deputations were tedious, but he certainly never let them interfere with his daily routine, often receiving them while shaving. His informality was startling to serious petitioners:

> What were they to make of [him] who received them lounging back

> nursing a sofa cushion; who . . . pulled a feather out of the cushion and began blowing it about the room; and who after they had finished, answered briefly and with a bland smile that he was afraid he could not help them as he knew nothing about the matter in question . . .[51]

Before the meeting, Evans and seventeen other members met at the rooms in Adam Street where Baring outlined their tactics, then they all proceeded to Downing Street, confident of a successful outcome.[52] But their first obstacle was Glenelg, whose opposition to colonial expansion was based on James Stephen's unshakeable belief that their sole motivation was 'gain'.[53] For 'nearly an hour' Glenelg stated his objections: the jealousy of foreign powers if Britain extended its colonies, that England had enough colonies, that they were very expensive to govern, and that they were not of sufficient value. When he had finished, Melbourne asked him if he had any other objections. Glenelg said, 'No.'

'Why', said Melbourne facetiously, 'you had an hundred just now!' Wakefield intervened at this point, telling Melbourne that many people had determined to emigrate. Since their positive interview with him in June, some 'had disposed of their property, or had quitted professions in which they were engaged'. One member in particular would 'suffer very seriously' if the scheme failed.

Melbourne was astonished, observing 'the man must be mad'.

Evans leaped to his feet, identifying himself as the madman. 'All this excited a good deal of feeling', Wakefield testified later. But Evans would not have stopped there. The Prime Minister of Great Britain might have found himself the recipient of a spirited speech of outraged sensibility if the conference had not been 'on the point of breaking up in confusion and disorder'. Melbourne was reminded again of his earlier reception of the Association's plans and he assured them he would reconsider their case, promising that if they visited Glenelg in a week's time, 'they would get an answer more to their satisfaction'. But the men were 'very much dissatisfied'.[54]

Evans's sacrifice for such a venture was unusual for the time. Most members of such organisations would have perhaps invested in land and been absentee landlords, sent members of their own family, or merely worked, as the directors did, from philanthropic or idealistic motives. Evans's commitment was driven by idealism and a strong belief in Wakefield's scheme of systematic colonisation. He stood to lose everything in a material sense, as his career prospects dimmed with each day he devoted to Wakefield's scheme. Such a risk makes nonsense of the theory that the Association's men had gain alone as their primary motive.

All the men felt 'hardly treated', but were still prepared to do battle. They decided Melbourne should be made aware of the connection between the Colonial Office and the Church Missionary Society – the court circular had informed them that within the previous six weeks the CMS had met with Glenelg six times. Later Wakefield would complain that, from the beginning, the CMS had treated all the Association's approaches 'not only with coldness, but with disdain'.[55]

Yet three days after their meeting with Melbourne, Glenelg told them he had had reports and opinions from Busby and Captain Hobson (the latter was in command of a warship in the region of New Zealand), and he now believed a measure could be carried into effect without applying to Parliament at all. The Colonial Office was prepared to grant to the Association a Charter of Incorporation. In late December, Glenelg sent Durham a letter outlining the conditions for the Charter. Briefly, the Association was to become a joint stock company with 'subscribed capital'. Durham was furious, saying it would drastically compromise the public and private interests of its promoters. Many of their supporters were members of the established church who could not be connected with any organisation that might gain pecuniary advantage from its activities. And the Wakefield principle excluded the formation of such a company.

As Glenelg's offer circulated amongst the CMS, the press and Members of Parliament, suspicions about the Association's motives grew. The press seized upon Wakefield's background, and it seemed all was doomed to failure. Tempers were frayed, and bickering broke out amongst the Association's members.

Three days after Glenelg's conditional offer, Betts Hopper observed Wakefield grill Robert Roy for two hours over his cousin Major John Campbell's rumoured claim that he should be appointed the first governor of the colony. This had arisen from a chance remark made by Durham to Campbell at a dinner, and Campbell's tacit response. Wakefield was sensitive to his past disgrace and believed that the episode – which had been discussed by several men – was threatening his future 'honourable distinction' and 'public life'.

Roy protested in vain and the haranguing continued until Evans entered, when the subject was dropped.[56] As secretary, Evans was asked by Wakefield to inform Campbell by letter that their conflict must be settled to avoid harming 'the great enterprise in which we are engaged'. On Christmas Day, Evans forwarded Campbell's reply, in which Campbell protested he was most 'desirous' to promote the 'great enterprise – I really know of no cause for difference between [Wakefield] and me'. He believed no meeting with so many members away 'could be competent to decide an important question'. Campbell did not think it was necessary to attend the meeting called by Wakefield, but if Wakefield were to inform the Committee members of the statement, 'I should be better able to determine whether I should "come to a different decision"'. Wakefield told Evans that, after the correspondence to that point, 'and so soon after [Campbell's] conversation with Mr. Rintoul', Campbell would know the nature of Wakefield's accusation. Wakefield would deliver the 'statement' to the Committee in just two days, '(but in any case if he is in doubt, I beg of you [Evans] to inform him that I intend to make against him a very grave accusation) and that I trust he will be present to hear it, and to repel, if he can'.[57]

Campbell's reply again asserted his innocence, saying he had acquiesced to Wakefield's insistence on refusing any appointment. He had never 'interfered with Mr. Wakefield's views whatever they might be; I have conscientiously avoided it'. He still refused to attend the urgent meeting, claiming it was his 'right to decide'. He would 'continue to devote his best attention to the work of the Association, 'which so far has been conducted with success and with perfect cordiality until this as it seems to me unnecessary and premature discussion was raised; but not by me'.[58]

Wakefield's position was unlikely to have been seriously under threat, but for him the timing was interesting, as the Association's setback was a crucial moment for him to reassert his pre-eminence. At the meeting on 28 December, which was attended by twenty-three men, Wakefield warned that the very existence of the Association was threatened. A representative for Campbell attested that Campbell did not wish to stand in Wakefield's way for the post of governor. Then Evans said Campbell had told him he believed the government would never 'sanction any scheme for colonization of which Mr. Wakefield was to be placed at the head'. Hutt and other members rushed to reassure Wakefield, praised his 'complete propriety', and confirmed that he was 'eminently qualified to fill any office in the proposed colony of New Zealand which may hereafter be at the disposal of the founders'.[59] Wakefield was mollified, if any mollification was needed, and claimed, without any objection from his audience, that 'the whole of the business of the Association had been transacted by himself with scarcely a single exception'.[60]

Both Roy and Campbell resigned in February after a belated attempt to dismiss the charges against the latter. Was Evans intimidated by Wakefield? To obtain a judicial role in the colony he would need to tread very carefully, and he was too committed to turn back.

ଓ

From 20 December to 29 December, including Christmas day, Evans had visited the Association's headquarters daily. Clearly worried, he must have sought reassurance from other visitors like Rintoul, Betts Hopper, Wakefield, Molesworth and Hutt.

But Glenelg insisted on the government's terms, and when his offer was withdrawn in February, Evans and Wakefield were forced to appeal to Parliament. To present their Bill, Evans immediately gave £1,000 of his own for fees, with Wakefield matching it.[61] But it was an uphill battle, not least because the Association had a significant percentage of dissenters and Catholics amongst its directors and members – a fact quickly seized upon by the hostile press. The Association was savaged by *The Times*, which branded Wakefield the 'experienced abductionist':

> How far the circumstances of Captain Cook having first landed at New Zealand compromises its independence as a free territory, or warrants the British Crown in asserting a preferable claim to it as a colony, is a question which, without committing ourselves to the views of these radical and popish philanthropists, we shall not now dispute with them . . . . Profit, of course is not the main object of such disinterested saints as Messrs [Henry G.] Ward and Wakefield.[62]

And at home there was tragedy. After suffering for eight months, Hiakai was taken to St George's Hospital where he eventually died.[63] After Hiakai's death, Evans conversed regularly with Ngaiti at Wakefield's house, consoling him. He was touched by Ngaiti's grief, saying it was to his credit that Ngaiti was found weeping over Hiakai's grave in Brompton churchyard, three weeks after the burial.[64]

In April, Wakefield announced that as a result of the Papineau Rebellion in Lower Canada, Lord Durham as Canada's new governor and high commissioner had invited him to be his secretary and advisor. Durham's offer gave Wakefield a chance to further his political ambitions, so in May he followed Durham, taking Charles Buller and Richard Davies Hanson with him. His departure was seen as an abandonment of the Association and its plans, but shrewdly Wakefield had left Evans in charge, knowing it was too late for the latter to turn his back on the undertaking.[65] If Wakefield distanced himself and the project failed, it would do little harm to his own prospects.

Evans concentrated on lobbying Members of Parliament to pass their Bill. The Association's directors asked for unprecedented powers to 'entrust New Zealand's administration for ten years to a Council elected by its founders, with full powers – and answerable only to the Colonial Secretary and Parliament'. They wanted authority to establish their own courts of law to administer their lands, and to make regulations for law and order. They also wanted to raise and equip a militia.

On 10 May, Evans, Hutt, Betts Hopper and others went to the House of Commons. After three hours, Hutt finally got an interview with Glenelg and showed him a list of MPs who would oppose him. Glenelg replied that he had no objection to the general principles of the Bill or to the commissioners. Next, the Select Committee of the House of Lords, chaired by the Earl of Devon, examined a variety of interested parties over nine days.[66]

Friday 18 May was reserved exclusively for Evans's interview as leader of the intending colonists. In attributing the formation of the New Zealand Association to Baring, Evans carefully omitted Wakefield's name. He assured the Select Committee that the Association was not a joint stock company. He intended emigrating to New Zealand, he said, as the 'Class of persons' who settled in other colonies would not provide 'the Society which would be quite necessary for our comfortable existence'. In Australia the 'emancipists' (released convicts) 'overran' the colonies, and in unoccupied Canada, there would not be found the sort of society he and his family 'should wish'. As well, New Zealand's climate was superior to other colonies, in spite of Maori dying from 'pulmonary complaints'. As it was their custom to move their sick outdoors in all climates, they died 'in great numbers of consumptive and scrofulous Diseases'.

Easy acquisition of land would mean the settlement's failure, he said, giving Western Australia as an example. The purchase of land should be restricted, and fixing a high price was the answer, so that labourers would be unable to buy their own land for some years after initial settlement. The fund created from land sales would pay for labourers' passages without calling on the public purse. Several gentlemen in New South Wales had complained of 'the inefficacy of the Colonial Office'. Even with £200,000 in the colonial treasury, landowners were still desperately short of labourers.

In New Zealand, their scheme allowed for land to be sold at £1 an acre. To own a farm, a man must acquire between 500 and 1,000 acres, which would 'prevent Labourers from setting up as independent Proprietors until they have saved Money, and thus the Classes of Society will be preserved'. Evans was the only witness called that day and there are sixteen pages of evidence. The questions and answers were detailed and paid attention not only to the motivation of the Association but also to the processes of government that must follow from colonisation, for example:

> Committee: You stated that a Part of your Plan was, that all the Money received for Land should be appropriated to Emigration Purposes; how would you propose to raise the money necessary for the ordinary Purposes of government, Courts of Justice, Administration of the Police, the Establishments of Religion, and so on?
> Evans: Our first idea was to appropriate the whole of the Land Revenue, after deducting what we paid to the Natives for the Purchase of Land, to the Purposes of Emigration; but we have now resolved on appropriating One-Fourth to what may be called local Purposes; – to the Benefit of the Aborigines, to the building of Schoolhouses, Places of Worship, and other Objects of public Utility in the Colony.[67]

Evans believed the absolute sovereign title to the two islands belonged to the Crown of England, according to the received 'Law of Nations'. He knew of the Declaration of the Independence of Northern Maori that was recognised by Great Britain, as he had read and translated the document from Maori. But it was not, he argued, 'a Declaration of Independence or Sovereignty, but merely of the chieftainship of those particular individuals who placed themselves under the protection of the Sovereign of Great Britain'.[68]

Warning bells sounded when the Committee was told the settlement would be overseen by a board of commissioners selected from the Association's directorate. Evans admitted 'no provision' had been made for the government to remove anyone in a position of power.

> Committee: All the appointments of every kind would devolve upon the board of commissioners at home?
> Evans: Yes. As that is only a provisional move, it was thought desirable that the persons employed practically in working it out should be those who have devoted a considerable attention to the subject.

When asked in what way were the commissioners to be 'responsible in every way to the Crown' if the Crown had 'no authority over the appointment of the persons in New Zealand', Evans replied that the Crown would be able to veto 'all proceedings of every kind; that they should never make an appointment without the permission of the

Crown; but the Bill does not give the Crown the power of originating measures'.

Maori chiefs were 'a sort of feudatories of the Crown, under its jurisdiction', he alleged. A board of commissioners could negotiate with the chiefs for a cession of their sovereignty and domain, as had been the case in Singapore when, seven years after Raffles established a settlement, the sovereignty of the Sultan of Johore was bought for a sum of money, while reserves of land were made for 'some of the Malay proprietors, and exceptional Laws . . . established out of deference to the Native customs and prejudices'.

Evans was certain he had an authoritative insider view, as Ngaiti and Hiakai had assured him that some of the chiefs would welcome 'a large number of settlers from England . . . residing in their neighbourhood', who would give them 'a sort of superiority'. They wanted to be employed by the settlers and learn their trades.

Evans told the Select Committee he believed the Colonial Office should have a separate commission for each colony so that prospective emigrants could gather information and make informed choices. Each commission should also have the power to sell intending colonists land or land orders in London. He also averred, 'From all the evidence . . . Cook's Straits will be the most favourable Spot for the Establishment of a Colony.'[69]

He could not 'speak too highly of the diligence and exemplary conduct of the Missionaries'. In civilising the Maori, 'The Missionary has necessarily been the Pioneer to the Emigrant'. Evans assured the panel that the emigrants on the Association's boats would be far superior to the Europeans already in New Zealand.

In France, one or two organisations had been investigating New Zealand's possibilities for colonisation. The Committee asked hypothetically whether, if a similar organisation from another country were to establish itself in another area of the country, that would be a problem. Evans supposed 'that the wisdom of Parliament, having established one Colony in New Zealand, would not permit another colony to be established'. But to prevent another government sanctioning a settlement in New Zealand they had 'inserted in the Preamble' [to their Bill] 'a Claim to the Sovereignty of New Zealand in Her Majesty . . . . We should hope that [as] in Australia, the first Occupation of the country, by means of a regular Colony under a Legislative Sanction, would be quite sufficient to prevent any other Country interfering.'

Had the discovery of New Zealand by Captain Cook given England a right of sovereignty, 'if not against the natives, at least against foreign Nations'? 'Unquestionably', Evans answered. Did their plan make it necessary to get sovereignty of both islands in the country? 'I think so, ultimately', replied Evans.

If Evans were told the government would not pass the Bill, instead merely sending out one or two vessels of war to the coast of New Zealand for the protection of British subjects, would that be sufficient security? Evans's reply was crisp:

> By no means; it would give me no security for the permanent value of my property in land. If I vested £4,000 or £5,000, which I propose to do, in land, I should want a Parliamentary guarantee that the same system for disposing of land which was established should be continued; and I should want also the confidence that a Board of Commissioners sitting in London would inspire me with, that the system would be worked with energy; that there would be a continual supply of labourers in the colony as they were wanted. I could not place myself and Family, nor do I think any respectable persons would place their lives and property, at the disposal of such a Court and such an administration of Justice as could be enforced by Ships of War off the Coast.

As Evans pointed out, two ships of war could never maintain a police force and the administration of justice within the colony; nor could they ever do what the Association proposed for the colony, in the way of providing churches, schools, hospitals, roads, bridges and so on.

The Select Committee suggested the settlers might instead form a club or association for that purpose. But, as Evans pointed out,

> I very much fear they will soon degenerate into what some persons have proposed to establish in New Zealand, which is a species of Republic, if we were left to govern ourselves merely under the authority of Ships of War stationed on the coast.

The Committee objected that they could not be a republic if the ships of war were 'watching over you, defending you and punishing you in case of aggression'. But Evans clarified the matter by saying the emigrants merely wanted 'the Power of a Local government vested in a body of Land Owners settled in the Colony'. He was adamant that their plan for two ships of war was flawed: 'It is doing a very small thing at an expense, when you have the power of doing a very great one for nothing.'[70]

He was vague on details of the Association's provision for taxation and duties, but he had every confidence the Association could sell 100,000 acres of land 'as soon as the Act of Parliament is passed'.

Evans also told the Committee that many people had expressed 'disapprobation' at the Association's seeking Parliament's sanction, arguing that with capital, and the 'energy to do it ourselves; why should we trammel ourselves with an Act of Parliament? We can go to Cook's Straits, and establish a colony there under the New Zealand flag, and be perfectly independent.' Evans assured the Committee they had rejected such suggestions, but they were so numerous he was convinced that with or without Parliament's sanction, 'a very great colony is on the Eve of being established in New Zealand, and that the question is, not whether New Zealand is to be colonized, but how it is to be governed'.[71]

The Select Committee handed the decision back to government. Francis Baring introduced the Association's Bill for a Government Charter to the House of Commons in June. But the Bill was flawed. Although the government had offered advice to H. G. Ward and other directors a year earlier, they had still provided few safeguards for the security and interests of both Maori and the emigrants.[72] Evans attended the Bill's readings, sitting below the bar of the House:

> One member opposed to the Bill said 'that as it was a money Bill, it could not be introduced without a message from the Crown' . . . . Evans was told by an Officer of the House that 'it was merely a matter of form . . . . The Prime Minister usually intimated in committee what course would be taken by the Government, as the . . . [Bill's fate] depended on the recommendation and advice given to the Crown.'[73]

The government threw out the Bill on 20 June by a margin of sixty votes, primarily because, as one historian has argued, the Association had displayed 'an extraordinary degree of political naivete'.[74] Yet MP Henry Ward said: 'during the whole of [my] experience in public life, I have never known so much uncertainty, oscillation, and change of purpose displayed by the Ministry towards those connected with the undertaking, whom I myself, relying on the faith of the Government, had been a party to deluding'.[75]

Another historian was more direct: 'Glenelg's complete capitulation to the anti-colonization lobby was, in retrospect, a political mistake. Stephen evolved a plan which might just have worked because, although it gave some scope to the colonizers, it provided for their control. Glenelg, by shutting the door on them, lost that chance of control and drove Wakefield and his supporters one step nearer to taking matters into their own hands and beginning the systematic colonization of New Zealand prematurely'.[76]

Lord Howick had condemned the Bill's inadequacies, but the Association believed he had betrayed them, in spite of his having qualified his support with insistence on adequate protection for the emigrants and Maori. Either the committee believed it had fulfilled his requirements, or it had ignored his warnings. Yet as one contemporary historian has noted, 'It is remarkable how much of the general sense of the Bill later became Government Policy.'[77]

Evans was furious and fired off a letter to Glenelg on behalf of 'more than 500 prospective emigrants' complaining that the government had misled them. He had been encouraged, he said, 'as much as twelve months ago, to believe that the principle of the Bill had received the sanction of Her Majesty's Government'.[78] Not content with that, he joined a society in London that had been formed to push for law reform of parliamentary procedures regarding private Bills. But he soon found that the 'chief difficulty was to get bankers and gentlemen engaged in commerce to interest themselves in the subject'.[79]

After the Bill's failure, many of its promoters 'gave up . . . in despair. It was very mortifying for [them]', wrote Thomas McKenzie.[80] Several moved on – John Abel Smith and Marjoribanks focused their attention on Australia. Others like Wakefield, Joseph Somes and Durham were considering the Beauharnois estate in Canada as a possible site for the Association of Ireland. Francis Baring had better prospects: he became Chancellor of the Exchequer the following year.

Evans and a few others 'were practically compelled to proceed with the undertaking', said McKenzie.[81] Evans took the lead, persuading Baring to chair one last meeting of the Association on 9 July. Ten members attended, resolving to 'persevere in their efforts for assuring to the inhabitants of New Zealand the blessings of Christianity and Civilization, and to this country the advantages of a well regulated system of colonization'. Evans was thanked for his additional work as secretary for five months and asked to continue. But most importantly, he was empowered to call meetings at the request of any two members.[82]

For the next two or three weeks there was a crippling hiatus when Evans and Riddiford were the only visitors to the rooms at the Adelphi. Then Riddiford cracked, telling his stepfather he had given the project too much time and money and they must consider abandoning it.

But Evans turned to his stepson and replied, 'By God, New Zealand shall be colonized!'[83]

And then, he did the unthinkable.

CHAPTER FOUR.

'A DAMNED PLUCKY SCHEME!'

> Hare awoke, and seeing Tortoise ahead in the distance, he raced after him.
>
> Aesop, *Fables: The Hare and The Tortoise*, c. 2500 BC

In late December 1837, Glenelg had suggested they create a joint stock company with subscribed capital, promising them a Charter of Incorporation in return. Leading members – especially churchmen like Dr Hinds – had rejected the idea, although it posed little risk for them. Apart from Wakefield and Evans, who had each contributed a thousand pounds for the Bill, no one else had yet been called upon to put forward their own capital.

Evans was now reconsidering Glenelg's conditional offer, which had expired six months earlier. In doing so, he must have recalled Brougham's successful actions in raising funds to found London University. And while he was aware of the risks to his financial security and reputation, Evans was determined. He withdrew £1,000 of his savings before approaching Captain Edward Daniell about raising capital of £40,000 in shares of £500. Daniell immediately agreed to invest £1,000, paying a deposit of £200, and another £1,000 on behalf of his sister-in-law, Miss Lawrence. An army man and a member of the 1st Gordon (75th) Regiment of Highlanders, Daniell would become a lifelong friend and ally of Evans.

Evans next approached Betts Hopper, Edmund Halswell, William Hutt, Lord Petre and John Heath, and outlined his scheme. All were reluctant, but saw little alternative and hoped their move might persuade Glenelg to grant them a charter.[1]

Several informal meetings followed, and eventually Evans and Daniell were asked to inquire about chartering a ship. They called first on Charles Enderby, who had no ship available and who declined to invest in the scheme. But he did introduce them to the wealthy shipbuilder Joseph Somes at the London Tavern, where Lloyd's was temporarily housed, the Royal Exchange having burned to the ground. When they outlined their plans to Somes, he made the 'laconic' observation that it was 'a d__d plucky scheme'.[2]

Evans managed to attract fourteen members of both the early 1825 Company and the later 1837 Association to a meeting at John Wright's Banking House in Covent Garden on 29 August, where his old friend, the lawyer and member of the Aborigines' Protection Society, Standish Motte moved, and Joseph Somes seconded, the resolution to form a joint stock company. Paid-up capital was to be £25,000 in fifty shares of £500 each – 'with the power of extending it to £500,000'. They planned to begin operations as soon as forty shares were subscribed.[3]

A sub-committee was formed with provisional chairman Motte, along with Evans, Somes, Wright, Thomas McDonnell, D. Ramsay, Edmund Halswell and Enderby, who had offered his assistance in enlisting subscribers. A week later each member was asked to pay a deposit of £200 before 17 September, and the remaining £300 by 1 November. On 19 September, Evans was appointed to revise the new prospectus for this New Zealand Colonization Company (the Colonization Company) and arrange for its publication. The draft he drew up set out their principles, and explained that while they expected Maori to sell their land cheaply, the real payment was not to be

> . . . the few perishable commodities which might satisfy them for a moment, but *colonization itself*, including the blessings of civilization, religion, education, as well as reserves of land for themselves and their descendants . . . and participation in all the rights and privileges of British subjects.[4]

A week later Somes brought some of his city friends – James Waddell, Walter Brodie, John Gordon, Arthur Willis and J. H. Luscombe – and offered the Colonization Company one of his ships, the barque, *Tory*. They moved cautiously on the offer at first. On Wednesday 10 October, at a general meeting in Wright's Banking House, Evans was asked to negotiate with naval Lieutenant McDonnell, a member of the 1825 Company who had offered the Company some land he had supposedly bought in the north of the North Island of New Zealand. He was not always reliable and negotiations with him had been waxing and waning for some time.[5] During the negotiations, Evans persuaded McDonnell to visit the *Tory* with Daniell; afterwards, both reported favourably.

Two weeks later they had thirteen subscribers, and Evans seconded John Wright's motion that as soon as twenty parties committed, the Colonization Company should be officially formed. A week later on 31 October, he was able to announce that the remaining seven subscribers had been found, including Somes and Lord Durham.[6] This last name was premature to say the least, and indicated Evans's misplaced optimism. Evans proposed, 'That it is highly expedient immediately on the arrangement being made with a retired naval lieutenant, Mr McDonnell, that an expedition should forthwith be sent to New Zealand to establish the settlement of the Colony on behalf of the Company.'[7] In November, the committee reported that the *Tory* was 'pre-eminently' suitable for their plans, and Evans and his colleagues began negotiations with Somes for the purchase of the *Tory* – 'to buy him and his city friends'.[8] Evans joined another sub-committee to draw up a list for outfitting the expedition, while assessing its 'nature, extent and necessary expense'. A three-page prospectus for the New Zealand Colonization Company, labelled Private and Confidential, listed the paid-up members, with additions and deletions added by Evans's hand; an outline of their ideals; and the fourteen resolutions adopted by the Company. The last resolution stated:

> That in all the transactions of the Company the protection and improvement of the Aborigines be regarded as fundamental principles, and every countenance and aid afforded to philanthropic exertions on their behalf.[9]

Meanwhile, the delicate negotiations with McDonnell continued, with Halswell and Motte assisting Evans. On 7 November he proposed crediting the earlier Company of 1825 with £20,000 worth of shares in exchange for their land. McDonnell would 'in substance' accept their terms, on being paid £1,000 in advance of the percentage on his territory advanced to the new Colonization Company.[10] But Evans was not entirely happy with the settlement, writing to Daniell of his fears that McDonnell's land might be worthless.

And in November, Wakefield returned.

In early December, Evans wrote to Wakefield asking for his assistance, but Wakefield's response dismayed him. The man seemed clearly unwell:

> I have done all I can in addition to what has been done before; but you must be aware of the feebleness in such a matter of one who has been dead for some months. I wonder what any one could do in any matter after being really buried for a year. Even into my

> grave however, there 'has penetrated' a hope that you will gain your object: and your success will be a great satisfaction to me.[11]

The use of 'you' and 'your' were indications that Wakefield had removed himself from, or lost interest in, his plans for colonising New Zealand. Possibilities for his own political advancement looked hopeful from his association with Durham, and the Beauharnois Project in Canada had supplanted New Zealand in his priorities. As Molesworth said later, Wakefield had 'too many projects afloat'.[12]

Through December the small committee negotiated with Somes for the *Tory*, finally agreeing to pay £5,250, half of which was handed over in a cheque signed by three trustees and countersigned by Evans. Another sum of £5,000 was approved for goods that could be exchanged for produce or bartered for land after arrival in New Zealand. A last meeting before Christmas to discuss the *Tory*'s refit was adjourned until Friday, 4 January 1839.

Meanwhile, the government had found its own solution in the form of Captain Hobson. Much earlier that year Hobson had suggested that the government buy restricted areas from Maori, and negotiate treaties with the chiefs to acquire jurisdiction by magistrates appointed by their organisation. His idea had lain dormant with Glenelg for some time, even though he had told Durham of it in February and had been pestered by Coates to consider a consular agent.[13] In December, Glenelg had contacted Hobson who came to London for further discussions.

In the New Year there were distractions at home in Pelham Road. Daniel Riddiford had been engaged to be married for three years, but when Harriot Stone's parents heard of his plan to take their daughter to New Zealand, they feared that in an unknown country at the end of the world she might be lost to them forever and withdrew their consent for the marriage. Undeterred, Daniel's mother worked swiftly, and helped the pair elope. They married on 18 January in Lewes, Suffolk. Harriot's family resigned themselves with good grace and gave them a generous dowry.[14]

On Saturday, 12 January, Evans was asked to 'fit up' the accommodation for the passengers on the *Tory*. It was resolved that a cheque for the sum of £382 5s be forwarded to Somes for the ship, to be authorised by the trustees. Evans added William Hutt to the committee and they prepared to communicate with the government, while negotiations continued with members of the 1825 Company. Evans wrote to Lord Durham expressing their determination to colonise New Zealand 'almost immediately' without government sanction:

> . . . and even without a Charter, trusting to each others' honour against risk of individual liability, and relying upon our own prudence and firmness to avert those troubles and disasters, which are apt to affect a society not sustained by any legal means of preserving order.

He acknowledged the years of work Durham had put into planning the colonisation of New Zealand and asked for an interview to outline their scheme and receive 'any advice that you may think fit to give us'.

Durham took time from writing his report on Canada to agree to a meeting, 'whenever you wish', but pointedly referring to the Company of 1825 and distancing himself from the new venture, he added, 'Of course you are aware that I have been long, and still am, connected with a Company, the object of which, like yours, is colonization and settlement in New Zealand.'[15]

Evans and his colleagues knew that the 1825 Company was applying separately to the Colonial Office for a charter. Impatient and fearful, Evans wrote a confidential letter to Glenelg from the Reform Club on 4 February, pleading not only for a 'judicial Office in the proposed Colony', but also for an interview to 'make explanations of some value on this subject':

> I have been allowed to pay all the expenses of the New Zealand Association, amounting to upwards of £800 and to work gratuitously for two years. After being abandoned by those who invited me into this, I have still persevered, and have raised, with the assistance of Mr. Wright . . . a subscription of £100,000 . . . . It is in my power virtually to place this at the disposal of the Colonial Office . . .[16]

Glenelg, who had been aware of the 'inconsistency, self-interest, and plain inadequacy of [the Church Missionary Society's] proposals', had hinted after the Bill's collapse that if the Association's directorate were Anglican, his office might yet co-operate with a joint stock company.[17] And Stephen apparently bore no antagonism personally to the Company: his attitude to their enterprise was more one of caution and realistic appraisal than decided prejudice. He could see that colonisation was inevitable, and he could also see it was possible for a colonisation company to work alongside the government, 'based on the model of the old New England constitutions'.[18] On 21 January he had suggested a company be chartered to handle finances, land sales and emigration.[19] Glenelg had dithered, but now he seemed to be 'more favourably disposed towards the Colonization Company than he had been towards the Association'. A week after receiving Evans's letter, he wrote a minute for Cabinet proposing the 'establishment of a regular form of government . . . to obtain by negotiation and cession of the chiefs, the sovereignty for the Queen . . . where the British are already settled'. He suggested the land policy be administered by the Colonization Company, and that a charter should be granted to 'the persons now applying for it'.[20]

Evans and the other members were so optimistic that a draft prospectus entitled 'New Zealand Bank, and Colonization Company' was drawn up, with spaces left for ten members of a provisional committee, and offices for the purchase of shares all over Great Britain. They were seeking capital of £500,000 in 10,000 shares of £50 each, noting optimistically that 'Capital may be increased to one million'. They were confident that an Act would be passed by the Legislature 'in the ensuing session'. Fortunately, it was merely a draft because time was not on the Company's side.[21]

Lord Glenelg – who had already been famously excoriated by Brougham for 'sheer laziness' – was replaced as Colonial Secretary by Lord Normanby on 20 February. But Normanby was even less effective than his predecessor.[22] Hutt and Motte approached him on 4 March enclosing a list of the members and directors of the company and informing them of having fulfilled the government's requirements for land, a ship, capital and emigrants.

Stephen then played the card of bigotry – no doubt urged by the CMS. He was horrified to see Catholic names on the list of the new company's directors – although in fact only Lord Petre was a Catholic. In a minute dated 6 March he wrote to Under-Secretary Labouchere:

> The leading members are now Roman Catholics. If the business is committed to them, New Zealand will infallibly become a Roman Catholic Country. As long as we have the choice of establishing Popery or Protestantism in any part of the world, I cannot understand how anyone, not a Roman Catholic, would hesitate what that choice should be.[23]

The Colonial Office then distanced itself from its former offer, telling Hutt and Motte that the list of directors differed from that of 1838, and 'much additional information . . . bearing materially upon the question' had been digested between the earlier offer of a charter and the present.[24]

Meanwhile, at their headquarters, Evans was discovering that 'buying the city men by buying the ships', as he later put it, had its drawbacks.[25] After the *Tory* purchase, many newcomers were trying to 'job' in different ways, angling for favours. Hoping Wakefield might become involved, and might also persuade Durham not to apply for a separate charter, Evans and his wife met Wakefield on Cornhill in February. Evans told him of his own Company's progress and its purchase of the *Tory*. He recounted how Somes had brought several city men into the enterprise, and their successful subscription drive. He and his wife persuaded Wakefield to visit the docks to see the *Tory* and afterwards they dined together at Blackwall. By the end of the evening, Evans had reawakened Wakefield's interest in the enterprise, but he consented to become involved only on condition that they set up a management committee that included him. On 12 March it was done, Wakefield being joined on the committee by Somes, Gordon, Hutt and Lord Petre.[26] Impressed by the rank of the men involved in the venture, Somes's desire for their esteem was greater than his interest in 'business dealings', so he needed little persuasion by Wakefield to surrender the contract for the *Tory*. Wakefield ordered Captain Edmund Chaffers, his brother Colonel William Wakefield, and his son, Jerningham, to make inquiries for other vessels, but after a short time, the City men were again accused of 'jobbing the expedition'. William Wakefield (whose rank was actually Lieutenant-Colonel, but who was more commonly addressed and referred to as 'Colonel') thought at first the *Tory* was too large, and suggested the *Sandwich*, which was not 'eligible'.[27] Somes re-offered the *Tory*, and he and Wakefield came to an arrangement on the purchase. Later, Wakefield would explain he had repurchased the *Tory* 'in a more business-like manner'.

Wakefield's hand in all this is evident. When he met Evans on Cornhill and was told of the influential men his scheme had attracted and the extent of the new Company's progress, he could smell success. The purchase of the *Tory* was a significant advance, and Wakefield, who had hitherto been able to claim every initiative or achievement as his own, knew this time he could not. By being placed on the directorate and wielding his power immediately under the guise of principle, he persuaded Somes to surrender the contract. He then undertook an elaborate search for a ship to replace the *Tory*, probably knowing it was unlikely they would find another on better terms. Their search was fruitless, Somes renewed his offer and, having proven his pecuniary disinterest, Wakefield seized it and claimed the vessel's purchase as his own achievement. The charade was exposed fourteen years later when his boasting caught him out.[28]

From this time, the confusing messages and reports Evans and his group of emigrants received from the Colonization Company's directors following interviews and correspondence with the Colonial Office are mirrored by the many interpretations since placed on them. After their interview with Normanby on 14 March, the directors told the intending emigrants that Normanby was 'gracious, even affable' – and, in fact, that he was extremely encouraging. On the one hand, Evans and his cohort were told that Normanby assured them their venture would 'be allowed if immediate steps [were] taken by the Association [*sic*] to form one or more settlements in New Zealand', but the directors omitted to mention that Normanby cautioned them that until New Zealand was 'wholly or in part' British, he was unable to recognise their proceedings. In fact, 'Normanby turned his back on the Colonization Association because, as Labouchere explained to the 1840 select committee', the government had decided 'that it could not, "consistently with the law of nations, exercise the rights of sovereignty without some previous arrangement with its inhabitants"'.[29]

On Wednesday, 20 March, Wakefield's forty-third birthday, Evans and others gathered for dinner at John Wright's home. It was not a happy occasion. Frustrated by the uncertainty, Evans grumbled that Colonel Torrens was sabotaging their chances by misleading people about which company had been offered a charter by the government, Torrens claiming it was his 1825 Company rather than their Colonization Company. Torrens and Durham had petitioned the Colonial Office separately with their own views on the joint administration of areas, juries and judiciary for New Zealand, thus jeopardising the chances of any settlement being arrived at with government or of any charter being drawn up.[30]

Then William Hutt revealed he had been informed by Henry Labouchere six days earlier that a clause would be added to the Bill empowering only the government to sell New Zealand land, which might raise the price of land 500 per cent above that of the Company's scheme. For Evans the shock must have been acute.

Wakefield was alert to the mood of simmering tension. 'Send off your expedition immediately', he directed. 'Acquire all the land that you can and then you will find that the Government will see the absolute necessity of doing something. Possess yourself of the soil and you are secure, but if from *delay* you allow others to do it before you – they will succeed and you will fail.'

When Wright challenged Wakefield over his commitment to the new venture, asking for his support and leadership, Wakefield's reply was evasive. He was busily engaged 'in other quarters'. He would 'decline taking any active part'. The new Company was 'an individual speculation of Land and Commerce' differing from his model, and he had no understanding of 'companies and shares [and] was therefore unfit to manage such matters'. He would 'pledge himself to raise five shares immediately the first expedition had sailed, but not a single one until something had actually been done'. This denial of any commercial acumen came from the man who would later explain he had stepped in to repurchase the *Tory* in 'a more business-like manner'.

It was a masterstroke. While urging immediate action as a prerequisite to his financial involvement, he managed to distance himself should anything go wrong. Yet while a more cautious man might have hesitated at Wakefield's ambiguity, Evans's desperate situation was his overriding imperative.[31]

On 26 March Evans was 'called in to act as secretary'. At a meeting of the five directors, he was asked to warn the original subscribers that they would lose their options if payments were not completed within four days.[32] A week later he advertised in *The Times, Chronicle* and *Herald* for a surveyor and a captain for the *Tory*. He made inquiries into the acceptability of a Mr Peppercorn and a Mr Giles for the ship's captaincy, and provided stationery for the committee. He was asked to write to Robert Whitfield and Mr Batts. He was also asked to write a formal letter of appointment to Colonel William Wakefield as leader of the expedition, which was fulsome in its praise of William's qualities, and an expression of confidence in his abilities to carry out 'the arduous nature of the duties to be performed at the extremities of the Globe, beyond the pale of the Law, where order will have to be maintained among bold and adventurous men'.[33]

Throughout April, as the purchase of the *Tory* progressed, Evans communicated with Messrs Foley, Moreing and many others. He was a workhorse, devoting every minute to the project, guided by a group of shrewd, clever businessmen and Wakefield, none of whom had as much at stake as he.

On 1 April, Evans watched his fellow founder of the Colonization Company, solicitor Standish Motte, become an early Wakefield victim when he objected to having been omitted from the management committee. Somes offered to stand aside for Motte, but Wakefield objected, saying he would not act without Somes. Wright attempted to soothe the Motte's injured feelings, pointing out that he (Motte) had been absent when the committee was selected. Three weeks later, Motte's failure to pay his subscription resulted in his shares being confiscated, and he appeared to fade entirely from the scene. However, from July that year to December 1840 he pursued his case, first by writing a letter of grievance asking for redress, then requesting a committee to consider his case. Both were declined, Wakefield referring to the 'continued importunities' of Mr Motte. In July 1840 the case went to arbitration, and the Company engaged 'to indemnify' his shares. Later Motte complained he had not been paid his £500, and the case went to a city court.[34]

Visitors came daily to the Colonization Company's headquarters. Evans haunted the premises, recording calls from leading London businessmen: the banker Isaac Goldsmid, John Gowen, A. G. Tollemache, Marjoribanks, Viscount Ingestre, Willis, John Boulcott and Alexander Nairn. Charles Buller too was a frequent visitor.

On 10 April, after reading an article in the *Glasgow Times* that hinted at another company being formed in Scotland, they resolved to send off the expedition within fifteen days. Wakefield was asked to propose a plan for a joint stock company, and Evans was instructed to have the draft prospectus printed and ready for the next meeting. He answered an inquiry from Dudley Sinclair, the son of Sir George Sinclair and a prospective emigrant, who had asked if anyone could buy land directly from Maori:

> . . . it is the opinion of the Directors that the Company will not be able hereafter to enforce any regulations prohibiting shareholders from purchasing land in New Zealand immediately from the natives; but that no person going out in vessels equipped by the Company will be permitted to do so, and that effectual means will be taken to prevent it.[35]

To Professor Knox in Edinburgh, who made a similar request, he confessed he was unable to give him any details, 'beyond stating the fact that considerable capital has been subscribed and paid up, and large purchases of land in New Zealand have been effected', a bold statement that referred to McDonnell's land up north. The agreement with McDonnell had been negotiated by Wakefield and signed only a few days earlier.

On 26 April Evans was 'authorized to go to Devonport to urge Captain Chaffers to come to London' to take up the command of the *Tory*.[36] Amidst all the preparations for the outfitting of the *Tory*, Evans found time to visit his parents at Mile End, where he found his mother and William prostrate with influenza. More than thirty years after the family had moved to Mile End, there was still no public drainage, fever was ever present and unemployment in the area was worse than ever.[37] Reverend Evans was sixty years old by now, still resolutely grappling with his large ministry and travelling tirelessly. A few days later his son scribbled off a hurried note to him:

> I have been laid up with influenza ever since I was at Mile End, and Mrs Evans is confined to her bed in the same way. I hope that my mother's illness is merely of the same description, and will pass away in a day or two; – indeed from what I saw I felt a high degree of confidence that it would be so. I will come to Mile End as soon as possible. In haste. (Etc.) Hope William is better.[38]

Four days later he had recovered enough to attend a grand luncheon at Lovegrove's Tavern at the West India Dock to publicise and promote the Colonization Company's intentions for New Zealand. Two hundred guests attended – 'the elite of London' – with George III's son, the Duke of Sussex, Lord John Russell, Lord Durham and Lord Petre among the luminaries. With William Hutt presiding, Evans condemned the dilatory conduct of the government, and invited prospective settlers to attend fortnightly soirées at the Company's offices in the Adelphi. Posters were displayed all over London. Pamphlets, illustrations and general information were also freely available at these '*conversaziones*'.

Twenty-four-year-old James John Taine was drawn there by a poster advertising the promotion, and met his future wife, Liocadia D'Oliviera, Wakefield's ward, who was accompanied by 'her friends' the Evanses.[39] On the streets there was a huge amount of public interest. A diorama of the Bay of Islands was exhibited in Leicester Square, which, according to twelve-year-old Thomas McKenzie, attracted 'crowds of people'. McKenzie was an enterprising and fearless young lad who had already saved a man from drowning in the Serpentine, and who intended emigrating with his widowed mother. He wrote of articles of Maori crafts on display: 'mats, baskets, fishing lines, spears, greenstone meres, ornaments, flax raw and dressed by Maori – "like silk", pocket handkerchiefs "almost like cambric", canvas, rope, Maori carving etc., etc.' The promotion was a huge success.[40]

Afterwards, three directors visited Normanby, Stephen and Parliamentary Under-Secretary Henry Labouchere to give a background of the newly formed New Zealand Land Company (later called the New Zealand Company) and tell them of the *Tory*'s imminent departure for New Zealand. Labouchere gave them no guarantees that any land they might purchase from Maori would stay in their possession, and said it would probably be re-purchased by the government; but Hutt assured him the Company had no intention of setting up its own government. They gave him a copy of the Company's rigorous instructions to Colonel Wakefield, the Principal Agent, and were given Normanby's assurance that the government intended to introduce a Bill.

Two days later, Colonial Secretary Normanby wrote asserting he had learnt 'for the first time, that a body of Her Majesty's subjects are about to proceed to New Zealand and to purchase large tracts of land there, and to establish a system of government independent of the authority of the British Crown'. He refused to give them letters of introduction to the governors of New South Wales and Van Diemen's Land.[41] This was astonishing, as after studying all the proposals from the interested parties, Stephen had suggested to both Glenelg and Normanby that the government favour a scheme that came very close to that of Evans's Colonization Company – a joint stock company with a body of governors in England and 'the Government of the Colony being the business of the Corporation abroad'. Yet Normanby preferred the idea of appointing a consul to the country.[42]

A day earlier, when the New Zealand Association and the Colonization Company had been wound up to make way for the New Zealand Land Company, Hutt proposed that as all expenses of the Association had been borne by Wakefield and Evans, 'each of them having expended more than £500, besides their unceasing attention to the business of the Association, an original share of £500' be given to the two. Wakefield refused the offer but approved it for Evans who, he said, 'had been led by the promises of Lord Melbourne and Lord Howick to make a considerable sacrifice of property, besides what he had laid out for the Association'.[43] A few days later when lawyer Edmund Halswell proposed a vote of thanks to Wakefield, the maestro suggested that Evans should be included in their gratitude.

In drawing up his list of expenses for the Association, Evans said his 'actual disbursement . . . including the outstanding debts which he undertook to pay off, amounted to more than £800'. But he 'cheerfully ceded the balance' to the Association and withdrew from 'active service of the Company'. Before resigning, he reminded the directors of Daniel Riddiford's 'diligence and perseverance' in acting as his assistant secretary 'for more than two years without any reward, on the promise and assurance held out to him of remunerating employment' as soon as capital was raised for the 'colonization of New Zealand'. In a gesture of good will, Somes immediately transferred one of his shares to Riddiford.[44]

On 2 May, Wakefield's prospectus was printed for the Land Company, and the sale of 99,999 acres of the town of the 'First and Principal Settlement' at £1 per acre began, without a single acre having actually been purchased in Cook's Straits. With his eye on a retirement of scholarly ease after his colonising work in New Zealand, Evans bought a total of fifty town acres, while Wakefield opted for a hundred shares.[45]

Durham and Torrens had been recaptured by Wakefield, Durham lured to govern the board of five directors who had absolute control of the Land Company's affairs for up to twelve months. Torrens, along with Petre and William Hutt, was amongst the nineteen-strong committee that supervised the financial, emigration and shipping tasks.[46] Somes was deputy governor. The New Zealand Land Company was split into two distinct groups, Evans being chairman of the emigrants' committee of the 'First Colony of New Zealand'.[47] At this point John Ward stepped in to replace Evans as secretary. Evans had known Ward for years, and could not resist boasting he had known him 'longer than anyone here'. 'No person living', he added grandly, 'could be better qualified for the office of Secretary to the Company.'[48]

Planning reached fever pitch in the Evans household. Harriet Evans had bought one of the first sections offered, as a perpetual endowment for an infant school for the 'children of the aborigines, and of the poorer class of settlers'. She guaranteed the salary for the first year of a master and a mistress, for whom she would provide 'free passage and accommodation on arrival'. Three trustees were appointed and 'donations and annual subscriptions' were to be received by Dr Evans. The bankers were 'Messrs Hankey and Fenchurch'.[49]

Her committee of Ladies Durham, Petre and Molesworth and Mrs Mabel Baring helped her draw up a list of educational resources and interview teachers. They selected twenty-year-old Miss Ann Tilke to teach the infants, with James Buchanan – aged fifty-five, with twenty years' teaching experience – as superintendent, guaranteeing both salaries for a year. They needed capital of £200 plus annual subscriptions, and appointed three trustees to handle the funds. Their goal was very ambitious: 'a system [of infant schools], which may hereafter extend itself over a large portion of the infant population of New Zealand', and might even 'be extended . . . to include an Infant Orphan Asylum for the native children'.[50]

On 5 May, Evans and his wife joined Wakefield, Somes, Molesworth and others at the Falcon Inn to farewell the *Tory* from Gravesend. Wakefield's younger brother Lieutenant Colonel William Wakefield was to be the First Colony's Principal Agent whose job was to 'purchase' tracts of land from Maori for intending settlers – much as the missionaries had done – and by living amongst them, introduce them to the benefits of 'British Civilization'.[51]

A year younger than Evans, William was of medium height, cool-headed, diplomatic and brave. He had distinguished himself during his fighting for six years in the Iberian Peninsula. He was a reserved man, who still mourned the death of his wife during his imprisonment in Lancaster Castle as an accessory to Gibbon Wakefield's crime of the abduction of an heiress.[52] With him were Charles Heaphy, draughtsman for the Land Company, surgeon John Dorset, Ngaiti, and nineteen-year-old Jerningham, Gibbon Wakefield's son.

Evans's committee of emigrants of the First Colony of New Zealand was indeed impressively and solidly establishment (apart from the Catholic Henry Petre): Francis Molesworth (Sir William's younger brother), Dudley Sinclair (Sir George's son), Captain Edward Daniell, Edward Betts Hopper, George Duppa and William Swainson. Daniel Riddiford acted as secretary. From 20 May they met daily at the Land Company's offices in the Adelphi to plan and 'lay the foundation of Charitable, Scientific, Religious and other Institutions for the Colony'.[53]

At their first meeting on 20 May, Evans copied an extract, in French, from *Le Commerce* of 20 March 1838, describing the qualities of New Zealand *Phormium tenax* – native flax. It might have been included as a reminder of the French threat or a suggestion for export. Two days later he approached the Church Missionary Society for a second time enclosing the Land Company's prospectus:

> In particular, I am directed to inform you that the gentlemen, whose sentiments I have the honour to express, are unanimous and zealous in their determination to sanction and promote, by every means in their power, all philanthropic exertions that are made for the benefit of the Aborigines. The missionaries, they will consider entitled to their especial consideration and support; and they respectfully request that you will favour them with your views on that subject generally, or with any particular suggestions you may think it desirable to make. Any communication from your Society will at all times be received with deep respect and consideration.[54]

Predictably, the offer was ignored. At the same time Evans wrote to Dr Hinds on behalf of the emigrant members of the Church of England, who wanted 'the administration of religious rites . . . to which they are conscientiously attached'. He hoped that Hinds's interest would encourage him to intercede for them with the governors of 'The Society for the Propagation of the Gospel in Foreign Parts'.[55]

While the directors wrangled with the Colonial Office, in turn demanding, reassuring and begging, Evans was in his element with the emigrants. Fizzing with energy and ebullience, he was ever the schoolmaster. His manner nettled some members and amused others, but he gave a positive charge to proceedings. And he got things done.

On the inside of a prospectus, Evans dashed off an urgent note to Betts Hopper in Dover: 'All goes on very prosperously. I could say a great deal about the Government, were I not bound to secrecy by the strictest ties of honour but . . . *all goes right*.' Come to London, he urged. Lord Petre had invited Betts Hopper to dine with him and Evans on 'Saturday next at 7 o'clock at his home in Mansfield Street . . . . Write immediately but pray, come on Saturday – you must, if you leave town again.'

On the letter's reverse, Betts Hopper's nephew, Edward Catchpool, later wrote wryly: 'Scripture text by Simpson in his lecture on Principles of Education –"If this counsel be of man, it will come to nought; but if it be of God ye cannot overthrow it, lest in so doing ye be found fighting against God".'[56]

The emigrants were determined to reach New Zealand for its summer, meaning they should begin the long voyage as soon as possible, so Evans and his ally Captain Daniell fired off urgent questions to the directors on 23 May, only three days after their first meeting.

What would be the fixed price for the land? What percentage would be used for sending labourers to the colony? Would terms be fixed? Would the Land Company guarantee not to lower them later? Would the original purchasers get any advantage over later purchasers? What percentage of the income from land sales would be spent on public works? They wanted a supply of maps, charts and books illustrating New Zealand,[57] and urged the directors to send out a survey party as soon as possible.[58]

Ripples of alarm circulated amongst some of the directors who suggested a 'great delay in sending out the first Colony'.[59] Wakefield began to attend Evans's committee meetings to keep a close eye on proceedings and answer their questions 'on behalf of the Directors'. But parties had already been sent to buy the land, and the emigrants were impatient. They were determined to set a fixed price for the land. Wakefield advised them against it, but Evans's committee voted for and reinstated the proposal.[60]

Evans wrote to the chairman of the Aborigines' Protection Society, forwarding copies of the prospectus, and advertised his Committee of Emigrants for the First Colony in the Edinburgh *Evening Courant*.

He responded to all queries promptly; there was one from a Geo Simpson, another from an Archibald Hillary. But he was struck by one thing:

> . . . he found the first fear on the part of the people was that the promoters were connected with the Government. The main point with the masses was the character and responsibility of those who were conducting the emigration scheme. The peasantry, so soon as they understood that the gentry had sufficient confidence in the new colonies as to send their own relations to them, flocked to those places, and no difficulty was experienced in securing thousands of most eligible persons.[61]

With the directors' approval, he sent out circulars broadly outlining Gibbon Wakefield's six points, the first of which was a highly dubious claim. The Land Company's acquisitions in New Zealand consisted of the entire land of the 'Hokianga and Kaipara belonging to Mr McDonnell to the extent of 600,000 acres, besides the land purchased by a former Company in 1825 at the River Thames. Maori had held the property "sacred" [for McDonnell] for fourteen years.'

The Land Company had sent a vessel to examine both sides of Cook's Straits with 'ample means to purchase the most eligible tracts of land, and prepare generally' for the first emigrants who would 'rendezvous in the Straits on 10 January next'. Land sales would follow 'the principles adopted by the South Australian Commissioners as closely' as possible. 'With one-tenth of the land reserved for [Maori], the rest would be sold in England for £99,999. Of this amount 25 per cent would be retained for the company's expenses, and the balance used to add to the value of the land by defraying the cost of sending labourers. Those who bought land orders were entitled to claim an expenditure for their own passage and that of their families and servants, equal to 75 per cent of their purchase money.'[62] '[N]o expense' would be spared 'in the Surveying Establishment', to ensure immediate possession for purchasers. The next point was also rather less than honest:

> The Company are in communication with Her Majesty's Government, and have no reason to anticipate any delay in the establishment of British authority in New Zealand – in the meantime a powerful body of Colonists has been formed, who feel perfect confidence in proceeding at once to settle in New Zealand, without the slightest apprehension of danger from the Natives or other persons.

Lastly, Evans promoted 'the most complete and authentic account of New Zealand' – *The British Colonization of New Zealand*, priced at 4s 6d. Members assembled daily, he told them, 'happy to make you thoroughly acquainted with their objects and plans'.[63]

By June, large numbers of visitors were attending the Land Company's headquarters. The directors told Evans's committee that Captain Hobson was being sent to negotiate with Maori for cession of their sovereignty to England. New Zealand would be a dependency of New South Wales, with Hobson answerable to Governor Sir George Gipps. Stephen had prepared draft instructions for Hobson – some of which were almost exactly those proposed by the New Zealand Land Company.[64]

Undeterred by the news of a government emissary for New Zealand, Harriet Evans met briefly with Captain Hobson, perhaps with her committee of women. Hobson was a frail, mild-mannered man, steeped in naval discipline. Privately, Hobson was also a man very reluctant to take up his new position as Lieutenant Governor of New Zealand.[65]

CHAPTER FIVE.
TAKING LEAVE

Polonius: This above all – to thine own self be true
And it must follow, as the night the day
Thou canst not then be false to any man.
Farewell – my blessing season this in thee.

Laertes: Most humbly do I take my leave, my lord.

William Shakespeare, *Hamlet*, I, iii, lines 78–82

In June or July, Samuel Revans (1808–88) was introduced to the New Zealand Land Company as a prospective emigrant by the reformer, Roebuck. Revans was in the printing trade and was known to be a 'militant radical'.[1] Years earlier, he had lived briefly in Canada with his friend Henry Chapman, founding with him the *Montreal Advertiser.* When Chapman went back to England on a political mission for the Canadian Liberal Party, the publication folded and Revans also went home, quickly becoming involved with Roebuck, Cobden and others in agitating for social and industrial change.[2] He had also worked on Wakefield's South Australian venture. In 1835, after Roebuck accused John Black of the *Morning Chronicle* of cowardice, the latter challenged him to a duel. Revans acted as Roebuck's second, two rounds were fired harmlessly, and 'in an altercation Revans offered to fight the other second'. The challenge was accepted, and the two men 'nearly engaged in mortal combat'.[3] The fiery Revans had then returned to Canada where he became engaged in the Papineau uprising in 1837, and was finally forced to flee the country for good.[4]

Back in London, Revans was soon introduced to and attended Evans's committee meetings. Revans clearly felt antipathy towards Evans, probably from the start. The two men were similar in temperament, both being volatile and easily offended by others, but Revans had also missed out on one of the prime positions for the colony, that of emigration agent. That prize was given to Daniel Riddiford by the directors to acknowledge his assistance since the inception of the New Zealand Association. Revans was not happy about this or about travelling with Evans, and expressed his reservations to Wakefield, who told him 'to hoist the flag of forbearance'. It was good advice, which Wakefield probably dispensed to all the passengers, but with Evans in such a commanding position Revans was not mollified. He was an independent man who resented being controlled by anyone.

Revans was encouraged to set up a newspaper in the new colony, and worked towards the first issue of the *New Zealand Gazette*, which was published in London on 21 August.[5] The major article in this issue was entitled 'Historical Sketch of the Colonization of New Zealand', which was chiefly a stinging denunciation of the government. It attacked Lord Howick in particular, whose earlier warm support of the New Zealand Association had encouraged several gentlemen to sell property, abandon their professions and make other sacrifices, only to be duped by the 'Anti-Colonial Office'. This was hardly fair to the conscientious Howick whose understanding of and sympathy for their cause did not necessarily guarantee a vote of confidence. The author of the lengthy article is believed to have been Wakefield, but Evans most definitely had a hand in the composition. It mentioned the appointment of Captain Hobson,

> . . . who . . . is to treat with the native chiefs for a cession of their sovereignty, – a thing for which their language did not afford a word until the missionaries coined one for the occasion – and then he is to become lieutenant-governor of the portions of the islands so ceded.

The very real sense of betrayal was indicative of the emigrants' mood, but the final paragraph of defiance is stamped all over with Evans's style:

> Lord Howick is unremitting in his expressions of hostility to the Colony . . . he [advises] gentlemen in the House of Commons to avoid all connection with it; and he goes about describing it as a bubble scheme, and Poyais project for cheating the public . . . . our consolation is, that all things and all men bide their time; and that, come what will, Englishmen carry with them, wherever they go, not merely the right, but the determination and the capacity to manage their own affairs. With these feelings and with this farewell, 3000 emigrants take leave of his lordship and the Colonial Office.[6]

Although he knew most of the details of the contract drawn up for his newspaper, Revans did not receive the terms until they were completed by the directors in mid-September and conveyed to him on board the *Adelaide* by Evans (see Appendix Three). Under the agreement, there were four trustees: John Ward, Evans, George Hunter and Richard Davies Hanson. Five hundred pounds was outlaid: £200 by the Company, with the balance coming from Revans and the trustees. The presses, type, machinery, paper and other equipment belonged to Evans, Hunter and Hanson, and at any time any of the men could demand their return. Revans was to be sole managing editor, replaceable only by serious default or breach of his contract. The paper would rely on advertising and subscriptions for revenue. For the first year Revans would reap all the paper's profits, and in the second year the Company would receive 5 per cent on its investment. Evans, Hunter and Hanson were to 'exercise a general control over the nature of the written articles and advertisements', and to ask Revans at any time to omit or not insert any material that 'may be injurious to the said newspaper or to the [Company's] ends for which the same was established'. Revans was to conduct his editorship 'under the general control' of the trustees 'for the time being', with the option eventually to buy out the shareholders.[7]

Letters to prospective emigrants flowed from Evans's pen. On 8 July he issued a new prospectus announcing the formation of 'Literary, Scientific and Philanthropic Institutions' for the benefit of the settlers and Maori. A public library, general museum and scientific institution, and dispensary and hospital were planned. Donations of books, manuscripts, maps, paintings and sculpture were sought. Each item would be publicly acknowledged, and the committee he chaired would reciprocate with 'New Zealand specimens'.[8]

By the end of July all the New Zealand Land Company's sections – which had not yet been purchased in New Zealand – had been sold, and another prospectus printed offering 50,000 more acres.[9] Nine weeks after Evans's urgent request, the survey ship *Cuba* with surveyor Lieutenant William Mein Smith, Richard Davies Hanson (journalist and lawyer who was replacing McDonnell as the representative of absentee landholders) and twenty labourers finally departed. When Lord Petre was denied a meeting with Normanby to inform him of the emigrants' imminent departure and discuss the government's arrangements for law enforcement, Parliamentary Under-Secretary Henry Labouchere had already told Reverend A. M. Campbell airily that the New Zealand Land Company was 'not recognized by H.M's. Government, who have given no sanction to the proceedings of that body and have no official knowledge of them'.[10] This assertion was repeated on 12 August and again a week later when Labouchere added that, although Normanby wished to protect the emigrants, the Colonial Office still declined to recognise the Company in the 'capacity in which they are assuming to act'.[11] The French, who by this time were preparing their own colonising expeditions to New Zealand, were 'astounded the Government did not support the New Zealand Company'.[12]

Meanwhile, the Union Bank of Australia, eager to set up a branch in New Zealand, asked the directors to select three men whose business acumen might qualify them to be appointed local directors of the bank, 'without responsibility and without pay until such time as the profit of the branch should justify their being remunerated'. The directors selected Evans, then Betts Hopper and George Hunter, and another frenzy of organisation followed.

A revised issue of the *New Zealand Gazette* was published on 6 September. Again it included the 'Historical Sketch of the Colonization of New Zealand', perhaps because of demand. Even two years later, when the settlers were establishing themselves in Wellington, they were still smarting over the government's perceived betrayal, yet forgetting the many qualifications and warnings that had emanated from the Colonial Office after Normanby took over in February. Instead they recalled:

> . . . how anxiously the support and continuance of the Government were desired and courted by Mr. Francis Baring, Mr. Hutt, Mr. Wakefield, Dr. Evans, and the other founders of the colony. They will also recollect how they were deluded into the belief that the Secretary for the Colonies [Glenelg], with Lord Melbourne's entire approbation, sanctioned their undertaking, and that it was not till all their preparations for departure from England were completed, that a change in the views of government was discovered, and measures for the establishment of British Law and Order in New Zealand, seemed to be indefinitely postponed . . .[13]

Meanwhile, the new Lieutenant-Governor, Hobson, with an annual salary of £500, had sailed from England on 25 August on the *Druid* to play his part in what would be 'a preordained tragedy of which Hobson and the New Zealand Company were the preordained victims'.[14] Another historical analysis points out:

> The great pity lay when Stephen's suggestions, first to Lord Glenelg, then to Lord Normanby, regarding the possibility of an official charter for the Colonisation Company [of Evans] had not been

> taken up by either Colonial Secretary. Even [Stephen's] proposal of consultation with all groups [interested in colonising New Zealand] could have borne fruit. If the Government had harnessed that frenetic energy so characteristic of the 'systematic' colonisers, and directed it into wholly rational channels, the future of New Zealand would have been very different.[15]

Today, the balance of sympathy has tipped the other way, with the New Zealand Company men portrayed as calculating opportunists with little regard for Maori but greed for his land. Had the Church Missionary Society set a trap, it could not have been better devised. But they did not, and nor did the government.

Evans fell somewhere in between the theorists and the capitalists by taking a leap of faith with Wakefield's principles of systematic colonisation, and his own ambition to 'civilise' the Maori. He was ethically supported by his philanthropic and humanitarian motives, and for him there was no apparent conflict between these strong sentiments and the purchase of land for his own and his extended family's futures. He was sacrificing everything, including his capital and livelihood, but he hoped that his investment would compensate for the risk.

For years he had struggled 'to maintain appearances, and had hardly a shilling to call [his] own; although [he] had the disposal of a large income', he told his parents.[16] As well as working gratuitously for over two years, he had invested his entire property: £1,000 of his own money in the form of scrip for 500 acres, £1,000 of his wife's money, and countless amounts on goods for his family and for public ventures in the colony. Evans had been officially appointed Chief Judge and Umpire of the First Colony's Council, second only to Colonel Wakefield. 'The Regulations for the New Zealand Land Company's first and principal settlement' stipulated that:

> George Samuel Evans Esquire Barrister at law shall be the first Umpire. That the Umpire shall preside in all criminal proceedings and, assisted by seven assessors shall decide on the guilt or innocence of the parties accused. That if the party be declared guilty the Umpire shall state the punishment to be inflicted provided that without the special approval of the Committee no imprisonment to be stated by the Umpire shall exceed three months and no fine to be stated shall exceed £10.

There was another regulation: that the Umpire preside over all civil proceedings.[17]

Evans immediately applied to the directors for a year's salary in advance.[18] For his services in the old Association, the directors had promised him 500 acres to compensate for his loss, but he was later 'compelled to take up a mortgage of £1,500', he told his parents. He amended this sum later to £1,750, having borrowed through a bank from a Mr Robert Monro, using the land scrip as security, and agreeing to execute a mortgage to Monro after selecting the land.[19] He arranged for £300 of his salary advance to remain in London – presumably to pay the interest on the mortgage – knowing he would not be paid again until the first quarter of the second year. On 11 October that year the directors wrote to Colonel Wakefield outlining Evans's financial situation: the Company's solicitor Robert Few had executed a mortgage on five of his preliminary sections, and none was to be transferred until instructed by the Company.[20] It was a huge gamble, although this was, said young Thomas McKenzie with considerable understatement, 'a most exciting time'.[21]

On 7 September Lord John Russell replaced Normanby as Secretary of State for War and the Colonies. He would gradually become sympathetic to the Company's plight, but it was too late for those in the Company who had defied the government in proceeding to New Zealand, and the hapless emigrants and labourers who accompanied them.

ᘓ

Evans found time to slip away from it all to visit his friends and farewell his colleagues from the *Morning Chronicle*. In honour of the occasion, Thomas Campbell had composed a poem, 'Song of the Colonists Departing for New Zealand', a farewell for his friends the Evanses as much as a salute to the enterprise.[22] Evans shared a final dinner with colleagues at the Reform Club, but felt unable to 'take a formal leave' of his parents or brothers and sisters, 'only because I could not endure it', he later told them.[23] After the tragic death of James's first wife Linnaea Lamb and their two young sons from an epidemic that had swept the school she ran, James had remarried that year, left his boys' school (possibly North End Academy) and taken up legal practice. Alfred at twenty-seven was busy setting himself up in practice as a doctor. William was a semi-invalid at home although he too would later take up medical practice. Hannah, at the ripe old age of twenty-four, and her sister Mary were employed as governesses, and Claudia at just seventeen was resigning herself to the same fate.

On 9 September, ever 'zealous and indefatigable', Evans chaired a departure dinner at the Thatched House Tavern in St James's Street, where ninety guests paid two guineas a head to attend.[24] With the departure date set for the sixteenth, they still had work to do and there were many last-minute purchases to be made for the colony. Thinking of every possible contingency, Evans asked the directors for a set of surveying instruments in case of emergency.

Because he was responsible for procuring a significant proportion of goods, he had been given a hundred tons of space in the ship *Adelaide* without charge. Almost everything that might benefit the colony was crammed in. There were a great number of bricks – no doubt ordered from his former neighbours in Spitalfields – 25,000 of which were to be sent as ballast by the *Aurora*.[25] Evans had purchased a large steam mill for the community's use, and Betts Hopper's nephew Edward Catchpool had it operating as a flour mill two years later. Three storeys tall, it was reputed to be the first steam mill erected in New Zealand.[26] A large number of books had been donated towards the Literary and Scientific Society and they were stowed in the holds as well. There were also 171 packages of his 'sundries', and 177 'deals' – quantities of planks of fir or pine, each six feet long, between seven and nine inches wide, and two inches thick; and two large Manning houses. An assortment of domestic animals and livestock was on board. A milch cow given to Mrs Evans by John Wright was permitted on condition her milk was used for all passengers.[27] To add to his menagerie of two Newfoundland dogs, one English terrier, one pug dog and some fine specimens of cats, Evans shipped twelve pheasants, only three of which were to survive the voyage.[28]

The *Glenbervie* carried the large safe for the bank, along with thirteen casks, four packages, two bundles of spades, a case of guns, a bundle of forks, six cases, two barrels, an iron frame, a crate, an iron roller and more bricks, together with 'building materials' for Evans.[29]

A day before the small fleet sailed, William Hutt dashed off a farewell note to Evans. Hutt knew that, for all his faults, Evans could easily be exploited. He had observed his punishing work schedule and the financial and personal sacrifices he had made, and had watched him keep the enterprise alive in Wakefield's absence. He assured Evans he would always be interested in his welfare and 'in everything which relates to you':

> . . . looking back on the long-protracted and trying difficulties in which I have seen you engaged in connection with the undertaking which is now leading you to New Zealand – after that they have been in a large part, surmounted, I never witnessed a stronger evidence of those moral and intellectual virtues which command affection and respect.

He was very pleased to hear that Evans had been assigned a position by the directors and told him, 'I shall not cease to exert myself as occasion may require it to cause you to be appointed to some similar office by the Crown . . . . Pray make my compliments and adieu acceptable to [Mrs. Evans] . . . . My best wishes will always attend you.'[30]

As a shareholder, Evans sponsored a number of young emigrants: James John Taine; Thomas Wilmor McKenzie, the printer's apprentice, and his widowed mother; and two other families, plus a couple and three labourers. Mrs Evans sponsored the teachers and took a household staff of a female cook, a housemaid and 'buttons'.[31] As Wakefield's 'great friends', they also had been entrusted with the care of his ward, Liocadia D'Oliviera, the daughter of Portuguese peasants who had cared for his dying daughter Nina in 1835 in Lisbon. Wakefield honoured a promise to Nina that he would look after Liocadia, sending her to 'the Misses Cheyne School for Young Ladies' at Twickenham.[32] Liocadia and Amelia Riddiford became friends as regular visits were made between the two households. Wakefield had not lost interest in her welfare, but probably had little time to spare for her, given his other projects and enthusiasms. Besides, it was more likely she would find a husband amongst the young emigrants.

On 14 September, the three ships, *Adelaide*, *Aurora* and *Oriental* were moored at Gravesend when the steamship *Mercury* arrived with some of the Company's directors and the official document of 'provisional regulations'. These rules were vitally important for the British emigrants, thundered the *Morning Chronicle*:

> . . . as the sanction of the Government has been withheld from the undertaking . . . as the infant colony has been left without the aid or protection of the Colonial Office . . . as no steps have been taken to secure the administration of English laws upon a soil which Englishmen are to inhabit . . . as all the hopes which up to the eleventh hour the Company had entertained of even a slight recognition from the Colonial Secretary had been disappointed . . .[33]

George Young read the regulations to the adult passengers on each of the ships (see Appendix Two), and obtained signatures of agreement from them. Five of the fifteen members of the First Colony's Council were on board the *Adelaide* with Evans: Daniell, Henry St Hill, Thomas Partridge, Major Durie and Samuel Revans.[34]

'Selected guests' enjoyed a feast on the *Mercury*, afterward returning to their ships, but Evans went back to London with the directors. The bottle circulated, Young toasted 'the Colonists with a lengthened but forcible exposition of the difficulties against which the

Company had had to contend', and Evans returned thanks, vowing:

> There are no men on the face of the earth who have a more sincere or heartfelt desire to preserve the rights of the [Maori] than we have who are about to depart to those distant shores. We feel they are our adopted countrymen (cheers); and that a wrong or an injury inflicted upon them would be an injury upon ourselves (hear hear). We will be parties to no transaction in which their rights are not consulted equally with our own (cheers).[35]

In London, Evans huddled with Wakefield and the directors, going over drafts of the First Colony's constitution and other matters. Somes gave Evans a letter confirming that, subject to certain conditions, he would succeed Colonel Wakefield as Principal Agent of the new colony.[36] The attachment is lost, but it is reasonable to assume that the conditions referred to would encompass the untimely death of Wakefield, his temporary absence from the colony or any matter of urgency arising in his absence.

When the *Chronicle*'s article appeared on the streets there was an immediate protest from the government. James Stephen wrote to Young asking for a copy of the colonists' agreement for the Crown's lawyers to examine. Young refused, saying he was prepared to justify every step that had been taken.

The Colonial Office had also heard that Evans was still in London and sent agents to detain him, McKenzie recorded. Evans was alerted, a coach was summoned and he travelled 'post haste' the 75 miles or so to the Deal Roads, where the *Adelaide* had put ashore the pilot and the Company's agent. The elements provided a fitting farewell for Evans from the land of his birth. After 8.30 on the evening of 20 September he was rowed to his ship 'in a gale of wind'.[37] Early the next morning, having fallen in the previous day with the *Aurora* and the *Oriental*, the *Adelaide* made for Falmouth, Cornwall, to collect the Daniell family, Mr Luscombe and others. The crew's efforts to bring the ladies on board up the high sides of the ship in mid-stream gave welcome amusement to the passengers; finally, they resorted to cutting a large barrel in the shape of a chair and hoisting the women aboard with a block and tackle.[38] As the day wore on, the passengers became silent and reflective, snatching a last glimpse of land at dusk.

And the great scholar and headmaster, Dr Evans, was about to learn the harshest lesson of his life.

CHAPTER SIX.
THE VOYAGE OF THE *ADELAIDE*

> No man will be a sailor who has contrivance enough to get himself into a jail; for being in a ship is being in a jail, with the chance of being drowned . . . a man in a jail has more room, better food, and commonly better company.
>
> Samuel Johnson, 16 March 1759, from George Kirkbeck Hill (ed.), *Boswell's Life of Johnson*, Clarendon Press, Oxford, 1971, Vol. 1, p.348

The first passenger voyages to New Zealand were gruelling tests of forbearance and endurance. Whether it was the five-month voyage of the *Cuba* carrying Surveyor-General William Mein Smith or the *Aurora*'s swift passage of 110 days, unhappy memories were formed on each. William Deans of the *Aurora* reported that there were two significant quarrels – 'one betwixt a Major Baker and a Mr. Palmer, which ended in an apology from the latter; the other betwixt the Major and the Doctor on board. The quarrels took place at sea, and there was a duel after our arrival here.'[1]

Yet for many historians, the voyage of the *Adelaide* has become one of the most intriguing of all the shipboard dramas that took place in those early years of immigration.[2] To uncover the mystery, most have relied on Samuel Revans's letters to his sister Eleanor and his friend Henry Samuel Chapman. But Revans did not come to the voyage with an open mind and his account was far from objective. It rankled with him that Daniel Riddiford got the position of emigration agent instead of himself, and that he was merely given 'the temporary office of Secretary' by what he called 'the general approbation of the Council and Colonists'.[3] Nevertheless his account has had a profound impact on Evans's reputation that resounds to this day. But there are other reliable accounts. Cabin passenger James John Taine wrote a memoir; Francis Thomas Yates, a steerage passenger brought out as assistant printer by Revans, kept a detailed diary; and Thomas Wilmor McKenzie, also in steerage, recorded events through the eyes of an alert young apprentice compositor for the *New Zealand Gazette*.[4]

From the outset, any voyage was never going to be easy. As Taine remarked:

> . . . the first week at sea entails the greatest trial and discomfort, for things are generally in a state of confusion and topsy-turvydom: most of the people are desolate at the recent parting with their friends; miserably sick from the unaccustomed motion and not caring to eat, drink, or converse. The general surroundings are of a nature never before experienced, and strange faces are everywhere.[5]

The *Adelaide* was the largest of the five ships, a teak vessel weighing 640 tons, and carrying a full complement of 186 passengers, of whom twenty men, eight women and nine children were cabin passengers. Steerage passengers numbered 144, forty-eight of whom were children.[6] Their captain, William Campbell, headed a large crew and was an able sailor, young, confident and debonair. The cabin passengers' quarters were in the stern and on the deck above midships. The two stern cabins were the largest – twelve feet by twelve feet – and could have accommodated four or five people. They were well ventilated, but 'the walls of the cabins were so thin that the creaking of the rudder and the voices of passengers on deck carried clearly into the cabins'.[7] The Evans family probably occupied these two cabins.

The other first-class cabins had been rebuilt – six up each side, all opening into the saloon dining room below the 'poop' or upper stern deck. These cabins could only accommodate two people comfortably. Revans shared a cabin with Thomas Partridge,[8] his intended business partner. Taine shared his with Captain Josias [Joseph] Thomas.

Forward on the lower decks and taking up most of the hull were the steerage quarters and male and female hospital wards. Accommodation in steerage consisted of a double tier of standing 'bed-places' or sleeping boxes six feet by six feet, with three feet of head room, all opening out to a common dining room. Some of the young boys had brought hammocks, which they slung in the small amount of free space in front of the berths.

The holds were stacked with goods that overflowed onto the decks, jostling against the crates and containers of livestock, and the ship's numerous ropes, small boats, spare sails and other paraphernalia. At sea all the sounds familiar to passengers from country and town were replaced by the discordant cries of livestock, the shrill screaming of infants and children, and the shouting and squabbling of adults.

The creaking of the rudder, the grinds and groans of stressed timber, and the harsh flapping of sails accompanied the rolling and pitching, heaving and shuddering motions of a vessel labouring under a great weight.

From the beginning passengers were seasick, but none more so than the Evans family, especially in the early part of the voyage, Revans wrote to his sister.[9] The seas were 'tumultuous' and there were gruelling challenges to the ship's new rigging as it rolled alarmingly. The stretching of ropes was so serious the captain was afraid of losing his masts. He fastened blocks and tackles to the rigging on both sides of the ship, managing to tighten the stays – but not before several animals and one unfortunate young man were washed overboard.

Evans's stepson Daniel Riddiford's post as emigration agent at £200 per year had gone to his head, and even while still in the English Channel his behaviour showed a want of judgement. Yates recorded what happened:

> A most remarkable event occurred on the evening of . . . [23 September] which created a considerable sensation among the passengers . . . . A 'jolly row' otherwise a 'rumpus' took place between myself and an important personage (in his own estimation) calling himself Riddiford, having reference to some alleged misconduct on my part towards his female servant. The gentleman was 'hot with the Tuscan grape', and hard words were exchanged between us. He threatened to 'throw me overboard' – dubbed me a 'liar' and a 'scoundrel', – to which I retorted by calling him a 'villain'.[10]

On 10 October, more than two weeks after the incident, Yates complained to members of the First Colony's Council, including the secretary Samuel Revans and other cabin passengers; but 'There was evidently a desire to HUSH UP the quarrel. [Dr.] Evans said he would put it to my good sense and good feeling, whether it would not be better, after so long a period had elapsed, to allow the matter to rest.' Yates was offered an arbitrator, but the next day he was astonished to receive a letter from Revans telling him 'the Council had thought fit to dissolve! [the matter]'.[11] There was no further reference to the event, so it can be assumed a rebuke from Evans was all that was necessary to quieten Riddiford and appease Yates.

Captain Campbell was another matter. McKenzie called him 'a plucky little man, [who] set a good example to the crew, by going aloft himself to take in the main top-sail. His conduct was firm and seamanlike.' But while Yates admitted he was 'a good practical sailor', he also believed him to be, 'in the strictest sense of the word, "a bad man"'.

This opinion was borne out when the steerage passengers presented a 'memorial' to the captain a week after they sailed, complaining about the 'unfair manner in which the rations had been served out. The *courteous* Captain ordered us away, threatening to "throw the [memorial] into the sea".' Yates wrote later that he knew of no single instance 'in which the Captain has spoken a kind word to the steerage passengers'. He had a 'bullying and authoritative manner'.[12]

On 6 October Yates refused to witness the 'brutalizing treatment' meted out to a young crewman who received a dozen lashes for stealing a knife from a sailor. McKenzie too was appalled, calling the treatment 'barbarous and brutal', but opinions about Campbell were mixed: Revans described him as 'a kind and capable officer', while complaining that he was 'not so severe a disciplinarian as I like'.[13]

After crossing the Bay of Biscay, the ship steered a course between the island of Madeira and the African coast. Then a minor quarrel broke out between two steerage passengers over a water bucket. Just as their differences had been settled amicably, the captain sent for the chief protagonist, Mr Wright, who resisted his attempt to shackle him, throwing the manacles overboard. Campbell and Chief Officer Pryce armed themselves, Campbell declaring, 'Let me see the man who will dare attempt to rescue him!' The outraged steerage passengers complained to Evans who quickly called the council together to prepare an apology for Wright to sign. He refused, preferring instead to spend the night imprisoned on the poop deck.[14]

The ship put into Santa Cruz, Tenerife, on 14 October. Half of the passengers went ashore one day, and the other half the next. Before they left the ship Evans addressed them 'in his gravest manner', reminding them that 'permission to go ashore was an act of kindness; that any misbehaviour would be visited on the Captain; and earnestly exhorting them to maintain the honour of England'.[15]

Evans presided over the cabin passengers' dinner for the British Consul, Mr Bartlett, at Richardson's Hotel in Tenerife. As chair, he took the opportunity to assuage Revans's injured pride by shrewdly asking him to propose the toast to their guest.[16] In all it seemed an affable and pleasant affair. The *Adelaide* was not due to set sail until 10 o'clock the next morning, after replenishing her supplies with eight bullocks, wine, fresh water and a large amount of fresh fruit, as McKenzie recorded, so Evans and his wife, the Daniells and others took advantage of the opportunity to stay the night at the hotel. But because the wind was favourable, Campbell momentarily forgot his passengers on shore and weighed anchor at 8 o'clock. McKenzie described 'the surprise and consternation' of the hotel guests' –

> . . . when they saw the vessel underweigh, with all sails set and a light favourable wind. Dr. Evans was the chief of the preliminary expedition and his loss to the settlement would be almost irreparable. The passengers hastened to the landing place and hastily got two rough-looking Spaniards with immense beards – their only clothing being a long woollen shirt with a belt at the waist, from which was hanging a large sheathed knife – to row them to the boat – for the double fare of 5/- each.

When Campbell was alerted he dropped anchor about a mile from shore, but the ship tripped her anchor and drifted another five or six miles out. After rowing for two miles, it became obvious the distance between their boat and the ship had increased, so the Spaniards turned round and headed for shore until the protesting passengers agreed to an increased fare of 10 shillings each. The sailors rowed for another two miles, 'stopped and increased their demands to 15 shillings'. Again the distance between the two increased, so the Spaniards demanded £1 per passenger, on condition the money was paid before they left the boat. By this time the men wanted to 'take the oars themselves, and certainly would have done so, if there had not been ladies in the boat'. They finally reached the ship, the sovereigns were passed down to the 'extortionate boatmen', the passengers handed over and the voyage continued.[17] The incident would have enhanced neither Evans's temper nor his opinion of the captain.

The next day one of the steerage passengers – possibly Yates – asked Revans to intervene in a dispute between himself and the captain. Instead of taking the matter to Evans and the council, Revans 'acted', he later told Chapman, 'reluctantly, with a view to keeping the peace'. This 'threw Evans into a passion with me . . . . He afterwards apologized.' Revans clearly felt his inferior position keenly, remarking to his sister Eleanor, 'All fear a war of words with Dr. Evans, because he is superior from education and practice.'[18]

Although Evans was aware of Revans's hostility, he did not know its extent. Revans retaliated in the most effective manner he could devise. His friend in London, Henry Chapman, was planning to print letters sent to England by him and other settlers in a new publication, the *New Zealand Journal*.[19] Chapman, a close associate of Wakefield, could act as informer, not only to the Company's directors, but also to members of the Reform Club. All of their friends and contemporaries would hear his story and his version of events. Eager to burnish his reputation, Revans kept a record of his impressions to post at the first opportunity.

'Dr. Evans', he told Chapman, 'has a headlong impetuous temper.'[20] His family 'seem to have got it into their heads that they were to be treated like the Governor General of India'. Like the other cabin passengers, they were dissatisfied with the stores, but 'their ceaseless complaints' had not only 'thrown a gloom over the passage' but also 'encouraged all to believe they all were ill-used'. But, he conceded ingenuously, 'the table was not so amply furnished with fresh meat as we could wish, and there was besides generally a scramble for the tarts . . .'. Revans said he had displayed 'great moderation when attacked by Dr. Evans in a most violent manner', and believed his restraint had been 'most beneficial' as he was 'held in the highest respect by almost everybody on board the *Adelaide* from one end of the ship to the other'. He gathered around him other cabin passengers who shared his animosity – Thomas Partridge, erstwhile reporter and his obedient cabin mate, and Henry St Hill, architect.

The Evans family had its own problems: everyone was seasick, Harriot's baby was expected imminently, and an unwillingness to adjust to the rigours of life at sea with good grace seemed to pervade their mood. Mrs Evans, as acutely perceptive as she had been at Mill Hill School when she challenged the Reverend March, was aware of the ill-feeling the men bore towards her husband. Not one to dissemble, her disapproval of them would have been made clear, and her imperious manner would have acted as a goad to Revans.

There was something else Mrs Evans and other cabin passengers began to notice. Revans had become a frequent visitor to Mrs Smith's cabin.[21] Louisa Smith was the wife of the Company-appointed Surveyor-General, Captain William Mein Smith, who had gone out in the *Cuba*. In Louisa's cabin, Revans met Liocadia who, he said, had 'fled' to Mrs Smith's cabin to avoid feeling 'truly wretched', because Amelia treated her 'in a way she dare not act towards a servant'. The attractive Mrs Smith had three lively children: Fanny aged five, George who was four and Wallace aged two. Although her maid Lydia Montague was a boon, she welcomed Liocadia's company and assistance in keeping the children amused. Of the eight women in the cabins, only Liocadia and Amelia were young and single, but unlike Revans, they could not roam the ship at will. Disagreements and squabbles were bound to occur between them in the confines of a small cabin, especially as the beautiful Liocadia was catching the eye of the gallant captain.

The pervasive bad feeling meant that it was easy for Revans and his supporters to form an alliance against Evans and to feed a campaign against him. Revans confided to Chapman:

> . . . from what I had been told by Partridge long since I had reason to believe Evans jealous of me – tho' why or wherefore I know not – being jealous and artful – and there being a feeling at the [Company] Office that I was an agitator he would have framed a story which might have placed me in an unfavourable position . . .[22]

Passenger forbearance was stretched as the weather became increasingly hot and uncomfortable. On 22 October the captain ordered the single women to be locked in their berths each night at 10, as two or three had been 'indiscreetly' sleeping on the deck. Eight days later a passenger caught his wife chatting to the third mate. They quarrelled, she refused to reconcile and he jumped overboard on a moonless night, frustrating all attempts to rescue him. More lives were nearly lost when the lifeboat became fouled in the davits and was launched with no bung. This, wrote McKenzie, caused considerable anxiety and panic.

They sailed inside the Cape de Verde Islands and finally crossed the equator on 14 November. They expected to make a straight run for New Zealand, but one passenger reported that the *Adelaide* had been taken so far off course that the Martin Vas Islands, 600 miles off the coast of Brazil, had been sighted. The deviation and stifling windless days frustrated the passengers and crew. Clothing chafed, livestock were loud in complaint, and in all parts of the ship British restraint and decorous behaviour were under pressure.

Revans complained publicly to the captain about the crew's conduct in throwing water over the steerage passengers when they crossed the line, which had alarmed the ladies. Yates agreed, and for his discourtesy was 'struck twice by the boatswain', ordered to the poop, and charged with 'calling the boatswain a "blackguard" and a "coward"'. The captain refused to listen to Yates's explanation and denied him his wine ration for the remainder of the voyage. Yates objected, was threatened again with the prospect of having all his rations stopped, and left the captain stating defiantly that he 'would seek [his] remedy on shore'. Yates's wine was restored to him a week later. In the meantime, Campbell's steward had jumped overboard but was 'saved'.[23] There was little Evans could do without usurping the captain's control, yet there had been a major downturn in the crew's morale and the passengers' mood.

For several days after crossing the line the ship was becalmed, her boats were lowered, and parties of men armed with harpoons and guns hunted porpoises for oil, and albatross. Trinidad was sighted on 24 November. Campbell ordered a stern sail to be lowered into the water to create a floating swimming pool where passengers could disport themselves in relative safety. Despite this thoughtful gesture, Campbell's ruthless dispensation of justice continued. The crew was ordered aft to hear charges laid against two crewmen. After a summary court-martial, they were sentenced to twenty-four lashes each on their bare backs. The ladies protested and mercifully the flogging was cancelled, but the men were clamped in irons to be handed over 'to the civil power on the first opportunity'. The next day a sailor got thirty-six lashes for refusing to work, and later the boatswain was ordered to his cabin, having been charged by a crewman with stealing canvas for a pair of trousers. He 'was not even allowed to pipe for supper, or call the watch for the night', wrote an incredulous McKenzie.

The steerage passengers by now were quickly forming cliques and developing resentments. One complained, 'The gentlemen . . . who got steerage passages given them out of charity, were always the men who created trouble. They always thought themselves a cut above us . . . they seemed to . . . think they did the Company a mighty favour by accepting the free passages.'[24]

The crew continued to quarrel amongst themselves and with some of the passengers. Revans was forced to remonstrate physically with a steward for 'striking Partridge's [sponsored] boys'. He added his own complaints. 'The Adelaide . . . has a weak crew . . . . Our food and its preparation is all coarse like a common St Lawrence vessel. There is no style about the ship . . . [it] compares in style and management sadly with a New York packet.'[25]

James Taine found a more serious cause of passenger dissatisfaction: Captain Campbell was favouring the pretty 'Scotch lassies in a very gallant and somewhat tender manner'. Jealousy was aroused not only amongst the young single men but also amongst the other young women who felt aggrieved at being 'not so favoured' – which provided a possible reason for the tension that Revans said developed between Amelia and Liocadia. The men approached the captain, who shrugged off their complaints 'with lordly disdain'. Inevitably, quarrelling broke out and sides were taken. The most offended parties separated on deck by going to opposite ends of the ship, 'and it behoved every male passenger who could sport a pistol or sword to strut the deck in a show of bravado armed with these accoutrements . . .'.[26] Henry Cole later told Alexander Marjoribanks that some 'actually carried loaded pistols in their pockets . . . to be ready in case of assault'.[27] In the midst of all this drama, Harriot Riddiford gave birth to a daughter, Ellen Chaffers, named after the *Tory*'s captain.[28]

When not in his cabin working or receiving visitors, Evans spent his time walking the deck, conversing with passengers, answering their queries and dealing with their complaints. In fact, he was beset by complaints – from members of his own family, from crew and from passengers. Some of them reached discussion in council and others, like cases brought before a legal hearing being considered insufficient to go to trial, fizzled out. Partridge wrote in frustration, 'He has instituted one frivolous proceeding after another, which he has successively abandoned.'[29]

For Revans, the only chronicler of the council's meetings, the real problems started on 7 December when Evans called a series of meetings of cabin passengers to discuss the inadequacy of the ship's stores.[30] Evans wrote to Dr W. Johnston, Company agent and ship's surgeon, complaining that the ship's undertaking to 'provide the best accommodation and provisions for the passengers had been . . . grossly violated . . . this is not only unjust and painful to ourselves but likely to be injurious to the Company whose Directors we are quite satisfied will feel as indignant as we do at the treatment we have received'.[31] Revans who acted as secretary – 'as usual', he told his sister – believed the letter was too strongly worded but remained silent: as he told Chapman, 'none felt able to cope with Dr. Evans in speech . . . many considered [the complaint] exceeded the bounds of truth. I did and would have supported any in a reasonable opposition – but none originated it.'

Evans again attempted to improve his relationship with Revans, this time by appointing him to his sub-committee with Daniell,[32] Captain Thomas[33] and Henry Cole[34] to examine Johnston's stores record, while telling Dr Johnston that he, Evans, had been given 'special powers' to advise him in his capacity as Company's agent. No one except Daniell knew about the appointment, although Evans insisted he had informed them. Evans apologised to Johnston, who asked if they wished to divert to the Cape to take on fresh provisions, as supplies were insufficient to meet their demands. On 11 December, the men decided they could proceed directly to New Zealand if the passage took no more than sixty days. If they did not make good time they could put into Van Diemen's Land to replenish their stores. But Evans warned them the decision was verbal only, and asked the committee to amend the rationing accordingly.

After dinner the previous evening, Archibald Millar, whose wife had recently given birth to their fifth child, had an altercation with Evans.[35] Revans told his sister Eleanor he had left the table 'immediately after the ladies, as the best mode of avoiding the rows which I knew from experience would most likely occur there'. He was told Evans had 'grossly' insulted Millar. In the heat of debate, fuelled by port, there was an unpleasant exchange between the two men. To the horror of the gentlemen present, Millar challenged Evans to a duel, which Evans accepted. Major Durie agreed to act as Millar's second. Thomas announced he would support Evans, but was confident the two protagonists would not meet because 'Evans was to fill a sacred office in New Zealand'. Evans was displeased with Thomas for speaking on his behalf, but the gauntlet was flung down when Durie responded that Millar was ready to duel 'at the first port' of call. The challenge was accepted the following day.

The next day Revans met with the committee but was informed they had decided not to alter the rationing. Angry at being overlooked, Revans returned to his cabin. Partridge found him there half an hour later and told him Dr Evans had sent instructions by Dr Johnston to put into the Cape. It is fair to conclude that Evans's decision was influenced by his desire to resolve the matter with Millar at the Cape rather than in New Zealand.

Next day, when Evans announced that the decision not to alter the rationing had been 'unanimous', Revans dissented, 'much to [their] annoyance'. Evans then produced his ace – the letter from Somes giving him permission to act as Principal Agent in exceptional circumstances. He 'claimed confidence, tho' the most inconsistent of men', and left the meeting 'with his supporters as well as those who declared they would be neuter [*sic*]'.

Now Revans was voted 'into the chair'. St Hill and Partridge had 'collected all the discontented and [begun] a protest', Revans told Chapman. They drew up a petition complaining about the delays, attesting to the adequacy of the stores, and expressing the fear of arriving in New Zealand too close to winter. Eleven men and Louisa Smith signed the petition. Understandably, Louisa wished to be reunited with her husband as soon as possible. Revans tried to involve Yates, instructing him to collect more signatures from steerage passengers, but although Yates agreed with Revans, the passengers refused 'to interfere in the matter'.[36]

For some time Revans had carried his animosity towards the Evans family throughout the ship, telling steerage passengers that Evans 'had assumed an authority he was not entitled to',[37] which was unsettling for those in steerage who looked to the cabin passengers for leadership and co-operation. Although speculation was rife, it was obvious to most that Evans and Daniell had ordered the *Adelaide* into the Cape 'for urgent reasons'. The crew was about to mutiny, said one group. No, said another, the captain was going to be forced off the ship.

In James Taine's account of events that led to the diversion to the Cape, there is an element entirely missing from Revans's account. The decision to change course, he said, was a wise one. The misunderstandings that arose could 'hardly be attributed to any one cause, except perhaps the slow rate of progressing reacting on the nerves of the passengers'. The jealousies caused by Campbell's conduct towards the young women on board made everything 'assume such a threatening look that Capt. Campbell was wisely advised and persuaded by some of the leading passengers to put into Capetown'. The crew *was* threatening to mutiny, and their captain, by now furious with the continual complaints, had also managed to find himself being challenged by a young man to a duel.

McKenzie believed he knew the cause of the argument between Evans and Millar: 'One lady thought that the Captain showed more attention to another lady than he did to her, and took umbrage in the matter. Naturally the husbands of the ladies took the part of their wives, and a quarrel was occasioned – only to be settled by an exchange of civilities at 12 paces distant.' William Deans, from the *Aurora*, was told a story that confirmed McKenzie's view of events. The cause of the ill-feeling, he told his father, was 'the ladies':

> The fact is that jealousies arose on board amongst the ladies. Parties were formed on board ship and the Captain put into the Cape to fight no fewer than four duels – he himself one of the principals; Dr. Evans another; Mr. Johnston, a Scotchman another; Mr. Miller [*sic*] another Scotchman, ditto etc.[38]

Another reason, more urgent, arose from the fact that some of the passengers were suffering from 'the fever', said Taine. Although Evans's decision that the captain must put into Table Bay had unsettled many passengers, it was his high-handed manner that annoyed some of them more. Revans, who had tellingly mentioned to Chapman that he himself was viewed as 'an agitator', constantly expressed the view that Evans was unable to handle men in a sympathetic manner. But others felt differently, and in begging Evans to forgo the duel, expressed their 'astonishment and indignation that a challenge' had been 'forced upon' him. Baron Charles Alsdorf,[39] Edward Daniell and Henry Cole appealed to Evans's position in the colony:

> We had hoped . . . from the extensive powers vested in yourself . . . from your peculiar position as one of the founders of this contemplated settlement, and from the uniform worthiness and

> placid line of your demeanour, you would at least have escaped messages of this description. We are aware that a high degree of moral courage is requisite to avoid invitations of this kind – but we . . . charge you by your sense of duty to the Company who has placed unbounded confidence in your wisdom, forbearance and discretion, and . . . in the numerous public trusts embodied in yourself, and by your conscience as a Christian man. Moreover as proprietors and representatives to a vast amount we do entreat you to discountenance this introduction of a system in an infant Colony, not only incompatible with the dignity and high public trust confided in yourself but subversive of all good rules and ruinous to our best interests.[40]

On the evening of 19 December, the *Adelaide* put into Table Bay. Early the next morning, the protagonists in the various arguments were ferried ashore, a suitable site was selected, and the seconds discussed the rules and primed the pistols. When Evans's duel was ready to be paced out, Thomas stepped forward, read aloud the three men's petition, and then announced that Evans refused to fight, instead electing to bring the matter before the court. Other versions suggested that Evans simply 'refused to fight. He was willing enough for his opponent to fire at him, but positively refused to return the fire. The seconds of course, could not allow this.'[41] There was no mention of the other duels. Evans evidently laid a formal complaint with John Wylde, Cape Town's Chief Justice, and Attorney General Mr Peter, who had the captain 'bound over to keep the peace'; an agreement to forget all acrimony was then drawn up and signed by Durie, Millar and Campbell.

The next day Revans 'stumbled on' Evans, who assured him that he took full responsibility for the diversion, which was why, he said, he had excluded Revans from the decision. He begged Revans not to interfere, as it had become 'a case of piracy' in the hands of the Attorney General. Revans offered his resignation, 'against which [Evans] protested. There was all the *appearance* of sincerity.' Revans's letter to his sister was unfinished, but he found time to scribble an instruction to Chapman on the first page, in pencil:

> Dear Chapman, Read this and send it forward afterwards. In this way it will serve as a duplicate and continuation of the subject . . . . I should like Falconer to know all the facts as he goes much to the [Reform] Club and also knows Wakefield.[42]

He told Chapman he wanted everyone in London to hear his story as soon as possible. His letter was full of contradictions: while saying there had been 'a few quarrels on board', he described the *Adelaide* as 'a quiet ship' compared with the other four. He portrayed the captain as too soft but also said he was a good man. Evans, he said, was going 'to justify the [diversion] to the Directors'.

The Evans family was 'detested'. He believed, 'if Col. Wakefield be lost and Dr. Evans take his place which he has power to do – the colony will be a scene of uproar . . . . we are none cast down, but had we had a man who knows men – like Wakefield – we should all have been in the highest spirits.'[43] Revans also accused Evans of having censored Liocadia's letter home and making her write another, an allegation later disputed by Chapman. Parroting his cabin mate, Partridge also wrote to Chapman from the Cape just before the ship set sail: 'Dr. Evans in my opinion is a rash and ignorant man . . . . I will never believe that it is for our interest to have such a man in office in the Colony.'[44]

Taine wrote of Evans, 'If there was one characteristic more than another in Dr. Evans it was the strength and heartiness displayed in his voice, and in after years the early colonists used to refer to it as having the "strength of a bull's"',[45] words that might indicate a dynamic, overpowering character but also an amiable man. James Taine later married Liocadia and throughout his memoir speaks highly of Evans and his wife. This esteem continued for generations. Taine's grandson, H. W. Fildes, edited the Taine memoir and wrote a favourable outline of Evans's life in 1927.[46]

Revans may have been frustrated by Evans's position, his superior education and his temperament, but by omitting to suggest that the captain was a major cause of the passengers' unrest, he obscured much of the truth and thereby dealt Evans's reputation a major blow. The emotional traumas and discomfort experienced by adults and children thrown together in a voyage which took six months to transport them from 'home' to a country at the end of the world required the most desirable qualities of patience, discretion and tolerance. Nonetheless, Evans, as leader, ultimately was forced to shoulder much of the blame, and there was an element of truth, although little charity, in Revans's summary of Evans:

> He is ambitious, laborious, energetic, of strong physical construction, without talent or originality – but has acquired a considerable knowledge of certain things, which entitle him to the title of being called learned. He is ignorant of men, tho' he has had much to do with boy – and the one and the other equally, but particularly united, disqualify him for the position which he now fills.[47]

The *Colonial Gazette* put the affair in perspective, commenting, 'the passengers in this ship had been deficient in the faculties of mutual forbearance . . . . It is not uncommon – for persons cooped up for months together in a ship . . . under circumstances not the most conducive to comfort – to be somewhat touchy and pugnacious.'[48] A further perspective is offered by Daniel Riddiford's great grandsons, Anthony and Daniel, who were told 'the captain, far from blameless . . . had already fought and killed a passenger aged sixteen! The crew mutinied at the Cape, and a new [crew] was shipped.'[49]

The only surviving record of any reference Evans made to the episode was when he told John Wright in April, with what was, at best, misplaced optimism: 'There was plenty of misunderstanding and something more on board of the ships, but we have taken care not to bring it into the colony.'[50] Evans was not one to bear grudges for long, but Revans kept alive his antipathy towards the family for months after the events on the *Adelaide*. Some time after disembarking at Port Nicholson, he lived with the Smiths, telling Louisa's husband William that Evans 'made life miserable for everyone on board' with his 'overbearing manner, high-handedness and rudeness'.[51]

After receiving Revans's letters from the Cape, Chapman replied with a severe rebuke, questioning his tactics and motives. Revans retorted:

> I read your letter and was greatly inclined to throw it in the fire . . . you have not hesitated to read me a long uncalled for and useless lecture . . . . I did not write the Company from the Cape because I did not consider my statements would have met their due and because I did not consider I was called upon to put myself in the position of making them a communication. In writing you it was without secret design and the letter . . . which I suppose E. G. Wakefield will write will if it comes be most unwelcome. I merely stepped in to prevent the Captain abandoning the ship and to obtain fair play for the injured. There was no jealousy on my part . . . and I cannot believe Evans could be jealous of me. Of him and his family I have a very bad opinion and their names are generally unpopular in the settlement – but tho' I held such an opinion I did not fail to reconcile the parties on board before our arrival out of regard to the colony. Miss Oliviera did write the letter in question, but it was suppressed and . . . making the girl write one of a different character convinces me that baseness must be added to their list of bad qualities.[52]

There are two small postscripts to the story. In June, Revans reported in the *Gazette* that at a special small ceremony, 'a number of the Cabin passengers presented Captain Campbell with . . . a small piece [of silver plate] as a testimony of their remembrance'. He was unable to give his readers a copy of their speech, as it had been 'unfortunately mislaid'.[53] And Captain Campbell, who had favoured Liocadia throughout the voyage, gave her a muscovy duck when she disembarked at Port Nicholson.

While at the Cape, the passengers including Revans enjoyed the diversions – the vineyards, sightseeing, dinners and dances. The Evans family with Liocadia, Captain and Mrs Daniell, and James Taine climbed some 1087 metres to the top of Table Mountain. They were told the *Druid* with Captain Hobson on board had passed through the Cape six weeks earlier, making good time for New Zealand.

After leaving Cape Town at 'about nine o'clock' on New Year's Eve, the cabin passengers were treated to two theatrical performances for the first time in the voyage: *Bombastes Furioso* and the *Innkeeper of Abbeville*. Taine observed that had the captain 'followed a course 5° south of the Cape, we should have been in the track of trade winds which blow nine months in the year'. Instead Campbell 'set a course South by East – into the region of variable winds and weather most unpleasant'. But his belief that the diversion to Cape Town 'restored harmony to the ship'[54] seemed to be vindicated, although Yates reported an argument between St Hill and Thomas on the poop deck on 28 January.

As the quarrelling all but ceased, the weather worsened. For several weeks the passengers and crew endured freezing temperatures for which they were ill-prepared; and rain, hail, sleet and snow. The ship struggled and 'staggered' under the great waves of the southern ocean which crashed on deck, sending freezing water cascading down hatchways and saturating the passengers' clothing.

On 19 February the *Adelaide* entered Bass Strait 'with a famous breeze which continued all through the night', wrote an exhilarated McKenzie, and here he takes up the story with authority. It took three days to pass through the Strait instead of the usual eight hours. Several times the ship was in danger of drifting onto rocks because of the strong current. Less than a week later they encountered another gale, and the ship sailed under close-reefed topsails. The next day 'a perfect hurricane raged'. The sailors took three hours to furl the fore topsail sheet against the wind and a raging sea, the captain urging them on tirelessly. Finally, 'when his patience was exhausted, he climbed up the rigging himself and lay out to the weather'. He was helping them to get in the sail when a 'fearful gust of wind split it to ribbons with a loud report, and the pieces were carried away by the wind'. The hatches were battened down, fires were banned and all cooking stopped. The hurricane lasted forty-eight hours, the worst experienced in the entire voyage. After it subsided, each passenger was given a gill of whisky.

There was more to come. When finally on 2 March the ship sighted Cape Farewell, she lay due west of Mt Egmont, where she was once more buffeted by a gale of almost hurricane strength. Early the next evening she reached Port Hardy, and beat in against contrary winds. While tacking in the narrow channel, the ship missed her stays, but finally she got into the port safely and anchored. The passengers caught a large number of fish and had their first encounter with Maori, who brought potatoes out to the ship. For the next two days the *Adelaide*, which had met the *Tory* and the *Bengal Merchant* off the port, lay becalmed with them in 'Cooks Straits'.

She beat against the contrary winds of the Strait all day on 6 March, McKenzie's thirteenth birthday. On the 7th, she tacked about off Cape Terawhiti with the *Tory* to leeward and the *Glenbervie* five or six miles windward. Close to shore, she 'missed her stays' and, once caught in a tidal rip, 'refused to answer her helm'. The captain was 'very anxious' as they were 'disagreeably close to some sunken rocks', wrote McKenzie.

After a voyage lasting nearly six months (170 days) and at about five on the evening of 7 March, the *Adelaide* finally entered the harbour of Port Nicholson. If nature is a harbinger of fortune, good or ill, then Evans had every reason to feel apprehensive. He had left the shores of England in a freakish 'gale of wind' and arrived in 'the country in which he had so long been interested', pursued by a violent storm. The sky became 'dark as Erebus', wrote McKenzie, 'and the flood gates of Heaven opened'.[55]

Then, in the midst of a spectacular thunderstorm and in a feat of remarkable skill, William Luxford and a voluntary crew rowed Evans, Alsdorf and Mrs Smith safely to Petone beach in a small boat in turbulent seas, nearly capsizing twice. After being given directions and stumbling towards the lights, Evans burst in to Moreing's[56] tent a little over a month after forty-six chiefs had been persuaded by Governor Hobson to put their marks to the treaty that effectively rendered the New Zealand Company's council obsolete.

Evans told the men of the events in England since their departure, and of his reasons for the ship's delay. In turn, Colonel Wakefield told him he had purchased the entire harbour in September from the two chiefs Te Puni and Wharepouri whose tribe, he said, owned it. In the three previous decades (between 1819 and 1836), the harbour had been invaded by hostile tribes six times, so the chiefs had seen Wakefield's arrival as an opportunity to strengthen their tribe's influence and their own mana, at a time when Ati Awa was involved in peace negotiations with Ngati Toa, whose chief was Te Rauparaha, based at Kapiti.[57]

Wakefield also mentioned the landmarks he had named after the chief colonisers. Of the two large bays in the harbour, he had named one Lambton after Lord Durham. The other, he had named Evans's Bay.[58]

PART TWO:
WELLINGTON 1840–1844

CHAPTER SEVEN.
THE SCHOOLMASTER ABROAD

Strong reasons make strong actions: let us go:
If you say ay, the king will not say no.

William Shakespeare, *King John*, III, iv, lines 1570–71

The next morning, Evans barely had time to marvel at the native trees and ferns cramming the hills down to the shoreline before he was borne off to Pitone pa to be introduced to Te Puni and his nephew Wharepouri.[1] He conversed with them in their own language, impressing Jerningham, who told his father, 'He speaks the language very well, with, however, much of the northern accent and phraseology.'[2]

Later in the morning the six ships lying at anchor between the beach and Somes Island displayed their colours and fired their guns. The chiefs and members of their iwi joined in the celebration.[3] Three waka manned by warriors rowed out to welcome the ships, Te Puni escorting Colonel Wakefield in the first, while the second was captained by the six-feet-tall Wharepouri. A third carried Te Rauparaha's nephew, Tuarau.[4]

McKenzie described the scene:

> About 11 o'clock three large war canoes came off to welcome Dr. Evans who was second in command of the first expedition [etc]; and the pakehas who had come with him across the seas. There were about 60 Maori in each canoe, nude to the waist, painted with red ochre and their heads liberally adorned with the tail feathers of the huia. There were two women in each canoe standing up; one near the bow and one near the stern marking time for the rowers. The women would say two or three sentences in a loud melodious voice of joyous welcome to the pakeha – then the Maori would dip their paddles in the water with the greatest precision and urge the canoes forward with utmost speed.

The waka skirted the *Adelaide* three times while the passengers leant over the sides cheering. Afterwards, the men performed a 'war dance' on the beach, 'again repeating with the greatest demonstration of joy and delight their heartiest welcomes to the white settlers'.[5] Although the chiefs were relieved the Europeans might protect them from hostile tribes, there was already some consternation about their presence: Wharepouri, for example, had spoken to Wakefield earlier about his unease at the large number of Europeans arriving. He had expected only a handful, but the passengers of the *Adelaide* and *Glenbervie* had brought their total to 854.[6]

The settlers had other problems.[7] When Surveyor-General Captain William Mein Smith arrived only a fortnight before the first immigrant ship, Wakefield had travelled north to Kaipara, but before leaving, had left instructions for Mein Smith to lay out the settlement on the shores of Lambton Harbour. Mein Smith found it impossible to squeeze the traditional English town of 1100 acres – envisaged in Samuel Cobham's prototype – into the slender flat strip at Thorndon.[8] But apart from the swampy land at Te Aro that was inhabited by hostile Maori, the rest of the area was hilly, steep and densely forested down to the sea.

So Mein Smith, a forty-year-old reserved, religious man, 'devoted to his duties', decided instead to establish the settlement on the mouth of the Hutt River where there was more flat land. Besides, Maori of Pitone and Waiwhetu pa were helpful and friendly, assuring him that the Hutt Valley was the 'high road to immense districts of beautiful land'.[9]

By the time Wakefield returned, Mein Smith and his surveyors had already marked out the 'boulevards' along Petone beach. Although his instructions had been superseded, Wakefield agreed that the habitable area at Thorndon was 'insufficient', but said somewhat vaguely that 'at some period of time, Thorndon must become the site of a commercial town'.[10]

So when the *Adelaide* dropped anchor, many of the settlers from the boats that had arrived between 22 January and 28 February – *Aurora*, *Oriental*, *Duke of Roxburgh* and *Bengal Merchant* – had made temporary homes on the foreshore, while others had moved inland on the western bank of the river. Betts Hopper, George Duppa and Francis Molesworth planned to set up a saw mill and timber business and Henry Petre wanted to build his house there, but others like John Wallace complained they had been 'induced' by Wakefield to move away from the beachfront.[11] What was worse, each time the river flooded after heavy rain, he and the other settlers on the bank were forced to rebuild their houses on higher ground.

The surveyors' progress was agonisingly slow, as the ground was swampy for the first three miles inland, and the removal of scrub and trees was gruelling work. When he heard their progress would be much slower than planned, the enterprising John Wallace, 'out of pocket' because of the delay in setting up his store, decided he and his assistant Robert Boon would join the surveying party to speed things up. They lasted only six days, Wallace complaining he had been 'obliged to be up to [his] middle in water the greater part of the time'.[12] Only five days before the *Adelaide*'s arrival, another flood had washed away valuable livestock and other goods. Some of the settlers had moved back to the beach and began pleading to have the town moved to Thorndon. Dr Dorset had already unsuccessfully approached Wakefield on their behalf, when the stormy night of Evans's arrival brought more flooding and damage.[13]

It took less than a day to persuade Evans of the folly of Mein Smith's decision. He was appalled by the settlers' plight. Everywhere he looked, from the pa at the western end of the beach to the mouth of the river three miles east, the beach was littered with the emigrants' belongings: pianos, ploughs, chests and casks were strewn everywhere. Possessions were perishing from exposure, others broken beyond repair and a few lay below high-tide mark. One family was living in an upturned boat; another under a ship's sail. Betts Hopper told Evans his chests and boxes had spent 'weeks out in the open air, night and day'.[14] The shallow water at Pitone meant the ships had to anchor a mile off the beach, so passengers, their livestock and goods were rowed ashore in open boats at the mercy of the weather, and offloaded at a small jetty. The river, which was supposed to be navigable for up to 128 miles according to Land Company literature, was found to be suitable only for boats 'drawing little water', and the trees and snags under its surface would take time and a great deal of money to clear.

The timing of the *Adelaide*'s arrival meant that the new immigrants saw at once it was a serious problem, and after listening to the settlers' complaints, Evans urged a reluctant Mein Smith and Wakefield to accompany him to Thorndon on Tuesday 10 March to reconsider its possibilities. There being only a rough narrow track at low tide to connect the two areas, they travelled by boat round the harbour, passing two 'picturesque' gorges – Kaiwharawhara and Ngauranga – through which several streams flowed.[15]

Meanwhile, on board the *Adelaide*, Amelia Riddiford was filled with excitement. 'I never in my life saw so splendid a country', she wrote to Mrs Ramsay in Brompton a few days later:

> The New Zealanders are a most interesting people; they build beautiful houses . . . . if you lend your gun to a chief, he will return in the evening, laden with game. I should say it is impossible to live among them without feeling a great interest in them . . . . they are extremely honest, not one theft yet having been committed. Dr. Evans, Colonel Wakefield and others have gone up the river to a part called Thorndon, four miles off, which is described as a second Italy, and a most picturesque spot, which unfortunately is too small for our town.[16]

For Evans and most of the other *Adelaide* passengers who were rowed ashore daily, Thorndon's advantages were obvious and the harbour's depth made it a natural port. Evans rebutted the arguments of Wakefield and Mein Smith, suggesting that the surveys might take less time if they went around and over the bushy hills rather than through swamp, a dangerous flooded river and impenetrable forest. As soon as they returned to Petone, Evans urged Wakefield to call a meeting of landholders, but Wakefield first ordered Mein Smith – who resented the interruption and Evans's interference – and his staff to explore Thorndon again for the town's possibilities. On Friday the landholders' meeting was held, 'although', wrote a sceptical Jerningham, knowing his uncle always preferred to make his decisions in private, 'I do not know how their opinions will be taken, or how far they will be conceded to'.[17]

So many settlers flocked to the meeting, it was held outdoors on the beach. Evans made a powerful speech, striding back and forth and insisting on the transfer to Thorndon, 'his stentorian voice drowning the sound of the waves'.[18] When the Thorndon group suggested the town acres be split between the Hutt and Lambton Harbour as a compromise, Wakefield was alarmed at the threat of rival towns and broke off the meeting. But Jerningham believed 'the difference of opinion on this point will give rise to some change in the matter'.[19]

Wakefield was in a dilemma. He had not told Evans that his translator Dicky Barrett – whose grasp of the Maori language was as limited as that of his native tongue – had expressed reservations about the validity of his purchase from the residents of two pa in Port Nicholson. Te Aro Maori had been left entirely out of negotiations, Te Puni having told Wakefield they were merely a group of slaves. And not all of the Pipitea chiefs had participated in the negotiations or agreed to the sale. Wakefield had also claimed he had bought eight million hectares from Te Rauparaha on both sides of Cook's Straits, whereas Te Rauparaha had given him only two pockets of land: Wakatu and Taitapu at Golden Bay.[20]

Wakefield knew he would be forced to deal with some Maori whose reaction to the occupation of their land would be less than welcoming. And his instructions from the directors had left no room for doubt: 'any act of aggression or affront from any of the Company's servants towards any [Maori would be] a sufficient reason for immediate dismissal from the Company's service, and in the most public manner'.[21] Evans knew nothing of Wakefield's underlying fears, believing at this early stage that he had made a clean purchase of the area, but both men knew the switch would incur more delays and extra cost. Wakefield turned again to Smith for a decision, but Smith, said Revans, 'very properly required [Wakefield] to assume the responsibility, which he did with very bad grace'.[22]

He had good reason to turn the decision back to the Company's agent. He knew, said Revans, that if he did not and the transfer proved a success, Wakefield would 'reap the approbation, and if otherwise, the condemnation would be thrown upon [Smith]'. Wakefield finally took the easiest route, informing Evans that as 'the main principle of their system was concentration . . . the town was to be at Britannia (the Hutt), the swamps . . . thrown out, and the survey would proceed as rapidly as possible'.[23]

Evans was never to be easily dismissed or dissuaded. Highly experienced in the adversarial role in any controversy, he rose to the occasion. With the support of Daniell and others from the *Adelaide*, he called a meeting at very short notice for Sunday, 15 March. Many were unable to attend, but he gave such a persuasive speech in favour of Thorndon that more settlers were convinced. Dorset wrote in his diary of the 'strong resolutions' passed, saying 'Great dissatisfaction was expressed' at Smith's action in changing the original site.[24] Surveyor Charles McGurk added, 'Dr. Evans spoke strongly, so did Daniels [*sic*] and St Hill; in fact the feuds they had on board the *Adelaide* seemed on the point of being renewed.'

As a sop to the dissidents, Wakefield had suggested that landowners could select 20 acres for cultivation until the country acres were ready, promising that if roads or lines later ran through crop-bearing land the owners would be compensated. Evans discussed this 'at great length', said McGurk, 'as being a thing hitherto unheard of, and mentioned it as a proof of the liberality of the Company'.[25]

Before the meeting broke up, Evans read a petition he had drawn up, circulated it for signatures and then sent it to Wakefield:

> As we have not yet received your determination on the important subject which was discussed yesterday, and firmly believe that the

> very existence of the Colony depends on the proper selection of a site for the first and principal town on the Company's territory in New Zealand, – we, the undersigned, very earnestly and solemnly press upon your attention our belief that our property and the prosperity of the Colony would be destroyed by fixing the town on the River Hutt; and that, on the contrary, a site eligible in the highest degree is presented in the land bordering upon Lambton Harbour . . . . We feel under the painful necessity of informing you that in the event of the location being made where now proposed on the banks of the river, a very large proportion of the colonists, both landowners and labourers, have made up their minds to abandon the undertaking altogether. We beg therefore earnestly to request that you will return to your original proposition to make the first and principal settlement at Lambton Harbour.[26]

The petition was perfectly timed – that day the river flooded so seriously that several houses were filled 'with three feet of water' – but Wakefield rejected it and, like everyone else, Charles McGurk believed it was a *fait accompli,* saying '[The petition] had no effect; the town is to be at Brittania.'[27]

Undeterred, Evans kept up the pressure on Wakefield as he and Richard Hanson worked with him on refining the rules of the settlers' constitution that was to be ratified by the Maori chiefs.[28] In their draft for a 'new and more effectual provision for the administration of justice', Umpire Evans would preside over and rule on all civil and criminal cases with the assistance of seven assessors. He had final discretion in sentencing – a fine not exceeding £10 or imprisonment for no longer than three months – and would be advised by arbitrators chosen by both parties; he could subpoena witnesses and examine relevant books and papers; he would rule on wills and probates, set dates for court sittings and direct the empanelling of juries. Aided by a sheriff and his deputy he would draw up a scale of fees to be approved by the settlers' council and the chiefs. There was provision for a substitute to preside in case of his illness, absence or in any case involving a conflict of interest.[29]

The jury lists were to include Maori with the chiefs' approval. Council members were to be elected annually, while Wakefield as president would retain his office for five years. No taxes or duties would be levied without the council's consent. Maori and European were to have equal rights, except that Maori would not vote for the first five years nor serve as assessors, 'except in cases in which the rights or interests of a native are concerned; and that in any such case, at least three of the assessors shall be natives'. For those five years no law affecting Maori would be passed without the chiefs' consent.

The ratified constitution was signed by the 'Sovereign Chiefs of the District of Port Nicholson' on 22 March (see Appendix Four).[30] It provides a window through which one can see the beginnings of this interracial relationship, with the Europeans purchasing land from and living peacefully amongst Maori, while protecting them and not disturbing their ownership of reserves; and Maori reciprocating by learning the British way of life and adjusting to the requirements of British law.[31] Although the Company had in reality placed its own interests above those of Maori, it believed that by living amongst them – each family 'adopting' a Maori who could share in their customs, even live with them – they would impart something more beneficial and less transitory than material gifts and payment. It was a utopian vision of exemplary race relations, its fourteen clauses since having been assessed as being 'of an equitable and comprehensive kind . . . really a well-conceived piece of government'.[32]

By this time Evans and his supporters had worn down Wakefield's resistance. Wakefield assured the directors that if the town's site were shifted, 'no harm' would have been done, since land already surveyed could be used as country sections, and it would take only six weeks to survey Thorndon. But Mein Smith was adamant about the Hutt being the only option and would not budge. Wakefield continued to agonise, asking Smith for assurance that a winter in the Hutt would not bring more flood damage. Meanwhile, with the manager of the bank John Smith, Evans, Betts Hopper and George Hunter moved on to set up the colony's branch of the Union Bank of Australia, opening it for business on 24 March at Petone.

At about this time the settlers were told it would be another two years before the country land would be available. 'When it is ready', a shocked Wallace complained, 'many of the landholders will not have sufficient capital to clear one acre' – at £25 per acre. The news brought more pressure from Evans's group, so Wakefield allowed them to rent 20 acres of land at Thorndon at a nominal rate. With that, the *Adelaide* weighed anchor and carried about thirty families to Thorndon.[33]

A little earlier, Wakefield's anxieties about reverting to Thorndon would scarcely have been dispelled by an incident involving a builder, Edwin Ticehurst, and a surveyor named William Turnbull, the latter being sponsored by Evans. The pair had been exploring Thorndon and decided to stay overnight. Turnbull became uneasy about the demeanour of Maori from Pipitea pa and returned to the *Adelaide*, so Ticehurst begged young Thomas McKenzie if he would keep him company for the night. Longing for adventure, McKenzie agreed, and as it was getting dark they decided to stay in the whare that Pipitea Maori had constructed for Evans on Thorndon Flat.[34] Built 'of poles interlaced with *kerewati*, daubed with clay in and out and thatched with *toi toi*', without windows or doors, the whare's interior was spacious, its walls 'lined with nikau palm, and divided into several large rooms'.[35] The pair gathered some native grass for bedding, piled it in a corner of a room and lay down to sleep. What happened next, McKenzie never forgot:

> In trooped a Maori chief and about twenty followers, his two wives bringing up the rear. All stood aside to give him room to perform. He threw off his mat and in a nude state, commenced his war dance – his posteriors were beautifully tatooed [*sic*] and he had a mere in his right hand fastened to his rist [*sic*] with a thong of leather which he flourished ominisly [*sic*]. His two wives moved towards us, and sat down at our feet, crying. The chief then ran up and down the room in the most excited state, jumping at times three or four feet from the ground, and smacking his posterior; the various contortions of his body, his tongue protruding and eyes rolling was one of the most diabolical scenes that could be witnessed. Just as he had wound himself up to the pitch of frenzy, sufficient to let us have the *mere* [kill them by scalping], one of his wives dexterously took off her mat, and threw it over us, and then submitted her own head to receive the blow. By this act she had saved our lives, for we were tabooed, and he dare not touch us. He turned from his wife with the utmost disdain, and with all his native dignity, marched off with his followers, his two wives bringing up the rear.

Their saviour was Ruhia, the daughter-in-law of Porutu, an old Ngati Awa chief residing at Pipitea pa.[36] Porutu had supervised the building of the large whare and was waiting for Evans's family before ceremonially lifting the tapu on the residence. After that night, Porutu 'was one of the best friends the settlers had'. When he met McKenzie later, he was 'most demonstrative in his greetings, calling me his brother, and giving as a reason . . . for his action that the house had not yet been paid for, and he thought we had taken possession, not knowing one white face from another'.[37]

☙

Throughout March, the settlers in Petone had endured ten days of heavy rain.[38] By 4 April, nearly three weeks after Evans's petition, when the council called a meeting for Evans and Hanson to present their constitution, there was another item on the agenda. Both Evans and Wakefield presided, and after more 'frank and full discussion . . . it was decided to abandon the proceedings already entered, and that the location of the principal town should be on the flat land of somewhat limited extent available at the south-western corner of the harbour'.[39]

It was a victory for Evans and the passengers of the *Adelaide.* Over the years the story has been blurred and Evans has been deprived of the credit, but James Coutts Crawford, an independent settler who had observed the company's immigrants from their first arrival, had no doubts about who was the catalyst for change:

> Colonel Wakefield, however, was a man not easily turned from his purpose, and . . . nothing would move him, until the arrival of Dr. Evans, who immediately took up the cause of the opposition. He called a public meeting . . . and worked up public feeling to such an extent that Colonel Wakefield was forced to give way . . . [40]

Wakefield could 'make himself a very pleasant companion . . . except when spoken to on business', he added.[41] In referring to Wakefield's 'remarkable reticence', Gisborne agreed, adding with insight, 'The man who speaks is at great disadvantage as compared with the man who persistently listens. No one [in interview with Wakefield] knew what he thought and what he meant to do.'[42]

Wakefield knew the delay was costing the Company dearly each day, yet he took a month to act decisively. His capitulation was 'a wise change', according to Jerningham, who then implied in his memoir that the decision was made very quickly.[43] Yet the delay in the *Adelaide*'s arrival had impeded the council's full representation by a month, and Wakefield's vacillation and Smith's obstinacy had cost the Company another month. Understandably, the overturning of Mein Smith's decision was 'a bitter pill' for him to swallow, for which he never forgave or approved of Evans. Revans had influenced Smith's opinion in telling him Evans had been 'high-handed', rude and 'overbearing' on the *Adelaide*, and because of the decision for Thorndon, Smith was convinced Wakefield was easily influenced by the opinions of others – especially those of Evans and Hanson.[44]

But Hon. Henry Petre spoke for many when he observed that 'if the mouth of the Hutt River had been carefully examined, if a competent exploring staff before the surveying party were placed upon it, it would certainly not have been chosen for the site of the first and principal town. Thus, six valuable weeks of unprofitable labour would have been saved, and Wellington would have been ready for selection and occupation at a much earlier period.'[45]

Once the decision was made, Wakefield worked with the committee that prepared for the town's removal. On 2 April he complained that he had been forced to change his mind by what he called 'the importunities of small capitalists' – thus absolving himself of responsibility and implying a lack of urgency. By 6 April he was able to write a despatch to the directors that in one stroke placed the blame, indirectly or otherwise, on Evans – for the delay in the *Adelaide*'s arrival, for the demurrage of the *Aurora* and other ships, and for the final decision to move to Thorndon:

> The detention of the *Adelaide* two days at Tenerife and twelve days at the Cape of Good Hope will put that ship on demurrage here which otherwise would not have been the case . . . . A lamentable state of disunion amongst the passengers and between some of them and the master . . . during the whole voyage (and continued here), seems to have been the occasion of this delay . . . . The accompanying copies of correspondence between the Surveyor-General and myself will inform you that it has been found necessary to fix the town on Lambton Harbour . . . . This decision has given universal satisfaction. My previous letters will have led the Directors to contemplate this change.[46]

Wakefield had resigned himself to Evans's determination to live in Thorndon and had written a somewhat rueful note to Harriet Evans on a 'Thursday Morning', perhaps as early as 12 March when Evans had announced he would camp at Thorndon, or two weeks later when the *Adelaide* had weighed anchor and taken its passengers there. 'My dear Mrs. Evans', Wakefield wrote:

> I am sorry that I am not to have the advantage of your neighbourhood, upon which I have been so long reckoning; but quite appreciate the motives of your preference of Thorndon as a residence. Pray make any use you please of my house and believe that I shall at all times be most glad to be of any service to your family to compensate for the poor reception you have found me prepared to offer you on arriving.[47]

The bank's large safe was uplifted and moved to Thorndon by raft, and the Thorndon settlers were soon scattered from the northern end of Tinakori Road to the junction of what is now known as Kate Sheppard Place and Mulgrave Street, and from there to Kumutoto Point. The back boundary was the northern end of The Terrace, which at the time was a forest with several streams running through to the sea. Evans's friend Daniell built his whare close to Kumutoto pa on the south side of the stream, which then ran through what is now Woodward Street.[48]

Maori were of invaluable help to the Europeans, saving them from great privation. The settlers paid them to build their raupo whare, shoot birds, and provide them with pork and potatoes, and their willingness to assist in other ways was deeply appreciated. But, like most Europeans of the time, Evans believed that New Zealand's 'waste lands' meant little to the tribes scattered in pockets throughout the islands, and could only become valuable through colonisation – with the settlers' work and capital. He agreed with Vattal's argument in *The Law of Nations*, which held that all uncultivated waste land in countries inhabited by largely nomadic tribes could be taken up legally by settlers crowded out of their own countries. The settlers did not understand the value of land to a people whose survival depended on their moving from place to place to renew their crops and replenish their meat and fish.[49] For most Europeans, Maori owned only the areas they held sacred, or occupied and cultivated. The complex question of communal ownership, involving iwi (tribes), hapu (sub-tribes) and rangatira (chiefs), was to be a revelation.

Porutu and Moturoa had been happy to build whare for Evans and Wakefield at Thorndon before Smith altered the survey site, but became uneasy when they saw the hundreds of settlers they brought with them. For Maori in all the pa in the area, the surveyors, armed with strange equipment to mark out their land, were also an unacceptable intrusion.[50] Arguing that they had not sold their land, Maori removed the surveyors' pegs every evening. Wakefield responded by arming the surveyors, and mounting the *Adelaide*'s four 18-pound guns on Somes Island. Local Maori were soon 'overawed'.[51]

Taringa Kuri, chief of Ngati Tama of Kaiwharawhara, said later when questioned about his people's impressions about what was happening: 'We never sold Kaiwarrawarra, Raurimu, Pakuao, Pipitea, this place, Te Aro. Colonel Wakefield and Dicky Barrett took Kumutoto – the European took forcible possession of this place.'

> Court: When did the Europeans take forcible possession and in what way?
> Kuri: After the Tory . . . – Dr. Evans took possession of the land – he was here and told the Europeans at Pitone to come here that this was the land of Colonel Wakefield.
> Court: Was there any violence or fighting used?
> Kuri: No.
> Court: Then what do you mean by saying they took forcible possession?

> Kuri: The Europeans came over here in such a body.[52]

Moturoa the Pipitea chief was angry with the surveyors:

> Court: Why did you interfere with the surveyors?
> Moturoa: We were served like Adam and Eve, we were deceived by Captain [Mein] Smith, Dr. Evans and [surveyor] Mr. Carrington, we were angry about our land. Our land is for ourselves till we die.[53]

In spite of their misgivings, Pipitea Maori welcomed the Evans family into their whare after the tapu was lifted. But barely had they moved in than Evans complained to Wakefield – probably at his wife's urging – that his chattels had not been delivered – due to the 'obstructiveness and incivility of Captain Campbell' – and demanded a sail to cover his wife's furniture lying exposed on the beach.[54] That done, he turned to council work, proposing at a meeting on 18 April that provision should be made for a public building to serve as both police court and town hall.[55]

The next day the missionary Henry Williams arrived to gather the signatures of the Port Nicholson chiefs to the Treaty of Waitangi. He called on Colonel Wakefield to inform him that Pipitea Maori had already sold about 40 acres of their land to the CMS for 'Church purposes'. The sale was negotiated by Richard Davis (Reihana Reweti) – a former slave from Taranaki who had become a Christian missionary – who, with Williams and others, had made the journey in July 1839 specifically to acquire land.[56] In exchange for the land – or to seal the deal – Te Aro and Kumutoto were given one blanket each and some clasp-knives and tobacco, and a blanket was given to Korokoro. Davis and two assistants, Barnabas and Mori, made Pipitea tapu, while Williams placed a tapu on a piece of land on the other side of Pipitea with four other chiefs. Davis later testified the land was made tapu 'to stop Europeans taking it'. With the land secure they then told Maori that if European settlers came, they would 'take all [their] land for things. Don't take their things there will be no land for you! If they take your land you will go and cultivate the sea, for you and your children!'[57]

When Williams informed Wakefield about this purchase, Wakefield swore at him, suspicious at the size of the church's estate, and Williams refused to deal any further with him. As the Company's legal advisor, however, Evans found a loophole. He told Williams that because Davis was a slave he could not represent the tribe that had sold the land. Williams insisted that Davis's claim was valid, as he, Williams, had bought the land to allow Davis to reside there instead of returning to his wife's iwi in Taranaki. Wakefield next sent Henry St Hill to try to negotiate with Williams. St Hill offered him money to negate Davis's claim and suggested that the matter should be resolved publicly. Both of these proposals were rebuffed, and once again Evans tried to find a solution. When he met Williams and assured him the Company held land in reserve for Maori, Williams capitulated and generously offered his land to the Company, reserving one acre for himself and another for Davis. Evans drew up the Deed of Cession, which described the land as extending from the beach 'to the mountain called Tinakore and bounded on the Southern side by the brook called Pipitea, and on the Northern side by the brook called Raurima'.[58]

Although Evans and Mein Smith assured Williams that his generosity would be acknowledged, Wakefield only grudgingly allowed an extract of his apology over his treatment of Williams to be published. He refused to believe Williams's reason for obtaining 40 acres, calling him the 'worst of the land sharks' who displayed 'selfish views, hypocrisy, and unblushing rapaciousness'.[59] Dudley Sinclair echoed this scepticism from the Bay of Islands in late May when he commented wryly to his uncle in London, 'The missionaries hold the best of the land.'[60]

The opposing views of the colonists and the missionaries were apparently at a stalemate, and the apparent focus of the conflict was Maori land, and more specifically, the holding of the land. The missionaries accused Wakefield of trying to dissuade Maori at Port Nicholson from signing the Treaty of Waitangi, but if Maori hesitated over signing the Treaty, it may have been because they had only recently signed the settlers' constitution, a different compact entirely. After ten days of negotiation Maori signed the Treaty, which ostensibly gave them possession of their lands, forests and other properties, while sovereignty was ceded to the Queen.[61]

The Crown had pre-empted the Company's attempts to buy land at a 'sufficient price' by ruling that, from 1 February 1840, Maori could sell it only through the government.[62] After reading the English version of the Treaty of Waitangi, Evans, who was 'well versed in any [legal] question' and a 'tower of strength in matters constitutional',[63] suspected that the Treaty was flawed. He continued to doubt the Treaty's efficacy and its adequacy for both races, which he was able to express more fully five years later when he returned to England (see chapter sixteen).[64]

CHAPTER EIGHT.
'UMPIRE' NO LONGER

> It is the most short-lived Council that ever existed. In fact, we have sat by its cradle and followed its hearse.
>
> G. S. Evans, June 1841

Within three weeks, nine hundred people were living in Thorndon, leaving only two hundred in the Hutt. A large row of whare paraded along the beach, and complaints were growing about the delay in the surveys. 'I believe myself that old Smith is a great dawdle', pronounced Jerningham, though Smith's task was not easy; he and his men were forced to adapt their plan to cover hills four miles long and two miles wide.[1]

Evans was exuberant about the success of the change to Thorndon, adopting a proprietorial tone as he told John Wright the decision was, in his 'humble opinion, the best that could be hoped for'. 'Everything has answered our expectations', and prospects were 'most encouraging', he said. The harbour, with upwards of 20 square miles of anchorage, was

> . . . perfectly land-locked, secure from all winds, without a single rock or land bar with prime holding ground everywhere, and deep water in almost every corner sufficient for a line-of-battle ship . . . . The country about here is more mountainous than we had supposed; but the sides and tops of the hills are as fertile as the level ground; and at the head of the harbour we have a valley extending up the country forty miles, and branching out laterally to an unknown extent, composed of alluvial soil from three to six feet in thickness, lying upon a bed of clay; a large proportion of the clay is potters' earth and pipe clay. There are from twenty to thirty kinds of timber already enumerated by us suitable for ship-building and other purposes, and water power in every ravine.
>
> The only drawback is that up to this moment, all the time has been lost in the surveys . . . . As [Surveyor-General Smith] was supposed

> to be in some measure independent of Colonel Wakefield, he was allowed to go on with the experiment at the mouth of the valley; but it has been found impossible to secure an adequate foundation on the alluvial deposit which I have spoken of, and the substratum of clay is for a great distance up the country below high-water mark . . . . Lambton Harbour is in the form of a horse-shoe, with deep water, and the table land round it closed in with an amphitheatre of mountains; so that every house will have a perfect drainage, and an abundance of fresh water from rivulets. We are all going on harmoniously; and there is no party question or difference of any kind among us. There was plenty of misunderstanding and something more on board of the ships, but we have taken care not to bring it into the colony . . . . The natives are a noble race of man; and far advanced from the savage state. They perfectly understand all that we are doing and intend to do, and help us to the utmost of their power.[2]

In July, Evans was forced to retract his boast of a sheltered harbour:

> . . . our winter really consists in our liability, during two or three months to tremendous gales from the south-east, or the north-west. These blow for forty-eight hours at the changes of the moon, then chop round suddenly, and clear up in sunny days of the most balmy freshness, equal to anything in the *same* months in England . . . .

Evans also told Wright of the enterprising nature of the Maori:

> The natives are spending the money they have hoarded for years . . . Mr Smith has taken great pains to calculate, and he concludes that the natives are in possession of at least £150,000 in money. Three natives here have bought horses at from £60 to £90 each. They sell you 300 pigs and 20 tons of potatoes in a lot.
>
> . . . They have built all the cottages we live in . . . perfectly water tight. We all prefer them to the trumpery wooden houses made in England. . . . [They] supply us with pigs, potatoes and fish, cut wood for us, fetch water, and do a hundred things, without which we should have suffered numberless privations . . . . They are quite as dirty as the poorest class in England though far beyond them as real civility and refinement. As I flatter myself I now speak the language, I associate with the native chiefs daily, and find endless amusement in doing so.[3]

On a personal level, a good relationship had indeed developed between the Evans family and the Maori of Pipitea pa. Evans's whare being so close to the pa, and his ability to communicate with Maori in their language, meant that many visited. James Taine noted that Maori designated Evans 'nui nui rangatira' – very important leader.[4]

In their turn the residents of the pa were enthralled by the family's menagerie of animals. They marvelled at the different breeds of cats and dogs, but their favourite attraction was Harriet's cow, which had given birth to a calf early in the voyage. The men enjoyed feeding her 'large quantities of native shrubs, besides cabbages and thistles'. For hours they would sit, exclaiming at the animal's 'peculiarities', laughing as she lowed. They watched her being milked as if observing a feat of magic, and were amazed by her abundant supply. At first the women and children were afraid, expressing their awe 'in a very marked way', but they were soon willing to taste the strange warm and creamy milk and butter. The family repaid their visitors for their gifts of cattle feed by supplying them with tobacco, meals and money.[5]

Evans may have enjoyed good relations with Pipitea Maori, but from the start there had been less harmony with the inhabitants of Te Aro pa. When James Taine explored Te Aro in early April, he found 'a low swampy area covered with flax raupo and toi toi, [where] one had to be prepared to wade knee deep to struggle over the land now known as Courtenay Place':

> The pa was stoutly pallisaded and the approach to it was through a long passage lined with palisades on either side. The natives there were a disreputable lot, they seemed to be the refuse of half a dozen tribes who had gone under to their more powerful enemies, but were left alone to make the most of their swampy lands . . . . We learned later that [they] were of an inferior type to those in residence at Petone and were informed that they were the remnants of a people who had been allowed by Te Puni to occupy this neighbourhood in sufferance, the main body having migrated to the Chatham Islands.[6]

As Evans would later testify, the reason for unrest at Te Aro pa was soon made abundantly clear. Only two or three weeks after his arrival, he spoke at length with its occupants and found they were angry and dissatisfied over the land sales that had occurred and the amount of goods given to their pa by Wakefield. He sent for Wakefield, who came to the pa with Barrett one Sunday morning. Several Maori complained that some of their chiefs had agreed to sell their land but had not been fair when they distributed the goods that Wakefield had given them. The Colonel asked what would satisfy them, and following more discussion 'they said they would take twenty blankets . . . and would give up the whole of their land to the white men'. Afterwards, Evans visited the pa 'frequently', and several of the residents acknowledged they had received the blankets. The council members had been given conflicting stories about the Te Aro Maori. Te Puni had not told the truth when he assured them they were slaves, but another chief and Barrett had also said they were slaves.

The good relations between Evans and Pipitea were marred when the chief Moturoa protested about the land sales around the harbour. Two years later Evans testified in Spain's Court of Land Claims:

> I heard a great deal of dissatisfaction expressed among the Natives, at the manner in which the goods had been divided amongst them: – and at the price which they had received for the land, but I never heard any Native dispute the fact of their having sold the land except Moturoa, until Reverend Henry Williams and Mr. Shortland arrived here, when the question was raised.

Evans blamed the government and missionaries for the change in attitude. He said that 'shortly after' his arrival in Thorndon, Moturoa told him 'he had not sold the land to Colonel Wakefield', then returned a short time afterward and 'told [him] a different story – he said that he had received "money-gold" from Mr. Tod and that he had done wrong, and was quite ready to give the money back again to Mr. Tod – because he knew the rest of the people had sold the land, though he had not'.[7]

Moturoa's sale to the Sydney merchant Robert Tod in January, following Wakefield's flawed purchase four months earlier, was the start of a bitter saga between Tod and the settlers' council. Tod had paid 30 sovereigns – £30 – for a large parcel of land at Thorndon, two acres, two roods and thirty-one perches in all. At Moturoa's request he had added a couple of blankets and a piece of printed cloth and for another 12 sovereigns bought a smaller piece of land of one acre, twenty-three perches. When Tod arrived at Thorndon, John Smith told him Wakefield had already purchased that area.

Pipitea Maori assured Tod that Wakefield had not in fact purchased the area. Davis later acknowledged that Wakefield had put up large signs at Pipitea and Kaiwharawhara giving public notice of his purchase, but excused the later land sale to Tod by saying that the area was still tapu. When he had told Tod of Wakefield's earlier purchase, Tod had asked, 'Did Moturoa go to the ship?' Davis had said, 'No.' 'Did he hold the pen?', asked Tod. Davis replied, 'No.' Tod then told him, 'Moturoa's land is his own because he did not write his name.'[8]

When the settlers' council first heard of Tod's purchase, they told him his claim was invalid because of Wakefield's purchase. A flurry of correspondence ensued, and Dicky Barrett pulled down the poles marking the framework of Tod's store.

Meanwhile, some Pipitea chiefs objected to Moturoa's sale of land to Tod and demanded Tod pay them for using one of their whare on the land for storage. Evans interceded on Tod's behalf when the chiefs Te Puni, Wharepouri and Tuhata were objecting to Tod's erecting a building on wahi tapu – sacred or tapu land. Not long afterward, on 20 May, Robert Tod went to Petone, but perhaps anticipating trouble, he left the title deeds to his property at Thorndon with his clerk, A. S. (Alfred) Farrar. Farrar arrived on the site with John Wade after eight in the morning to find Mein Smith, Evans, William Carrington, Robert Stokes and several others already there. They were intending, Farrar said, 'to pull down' Tod's house, which then consisted of 'posts . . . all around'. Farrar showed Smith the deeds of title, and after perusing them Mein Smith handed them to Evans for a legal opinion. Evans read them and was 'satisfied that it was good law'. Smith immediately insisted he would have nothing more to do with the matter, and went to fetch Wakefield, saying, 'If he wishes to pull down Mr. Tod's house, let him come and do it himself'. Seeing how restless the Maori were, Evans accused Farrar of having made them drunk that morning, which Farrar denied. Evans said, 'Then we had all better go quietly away and get our breakfast', and Farrar was left undisturbed for the rest of the day.[9]

On his return, however, Tod was told that Evans and a party of men had 'attempted to pull down his house', Maori had driven them off the land, and Tod's housekeeper had rewarded them with a breakfast of rice and sugar. Immediately, Tod wrote to both Hobson and Governor Gipps complaining that 'Colonel Wakefield and Dr. Evans had tried to pull down his store'. This accusation against Evans may have dealt a blow to Evans's reputation with both men. No doubt he protested his innocence to them, but it was two years before Tod's story was exposed as seriously flawed, based as it was on hearsay.[10]

Wakefield continued to harass Tod, but Tod ignored him and appealed instead to Pipitea Maori. The council condemned him for attempting to 'produce a rupture between the native and European population at Thorndon', adding that he would be singled out to the police as a 'dangerous character'.[11]

But the damage had already been done. Earlier in April, Richard Davies Hanson, the Company's agent for absentee owners, and Baron Alsdorf had observed that the missionaries were 'endeavouring to excite the natives against the English settlers', jealous of 'the interference of the Company, in a place of which [the missionaries] desired to secure the monopoly'.[12] A few, like Richard Davis, had warned Pipitea Maori that the New Zealand Company's men were 'devils', intent on stealing their land and sending them 'into the mountains and into the sea'.

Meanwhile, John Wade had chartered his vessel *Integrity* to a man called Captain Pearson, but after an altercation with him, he laid a complaint of violence against Pearson before the council. Major Baker, a twice-decorated soldier who presided at the hearing, sentenced Pearson to a month's imprisonment for contempt of court after the latter refused to acknowledge the council's authority, and placed him in the custody of Captain Chaffers on the *Tory*.[13] But the *Integrity* sent a boat to rescue him and, vowing revenge on the 'democrats', Pearson immediately sailed to the Bay of Islands.

He arrived at the Bay of Islands on 21 May to lay a formal complaint of illegal detention before Hobson. Samuel Martin, an Auckland visitor to Port Nicholson, had been shocked but somewhat amused by the settlers' council, derisively describing it as being headed by 'King' Wakefield, with Evans as 'Lord Chancellor or legal adviser to the Wakefield Government'.[14] But when Pearson told Captain Hobson they were 'a turbulent set of rebels who [were] establishing a republic at Port Nicholson', he achieved a response far beyond anything he might have hoped for. The frail Lieutenant Governor, who was recovering from a paralytic stroke, had been instructed by Lord John Russell to treat the New Zealand Company's settlers with benevolence, but he reacted to Pearson's news by extending British sovereignty over the lower North Island and the entire country. He wrote to Normanby and Lord Russell accusing the Wellington settlers of high treason and of attempting 'to usurp [his] powers',[15] and declared all purchases of land from Maori after 1 February 1840 to be null and void. Many Maori chiefs in Cook's Strait and the South Island had still not seen, let alone signed, the Treaty and, as the settlers were discovering, Maori guarded their rights jealously, resenting anyone meddling with their property. Maori were, said Martin, very uneasy that Hobson 'should forbid Europeans to purchase their lands'.[16]

A contemporary historian confirms 'it was the Port Nicholson [Pearson] affair . . . that pressured Hobson to make his proclamations of sovereignty' over the entire country. By May, he adds, the Treaty 'no longer served a tangible purpose for Hobson's regime, beyond any pacifying effect it might have had on some tribes'.[17] Hobson sent his Colonial Secretary and Police Magistrate, Lieutenant Willoughby Shortland, on the *Integrity* to Wellington, together with a detachment of the 80th Regiment, warning him 'not to use any irritating measures or language, but . . . to act with becoming firmness and discretion'.[18]

Shortland had graduated from being an officer for the Botany Bay convicts to his appointment as Colonial Secretary purely by the vagaries of the New South Wales' government.[19] Martin predicted that he was 'likely to discharge [his] duty in the most obnoxious manner', and would 'most likely create a feeling of ill-will on the part of the Company's people towards the Government, which is not by any means difficult to be done'. He found it incredible that Hobson could think 'a person so very ignorant of business and so totally destitute of the elements of an ordinary education could have discharged the duties of a Colonial Secretary'.[20]

Yet Willoughby Shortland, with a detachment of thirty troops, five mounted police (without horse) and Lieutenant H. D. Smart of the 28th Regiment, sailed into Port Nicholson on the evening of 2 June. He put Constable Cole ashore with a letter for Wakefield, together with the written proclamation of British sovereignty over the islands of New Zealand.

The next day Wakefield sent a highly dismayed Evans with Harbour Master Chaffers and, strangely, Robert Tod – who was probably anxious to lay his own complaints – to greet him. Forced by gale-force winds to be rowed out to the ship, the trio welcomed the official party with due deference, Evans hastening to assure Shortland that they had been 'greatly misrepresented'. He swore the settlers' council had been formed merely 'to keep the peace and for mutual protection until the arrival of [Hobson], or any persons appointed by [him]', pledged their loyalty, and agreed to remove their flag and disband the council immediately. Although he was disappointed that after years of preparation his judicial role had been so swiftly snatched from him, Evans had no choice but to capitulate.

The following afternoon when Shortland stepped ashore with his entourage, he was greeted again by Evans, as well as by Wakefield, Captain Smith and all the leading settlers. Hobson's orders were read and received with three cheers. There was a royal salute, a haka by Maori, and everyone saluted the flag.

But Dudley Sinclair, a member of Evans's 'Committee of the First Colony' in London who had travelled in the *Adelaide*, was rumoured to have told the Auckland officials – presumably in a fit of bravado – that the Port Nicholson settlers were prepared to resist, 'even to the knife the authority of the British flag'.[21] Before breakfast the next morning, Ensign Best discovered Evans 'in close confab' with Shortland. He was struck with Evans's demeanour. 'The poor man was dreadfully down in the mouth' at the council's demise, yet at the same time he was 'loyal to the backbone, denying everything

Dudley Sinclair had said'. Evans even told Shortland and Best that the sentiments expressed in the *Gazette* against Hobson's proclamation of sovereignty were not shared by 'a single individual in the place', but Best was not fooled, concluding, 'Altogether he was as pretty a specimen of humbug as you could meet in a day's march.'[22]

Jerningham Wakefield, whose views agreed more with his uncle's, had wanted to fight to retain the council. He said Evans was 'completely frightened, and would make any sacrifice to secure the co-operation of the Government . . . he gives in entirely to [Shortland] who of course wishes no mention to be made of the authority granted by the sovereign chiefs to the Council'.[23]

But Evans took the only sensible course. On behalf of the settlers he was anxious to disabuse the government of any suspicion of treason. Reconciling the New Zealand Company's interests and those of the government was almost impossible. It was mortifying and embarrassing for Evans and the council's members, who must have felt like errant schoolboys caught tinkering with dangerous chemicals in a school laboratory. Evans's dual role as Wakefield's legal advisor and settlers' advocate was reduced to a juggling act, fraught with hazards that would mar his career in New Zealand.

Shortland did not make their discomfort any easier. He was particularly hostile to anyone connected with the Company and disliked Evans for his outspokenness, preferring men who were suitably deferential and kept their own counsel. When Evans later approached him on the settlers' behalf for an interview to discuss the government's intentions for the land, Shortland's brief reply echoed round the community. '"Sir!" he barked, "You are here as squatters, and I expect shortly to receive instructions to warn you off the Crown lands."'[24] His outrage was skin deep. Afterward Shortland made many 'irregular land deals in Auckland, was rebuked by the Secretary of State and forced to surrender them' – but not before making a good profit from a section 'with an excellent frontage'.[25]

Revans dismissed Shortland as 'ignorant', accusing the 'silly vulgar fool' of perpetrating 'great mischief', especially since he, Evans and the settlers had detected a noticeable shift in Maori attitude to them after his arrival.[26] The mana reserved for them was transferred to the government's representatives, as they clearly wielded more power. And Maori resentment was not discouraged by the Auckland visitors.

Major Bunbury proclaimed the Queen's sovereignty over the South and Stewart Islands, and by the end of June, Wakefield was nervous about Hanson's delay in returning from 'purchasing' the entire

Chatham Islands on behalf of the Company's absentee owners.[27] At about this time, he received the despatch from the directors informing him their council was illegal, which also meant that Evans's role as Umpire came to an abrupt end.[28] In July, Evans asked Wakefield to petition the directors for a year's salary, but the request was merely tabled at a directors' meeting late in November, as being 'under consideration as others were also pending of a similar nature'.[29]

To pre-empt the government, Wakefield and Evans decided to call a meeting for 1 July to propose Britannia (Wellington) as the colony's capital. Evans drew up the address of loyalty to Hobson, prefacing its reading with his own views. He emphasised the town's qualities as the seat of government: its harbour, its geographical centrality and the fact that it contained 'by far the greatest European population in the Islands'. After praising Colonel Wakefield's leadership, he said of the council, 'There were periods in men's lives when they ought to sacrifice their feelings, and this was one of them. It was impossible that 1,500 people could live together without some sort of authority being established, and, right or wrong, the Council had protected their persons and property . . . (Hear).'

At first, the petition was suitably placatory, assuring Hobson of their loyalty to the Crown. But it was followed by the bold assertion that by reserving the 'most valuable sections of land for the convenience of the public offices and the personal accommodation of your Excellency, we [feel assured] that sooner or later this must . . . become the seat of Government'. After it was unanimously approved, Revans proposed Wakefield carry the petition in person to Hobson.

A few days later, the New Zealand Company's barque *Platina* anchored off Petone beach bearing the wooden mansion the Company intended as a gift for the governor as his residence. Wakefield presumptuously ordered it to be unloaded at Thorndon. But Captain Wycherley's orders were to deliver the house directly to Hobson, so he contacted Shortland for confirmation.[30] Shortland's reply was a terse 'No'. He sent for Evans, accusing the settlers of blackmailing Hobson into making Britannia the capital. Evans agreed that the action was illegal and, exasperated by Wakefield's transparent move, he wrote urgently to him recommending he reconsider landing the house without merely storing it:

> I fear that the Governor's house will prove a cause of ill-will to this settlement. The end proposed by the manouevre, for everybody sees through it, will be most effectually defeated . . . . Nobody likes to be entrapped . . . Mr. Shortland desires me to say that he declines all responsibility . . . . I . . . most strongly urge upon you to go to

> Captain Hobson himself in the vessel and have it all out personally and you might greatly benefit us all.[31]

Wakefield took this advice in bad grace. Six days later, a fortnight after the meeting that had urged his departure, he left for Auckland – but not before appointing Hanson, who had finally returned from the Chathams, as his acting Principal Agent. Evans and Hanson soon formed a legal partnership. Like Evans, Hanson was a very clever non-conformist, a purposeful, thinking man, but he had strengths Evans lacked: he was even-tempered, reserved, patient and pragmatic.

Revans resented being passed over for acting Principal Agent, and told Chapman that in Wakefield's absence the 'temporary power' had gone to Hanson's head. Hanson was 'a firebrand . . . a remarkably rude and offensive man' who, with Evans, had turned the 'whole place into a state of turmoil'. They were all 'firmly convinced [Hanson] is dishonest and fear under each good some great evil is concealed. He and his friend Evans are nearly isolated', he gloated. Revans told Chapman he believed 'that the Company had not been fortunate in appointing [Hanson], in preference to me, as their agent. And though it may be considered vain, I remain to this hour of that opinion.'[32]

Some settlers pursued more modest ambitions. In exploring Port Nicholson, James Taine had found himself by 'singular coincidence . . . strolling in the same direction' as Liocadia as she walked the occasionally 'unruly' Evans family dogs. On their perambulations they watched Maori haul their fishing nets onto the 'fine sandy beach' of Evans's Bay. Behind the bay the even land was dense with turnips and parsnips or, as Maori called them, 'Captain Cook's cabbage'.[33] Taine often dined with the Evans family and their friends the Daniells, concluding the evening with a game of cards. The young couple spent many evenings by the 'warm fireside' where Harriet would suddenly recall that she and her husband 'had engagements elsewhere', and they were left alone. When they became engaged, Harriet gave Taine advice for furnishing his house, and later complimented him on 'many details, particularly the sleeping room', proclaiming it to be 'one of the most comfortable *whare* in the settlement'.[34]

On a Sunday morning late in June, Evans gave the bride away on behalf of Gibbon Wakefield, and James Taine and Liocadia were married at his home by the Anglican minister J. F. Churton. Colonel Wakefield was best man and Amelia Riddiford bridesmaid. Mrs Daniell made the wedding cake, and Harriet prepared the wedding breakfast at her home, whence the guests returned in the early afternoon.[35]

Since early May, with no end to the survey in sight, Evans had been feeling the financial strain. Dicky Barrett was happy to give him £400 in exchange for the Manning house he had bought for his wife's school, and had soon assembled it on the site opposite the old government buildings as his hotel.[36]

By July, Evans wrote again to Wright, at first proudly commenting on 'the schooners, luggers, whale boats and small craft of all description' that 'every day' crept 'into the harbour, from various parts of the coast for hundreds of miles; and then [departed], laden with sugar, flour, tobacco, spirits, blankets, etc., etc.'. He spoke of the abundance of pigs and potatoes, but added that 'blankets, flour, shop-clothing and all articles' were in great demand, reaping 'very large profits' for the importers. For unemployed people like himself, prices were 'quite distressing', he complained. There was already a labour shortage, employers were 'ruined in wages', and three of every four capitalists might be 'forced out' unless 'four or five thousand' labourers such as 'sawyers, carpenters, tile makers, wheelwrights and boat-builders' were 'speedily sent out'. There was also an urgent need for roofing materials and 'iron pipes for chimnies'.[37]

But by the time Wright received these requests, his bank had collapsed under a debt of £900,000. With assets of just £500,000, he was a ruined man. The Duke of Norfolk lost £60,000, and large sums were owed to Lord Petre, Somes and William Hutt. Several members of the Catholic clergy were creditors – Reverend Henry Burton of Saklop was owed £22,850 – and the New Zealand Company also suffered loss.[38] It had been Evans who had first asked Wright for the advance of £100,000 for the colony, and the news must have been a deep shock for him.

ᴓ

It was not until late July that the town sections were displayed for their 'owners' inspection. Evans was one of the largest landholders, owning a total of 51 town acres that were dotted between Riddiford Street, Oriental Parade, Mount Victoria and parts of today's inner city and the Hutt. Two sections extending from Guildford Terrace to Golders (Eccleston) Hill were earmarked for his future home.

But on the third day of inspection of the plan, an error over two sections held by Hanson and Evans was discovered. Evans's section began at Kumutoto stream (now Woodward Street), and extended about 250 feet south. From that point, 'Hanson's' section was to continue another 250 feet south. According to the plan drawn up, Evans might have benefited by an extra frontage of about 180 feet, but Hanson objected that his absentee owner would have 'sustained an uncompensated loss', presumably as Evans's section encroached on that of the absentee owner. Evans, like everyone else, did not realise the true value of the two beachfront sections and was prepared to surrender his section and choose another. Mein Smith suggested as a compromise that the north and south boundaries remain unchanged, 'but the front boundary of each section should be brought down to high-water mark'. Hanson was sent to persuade Evans to accept the option. There was an argument – with Evans being irascible and difficult – but when Hanson assured him that his absentee client stood to lose more with the alteration, Evans submitted, believing that he was making a significant sacrifice.[39]

Two years later, Revans accused Hanson of an 'iniquitous act' in the distribution of these sections. Hanson was furious in reply, protesting he had accepted '260 feet with a frontage to high water, instead of 520 feet to the road!' He had been 'frequently subjected to charges almost equally frivolous', but 'none [had been] so palpably baseless. I neither feel surprise nor disgust at your suppressions and misrepresentations, [but] leave the public to judge between us.'[40]

In early August they were all stunned to hear that the Legislative Council in Sydney had passed a New Zealand Land Bill, declaring all land titles not 'derived from' the Crown null and void. Anyone wishing to claim land had just six months to present their case to the Colonial Secretary of New South Wales, when a Board of Commissioners would decide each case. The Port Nicholson colony seemed doomed as it broke three rules of the New Zealand Land Bill: it was the site of a town exceeding 2560 acres, it was within yards of high tide mark, and it was situated on a port. Evans was not the only one whose life investments were under threat, and everyone felt betrayed by the British government. Many even threatened to move to Chile.[41]

On 19 August, after Wakefield's return from Russell, Evans presided over a public meeting at Barrett's to hear the governor's reply to their petition. Hobson politely but firmly refused to consider Wellington as the country's capital, telling them he had decided to form the seat of government 'upon the south shore of the Wai te

Mata', adding that the New Zealand Company's description of land available at Port Nicholson was 'very incorrect'. On the topic of the New Zealand Land Bill, Evans proposed Gibbon Wakefield for the colony's agent, presumably to seek intervention on their behalf. Hanson read the resolutions for a 'memorial' or petition to Governor Gipps, and George Hunter's motion that a deputation comprised of Evans, Hanson and Moreing present the memorial personally was unanimously approved.

Evans had written earlier to Hobson begging for a judiciary role, but Hobson informed the settlers that Gipps alone had the power to make official appointments, and was sending two police magistrates from Sydney. Hobson's personal reply to Evans did not arrive until September, confirming that he was unable to help and appealing for Evans's understanding and sympathy. He stressed the poor state of the finances of his jurisdiction and role, writing 'we have not a shilling, except what we borrow from others who are very unwilling to lend'. He said he was glad to hear from Wakefield that Wellington's community enjoyed 'so good a feeling' and that he hoped 'to see some of the enterprising Gentlemen' in 'the Thames before long. The land there is well worthy of attention'. He sent his compliments to Mrs Evans 'with whom I had a very short acquaintance in London, which I shall be most happy to renew, either here or in Port Nicholson'.[42]

It was a sincere and kindly letter, but Hobson's plea of lack of funds rang hollow to Evans. The settlers had already heard many of Martin's accusations: that 'Money was being thrown around by ignorant and reckless servants of the government'; that Hobson had created many 'useless and unnecessary appointments'; and that he had undertaken other foolish actions. In fact, Martin went so far as to say that he believed Hobson's 'mind had become seriously impaired' from 'disappointment, anxiety and an extremely nervous temperament'.[43]

The presence of the troops, the bullying constables and the tough magistrates imposing harsh (£5) fines for inebriation made everyone miserable, but after nine men drowned in late August,[44] the collective mood of the settlers sank even lower. Evans was alarmed people might leave, which would be a huge setback to the colony's success and cause serious financial loss. But Evans had explained the arguments the men would present to Gipps at the meeting on 19 August 'with great clearness and ability': 'The case of New Zealand was essentially different as the dominion of the country was not claimed by Great Britain. The chiefs of New Zealand were admitted to possess sovereign rights; and these rights have not been extinguished, but are vested by purchase in the English Crown.'[45] On this occasion he might have gone further to bolster their spirits and rally them against the arbitrary rules of Shortland and Smart, who had taken over the magistrates bench in July.

At the time his words were music to the embattled colonists' ears. Young Captain George Moore was present on at least two occasions when Evans spoke, and he was so deeply impressed by Evans's fiery oratory that he recorded the experience nearly fifty years later. For him, Evans was the 'fine old English gentleman . . . politician and classical scholar'. Although Moore's memory of the timing of the speeches is confused, and the speech he recalled was made a year later, he was particularly impressed on this occasion because throughout it he was aware that Shortland was listening on the other side of a calico partition, which added even greater drama to Evans's defiant words.[46]

'As long as I live', Moore wrote,

> I shall not forget some of [Evans's] introductory remarks . . . . [when he] said 'we find it necessary to gather together to meet a Government whose deputy . . . has the assurance to tell us we are unlawfully in possession of any part of New Zealand, and that the newly appointed Governor would closely watch and check our daring movements . . . . We, the free and enterprising Englishmen who have at our own cost and personal risk, sought these shores with honest and liberal intentions, to found a new colony for ourselves, our friends, and all that may follow. Who is this Mr. Shortland that comes from afar amongst us – secretly, like a detective – escorted by a "mighty army" . . . to overawe us into a subjective state of mind and purpose, foreign to our wishes or intentions, as honest men and free Britons?'
>
> Altogether this meeting was an earnest and effective one, for Mr. Shortland, sitting in the next calico room, of course heard all, and found undoubtedly he had entered into the wrong box. Next morning he became less official [*sic*] and bumptious, and soon rather anxious to remove himself and his army where he could uninterruptedly report to His Excellency the daring and marked independence of the Port Nicholson early settlers.[47]

In early September, Evans and his wife, Moreing and Hanson left for Sydney to present the memorial of Port Nicholson settlers, asking for Gipps's intervention in the New Zealand Land Bill in the form of a plea to treat theirs as a special case. And on 16 September, three months after his arrival, Shortland returned with Lieutenant Smart to the Bay of Islands to make his reports.[48]

CHAPTER NINE.
A GLIMMER OF HOPE

Cheer up! Cheer up! our course we'll keep
With dauntless heart and hand,
And when we've ploughed the stormy deep,
We'll plough a smiling land.

Thomas Campbell, 'Song of the Colonists Departing for New Zealand', 1839

Before he left for Sydney with Harriet, Hanson and Moreing, Evans arranged to leave his house and goods in the charge of a chief from Pipitea pa who had become attached to the family. Just before their departure, the *Britomart* arrived in port with the newly appointed Police Magistrate, Michael Murphy. Murphy's credentials seemed singularly uninspiring to the settlers. As a clerk to the Police Magistrates at Paramatta, he had once edited a work by the Attorney General. Gipps transferred him to Hobson, who promptly sent the twenty-five-year-old to Port Nicholson on a salary of £250 a year.[1]

Two days after the deputation arrived in Sydney on 22 September, the men met Gipps to deliver their petition. They gave a detailed account of the background and operations of the New Zealand Company that had spent £75,000 in promoting emigration to New Zealand, and described Wakefield's purchase of land in 'Cook's Straits'. Gipps, described by historian Robert Hughes as a 'fair-minded' and 'diligent' man and 'a strikingly prudent and humane Governor', was courteous and interested.[2]

Evans was so buoyed by their reception he wrote to his friend, Edward Betts Hopper, addressing him as his 'oldest coadjutor in Port Nicholson, and as one who will not put any forced interpretation on what I may have to say':

> [Gipps] is favourable to us and is quite sincere and candid in all he says. Altogether he has made a conquest of our good opinion, and I dare say he will be as successful with you all – if he will give us what we want. He admitted several things –

> 1 That if the Company could fulfil their pledges they would confer a benefit on New Zealand. – but, 'he thought that impossible; they would lose money'. 2 That it could be no more desirable for the public, than for the settlers themselves that any check should be given to industry by a panic or uncertainty about land. 3 That we certainly should not be disturbed by him, at present, without instructions from the home government. 4 That all he could do was to recommend the home Government to confirm our grants with some modifications of the plan – He said that, after considering this, he would see us again, in the mean time pledging himself to nothing. He then produced the [returns?] of land sales at Port Philip, and particularly insisted on the superiority of the Government plan of half acre towns with suburban allotments of 15 to 20 acres.

He was apprehensive that Gipps would insist they alter their plan as a condition of his clearing the way for the British government to give the New Zealand Company a perfect title.

> He says that the Govt. might have sold our township for £150,000 more than the Company have, and that as that surplus would have been available for roads, bridges, etc. etc. we must suggest some method of supplying the deficit. It occurred to me that a municipality pledged to these expences (which are all for our own benefit) with a power of local taxation – would meet the case. We have therefore made the proposal, and the whole case is before him. We expect an answer in a few days. On Tuesday we are to dine with him. We meet with general sympathy.

He extolled Sydney's benefits and harbour, adding 'as for the convict system, we neither see, nor hear any more of it than we did at Hampstead'. Finally, he urged Betts Hopper to 'show' the letter 'to Colonel Wakefield, Captain Daniell, etc – but consider it strictly private'.[3]

But the news was bad for Evans. A fortnight earlier his 'coadjutor' Betts Hopper had drowned tragically in the Hutt River. The loss for Evans was incalculable. Betts Hopper had been his most trusted friend and companion for the past decade, serving on nearly every committee with him since the New Zealand Association's formation. Had he lived to record events in the settlement without 'putting any forced interpretation on what [Evans] may have had to say', we might have a more rounded view of Evans.[4]

When they met again with Gipps, Evans outlined his idea of a charter of municipality for Port Nicholson, and by 20 October Gipps had drawn up an eight-point proposal, based on three 'fixed' principles: that the land, 110,000 acres, was to be taken in one continuous block; that of the 110,000 acres, one tenth was to be reserved for Maori, with their lands being selected by lot as provided for by the plan of the New Zealand Company; and that twenty acres were to be reserved for the purposes of government in no more than four localities, which should include a frontage of not more than two hundred yards to deep water in the best commercial situation of the town. Overseeing the application of these terms would be a person nominated by the Lieutenant Governor, and approved by him.[5]

Gipps said the government would never 'admit one pound per acre to be a sufficient price for any land, unless it be taken in the block, good and bad together'. He believed not even £100 per acre would be sufficient for land in Wellington, which had 'a seaport commanding one of the best harbours in New Zealand'. The entire area was worth far more than the Company's estimate of £110,000. Gipps suggested they follow the model of Port Philip, where land sold at the discretion of the government had realised £312,700.

For three weeks they debated the issues. Gipps finally told them the government would allow them to take 110,000 acres in one continuous block, reserving one-tenth of it 'for the use or benefit of the [Maori]'. He instructed them to honour the rights of Maori and added that Hobson would designate someone to select Maori land and approve all the selections. Twenty acres were to be put aside in four lots for the use of the government, and thirty for a barracks 'within reasonable distance of the town'. Gipps also made it clear that the government did not guarantee possession of any land to any settler that might be claimed by others. Should anyone claim 'prior purchase', the commissioners would enquire into their validity. He assured them that the local government would work towards giving them a municipal charter.

The men had demurred over a few issues, their main worry being that waiting for Hobson's approval of their selection of public and native reserves would cause unnecessary delay – at least a year, and probably two to lay out the settlement. This would seriously impede the business and development of the settlement. They also pointed out that taking 110,000 acres in one continuous block would be unfair to later immigrants whose land would, inevitably, be further away, poorer and 'absolutely worthless'.

They reminded Gipps that the claims of the Company's settlers rested, not on land purchases from Maori, but on the 'large sum' they had contributed for immigration, which was why they wanted the Company's purchases to be exempted from the Act. They worried too about Maori resistance to Wakefield's claim:

> . . . where it is not known whether any precise rule prevails as to the degree in which individuals are bound by the acts of the tribe, in a sale of land, [any claims] which might be urged to detached portions, by persons who had by removal or otherwise forfeited all claim to any portion of the land as against their tribe, but might attempt to establish such a claim as against the settlers.

They believed the benefits of colonisation would make the value of the Maori portion ten times that of the whole area before European settlement, and stressed that they thought it 'highly unjust', if considering they had paid £100,000 'to what is in reality a town, and 20,000 acres of land' (about £5 per acre), that they would be subject to counter claims brought against them by latecomers who had purchased land from Maori, knowing a settlement was being already formed. These people would have 'contributed nothing to any public purpose; and . . . if the town [had been] founded by Government, would be only entitled to compensation in land'.

Gipps assured them the government would interfere only in cases of 'glaring injustice', but said that while assuming the Maori title had been 'fairly extinguished', it reserved the right to 'inquire into' and redress 'any injury that may be proved to have been committed'. The Government would not interfere with the Company's selection of lands for Maori except 'in any case where injustice might appear to have been done to the natives . . . . The Official Protector of the Aborigines would be, moreover, a more fit person to judge in the first instance of such injustice than the Surveyor-General'.

Gipps added that any compensation awarded to any individual whose claim had been rejected 'must be made by the settlers collectively or by the Company'. He reminded them the government had been 'in no way a party' to the Company's purchase of land, and could not guarantee it, as his instructions to them were, of course, subject to the approval of her Majesty's government.[6]

But Gipps had at least nominally approved the Company's purchase of 100,000 acres around Port Nicholson for the time being – subject to the British government's approval. In Wellington, the *Gazette* had already reported that while Gipps 'would apply the New Zealand Bill to the Company's territory', he would 'refer theirs as a special and most peculiar case to the Home Government'.[7] Before the three men left him, Gipps appointed them all magistrates. He also promised to recommend a Charter of Incorporation for their settlement,[8] but told the deputation he disapproved of the actions of their Council of the First Colony.

There had been one disagreeable surprise. The redoubtable Captain Pearson, who had escaped from custody to tell Hobson of the Company's independent state in Wellington, had had the magistrate Major Baker arrested for 'false imprisonment' when the latter visited Sydney, and the press had seized on the case. It was too late by the time Hanson and Evans arrived to have the case dropped. If the two men had not instructed Baker to pay Pearson £100 in lieu of damages, there would have been a highly publicised trial with damages amounting to £1,000.

Both Hanson and Evans believed that, as Baker had represented the Company when he arrested Pearson, he should not be expected to pay the fine or the fees, so they asked Wakefield to apply to the Company's directors for compensation to the tune of £369 9s 1d, which they had borrowed from the bank to pay the costs. They reminded Wakefield that interest would accrue until the Company's reply was received.[9]

It had been an expensive lesson, for the Company, the settlers' council and the individuals concerned; and one that would not have endeared Evans to the New Zealand Company's directors.

Evans found time to write to his parents from Botany Bay about the delays and 'pecuniary loss' most settlers had suffered. His letter was a model of all that might please his father, Evans saying he hoped to return to Europe with the means to live there for the rest of his life. He missed the 'religious, the literary and political society of Europe', and renewed his vow to look after his parents' 'comfort in their old age', and the promotion of the 'happiness and prosperity' of his brothers and sisters. He hoped to realise a profit of eight or ten thousand pounds on his investment in land in a year, investing the money at 12.5 per cent, on security 'of the very best freehold property in front, I mean on mortgage'. He couldn't return with enough income 'for a studious man in England', but was considering leasing his land. His health was good but, he confided, his experiences had made him 'feel almost an old man'. He and his wife felt keenly the 'privations' of a colony. He had had 'strong inducements to come up [to Sydney] to reside', but did not intend to change his plans.

For young people, New Zealand was an 'El Dorado – a paradise where food will drop into their mouths', but Evans had begun to see that the dream was far from reality:

> I have encountered perils of all kinds, and have seen much wickedness of men – my conclusion is that the first lesson which you taught was the right one, and that the 'fear of the Lord is the beginning of wisdom', but I feel that I am following the course of providence in a private station; although I am at times in the hands of God.[10]

On their way back from Sydney the party stopped first at the Bay of Islands, where they called on Hobson and Shortland. They had been told Hobson was openly offering incentives to Wellington's (Company-sponsored) labourers to move to Auckland, and they berated them both for the manoeuvre. Evans argued for two hours, using language 'he was sure [Hobson] would never forget or forgive'. He told Hobson that 'he feared he was being advised [by Shortland] to do "that in his public capacity, which he would not do as a private gentleman"'. When the rattled Hobson read the despatch from Gipps, he exclaimed: 'What does Sir George Gipps mean by this; he might as well have given up the government of the country to the Company.'[11]

They arrived in Port Nicholson on 8 December to find the town had been officially named Wellington.[12] It was evolving into two areas: to the north and south of Windy or Clay Point (Stewart Dawson's corner); and the Te Aro Flat and Thorndon Flat. There were traders on the beach, but Thorndon was the administrative heart, containing the immigration barracks, military barracks, the barn which served as post office, court house and jail, Barrett's Hotel – the hub of meetings – and Wakefield's house. Te Aro was becoming mostly commercial, with the Exchange and businesses like Revans's and various mills being constructed, such as Catchpool's steam flour mill and Hoggard's wind mill.

The settlers had been told all their taxes were to be sent to Auckland – 'none [of which] was to be spent on roads or other public works in Wellington', complained Wakefield to the directors. In October, Dicky Barrett's hotel had been officially opened with a grand dinner, and Evans was told the toast coupling his name with Gibbon Wakefield had been greeted with loud cheers. In his absence there had been a meeting to form the Port Nicholson Exchange and General Library. A committee had been appointed and had decided to buy Barrett's old whare on the Wai Peraro Reserve for £30; Dr F. J. Knox was elected librarian, and members paid a subscription fee.[13] The books Evans had collected before leaving London were donated to the library. Later, Evans proposed they build a house for the library that they could rent at 3 per cent on outlay, paying for the ground at the same rate as he was getting from his tenants.[14]

After the *Gazette* published the exchanges that had taken place in

Sydney, the settlers were read Gipps's instructions at a meeting on 12 December which led to a debate. Some were in favour of demanding more land – they had expected 200 square miles instead of the 15 square miles Gipps had allowed. Hanson and Evans suggested resurveying the town and allotting it in half-acre sections as Gipps had suggested, so that each landholder had at least a portion of the land he had purchased in England. The country lands could be divided into 20-acre lots. But the settlers rejected the idea, believing the delays and extra expense would make it impracticable. At a further meeting on 15 December, a resolution was passed to convey their gratitude to Gipps – especially as he had agreed to Evans's suggestion of a municipality – and the deputation was thanked 'for the zeal and ability with which they represented the interests of this settlement'.[15]

A week after the New Year celebrations, Evans received a note from Colonel Wakefield, a letter from the directors, 'and a memorandum respecting your conditional appointment as Principal Agent of the New Zealand Company'[16] that made his position in the colony clear. Company secretary Ward had explained to Wakefield that Evans's appointment as Principal Agent had been only to cover the possible loss of the *Cuba* and the *Tory*. In fact, Captain Smith alone was authorised to act in Wakefield's absence:

> . . . the Directors do not deem it advisable to fetter their own discretion by continuing any longer the appointment of a third person to be Principal Agent. The Court of Directors therefore have revoked all the conditional powers and authorities conferred upon Dr. Evans . . . . As the reasons of the revocation (which are previously stated in this letter) will be sufficiently apparent, the Directors do not see occasion to add any remarks in this place.[17]

The reasons were stated as follows: they had received 'numerous' letters written by passengers from the Cape of Good Hope; the ship's deviation had cost the Company 'great expense, and not . . . without serious damage to the Colony'; and the delay in the *Adelaide*'s arrival had impeded the 'first proceedings of the colony'. Smith having caused the first and most serious delay by surveying the Hutt in direct contravention of Colonel Wakefield's wishes, and Wakefield's own vacillations, were ignored. Evans was their scapegoat.

Colonel Wakefield was given 'undivided authority', the directors telling him pointedly he was free to act 'without consulting anybody . . . . [You are] authorized to dispense with the services of any of them without assigning any reason . . . and to engage others as you may please.' The onslaught did not stop there. Alfred de Bathe Brandon had been sent from the office of the Company's lawyers, bearing the despatches for Colonel Wakefield and offering his services. Wakefield was urged to employ him 'as the legal adviser of the Company in any cases which may require the aid of a solicitor particularly . . . in the event of any enquiry or proceeding of the Government with reference to the Company's titles or possessions . . . . this letter is not to be understood as in any way interfering with the unlimited discretion committed to you by the Directors of employing in the Company's service those persons only whose conduct should give to yourself unqualified satisfaction.'[18] In addition, the directors forfeited two hundred of Evans's shares. Others, including Riddiford, Hanson, Daniell and the late Betts Hopper also lost some shares.[19]

Evans was severely rattled by this, but he needed income and probably met with Wakefield to discuss his role of counsel in Company matters. Wakefield knew he would be foolish to dispense with Evans's services altogether, as few could equal his legal skills. At times he even called Evans in to write important letters. Two such letters to Gipps and Hobson certainly stand out as having been written by 'one skilled in the law'.[20]

The success Evans and Hanson had secured in Sydney had enhanced their status, so the fact that Evans had been stripped of his extra powers delighted Revans, who gloated over his rival's fall from grace. When Evans was told the directors had revoked his shares, he had made, according to Revans, 'insinuations against the Company at a public meeting'. Revans then accused him of using any excuse to discredit the Company, and Evans was 'compelled to retract his charges publicly . . . to our amusement'. He told Chapman that Evans had been betrayed by John Ward over a confidential letter. Although everyone was affected by Chapman's publishing their letters without discretion, and Revans was soon far from happy about the practice himself, he warned: 'The Times newspaper is to be addressed upon this Port Nicholson grievance so old Evans told me, and sundry other modes of redress are to be sought, so prepare yourself for the storm. Your warning against Evans I thank you for, but we had all become too well acquainted with him to need it.'[21]

Revans reserved his most bitter venom for Harriet Evans, whom he had decided was behind the rumours gathering momentum in the settlement about his unorthodox relationship with Mrs Smith. Captain Smith was often absent for days – sometimes weeks – surveying, and soon even Colonel Wakefield, whom Henry Chapman believed was 'as great a scandal-monger as an ill-educated woman', listened. Louisa was a free spirit who flouted convention, having no time for 'idle social calls'. And certain ladies who believed themselves superior to Louisa Smith sniffed when she swirled past them in Molesworth Street in her 'beautiful watered taffetas, velvets, silks and satins hooped, cut and trimmed in the newest French style', on the arm of the 'turbulent and rather coarse' Revans, himself carelessly dressed and always wearing a large panama hat.[22]

Revans believed Harriet resented the 'agreeable warm-hearted' Louisa and was determined to do her worst by her. 'Mrs. Evans would really make the mischievous woman of a book to great advantage', he declared. '[Evans's] wife rules him; and this old devil may be considered the cause of all mischief and bad feeling here. Were she dead even Evans would act better than he does.'[23]

Revans also accused Daniel Riddiford of going on board ships in the harbour, drinking in the cabins and spreading 'scandal'. He intended reporting this to Wakefield, 'who always disliked this drunken brawler, and who has much the same opinion of the Evans as the rest of the community have', he added airily.

Revans then turned on Colonel Wakefield, boasting that it was he who had persuaded Mein Smith and his surveyors not to leave Wakefield in disgust. At the same time he accused Wakefield of finding his task as Principal Agent 'distasteful', loving as he did only 'ease and retirement'. Revans concluded that Wakefield had 'no go' and that the colony's affairs were being handled inefficiently. Hobson was 'double faced', 'extravagant and wasteful'; and his men 'unmitigated' in their 'hatred and jealousy of this place'. Revans the republican longed to 'beat Auckland out and out', with a corporation or a revival of the settlers' council.[24]

Revans's criticisms did not merely relate to those in positions of power. Less than three months later, he was the outsider, quarrelling with settlers on all fronts. He rebuked Chapman, complaining he had been harassed by his 'enemies' and 'given nicknames'. He feared now that the publication of his letters 'might cost me my life'.[25] Partridge confirmed his fears, telling Chapman, 'You have no idea what a row some of the allusions in people's letters here have made in a small society'.[26] Two years later Chapman was dismayed when he saw for himself how Revans's quarrels had isolated him from the community. Revans would later form more balanced opinions, but historians continue to accept his rancorous observations unquestioningly.

Like others, Evans was concentrating on the colony's prosperity. In the new year of 1841, Coutts Crawford arranged a meeting to discuss investing in the development of the flax industry. Usually, Maori women cleaned and stripped flax by using mussel shells as tools, but there was a scarcity of Maori labour. Evans was appointed to a committee with Hanson, Daniell, Crawford, Hunter and others to examine proposals and raise capital from subscription. His financial pressure had eased somewhat after he leased out his beachfront sections for 30 shillings per foot annually (from Woodward Street almost to present-day Stewart Dawson's Corner on Lambton Quay).[27] Hoping to raise £2,000, Evans was one of twenty-three who invested five guineas each to start the ball rolling. A reward was offered for a machine costing no more than £5, which could prepare and produce 50 pounds of flax daily for export.[28] Two months later Messrs Pratt and Golder had produced flax in a 'perfectly marketable state', and £20 was voted to them to produce samples for England.[29] Eighteen months later, Evans designed a machine that initially appeared to overcome all the obstacles. A working model was to be built and hopes were high that the 'learned gentleman' would succeed, but it appears to have defeated its inventor's efforts.[30]

Meanwhile, Wakefield was eyeing Porirua for settlement, in spite of warnings from local Maori about Te Rauparaha and Rangihaeata and the fierce Ngati Toa tribe. Jerningham had met Rangihaeata at Paremata. He was reported as demanding 'spirits as usual' and abusing Wakefield for 'buying' their land. The formidable warrior vowed he would never let white people live in Porirua. He complained bitterly about the loss of Manawatu, Whanganui and Taranaki, which he claimed as his. The settlers underestimated his warning.

On behalf of the settlers Evans wrote to Wakefield in late January complaining about the state of the 'roads' linking the main settlements – the Hutt, Karori and Owhiro – where no carts or carriages could negotiate the rough paths that ran between the three valleys. He told Wakefield it was hardly worth the trouble and expense of cultivating the land when produce could not be transported to any market. If government did not provide the funds, would the Company help? He was worried the surplus of labour over land and capital might 'induce' labourers to move to neighbouring settlements. As it stood, the survey's delay meant that only a tenth of the land was allotted, a tenth of which was available because of the state of the roads. If Wakefield employed extra labour to widen and improve the roads, the Company would benefit. When the roads were cut, surveyors' lines would be unnecessary, the surveys would accelerate, and labour and transport would be cheaper. The settlers would pay some of the cost. He suggested writing to Gipps and possibly the English government, asking for a clause to be added to their Charter of Incorporation that reimbursed the Company for any expenses.

It took a fortnight for Wakefield to reply, when he confirmed that the road from Thorndon to the Hutt was under way and lines were also being cut from Porirua to Ngauranga and the Hutt Valley. But the Company's funds were 'limited', and the directors believed the settlers should pay a proportion of the costs of public works. Wakefield promised to send their petition to the directors – but asked for more details.[31]

Several landowners were trying to recoup their losses by renting out sections. Evans was building up his practice with Hanson, but the cost of maintaining his large household and building his permanent home was considerable. Between February and June his London agent sold seven of his land orders – five of which were snapped up by Secretary Ward in London, but Evans's temper was not improved when, in spite of his protest to Hobson, the police magistrate Michael Murphy advertised in the *Gazette* for carpenters, sawyers, bricklayers and stone masons to work in Auckland. The settlers complained that Hobson had not only sent his men to smash their organisation, stir up Maori grievances and force the laws of a convict colony upon them, but that he was also poaching labour brought out at Company expense. As proof of this, the Company's chaplain Reverend Churton moved to Auckland to become Colonial Chaplain at a salary of £325 per annum, and twenty mechanics also responded to the lure of Auckland, travelling in the *Tyne* sent especially to collect them at the government's expense.[32]

It was only a matter of time before Evans would have a run-in with Murphy over the issue. Hanson had drawn up a memorial asking Hobson to stop taking their labour and to put money aside for a separate government in Wellington; and at an 'Indignation Meeting' held on 15 February, Revans, Daniell and others read a petition for the recall of Hobson or, as they called him, 'Captain Crimp'. The petition was given to Henry Petre to take to Britain as he was sailing there shortly. Evans did not attend the meeting, his excuse being that, as a magistrate appointed by the Crown, 'it would have been most unseemly for him to call the conduct of the Lieutenant Governor into question'.[33] At first persuaded to sign it, he withdrew at the last moment because, as he explained, 'he objected to the language used'. He also alleged he had signed it only under sufferance 'at the suggestion of his wife, whilst labouring under the influence of an opiate', an incredulous Murphy told Hobson:

> People here say that is not true, but that he is looking for a Government appointment; from what I have seen of Dr. Evans

> I place little confidence in his assertion . . . . with good natural abilities, Dr. Evans wants what would make him an useful member of society, namely, stability of principle and character.[34]

At the time, Evans was building a mill on a piece of land near the Kaiwharawhara stream. Taringa Kuri arrived and demanded payment, but when Evans reminded him that Wakefield had already bought the land, he replied 'Colonel Wakefield had bought the land but not the water'. Kuri's men then interrupted Evans's workers so often that he gave them 'a double-barrelled gun to pacify them'.[35] But two of his sawyers were frightened enough to leave and were hired for Auckland by Murphy. Evans confronted Murphy, accusing him of poaching his men, and Murphy told the sawyers he could not hire them after all. They assured him they would find replacement sawyers for Evans and later told him Evans had released them. The next morning Evans called on Murphy:

> . . . in a great passion, and commenced a violent tirade of abuse against me for having . . . 'seduced his men away' . . . . I endeavoured to explain . . . he would scarcely hear me, indulged in a deal of personal abuse both to myself and [Hobson] and stated that <u>he had not released them</u>, that they had deceived him and taken two men of straw to him.

Murphy assured Evans he would not hire them if that were the case, and asked again if they were still his employees. 'Instead of replying, Dr. Evans turned on his heel and walked away . . . . I again sent for the men . . . [and] <u>they produced the release in Dr. Evans's own handwriting</u>. After such conduct of Dr. Evans, I cannot place reliance on what he states.'[36]

This sort of erratic behaviour plagued Evans all his professional life. When out of temper, he was uninterested in popularity or others' opinions. He wrote peremptorily to Major Durie who had built a house on one of his sections:

> In the event of your continuing to occupy the said piece of ground after the receipt of this notice without agreeing to pay rent to me for the same, I shall claim rent from you . . . at the rate of two pounds per annum for each lineal foot of frontage to the road in front of the same and shall demand payment of such rent from the 1 September, 1840 and shall enter upon the said piece of ground, take and retain possession of all improvements that may have been made upon the same without allowing any compensation therefore, and shall take such other proceedings to enforce my claims as I may be advised.[37]

In March, Wakefield sent Evans and John Wicksteed to research Porirua's scope for settlement, to deal with the chiefs and to negotiate with Joseph Thom, a Pakeha related by marriage to the local chiefs who held a valuable site at a whaling station. It was rumoured that Thom ran 'a house of the greatest disorder, [which was] the scene of constant drunkenness'. The two men attempted to bargain with him, but a settler later wrote:

> Dr. Evans has selected Porirua as a suitable place for a township, and has selected 640 acres of land there; and Dr. Evans, who is the Company's legal adviser, has done (as might be expected) everything he can in the way of turning Mr. Thoms out, and probably in giving him a bad character; but at present [1845] Thoms remains in possession of his land, which he has resided upon for twelve or fifteen years; and I hope if he is turned out that he will be amply compensated for the same.[38]

But it was Wakefield who was advertising land in Porirua for selection. Again, Evans wrote to Colonel Wakefield in March complaining about the premature move:

> In common with many other persons I have been watching the progress of the bridle road to Porirua with great satisfaction; but as I presume it cannot be completed within two or thee weeks, and as I am one of those who have not the physical power to examine some ten to fifteen thousand acres of forest land without seeking for the facility which a road would give, if it can be obtained, I do hope that you will postpone the selection advertised for the 1st. of April another month, in order that we may enjoy the great advantage of riding to Porirua. Added to this consideration, I think that we may very shortly expect some intelligence from England which may enable us to interpret Sir George Gipps's despatches to us with more latitude than we are at present warranted in doing. This would be a great boon and encouragement to the landowners, and would be fulfilling the original intentions of the Company.
>
> At the same time – I venture to give my opinion emphatically that any wide departure from the spirit of those despatches would violate a fundamental principle of our Colony, which is concentration, and would be as injurious to the landowners themselves as it would be embarrassing to the Company.
>
> I am, my dear Colonel Wakefield, yours very faithfully etc.[39]

The settlers met in late March to discuss the actions of the police in manacling inebriated men and meting brutal punishment to them in the jail; they had also heard that Murphy had ordered the police to spy at public and private houses. Wade proposed to rein in Murphy's power by having Evans and Hanson join him on the bench; the motion was carried '*nem. con.*'.

Two days later, Evans was visited by a deputation of several gentlemen. They assured him that his competence, 'integrity and impartiality' inspired their 'utmost confidence':

> . . . we know, that where the interests of the colony are at stake, you will consider the hours devoted to our welfare to be well spent, and although we have no direct recompense to make, we feel certain that you will esteem the reliance of your fellow citizens to be of more value than any thing else in our power to offer . . . . With assurances of our esteem . . . etc.

Evans regretted they felt the need to ask for protection, but explained that the police were being 'unjustly compelled to bear the odium of those laws, which they were only called to administer and for which they are in no degree responsible'. He explained that the laws were 'framed exclusively for a penal settlement and totally unfit for a community of Englishmen untainted with crime'. He encouraged them to think the laws framed for a convict settlement would soon be replaced by municipal laws specifically created for their town. He added gravely,

> I cannot deny that there are serious grounds for complaint. With that admission, I am bound, as a faithful servant of the Crown and of the Public, to make every sacrifice that may be necessary, in order to [undertake] the performance of a very onerous and painful duty. Gentlemen, . . . relying upon your support in the conscientious discharge of my duty as a Magistrate, I shall endeavour, according to my humble ability, to secure for you what you seem now to require – a just and lenient administration of the Common and Statute Law of England.[40]

His equilibrium restored, Evans's resolve never wavered. Thereafter he represented the interests of the settlers as well as those of the Company.

CHAPTER TEN.
MEETINGS REPAIRED

Advantage is a better soldier than rashness.

William Shakespeare, *Henry V*, III, vi, line 120

Murphy viewed Evans's acceptance of the settlers' request as a deliberately provocative act. On 31 March 1841, as soon as they arrived together on the bench, the two men held what the *Gazette* called a 'dignified exchange':

> Murphy: Is it your intention to sit here in your magisterial capacity?
> Dr. Evans: Such is my intention.
> Murphy: Then sir, in consequence of the proceedings of a public meeting and a letter inserted in the newspaper last week, I shall be compelled to leave my seat.
> Dr. Evans: You can do as you please sir. It is my intention to sit here for the purpose of administering, to the best of my ability, justice to the public.

Murphy added that he would abstain whenever Evans took his seat on the bench except in cases 'where two magistrates were required by law'. Evans calmly proceeded to deal with a case of drunkenness, reminding the police that it was their duty 'when they found a man in a state of intoxication, if he was not disturbing the peace by riotous conduct . . . to see him to his house in preference to using violence'. He warned them that while they had his support and protection 'in the discharge of their duty; if unnecessary violence was used, such conduct would not go unmarked by [him]'. The defendant was found guilty and fined five shillings.[1]

Apart from the magistrates' conduct, the British justice system enjoyed little dignity in its antipodean environment. The large draughty barn that housed the court also served for the post office, the police station and a church. The jail on the beach was a filthy rat-hole crammed with drunken brawlers and worse. Lamps shed their flickering light over the doors of the many hotels and inns in the vicinity. Roads were rough tracks that became muddy and difficult to negotiate after heavy rain. Barrett's Hotel, situated a little back from the beach, near the corner of Molesworth Street and Lambton Quay, was close enough to Evans's home for him to visit it without difficulty, but trips to the Exchange at Te Aro, where many meetings took place in the evening, meant the horse had to be saddled up. On clear nights Evans walked from his whare to his numerous meetings with the aid of a lantern.

Things were looking up. By early April the community heard that New Zealand was going to be declared a separate colony. After the road from Wellington to Petone was opened for traffic, numerous bullock wagons drawn by oxen brought goods to town. Coal was discovered at Evans's Bay on Revans's section. A blacksmith said it was the best he had used for welding iron, and this, Robert Stokes proudly told a friend in England, was only the stuff found on the surface – 'a few feet deeper it is expected to prove of the best description'.[2]

Wellington was abuzz with activity. Men swarmed over pockets of land, eagerly plying the tools of construction.[3] By this time there were 2500 Europeans living in the area.[4] Amongst the scores of houses being erected was Evans's home, which was built on the crest of a rise leading from Hill Street, which Evans named Golders Hill after his favourite hiking area in London. The site commanded an impressive view of Thorndon Flat, and across the harbour to Kumutoto, Te Aro and Mount Victoria and, in the distance, the entrance to Evans's Bay and the Hutt Valley. It was also conveniently close to Wakefield's house, where Parliament now stands. When the family moved into the house, their whare near the pa was used for Harriet's school by teacher Miss Tilke.[5]

The long two-storeyed wooden house was hugged by a pillared verandah and boasted shutters at the windows and a dormer upstairs. Behind the house were the stables, in front was a swathe of grass on which the cows grazed, and the section was terraced with a pretty garden planted earlier with 'camellias, olives, and other delicate plants'.[6] More than one person commented on his house. Heaphy remarked that it was 'the best and is an ornament to the place', while Francis Bradey, who acknowledged Evans as 'one of the principal props of the Colony', commented on his 'splendid house and pleasure grounds'.[7] Samuel Brees later chose Evans's garden from which to record his famous panoramic view of Wellington.

William Curling Young, the son of director G. F. Young, was one of the first to dine at Evans's new home. He was struck by the level of refinement in the ladies' dress, the furnishings and the entertainment, saying the party was 'somewhat ostentatious. The style of the thing, as well as the fittings and size of the room, the beautiful London furniture and the profusion of the table reminded me of such parties as Warner's or Mitcalfe's.' This was not unusual for Wellington society, he added, noting that 'the general appearance of the place resembles Hastings or Brighton'.[8]

Evans's household was a boisterous hive of activity, with dogs hurtling everywhere, cattle lowing outside, staff bustling about and, when visitors called, Evans's voice booming through the house in animated conversation.

☙

In April there was a public meeting to present an address to the Queen drawn up by Evans, and a petition and letter of congratulation to Governor Hobson. The address to the Queen congratulated her on the birth of the Princess Royal, and continued:

> We presume to remind your majesty that we have founded this colony without the slightest aid from the public treasury . . . and, disclaiming all bounties, all privileges and pecuniary assistance, we pray only for the power of managing our own local affairs, by means of such municipal institutions as have already been promised to us by one of Your Majesty's representatives, The Governor of New South Wales . . . . We can derive but little benefit from the administration of a Government which is fixed at a remote part of this island, in a place at present uninhabited and distant at least 500 miles from the district preferred for settlement [Wellington], and now occupied by the great mass of the British population. We pray for Her Majesty to instruct your representative and his officers to take up their residence, and which nature points out as the proper seat of Government, or that Your Majesty will . . . provide a sufficient substitute, by granting us the most ample power of legislation and administration, as a municipality, or by such other arrangement.[9]

The petition to Hobson congratulated him on his new status and that of the colony; assured him of their warmest support; gently reminded him of the impracticality of his choice of the seat of government in the north of the North Island, which would be 'in ignorance of the state of three-fourths of the British population of the Islands'; and reminded him that the settlers at Port Nicholson were no longer an 'assemblage of individuals' scattered randomly in a 'foreign country, beyond the protection and control of Great Britain', nor were they 'squatters upon Government Land liable to be dispossessed of their property and having no claim to recognition by the government'. Their population was six times that of any other settlement in the country, the petition continued; they held their lands under a title from the Crown, had 'contributed largely to the public revenue' and 'above all form the nucleus of the only extensive and systematic scheme for covering with an active and industrious population the fertile wastes of the Island'. It would be 'invidious' if the concerns of their community of eight thousand people should be administered by individuals selected from a population of three hundred who had different needs and 'perhaps opposite interests'. Relations between the Port Nicholson settlers and Maori were 'undefined and uncertain' – Maori numbered perhaps two thousand. If Hobson were to hand over the disposal of the waste lands of the island to the Company – under his close supervision, of course – then he would be freed up to go about his business as governor and preferably make Port Nicholson his seat of government. This would eliminate all rivalry and ill-feeling.[10]

At the dinner to celebrate New Zealand's becoming a colony separate from New South Wales, all acrimony was forgotten as Revans smoothly proposed a toast to 'the memory of the deceased Council and the healths of Dr. Evans and Richard Hanson, the authors of the constitution under which it had its legal existence'. Evans thanked Revans, quipping he wouldn't say much about:

> . . . the annals of the most short-lived republic that ever existed; we have literally and in fact 'sat by its cradle and followed its hearse'. Suffice it to say, it was conceived in a moment of difficulty, and fully answered its purpose. (cheers) . . . . the most eminent men had acknowledged that the colonists acted legally . . . . Mr. Hanson, in common with himself, was looking forward to better times; such as when they should have the honour of addressing many of those around them as 'gentlemen of the jury', 'members of the Council', or 'most potent, grave and reverend signiors' – (cheers and laughter). They should pay 'tribute to whom tribute is due' . . . . Edward Gibbon Wakefield whose never flagging zeal and the untiring energy of his master mind had led them on to triumph – (cheers) . . . there was no contretemps – no discordancy between the Directors in London and the settlers in the Colony – (hear). While this good feeling existed, the Colony could not fail to prosper (loud cheers).

In toasting 'the Independence of the Press', he said that of the public principles, the one 'most dear to Englishmen' was 'the liberty of the Press':

> One of the most powerful writers, who had pleased to veil himself in the mantle of mystery – Junius – had said – : 'Let it be impressed upon your minds, let it be instilled into your children, that the liberty of the Press is the palladium of all the civil, political and religious rights of an Englishman.' In a colony, liberty of the Press is more important than anywhere else. (hear) It is the means of calling governors, secretaries and officials down to a state of subordination to public opinion. (cheers).

He reminded them also of the 'working classes' who were 'a very valuable portion of the community . . . those who produced everything, who were the real pith and substance of every community, and without whom nothing in society would flourish or even exist'.[11]

Only a fortnight after their petition to Hobson, New Zealand was officially declared a separate colony and Port Nicholson a municipality. The Commission of Peace was enlarged with the addition of Wakefield, Hunter, Daniell and St Hill. Evans joined the committee to review Hanson's draft of their Corporation Bill. As Wakefield was about to travel north for the Legislative Council's first meeting, there were time constraints. Nevertheless, there were countless resolutions and amendments – not to mention several tense moments – as the legal minds amongst them argued the finer points.[12]

Towards the end of May the Legislative Council sat for the first time in Auckland, passing six Bills establishing customs, courts of quarter sessions and courts of requests, and filling key positions. Shortland's salary as Colonial Secretary was £600; Chief Justice William Martin received £1,000 per annum; Attorney General William Swainson, old friend of Gibbon Wakefield and barrister of the Middle Court, earned £400; and the registrar of the Supreme Court £300 per annum. The chief Commissioner of Lands received £1,000.[13] It is little wonder Auckland was increasingly being seen as the preferred destination: by the end of that year its population had soared to well above 1500.[14] But Hobson and his system of government were soon condemned by Evans, as well as by Gibbon Wakefield and other reformers in London, writing in *The Spectator*.[15]

The Wellington settlers had good reason to complain, and with all the evident injustice, it is hardly surprising their anger was so easily inflamed. The jail heaved with heavily chained prisoners, some of whom had been languishing for as long as eleven months, because no Wellington magistrate had the power to hear serious offences. The dangerous harbour had no beacon at its entrance and was manned only by volunteers. And their customs tax was being reserved for Auckland. It seemed to them that they were being snubbed.

As seasoned reform supporters, Evans, Revans and others had already learned in Britain that agitation in the form of speeches, meetings, petitions and articles in the press appeared to be the only means by which results might be achieved. They made it clear in all the ways they could that Wakefield, as Senior Magistrate, should advocate on the settlers' behalf with Hobson, who bore the brunt of their frustration. Wakefield was expected to attend all the Legislative Council's meetings in Auckland, and when he returned in June he reported only that Hobson had given a vague assurance that he hoped to remedy the settlers' many complaints.[16] The settlers were dissatisfied with this response, and turned their disillusion on Wakefield as well as Hobson. Wakefield, unwilling to travel as often as the role required him and unused to such work, lasted only a few months, resigning in September.[17] His feeble surrender must have seemed like a betrayal to the settlers and a breach of faith to Evans and others.

Competition amongst the legal fraternity was fierce, but Revans typically dismissed them all in a bid to attract Chapman to come over. 'The lawyers here are Strang, Brewer, Hanson, Evans and Brandon. The last named is a flippant fool.' Evans was 'no lawyer and will not attempt to practise', he declared confidently. Hanson barely knew the principles of law, being 'only a solicitor'. He was 'disliked', too 'absorbed in his own business' and unlikely to 'attend properly to [it]'. William Brewer was 'no lawyer', 'improperly educated', and a 'wretched speaker and pleader'. Robert Strang was a 'Scotch attorney, not over bright and abundantly fat and idle'. Partridge chimed in, telling Chapman that Evans was 'strongly suspected of having NABBED' some of the books and scientific objects sent from England for the library.[18]

Later, when Chief Justice William Martin and Attorney General William Swainson arrived with the new charter, they checked the credentials of Wellington's legal fraternity. They were told, correctly, that Brandon had been a copying clerk for a firm of London solicitors. Martin wrote to Brandon to confirm this. Brandon suspected Evans and Hanson of having belittled him, and retaliated with his own appraisal of their skills. Evans, he declared, was a 'Barrister and Dairyman', and Hanson a 'Solicitor and Land Agent'.[19]

In early June, Rangihaeata broke up the Porirua road. Wakefield sent a formal letter of complaint to Murphy and another to the directors, who protested to Lord Russell about the local government's inability to offer protection to the settlers. The warning signs were still ignored. Molesworth, Swainson, Evans and others wrote to Wakefield on behalf of the settlers, pleading for funds to create a new road from the Hutt into Wellington, and another from Petone to Porirua, for transporting agricultural produce and timber. In a few years, they said, the new district might produce goods 'sufficient for the whole city . . . timber, corn, potatoes and grain of all sorts'. Owners and renters would pay for the breaking up and clearing of the land. Meanwhile, in a thinly veiled criticism of the Company, Evans asked Wakefield to petition the directors to give some of their 'large profits' for the 'formation of such roads'. In January the following year, Wakefield sent Evans their reply. The Company would pay only after the district became a municipal body.[20]

Wakefield gave four new arrivals their licences to build in Porirua but, although Murphy's constables had been sent to protect them, there was a fierce confrontation with Rangihaeata and fifty warriors and they were driven off. Rangihaeata's men destroyed the Europeans' huts, but returned all the nails and other 'fastenings' to them.

When Halswell pointed out to Rangihaeata the benefits of allowing Europeans to live amongst them, giving Richard Davis as an example, the chief was adamant in his opposition, setting fire to several buildings and destroying a bridge.[21] The offer of £200 was not enough to appease Te Rauparaha and Rangihaeata. The settlers demanded Rangihaeata's arrest, and the *Gazette* called for them to be punished. But, as Hanson pointed out, Rangihaeata had consistently 'refused to acknowledge the right of the Company to any of the land around the harbour of Porirua', and Murphy declined to intervene until Commissioner William Spain had investigated the land question.

There had been some good news from England. The government had granted the New Zealand Company a charter of incorporation on 12 February 1841.[22] In July and August there was a flurry of meetings concerning the Corporation Bill and the kind of reception Hobson should receive when he visited the settlement. At the first such meeting, Wade and Davis, who had signed the petition for Hobson's recall, were opposed to welcoming him, but Evans suggested adjourning the meeting until settlers who lived miles away were able to express their opinions. In the meantime, he presumed nobody wanted to 'pour out a fulsome effusion' on Hobson. 'They were not, as free-born Englishmen, about to commence a new career in politics, and fall down in adulation before His Excellency. (Hear, Hear, and cheers).' They first needed 'evidence' of Hobson's 'public principles'. If the government were determined to 'enforce the laws of a convict colony here, he . . . would be cautious' about the manner in which Hobson should be welcomed. 'His Excellency had contrived, somehow or other, to spend £62,000, and . . . what benefit had the inhabitants of Port Nicholson derived from its expenditure?' He said he had consulted the earlier numbers of the *Government Gazette* and found that 'Their duties were 10–15% higher than in New South Wales. Tea, sugar, etc. was taxed 5% higher and all other articles 10% higher.'[23]

At the adjourned meeting on 30 July, which was attended by two hundred and fifty men, Wade had had a change of heart. He proposed welcoming Hobson and professing 'unfeigned loyalty' to the government. In a 'masterly and eloquent speech', Evans gave Wade 'full credit for his sincerity and patriotism', but believed it was 'preeminently a question of prudence'. He advised that they should wait and see what the governor would do, adding that he believed their difficulties were due to 'jealousy, almost overwhelming jealousy, rivalry and animosity from those who ought to have protected them'. He reminded them of Shortland's arrival:

> . . . no one can forget the first arrival of Government authority amongst us. No one will forget the fetters and the manacles dangling from the pockets of the mounted police as they paraded the beach at Petone; nor the threats of the thousands of the ball cartridges in store for them! He [Evans] made an appeal to Mr. Shortland, respecting the occupancy of the lands they were now located upon and what was his answer? 'Sir, you are here as squatters, and I expect shortly to receive instructions to warn you off the Crown lands.'

He reminded them also of the 'general gloom throughout the official circle' and how Hobson had reacted to Gipps's despatches 'with displeasure'. But his opinion that the government had poached the Company's labour had softened. He did not believe in using 'undue influence to confine' those who wished to move north, but he would feel 'ashamed' and 'astonished' if the colonists were to meet His Excellency in the 'servile and disgraceful' manner of the people of Kororareka:

> They were in a British colony; they were not in Turkey, or any other part of Asia; nor was Captain Hobson, 'Lord of the twenty-four umbrellas' who had come down to shade them with his greatness. They had not yet lost the effect of living in the

> mother country, and they had some notions of trial by jury and representative government; and they did not understand how six men could meet in a room, and declare the Sydney laws in place here until such period as they should think fit. Another Act which had been passed was the Act of indemnity, which went to screen magistrates, etc., from official acts which they had committed previous to 1st January, 1841. Now, he had no doubt if gentlemen referred to their memoranda, they would find out what particular case this would meet; for himself, he had been retained in several cases against Mr. Shortland, and by this Act, they were deprived of their constitutional remedy.[24]

Wade had suggested meeting Hobson in a 'friendly spirit' but Evans disagreed. His proposed amendment that 'any public expression of opinion [without first knowing Hobson's intention toward the settlement] . . . would be premature and inexpedient' was supported by Wicksteed and Revans and carried by a large majority, 'amidst loud cheering'.[25]

But when, six days after the meeting, the body of a Maori was discovered behind Te Aro pa by two Europeans, other matters concerned the colonists. Two doctors confirmed after an examination that he had died of 'apoplexy' and Kaiwharawhara Maori requested an autopsy. Then Wharepouri appeared, alleging Pakeha had killed the young man. This caused a sensation and Maori called for utu or revenge. Murphy ordered a number of Europeans to go to the pa to quell any signs of violence. The arrival of so many men defused the situation and the pa's inhabitants 'returned to their houses'.[26]

This episode was so unsettling that on the same evening defence became the major topic at the meeting originally called to discuss the Corporation Bill. With memories also of Rangihaeata's men obstructing them from exploring Porirua still fresh in their minds, Evans, Wakefield and others all complained of Hobson's failure to provide adequate safeguards for them. Appropriate resolutions were passed.[27]

At a meeting on 16 August to discuss the adoption of the Corporation Bill, Hanson submitted the Bill, including a request to vote by ballot, and Evans quickly advocated its adoption 'in a speech evincing great ability'. He also recommended presenting a 'memorial' to Hobson outlining their principles, 'which under any circumstances they were determined to maintain'. Both proposals were approved unanimously.[28] News arrived that the brig *Victoria* with Hobson aboard had been seen entering the harbour and the meeting was hastily adjourned.

Evans's financial situation had not improved. He spent much of his time conferring with Wakefield on legal and Company matters, and although he attended meetings, acted in court and drew up petitions, his work for the settlers and as Company's advocate did not cover his expenses The next day Evans was dealt a stinging blow when he was formally advised that he, Moreing and Hanson had been removed from the Commission of Peace. He became ill, the news of the demotion spread quickly and the settlers' anger was revived.

The brig arrived at port on 19 August and Shortland, who was in Hobson's party, was ferried into Thorndon. The official party would be residing at Barrett's Hotel, where, coincidentally, the adjourned meeting was to be held that same night. Four hundred men attended the meeting to hear charges against Hobson for his neglect.[29] Rumours were rife. A government official had warned a merchant not to buy town acres in Wellington as Hobson planned to 'seize more than twenty acres of the best water frontage'. No one could be trusted. When George Earp alleged there was a government spy in the room, the furious men shouted, 'Turn him out! Turn him out!', and when Evans's apologies were given, a wit called out, 'He has taken shelter under one of the twenty four umbrellas!'

As Hanson began reading the 'cautious' version of the memorial he had drawn up with Evans and Wicksteed, he was interrupted by the arrival of Evans. Clearly frail and unwell, Evans was greeted by cheers. Wicksteed took the cue, explaining that he and Evans had wanted another clause added objecting to their labour being exploited to line government pockets, and complaining that the several hundred miles between the settlements caused 'a virtual denial of justice'. Their amendment left no doubt:

> The inhabitants of Port Nicholson would be guilty of deception were they to dissemble their full intention to obtain, by every lawful proceeding, not only the powers of local self-government incident to a Municipal Corporation, but the more extensive Constitutional rights and privileges which are the birthright of Englishmen, and which they feel themselves as competent to exercise and maintain in New Zealand, as in the mother country they have left.

In a 'forcible speech', which the *Gazette*'s reporter omitted with 'regret' due to the lack of space, Evans struggled through his endorsement of the amendment, but common sense prevailed and Hanson's memorial was passed to 'loud cheering'. Evans's strategy in adopting the less conciliatory approach toward the embattled Hobson had failed. But as soon as Evans departed, Wade pointed out that

Evans had 'suffered in their cause' by taking his seat on the bench on their behalf only for justice to 'be impartially administered'. Evans had been publicly humiliated by Hobson by having his magistracy stripped from him. They should make an appropriate gesture to 'testify their respect' for him. Accordingly, Brewer suggested that a petition of protest from the settlers should be presented to the governor when he arrived; and Earp, Wicksteed and W. A. Cooper were selected to present it.[30]

Hobson disembarked the next day and Evans and Hanson duly presented him with their Corporation Bill and memorial, which proposed rules to meet their special needs as a settlement based far from Auckland. Their arguments were sound: there were six times more British subjects in Port Nicholson than anywhere else; with Maori numbering 20,000, the governor's presence might prevent potential hostility between the two races; and the settlers made a huge contribution to the public revenue, and were pushing further north in their 'exploration'. Instead of rivalry between them, they might combine in the colonisation of New Zealand 'in the briefest period and in the most advantageous way', with the Company operating under Hobson's aegis.[31] Although they assured Hobson they were merely proposing rules to meet their special needs as a settlement far removed from government, he was unsympathetic, insisting they were seeking 'exclusive privileges'. They must wait until his Legislative Council met in Auckland and the charter was 'legally provided for'.

He also accepted 'the sole responsibility of dismissing the Port Nicholson magistrates'. Still smarting from Evans's rebuke at the Bay of Islands nine months earlier for luring labour to Auckland, and from Hanson's petition for his removal, Hobson felt unable to accept any of Evans's and Hanson's demands.[32] When pressed by Evans for the reasons for their dismissal, he replied coldly: 'Whatever gentlemen holding office under [my] Government might think, they could not be allowed to speak.'[33] The *Gazette* recorded that throughout the encounter Hobson seemed 'alternately nervous and confident . . . [and] distressingly powerless' and 'in delicate health'.[34]

The famous banker Walter Bagehot (1826–1877) would sum up the dilemma of men like Evans:

> Public opinion is a permeating influence, and it exacts obedience to itself: it requires us to think other men's thoughts, to speak other men's words, to follow other men's habits. Of course if we do not, no formal ban issues; no . . . penalty is inflicted on the offender: but we are called 'eccentric'; . . . 'most unfortunate ideas', 'singular young man', 'well-intentioned . . . , but unsafe, sir, quite unsafe'.[35]

For Hobson, Evans was worse than 'unsafe'. But Hobson was hardly 'safe' in his dealings with Maori and the Company's servants. While he recorded that the chiefs had sought protection from the Company because it had 'unscrupulously appropriated their lands', and that he had assured them their unsold pa and cultivations would be protected, a month earlier he had told Wakefield he would sanction 'any equitable arrangement' that persuaded Maori to surrender their villages.[36]

Hobson was a beleaguered man. He was well aware of the success of the Wakefield system of colonisation in Wellington and the considerable skills of Wakefield's officials. Before visiting the town he had even acknowledged they were 'from their rank, their numbers and their wealth, by far the most important in the Colony'.[37] For his own part, he felt he was being sent second-class officials from New South Wales, and he cannot have been unaware of their venality and the plethora of land deals taking place in Auckland. In Wellington the *Gazette* had reported in July that James Clendon had sold the property he had bought in Okiato for £20 'a few years' earlier to Hobson for a staggering £22,000.[38] And Taine alleged Shortland had obtained four sections, paying £315 for the largest and selling it on for £1,500.[39] The Secretary of State for the Colonies, Lord Stanley, severely rebuked Hobson when he heard of this, telling him, 'You will understand that you are positively prohibited in future under any circumstances from purchasing land from any individuals without the previous sanction of Her Majesty's Government.'[40]

Hanson had shrewdly assessed his options and defected from the Company camp. Earp too switched sides, apologising to Hobson for his 'violent views' in petitioning for his removal, and assuring him others regretted it too. Hobson told Lord Stanley that the Port Nicholson settlers were 'by far the largest and most influential body of the colonists', adding that Hanson and Earp 'were the warmest and most zealous supporters I had in the colony.'[41] Hanson had an advantage over Evans. It was easy for him to leave the Company and to defy Wakefield: he had refused to hand over to Wakefield the deeds for the purchase of the 200,000 acres he owned in the Chatham Islands,[42] instead, keeping them as security against the 'uncertainty of the Company honouring his bills'; and his position as representative of absentee buyers also gave him a degree of invincibility.[43]

He and Earp were well rewarded. On 9 September, Hanson was named Crown Prosecutor on a salary of £250 a year and thus ended his partnership with Evans. George Butler Earp became one of the three senior magistrates and a member of the Legislative Council.

(This latter appointment did not last long, as he broke Hobson's golden rule by speaking out at a Council meeting in Auckland, asking that Wellington be given due consideration.) Edward Chetham, a well-connected solicitor and recent arrival from London, was similarly honoured.[44]

Evans was conspicuous by his absence from Hobson's levee at Barrett's on Tuesday, 24 August, which was attended by only a few of the 'leading settlers'. The snub was deliberate, Colonel Wakefield attributing it directly to the removal of the three magistrates.[45] The *Gazette* dismissed the levee by noting, 'The whole ceremony was over in about ten minutes.'[46]

In fact, there was more urgent business to attend to. Hobson had denied the New Zealand Company a second settlement at Port Cooper or Lyttelton Harbour, as it is now known, offering instead to compensate the landowners with an area of North Auckland. Wakefield had refused the offer, and eventually a compromise was reached, with Nelson being given to the Company.

Then Hobson refused to believe that native title had been 'fairly extinguished' by the Company's reserves, arguing that under the Treaty he was bound to purchase all lands necessary for settlement. Any land that Maori had 'abandoned – no matter to whom', was 'the property of the Crown'. The owners could be compensated with land elsewhere. Wakefield tried to dissuade him, but even Chief Justice Martin could not budge his resolve.

A draft of Hobson's imminent proclamation was rushed to Wakefield, who immediately sent for Evans. Wicksteed and a few others joined them and they hurriedly drew up a letter of protest. It was the worst scenario. The consequences were dire: the banks would be in turmoil and it could ruin them all, as well as the Company.

Their letter to Hobson reminded him that the Colonial Minister had (in November) authorised them to select land on both sides of Cook's Straits in excess of 600,000 acres. They asked for an extension of time for the Company to select its lands, and a guarantee of a 'sure and indefeasible title to all such lands as have been surveyed or may be surveyed' to allow the Company to fulfil its obligations as vendors. If, in any case, any purchase should be found to be invalid, 'full compensation would be made to the Maori, or the previous purchaser, by the New Zealand Company'. The Protector of the Aborigines and a Company agent would decide on the amount of compensation for native titles, and would pay owners the amount fixed in Gipps's Act. They pledged that 'until the decision of the [Land] Commission', they would not 'interfere with the site of any pah actually occupied by the natives, or with any place held sacred by them on religious grounds, or with any land hitherto unsold by the natives, and which they absolutely refuse to dispose of'.[47]

To their relief Hobson capitulated and cancelled his proclamation. The Crown's rights to land were suspended until title was given and a Crown grant issued to the Company, excluding land for public purposes and reserves for Maori. No Crown grant would be made of any land which then – 3 September 1841 – was 'in the actual occupation of [Maori] by residence, cultivation, clearing or substantial inclosure, or which shall by them be held sacred, and which they shall be unwilling to alienate'. A grateful Wakefield told the directors of Evans's and Wicksteed's assistance, adding that he believed Hobson was 'sincerely anxious to satisfy [their] feelings'.[48]

After this breakthrough, some confidence was restored to the settlers, the bank was able to 'continue advancing lands on its security' and the merchants could continue trading in Wellington.[49] After twenty-seven days in Wellington, Hobson left for Akaroa. In December, addressing his Legislative Council, he commended the 'zeal and vigour with which the Company have conducted their operations' and the 'enterprising energetic and independent character of the settlers'.[50]

Soon after this, Evans's old colleague from the earliest days of the Association, Captain Arthur Wakefield RN, arrived in port with Captain Francis Liardet, also of the Royal Navy, to take up duties as Principal Agents: Wakefield in Nelson, and Liardet in New Plymouth. Evans presided at the formal dinner given in their honour at Barrett's on 21 September. Seventy men sat down to dine in a room festooned with flags, with the Union Jack and Tricolour suspended over the centre, where Evans sat with guests on his right and left. Over the assistant chairmen were suspended the bust of Gibbon Wakefield and a New Zealand flag. After toasting the Queen and Louis Philippe, the governor's toast was offered without comment. In a direct snub to Hobson:

> . . . only about half a dozen persons beside the Company's officers rose to do honour to the toast, and made a feeble attempt to raise a cheer, which was drowned in the respectful silence of the great body of independent settlers, who sat still with their empty glasses upturned on the board.[51]

By contrast, in toasting Arthur Wakefield, Evans pointedly spoke of his 'calmness of temper . . . conciliatory habits . . . industry and perseverance and . . . thorough acquaintance with the sound principles of colonization'. He also referred to Liardet's exploits at the siege of St 'Jean D'Arc'. He was sure Liardet would find more satisfaction in 'transplanting Englishmen to a land surrounded by the bounties of nature . . . than the work of destroying, however just and honourable the cause of the warfare might be'.[52]

CHAPTER ELEVEN. TRIALS AND TRIBULATIONS

> [Mercy] is enthroned in the hearts of kings,
> It is an attribute to God Himself;
> And earthly power doth then show likest God's
> When mercy seasons justice.
>
> William Shakespeare, *The Merchant of Venice*, IV, i, lines 189–92

On Tuesday, 5 October 1841, at the first Court of Quarter Sessions, Evans represented a Te Aro Maori named Pakewa, alias E Tonghi, who was accused of having stolen a blanket from a Mr Hornbrook. Before the jury could be sworn in before Justice Halswell and five magistrates, Evans presented a plea based on the Treaty of Waitangi. Specifically, he reminded them that 'all the rights of chieftainship were reserved to the [Maori] New Zealanders; and that among those rights was that of administering justice among the inhabitants of their own tribe'.

For the Crown, Hanson objected to Evans's argument on three grounds: as the Treaty had not been produced, the court could not examine it; 'there was no evidence to show that the right of administering justice was among the rights of chieftainship'; and the case involved a dispute between a Maori and a European, not between members of a tribe. Nevertheless, the ingenuity of Evans's plea caught the justices by surprise, and after a quick discussion, they adjourned the case until the following day.

Evans had always believed it would take time, patience and education before Maori would understand the implications of breaking the law under the British system of justice. It was unfair to expect otherwise. He had seen prisoners in the jail chained and handcuffed, sweating in the fœtid confines of dirt and waste, and had no wish to see his young client shackled for months in such a way.

The next day, having studied the Treaty closely (the English version), he exchanged one plea for another, this time claiming for the defendant a jury *de mediatate lingua*, that is a panel or jury, composed half of Maori and half of Europeans. The prisoner was not a native-born British subject and, under British law, an 'alien' could acquire certain rights – with restrictions – only by an Act of Parliament. The defendant 'was not even a denizen'. As an alien he was entitled to half a jury made up of his own countrymen. If he were deemed to be a British subject, then Evans would challenge each member of the jury, 'as there was not a single native among them'.

> He adverted very strongly upon the circumstance that while the [Maori] were subject to British law, and liable to all the duties and restraints to which British subjects were liable, they were deprived of their share in this great constitutional privilege. [They] certainly were fully equal to the exercise of this franchise; and it would be felt by the whole world, that the pretences upon which their country had been settled, and their land located upon, was but a solemn farce, if [they] were excluded from the enjoyment of this right.

Whilst the men on the bench were left to muse upon this reasoning, Hanson objected on the grounds that the prisoner was, in fact, 'clearly a British subject', having become so as soon as New Zealand was proclaimed a British colony. There were no grounds on which to dispute the jury's partiality. If Evans chose to do so, he should challenge the 'poll' (the list of citizens) rather than the 'array' (the jury). The judges agreed and dismissed Evans's plea.

An interpreter assisted Pakewa throughout the five-hour hearing. The poor man was apparently guilty of having hidden the blanket under his clothes when challenged by the shopkeeper, but Evans did not let the case rest. He closely cross-examined an eleven-year-old witness. At first the boy said no other Maori was in the shop during the theft, but he finally admitted seeing Dr Fitzgerald's servant there. He denied having been coerced into 'rehearsing' his evidence, but admitted he had 'repeated' it five times.

In his summing up, Evans made a 'powerful address to the jury', pleading for their 'merciful consideration', and reminding them that Pakewa did not understand one word of their language or customs. He argued also that Hanson did not have a sufficient grasp of the language to understand Pakewa's explanation of how he obtained the blanket. The jury returned after only a few minutes with a verdict of guilty, but mindful of Evans's pleas it made a strong recommendation for mercy.

Pakewa was given seven days' hard labour, a sentence significantly lighter than that of a Pakeha found guilty of similar offences.[1] This was an historic case in two senses: it was the first of a Maori to be tried under British law in Wellington, and the only one for a very long time in which the plea *de mediatate lingua* was offered in defence. Evans's small victory in obtaining the reduced sentence resonated through the town, and many Maori viewed Evans as their champion in court. It was perhaps at this point that they marked their esteem with the gift to Evans of a Maori cloak.[2]

When Evans was invited by the traders and merchants of Wellington to chair their opening dinner at the Exchange on 4 November, he made several 'excellent' speeches during which he suggested they establish a Chamber of Commerce. After he pointed out the benefits it would bring the community, his proposal was immediately hailed.[3] However, there were many obstacles to be overcome before it could be officially formed – the uncertainty of land titles being one, the lack of a corporation being another. In fact, it was fifteen years before the official Chamber of Commerce was formed.[4]

A fortnight later he was informed he had been reinstated onto the Commission of Peace, but his anger returned when he was told Hobson had removed Earp from his Legislative Council in Auckland for daring to suggest that the Municipal Corporation Ordinance be adapted to meet Wellington's needs.[5] Hobson would brook no opposition: he had also ordered the editor of the *Bay of Islands Gazette* to suspend publication for two weeks after the paper criticised his measures.[6]

In Wellington there was goodwill amongst the settlers, many of whom were determined not to bring the bigotry and prejudice from the old country into the new colony. When contributions were sought for a Roman Catholic chapel and schoolhouse, Bishop Pompallier offered £15, Henry Petre £20 and Baron Alsdorf £10 – which was matched by Murphy's annual donation. Wakefield, Hanson and Evans gave £5 each, Partridge offered three guineas and Revans two.[7]

Local problems were more urgent. Violent storms and fatalities in Wellington's harbour had highlighted its perils, but after nearly two years, there were virtually no resources: there was no lighthouse and no pilot. In the Legislative Council's estimates for that year, over £1,000 was proposed for the harbour master's department at Auckland, £60 for the salary of a signal station conductor at the Bay of Islands, and nothing for Port Nicholson. A well-attended meeting on 14 December decided that the government should appoint a harbour master and that the settlers should subscribe to a lighthouse. Evans seconded Brewer's motion for a petition to be sent directly to MPs Francis Baring and John Temple Leader, asking them to 'bring the subject under the notice of the House of Commons, and of the Queen's Ministers'. But after Evans and Hanson were voted to the committee to compose the memorial, Hanson provoked uproar by accusing the Company of having 'done nothing' for the colony with its profit of more than £30,000, while praising the government which had given the settlers a 'large grant of land' without obligation.

Evans picked up the gauntlet in what the *Gazette* called a 'triumphant and crushing reply'. He countered Hanson's jibe that the Company was 'fitly' represented at the meeting by observing that 'the Governor too was not without an efficient representative, and that on no occasion, past, present and to come, could his learned friend more efficiently perform his duty'. Everyone had a duty to put his own interests behind him and 'look with a single eye upon what was most necessary for the welfare of the colony'. The Company's funds were purely for emigration purposes and not for resources that the government should provide. He reminded Hanson that the Company's harbour master (Chaffers) had been laying buoys in the harbour when he was dismissed by Hobson for having signed 'a document drawn up by a certain member of [their] Council' (a clear reference to Hanson's earlier protest to Hobson). Cheers greeted this sally.

Evans also stressed that it was unfair to blame the Company, which – in addition to all its responsibilities to the settlers and prospective immigrants – had arranged steam communication for them from South America. He also reminded them that the government had made it clear to the Company that

> You must confine yourself to sending out emigrants; we will do all works necessary for public purposes, and it must be remembered [that the government] had not forgotten to tax them also. (cheers). The estimates were grossly inflated for an infant colony. It was unnecessary to call up the name of Gawler – but it would be some satisfaction to him to know that his name would not be handed down to posterity alone. (Laughter and cheers.)

The recent fatalities were not merely casualties, but were 'public calamities'. Evans called on the settlers 'to fly from petty tyrants to the throne' and 'to seek redress at the hands of Her Majesty's Ministers – who . . . had treated this community with great consideration, which was denied by the local government'. The reference to Gawler was appropriate, as Colonel George Gawler had been accused of wasteful expenditure as South Australia's second governor (from 1838 to 1841), having bankrupted the colony after spending £200,000. There were mitigating circumstances, drought being one of them, but Gawler's successor, George Grey, made much of his wastefulness.

The result of Evans's speech was inevitable: Brewer's and Evans's motion for a petition to be sent directly to Baring and Leader in London was carried by a large majority.[8]

His energy made Evans the obvious person to found a club for his colleagues and friends in Wellington. There was already the Wakefield Club, established in October 1840, after Evans, Moreing and Hanson had left for Sydney. This club had probably risen from the ashes of the Pickwick Club after the death of several of its members by drowning. One or two historians have associated Evans with the Wakefield Club, but although Murphy became a member with the likes of Francis Molesworth, Jerningham Wakefield and Partridge, it appears Evans never joined the Wakefield Club. The Wellington Club was separately formed, although some members of the Wakefield Club left to join Evans's club – including, interestingly Partridge, whose business partnership with Revans had been dissolved.[9] This suggests there was disquiet about the conduct of some members of the Wakefield Club, as it gained a reputation for being a den of gambling and drunkenness. A more gentlemanly club along the lines of the Reform Club was envisaged, and so the Wellington Club was launched in December 1841 'to promote a spirit of social intercourse among the Colonists, and afford a means of shewing [*sic*] hospitality to strangers'. Evans chaired the first meeting of its committee. Rules were drawn up: a weekly dinner was held at the Southern Cross Hotel on Thursdays at six o'clock, chaired by members in rotation; at eleven o'clock when the chair was vacated, card games – excluding games of chance, which were banned – could be introduced; membership was restricted to twenty-five, with new members balloted, and a fee of £5 was to be called in when the majority voted for it. The committee of five comprised Evans as the first chairman-president; with members Hanson, Major Durie and Robert Waitt; and Edward Chetham, who was its secretary for the time being.[10]

Just before the New Year, Evans worked on a committee of thirty-four men to organise a 'fete' to celebrate the colony's second anniversary. Sailing and rowing matches, horse races, rifle matches and running races would conclude with two balls: one at Barrett's, the other at the Exchange.

In between there was plenty of court work to keep him busy. Exactly three months after representing Pakewa in court, Evans found himself defending him again – this time for the theft of two blankets worth 15 shillings. In spite of another 'lengthened address' and plea to the jury, Pakewa was convicted. Having been found guilty of theft twice in three months, no leniency was allowed for the hapless young man. He was sentenced to seven years' deportation to Van Diemen's Land.[11]

Evans's father had written again, clearly upset at not having heard from his son. He and Hannah had moved from Mile End Road to Gretton Place North in Bethnal Green in the spring. Hannah's health was fragile, and he reminded George that she had always been sceptical about the New Zealand enterprise: 'I do suspect that her fears will not quite subside until she sees the waggons and the horses.' His sisters cherished the letters he wrote them, 'although, like angel visits, they are very few and far between'. The family had suffered when one of Evans's private letters had been circulated. 'There is a want of discretion on the part of Chapman in publishing private letters in the Journal', his father wrote with considerable understatement. His demands and paternal strictures had not waned. He wrote pointedly:

> There is one thing in the history of Joseph, which I have never been able to understand, or reconcile with his general character, namely, omitting to communicate with his Father for a long period. Perhaps it arises from my ignorance of the Hebrew language. I am going to send the Hebrew Bible to you. Perhaps you will enlighten me on this point. You will be expected to write and publish in two handsome volumes illustrated with maps and drawings, a History of the Rise – Progress – and Prosperity of the Colony of New Zealand. Preparatory to this a good article occasionally from your pen, would be very useful. Your credit requires it. They will publish your speeches now you are on the Bench.[12]

The two men now existed in separate worlds. Nothing was settled and orderly in his forty-year-old son's environment, whose silence spoke volumes. Ten months later the Reverend Evans wrote again, complaining of not having heard one word since May 1841. His letters might have stirred up Evans's guilt in having disappointed his father, and fuelled his anger – at himself and anyone he believed stood in the path of the colony's success. Meanwhile, back in London, Evans's deeds of mortgage over forty sections were delivered to his London solicitor by Bradey when he returned there to collect his family, and transferred to Robert Monro under mortgage. A year earlier, a contract for this had been drawn up between John Wright, Evans and Monro.[13]

The settlers were still fuming at the infrastructure provided by local government – there was no decent jail or even a post office. William Brewer told Chapman that Hobson was 'a foolish and weak minded man' and that:

> . . . the clique of officialdom who surround him are shameless jobbers . . . there is not a man among them who is not deeply involved in speculation and land jobbing at Auckland. Boys of 14 and 15, sons of the missionaries and officials, are filling the several departments of Government with large salaries, and the lower departments . . . are filled with their creatures.[14]

Brewer had been in partnership with Edward Chetham, but after Chapman told him of Chetham's reputation for scandalous conduct in London, he was secretly pleased when Evans informed him he had asked Chetham to join him in partnership. Although Brewer upbraided Evans, calling it 'a very unhandsome thing on his part', he told Chapman he was not sorry to lose Chetham and thanked God he was 'quite free of him'. Evans, he asserted, had wooed the man, and after 'hearing that he was likely to come into a good property, [had] invited [Chetham] to his house [where he] and Mrs. Evans threw their daughter in his way, flattered his vanity', and 'effectively hooked him into a marriage'.[15]

Hanson had been the first to court Amelia, but his efforts had been ruined by Colonel Wakefield who had referred to him in her presence as 'Dirty Dick' – probably for having switched allegiance from the Company to the government. Hanson got his revenge later when, again in front of Amelia, 'someone expressed satisfaction that this was not a convict colony'. Hanson retorted, 'Don't let us say too much on that score. Have we not an emancipated convict at the head of us?' The remark was repeated to Wakefield, and afterward both men barely spoke to each other.[16] Although Hanson's suit was unsuccessful, he would not be the only one to harbour regrets about Amelia's choice.

Since the arrival of the first five ships, hundreds more settlers had disembarked on the shores of New Zealand. But the halcyon days of Maori–Pakeha relationships were fast fading. A common complaint aired by Company and independent settlers like Crawford centred on the patent hostility of government officials who had taught Maori to treat the settlers with little respect, and even with 'contempt'.[17]

In late March 1842, there was a public meeting to discuss government neglect. Wicksteed had drawn up a memorial to Lord John Russell, arguing that the Supreme Court's Ordinance, which allowed a full eight months every year for sittings in Auckland, would be harmful and expensive for courts in other districts, causing unfair delays. 'An imprisonment of several months before trial must frequently be endured by persons whom the law presumes to be innocent', he complained. Another grievance was the Raupo House Ordinance, in which all houses constructed even partially of thatch, reeds or flax were taxed at £20 per annum. It had been passed without consultation, and the settlers' right to petition had been virtually cancelled by distance and ignorance.

At Evans's request, Earp was brought to the meeting. He declared that he believed Hobson was determined 'to ruin this place if possible'. Evans proposed amending Wicksteed's resolution by including a request to Lord John Russell to suspend judgment on all Ordinances passed by local government until the residents had expressed their opinions. In spite of Wicksteed's objection that it would mean suspending the Corporation Ordinance, the amendment was carried.

But at another meeting on the Corporation Ordinance less than a week later, when Murphy – who had clearly been tipped off – invited everyone to have a free say, there were long awkward pauses. Evans remained silent and only Wakefield spoke. Evans may have tired of speaking out for Wakefield and chose – temporarily at least – not to court further government disapproval, or perhaps Wakefield had told him to hold his fire.[18]

After the renewed disturbances at Porirua, Evans had quickly advised Wakefield against sanctioning its purchase or guaranteeing title under the Company's name. But the backdown infuriated many, including Revans and other frustrated would-be farmers, who turned their ire on Wakefield.[19] In late April when a meeting was held to consider the 'recent outrages' in Porirua, several were clearly disenchanted with Wakefield's handling of the affair, but Evans successfully defused their anger by turning it back on the government. When Stokes asked Wakefield if he had notified Murphy and the directors of the attacks, Wakefield replied that on every occasion he had sought Murphy's protection they had received it. Wade had planned a vote of censure on Wakefield and wanted to propose a modified version, but Evans moved in adroitly, suggesting he substitute what was in fact a stalling tactic:

> That in consequence of the late reported aggressions on the part of the natives, on the property of the settlers of Port Nicholson and Wanganui, a deputation be nominated to wait upon [Murphy], to express the willingness of the entire population to assist him . . .

In seconding what was in fact his own motion, Evans 'dealt several hits at the Auckland Government', whom he said, 'just did enough for the inhabitants of Port Nicholson to keep them in a taxable state'. His speech was hugely entertaining – 'almost every sentence was greeted with cheers and laughter'.[20] The motion was carried by 'acclamation', and when Murphy was presented with the petition the following day by Evans, Wicksteed and others, his response was diplomatic but guarded: he relied on their assistance in upholding the law, and would 'avail himself of it, when . . . recourse to it was expedient'.

By May, Hanson was so concerned at Wakefield's handling of the land issue that he wrote to the Aborigines' Protection Society in London alleging that land sales had 'been widely departed from'. Reserves had been made 'in such a manner as to produce few or none of those immediate results anticipated by the intelligent and philanthropic individuals who devised the plan' of the Company's tenths agreement with the chiefs, he complained. Of the nine pa in Port Nicholson, only three had been selected as native reserves, and one had become 'a public reserve, leaving five which have become the property of private individuals'.[21] Only Pipitea, Kumutoto and Te Aro were held by Maori. Hanson must have discussed these issues with Evans in private as he was a frequent guest at the latter's home. The wide departure from their utopian scheme probably unsettled Evans, although if he protested to Wakefield at all, his words fell on deaf ears. As the Company's Commissioner for Native Reserves, Edmund Halswell had been given the task of letting the reserves, but Wakefield bore full responsibility for the betrayal.

When Land Commissioner William Spain arrived in Port Nicholson on 22 April to examine the titles of land claimed by the Company and individuals, his task looked relatively straightforward to the settlers. But in reality Spain had to unravel the complex question of Maori land tenure, with its history of tribal conquest, enslavement and peaceful land use that could involve several tribes in any one district. The most difficult questions arose in relation to the Maori view of their land and their laws of tribal possession. Most land had been inherited but their law of possession by conquest was complex. Permanent occupancy meant permanent possession: it was not enough to ravage an area and drive out the residents. The victors had to stay on the land they had taken, and pa and cultivations were therefore signs of permanent occupancy.[22] Once he had made his decisions about the claims, Spain had to separate land sold before 1840 from that sold afterward. It was a difficult question but Spain was a solicitor who, like Evans, had been a very active supporter of the Whigs during the period of the Reform Bill. He was a calm, decent man, methodical and conscientious.[23] It was his assistant who raised eyebrows.

George Clarke Junior was the son of the missionary George Clarke who was Chief Protector of Aborigines and a close ally of Hobson. Clarke Junior had lived for several years in Australia under the guardianship of the Reverend Samuel Marsden – nicknamed 'the flogging parson' for his brutal treatment of convicts – before returning in 1837 to Auckland. His championing of Maori rights was fuelled by zealous righteousness and a remarkable self-assurance for a young man only eighteen years of age.[24]

He believed Wakefield's annoyance with the government stemmed from Hobson having listened to the complaints of the chiefs of Te Aro pa, 'and that my father interpreted their complaints'. But he was unaware of his father's infamous ploy to shame Wakefield.[25] The previous year, at a meeting at Te Aro pa with Hobson, George Clarke Senior, with several Company men in attendance, translated the chiefs' testimony and implied in the transcript that Wakefield had had a 'woman' brought out to the *Tory*. When his translation was discredited and the accusation proved groundless, Hobson was momentarily embarrassed while Wakefield had been outraged.

In his memoir of his life in New Zealand, Clarke observed that Maori 'were savages, pure and simple'.[26] Although he had no legal training, he was put forward in Auckland for Maori advocate and interpreter by Chief Justice Martin and Attorney General Swainson, as he had a good knowledge of Maori language and culture and understood their tribal laws of possession. His view that if Maori gradually modified their system of land tenure then their land law would gradually merge with that of Europeans was not far removed from the Company's idea of education through co-habitation – but Clarke's was more equitable.

At 11 o'clock on 15 May, Evans duly turned up at the Court House on Lambton Quay and handed over the six Maori deeds of sale to the Company.[27] Spain encouraged the Company's advocates to find witnesses who might prove their cases in court. Evans's adversary was Hanson, and although their friendship was to be seriously tested in the first few weeks of the hearing, after all their legal tussles in the colony, Hanson and Evans proved to be exemplars of the bard's advice: 'Do as adversaries do in law, strive mightily, but eat and drink as friends.'[28]

At first there was a difference of opinion between Evans and Wakefield regarding the order in which their cases should be heard. Wakefield had instructed Evans to ensure claims registered before 1840 were heard first, 'to put [their] opponents to the proof'. Yet when Hanson asked for the Company's claims to precede the others, Evans agreed. Wakefield objected, and Spain adjourned the court for Hanson and Evans to confer.

Two days later, when Spain asked Evans to begin, Evans objected, saying he had agreed with Hanson 'that the minor claims of others should be heard first'. Hanson angrily 'denied any such understanding'. Evans, surprised, asked Hanson for whom he appeared. According to Wakefield, Hanson replied, '"For the natives. At least I understood I was retained for the natives." He then corrected himself and said, "For Mr. David Scott who opposes the claim." Spain reminded Hanson, "There is a fee of £5 for opposition." "Oh yes, certainly", said the Crown Prosecutor.'[29]

Both men refused to budge, so the court was again adjourned, giving Evans two hours to decide his course. Evans and Hanson had at best crucially misunderstood each other, and the matter was urgent. Wakefield recorded that in conferring with Evans,

> ... the learned Doctor very honorably and disinterestedly determined to give up the advocacy of the Company's claim on the ground that the position Mr. Hanson had taken and Mr. Spain had allowed, precluded him, Doctor Evans, from bringing on advantageously the claims of the Company, and that viewing the hostility evinced by Mr. Hanson to the Company's interests, and the factious and litigious spirit shewn by him to their advocate, any professional assistance would embroil and entangle the question on points of law and evidence, whereas [Wakefield] wished to treat it as one of equity and conscience agreeably to the instructions binding the commissioners to the same course.

In resigning the advocacy of the Company's case, Evans accused Hanson of not having honoured their agreement, and there was no lessening of animosity between Hanson and Wakefield. At the

Exchange three weeks earlier when supporters of the government attacked the Company, the political and personal feeling between the two had been noted by the *Gazette*: 'Mr. Hanson was in the room, but though so prompt to attack Colonel Wakefield in his absence, preserved a moody silence when he met him face to face.'[30]

Wakefield took up the Company's case, examining a few of his witnesses – Jerningham, Dr Dorset and Te Puni. He was questioned himself, but a few days later he was unable to cope with the stress any longer. In an action that mirrored his brother Edward Gibbon Wakefield's excuse four years earlier when Evans had asked for his assistance in reviving the Association, Wakefield left the court early complaining of fatigue. While his excuse may have been valid, the outcome was that he divorced himself from the proceedings; he had also realised they would be more than a mere formality.[31] The court, he complained petulantly, had 'more the appearance of an inveterate family law-suit than that of an equitable court-of-conscience-enquiry into the real merits of a treaty between a colonizing body and aboriginal tribes desirous to see their country settled'.

Spain needed further evidence, which required more witnesses. Halswell stepped in to assist Hanson in cross-examining Wi Tako. Wakefield was deeply suspicious of Wi Tako's evidence, saying he believed he had been 'tampered with'.[32] Then Te Puni finally admitted that the land he had sold to the Company was not his to sell, nor was it Wharepouri's. Only the Pipitea chiefs Moturoa, Wairarapa, Porutu, Ngapuna, Koaka and Tute had that right.

Wakefield again begged Evans to take up the reins. On Monday, 23 May, Evans entered court, again complaining of 'a dishonorable and discreditable breach of compact in Mr. Hanson'. Before calling witnesses, he spoke of his own experience, telling Spain he was one of the earliest to take up residence in Lambton Harbour. He told of Te Aro Maori dissatisfaction, of Barrett's and Te Puni's assurances that Te Aro Maori were slaves, of Moturoa's denial of having sold his land to Wakefield and admission of having sold to Tod. And although he believed the hearing of the case of Robert Tod in the midst of the Company's claims was 'informal and *ex parte*', Evans finally had his chance to examine him over two days.

Tod testified that he had been informed of Wakefield's claim on the area, having heard it at Queen Charlotte's Sound and then later from Smith. After telling his story of how Evans and others tried to 'pull down his store', the Sydney merchant was grilled by Evans:

> Evans: You say, 'When Dr. Evans and a party of men came to this piece of ground'. Do you persist in stating on oath that Dr. Evans came accompanied by any other individual than Colonel Wakefield?
> Tod: I was informed there were –
> Evans: Are we to understand that what you have stated on the subject is derived from hearsay?
> Tod: I mentioned in my evidence that on the day of the disturbance I was down at Petone, consequently it was from others that I received the report.

When Evans asked Tod to produce copies of his letters of complaint to Hobson and Gipps, Tod replied, 'I have not got, nor can I get it.'

> Evans: Did you or did you not endeavour to convey to Sir George Gipps and Captain Hobson the impression that Colonel Wakefield and Dr. Evans or Dr. Evans and a party of men went to that ground and attempted to pull down a store, and were driven off by the Natives?
> Tod: I do not remember.
> Evans: Did your letters agree in substance with what you have told the Court of the attack?
> Tod: My reminiscences are indistinct and I will do all I can to produce them.
> . . .
> Evans: You say, 'I employed Moturoa and Mangatuku to take care of this piece of land from the time that Dr. Evans attempted to pull down the second building until the arrival of Mr. Shortland in this place.' Do you persist in stating on oath that Dr. Evans attempted to pull down the second or any other building?
> Tod: I can only repeat what I have already stated in evidence, and that I was at Petone at the time and that I was informed of it by Alfred Farrar and two natives, but that in consequence of the positive denial of Dr. Evans, I am unwilling to occupy the time of the Court in this matter and I am willing to admit that I must have been mistaken in my information.

Tod admitted he had told Mein Smith he was willing to sell his entire land for £500 or a selection of it, and that there were others in whom he had confided his willingness to barter. Evans asked him to explain how the land which had cost him £12 had risen to the value of £500 by the time of Hobson's proclamation and was currently worth £1,500. After citing various reasons, Tod finally admitted that the value of the land had been created 'by the expenditure of the New Zealand Company' and its settlers.[33]

The dissolved settlers' council had been right in questioning Tod's motives. After that confrontation on the beach in 1840, Robert Tod had not let the grass grow under his feet. He had moved to Auckland in time to buy three acres from the government on 1 September 1841, and within three days had subdivided the land into 36 sections that he advertised for sale as 'the Village of Parnell'.[34]

Clarke's role in court was to transcribe the evidence of Maori in both te reo Maori and English, which meant that the record of all evidence rested entirely on his skills in interpretation and translation. But when he took it upon himself to examine witnesses, Clarke said the Company's agents began by 'shaking their fists in his face, grimacing to their utmost power of contortion, and defying his authority in a very larrikin [way]'. He believed the 'outward bluster' masked the 'inner trembling'.

Evans's view of Clarke, a youth less than half his own age with no legal qualifications but with all the powers of an English barrister bestowed on him, can be imagined. It was an egregious insult to Evans for a young man of eighteen to assume the moral high ground while metaphorically donning wig and gown, and taking on the key role of translator in court. Besides, Clarke had inherited a jaundiced view of the Company from his father. His hostility was heartily reciprocated, making relations between Spain's Commission and the Company extremely tense. For Clarke, all Company men were evil, their proceedings all 'vile'. Port Nicholson itself embodied the 'nest of Belial'. Wakefield was a 'designing, crafty, unprincipled fellow'; and Clarke was determined not to let any of Wakefield's 'minions "come paddy over me"'.[35]

For Maori from the various pa around Port Nicholson, especially Pipitea, Evans as barrister was an entirely different figure from the companionable, appreciative man they knew as a neighbour. For most it was their first appearance in a British court of law, but they were not easily intimidated. In fact, they regarded their appearances in court as opportunities to seek redress, or at least, to express their grievances and their dissatisfaction with the colonists.

Evans examined Taringa Kuri of Kaiwharawhara on 28 May, the chief who had claimed the stream for his tribe when Evans was building his mill. Kuri was the 'principal chief' of Ngati Tama, which formed one tribe with Ngati Mutunga. Spain believed Kuri was a 'crafty and troublesome native – Rauparaha's first lieutenant'.[36] But Kuri told another story: when his tribe arrived in Port Nicholson they had defeated Ngati Kahungunu. They were later joined there by Wharepouri, Te Puni and Moturoa. He said when the great chief Pomare went to the Chathams, he told Wharepouri, 'here is your land, Poneke' (Port Nicholson). After Pomare's departure, Kuri kept his own land, and all Pomare's land became the property of Wharepouri and his people. Kuri admitted to the court that the land was sold to the Europeans in case Te Rauparaha should come and fight, but he was angry when the Europeans settled on it. He then reneged on the sale in spite of having received one-sixth of the goods from the *Tory*. Although he assured Clarke that his people would return the goods, he never honoured the promise.

John Brooke, the Company's interpreter during the 'purchase' of Whanganui, recalled being told by Maori that they had sold their land to Colonel Wakefield. Wharepouri, Te Puni, Wi Tako and the other chiefs such as Ponga from Te Aro and Wairarapa from Pipitea all appeared to be satisfied.

When Pipitea chief Moturoa gave evidence on 1 June to prove Tod's claim to the acre on Thorndon Beach, the *Gazette* claimed that Clarke grilled the chief 'on every point connected with the Company's claim to the whole district of Port Nicholson . . . [which had] not the remotest connection with Mr. Tod's claim'.[37] A proud chief of Matehou, Moturoa belonged to a branch of Ngati Awa originally from Taranaki. He gave a breakdown of the history of Ngaki's ownership of Pipitea, and of his continuing quarrel with Wharepouri over Pipitea's ownership. Wharepouri claimed that Poki had given him the land, but Moturoa told him Patu had given him the land earlier. He had cultivated it and lived there 'ever since'. Of the blankets given them by Wakefield, all the Pipitea chiefs had kept them except Ngakurae, who wanted to return them. 'After each man got his blanket he was warm.'

Moturoa told Hanson he had built a house for Tod on his land, ignoring Wakefield and Evans's offer of a double-barrelled gun if he stopped building it. He had not signed the deed nor gone aboard the *Tory*. Moturoa's land included Te Aro, Waikoukou, Pipitea and Raurimu, all of which belonged to him and his deceased brother Patukawenga. He said that of the twenty-two Pipitea chiefs, whose names he recited, only Wairarapa and Wi Tako had signed the deed. He also claimed that Mahau had sold his land at the Hutt. 'We were angry', he said with considerable understatement.

Barrett had not discussed the land sale with him, and Wakefield pressed him to take payment for it only after the deed was signed. He wanted to send Wakefield back to Petone. He clarified the position of Te Aro Maori, saying that all the inhabitants of Te Aro had once been slaves – mokae – to Waikato, but when released to return to their own land, they became chiefs.

When Evans asked him why Wairarapa and Wi Tako were sent to the *Tory* for the goods if they were not the principal chiefs of Pipitea, Moturoa replied that they were merely returning the boat to the *Tory*. Wi Tako belonged to another tribe. Wairarapa had brought things back for Pipitea, but Barrett had said that they were for the purchase of the sea. Moturoa explained that he had not expected 'white men from Europe to settle here'. He had not taken any of the goods:

> Evans: Have you not over and over again acknowledged to Dr. Evans you had received a portion of the goods at that time or shortly afterwards?
> Moturoa: When Mr. Tod's house was broken down Barrett said to me, 'Some blankets will be given you by Warepouri' – I took them to my place; after two months I returned all the blankets to Richard Barrett; I returned the blankets of his disputing about Mr. Tod's land.
> Evans: For what were the blankets you took from Mr. Barrett, a consideration?
> Moturoa: He made a present of them to me.
> Evans: Do you remember pulling up the stakes that marked the boundaries of Mr. Tod's land, and burning them in Dr. Evans' house?
> Moturoa: Colonel Wakefield talked about pulling up the posts: some of the Europeans pulled them up. I took two posts to Colonel Wakefield and Dr. Evans; to the house of Dr. Evans; and I burned them in the fire.

Clearly, Moturoa had thought he would please Evans by burning the posts. When Spain asked him why he had done so, he replied: 'I went to Dr. Evans's house because I was hungry and wanted food. I burned them because I wanted him to give me some food.'

> Evans: Did you not say at that time you had done wrong in these transactions with Mr. Tod, and were sorry for it?
> Moturoa: No, I was not ashamed, I did not say so.
> Evans: Did you not say that if Colonel Wakefield would give you £12 to return to Mr. Tod, and would give you a double-barrelled gun for your trouble you would prevent Mr. Tod from keeping the land?
> Moturoa: No. I did not say so.

He denied having asked Richard Davis to draw up a paper admitting he had erred in selling the land to Tod, and denied verbally admitting his error. He had heard Maori had one-tenth part of the land in the town and country put aside for them when they sold their land, but he 'did not consent'. He asked Halswell to point out the native reserves and large fenced off sections of them, 'because, as the Europeans had occupied all our land, I wished to know what was left for us'.

He denied that there had been constant disputes between the tribes regarding the boundaries and ownership of land. Of Te Puni, Wharepouri and Taringa Kuri he said, 'They will not come to Pipitea to dispute my land, and I will not go to Petoni to dispute theirs.'[38]

As Evans continued his examination of the Maori chiefs, everything seemed to point to Maori being victims in the contest between the government, the missionaries and the Company, and it did not assuage his temper.[39]

The meeting on 7 June at the Exchange to discuss the Court of Land Claims soon degenerated into a slanging match. Hanson had an 'altercation' with Revans, who had protested that Spain and Clarke had created the impression that the court believed 'the Company to have been guilty of some gross acts of fraud'. David Scott sided with Hanson and rebuked Evans for 'the spirit' he had displayed in court 'by calling in question [Clarke's] motives, integrity, and ability', when his 'speaking and interpretation of [the Maori language] was the most correct he had ever heard'.

Wade supported the missionaries, but complained that it was undignified to watch 'a mere boy, cross-examining witnesses as [he] does, and although we have heard it denied that he is advocating any side in the question, I can say that he does not confine himself to the office of interpreter, for I have been present when I have seen him examine natives at some length, and I never heard any questions detailed to him by the Court'.

Clarke then replied in a speech that Evans immediately 'unravelled and robbed of its false colours in a masterly manner', boasted the *Gazette*.[40] Evans proposed that copies of the resolutions be sent to Hobson and the Company.[41]

During this period, in a series of very well-written articles, the *Gazette* pointed to the irregularities in the court's proceedings and queried Clarke's interpretations:

> . . . he still managed to throw over the evidence a very different appearance to that which it would present, were he not an advocate for one party, as well as an interpreter bound to translate impartially for both. If a native witness lengthens out his answer in a way favourable to the cause which Mr. Clarke is instructed to support, the whole answer is taken down and translated; but should he, on

> the contrary, be inclined to add any circumstances of an opposite tendency, he is immediately confined to the question, and a plain 'yes' or 'no', which would probably have been materially qualified, is recorded as the answer.

The effect on Maori had been 'mischievous'. 'The most extravagant notions [had] been spread among them', some proclaiming they would be paid again in 'money gold', and most believing the settlers would not be 'allowed any more land'. Since Spain's arrival, they had 'forcibly expelled settlers from spots close to the harbour – even pulling down the houses; which they had earlier ceded peacefully':

> Should the forbearance of the settlers be once exhausted, and a collision take place, it would cause reprisals on either side, which can end in no other final result than the total extermination of the aboriginal race. The mere contemplation of such an event must ever be a foul stain upon that Government which has pointed its strongest efforts at destroying the good feeling once subsisting between the two races, and has perversely thwarted the excellent arrangements made, by means of the reserves, to prove to the natives that the purchase of their land was a benefit and not an injury.

The articles accused Hanson – originally retained to help Clarke defend the rights of Maori – of abandoning the task once he found out his pay 'would be somewhat doubtful' and becoming 'the advocate of nearly all the white claimants in opposition to the Company'.

Knowing Evans contributed occasionally to the *Gazette*, Hanson was suspicious of the author's identity. It was believed to have been Jerningham, but it also had the stamp of Evans's style on it. Hanson wrote to Revans threatening court action if he did not divulge the author's name and retract the allegations. The *Gazette* replied that it wanted to prove that Clarke 'filled incompatible offices, and necessarily laboured under a bias, from which the most able man, under similar circumstances, would find it difficult, if not impossible, to relieve himself'.[42]

CHAPTER TWELVE.
THE SMILING LAND

> '"But", said Alice, "the question is whether you *can* make a word mean different things."
> "Not so", said Humpty Dumpty, "the question is which is to be the master – that's all."'
> We are the masters at the moment and not only at the moment, but for a very long time to come.
>
> Hartley Shawcross (1902–2003), British Labour Politician, Speech to House of Commons, 2 April 1946, quoting (almost exactly) Lewis Carroll, *Through the Looking Glass*, Chapter 7

Towards the end of June 1842, Spain had a meeting with Evans and Wakefield to discuss their attitudes to Spain's Commission of Inquiry into the Land Claims of the New Zealand Company. In the heat of discussion, Evans evidently lost his temper, but by the next morning Spain told Wakefield that he had 'had an explanation with Dr. Evans which will render it unnecessary for you to communicate with him upon the subject, and will, I trust keep him more quiet in future'.[1] A little later, Wakefield told the directors that court proceedings were 'extremely slow'. There were no counsel in the police and county courts – the Land Court was 'almost deserted and the affair is treated as a burlesque by the counsel and spectators'.[2]

Evans continued examining witnesses. In July, after Richard Davis had described the transaction between himself, Moturoa and Tod, Moturoa gave an account of an incident involving about forty Europeans and fifty Maori. He said 'We saved the house of Mr. Tod'. He said that only Dr Evans took hold of Tod's house to 'pull it down'. But just before this he had testified to Halswell that Evans, Colonel Wakefield, Captain Smith and forty Europeans had attempted to do so. Halswell asked, 'Was Mr. Park present?'

> Moturoa: Mr. Park was there but it was only Dr. Evans put his hands on the part of the house.

> Court: Were any attempts made to stop the building of the house or to take possession of the land?
> Moturoa: No. No one tried to stop the building of the house or to take possession of the land.

Moturoa's recall of episodes of the heavy-handed approach of the settlers' council to Tod's claim on land had clearly become hazy. Tod's house at the time had been a series of posts, but as soon as Evans had seen the deed of purchase he had withdrawn the council's protest. Tod's clerk Mr Farrar made a statement that confirmed Tod's evidence and Evans's cross-examination, which rebutted Moturoa's evidence.[3]

When Moturoa was recalled in September, he admitted that Ngaki was owner of all Pipitea, but added that Ngaki could not sell it without his consent or that of all the chiefs. Pipitea was divided between different members of the tribe, and each could sell his own portion without consultation. No chief could interfere with another, 'or else we should quarrel'. Yet he said he could sell his own land at Pipitea 'without the consent of any other person'.[4]

The giant jigsaw of possession and doubtful purchase remained unsolved for Evans. Yet in spite of his irascible conduct in court, he was occasionally helpful to Clarke, advising him discreetly on legal requirements. Early the following year when an action for debt had been brought by Wi Tako against a European before the county court, Wi Tako did not appear. Clarke begged for an adjournment, which was granted. Worried about the anomaly of his roles as protector and advocate for Maori in the courts, Clarke told his father:

> Evans who was appearing for the defendant immediately stood up and asked in what capacity I appeared in the Court. I replied, 'as the official advocate for the natives' he said very quietly that the rules of the Court did not allow 'anyone except barristers and solicitors to act' – the only reply I could make was that I remembered a claim on Lord John Russell's printed instructions to the late Governor which stated that the Protector of Aborigines and his officers should have free access to all the ordinary tribunals of the Colony . . . . I afterwards spoke to [Shortland] and he spoke to the County Judge on the subject . . .

Clarke asked his father if there was a law covering the provision 'about to be passed? – because if not, all my proceedings in the county court as counsel for the natives will be illegal – I wish . . . you would mention it to the Chief Justice.'[5]

A couple of months later he was forced to seek help again from his father after the case of Martin and the Maori plantations had been brought before the court. Evans had appeared for the defendant, but when Clarke introduced new information Evans reacted with 'personal abuse', which Clarke 'threw back in his teeth, and would not condescend to notice'. Because of the 'illegality', the case was dismissed. When Evans appealed for costs against Clarke, Police Magistrate McDonough promised to consider it. Clarke was totally ignorant of 'certain legal technicalities' and knew that only lawyers could decide the finer points associated with trespass actions. Painfully aware of the 'curious indefinite position' he held as protector, he confessed he felt inadequate in court with professionals, and urged his father again to consult Martin and Swainson on the issue. Clarke was also arguing with Spain, confiding he preferred 'to do things his way without the interference of Spain'.[6]

Although zealous in court, Clarke did not always behave in ways that matched his convictions. He wrote of a spat that developed between a Maori and a Pakeha at Pipitea pa. The Pakeha had struck out and the Maori retaliated with 'a good thrashing with his fists'. The Pakeha fled, calling out he had been nearly killed by a Maori, a crowd gathered and soldiers were ordered out. Clarke raced to the pa to find the soldiers 'on the edge of a bank, which half surrounded the pah', with their muskets loaded and bayonets fixed. When he discovered that 'the most aggressive troublemaker' was his own Maori servant 'boy', Clarke attacked him, knocked him down, wrested his musket from him and 'kicked him into the nearest house'. The court hearing took place the next day, but the case was dismissed after it was proven the Pakeha had begun the assault. Maori were pleased at the outcome, but Pakeha were 'intensely disgusted', wrote Clarke.[7] They would have been more than disgusted had they witnessed Clarke's treatment of his servant.

Spain was, as ever, conscientious and methodical, and determined to examine every chief and witness. But as the days turned to weeks and then to months, Evans's private practice began to suffer. He was considerably frustrated by the distractions of Spain's court. Chetham was no barrister, and it was left to Evans to represent his clients in the county and police courts. His frequent absences from and late arrivals in Spain's court were matched by those of Hanson, whose duties as Crown Prosecutor similarly suffered. Inevitably Clarke and occasionally Spain complained of deliberate obstruction, but in this case their complaints were ill-founded.

When Evans appeared in the county court in late June, the court was crowded with Maori as he defended Te Kopo and E Pokai on a charge of stealing two pieces of pork from Henry Brown the butcher. Evans had found witnesses to attest to their good characters, but Hanson objected and Halswell asked the prisoners to speak for themselves – a daunting task for two young Maori who had little English. They were found guilty, but after Evans's final address the jury again added a strong recommendation for mercy. They were sentenced to one month's imprisonment and hard labour.[8]

In the midst of the unremitting stress, there had been one occasion for celebration. Towards the end of June, in front of a large number of guests, Amelia Riddiford and Edward Chetham were married at the Evans's residence. The Reverend J. Macfarlane officiated, Evans gave the bride away and Harriet prepared a splendid wedding feast. Chetham had bought the section next to the Evans house, on which Evans had a handsome home built for them as part of Amelia's dowry. Chetham's father sent a wedding present of a box of gold by the *Thomas Sparks*, but on its arrival they found the gold had been replaced by iron – probably by crew members who had left the ship at Panama.[9] It might have served as an omen for what became a barren, lonely and unhappy marriage for Amelia.[10]

Evans had told Chetham of his mortgage agreement with Monro, and not long after the wedding when Monro pressed for payment, Chetham offered to go to England to persuade his father to take over the mortgage and re-lend it to Evans on more reasonable terms. Evans accepted the offer, but just before sailing Chetham asked Evans to sign a document giving 'certain property' – several of his sections – to him in lieu of settlement on Amelia. Hanson advised Evans to sign, saying the document would be useful to Chetham for his negotiations in England. In spite of his misgivings, Evans signed and gave Chetham £300 he had borrowed from the Union Bank.[11]

Back in Spain's court on 6 July, Henry Ware testified that he had signed the deed on the *Tory*, having been told the payment was for Port Nicholson. He had been assured that Wakefield would not take all the lands from Maori and no one had said the payment was only for the water. When they all danced at the 'war dance' afterward at Petone, no one expressed dissatisfaction.

Moses Ngaponga relayed a different story, confirming Mohi's evidence that Wi Tako had first told him that Wakefield 'only wanted to purchase the sea'. He had realised only later that the payment was for the land.[12]

On the stormy night following this evidence, the whare that had served as post office, police office, court house and a Maori church was totally destroyed by fire. It was a mixed blessing, as five weeks earlier Evans had objected to the state of the court on behalf of his colleagues on a day of atrocious weather. 'It blew hard from the North-west with rain; papers were seen flying about in all directions, and at his honour's request all persons were permitted to wear their hats. The jury, Bar and the Public, were mostly wrapped up in stout pea jackets.'

Evans, always susceptible to infection, had pleaded:

> Notwithstanding his Honour's known character for patience and perseverance, he could hardly conceive how any human being could endure the hardship of sitting there from ten o'clock in the morning until six at night. The cold, the wind and the rain penetrating in every direction . . . he trusted something would be done to remedy these monstrous evils, and the abominable neglect, and indifference with which this important part of the colony had been treated.

Spain had promised to plead his case in 'the proper quarter'.[13] After the fire, the court was transferred for a time to a hotel and the Land Court moved to Spain's offices in Manners Street.

Soon there was disagreement amongst Maori over the ownership of Port Nicholson. In July when Evans examined Te Puni about his relationship with Pipitea pa, Te Puni said he had cultivated the land there for three years but not taken possession of it. He had never given or sold any land to Richard Davis or to any Maori, but he claimed the piece where Davis now resided. Moturoa, he said, had been living at Pipitea for six years. Apart from Kaiwharawhara, all other pa in Wellington were given to Wharepouri by Kotiriki.

There had been squabbling amongst them. Wairarapa and Ngapuna had taken the goods from the *Tory* to Pipitea, Wairarapa asserting they were also for other pa. Wharepouri had corrected him saying, 'No, the goods are [solely] for Pipitea.' Te Puni had told Wairarapa to return the goods, telling him, 'You go without, Wairarapa!', but Wairarapa took a case of guns. As far as Te Puni was concerned, Wairarapa having boarded the *Tory* meant that all Pipitea Maori had consented to the sale.

Te Puni said other Maori had disputed his claim to be their chief, but only 'After the Europeans came and after the Court came here'. Te Puni endorsed all of Wakefield's evidence on the purchase of Port

Nicholson. 'When Colonel Wakefield arrived', he told Evans, 'the land belonged to Warepouri, Puni and all my tribe.' Yes, he had sold the land to Colonel Wakefield. 'The Matehou tribe lived at Pipitea – Wairararapa, Moturoa, and the others.' They were a branch of his, Te Puni's, tribe. He had sold, he said, 'the whole of Port Nicholson'.[14]

When Wairarapa took the stand, he accused the Europeans of taking Pipitea's cultivations. After Shortland's visit, he and an angry Moturoa had told Wakefield to 'go and live at Pitone' and challenged the surveyors, saying 'you must cut the throats of the Maoris first and then take our land'. Wairarapa believed that the payment was for the sea but Te Puni told him it was for Pipitea. He objected as Pipitea had been made tapu by Davis. Wairarapa had never acknowledged to Wakefield, Evans or anyone else that he had sold Pipitea and he had told Shortland as much. He was adamant that Waiwhetu and Pipitea belonged to him. Henry Williams had given him, Te Puni and Wharepouri a hundred blankets, some shirts, trousers, waistcoats and other goods to ensure the Europeans 'might not purchase our land'.

But on 7 September, Mahau of the Ngati Tawuaikina [*sic*] tribe at Petone testified that it was his right to sell Port Nicholson. At first he was glad to have Europeans living amongst them, as his tribe were 'afraid of the Ngatiraukawa and the Ngatikahungunu . . . I said, "Here is Poneke, land for you."' He had signed the deed selling Heretaunga to Wakefield and received goods which 'were divided into six heaps: two for Heretaunga, one each for Ngauranga, Petone, Kaiwharra, Pipitea and Te Aro'. 'Warepouri gave Tako the guns for Kumutoto.' The deed was not explained to him, but he had sold 'all Port Nicholson'.

> Evans: What do you mean by the term all Port Nicholson?
> Mahau: Heretaunga and Petone and Pipitea, Kumutoto and Te Aro, those are the places that I claimed. I had cultivations here when the Ngaturutunga were here – these are the places I sold to Colonel Wakefield. I left Ngauranga to Warepouri and Kaiwharra to Tangakeni. I did not sell them.

Mahau had been present at the 'war dance' at Petone after the execution of the deed, as he believed Wakefield wanted to see how many Maori belonged to the various pa of Pipitea, Kumutoto, Te Aro, Kaiwharawhara and Ngauranga. He told Evans, 'All the Pipitea's natives were there.' Evans asked if Moturoa was present. 'Moturoa stayed by himself at Pipitea', said Mahau. Evans asked him, 'Which of the natives had a right to sell Pipitea at the time of the arrival of Colonel Wakefield?'

> Mahau: These places all belonged to my tribe. I sold Pipitea and Kumutoto and Te Aro. They said nothing. [It was] on me to speak. It was on account of my word that these places were all sold.
> Evans: When did you agree to sell all these places?
> Mahau: It was on board the Tory . . . when the natives of Pipitea and Te Aro and Kaiwarra saw that all the goods were for us they came for them it was this my word that Port Nicholson was sold.
> Evans: Did Ngakurae and Wairarapa concur in the sale?
> Mahau: Yes.
> Evans: Did all the persons whose names append to the deed now produced as sellers of the land perfectly understand at the time that they were selling all Port Nicholson?
> Mahau: They all knew that they were selling their land except Te Aro. We were not going to give Te Aro anything we were going to take away the guns to Petone but Tako brought them things in the boat.

Nothing was given to Te Aro Maori because they had cursed Te Puni two years before the *Tory*'s arrival. They had long been slaves 'of Ngapuhi, Waikato, Kawia and all the tribes'. Spain asked him:

> Court: Was it right and just to sell to Colonel Wakefield without permission of the Matehou tribe?
> Mahau: It is right. It is for me to say that it should be sold. If they get angry I take the payment and sell the land.

He could sell Pipitea without Matehou's consent as he had allowed the tribe to settle there and cultivate the land. He had no right to sell without the consent of the other chiefs, but added, 'If I had said don't sell it, they would not have. If I had said sell, they would.'

Te Puni, Wharepouri and he were the 'great speakers of our tribe'. He told the court his tribe had consented to sell all the land. Even if they had not consented, he said, 'I by myself could have sold it all to Colonel Wakefield'.

> Court: Do you, Puni and Warehou have a right to sell all Port Nicholson to Colonel Wakefield without the consent of the natives living at the pas – Te Aro, Kumutoto, Pipitea, Kaiwarrawarra and Waiwhetu?
> Mahau: Have I not told you that it was for me to sell the land! It was on account of my word that Port Nicholson was sold! If I had said it should not be sold then it would not have been sold.

Port Nicholson was different because its land did not belong to their forefathers. Of right it belonged to the Ngati Kahungunu, 'but the people here have taken the land'.

By this time Evans was aware that the Company's titles were very shaky. More rumblings were being felt outside the court. From June to August, Te Rauparaha had sent some of his followers from Porirua to the Hutt to prevent settlers from clearing their sections. Another party headed by Taringa Kuri demanded extra payment for the land. This sort of confrontation was becoming increasingly common, and Wakefield and Halswell told the directors that Maori had become 'extortionate'. Wakefield also complained to Spain that, although he had purchased the unoccupied land of Port Nicholson with the approval of the chiefs, Maori had now moved 'on the pretext of cattle intruding on their land and seized possession of land in which they have not or do not claim'.[15]

Evans continued commuting regularly between Spain's court and the county court. He successfully defended Robert Wyeth on a charge of stealing a cock and hen worth eight shillings, and a week later obtained an acquittal for local trader William Fitzherbert who had been charged with assault.[16]

ꕤ

The continual fulminations of Evans and other Company servants against the government were receiving negative feedback. There was a slide in popularity for Wakefield, and anger against the Company's representatives was steadily growing.[17] In early August, Richard Hanson mustered a committee of more than fifty men from the pastoral and commercial sectors to counter the anti-government feeling, and launched the *Colonist and Port Nicholson Advertiser.* This act might have piqued Evans as he was contributing articles to the *New Zealand Gazette and Wellington Spectator* at the time.[18]

When Murphy presided at a meeting in the Exchange on Tuesday 9 August to discuss an address to greet Dr Selwyn, the Bishop of New Zealand, there was a rare harmony. Evans was charming. He was pleased to see that all denominations were represented that evening, and that their equality had been ensured by legislation. He remembered their cordial welcome of the Catholic bishop on his visit to Wellington and trusted Wellington might be selected as Selwyn's future home. His address to the Bishop was 'drawn up on principles so perfectly unobjectionable', it was immediately seconded by Hanson, adopted unanimously, and given to a committee of seventeen men, headed by Murphy, Evans, St Hill, Hanson and Wakefield, to sign off.

In Evans's vote of thanks to Murphy he congratulated him on having chaired the first meeting that had unanimously approved all resolutions, but Murphy was wary of Evans's conciliatory mood.[19] A few days later when they met again to hear the final draft, Henry St Hill – no friend of Evans – was asked to read his alternate address. Evans was surprised, observing that it was almost identical to his. The committee was asked to blend the two, with the second and fourth paragraphs of Evans's address replacing those of St Hill. The following day, although no reason was given, Evans, Hanson and Wakefield were pointedly excluded from the deputation to present the address to Dr Selwyn. This is unlikely to have been because of Hanson's and Evans's dissenting background, but Evans was disappointed, having hoped to take the deputation to Selwyn himself.[20] However, he achieved a victory of sorts when the Bishop's first christening of a Pakeha child in New Zealand was that of Daniel Riddiford's second child and first son, Edward Joshua.

Evans was not without friends. Isaac Featherston, Daniell, Taine, several merchants, Halswell and Hanson were regular guests. Wakefield also regarded him as a friend and relied heavily on his assistance, as it might take up to a year to receive instructions from the directors and he frequently needed advice on the ground. In early August he asked Evans to give his opinion on a subject that had been worrying James Kelham, his secretary and accountant. Kelham referred to a clause in the Company's Charter, which prohibited the Company's agent to 'carry on the business of Banking, by keeping Cash of or for any person payable on Demand, or by borrowing, owing or taking up money on their Bills or notes payable on demand or at any less time than 12 months from the borrowing thereof, or for a sum less than One hundred Pounds'. Kelham believed that Wakefield's practice of 'borrowing money from the bank' to pay Company bills was 'contrary to the meaning of this clause'. Wakefield immediately turned to Evans for legal advice. After consulting the bank manager, Evans confirmed his own view on the matter and wrote to Wakefield, explaining his borrowing was 'not contrary to the clause in the Charter recited by Mr. Kelham', and in fact that drawing on money for 'the purpose of carrying on the proper business of the corporation is no more banking than the buying and selling of a gentleman for the purposes of his household will constitute him a trader within the bankrupt Laws'. He recommended Wakefield should get confirmation from Crown lawyers in London, adding: 'But I repeat that I have no doubt on the subject, and am confident the directors will have none. In the meantime', Wakefield should continue to draw 'as usual' on the Company's account until he 'received other instructions'.[21]

Wakefield waited nine months or so for the directors' reply, which confirmed Evans's advice: 'The mere act of obtaining cash in New Zealand for Bills drawn upon the Company for its Agent does not constitute the business of banking within the meaning of the Charter – you will, therefore, act upon this matter according to Dr. Evans' advice.'[22]

Meanwhile, Wakefield wrote to Hobson in late August, admitting that the Company's titles were imperfect and suggesting that he and Halswell should review them, with Spain acting as mediator. But the conciliatory gesture was too late. The sick and exhausted governor died on 10 September. To make matters worse for Wakefield, Clarke superseded Spain's authority by writing to Maori, promising that the settlers would never remove them from their pa and cultivations unless they wished it. Of course he was correct, but he pre-empted Spain, and his letter implied that the Company's officials had every intention of evicting the Maori inhabitants. Naturally, some responded by putting barriers round land 'that had not been previously occupied by them, but had been chosen by the holders of the Company's section orders. The Colonel was in despair.'[23]

When the news arrived of Hobson's death, most of the Wellington settlers would have agreed with Gisborne's judgement that his 'gravest fault' had been 'his treatment of the New Zealand Company'. Instead of appreciating the Company's 'struggle' in implementing its ideas of systematic colonisation, he had 'regarded it with unmitigated aversion, and pursued it with increasing enmity'.[24] As early as 29 July the previous year, Somes had written to Lord Russell complaining about the 'very unfavourable, not to say hostile, view which Governor Hobson appears to take on all occasions of the proceedings of the Company, and of its agents and officers in New Zealand'.[25]

Colonial Secretary Shortland assumed the powers of governor for fifteen months before Governor FitzRoy arrived in the country. Shortland was as unpopular in Auckland as he had been in Wellington – wasting precious funds on numerous employees and using his position to purchase town acres before the public could do so.[26] During the recession that continued into the year ahead, the settlers' complaints of exorbitant taxes were well founded; in the entire period 1840–45, the income from Wellington customs was £22,702 2s 2d, while Auckland customs for the period yielded £14,916 9s 6d. In that year alone, 1842, Wellington fed £8,967 3s 2d into the government's coffers, while Auckland contributed £5,496 19s 11d. The press suffered from the prohibitive costs of pen and ink, as did legal practices like Evans's.[27]

In late September a letter arrived in Wellington from Acting Governor Shortland. It was addressed to 'a gentleman', and suggested that if Colonel Wakefield 'would meet him halfway, he thought the settlers under the Company might forthwith be put in possession of their lands'. The 'gentleman' (probably Evans, as Wakefield's counsel) was 'urged to go immediately to [Wakefield] and suggest the propriety of showing [Shortland] how anxious he was to avail himself of any overture of the kind by proceeding forthwith to Auckland'. On 12 October, Wakefield and Spain boarded the schooner *Elizabeth* and set sail as requested.[28]

CHAPTER THIRTEEN.
'A GOOD AND PIOUS MAN'

Ac veluto magno in populo cum sæpa coorta est
Seditio, sævitque animis ignobile vulgus,
Jamque faces et saxa volant, furor arma ministrat,
Tum, pietate gravem ac meritis si forte virum quem
Conspexêre, silent, arrectisque auribus adstant;
Ille regit dictis animos, et pectora mulcet.

Virgil, *The Aeneid*, Book 1, lines 148–53, quoted in the *New Zealand Colonist*, 23 September 1842

In late March, Murphy had published Hobson's instructions to draw up a 'Roll of Burgesses' (resident voters) for the district. Wellington was officially proclaimed a borough on 4 August, and the settlers were preparing to elect their first council on 4 October.[1] Murphy was the enrolment officer, charging £1 for each man to enrol.[2] The last date for enrolment was advertised as 30 August, Murphy giving notice in the *Colonist* that registration could be completed at the police office between 11 a.m. and 4 p.m. each day. As interest in Spain's court had evaporated, the community's focus turned to the selection of candidates. The embryonic political makeup of Wellington was an indication of the social and class interaction in New Zealand pioneer society. Ultimately, there were three groups connected by common interests: the mechanics, labourers and 'working settlers', who formed a committee of twenty-one members and held regular meetings; the 'popular' group of merchants, publicans and artisans; and the 'elite' group of landowners.

By the time the first labourers' group met to approve a list of eighteen candidates for council on 15 August, the 'elite' had splintered into the Wakefield faction and the government supporters. One wit divided them (the elite) into 'government', 'Company' and 'colonist'. The 'wide-awake' were Wakefield's followers such as Evans, while men like Hanson, Rowland Davis, Wallace and other government sympathisers were 'as the wind blows'.

The labourers had agreed to exclude lawyers from their list, so when Hanson's name was called, many objected that he was 'a slippery person', while others pointed out that he was the largest landholder in the settlement and as such represented most of the absentees, 'whose interests . . . [would have] the effect of utterly ruining the settlement'.[3]

Evans's name was amongst others suggested to replace Hanson's, despite the fact that he was also a lawyer, and although he was included it would be fair to assume that many may have felt intimidated by him, disliking his dominance at meetings and his evident superior education. Evans also had the unhappy knack of making himself unpopular, and he could not be trusted to hold to any one principle, falling into the lawyer's trap of agreeing with certain aspects of one side of an argument and certain aspects of another.

After yet another preliminary vote, Hanson was selected as 'the sheet-anchor of the Government party'.[4] Some were suspicious of the committee's motives and the group split, an overwhelming majority voting for a new committee altogether. But Davies wrote to the *Colonist*, defending Hanson as 'the liberal and firm friend of the people when their best interests are at stake', adding:

> And in justice to Dr. Evans, he displayed the same enlightened feeling for the extension of the suffrage and a tax of some description on absentee property, for by so doing [Hanson and Evans] considered that improving the colony would better their own and [their] clients' interests.

By late August, emotion over the election had built, leading to accusations of bribery and personal abuse. Advertisements on behalf of various interest groups flooded the papers, together with near-defamatory letters suggesting that certain parties were using bribery to gain support. John Wade came close to accusing the ambitious Henry St Hill of backing government men just to get 'some more substantial Government favour conferred on him'. He also accused 'certain' committee members of attempted bribery, and vowed he would publish their names if necessary.[5] Nathaniel Levin attacked Wade for 'perpetrating a gross untruth', and Halswell, Moreing and Jerningham suggested that several of the men who had registered had paid for others to enrol in order to buy their votes.[6]

Not everyone read the notice in the *Colonist* of 19 August making it clear that registrations would close on Monday 29 August (rather than 30 August, as initially advertised). No time of day was indicated in that notice, so the *Gazette* of 31 August spoke for many when it complained that registration had, in fact, closed at 4 p.m. on the

29th, catching many people unawares. Over 350 men had managed to enrol in time, but Revans, who had a fair chance of being elected, was absent in Nelson. And Evans was irate that he had 'tendered his £1 and the usual declaration to the Police Magistrate, and he was refused, he was informed he was too late, it was after the hour which Mr. Murphy had appointed to receive the names of burgesses'.[7] It is possible he had just learned of the altered date, but he was frequently late for appointments all his life. However, there does remain a doubt. The man who could justifiably argue he had done as much as anyone to bring about Wellington's Corporation Act had sensed the groundswell of suspicion and resentment forming against the Company's men. He must also have realised that the size of the labourers' group gave them a power hitherto denied them. Knowing bribery had taken place and 'lists' of favoured candidates were circulating, he must have seen that he had little chance of being elected.

Many were aggrieved at missing out, and feeling in the community was at fever pitch when a public meeting for 'Burgesses' was advertised for 18 September at Barrett's. That evening, Hanson dined with Evans, listening to his friend's storm of protest at Murphy's management of the registration process. Hanson may also have suspected Evans had deliberately failed to register in time in an attempt to highlight the 'illegality' of Murphy's closing the register early, but Evans had worked himself into a fury and nobody could calm him down. He grabbed his coat and lamp and took off into the night for Barrett's Hotel, leaving Hanson to make small talk with Harriet.

The reporter from the *Colonist and Port Nicholson Advertiser* was struck by the peculiar appropriateness of one of the most famous extracts in Latin literature when he witnessed the chaos that erupted at the meeting of the burgesses of Wellington.[8] The room was 'crowded to excess', the mood ugly, the air close and fœtid. By the time Evans entered, out of breath, the chairman, William Lyon, had just arrived. 'Workingmen' jostled alongside Company men, their feelings of hostility barely repressed. Many, if not most of them, had been drinking. Lyon felt sufficiently alarmed to beg for their support in his efforts to maintain order.[9]

Evans shouldered his way through the crowd. The atmosphere was strained as St Hill held the floor, complaining that Wade had boasted he could enlist 150 whalers to vote for him, while Wade shouted he had merely been responding to Molesworth's boast that he could get 120 voters from the Hutt. As soon as St Hill left the floor, Evans attempted to address the crowd but was greeted by a 'diversified mélange of cheers, hisses and groans'. Making 'a footstool of one gentleman' and using 'the shoulder of another' to mount the table 'amidst roars of laughter', he ignored the tumult and began to stride back and forth along the table 'with great dignity, folding and extending his arms alternately, and going through every variety of gesticulation'. Above the 'most deafening uproar', not one man could hear a word he spoke. Lyon tried in vain to bring the meeting to order but vacated the chair after warning Evans that he would be responsible for any damage or breach of the peace if he continued. Wade, Roots and Dorset added to the spectacle by joining Evans on the table, all trying to distract the audience's attention.

Evans had participated in countless stormy meetings in London and was not in the least deterred by the catcalls, whistling and cheering, mingled with cries of 'No burgess!', 'Off! Off!' and 'Hear the Doctor!' Then, quite suddenly, he felt his legs being seized. He lost his balance, toppled backwards and disappeared into the crowd. He had been pulled from the table by a 'rough stockman from Australia', but he struck back 'furiously' at his assailant from all directions, and others rushed to his rescue, carrying both men bodily out of the room. Those closest to the skirmish forced Evans's assailant to flee from the building.

Shortly afterward an unperturbed Evans reappeared at the head of the table, and after minutes of 'prolonged uproar', finally gained control, as the crowd quietened.

> Just as so often it happens, when a crowd collects, and violence
> Brews up, and the mass mind boils nastily over, and next thing
> Firebrands and brickbats are flying (hysteria soon finds a missile) –
> That then, if they see some man whose goodness of heart and conduct
> Have won their respect, they fall silent and stand still, ready to hear him;
> And he can change their temper and calm their thoughts with a speech.[10]

Evans knew how to 'change tempers' and 'calm thoughts', and his address was a dazzling tour de force. He reminded his audience that he was 'a burgess as much as anyone in that room'. He had spent 'largely', in spite of not having gained possession of his land, and the money he had invested had benefited two hundred emigrants. He ferociously assailed 'that government stipendiary' Murphy, whom he was determined to bring before the Supreme Court – 'so help me God!' – for closing the roll at 4 p.m. and not at the end of the legal day (midnight), and for having closed it a day early.

He had been chary about enrolling as a burgess at first, but 'was told that on this first occasion of exercising our high municipal privileges, it might seem unmannerly and cowardly to shrink from the task'. For 'five and twenty years he had fought long and hard for the cause of radical reform'. In Port Nicholson he had never 'advocated this party or that party, but the only cause I have ever supported has been the substantial welfare of this colony, and the happiness and prosperity of the universal people'. He reminded them it had been he who had 'the honour of proposing the Corporation Bill to Sir George Gipps' in 1840, and 'having been instrumental in framing and bringing it about, having been the first to press upon you the expediency of adopting it'.

He warned the men not to pledge themselves to any list or to any man until their conscience dictated their choice on the day. He respected St Hill 'as a man' but begged them not to 'return to the Council, [any] agent of absentee landlords – no officer of the New Zealand Company – no stipendiary of Government!' He believed the British and local governments wanted to deny them their land by stirring up 'the [Maori] mind in opposition to the settlers', and urged those present not to support the representatives of absentee landlords who owned 'tens of thousands of acres . . . which they have never seen, and for which they have done nothing – men who are only connected with the colony as a profitable speculation – who have done nothing for you or for the colony'.

> And, there is also another man, whom I respect and admire in his private capacity, and whom I have left a few minutes since in my own family circle, but who, from his connection with that local government, whose every effort and wish is for your oppression and destruction, is unfit to represent you in the council. I mean Mr. Hanson! (Cries of oh! Oh!–now, it's coming out!) . . . . act upon your own judgment – think for yourselves . . . . Once more I entreat you, pledge yourself to no man's lists – Mr. Sutton's list, or Mr. St. Hill's list, or the working-men's list or Mr. Anybody-else's list. Scatter your lists to the winds of heaven, and dare to think and act for yourselves!

Evans concluded by paraphrasing the parable of the faithful steward.

John Roots, who had assumed the chair, made some remark that was inaudible, but Evans responded with asperity, 'We want no slaves to power here; we will not be dictated to by the baseborn slave of an arbitrary faction!'

In one stroke, Evans had vilified Michael Murphy, risked his friendship with Hanson, alienated his colleagues and angered John

Roots, who scorned his address as an opportunity to 'have a slap at Mr. Hanson'. Roots had opposed the Corporation Bill, urging the assembly to vote for those who would be 'most likely to support the working men's interest'. This advice was greeted with loud derision, which continued for many minutes.

Evans had an unexpected ally. After attempting for some time to be heard, Revans said he was appalled at the reception given to Evans. 'Class representation', he said, 'was the curse of England.' He agreed with Evans that they should tear up all lists and think for themselves, and expressed his disgust at the attempts to stifle discussion that evening, saying it 'was a disgrace to the town'.

Mr Fitzherbert said he was sorry for the way Dr Evans had been treated. He did not know him well, but respected his public spirit and admired his talent. In his opinion there was nobody better equipped in the colony to address them or represent them. Evans had defended him recently in court, and he had benefited from his 'benevolence, determination and talent'.

The *Colonist* reported that 'Mr. Forster' – in reality it was J. H. Greenwood – moved a vote of censure on Evans for resisting the authority of the chair and causing a disturbance by his obstinacy.[11] Someone then moved an amendment to Greenwood's resolution: to censure those who wished to censure Evans. Roots put both motions to the meeting, saying he thought Evans was merely guilty of a breach of etiquette, 'which might be considered pardonable under the circumstances'.

Evans then reappeared at the back of the room and proposed an amendment to the first two motions: that the assembly pledge themselves to vote only for each man they considered worthy of their confidence, one who 'would conscientiously discharge the duties of a Councilman'. Many objected, saying a similar resolution had been put at a previous meeting, so Roots asked Evans if he would withdraw his amendment. Evans refused. His amendment was seconded, and in being put, carried by 'acclamation'.

Virgil's man may have left the meeting in triumph, but the fallout from the meeting was considerable. Even John Roots felt obliged to insert a notice in the *Colonist* protesting that 'some evil-disposed person has reported that Dr. Evans, Mr. Revans and myself have lost caste. I most emphatically deny that I have lost caste, and I leave it for the other gentlemen to justify themselves.'[12]

Hanson – well aware of his image as 'slippery' and 'as the wind blows' – had been stung by Evans's criticisms, and he was clearly behind the *Colonist*'s editorial about the meeting. Clouded by antipathy towards Evans's slur on Hanson, and keenly aware of Evans's role as advisor to Colonel Wakefield, the editorial clinically dissected Evans's motives and character. It also presented a view entirely opposing that of Evans.

The *Colonist* alleged that Evans had never intended enrolling, let alone standing as a candidate, but had abstained merely to pour scorn upon Michael Murphy and to 'represent his [own] exclusion from the [candidates' lists] as the result, not of his unpopularity, but of what he would . . . characterize as the partial conduct of [Murphy]'. The *Colonist* reasoned – rather speciously – that by condemning the government's servants and the agents for absentee landlords, and urging every man to scatter his votes, Evans and the 'Wakefieldites' planned to capture the vote.

As an orator, the article continued, Evans was unequalled in the colony. Few could better him in 'convincing by argument or guiding by counsel'. In the 'soundness of his deliberate judgment' he had few peers, yet there was just one thing necessary to ensure he became 'one of the most influential persons in the colony'. And that was 'that he should argue for truth, not for victory'. He should be above 'petty contests', pursuing instead 'by consistent means, a worthy and intelligible end'. The *Colonist* 'always regretted . . . detecting and disclosing the artifices which, for unworthy ends, he so often stoops to employ'. Evans possessed:

> . . . great strength of lungs; imperturbable self-possession; unequalled fluency of vituperation; a great readiness in selecting and enforcing such topics as are likely to suit the taste and temper of his auditors; . . . he lacks nothing but steadiness of purpose, and that weight which consistency gives, to carry with him almost any public meeting. For his sake, and for the sake of the colony, we regret that his valuable qualities are clouded, we might say utterly neutralized – by the lightness with which he adopts and abandons opinions – by his at least seeming willingness to sacrifice consistency and principle in order to carry his point – and by the absence of any intelligible motive of public policy or general interest as the rule of his conduct. With every respect for the learned Doctor in his private capacity, with the highest opinion of his talents, and with great admiration for his social qualities, we must say, that as a public man, we are unable to place confidence in him; and we imagine we are not quite solitary in [this] sentiment . . . [13]

The criticisms levelled against Evans were very similar to the observations Henry Cockburn and William Hazlitt made of Lord Brougham. Cockburn had said Brougham was:

> . . . an instance of the blunders men commit about themselves. Could he retain the esteem of men half as well as he provokes their hostility, he would be omnipotent. He has as yet always espoused right public causes, and always displayed talents of the highest order and the greatest variety, yet he has never had any moral influence, but is a mere intellectual machine.[14]

While Hazlitt spoke of Brougham's 'loftiness', he highlighted his lack of sympathy with other people: 'It is not that he thinks too much of himself, too little of his cause: but he is absorbed in the pursuit of truth as an abstract inquiry; he is led away by the headstrong and overmastering activity of his own mind.'[15]

Evans would have argued his advice had been sound – after all, he had nothing to gain – but his character had been shredded. As he wrestled with his divided loyalties, attacking his real or imaginary foes, the split between the values that informed his character and the necessity for expediency in a hostile environment widened and was to dog him throughout his colonial career. His powerful personality and determination might have been well-suited to the cause of reform in the old country, but they were not so attractive in a smaller community, where men of differing temperaments were forced to deal with one another on a daily basis. His failings were all too evident: almost invariably he acted impulsively and alone, and was seemingly heedless of others' opinions of him. While Hanson and others with cooler heads measured, sifted and manipulated before acting, Evans often appeared in the public domain as a figure who could not be ignored, parading his failures as well as his virtues.

Over a week later, Evans was working in his office when he received a letter from John Wade, accusing him of having made some very 'unjustifiable and highly injurious' remarks to him at the meeting in front of others. He had waited some time for Evans to cool his hasty temper and write an apology, but as none had been forthcoming he felt compelled to bring an action against him for slander. Wade had been a key figure for Evans, bringing him a great deal of business and championing him after his removal from the Commission of Peace. Although he had no recollection of having abused Wade, it seemed Evans had lost a valuable client and supporter.[16]

Evans spent several days in bed with a feverish cold, returning to his office on Lambton Quay on 1 October. He was unsettled enough to fire off a letter to Colonel Wakefield asking for a 'check on account of fees' for acting as Company's counsel in the Land Claims Court. At a rate of 5 guineas per day, £200 was 'insufficient' to cover the days he had spent at work.[17]

At two o'clock that afternoon, a clerk arrived, asking for all the papers relating to Wade's cases pending trial in the Supreme Court, and an account of costs due. Evans was astonished. He still could not recall having said anything to upset Wade.[18] In his dilemma he turned to Hanson for assistance, suggesting the matter could be resolved by an informal discussion. Hanson approached Wade on Evans's behalf, but the aggrieved Wade replied, 'it clearly shows the unjustifiable length to which [Evans] will proceed, and the reckless indifference with which he will assail the character of those who have in no way injured himself'. He rejected Evans's overture, threatening to take the matter to the Supreme Court, but the case seems to have been dropped, perhaps after an apology and reparation from Evans.[19]

The elections duly took place. Hunter topped the poll, becoming Wellington's first mayor, and of the seventeen councillors appointed with him, Hanson was the thirteenth most popular with 126 votes.[20]

Evans was very busy in the county and supreme courts, acting for the defence. Only two days after the burgesses' meeting, he acted for Edward Thomas Fox who was accused of rape. He produced a surprise witness, Henry Cole, who testified he had been in the next room to where the alleged offence had taken place. Hanson, for the Crown, objected that had he known of this, the case would probably never have come to court. Justice Halswell agreed, but added that it was possibly a good thing, as it gave the accused a chance to defend his character. Evans declared he had purposely kept back the witness as he was 'anxious to put a stop to a system of extortion which had been going on to a most frightful excess', and adding another empty threat: 'most likely the matter would not stop [there]'.

At the Supreme Court's first sitting on 4 October, Evans succeeded in defending Dr Francis Healy against his young brother John who claimed half of the value of Dr Healy's land. On the second day, when William and John Wallace brought an action against Mr Guard to recover the cost of nine casks of oil, Hanson acted for the Wallaces and Evans for Guard. There was a great deal of evidence and the case went on until late. When the jury awarded damages to the plaintiffs, Evans was dissatisfied, saying he would make a further 'communication'. The foreman re-evaluated the damages and agreed to lower them, but Evans hinted he would apply for a new trial 'altogether independent' of the jury's error.[21]

Revans had changed his view of Evans markedly since the voyage of the *Adelaide*. Having observed him in court on many occasions, he decided that, far from being 'no lawyer' who 'will never practise', Evans was just the man to defend him on two charges before the court. In the first case, Postmaster Walter Mantell claimed damages from Revans for an article he had printed in July. Revans denied writing the article, but accepted responsibility as editor and was ordered to pay damages and costs. Evans was also unable to save him from paying £160 and costs to Mr Mercer over a disputed bill.[22]

Brewer renewed his application for a warrant to arrest Rangihaeata. The chief had 'violently and illegally' demolished several buildings in the Porirua district earlier in the year, and had actively obstructed several settlers, including a servant of Evans.[23] When Justice William Martin asked if any counsel at the Bar would represent Rangihaeata, only Evans offered his assistance. It was considered a magnanimous gesture. Evans then engaged in a lengthy discussion with Martin, during which the Blue Book (a legal citation guide for lawyers) was consulted more than once. Evans pointed out that Rangihaeata had not signed the agreement between the settlers' council and the confederate chiefs, while Brewer argued that the proclamation of 21 May 1840 'clearly made Rangihaeata a British subject, amenable to British Laws'. Evans countered that the onus lay upon Brewer to show that Rangihaeata had ceded possession by signing the agreement entered into by the confederate chiefs, and 'suggested that Rangihaeata was now in the hands of the Land Claims' commissioners, and in fact had never ceded the land to any one, or parted with the rightful possession thereof, as a free and independent chief'.

The court reporter noted that at that point Martin closed the proceedings rather abruptly, after assuring counsel he would seriously consider the case before leaving the harbour. A 'patient, just, sagacious and firm' man, Martin felt keenly for Maori, and his acute mental discomfort when he dealt with their rights featured strongly in his hearings.[24] In February the following year Martin found in Rangihaeata's favour, his reasons hinging on two points. There was a doubt about the 'true construction of the 4th section of the Police Magistrates Ordinance, Session 2, No. 4' – the Act under which Brewer's application was made; and 'the discussion was, from the nature of an *exparte* application, less complete than was desirable. Under these circumstances . . . I do not think I should be exercising a sound discretion if I were to issue this warrant.'[25] Although Evans was gratified by it, Martin's judgment was not welcomed by others who feared the worst, and when the inevitable confrontation occurred, pointed to this case as a key factor.[26]

In the early morning of 10 November when a fire broke out in John Lloyd's bakery on Lambton Quay, Evans's office was one of the forty-three houses and huts razed to the ground. Nearly all of his records were destroyed, including one of the original deeds signed by the Maori chiefs. Fortunately, Colonel Wakefield had made copies for the Company in London, and was able to retrieve them from the post office before they were sent.[27] The damage overall amounted to £16,000 and everyone rallied with donations for the victims. Evans and his clerk Thomas McHugh sifted through the ashes, retrieving what remained of precious documents and correspondence, and cleaning up and rebuilding in brick.

At about the same time Michael Murphy was forced to resign from his thankless role. In spite of his qualities as a magistrate, he had been expelled from the Wakefield Club on the 'well-established charge of filching money from the pool at a card table'.[28] The *Gazette* claimed that 'everybody in the community' knew Murphy had appropriated money – even the 'convicts'.[29] But his downfall came about when one night he ordered the gaoler to call out all the constables for duty from midnight till four in the morning, so that he could 'obtain access to one of their wives'. The constable stayed home and foiled Murphy's plan, attacking him with a stick or a horsewhip. In spite of Murphy's pleas, and promises of promotion shamelessly made in front of witnesses, Murphy was exposed.[30]

George Clarke admitted ruefully to his father:

> Poor Murphy I am afraid has ruined himself irretrievably in this place by his unguarded immoral proceedings, and has been compelled to give up his situation . . . the circumstances are bad enough but I believe it would never have been known were it not that a conspiracy had been found to ruin him. Colonel Wakefield has been playing a sharp game. I am afraid he has succeeded too far in his game with S--- [Spain] the latter is too fond of money . . . [31]

Outside court, Evans was still passing on donations to the Mechanics' Institute and Library, including thirty-five volumes sent by Archbishop Whately of Dublin.[32] His father had written again, hurt and angry the family had not heard from him in fourteen months. He told Evans pointedly he had given the Hebrew Bible to William Young to deliver to him. Hannah's health had suffered severely in the winter – for four months she had been too ill to leave the house and was still unwell. 'We have learnt from other sources that you and your wife continue to enjoy a good state of health', the Reverend Evans added accusingly. Francis Bradey, whose daughter was in Evans's domestic service, had visited Reverend Evans to convey his gratitude for Evans's kindness to him and his family. Bradey had spoken 'in very strong terms of respect for you and Mrs. Evans'. The Reverend was sorry to hear that Hobson harboured 'hostile feelings' toward his son. With their Charter of Incorporation the settlers would have the 'opportunity . . . of manifesting their regard for you', he added confidently. 'You must be Recorder [District Magistrate, holding courts of quarter sessions] of Wellington.' There was no common ground between the father's ambitions and the son's reality.

Evans replied immediately, assuring his parents he had written more than once, but 'it was a common complaint' that letters 'miscarry'. He was concerned for his mother but 'cherished the ardent desire and hope of returning to England and seeing her again'. He complained to his father of the frustration of his hopes and plans caused chiefly by the 'backwardness of the surveys'. Although he had expected to have received all his land within a year, he had still not secured it nearly three years later. The Crown had not issued any grants, his plans to discharge his mortgage had been dashed and he had been forced to borrow more money. But things were improving. He had contracted to sell four country sections for £800 and intended to have shed his debts within the year. His property would be 'put in a train to give me a small independence for the rest of my days . . . . I shall not lose an hour in returning to take my part in the good old cause of civil and religious liberty', he promised:

> Such is the difficulty of getting money here and so severe the struggles I have gone through. Not that I am disappointed with the country – for a man who has a family, and will devote himself to agriculture, I can say conscientiously I believe it presents the finest opening in the world. But my position – my studies and my feelings lead to different pursuits and an old country is my proper sphere. You speak of my brothers and sisters – the scorcher of hearts knows that nothing weighs more heavily on my mind than my present inability to help them – but why do they never write to me? – I should be delighted to hear from them and to answer their letters.

He was pleased James was studying pleading, the 'foundation of everything in law'. New Zealand's Chief Justice and Attorney General – Martin and Swainson respectively – were, in his opinion, 'utterly ignorant of the science of pleading, instead substituting *viva voce* statements', which had resulted in confusion. Their 'alterations' had hurt lawyers' incomes, he added, which would lead to 'uncertainty and litigation'.

Evans knew that the Company was in dire straits financially and relied on the goodwill of government. The directors had a prime scapegoat in Evans, who told his father he was sorry to hear that 'any one belonging to me had been near Gibbon Wakefield or the Company. I am too powerful here to be attacked, but I well know their feelings at home. All this is said in confidence.'[33]

In the new year of 1843, when Wakefield returned from Auckland with Shortland, the interim governor made a promising start. Evans had 'sent a letter' on behalf of the settlers that proposed the district become a county and be sub-divided to give them 'the power of making roads and bridges' and to raise funds for the cost. He argued that 'all the property' would benefit 'by such improvements'.[34]

On 21 January, when Shortland met the deputation, Evans read his petition, and expressed the 'deep anxiety with which the settlers had awaited [his] arrival, and the almost exhausted hope' of using 'the remnant of their capital and their paralysed energies in the profitable employment of their property'. Shortland was confident of a 'satisfactory conclusion', assuring them he 'would spare no time, labor or exertion, to bring about so desirable an end'. According to Jerningham Wakefield, he also promised the settlers that their land claims would be quickly settled and a more suitable jail for the prisoners would be built.[35] But they were not reassured, and continued to wonder if any arrangement had been made between Shortland and Wakefield for the settlement of the land claims.[36]

On 8 February when Commissioner Spain reopened his court, Evans explained that the original deed of sale of Port Nicholson had been lost in the fire of November. It had been stored in a desk in his office after Mr Yates had lent him the deed, which had been examined and attested by Evans and his clerk McHugh.

Whilst Evans suspected Maori had been 'tampered with' by Clarke before they gave evidence, he could not make such an assumption about the Company's translator Richard Barrett, when he cross-examined him. Barrett told him Maori understood the deed they signed. He had never said the payment was for the anchorage or the sea, and not the land. No Te Aro Maori had signed the deed. He had not told the tribes they would get one-tenth of the land but had said, 'A certain portion of the land'. When Maori had told him all the land was bad – that it was all hills – he had said in Maori, according to Clarke's translation, 'What consequence about the mountains, the harbour is good.' He admitted the blankets he had given Moturoa had been returned, and said he had told Wi Tako the blankets were presents for the Maori at Te Aro – he did not say they were given in exchange for the land. He, Richard Davis and Shortland had gone to Te Aro to persuade the Maori there to sign the deed, reserving land for Queen Victoria on behalf of the white people, and had told them Spain would settle the question.

Evans reminded Barrett of the time he had gone with Evans and Wakefield to meet with Te Aro Maori. 'Yes', said Barrett:

> We went ashore on the beach . . . we walked about the pah and conversed with the Natives and then left. The Colonel had told him to tell the Maori he would send blankets – for the people who had received no payment for the land. On that subsequent visit, the natives of the same pah had told him, when blankets were offered in payment for their land, they declined to accept them.

Evans asked, 'Who did they complain of, Colonel Wakefield or the other Natives?' Barrett answered: 'Of both Wakefield and the other Natives.'

Evans asked Barrett why Wakefield had ordered the 'war dance' and donated a pig for the feast. When word had spread, Maori came the next day 'from every part of the Bay and Port Nicholson, with fifty visitors from Wanganui – about 150 in all'. Barrett said the dance was not connected with the land sale. Wakefield wanted to meet them all and part as good friends. 'To avoid disturbance', Wakefield gave Barrett about thirty blankets to distribute when the settlers arrived.

Barrett assured Evans he had searched for the parties who had the power to sell land in each of the pa, and could not recall any Maori complaining after the goods were distributed. He had given them 'a week to consider'. Some of the Europeans had gained possession of the land 'by making presents and the greater part got possession themselves without any trouble'.[37]

The following day, Evans asked him to explain 'the groundwork of the Treaty of Sale . . . embodied in this Deed'. Barrett told him different divisions of the Ngati Awa tribe had claims on the land. Their claims resulted from both conquest and occupancy.

Evans persisted. Did Barrett make it clear to Maori that they were surrendering their lands? Did they understand? Barrett answered he did, 'as well as he could – the Maori were so anxious to get the trade on shore, but I thought they understood they were giving their land in exchange'.

Did Barrett explain the land that was reserved for them, their wives and families forever?

Barrett: Yes, I did as well as I could.
Evans: Do you mean that subject to those reserves of land for themselves and families for ever they were willing to sell the rest of the land for the purposes of colonization?
Barrett: I thought they did.[38]

At this point, Clarke took over. His probing uncovered no utopian scheme of benevolent settlement, but something that appeared more like a rushed grab for land. As Wakefield's and Barrett's carelessness, lack of rigour and paucity of negotiating skills were revealed, Evans could only look on while Clarke exposed the flaws in Barrett's interpreting skills, the misapprehension of the Maori, and the wide gap between the Company's instructions to conduct a thorough purchase with the full understanding and co-operation of all the tribes, and what had in fact taken place. The undue haste, the Europeans' ignorance of the complicated relationships in the area, and the width of the gap between the uttering of a few careless phrases and the literal meaning Maori took from them had provided the government and the missionaries with plenty of fuel to attack the Company's purchase.

As the flaws were exposed, Wakefield distanced himself again, and Spain's frustration in communicating with Wakefield, Evans and even Clarke grew. Wakefield received a letter from Clarke about Maori pa and cultivations, and he instructed Evans to reply on his behalf. Evans had already clarified a few points in discussion with Spain on the issue, but knew that on paper Wakefield's view would be clearly understood. Evans must have been wary of any opportunity Wakefield might take to blame him for events.[39] As the Company's advocate, he wrote to Clarke:

> Colonel Wakefield is prepared to go into conference with you, in order to make an adjustment of the claim made by you, as Protector of the Aborigines, on behalf of the natives resident in the Pah Te Aro. In so doing, Colonel Wakefield will not be understood as admitting the invalidity of his purchase, which he believes that he effected in good faith and as completely as was practicable in the rude state of the country and its inhabitants.

Wakefield realised that some chiefs might have been absent from the sale, and had learned of the ancient feud between 'two subdivisions of the pa', one accusing the other of having defrauded them. Some Maori therefore might complain of not having been compensated for the sale of their lands. Evans added:

> Without adverting to the great value of the native reserves in that quarter of town, or to the numerous payments that have subsequently been made by Colonel Wakefield and individual settlers, in order to satisfy the natives upon the surrender of various parcels of land, I would remind you that the natives of Te Aro, as we learn from official papers, have actually made a cession of the whole of their lands to the Crown, as represented by the Colonial Secretary, and that on principle, and in terms of the arrangement between Her Majesty's Government and the Company, we are entitled to consider them as *demesne* lands of the Crown [land owned and occupied by the Crown].
>
> Nevertheless, in the spirit which has activated the New Zealand Company throughout in its proceedings with the natives, I have recommended Colonel Wakefield to adopt the suggestion that has been made by the Commissioner with a view to a just and amicable arrangement, and have to request an early appointment for that purpose.[40]

Clarke showed Spain Evans's letter, and an exasperated Spain wrote to Wakefield complaining that Evans had 'gone into matter [*sic*] with which [Clarke] the Protector has nothing whatever to do, and which is calculated to retard rather than assist us in carrying out the object we have in view, and with respect to his last observation as to the land of the natives of Te Aro having become *demesne* lands of the Crown, I clearly explained to Dr. Evans yesterday morning that such was not the case'.[41]

Wakefield replied that he could not accept any solution that excluded land already set aside for the settlers or public use and sanctioned by the government, and asked for a proposal that included 'all claims for the Port Nicholson District' on unequivocal terms, leaving 'no question as to the surrender of the pahs and cultivations required for the settlement so soon as the Natives can be reasonably expected to leave them'. Clarke replied, quite correctly, that under no circumstances would he sanction the Maori pa and cultivations being ceded to the Company 'without [Maori] consent'.[42] He assessed the value of all the Maori land within the limits described in the Company's Port Nicholson deed at £1,050 and later increased it to £1,500.

Wakefield was 'shocked' at the amount, saying Maori had considerably exceeded the compensation offered. The Company had allowed Wakefield £500 and a thousand acres of its land to settle land disputes.[43] He wrote again to Clarke on 1 March, noting the latter's observation that the Maori demand for their land was 'exorbitant'. He advised that there should be some 'permanent provision' for Maori as any goods or money would be 'speedily squandered'. At the same time he was 'prepared to make that gesture'. The value of land had risen with colonisation, the various pa were disease ridden, Maori housing was inadequate, and their high rate of mortality coupled with the danger of fire meant pa should be abandoned and their inhabitants moved to reserves chosen for them. The threat of fire and disease was very real but the excuse seemed all too convenient. Clarke argued that Wakefield's choices for the reserves were inferior and Maori were unlikely to accept them as alternatives, but Wakefield merely protested that some of the land was first choice.[44]

At about this time the bill for court costs of £55 15s was sent to Messrs Evans and Chetham and paid under protest. 'Wakefield looks very bitterly at me', wrote Clarke to his father, but that was not all. Spain and Clarke were quarrelling, Spain calling Clarke obstinate, accusing him of having little interaction with Maori and complaining that it was difficult to get him to meet with them.[45] The Maori chiefs had little confidence in Clarke, whom they regarded as a mere child and incapable of advising them. And the settlers had believed for some time that Clarke was deliberately stirring the Maori into a mood of fear and bitterness against them. Brewer had written to Chapman a year earlier:

> [Mr. Clarke] is a man from education and previous pursuit wholly incapable of filling that office. He receives a salary which . . . amount[s] to a sum . . . exceeding by far that of the judge – he is a mischievous man very indifferently acquainted with the language of the natives and acting with the greatest animosity to the interests of the company and its settlers by inviting the natives to resist the settlers from settling on their lands on the plea that their lands were not fairly purchased from them – to which the Governor lends his hearty cooperation.[46]

And in late 1843 Dr Isaac Featherston was telling his brother the same story:

> Mr. Clarke junior is a most terribly mischievous boy for his age. He has done more mischief, by his evil counsels to the natives than years can remedy . . . so great is the mischief done by these protectors that I utterly despair of order being established amongst the natives without considerable bloodshed; and on their heads will, in a great measure rest the heavy responsibility of having excited such feelings between the two races . . .[47]

Over a year later, Wakefield told the directors he had inferred from Spain's letters that he had only to compensate Maori who had not been paid in 1839, rather than make a fresh purchase. He explained his dilemma to Evans and with his help tried to persuade Clarke to make a lesser estimate of the native claims. He failed.[48] In all these negotiations Evans could only follow his client's instructions, but his private views are unknown.

After Wakefield's flurry of correspondence with Clarke and Spain, he waited. He had not heard from the directors since November the previous year and was convinced it was best to be patient. Spain had reopened his Land Court on 24 May in Wellington, and the land claims dispute between Wakefield and Clarke remained unresolved. The rift between them widened when Evans wrote to Clarke on Wakefield's behalf asking for a postponement of correspondence until Wakefield received his advice from London.

Revans found another explanation for Wakefield's reluctance and the eventual standoff. When he saw Spain at the home of a mutual friend, Revans was told that when Wakefield met with Shortland in October 1842, he had withdrawn his demand that land be given to settlers in blocks without reserving for Maori their potato grounds and pa. In fact, Wakefield had capitulated to the government in Auckland. He would have excused himself by blaming his legal advisors, said Revans, but, 'As the leader gets the merits of success, so he must take the censure of failure, whether he was in either case, or in both cases governed by the opinion of another or others.'[49] Wakefield had not told the settlers about the concession, but the 'legal advice' given him was sound. Wakefield continued to stall as he waited for the directors' instructions. He failed to attend Spain's court in Whanganui, although Spain waited for him for three weeks. Jerningham eventually arrived with his uncle's apologies and an empty promise to supply witnesses. Days went by. Spain told Revans that if Wakefield had kept his appointment, the settlers might have been given their land after Wakefield had paid 'a moderate sum'. Instead, local Maori were abusive when their compensation failed to materialise, eroding the goodwill between them and the Europeans, and their faith in Spain's court.[50] Whatever his part in this episode, Evans was anxious to solve the land dilemma for personal reasons and must have been beside himself with frustration.

For land was indeed becoming valuable. The sections along the waterfront from Pipitea Point to the south-east end of Lambton Harbour were most desirable. Captain Smith and Revans ran a large cattle station near the coast between Owhiro and Karori, and sent butter and cheese regularly to the market. Revans had imported between seven and eight hundred sheep from Sydney, only seven having died in transit. The flax research was continuing and Maori were getting 15 shillings a ton. Provisions were cheaper.[51] A mini boom had been created by the settlers' capital and the employment provided by surveying, the timber industries and speculative enterprises. Merchants were slowly building their fortunes, but in England the Company was in dire straits.

When Henry Petre returned from England with his seventeen-year-old bride, Mary Ann Eleanor Walmesley (Eleanor), he was amazed at the colony's progress, and the visibility of many expensive houses, as well as merchandise and provisions.[52] He set to work on his new house 'Herongate' in the Hutt with the help of his friends William Vavasour and Dr Fitzgerald. Evans and his wife visited. The men had a great time chasing Harriet Evans's dogs while she offered assistance and advice to the young bride. Eleanor Petre soon picked up the habit of riding daily into Wellington to call on Harriet and other friends.[53]

The legislative infrastructure of the colony was a focus of concern, especially as it affected both security and landholdings. Evans was voted onto a committee of thirteen men to draw up a memorial to the government addressing the problems of delay and costs in the running of the existing County Court in Wellington. They proposed the establishment of a separate Court of Requests for the recovery of debts under £20, with cases to be tried before a commissioner and two assessors.[54] This would free up the County Court to tackle its business more efficiently and to strengthen the arm of the law.

However, some of the local legal provisions were controversial. When William Fox, a barrister of the Inner Temple and Oxford graduate in classics, arrived in the colony with his wife, he and Evans soon became friends. On 1 April, on his first appearance before Martin's court in Mulgrave Street, the thirty-year-old barrister was asked to make a 'declaration'. The 'declaration' read, 'I have not at any time before or since my leaving England done any act whereby I should be precluded from practising as such Barrister at Law.' Although Evans and others advised him to make the declaration under protest, Fox refused to co-operate, 'on the ground that it was derogatory to the character of the English Bar to suppose such a declaration necessary'. Because of his refusal, Fox was temporarily denied the right to practise.

Fifty-nine men, including Evans, drew up a protest supporting his stand.[55] Martin told Wakefield he would remove the regulation 'only when the authorities at Home shall tell me that I have acted erroneously'.[56] Battles raged about the question in the press.

The press was an important instrument of argument and opinion in Wellington. At about the same time that Fox's stand was being debated, Revans relaxed his hold on the *Gazette* to devote more time to his business interests and to launch the *Wellington Almanac*. The *Gazette*, however, gained strength, with one historian remarking that 'The *New Zealand Gazette* was not at all a pretentious production in any sense of the word. But when Dr Evans and the three Fs of Wellington – Fox, Featherston and Fitzherbert – took it up, it became quite a shining light, both in a literary and political sense.'[57] (The contribution by Fox and Evans would have been relatively short, as Fox left for Nelson in November, and Evans a little over a year later.) The *Gazette* had been balanced by Hanson's *Colonist* until the latter's demise a little later, its last issue appearing on 1 August.

The *Colonist* was damning about the Company's role in and commitment to the colony. It had spent £15,000 of its £100,000 on the purchase and outfitting of the *Tory* and *Cuba* in July 1839, and it was only after receiving news of the 'acquisition of Port Nicholson' that it had expended the 'major part of the purchase money'. The Company had 'never actually incurred [any risk] except with regard to a portion', and subsequently it had donated only £2,000 for public works. In contrast, the settlers had 'risked everything'. The paper concluded that the Company could have 'no reasonable claims to compensation from the Government arising out of the Port Nicholson Settlement beyond, or in opposition to the settlers'.[58]

When Mayor George Hunter gave his first dinner at Barrett's on 24 April to the aldermen and officers of the corporation and the bench of magistrates, Evans promised that the Company was determined to build a road up the Hutt Valley that would extend over the hills to the Wairarapa and open up 'millions of acres of fertile land'. Of course this went down exceedingly well.[59] And less than a month later Evans was at his most charming at the Corporation Dinner held by Hunter in honour of Commodore M. Berard and officers of the French man-o-war stationed off Banks Peninsula. France was very popular amongst educated Englishmen, and Evans could be relied on to cite appropriately flattering references. The *Gazette* noted:

> . . . we never heard him more happy in the delivery of his sentiments than he was on this occasion . . . . he compressed into the shortest possible period a splendid reference to the grand principles of civil and religious liberty . . . . [R.T. Edmonds, Trinity College, Cambridge] a very intelligent writer on practical, moral and political economy,

> [had said that] in social pleasures of all kind, the experience of the French nation is vastly superior to that of the English nation. The opinions of France, he observes, regarding happiness, are more true than the same kind of opinions current in England, and the French nation are consequently happier than the English nation.[60]

In June 1843 Wakefield finally heard from the Company. Spain's Land Court was illegal. He could now complain 'formally and publicly against the whole of Spain's proceedings' and 'abstain from taking any part' in them.[61] Wakefield replied that he had 'been advised by Dr. Evans not to continue with arbitration until the result of negotiations in England between the Directors of the New Zealand Company with the Colonial Minister on the subject of titles to land' had arrived. Besides, he 'had his own convictions of the duties of an agent' and would not 'be hurried into any measures which may not be in accordance with the view taken of the subject by the Directors'.[62]

But then there came a tragedy of such far-reaching proportions that the settlers' concerns about land ownership were forgotten.

CHAPTER FOURTEEN.
WAIRAU

Of contumelious, beastly, madbrain'd war.

William Shakespeare, *Timon of Athens*, V, line 174

Early on the morning of Sunday, 18 June, Evans was summoned urgently to attend a meeting of magistrates at Barrett's. The *Victoria* had arrived in port at midnight carrying several men, some of whom were wounded. At Barrett's, a very frightened Nelson surveyor, Frederick Tuckett, told them of dreadful conflict between Maori and Pakeha at Wairau in the Nelson area.

A week earlier, after Te Rauparaha had burnt a raupo hut that surveyors had built on land they were marking out for settlers in Cloudy Bay, magistrate Henry Thompson, a petulant, quick-tempered man, had gathered a group of special constables together to arrest Te Rauparaha on a charge of arson.[1] Tuckett had gone with Thompson, Captains Wakefield and England, and forty-five other settlers – thirty-three of whom were armed with muskets but had never handled a firearm – on what was to have been a peaceful mission.[2]

They found Te Rauparaha with about eighty men and some women and children on the right bank of a deep rivulet in the Wairau River, thirty feet across from where they were positioned. While the Europeans waited on the left bank, Maori bridged the water with a canoe to enable Thompson, his interpreter and some of his men to cross and negotiate with them.[3] But when informed he was being arrested, Te Rauparaha insisted on waiting for Spain's decision regarding the Wairau as he had promised. The land in contention was his, he said, and the hut he had burnt was his own property, although he offered to make compensation for it. 'Thompson inquired peremptorily whether he would go or not, to which he replied he would not.' He refused to be handcuffed, marched to the *Victoria* and 'tied up like a slave for nothing'. Thompson ordered his men to fix bayonets. A few moments of indecision followed as the men were surprised at the order. A tense confrontation followed,

Rangihaeata came forward and gestured aggressively, while Tuckett and Captain Wakefield suggested they discuss the issue openly with the Maori who were present. Wakefield asked Puaha, a local chief who was a nephew of Te Rauparaha, for the use of his canoe to cross the stream. Puaha helped him place the canoe across, but, perhaps while clambering aboard, one of Thompson's civilians discharged his musket accidentally.[4] Maori crossed the stream in pursuit, and the fire and counter-fire that ensued was chaotic. Some Europeans stayed to fight while others retreated in confusion. A white flag (a handkerchief) was held out towards the Maori, 'but someone said, "they won't understand it"'.

The men who took flight ran in panic along the ridge, around the sides of the hill, and out of earshot of the conflicting orders being screamed by Thompson – now hysterical – and Captain Wakefield, who urged them all to gather on the top of the hill, lie down and surrender – 'to stop the useless sacrifice of life'. Those too far away to hear his orders continued firing. Tuckett scrambled with others over the hill to White's Bay and escaped to the brig.

After listening to Tuckett's account, the Wellington magistrates decided that a group comprising Police Magistrate McDonough, Colonel Wakefield, Mein Smith, St Hill, Charles Clifford and Spain should go to Cloudy Bay with police volunteers.[5] Soon afterward Evans, Edward Meurant (Spain's interpreter), Clarke and Hanson were added to the deputation.

Once the men returned to their families, the news spread rapidly and Wellington was put on alert. The town was unguarded and all the troops were stationed in Auckland, leaving 10,000 settlers in the Cook's Straits region defenceless against Maori.[6] At a crowded meeting the next morning, a petition to Governor Gipps was drawn up, begging for military assistance. Nearly seventy men volunteered to go to Wairau, but adverse weather caused the mission to be abandoned on Tuesday morning. Only McDonough, Spain, Clarke, St Hill and Wakefield were to go south while the others were to stay to control the residents, but the frightened settlers begged McDonough to remain behind as well. Evans replaced him and the next morning at ten they sailed south, reaching Cloudy Bay later that day. They were met by the missionary Samuel Ironside who told them of the nineteen men he had buried, including Captains Wakefield and Richaard England.[7]

Some of the survivors were interviewed on board, and their evidence recorded. Parau told of the desire of local Maori to avoid a fight at all costs; how the local chief Puaha had begged Brooke the interpreter, 'Don't Johnny, we don't want to fight!'; how 'Puaha's wife had pleaded with Rangihaeata to save some of the [European] chiefs. But Rangihaeata killed them all.' Rangihaeata had tried to speak with Captain Wakefield, but Wakefield did not understand him. When the brig arrived at Wairau, Te Rauparaha had thought it was Spain. During the heated exchange Rangihaeata had said: 'Do I burn your tents, have I stolen a single nail, have I gone to England or to Port Jackson to take away your land from you?'[8]

James Grant told how G. R. Richardson called out, 'For God's sake, Thompson, mind what you're about!'; how the wounded Thompson cried, 'For God's sake, come back men! The Maoris are upon us!' Grant described the temporary stand and retreat, the sounds of firing, the groans of the dying. After Captain Wakefield had ordered his men to surrender, thirteen had turned back. He waved a white handkerchief, and while the men surrendered their arms, Rangihaeata, whose wife Te Ronga had been killed in the conflict, said to Te Rauparaha, 'Don't forget your daughter.' 'Te Rauparaha sat still and consented, and Rangihaeata, with his own hand, put to death the whole of the prisoners', splitting their skulls 'with great ferocity'.[9] Four Maori had died and four Europeans were still missing.[10]

The magistrates went on to Wairau, found and 'buried another body or two', recorded Clarke,[11] and returned to Wellington on the evening of 27 June. Evans had lost an old friend who had struggled with him since the formation of the New Zealand Association six years earlier, but was appalled at the lack of wisdom on Thompson's part. Two days later he read aloud the witnesses' depositions of evidence at the magistrates' meeting at McDonough's house attended by Attorney General Swainson, after which he proposed that:

> Mr. Spain, the Commissioner of Land Claims, be requested to go in his capacity as one of the magistrates to communicate to the native chiefs and tribes in Cook's Straits their determination, which is not to make or to sanction any attempt to take vengeance for the death of the white men at Wairau, but to leave the whole matter to the decision of the Queen's Government, who will inquire into it and decide according to law.

His motion was immediately approved and it was unanimously agreed that he travel to Auckland and tell Shortland of the 'catastrophe at Wairau'.[12]

Acting on Evans's advice, Spain and Bishop Hadfield went to Otaki to assure the two chiefs that no action would be taken. Te Rauparaha had returned to Waikanae, upset. He had attended Spain's court in Porirua daily, he said, 'degrading himself and answering every question'. After agreeing to wait for his claims to Wairau to be investigated, he had gone back to find people had taken possession of his land, cutting roads and erecting huts. While he awaited 'impartial justice', the armed party of Europeans had arrived. He had resisted fighting until – he said – the white men killed or wounded seven of his group; before that not a shot was fired in their own defence.

Henry Petre and Clifford were alarmed at the prospect of Evans going unaccompanied, and suggested to Wakefield that he go with Evans 'to keep the old Doctor in order'; but there was no time to deliberate and Wakefield was always loath to leave Wellington. Before sailing on the government brig the following day, Evans asked one of the Pipitea chiefs to look after Harriet in his absence. Eleanor Petre called on her to find her 'left in [the] charge of an old Maori who has promised to carry her off in his care in a vessel on the harbour if the town is attacked'.[13]

More than one person shared Petre's disquiet about Evans's journey. Clarke misjudged Evans's intentions when he warned his father:

> A secret – Evans is going up – be careful of him it was the maddest act I ever heard of – sending him to Auckland to represent impartially the case to the Government. He has been acting as a magistrate but in my opinion has conducted the case with great partiality – I am afraid lest he should give such a coloured story as to induce Governor Shortland to take some rash step.[14]

Another government sympathiser and visitor to Wellington was also sceptical:

> One of our great guns here has been selected to represent this affair to the Government . . . . he is one of the original Company, or *Forty Thieves* as they are called, completely in the Company's interest, though he may not appear so, and is deeply interested in land here; so that he will, no doubt, throw the whole blame on the natives, and justify the Company's Agent's proceedings as far as he can, no doubt blink the question, being owner of land not purchased and throw the *onus* on the Government to support the farce of enforcing a warrant against a Maori, who does not understand what it means . . .[15]

The *Gazette* gloomily reminded its readers of Earp and Hanson's defection to the government's side, wondering if Evans too would be tempted to 'take the pledge' and join the government whilst in Auckland.[16]

As Evans sailed north, Major Baker gave the newly formed Cavalry Corps their first military drill. 'Henry bought an immense long sword', wrote Eleanor Petre proudly. She rode the twelve miles every day into Wellington, excited by the displays at Thorndon and Te Aro. 'I wish we could have some fighting', she wrote:

> They looked today such a brave lot with their bayonets glistening in the sun – with the English colours carried in their centre. When [the Maori] saw this general muster of about eight hundred men, [they] retired to some little distance and sitting down watched the English with very grave faces. We will give the rebels a warm reception if they will only attack the town.

Evans was more realistic in assessing their situation while travelling north. Wakefield's scheme for their colony seemed doomed, as the three vital elements for its success were absent: land, labour and capital. Few land sales had brought little income, so that emigration from Britain had virtually ceased. Without the labour so urgently needed, it was most unlikely capital would be invested in the country. In that year alone, colonial expenditure was £39,000, but the income only £22,000 – land sales accounting for only £1,613.[17] Business and agriculture were at a standstill. Their plans for settlement had been frustrated by the communication lag of nine months if they were to act only on instructions from the Company in England. Wakefield still heavily relied on London, and his dilatoriness added to their problems. The hostility of government and missionaries, the careless 'purchase' of Port Nicholson and the unexpected reluctance of Maori to part with their land had exacerbated the situation.

The Wellington settlers depended on Evans's presentation of the tragedy and on Shortland's decision.[18] Evans wanted 'not less than two or three garrisons, together with two or three small armed vessels' for the town. He hoped that in Auckland he might be able to control his emotions, but the letter he penned to his parents on board the *Victoria* reflected his fear. Over three foolscap pages in close, neat script, he poured out his heart to them. As a consequence of the tragedy, he said, the affairs of the colony were being brought to a '*crisis*'. He believed the fault lay with the government, which now would 'be compelled to do what they ought to have done three years ago – establish a military force in the country [to] keep the [Maori] in subjection to the law'. The whole affair, he stated,

> . . . has arisen out of the land question and the state of feeling in [Maori] brought about by the intrigues of the local government, the Church Missionaries, the protectors of aborigines, the land sharks and the whalers, all of whom are combined in a deadly conspiracy against the New Zealand Company, and the purchasers of land under it.

'Captain Hobson and his retainers and adherents have been a set of desperate gamblers in the land', he alleged, believing that as soon as they found they had been forestalled by Wakefield's purchase of Port Nicholson they had 'set up' in Auckland 'as a rival speculation'. Then they had begun 'destroying the property and breaking the hearts of the settlers, in order to attract all the people and capital to Auckland'.[19] Evans accused the 'philanthropists'[20] of having 'infused' Maori with 'ideas beyond their dreams'.

The complexities of the Maori view of their land – that over many generations, members of different tribes could have equally valid claims to the same piece of land – appeared vague and possibly spurious to the colonists.[21] To British eyes, land that was unused or undeveloped was waste land to be bought for 'a sufficient price' and developed. The idea of hunting and fishing grounds, of land lost by tribal war but still claimed by the same tribe, seemed incomprehensible. If land was not in use, the Crown should buy it and sell it on, they believed. The remainder – the living areas, the burial grounds and the gardens – should be retained by Maori. Evans was bitter and angry that the 'principle' had been 'laid down' –

> . . . that all New Zealand (about ninety millions of acres) belonged to some or other of 100,000 savages who live in little nooks and crevices on the sea coast, and that civilized men could not 'replenish the walk or subdue it' without their consent . . . . [The Maori] notion of property was a simple and just one, that they had a right to all that they could cultivate or improve, – but this did not suit the humanity mongers, and out of their theories have sprung the terrible disaster we are brooding over and all the possible consequences.

He believed that with the government's refusal or inability to purchase all the unoccupied waste land in the colony, Maori had 'been played upon as instruments in the hands of our enemies'. He visualised the worst scenario – the country being deserted by the 'quiet people', leaving the colony in the hands of a 'small band of heroic and fearless desperadoes who will soon acquire a military skill which will not leave one native soul alive'. The idea of the extermination of Maori filled Evans with horror. His reference to 'native souls' in a private letter to his parents belies the concept advanced by some modern historians that the Company's representatives in Wellington desired such an outcome, if not actively plotted it.[22]

He condemned the 'Nelson people' – Thompson and other government employees – for the tragedy at Wairau, calling it 'a species of infatuation [extreme folly] for the group to attempt to take the two most warlike chiefs in New Zealand into custody like common felons'.

He excused Captain Wakefield's lack of understanding of Maori customs and language, as he had been in the country for only a short time. At the same time, he was shocked at Rangihaeata and Te Rauraparaha for 'murdering their prisoners in cold blood', believing it to be unjustifiable. In Wellington, he said, 180 riflemen were being mustered daily with 500 able-bodied voluntary infantry.

His frustration and irritation with the judgemental Englishmen at home spilled over in a heartfelt cry:

> Ah my dear friends, at home by the fireside, it is easy for you to dream justice and humanity, and to go to Exeter Hall, and listen to romantic tracts, and condemn your unhappy countrymen, who have to bear the brunt of it in real life; it is a very different matter to go to bed at night with the knowledge that before morning, in the dead of night, five hundred armed savages may surround your home, set fire to it, and tomahawk you as you rush from your slumber. You may tell the philanthropists that if the Government leave us unprotected, and these men become thoroughly disciplined, we will not become so for nothing. If they are provoked, I am sure they will fight; and when they begin, who shall say where they will end?[23]

He arrived in Auckland on 7 July, met the next day with Shortland, outlined the facts to him and gave him McDonough's despatch, together with the depositions of evidence. But he had little chance of influencing Shortland, who had already been briefed by Swainson. Swainson had no sympathy for the European victims, calling their actions illegal and unjustifiable according to the government's obligations under the Treaty of Waitangi. George Clarke senior had also heeded his son's warning to avert any weakening of Shortland's resolve, or to harbour any sympathy for the Europeans involved in the conflict. One historian wrote of the two deputations from Wellington and Nelson:

> There was an unhappy want of accuracy in the statements made by [them], and a manifest concern for the reputation of the dead at any sacrifice of justice to the living of either race. These careless

> assertions were replied to with a dignity, taste and ability which leave no doubt that the replies were dictated by abler heads than that of Shortland, probably by . . . Swainson and Chief Justice William Martin . . .[24]

Evans asked for troops to protect the southern settlements, pointing out that since the tragedy, Maori in the Hutt and Porirua were becoming restless. The lack of any retaliation for Wairau had brought about a great deal of aggressive talk, and Maori were making menacing speeches and discharging their muskets without restriction.[25]

After reading the accounts in the Auckland papers he was horrified at the near flippant dismissal of the tragedy.[26] The 'soldiers' (most of whom were inexperienced, and had been pressed into service by Thompson) were ridiculed as inept cowards who had sullied the glorious reputation of British military prowess. Evans's attempt to convey the Wellington settlers' indignation to Shortland, believed one historian, could be summed up in one phrase: 'When Clarke expressed in Maori [Shortland's] horror at the massacre of the prisoners at Wairau, Dr. Evans retorted by expressing his "horror at the infatuation of the authors" of the papers emanating from the Government.'[27] This was a clear reference to Swainson's editorship of the *Auckland Chronicle*, which was effectively as much the government's paper as the *Gazette* was the Company's. In one stroke Evans had killed any chance of the government offering him the magistracy at Nelson, or indeed any post anywhere.

Like Evans, Shortland deplored the misguided conduct of Thompson. Of Captain Wakefield he had only praise, describing him as a man of 'urbanity, good feeling and good sense, loved and respected by all', and excusing his part in the tragedy by his ignorance of 'the state of land question' and of the 'native character'.[28] But it was Shortland who had extended Thompson's powers by appointing him County Judge and Protector of Aborigines. Two and a half thousand of the three thousand Nelson settlers had petitioned Spain for Thompson's removal, believing he was insane, 'a lunatic to all intents and purposes'.[29] And Evans was not alone in saying the government and missionaries had incited Maori by convincing them the Company settlers were out to steal their land. Featherston said as much in private letters, and testifying before the Committee on New Zealand, George Earp and Coutts Crawford swore to the good relationship between Maori and settler before government hostility forced a wedge between the two.[30]

Just before he left Auckland, Evans was alleged by the *Chronicle* to have said the affairs of the Company's settlements 'had come to a crisis before the late unfortunate collision at Cloudy Bay'. Evans had also represented the settlers as being 'disgusted at having been entrapped into the purchase of what had not been alienated by the Natives', and had confided while praising Auckland's 'open district' that he and others were seriously considering abandoning Wellington as a settlement.

Evans was 'astonished' at the blatant libel, believing it to be a deliberate attempt to damage him 'in the estimation of [his] fellow settlers'. He called on Swainson, demanding to know the author and threatening to bring an action for damages against the '*real* editor and proprietor of the Government organ'. Swainson demurred, but 'after much consideration' accepted responsibility, promising to 'insert any contradiction'. Evans wrote a vigorous refutation before boarding the brig to return to Wellington on 15 July, calling the accusation a 'deliberate misrepresentation'. He had merely said the settlers were 'disgusted at the delay in settling the land claims, and that . . . they considered the government more to blame than the Company as having created the difficulty, by means of its interference with the Natives. I have never doubted of the ultimate prosperity of the settlement of Port Nicholson; and I have said that if I left it, one object would be to drag our local Government to the Bar of public opinion, in the Mother country.'

He also protested on his own and the settlers' behalf at what he derisively referred to as the *Government Gazette*'s (actually the *Chronicle*'s) reports of the events at Wairau: 'Their tendency, [being] to bring on a war of extermination between the European and the Native races.'[31]

Samuel McD. Martin, former editor of the *New Zealand Herald* and *Auckland Gazette*, confirmed the consistency of Evans's attitude when he wrote to a friend:

> Dr. Evans . . . has been here on a visit to Mr. Shortland. It is said that he made supplication for some of the vacant offices at Nelson, and that his application was not entertained: at all events, he is very wroth with the Government of which he speaks in no measured terms.[32]

The *Southern Cross* condemned the conduct of the editor of the *Chronicle* in his 'insidious attempt to injure' Evans, saying it was only natural that Evans had complimented his hosts on Auckland after 'enjoying the splendid prospect from Mount Eden':

> But that he would so far lose sight of his own interests as to abuse Port Nicholson and the New Zealand Company, we would not believe, even if the *Leader of the New Zealand Bar* were to assert it . . . . May not they and Dr. Evans at least ask why a member of the Legislative and Executive Councils should have been allowed to be the editor and part proprietor of an Auckland newspaper, and why nearly all the members of this government have combined to suppress public opinion by purchasing the materials of the only free press in the colony at the time, and starting with the same a newspaper of their own? We doubt not Dr. Evans will bring several things to light before he has done with this affair.[33]

The local government's unpopularity was at an all-time high. The Land Commission had not granted one title in the southern settlements, yet six hundred claims had been 'disposed of in Auckland, with a population of only 4,000 people'.[34]

Evans may have missed out on the Nelson appointment – but he got his troops.

The brig arrived in Wellington on 24 July with a garrison of 53 soldiers of the 96th Regiment. The new Police Magistrate for Nelson, Major Matthew Richmond, immediately ordered Major Durie to dissolve the volunteer corps and posted a notice, warning the settlers of the illegality of their military exercises.[35]

The settlers in Wellington and Nelson convinced themselves there was one 'law against the white and none against the Maori' – a view hardly conducive to good relations between the two races.[36] 'No longer does each house maintain and succour its native dependent', wrote Wakefield gloomily to the directors. He believed the blame for the conflict at Wairau could be laid at the door of Pakeha men married to women in Te Rauparaha's tribe who were eager to make a land claim in the Cloudy Bay area in anticipation of Spain's land hearings there.[37] The part the local government had taken in Wairau was 'pusillanimous and treacherous'.[38]

In early August, the magistrates had met to draw up resolutions to present to Major Richmond, protesting at his 'tyrannical proceedings' in disbanding their military drills. Evans was selected to present the chief resolution, but he 'allowed himself to be won over by [Richmond's] smoothing manner, and kept the resolution in his pocket', wrote Jerningham in disgust.[39] Clearly, Evans was having second thoughts.

By this time, word had spread of Wakefield's dilatoriness in the land claims saga, and a deputation met him, urging him to proceed with land settlement on the terms he had agreed at Auckland in November 1842. Spain said he was happy to reopen his court if there were no further delays. Wakefield assured them he would co-operate, but they were alarmed to hear the next day that Spain was about to leave for Auckland, Wakefield having informed him that 'nothing short of a "final and conclusive settlement of all claims of the natives resident within the limits described in the New Zealand Company's Port Nicholson Deed"' would satisfy them.

Spain refused to negotiate any further. The men again visited Wakefield, who announced he would not proceed 'because he did not consider it would be final and satisfactory'. A petition was then hastily drawn up at an urgent public meeting urging the Auckland government to settle the land question, and Spain agreed to deliver it.

At about the same time Wakefield received another Company directive contradicting the first: Spain's Commission was no longer considered illegal. They ordered Wakefield now to co-operate with Spain. All land sales were to be suspended, as the government in England had refused to give the Company legal rights to its land until Spain's Commission had released its findings. Wakefield's salary was halved to £500 and all the surveyors were sacked. Many were made nearly destitute.[40] Wakefield had never been popular with the surveyors, an aggrieved Frederick Carrington having told him years earlier that his actions were 'unparalleled in any colony'.[41] He was also accused of deliberate delay and of 'favoritism'.[42]

Everyone was bitter, the Company was nearing crisis point and the rumour that Clarke had told Maori to eject colonists off the land flew around the settlement. Residents had armed themselves as early as May, and their relationship with Maori was becoming increasingly 'rancorous', Clarke told his father. The Company's headlong rush into the country was bearing a bitter fruit. Evans's dream had turned to nightmare.[43]

After Wairau, a significant number of Whanganui Maori had moved to the Hutt. They cleared hundreds of acres and provided a large and cheap supply of food to the 'labouring classes' in Wellington.[44] It was rumoured that Te Rauparaha and Rangihaeata were forming a pa at the entrance to Porirua harbour with a force of two hundred men. They were 'mustered within fifteen miles of us at Porirua – the man-o-war in the harbour is no deterrent', fumed Wakefield.[45]

Wakefield could not afford to lose his counsel Evans, and appointed William Fox as the Company's resident agent for Nelson. Although it would take another year before Evans resolved his struggling loyalties, he was irrevocably yoked to the Company. But away from that role, in conversing with the settlers, in private conversation with Hanson and others, and in considering his own career, Evans expressed conflicting views – thus contributing to his reputation for inconsistency. Many of his peers were wary of his motives and Wakefield was no fool. He kept his cards close to his chest and in his confidential correspondence with the Company he could pin the blame for any wrong move on his advisor.

In London the Court of Directors now consisted mostly of moneyed merchants who barely knew Evans – some not at all. Ward wrote to Wakefield asking Evans to pay £19 11s for the printing of a hundred statements and six hundred pamphlets in 1837. The bill was addressed to Gibbon Wakefield, whom the directors 'would not allow' 'to suffer', because Evans had undertaken to satisfy all outstanding claims of the Association, in return for which he had received 'an original £500 share'.[46]

Evans's reply was brief. He declined to pay, reminding them of his waiver of the Company's additional debt to him of £300. The directors were 'under a misapprehension as to the nature of the arrangements' under which Evans was paid 'the £500 on the occasion referred to'. He continued, 'and I must decline the amount now claimed. I could go into the subject at great length and with much earnestness, but I shall not do so, as I hope to have an opportunity of personally communicating with the Directors on much graver matters, when this also may be thought worthy of some attention.'[47]

At the public meeting on 14 October to raise funds for a memorial to the victims of Wairau, Evans told the men who attended that the Auckland settlers did not harbour ill-will towards them. They differed –

> . . . on some fundamental principles relating to the disposal of waste lands and the mode of acquiring territory from the [Maori] by the Crown, and on other matters; but on [the subject of the Wairau affair], they took enlarged views, and freely confessed they saw nothing of whether the Queen's Government was to be established in these islands *de facto* and *de jure* or not.[48]

He reminded them that the only legal action of the police magistrate at Wairau was in serving a Queen's warrant on the chiefs. But he alleged that the government's policy on the native question was crooked. 'Any man who held the Queen's commission, and who dared to raise a doubt on whether the Queen's authority extended over every Maori' in New Zealand, 'when so many acts of the Crown and Legislature had affirmed the fact, and so many thousands of her Majesty's subjects had ventured their lives and fortunes upon the assurance of it', was 'disloyal and traitorous'. Leading members of the government were 'most deadly enemies of the prerogative' whilst they 'posed under the veil of philanthropy because it suited their private views in their own land speculations'.[49]

He also cautioned them not to condemn all Maori. The memory of the fallen men at Wairau 'must be vindicated, the majesty of the Law must be asserted', he said. If those responsible were brought to justice, he predicted that other Maori would be 'ready to submit, and to become as peaceful and as industrious as we had ever contemplated in our most sanguine moments'. He called for the co-operation of the Company and its colonists, a motion that was carried unanimously.[50]

Later, Evans was dismayed to hear of FitzRoy's actions after leaving Wellington in February with Richmond and Clarke to visit Te Rauparaha and 'several hundred' Maori at Waikanae. Te Rauparaha reiterated that he had kept his bargain with Spain not to move onto the land until his claim at Wairau had been heard, and had believed the Company would do the same.[51] FitzRoy told them:

> The English were wrong for having provoked the conflict by trying to take forcible possession of disputed land, while the case was under debate in the Commissioners Land Court; they were to blame in sending an armed party to arrest the Chiefs on such a pretext as burning down a temporary surveyor's hut; and because at the last moment they had been the first to fire. He, the Governor was deeply grieved, especially at the slaughter of the English prisoners when Ronga [Rangihaeata's wife and Te Rauparaha's daughter] was killed, but looking at all the circumstances, he felt that it would not be just to use the British power merely to avenge the death of those who had fallen.[52]

Although Evans agreed with FitzRoy's judgement on the inept conduct of the affair, he was angry at what he viewed as capitulation on the government's part. He was not alone. Many Maori who expected utu of some sort were even contemptuous of FitzRoy, some calling him 'Pumpkin-Head'. Even the missionary George Clarke noted:

> The [Maori] say they have no occasion to sell their land if they do not like; agree with Rauparaha in almost everything he says; very suspicious, obtrusive, boisterous, thieving, plundering, taking advantage of the white men in dealing; impudent, asking

> for anything thinking you will give it them through fear, trying to frighten you, firing off muskets, . . . laugh at the white people, say that they are cowards, the Queen is but a girl; they are ready to fight the people in Port Nicholson.[53]

Bishop Hadfield believed the government was remiss in not giving a 'sufficient demonstration' of military power after Wairau.[54] And Bishop Selwyn later wrote, 'all good governments have two elements of strength, moral influence and physical force . . . neither of [these] had been present to a sufficient degree up to the time of the trouble with Heke' (1844–45).[55]

Today, the view of the Wairau affair is more measured. As Michael King said in his *History of New Zealand*, the Company's land deal was fraudulent from the start. Colonel Wakefield had 'bought [Nelson] from the widow of a whaler who claimed in turn to have bought the land from Te Rauparaha of Ngati Toa'. The events that followed were tragic, but FitzRoy was right in his verdict that the settlers were more to blame in continuing their land possession despite Spain's pending Land Commission of Inquiry.[56] He had rebuked Te Rauparaha and his nephew for their act of revenge, but it was not enough for the settlers.

But Richardson's desperate cry of alarm, 'For God's sake, Thompson, mind what you are about!', matched by Rangihaeata's cry of grief and fury in finding his wife Te Rongo shot dead, still echo down to this day.

Evans was desperate for income, for he was receiving half what he had earned the previous year. Lawyers' fees had slipped from 16 shillings per hundred feet of print in the July–October quarter of 1842, through the 10 shilling mark in March–April until reaching a low of 8 shillings in May–June 1843.[57] In London, Henry Chapman had been appointed Chief Justice and was expected to arrive soon. Harriet was becoming increasingly anxious and querulous: the best judicial posts had been filled and Evans was a worried man. In late 1843, they were all disappointed to find they were under Crown Colony rule again, their Municipal Corporations Act having been disallowed.[58]

In early November Evans wrote to Colonel Wakefield begging for £100 'on account. I am not aware of the exact amount due to me', he continued, 'but on the score of the peculiar circumstances of the colony, and the very painful situation in which I am placed, and which I have explained to you in conversation, I trust you will oblige me without delay, subject to an account hereafter.' Wakefield paid, entering it on his Bill of Costs for the directors.[59]

On 6 December a public meeting was held at the Exchange to consider the reception for Governor FitzRoy. Evans joined the committee of seventeen men to draw up a petition. There were several grievances and the document he eventually completed was lengthy and detailed. The settlement of the land claims was the most urgent grievance. Maori were being treated inappropriately by the government. They were being 'conciliated and gratified in the childlike and semi-barbarous feelings of the moment', whereas the state should act more as a guardian, providing for them on more permanent and comprehensive principles, which 'could only be fully appreciated in two or three generations'. If their behaviour continued to be treated leniently by government, they might descend to lawless violence. A set of absolute rules drawn up for them might ameliorate the differences between the two races. The fortification of the harbour entrance together with 'a sufficient force' might also ensure the 'ready obedience to the Law' of Maori. FitzRoy might appoint someone – preferably, one of their own – who had 'struggled with them through all the difficulties of their first establishment, and who by his stake in the settlement would do his best in the settlers' interests'. The appointment should be filled by 'a person with a competent knowledge of the law'. Clearly, Evans had a specific candidate in mind.

The Wellington settlers raised a greater proportion of the revenue – some £9,000 annually – most of which was spent at Auckland, while money was desperately needed in Wellington for creating roads, and vital improvements such as a custom-house, a lighthouse and a powder magazine. They could not afford to pay direct taxation because of the non-settlement of the land. Evans suggested dividing the settlement into districts or counties with annually elected officers placed in charge of roading. The dangerous and frustrating delay of the erection of a beacon and lighthouse was due to both police magistrates – Murphy and Major Richmond – having postponed their decisions. The Company was prepared to pay £1,500 and yet the local government only £100.

And so the list went on. The settlers' petition begged FitzRoy not to be 'precipitate', but to apply for an accurate survey of their settlement and its surrounding area to the home government. Not only did they ask him to remedy their problems, but they also suggested he encourage them to develop their resources and extend their trade, establishing 'their prosperity on the firmest basis'.[60]

❧

At about this time, William Charles Cotton (1813–79), Chaplain to Bishop Selwyn, arrived in Wellington for the first time. He was immediately impressed by the 'splendid landlocked harbour' as he approached the town from the bush, and more than a little amused by the settlers busily 'getting up memorials' in preparation for the new governor's imminent visit. He was struck by their 'seriousness' in preparing 'regular proses' and instructing the governor in all his duties: 'There is something very original in the way in which these things are done in the good town of Wellington. Dr. Evans writes the memorial and then seconds the amendment.'

He listened to stories circulating amongst the gentlemen in the community. Evans's pompous manner and sesquipedalian phraseology were ripe for mimicry. Cotton was amused by a story told him by Colonel Edward Godfrey, who had approached Evans at a recent meeting and had said 'in his blandest manner', 'Dr. Evans, there is one of the greatest grievances of Port Nicholson which is not included in the Memorial!'

> Oh Colonel Godfrey, we shall be very pleased to receive any suggestion from a person of your intelligence – I thought we had pretty well exhausted the subject, but anything that you can suggest shall certainly be inserted.
>
> Then put in this plaguey North-West wind, for it is the greatest nuisance in the place!

As Cotton toured the leading settlers' homes, accepting their generous hospitality, the Anglican cleric had a keen eye for their material assets. He approved of Colonel Wakefield (his house was in the very best situation in town), Molesworth, Major Richmond (who had a most beautiful table made of curled totara), and Daniel Riddiford, whose house impressed him as 'a regular squire's house, beautifully situated'. Evans, he noted, was 'a singular character but whether one which it is worth studying except to fill up an idle hour is another question'. But Evans's material prosperity was a bitter disappointment. '*Dirta misera*',[61] Cotton exclaimed, after dining at Golders Hill on 9 December, adding, 'which in this case means, I fancy poverty in disguise'. He was highly entertained by an apologetic speech of Mrs Evans, who told him, 'I do not like to get out our champagne.' He went on: '(I begged she would not). "It is not at all up or good. The [real] Champagne cost an enormous price!"'

He had 'peeped about' the drawing room before dinner, and seen 'it' in the window trying to 'get up'. After drinking 'it' he declared it to be the 'most abominable gooseberry'. He noticed when the maid climbed a chair to choose more refreshments that she revealed 'a large portion of stocking between her foot and down-at-heel shoe'. And the next drink offered, he declared, 'proved to be stale ale'. The hapless doctor rang again and the ritual was repeated. This time Mrs Evans's 'peculiar cherry brandy' was produced. Cotton intervened at this point, rejecting any further offers of the cupboard's contents, and the gentlemen joined the ladies.[62] It was a far cry from the sumptuous entertainment the Evanses had provided just two and a half years earlier.

On 19 December Cotton accompanied Bishop Hadfield, one of the few missionaries revered by both races, to observe the trial of a Maori called E Wahu, the great-nephew of E Puni. The settlers believed E Wahu had murdered an Englishman two years earlier as utu for a quarrel the man had with the Maori, but this time he was accused of stealing women's clothing. Maori believed Pakeha were determined to put E Wahu to death. The jury retired at six o'clock, and brought in a verdict that, Cotton said, the judge 'could not receive'. After an hour the panel returned its final verdict. The trial had lasted ten long hours, and it was now dark. During this time, Cotton noted 'Dr. Evans, who flatters himself that his influence with the Maori is very great, was waiting outside the court on horseback to carry the first news of the verdict to a vast body of natives assembled at Pipitea pah. The old chiefs were sitting close by on the ground. "Just as they do", said Bishop Hadfield, "when they intend mischief."'

The air was charged with tension until the verdict was carried outside:

> 'What is it?' Evans asked.
> 'Guilty'.
> 'Then I'd better wait for the sentence . . .'
> 'Two months. [With hard labour]'
> 'Then I think I'd better not go'.

But of course Evans did go. He returned a little later from the pa to tell Hadfield and Cotton that its residents were in a state of great excitement. Hadfield decided to take Cotton to the pa, but as they entered, 'a great tall fellow rushed up and brandished a tomahawk over [their] heads, pushing [them] back as tho' to prevent [their] entering'.

It was dark but the only light coming from a large fire in the enclosure lit up the crowd squatting all around. On hearing Hadfield's voice raised in greeting, they allowed the pair to enter and the bishop to address them. Clarke and Dr Fitzgerald the Maori doctor also offered to intervene, but they were turned out of the pa.

Evans was then told that a large group of Maori from the north had assembled at Petone and were planning to rescue the prisoner. They had advanced as far as Kaiwharawhara. It took great courage, but unhesitatingly in the dark he rode out to them alone and advised them to retire. They refused and he accompanied them on their journey to the pa. In the morning the three hundred Maori fired off their muskets, which they had kept loaded all night, and peace, for the time, was restored.[63]

Apart from the two missionaries, Evans was the only Pakeha allowed entry to the pa to bring the verdict and offers of intervention on behalf of the prisoner. Whatever their grievances, Pipitea Maori respected Evans, his work on behalf of Maori brought before the court and his offer a year earlier to act for Rangihaeata. In turn, he respected their willingness to co-operate and their forbearance in confusing and difficult times. Cotton may have mocked Evans's special relationship with the Maori of Pipitea pa, but Evans was not called 'nui nui rangatira' for nothing.

Cotton's attitude to Maori is reflected in a letter he wrote from Waimate to a friend at Windsor, on 18 August 1842: 'I must say the Blackies are very civil. I am in no great danger of being eaten, for they are all Christians here . . . an old pagan chief called Teraina, whom I saw on the river, made a meal off some of his enemies the other day.'[64]

CHAPTER FIFTEEN.
FITZROY

A ruler, however despotic, almost always encounters an opposition, and the more despotic he is, the more dangerous the opposition becomes.

William Gisborne, *New Zealand Rulers and Statesmen*, Sampson Low, Marston, Searle & Rivington, London, 1886, p.16

Evans's mana remained relatively intact at Pipitea, but it was a different story with his peers. In the new year he proposed and read the draft of a congratulatory address to welcome Governor FitzRoy. Several men disagreed with its content, the committee was dissolved and another appointed. Evans, Hanson, Revans, Smith and Partridge were all jettisoned, their exclusion mostly reflecting the now prevailing mood of disenchantment of the settlers toward the old faces of the Company. By 8 January the deputation to present the memorial had been chosen 'with care', reported the *Gazette*.[1]

Naval Captain Governor Robert FitzRoy arrived in Wellington on Saturday, 20 January 1844, and two days later received the deputation at Major Richmond's house. At first most of the settlers had immediate confidence in him, admiring his straightforward manner. But they smarted when he told the settlers he believed the affair at Wairau was the fault of the British, that Magistrate Thompson had acted illegally, and that Captain Wakefield and his men who were slaughtered were victims of the 'ferocious passions' of the Maori who were 'still wild with savage fury'.[2]

A few days after FitzRoy's official welcome, Evans was urgently summoned to a meeting at Richmond's house to assist Wakefield as his 'friend'. There he also found FitzRoy, Spain, J. W. Hamilton, Protector Clarke and Thomas Forsaith, Protector and Interpreter. FitzRoy was questioning Wakefield on his views of the land claims. He said they were the same he had always held, but added he had been ordered by the directors to leave the matter entirely to FitzRoy. He believed 'the arrangement between Lord Stanley and the Directors points out the precise plan upon which this question is to be adjusted'.

When FitzRoy made clear that the Spain Commission and the correspondence between the home government and the directors were 'entirely distinct', Wakefield explained that his breaking off of negotiations with Spain's court in Porirua was not a snub. His excuse was that he could not proceed without 'definite instructions' from the Company. FitzRoy accepted his explanation.

After assuring them he wanted 'a fair and open arrangement, which would be satisfactory to all parties', FitzRoy said he believed the main question centred round Maori surrendering their pa and cultivations, a policy Spain refused to support. Wakefield and Evans were surprised at this conclusion and denied it, saying they thought they had been summoned to discuss the amount of compensation the Company should pay. The correspondence between Evans, Clarke and Spain was referred to. Wakefield pointed out that the buying of pa from Maori did not constitute dispossession. Both Clarke and Spain believed Maori would never surrender their pa under any circumstances.

FitzRoy asked Wakefield if he was prepared to make 'a fair compensation' to those entitled to it, without including 'their pahs, their burying places, and their grounds actually in cultivation'. Wakefield hedged, remonstrating for some time and quibbling about the precise meanings of the 'cultivation grounds – were they to be those cultivated after European settlement?' He alleged that Maori were moving onto settlers' lands, then claiming them as cultivations. FitzRoy said that whatever 'ground is in actual use and occupation of the Natives must be considered as theirs. They were not to be dispossessed unless they had encroached on land which carried a valid title proven by the Company.' Wakefield objected again but was silenced when FitzRoy pointed out that anybody who had bought land from the Company 'at home' (meaning England), only to find they could not take possession, could bring action against the Company.

He repeated his question and – probably with prompting from Evans – Wakefield capitulated, agreeing to provide compensation immediately. The meaning of the word 'pa' was then discussed in earnest, Evans agreeing with Forsaith's view that a pa was 'more particularly a fortified village – or houses within a fence. Houses without fences he termed Kaingas.' But the argument turned on the cultivation grounds. Many more had been added by Maori since the settlers had 'purchased' the area. Wakefield argued that the new cultivation grounds should not be part of the agreement. FitzRoy asked again whether Wakefield would be prepared to pay as soon as an amount of compensation was decided. Wakefield said, 'I am.'[3] Evans had clearly encouraged Wakefield to co-operate with FitzRoy, as later Wakefield told the directors that he had submitted to FitzRoy 'under compulsion', merely to prevent the possibility of being refused Crown grants.[4]

FitzRoy ordered Clarke to compensate Te Rauparaha and Rangihaeata for their claim on the Hutt. Spain later objected to the large amount Clarke paid the two chiefs, as no claim had been lodged or argued in his court by them or any of their tribe. Some years earlier, he reminded FitzRoy, the two chiefs had fought their way from Taranaki to Port Nicholson conquering, but without sufficient force to keep possession of, the places they had taken.[5]

Spain suggested a compromise. If Hutt Maori as well as those in Port Nicholson were paid compensation by the Company, the Europeans could remain on the land. The Ngati Awa at Petone and Waiwhetu accepted his offer but the Ngati Tama of Kaiwharawhara and Ngati Rangatahi tribes stayed on their land, evicting settlers and building fortified pa, partly because the Company's reserves were insufficient and in some places inaccessible. In the Hutt Valley, Maori were granted only fifteen sections. A block of land at Kaiwharawhara was grudgingly handed over after the governor intervened – possibly the same block Evans had developed into a mill – as well as three sections at Pukuratahi in Upper Hutt. In all, Maori were given twenty-three sections, nine of which were impossible to cultivate, and the Company's servants were regarded as little more than swindlers.[6]

While FitzRoy was in Wellington he decided to appoint two men to the Legislative Council. Several magistrates declined, saying their official duties would conflict with regular travel to Auckland. FitzRoy approached Evans, who called on Wakefield to tell him that FitzRoy wanted to appoint a permanent Company agent who would live in Auckland and disperse funds on emigration and public works on its lands there. If Wakefield elected 'Dr. Evans as that agent, the Governor would be happy to place him in the Legislative Council', FitzRoy wrote in his proposal. Evans told Wakefield that FitzRoy had suggested that both the southern settlements and the Company could be represented in Council, and that if no second person could be found for Auckland this arrangement might meet both goals.

The timing of FitzRoy's offer was unfortunate. Wakefield was becoming more unpopular with the settlers. His tendencies to 'capriciousness, ruthlessness . . . [and] vindictiveness' had isolated him.[7] Wakefield had relied heavily on Evans's legal acumen for over four years, and if he lost him to Auckland he would have few supporters left. Yet he had frequently ignored Evans's advice. Evans, on the other hand, had expressed his frustration with Wakefield's machinations several times – over Hobson's house, over the town's siting and over compensation to Maori. This disenchantment, coupled with a healthy dose of opportunism, had led to his seeking the government post at Nelson and now agreeing to FitzRoy's suggestion.

However, under intense strain and wary of Evans's motives, Wakefield declined FitzRoy's proposal. As he told the directors, no-one could fill the role as resident agent of the Company and take a seat in the Council, because it would be 'assenting to the delusive doctrine that the Legislative Council as at present constituted is a representative body, which it is not'. The governor had a casting vote, and three official members together with three magistrates in rotation meant FitzRoy would always command a majority. By having a nominee in Council the Company would be sanctioning its proceedings. Lastly, and most importantly, 'the public in England would suppose that [with a Company and southern settlements' representative on the Council] . . . there was no necessity for placing the seat of government in the center of population of these islands'.

An agent at Auckland could not know the directors' 'opinions', those of the constituents, or 'the interests which some particular measure might affect'. In short, Wakefield believed it would be a 'nominal representation' at best, 'which might, in bad hands, be made most injurious to the Company'. All this made good sense. But, he confided:

> I must frankly add that, although I entertain a high respect for the talents of, and a personal friendship for [Evans], I had no faith in the advocacy of the Company's interests in the Council or the management of its affairs out of it by the gentleman proposed. If the proposal were not made with the intention of making the Company and the settlers under its guidance apparently parties to all the measures of the Legislative Council, whilst in reality the Governor would have the power exactly as at present, it has very much the appearance of it.

In believing Evans might support the government rather than promote Company interests, Wakefield had picked up on Evans's dissatisfaction with the lack of support from the Company, but he also misjudged him, as Evans would not have sacrificed the settlers' interests. Wakefield told Evans the Company had made no provision for an agent in Auckland and until such time as the Company's plan for land sales there was 'matured', it was unlikely there would be one. He could not name an agent who would have a seat in the Council 'even if I were more inclined than I am, to consider such an arrangement possible'.[8]

Evans wrote to Wakefield to clarify his misconception that the Auckland agent would also have a seat in the Legislative Council. 'My statement related entirely to myself and certainly was not designed to have any more general application', he added.[9] In fact, he doubted the governor would allow him a seat on Council. But Wakefield was adamant.

After Wakefield's refusal to relinquish him to Auckland, Evans's last hope was extinguished. He was the premier barrister in the town, but it was not enough for a man of his skills. For four years he had kept up the settlers' spirits with his fighting talk, urging them to stay, to persevere and to build for their families a new life. In the face of an inept and hostile government and few resources, his efforts appeared not to have enhanced his popularity with the Company's settlers and their leaders. The best hope for the country, he knew, was to work for its self-governance with proper representation.

FitzRoy returned to Auckland after visiting Nelson then Kapiti to hear Te Rauparaha's evidence. Under great strain, Evans struggled against the onset of illness. His gloom must have deepened when he received news that Chetham's father, Admiral Sir Edward Chetham Strode, had paid off a portion of his mortgage to Monro. In April he looked on bitterly as Clifford was chosen to replace Earp on the Legislative Council in Auckland. He attended court to hear Henry Chapman, Wellington's new Chief Justice, address the jury for the first time.[10] And later he had to congratulate Hanson who had been appointed Commissioner of the Court of Requests. Like Revans, Hanson was also dabbling in business ventures and his prospects looked remarkably good.

When Evans finally succumbed, his illness was enough to restrict his usual activity for some time. Between March and September the *Gazette* barely gives Evans a mention, even in reports from the law courts where he seems to have made his last appearance on 24 April. James Taine spoke of the seriousness of his illness.[11]

It may have been coincidental that, with Evans out of circulation, the *Gazette* – under Revans's editorship – again attacked the Company in the press for weeks. Many of the articles were particularly well written and some were savage and to the point, calling the Wakefield experiment a 'vicious game of chance, instead of a sound system of colonization'. Gibbon Wakefield was 'the scatterer of settlements, the enemy of cheap government and the curse of all colonies', who headed a Company that had committed a 'gross public fraud' by 'pretending' to colonise the country under the 'Wakefield Principle'.[12]

Colonel Wakefield was accused of neglecting to 'conciliate' the most powerful chiefs, Rangihaeata and Te Rauparaha. He had not seen Te Rauparaha at all after September 1839, and had made a personal enemy of Rangihaeata in 1842. Wakefield seemed to believe his role consisted of 'sitting in a comfortable office, and writing plausible despatches'. Instead of undergoing 'the fatigues of a journey to Porirua, (only eight miles away) and the irksomeness of a few days conference' with Rangihaeata and Te Rauparaha, it took the Wairau tragedy to 'rouse him from his lethargy, only to find that the favourable moment had been irretrievably lost'. Had he 'attended Spain's Courts and paid compensation to the Maori, the tragedy at Wairau would not have taken place'. In May 1844, his 'very name appears hateful to the native population of New Zealand'.

Colonel Wakefield was rude to the Company's servants and blamed his advisors for his own failures and decisions, sending harsh criticisms of them to London, while praising them for their efforts in public. Revans alleged that Mein Smith was one of the victims of Wakefield's criticism.[13] If he had 'been regarded as an example, the Company's servants and the settlers would have all lain down and gone to sleep'.

Wakefield's response to this diatribe was a complaint to the directors. He told them that Revans had 'denounced' him 'as agent for various sins of commission and omission, for indolence, apathy, fear of responsibility, and general inefficiency in the administration of the Company's affairs'. Wakefield said Revans was furious with him as he, Wakefield, had refused to subsidise Revans's private ventures. After these attacks, Wakefield had discontinued his subscription to the *Gazette*, whereas previously he had sent fifty copies to England.[14]

At last in early June the settlers had something to celebrate when Spain awarded large tracts of land to the Company, allowing thirty-nine native reserves of a hundred acres each.[15] In Taranaki the Company received 60,000 acres. But when FitzRoy reversed the latter award on 4 August, giving the Company only 3,500 acres in Taranaki, Evans and others were furious, believing FitzRoy had an agenda to attack the Company even at the expense of British law.[16] Evans agreed with Spain that those Maori who had been driven from Taranaki by war but returned to claim possession after those left behind had sold the district to the Company should have no rights. They were arguing, of course, from the viewpoint of English law, rather than from the tribal and ownership laws of Maori.[17] As Keith Sinclair notes in his *History*, for some time the leaders in Wellington as well as the Company directors in London had been acting 'more like a group of anxious speculators than determined idealists'.[18] But for those like Evans who had invested their capital in a utopian vision which had never been put to the test, it must have been an unbearable burden.

ঔ

In July war erupted in the North. The Ngapuhi chief Hone Heke chopped down the flagstaff at Kororareka for the first time, while Maori demanded the withdrawal of police at Russell and threatened 'a bloody war of races'.[19] On 19 August Wakefield announced that the Company's coffers were empty, and all surveys and expenditure on roads, bridges and civil contracts were stopped. The road into the Wairarapa over the Rimutaka hills had been mapped, surveyed and two-thirds developed, as far as Mungarao, but just as the survey party reached the summit the project had to be abandoned. Two and a half miles were left unsurveyed. The farming settlers in the Wairarapa were furious, having hoped they could drive their stock over the hills instead of along the coastline to Palliser Bay or shipping them to the anchorage at Te Kopi.[20] Revans passed on his press to others at the end of September and prepared to take up sheep-farming in the Wairarapa with Mein Smith.[21] Others drifted away to Chile or elsewhere in New Zealand.

It was not until 22 September that a considerably weakened Evans was well enough to attend a farewell dinner for the Reverend Macfarlane to offer a toast to the Church of Scotland.[22] In the same month he attended a meeting at the Aglionby Arms in the Hutt to discuss the destruction of farmers' crops there by Maori. Although Spain had given them compensation and told them to leave by March the following year, Rangihaeata had decided the land north of Boulcott's farm should be reserved for the chief Kaparatehau. Armed members of Ngati Rangatahi led by Kaparatehau were sowing fresh crops with the assistance of Ngati Toa. Evans had a personal interest in the Hutt – in Upper Hutt he owned the hundred-acre section on which the Trentham Rifle Range was later situated.[23] At the settlers' request, Evans drew up a memorial to FitzRoy begging him to resolve the issue, but FitzRoy could spare only a meagre two companies of soldiers, as he had to cope with unrest in the Bay of Islands.[24]

FitzRoy left Auckland and visited Wellington again in October when the Hutt deputation presented him with their memorial. FitzRoy offered those who had not got their land the chance to exchange their titles for similar land in Auckland – any difference in value would be settled by arbitration. He also proposed buying the lands from absentee owners and offering them to residents. This proposal was vetoed by the settlers who had sunk so much of their capital into improvements at Port Nicholson. Land could not be exchanged at an equivalent value, as FitzRoy had reduced Auckland's value to 1s 6d an acre. The settlers also pointed out to him the 'impossibility of uprooting in that manner a population of 10,000 people, who would resist to the last extremity'.

When his suggestions were rejected, there was 'an explosion of childish passion' from FitzRoy that shocked everybody. Not long after, FitzRoy returned to Auckland.[25] Evans later sold his Trentham block to Mr McCullough, and was eventually compelled to exchange the sections he and Mr Northwood held at Horokiwi for land at Upper Hutt because of Maori resistance. His allotment was transferred to Pakuratahi.[26]

FitzRoy believed New Zealand was not fit for the Wakefield system of colonisation. He thought the Company's activities had forced the government's interference, while it tried 'to carry out a legalised system, – similar in principle, though differing essentially in practice'. He conceded that the government had been guilty of 'serious practical errors', and recognised that the Company was unable to continue its operations. The Company's settlers would suffer 'disadvantages and pecuniary loss'. They were, he believed 'under a delusion, [and] are still mystified about [New Zealand]'.[27]

FitzRoy's own undoing partly came about when he issued an edict announcing he would waive the Crown's right of pre-emption and allow Maori to sell their lands to individuals at any price ranging from one penny to 10 shillings an acre, with protectors supervising each sale. The Act not only seriously affected the Company's plans, but also defied the Colonial Office's Ordinance of 1842, which stated that waste lands were not to be disposed of for less than 20 shillings an acre.[28] Everyone was furious. Before Evans could act, he was momentarily distracted by the published Report of the Aborigines' Protection Society in London at their seventh Annual Meeting. The article alleged:

> . . . not even the slave trade itself, with the atrocities of the Middle Passage, was so destructive of the aboriginal population of a country as colonization, such as had been carried out by civilized nations.

> Persecution and injustice to a great degree were also suffered by the New Zealanders . . . but the [Aborigines' Protection Society] Committee had exerted themselves with the colonial authorities, and were not without hope that they [Maori] would ultimately receive the protection of Government.[29]

A public meeting was called for Monday, 28 October, and in spite of being still physically very frail, Evans struggled through the foul weather and addressed the crowded hall at length. The 'particular charge of persecution and suffering' was, he said, 'a flagrant falsehood', with the Aborigines' Protection Society having 'either invented or adopted the lie'. He knew several members of the Society – some since childhood – and he vouched for their 'religious and moral character', saying he had been 'educated in the same principles' and 'worked with them in their many good works for others'. He was sure they would apologise when they realised their mistake, but he was angry they had accepted rumours without inquiry or evidence, and he would pursue them to the end to 'convict them of a violation of the great command – "Thou shalt not bear false witness against thy neighbour"'.

He could easily disprove their charge by calling several Maori to the Bar, he said dramatically, displaying and reading from twenty-two letters written by Hawke's Bay's 'principal chiefs' to Wakefield, begging him to buy their land and send Europeans to live amongst them. Evans then announced he was returning to England to 'render the colony far more essential service'. He would attend meetings at Crosby and Exeter Halls, and tell all 'the tales of their toils and privations, their sufferings and forbearance' in the hope that ultimately the settlers would receive government protection. At this point his voice gave out, but Evans assured them he would continue his speech in England.

Some who had disagreed with Evans or mistrusted him in the past now sympathised and came out in his support. Hanson promised to write to the Aborigines' Protection Society with his history of events and hoped it would take up the land question on the settlers' behalf. He believed there had been 'the greatest forbearance shown towards the Maori', and reminded them of all they had endured over almost five years of settlement. They had seen the Company fail in its obligations; and they had seen many settlers leaving, and several reduced to poverty, 'their resources wasted from inability to obtain land'.

Mr Roots said he approved of Dr Evans '*at last*' and trusted that the 'half to be spoken in England would correspond with the half spoken here, and thereby prove that the learned Doctor had found out the meaning of consistency at last'. Revans backed Evans, proposing he convey their sentiments to the Society and take 'any other means in his power to inform the English public of the truth . . . particularly by means of the public press'.[30]

Evans's announcement was no snap decision. His return to England had become absolutely vital on personal grounds. Monro was threatening to foreclose on his mortgage and Evans already owed a considerable sum of money to the Union Bank – £3,000. Chetham had returned to Wellington after persuading his father to pay the arrears of interest and some principal, but nothing in Wellington pointed to a quick solution to Evans's problem.

By temperament Evans was no natural colonist. Relying on the traditions and rules of the old country and mutual goodwill between the races for the colony's success, he had been stymied by inept officialdom, and limited by few resources, the hostility of missionaries, and a proud and determined native people who had their own rules. Personally, as Evans himself had admitted, an old country was his 'proper sphere'. The privations and social limitations had not suited his wife either. Her dissatisfaction and his political impotence had only served to fuel his discontent.

After FitzRoy's edict, sales suffered. He reduced land tax in October then compounded the problem by creating debentures as legal tender to save 'the colony from an extremity of disorder and distress'.[31] His own coffers were bare, but as Wellington settlers had long bemoaned the profligate use of their taxes in Auckland, there was little sympathy for the man who had been so dismissive of their needs. The problem was not created by FitzRoy. Shortland's predecessor Hobson had invented 'a proliferation of official posts' that seriously depleted 'the meagre finances of the colony'. His officials were incompetent and many proved to be corrupt. Hobson had made a 'reckless decision to allocate sections in Auckland' to them 'before the land was made available for sale to the general public'. They were then able to sell them on, making large profits.[32]

Wairau was still fresh in the settlers' minds and Evans was seriously alarmed for the colony's future. If Wellington were to gain any sort of political autonomy, it would never achieve it from the Council. Only the British government could act in their interests.

And the missionaries' land purchases still rankled. Full credit was given to their courage in arriving to convert an 'uncivilised' native race to Christianity and to guide them towards embracing the habits and traditions of a 'civilised' British society, but it was generally known that the Church Missionary Society had authorised the expenditure

Edward Betts Hopper was a close friend and neighbour of Evans from 1832. He was involved with Wakefield in colonising South Australia, and was an active member of the New Zealand Company. Shortly after he established a flourmill with his friends Francis Molesworth and Hon. Henry Petre, he drowned in the Hutt River in September 1840. 'Self portrait 1835–39', by Edward Betts Hopper, A-001-055, Alexander Turnbull Library.

One of Evans's oldest friends, Richard Davies Hanson was appointed Crown Prosecutor by Hobson. He strongly disapproved of Governor Grey's native policy, and left Wellington for South Australia in 1846. Sir Richard Davies Hanson, Chief Justice of the Supreme Court, South Australia, from the *Illustrated London News*, July–December 1869, Vol. XV, p.117, National Library of New Zealand.

A close friend of Evans, Dr Isaac Featherston worked tirelessly for Wellington from his arrival in 1841. A popular leader, he was Superintendent of Wellington from 1853 to 1870. With Evans's assistance, he established steam communication between Wellington and Melbourne. Photograph by kind permission of Mrs E. A. Riddiford.

Samuel Revans edited Wellington's first newspaper, generally referred to as the *Gazette*. Revans's trenchant criticisms of Evans's family, other settlers and those in authority mark his correspondence with Henry Samuel Chapman. Henry Sewell thought he was 'a specially disagreeable man'. Samuel Revans, A. H. & A. W. Reed, photographs, ca. 1860, 1/2-038720-F, Alexander Turnbull Library

Panorama taken from the terrace in Dr Evans's garden, showing his house (far left) with cows
Left-hand section of Panorama of Wellington, Port Nicholson, taken upon Thorndon Flat

Part two of the central section of a sketch taken from the ship *London* on Lambton Harbour, showing Evans's newly built distinctive house (above all of the other houses) on Golders Hill, now Eccleston Hill. Many more trees would be felled to develop this part of the settlement. Luke Nattrass, City of Wellington New Zealand: Sketch of Thorndon Quay and Beach, 1841 (W. Richardson, lithographer), C-029-004-2-3, Alexander Turnbull Library.

grazing on the front lawn. Samuel Charles Brees, from an engraving by Henry Melville. [1847], PUBL-0020-22-1, Alexander Turnbull Library.

Part three of the central section of the sketch. North of Evans's house, on the beach, is Pipitea pa (far right), adjoining a chief's house. Luke Nattrass, City of Wellington New Zealand: Sketch of Thorndon Quay and Beach, 1841 (W. Richardson, lithographer), C-029-004-3-2, Alexander Turnbull Library.

Ngati Toa chief and the most feared warrior in the southern area of the North Island, Te Rauparaha was defiant after Wairau, but took no further action against the settlers. He was arrested on Governor Grey's orders in July 1846. 'Te Raparaha, Chief of the Kawias' [*sic*], A-114-047, Alexander Turnbull Library.

Rangihaeata, nephew of Te Rauparaha. When an application for a warrant for Rangihaeata's arrest was issued in court, Evans successfully defended the warrior. Less than a year later, Rangihaeata took terrible revenge on the Company's settlers at Wairau in Nelson for the death of his wife. 'Te Rauparaha's fighting general', by Isaac Coates [1843?], A-286-014, Alexander Turnbull Library.

Evans Bay, named after Dr Evans, one of the two large bays in Port Nicholson, the other being Lambton Harbour. This is an early view when the bay was still known as Evans's Bay, showing sailboats in the fore and background, and heavily bush-clad hills. 'Evans's Bay near Wellington, New Zealand, 1857', by Henry Stratton Bates, Private Collection, copy held in Alexander Turnbull Library, 052726 1/2, Alexander Turnbull Library.

The Courthouse where Evans spent much of his time was in the lower part of Mulgrave Street. A knot of lawyers and others can be seen outside with a man on horseback. The Thistle Inn is below the Courthouse on the street. Below the hill close to the shore is a European house. Courts of Justice, Wellington, 1843, by Samuel Charles Brees, B-031-009, Alexander Turnbull Library.

Bird's-eye view of Wellington Harbour from the southern entrance, with Evans's Bay scooped out in a u-shape in the foreground. In the far distance the flat stretch of shoreline is 'Pitone', where the passengers of the first ships disembarked in 1840. Somes Island is prominent in the harbour. Charles Heaphy, C-029-006b, Alexander Turnbull Library.

of £50 from its funds on land as a provision for the maintenance of each child born in New Zealand to one of its missionaries.

> Some . . . had excellent prospects. Twelve of them were said to have eighty-four children [amongst them] . . . . Since land was [then] to be bought for a few blankets and axes, £50 would purchase a large farm, while a large family was security for an estate. When the early land purchases were investigated in the 1840s, several Anglican Missionaries claimed ten or twenty thousand acres [each].[33]

There was one small victory. When Richmond allowed some labourers who had bought land from Maori in an area reserved for Taringa Kuri to take possession, Evans and others visited him to protest against the 'injustice and illegality of allowing land, of which the preemption had been waived in favour of the New Zealand Company, and which an Act of Parliament prohibited from being sold at less than £1 an acre, to be bought at a penny'. Richmond immediately backed down and cancelled the sale, while Evans, assisted by a sub-committee, drew up a memorial to Lord Stanley. Soon after, at a general meeting of landowners held on Friday, 29 November, Evans agreed to 'carry the Memorial' to London.

He wrote the memorial in a little over a week and displayed it for signatures in the week 7–14 December. Wakefield was clearly impressed, writing to the directors, 'A memorial most ably drawn up by Dr. Evans is now in the process of signature for [him] to lay before the Colonial Minister, praying that the principle [of FitzRoy's proclamation] be not recognized.'[34]

The memorial covered nearly six columns when published in the *Gazette*:

> The undersigned landowners . . . beg respectfully to call your Lordship's attention to a proclamation published . . . on the 6th of October last, by which we conceive that an Act of Parliament, the 5 and 6 of Victoria, c. 36, is attempted to be set aside or evaded; a fundamental article of what is called the Treaty of Waitangi, in favour of the prerogative and essential to the well-being of the Natives no less than of the Europeans, abandoned; the Land Claims Ordinance of this colony (Anno 4 Vic. No.2) virtually repealed, and new principles introduced for regulating the acquisition and disposal of waste lands, subversive of those established by the Act of Parliament, and pregnant with all the evils with which that Act was intended, and so well calculated to remedy.

There were frequent references to the Treaty and to Victoria's instructions to Hobson which stated that 'nothing . . . shall affect or be construed to affect the rights of any [Maori] . . . to the actual occupation and enjoyment, in their own persons, or in the persons of their descendants, of any lands in [New Zealand] then actually occupied or enjoyed by such natives'.

The settlers' legal interpretation of the Queen's edict, 'which is in strict accordance with the usages of the natives, the law of nations and the common law of the plantations, is not in any sense repugnant to the Treaty of Waitangi, which we acknowledge as a fundamental law in this colony':

> This treaty simply and absolutely confirmed and assured to them all their territorial rights, as they existed prior to the acquisition of the sovereignty by the Queen; but it never undertook to confer upon them new qualities which they did not possess before.

The government was asked to pass another Act 'indemnifying us, by refunding the whole of the capital which we have invested in these islands':

> . . . we are some of us members of the original New Zealand Association, and we claim some portion of the credit for the invention of a scheme of colonization more favourable to the aborigines than any that preceded it. We first suggested the application of a principle of 'definite proportions', to be observed between the land to be reserved for the natives and the amount of population . . . we claim to be, not only the most accurately informed, but the most zealous of the friends of the aborigines; and . . . in their name and on their behalf, we . . . protest against this proclamation.[35]

In the letter to Lord Stanley that accompanied the memorial, Evans spoke on behalf of the 'memorialists' of Port Nicholson. The letter summarising FitzRoy's actions was a devastating tour de force. Fourteen accusations against FitzRoy were written in the rhetorical style used so effectively a century later by Churchill during the Second World War:

> He has, with an infatuation like total loss of judgment, publicly caressed the perpetrators of the massacre of Wairau, and reproached the memory of his countrymen who fell there.
>
> He has suddenly destroyed the currency of the colony, and exposed every man in it to ruin, by issuing a paper money in very small amounts, and making it legal tender by Ordinance . . . .
>
> He has saddled the colony with the expense, and exposed his own authority to the ridicule of having sent to New South Wales for a military force in order to punish the authors of an outrage against the Government at the Bay of Islands, whom, having first sent away

> the troops, he rewarded by abolishing all customs duties, for the avowed purpose of gratifying the rioters.
>
> He has . . . abolished all duties of customs in New Zealand, thus destroying nearly the whole public revenue of the colony at the same time that he destroyed its currency.
>
> He has, with the intention no doubt of benefiting the natives, made exceptional laws so greatly to their disadvantage as to preclude safe commercial intercourse and almost every kind of legal bargain between them and the colonists, and thus preserve them in a state of social inferiority.[36]

On the eve of Evans's departure for England, when Wakefield's office sent him an overdue account for £87 8s 2d, Evans replied immediately, reminding Kelham of the 'quantity of bricks' omitted from the bill. He promised payment 'at the earliest possible moment' but added a postscript begging for time, owing to 'the colony's peculiar circumstances'.[37]

He put his affairs in order, remortgaging his property to the bank for the sum of £3,000 on equity of redemption to property previously under mortgage to Sir Edward Chetham Strode, and signing an agreement in which he owed Harriet's estate £2,000.[38] He leased his house to James Coutts Crawford, leaving Harriet to stay with Chetham and Amelia, and promising he would send for her when he was settled in London with regular employment.[39] He had appointed Chetham as his agent to dispose of his rentals, but after Evans's departure Chetham made no arrangement for the bank to receive the rents of his property, which would have given Harriet £100 a year.[40]

Just before he left, news reached Evans of the death of his old friend and mentor, Thomas Campbell. On Saturday, 14 December 1844, he boarded the brig *Nelson*, which was laden with black oil, whalebone and wood for furniture. He might have taken with him that day's *Gazette*, with a description of Campbell's funeral and interment in the Poet's Corner of Westminster Abbey. He would have been touched to read that one of the two 'jewels of [Campbell's] property' was the bowl presented to him by the students at Glasgow University when he was rector.[41]

In the same issue it was announced that the Commons Committee on New Zealand's Affairs 'had decided every point of importance in favour of the New Zealand Company', ruling that all land not in the actual possession and occupation of Maori was to be considered 'waste land' belonging to the Crown. The Company was commended for being 'sound and judicious' in 'making reserves for the natives . . . and in making suitable provision for spiritual and educational purposes'.[42] Forty-four and a half thousand hectares in Port Nicholson and twenty thousand at Nelson were awarded to the Company – subject to the Commissioner's report. Of the nineteen resolutions, the first was disapproving: 'That the conduct of the New Zealand Company in sending out settlers to New Zealand, not only without the sanction, but in direct defiance of the authority of the crown, was highly irregular and improper.' The rest were favourable to the Company's philosophy and actions. As the editorial pointed out, 'after five years suffering, the settlers in Cook's Straits have a prospect of enjoying what they have purchased at an expense of life, money, vexation and harassing delay, at which it is frightful to look back'.[43] The Report of the Commons Committee was not acted upon, but dismissed by the Colonial Office.[44]

While his ship laboured on towards England, Evans's fears for the future of race relations in New Zealand proved well-founded. On 17 January 1845, the first battle on New Zealand soil between Pakeha and Maori began – the Hone Heke war, and in March, Kororareka was destroyed by fire.

In the same month, Spain sent his hand-written, 103-page report to FitzRoy, alluding to the imperfect translation of the deed of sale of Port Nicholson that had brought about the collapse of the Company's plans. Compensation had to be paid to the tribes that had no part in its sale before the Company was given a Crown grant.[45] The Company had paid £1,500 after FitzRoy's meeting with Wakefield in January 1844; but although Clarke and Wakefield were to negotiate its dispersal with Spain, over a year later no such discussion had taken place. 'The whole site of the town of Wellington upon which thousands of pounds have been expended by the settlers, and to which the Company's title was most defective, has been secured to the Europeans – together with a considerable country district', he told FitzRoy.[46]

Four years after Evans sailed for England, in an irony that would not have escaped him, George Clarke Junior took the same journey – to study for the ministry of the Congregational Church.[47]

PART THREE:
ENGLAND AND WELLINGTON
1845–1852

CHAPTER SIXTEEN.
'A PROPER SPHERE'

> The new management of the New Zealand Company were more mercenary and less patriotic. There was a want of unanimity amongst them.
>
> J. J. Taine (ed. H. W. Fildes), *Reminiscences*, Vol. 2, p.286, qMS-1974-1975, ATL

After Evans's arrival in London on Friday, 2 May, he moved into 44 Hans Place, one in a row of brick terraced houses in Chelsea that overlooked the vast expanse of fields leading to Westminster.[1] After reuniting with his family, he was eager to catch up with his former associates, and dined on Saturday evening with William Guyton and the naturalist Percy Earl who had collected moa bones for the British Museum.

On Sunday he found Gibbon Wakefield at his cottage in Burstow Park. His nephew Charles Torlesse and son Jerningham (who had launched his book *Adventure in New Zealand* only about a fortnight earlier) were already there, with the banker and director of the New Zealand Company, Sir Isaac Goldsmid, along with Joseph Somes, the Company's governor, and Robert Rintoul of *The Spectator.*

The group had been discussing the proceedings of the Company's 'Secret Committee' when Evans, who could barely contain himself, exploded with 'an escape of bitterness and bile', wrote Jerningham in his *Journal.*[2] They were well used to Evans's highly strung temperament and to his fulminations against the government, but this time Evans preferred to discuss the long desperate struggle of his family and his fellow settlers in New Zealand, and the trust they had placed in the Company to address their problems. They managed to calm him down only gradually, but he had riled Gibbon Wakefield, as the Company was beset by financial problems and under intense scrutiny from the public.

The next morning, Evans and Wakefield were left alone to 'confabulate and have it out'. Evans's grievances included criticism of the Company's use of its funds. Wakefield was unwell and, probably annoyed at Evans's criticisms, might have shafted home some of the blame for its misfortunes to Evans himself. It has also been surmised that the talks centred on Evans's supposed ill-treatment of Liocadia, Wakefield's ward, and an apparently weak defence of Captain Wakefield's actions at Wairau in Auckland.[3] But apart from Revans's complaints on board the *Adelaide*, there is no evidence to suggest that Evans was ever anything but courteous and hospitable in his treatment of Liocadia. The highly favourable view of Evans carried through from her husband James Taine and her grandson, the amateur historian Horace Fildes, gives the lie to this contention.[4] Nor had Evans been anything but defensive and supportive of his colleague Arthur Wakefield, who had died so tragically at Wairau. We know that it was for precisely this reason that Evans had been roundly criticised for his representation of the affair in Auckland. It says something of the mutual respect between Gibbon Wakefield and Evans that their discussion ended amicably.

Afterwards Evans travelled to Bletchingley, Surrey, where he wrote to the Secretary of State, Lord Stanley, enclosing the settlers' memorial. He had heard rumours of FitzRoy's recall, but would not have known that only two days before his arrival in the country, Stanley had signed the necessary papers – although they were not dispatched until 29 May. This was possibly to give Stanley time to hear the new evidence from Evans and read the plethora of petitions from other parties.

Evans told Stanley he had not followed the correct procedure of sending the memorial to FitzRoy as it was too expensive for the impoverished settlers and the delays would have ruined the colony. In addition, there was widespread belief among the settlers that FitzRoy was likely to 'throw our memorial into the fire, or send it back to us with an insulting message'. While initially they had high hopes of FitzRoy, as the Company had reported favourably on him, they had been shocked by much of his behaviour. But these complaints, continued Evans, were petty compared to Wairau:

> [FitzRoy] has, with an infatuation like total loss of judgment, publicly caressed the perpetrators of the massacre of Wairau, and reproached the memory of his countrymen who fell there; pretending to found his opinion of the conduct of both parties on a speech delivered to him by one of the murderers [Te Rauparaha], but actually reading that opinion from a paper which had been got ready for his use before the speech of the savage commenced.

He wrote of FitzRoy's manufacture of money and his destruction of the country's currency and its revenue by the abolition of customs duties, and pitilessly portrayed him as a man who had exhibited:

> . . . a degree of inconstancy of purpose and inconsistency in action, of suspicion, of inordinate self-esteem, and contempt for others; of fretful irascibility at one time, and of inexplicable self-complacency at another; of forgetfulness of his own recent acts or promises, and of general infirmity of apprehension or conception.[5]

For his own character reference, he referred Stanley to the Commissioner of Bankruptcy Joshua Evans (who was unrelated). After receiving a prompt reply summoning him to a meeting with George Hope, Under-Secretary for the Colonies, he called on Gibbon Wakefield again at Burstow. This time Evans was in a happier mood, prompting Jerningham to describe him as an 'inconsistent and flighty soul!'[6]

But after the lengthy meeting with Hope on Friday, 16 May, he emerged disappointed and more than a little puzzled. Of the settlers' memorial there had been no mention. And instead of discussing the disposal of New Zealand's waste lands, Evans had found himself being grilled on every facet of FitzRoy's actions and behaviour. He felt he had been placed, he said later, 'in the position of a witness whom an attorney was examining for the purpose of preparing a brief for the plaintiff, Captain FitzRoy being the defendant'.[7]

Five days later he dined again with Wakefield and told him of his unsatisfactory meeting with Hope. Whether prompted by Wakefield or not, he wrote to Stanley the next day, complaining he had been left 'completely in the dark' about the reasons behind the interview, and hoped he would be able to present written evidence from other petitioners.

At the time, articles on New Zealand were featuring prominently in the press, which was unanimous in its condemnation of the 'blunders and imbecilities' surrounding New Zealand's colonisation. The publicity nettled Stanley, so it was not surprising that Evans received a peremptory reply – again from Hope – who said Evans had mistakenly interpreted his 'language and demeanour' during the interview. Stanley had read all the letters and his memorial, and had decided to appoint a successor to Captain FitzRoy. It was his 'intention to reserve for [the future Governor] whatever instructions he may think it right to give, as well upon the question brought under his notice by the memorial you refer to, as on others'.[8]

Hope had neatly put Evans in his place, but Evans was frustrated that the settlers' grievances had not been given more priority. In letters to his friends in Wellington he also fumed at the treatment he had received from the Colonial Office.

He got his chance to air his frustration three days later, when he attended the annual meeting of the Company at New Zealand House in Broad Street. His letter to Stanley telling of FitzRoy's blunders and shortcomings was read aloud, and when he rose to speak, he was greeted with loud cheers. He read the letter he had written to the directors appealing for them to 'procure that justice for the settlers, which has never yet been accorded to them by Her Majesty's Government', and expanded on the theme. FitzRoy had waived the government's right of pre-emption, as long as prospective buyers –

> . . . pay a registration fee of 10s. per acre to the local government. The proclamation did not satisfy the gentlemen in . . . Auckland – gentlemen who formed what was called the landshark interest. (Laughter). They were exceedingly desirous of having the price reduced still lower – in fact abolished altogether.

These 'landsharks' had encouraged 'a considerable body' of Maori in the north to march to the Governor's house armed with muskets and tomahawks, object to the proclamation and demand all registration fees be abolished. This had been duly done, so that the approval of the Governor and the Protector of Aborigines was the only requirement for buying land. FitzRoy's capitulation was, Evans alleged, 'a virtual repeal of an Act of the Imperial Parliament'. The government's pledge to keep the minimum price of land at £1 per acre had been effectively reduced to one penny per acre. Evans was there 'to implore of them not to relax in their exertions', but to compel the government to tell them its plans, 'and whether they intended to destroy the colony and ruin every man in it'.

When he left the colony, said Evans, the effect of the combined actions of the local government, the missionaries and the protectors over the previous four years 'on the minds of Maori was apparent in the almost complete alienation of them from the Europeans'. The 'mistrust, coldness and jealousy . . . convinced him . . . the colony was on the eve of some very serious catastrophe'. He was most worried about the fate of settlers in the remoter areas, believed danger threatened both races, and added that unless something were done New Zealand might suffer a disaster 'which might be recorded in history as inferior only in its magnitude and its deplorable consequences to the Sicilian Vespers'. Maori were arming themselves, 'convinced they were in danger of something utterly undefinable, utterly incomprehensible by them'. He believed the Maori mind had been captured by 'extraneous influences, [and they were] brooding over unintelligible wrongs, of which they possessed only a dim and cloudy consciousness'. They were in a state of 'restlessness and excitement', which 'often obtained among the ignorant population of great cities previous to the breaking out of some pestilence or other grievous calamity. (Hear Hear!)'. In the last two years, Maori 'had retrograded in civilization and religion' – many had 'apostatised to heathenism'. Evans spoke at some length upon the Treaty of Waitangi, 'declaring that the natives, in ceding the sovereignty of the country, gave to this country the appropriation of the public domain'. He believed that:

> . . . such was the opinion of the natives themselves before a different interpretation of the treaty was suggested to them. The natives originally had no idea of being possessed of millions of acres of waste land on which no human foot had ever trod. If this land were sold at the minimum price of £1 per acre, the aborigines would be benefited, the roads and bridges of the colony provided for, and emigration promoted. If, on the other hand, the opposite course was adopted, then he was sure they would be prevented from permanently benefiting the aborigines, and it would be impossible that roads, or bridges, or other public works could be constructed in the colony.
>
> If it were true – which he did not believe – that such alterations had been made in the treaty of Waitangi as would deprive her Majesty of the most important functions she could exercise for the benefit of the colony, then there had been treachery, most shameful treachery, on the part of those who had acted in Her Majesty's name; that her Majesty's hands were tied up, and she must look silently on while the whole territory was jobbed away under the pretence of protecting the aborigines. (Hear)[9]

The meeting – and Evans's speech – received extensive coverage in the press. It featured prominently in *The Times*, which used it as a warning to Stanley.[10] Although Stanley had suggested the government buy up the interests of the Company, two months of the parliamentary session had been wasted on 'overtures and treaty'.[11]

By 2 June, when Company director and Whig MP Henry Aglionby presented copies of the correspondence between the Colonial Office and Evans, together with the settlers' memorial to the House, Evans had joined Buller, Rintoul and Somes in lobbying government members on the Company's behalf.[12] He had also met with many of his contacts from the press, knowing there was considerable public interest in the pending Commons' debate on New Zealand.[13] Buller's

Motion for a Debate had suffered setbacks and delays that proved to be a blessing in disguise, as they had allowed Buller to listen to Evans's speech, and to draw on his and others' accounts of the most recent events in New Zealand.[14]

In early June, after Evans and Jerningham had made appointments to meet with Members of Parliament, Evans arrived half an hour late for a meeting with Sir John and Lady Easthope at Jerningham's residence in Jermyn Street. As the new owner of the *Morning Chronicle*, Easthope would be a useful ally in their work for the government's co-operation. After being assured of his support, Evans and Jerningham visited James Matheson, an influential MP and retired merchant of Jardine, Matheson and Co. of Hong Kong.[15] He was supportive and suggested they lobby two moderate Tories, Lords Egerton and Sandon. The next day Evans, Guyton and Jerningham visited the directors[16] to discuss the best way to present the settlers' and Company's interests at the Commons debate on 17 June.

Evans spent the next two weeks with Jerningham feverishly lobbying, but he had other matters to attend to as well – finding employment being the most urgent – and punctuality was never one of his virtues. He was so late for one meeting that they were able to see co-founder of the Reform Club William Ewart only briefly. They called on Easthope again, who was accompanied by Andrew Doyle, John Black's replacement as editor of the *Morning Chronicle*, and his leading reporter Eyre E. Crow.

Easthope may have commissioned some articles from Evans, as by this time he was writing for a few journals. Perhaps through the recommendation of his brother James Cook Evans, who was reporting from the Law Courts for *The Times*, Evans joined its staff. He took full advantage of its new stance, writing articles on New Zealand and influencing other reporters like Gilbert Beckett, with whom he conferred on the subject of New Zealand many times.[17]

After time spent lobbying with Evans, Jerningham was fed up with his 'fearful impracticability', complaining that while he and Moreing had called on key people, Evans had 'converted M. J. O'Connell, Serjeant-at-Law Murphy and others by drinking sherry cobbler with them in the smoking room' of the Reform Club. Jerningham's momentary righteousness belied his own reckless, scandalous life in London. To read his *Journal* is to be taken on an incessant whirlwind tour of high and low spots, to hurtle from lobbying to socialising, personal intrigue and promiscuity.[18]

Easily distracted and easily bored, Evans did not like to be managed (particularly by a young blade nearly twenty years his junior) and always preferred to do things his own way. He was nothing if not a shrewd networker of his own influential contacts within and outside the Reform Club, visiting men such as Brougham, and especially his old mentor and friend, John Black.[19] He also continued on the rounds with Jerningham, calling on Disraeli, Captain Rous, Arthur Wellesley, Howick and Russell, and the Hon. George Anson, and enduring 'the humbug of [Secretary] Hope' again. It was an exhausting schedule.

On 17 June, almost exactly two years to the day since the events at Wairau, Buller rose to the occasion in the Debate on New Zealand in the House of Commons. His opening speech is generally regarded as an inspired, brilliant effort: it reads today as an eloquent, persuasive piece of rhetoric, still capable of stirring outrage at his portrait of the injustice of the government, the suffering of the settlers and not least the careless disturbance of Maori. Throughout, Buller excoriated the actions of the government and the church missionaries. In discussing the impact of the Treaty of Waitangi – which he confirmed was consistent 'with the common-law rights of the crown' and agreed 'with the Company's claims' – he qualified his support of it by echoing Evans's reservations about the impact it would have on Maori:

> Was it for the real well-understood interest of the natives to put them in possession of a property which they had not before – to place this large extent of land at their disposal? Why, suppose . . . they were to get, in one or two cases, large prices for some land; I say that every such large price given to the savage, to be spent in the gratification of his passions, is so much poison administered to him. But the evil would not stop there.
>
> The speculators would find that such bargains did not answer, and the sales would cease. The settlers would find the rights of the natives interfere with the one great necessity of their existence, namely the extension of their cultivation; they would learn to regard them with hatred . . . . The white people would become unscrupulous in their mode of acquiring land; . . . [they would] beat down the price; they would tempt him by the means of instant gratification; rum and gunpowder would become the direct instruments of exchange, and, as the extermination of the native would be the interest of the settler, every act of superior intelligence would be directed to [that] end . . .

Buller asked the House to compare that scenario with the Company's scheme of native reserves:

> . . . and tell me which was conceived in the wisest spirit of kindness to the native – the plan which assured him forever a property ten times as large as he had ever occupied, with a value given to it by the

> labour of the Europeans and a peaceful amalgamation with these Europeans; or that which, by nominally investing him with the brief possession of a useless property, brought him into fatal collision with the race which must be the master of New Zealand?[20]

He also echoed Evans's warning that FitzRoy's follies would lead to open conflict with Maori.

But the government had its own weapons at the ready. Hope did his best to paint the Company's actions in the most cynical light, blaming its precipitate entry and careless purchases for all the colony's problems. He also cast doubt on Buller's reference 'to the state of New Zealand as being in the most perilous and critical condition'. Buller, he said, had –

> . . . quoted the authority of Dr. Evans, who had lately arrived from the colony. Now, Dr. Evans had left about the 7th or 8th of December; and when he left, the impression was, that some great and general rising was about to take place. [Hope] had seen a gentleman who had brought letters from Wellington dated the 19th of Feb., and up to that date, no collision had occurred . . . . [Hope] was, on the whole, justified in saying that the apprehensions, founded on the representations of Dr. Evans, were not verified by the experience of two months afterwards . . .[21]

Angered at the inference behind his remarks, Evans sent word to Hope citing Colonel Wakefield's recent despatches that had agreed with his own views. The next day, Hope rose and 'in a tone scarcely audible', admitted that he 'ought not to have stated' his 'opinion of the natives on the authority of Dr. Evans':

> He had received his information from several other persons; and also with respect to the land Dr. Evans's information did not agree with his, though the dispatches of Mr. Wakefield of the 8 October 1844 and 1 December to the Company bore him out.[22]

It was obvious Evans and Wakefield had firmer fingers on the pulse of the mood in New Zealand, for war had already broken out in the north.

That day, Aglionby also spoke out at the treatment Evans had received from the Colonial Office. Evans had expected Lord Stanley to discuss the contents of the settlers' memorial, especially the effect FitzRoy's 'Penny-an-acre Proclamation' would have on both the settlers and Maori. He also expected to be informed on 'the course being taken for affording redress, [but] Lord Stanley only informed him of his appointment of a new Governor':

> Was that, he would ask, a conciliatory or satisfactory answer to return to those who had embarked [*sic*] their fortunes in the colony? Would it be too much to expect that some information might be given them on a subject which so vitally concerned their interests?[23]

During the course of the debate, which raged for an unprecedented three days, Evans met other speakers who supported Buller's stance, including a young Henry Barkly, whom he would encounter again many years later. The measure was defeated by fifty votes (223 to 173), but the die had been cast. Chartism, factory conditions and the push to repeal the new Poor Laws were the political topics of the moment, but the debate on New Zealand carried on in the salons and studies of private houses, and the dining and drawing rooms of London's clubs.[24]

The Reform Club in particular was a hive of activity, abuzz with fervent discussion, speculation and interest. Evans found himself seized and questioned, the centre of attention, and he entertained his audience with stories of his experiences, with bitter denunciations of the government, and with his fears for the future of Maori–European relations. Members of the club had been told of the swathes of land the missionaries had accrued privately. The news had been corroborated by the *New Zealand Spectator and Cook's Straits Guardian* of 28 December 1844, which listed the 'Missionary Slices': in one purchase alone, Henry Williams had managed to garner 9000 acres in six titles, while his brother William had gained a more modest 890 acres.[25] That year Alexander Marjoribanks pointed out the contrast between the Wesleyan missionaries and the Anglicans. The Wesleyans were 'as zealous in their heavenly mission as the Church of England missionaries are in their earthly mission'.[26]

When the information on the missionaries' purchases was passed on to Buller's and Jerningham's mutual friend William Makepeace Thackeray, he wrote an article for *Punch* under the guise of the Reverend Stiggins, which was reproduced in *The Times*. Thackeray marvelled at the 'miracles the Missionary Fathers had performed in New Zealand':

> Father Kendal had purchased forty square miles of land with thirty-six axes. Was not this working wonders? Father Williams . . . got 11,000 acres of land out of the natives . . . . Mr. Dandeson Coates declares this is what every family missionary ought to do. Father Taylor got 55,000 acres, Fairburn got 4,000. (Dandeson says they are going *to give it back again* . . .) another little army of twenty-three martyrs put in their claims for 86,000 acres . . . . These proud achievements belong to the Church alone. The Roman Catholics in

> New Zealand have not asked or taken one acre . . . . [Jerningham Wakefield] tells us that the admirable [Anglican] fathers have taught the natives not to put their trust in any man of the world . . . and they call all the non-missionary colonists *devils*. Devils of course –, and what is the duty of their reverences? Why, to cast out the devils to be sure, and to keep the natives from all dangers.[27]

In early July, Evans's petition from the settlers was finally presented to the House by Lord Howick, together with other petitions from the Company, absentee landowners, former settlers resident in England, and London's influential bankers and merchants.

When news finally reached England of the conflict in the upper North Island, Evans was not the only colonist to feel alarmed at Wellington's vulnerability in being so close to Te Rauparaha and Rangihaeata. He accompanied Jerningham, Guyton and Moreing to visit Edmund Halswell's son Beauchamp in Brompton. Beauchamp and his wife had taken Pirikawau of Ngati Toa under their care for over two years. Pirikawau, who was closely related to the most influential chiefs at Waikanae, needed little prompting to write to Chief Wiremu Kingi, urging him to steer clear of Hone Heke's war and to advise Rangihaeata and Te Rauparaha to do likewise:

> Listen to what I am about to say to you. The maories will certainly be destroyed by the pakehas, if they adopt the principle of John Heki . . . . O William King, have nothing to do with the proceedings of that fellow. I have a word more to say to you (tell it to our relation Rangihaeata, also to Te Rauparaha): Let not our relation imagine that it was because of his size, or his power, or his tallness, that the pakehas were afraid of him; – no, they were not afraid of him, but the considerateness of the chiefs of England induced them to let them both live. The leading men of the New Zealand Company are sufficiently powerful to avenge the death of Wakefield; that they do not do so arises from their good feeling. But I will explain more fully to you, when I return, the kind consideration of the people of England. Governor FitzRoy is to return and Captain Grey is to be Governor there. Here are Tiraweke [Jerningham], Guyton, Moreing and Dr. Evans. This is all I have to say to you.
>
> Your loving relation, Pirikawau[28]

In January the following year, the *New Zealand Spectator and Cook's Straits Guardian* rejoiced that this letter had had a salutary effect. Maori at Waikanae under the aegis of Bishop Hadfield were beginning to prosper in European skills such as growing wheat. They were reportedly writing a memorial to Governor Grey begging to be 'treated as British subjects and to be instructed in the customs and the laws of the pakehas'. Rangihaeata held out in opposition but Te Rauparaha was cautioning his followers to obey the governor.

A week after his visit to Pirikawau, *The Times* editorial deploring the news from New Zealand bore Evans's influence:

> The news from New Zealand . . . [proves] that the fears which we long ago expressed were not those of idle alarmists . . . . we speak in a sad, and not in a boastful spirit . . . . it needed but slight ability in connecting cause and effect to arrive at the moral certainty that to provoke and ill-treat a savage race, and then to make a parade of weakness and inability was a sure method of inviting them into the wild justice of revenge . . . . At how high a price has Lord Stanley bought the gratification of thwarting the New Zealand Company! Had he supported its rights while controlling its rapacity – had there been union between them – the native race, instead of being egged on into the competing line, would have fulfilled its destiny of being adopted into the family of civilization peaceably and advantageously. Government have taught the savages to treat the colonizers as though they are a railway company, and to ask a fancy price for their land. If however the New Zealanders have shown an aptness for European arts in selling their titles for the same land two or three times over, they have also displayed in their warfare a spirit worthy of civilized nations. We are assured even by the sufferers that Heki showed himself a generous foe; he sent notice beforehand of the intended attack; he allowed townsmen who were popular with the natives to bring off their property; in destroying the settlement he made a point of excepting the churches and the houses of the missionaries; and we are not surprised to learn that people capable of such conduct displayed courage in action.[29]

Evans was also chipping away at the government in other ways. Only three days after Joseph Somes's sudden death on 25 June, Company secretary T. C. Harington was instructed to ask the Company's solicitors, Few and Co., to 'take the opinion of two counsel of eminence' on a case that Evans would lay before them. The two questions Evans wanted to explore regarding the Acts of Parliament, 3rd and 4th Victoria, clause 62 were: firstly, whether New Zealand came under the provisions of the Acts – in particular clause 62 – giving Victoria the power to appoint a Legislative Council of seven members, including the Governor, who were 'empowered to make and ordain "all such laws and ordinances as may be required for the peace, order, and good government of the colony"'; and secondly, if New Zealand were included in the clause, did the Colony's Legislative Council have the power to impose taxes? He wanted also to examine the Company's Charter, dated 16 November 1840.[30]

At the time, Winchester's 'Recorder' was William Burge, probably the most eminent expert in colonial law, as for some years he had obtained 'more practice . . . than any other member of the English Bar'.[31] He and Evans met several times to mull over the Acts and Charter, and even before he sent his opinion in writing, Burge's findings detailing the illegality of the government in New Zealand had found their way into clauses thirteen and fourteen of the Petition to Parliament of 'the Settlers of New Zealand at present sojourning in England':[32]

> . . . the act of Parliament under which New Zealand purports to be governed is wholly inoperative in that country, and that its inhabitants, – the colonists by their birth, and the natives by the Treaty of Waitangi, which confers on them all the rights and privileges of British subjects, – are entitled to a free government, and may lawfully resist the despotism to which they have been subjected.

Burge's decision was given due prominence in *The Times*. The editorial acknowledged that the news of war in the colony would normally put such questions into the background, but:

> . . . *inter arma silent leges* [in times of war the law falls silent]: . . . . Injurious as the change may have been from a revenue raised by customs duties to one obtained . . . by the imposition of an income tax, it would complete the climax of misrule if it should be legally established that both were absolutely illegal . . . . [Burge] declares that he has formed [his opinion] with no inconsiderable anxiety, because he is well aware that an opinion which imputes to an Act of Parliament insufficiency and imperfections in its structure is likely to be controverted, and to be regarded with prejudice.

After comparison with other colonies, Burge had decided that as New Zealand had no House of Assembly or body 'analogous to the tax-imposing part of our English Government . . . the Crown, having itself no power to impose taxes, could not grant such powers to [its] nominees'. Therefore:

> . . . we insist that representation shall go along with taxation . . . . this matter will come in with others to be settled, and the affairs of the colony will now secure attention. The recent fatal occurrences will have the same kind of effect which an accident has upon the dangerous bridge or precipice of a highway. When the mischief is done the bridge or road is indicted.[33]

The *Colonial Gazette* waded in, pronouncing 'every act of the New Zealand Government has been *ab initio* illegal . . . . Government dare not introduce a bill of indemnity [without] a bill giving New Zealand a constitutional government for the future.'[34]

On 7 July the Company forwarded this decision to Lord Stanley, who took it seriously enough to seek the government's advice on the issue. He sent it to the Attorney General, the Solicitor General and to Sir Thomas Wilde. 'FitzRoy Kelly, F. Thesiger, and Thomas Wilde, vouched that neither Mr. Burge's "reasons, nor any other that occur to us, furnish any well-founded doubt upon the subject". Lord Stanley directed Governor Grey to be guided by their opinions in New Zealand.'[35] During the second debate in late July, *The Times* accused the government of treating the management of New Zealand purely as a party question, making it easy for Stanley's 'egregious, habitual, systematic mismanagement of the colonies in general and of this colony in particular, [to] escape censure and a reproving vote'. The Colonial Office's policy affected four parties: Maori, the settlers, the Company and the Crown. What the Maori occupied 'ought to be secured to them':

> Nor can we recognize the proper spirit of protection in Lord Stanley's *avowed* design of getting possession of those lands which they make least use of, by taxing them and compelling them to register these uncultivated acres. It would be more direct and more fair for Government to assume to itself all the land that cannot be known to have been under occupation.

The Company had been driven into a breach of contract with the settlers, and the Crown's right of discovery was more valid than its cession by treaty. Stanley had:

> . . . ruined the company as a speculation, exasperated the natives and driven them to arms, sacrificed the prosperity and the property, and in some instances the lives of the settlers . . . . We can admire Lord Stanley's dexterity as a skirmisher in debate . . . but he is woefully deficient in weight and stability, in comprehensiveness, in fitness for responsible office . . . . He bears about the same proportion to a statesman that Lord Anglesey in the field did to the Duke of Wellington, or Ney to Napoleon.[36]

Evans played no small part in the publicity surrounding the illegality of New Zealand's measures – which may well have hastened the agreement between the two parties. The Company had been making plans for two further settlements in New Zealand – one Anglican and the other Church of Scotland – and after the second debate the directors' hopes were raised by the government's softening stance and willingness to give the Company concessions.

But just as they were considering co-operation, in early August Evans wrote to the Company's directors from the Reform Club, maintaining that the settlers deserved to 'be indemnified in some way' by the Company or the government:

> As it is understood that negotiations are going on at this time between the New Zealand Company and the Government, with a view to the settlement of the differences between them, I feel justified, by the deep interest I have in the question, and under an obligation to my fellow settlers, to remind the company that we have a just and unanswerable claim to be indemnified in some way for the ruinous consequences of the long delay in the fulfillment of the New Zealand Company's contract with us.
>
> To give us at this late period a bare fulfillment of the original contract, after the lapse of more than six years since you received our purchase money, would be of little value to the majority of us. Having been a director of the Union Bank, I know that there is scarcely one of the original land orders that has not been mortgaged at the rate of 10% per annum; and that men like myself have made ruinous sacrifices in the hope that ultimately they might redeem their property. I do not now presume to say whether the company or the Government is morally responsible for this state of things; but it is clear that the settlers ought to be indemnified, and my sole object now is to prevent that subject from being overlooked in the final settlement of the question.
>
> I trust that the part I have taken in the late controversies will be a sufficient pledge that I make this communication from a sense of duty, and not from any distrust in the honour and generosity of the directors . . .

This flew in the face of the united front of the Company and its settlers against a hitherto hostile government. At a meeting on 7 August the directors turned on Evans in a fit of moral outrage. Far from repaying him or being indebted in any way personally, they countered:

> With respect to your own case, it is to be observed that, from the active share which you took in the earlier proceedings, they have always been in the habit of considering, that with the transactions of the Company and the responsibilities it incurred, whatever these may have been, there was scarcely any one person so thoroughly and essentially identified as yourself.
>
> With respect to others . . . . Deeply as they lament the state

> of circumstances which you describe, they conceive that they are not responsible for it, and cannot justly be expected to make compensation; produced, as it has been, by causes under which they have themselves been fellow-sufferers with the colonials, over which they have had no control, and against which it has devolved upon them, in behalf of all, to struggle, without intermission of exertion, and, unfortunately, without prospect of success . . . . In conclusion . . . occasion will be taken from your letter, to bring the subject again under the immediate consideration of Her Majesty's Government.[37]

A copy of Evans's letter was forwarded to Lord Stanley. The directors had shunted their responsibilities to the settlers onto the government, making Evans the whipping boy of both, and he retreated in fury to the company of his friends. Just what had he been doing this last decade? Only sacrificing two promising careers and enduring hardships and privations the directors could not even begin to imagine. Yet in their condemnation of Evans, the Company had also recognised his pivotal role in Wellington's colonisation.

When news reached Wellington of the directors' response, the furious settlers held meetings from July through September 1846. In late July, at a meeting of the landholders, Featherston spoke for them all when he said:

> . . . the Company had grasped everything for themselves and after having by means of the settlers obtained great advantages, had thrown them completely overboard. Again, when Dr. Evans, on their behalf, applied for compensation for the losses incurred by them from the inability of the Company to fulfil their contract, the Directors not only denied their liability, but coolly referred him to the Government. The Directors had received their (the settlers') money for goods to be delivered on their arrival in the Colony – had been paid a handsome commission of 25 per cent. – and yet when at the end of six years, they, [the Purchasers] complained that the goods had never been delivered, and claimed compensation, the Directors (who might be regarded as their brokers) denied the justice of the claim, and referred them to a third party [the Government] with whom they had never had any dealings whatever.[38]

Several meetings followed, and in November the main body of the letter to the directors, signed by fifty-five men, complained that for six years, instead of having followed Sir George Gipps's 'arrangement' that would have given the government the task of managing the accounts between the settlers and the Company, they had become 'the victims of the unhappy differences between the

Company and the Colonial Office'. They cited clause 12 of Lord John Russell's agreement, which disclaimed liability of the Crown for the Company's land sales, leaving it to the Company to 'fulfil and carry into effect'. 'How', they demanded, 'can you now deny your liability?' The letter continued:

> . . . [we] claim from you compensation . . . . we are smarting under a sense of wrong: . . . we have been inexpressibly grieved, mortified and surprised at the unaccountable determination so openly announced in your reply to Dr. Evans – your determination to repudiate your most solemn and sacred obligations.[39]

In spite of its irregularities, the early Company still had its supporters. An 'Old Correspondent' from Auckland who wrote to *The Times* was no fan of Wellington becoming the capital, dismissing the notion as 'preposterous', but spoke for many who believed at the time:

> There can be no question that to the New Zealand Company England is indebted for the sovereignty of these magnificent islands; and on that account alone, great allowances ought to have been made for the irregularities of their first proceedings. The Company has 'done the State good service', and ought to have been encouraged instead of thwarted in its unexampled efforts; and I am rejoiced to see Sir Robert [Peel] proposes a co-operation for the judicious settlement of this colony.[40]

This was cold comfort for Evans, who knew at forty-three that his prospects in any field were narrowing daily. He had privately tried to address the problem of Monro's threat to foreclose on his mortgage, but the pressures were mounting. In some way he had to realise on his property that lay idle, awaiting the decision of the Land Court. And the interests of the Wellington settlers weighed heavily on his mind.

When a position was advertised for Judge of the Court of Bankruptcy at Tower Hamlets for the following year, Evans jumped at the chance, canvassing his colleagues and friends for testimonials in late August. Less than a month had passed since the directors' rebuke, but George Young apparently felt no qualms in picking up his pen and swearing:

> . . . from the manner in which Dr. Evans has discharged many responsible and delicate commissions entrusted to him by the New Zealand Company, *he has acquired the confidence of the Directors in no ordinary degree*; and that I know from the most unimpeachable authority, that his conduct as a magistrate and in various difficult

> and important positions into which he was thrown in New Zealand, equally obtained for him the respect and confidence of the Colonists . . . it would be difficult to find a Gentleman better fitted for the office by character, information and habits.[41]

Aglionby testified to Evans's 'general information and knowledge of the world, integrity, discernment, vigour and industry . . . in a high degree'. Evans had enjoyed 'great practice in the Courts of New Zealand', earning 'the reputation of being a zealous, industrious and able lawyer'.

After returning from dining with Thackeray at Vauxhall, Jerningham agreed, attesting that Evans had attracted the 'leading business, among the ten or twelve barristers in the Supreme and other Courts of law' in Wellington, acquitting his duties as magistrate 'not only to the satisfaction of the Local Government, but, also, in such a way as to merit the general approbation, which was, in one instance, especially and emphatically expressed, of [his] fellow colonists'.

The Right Honourable Stephen Lushington, DCL, Judge of the High Court of Admiralty, and former tireless campaigner for the abolition of slavery, parliamentary reform, Catholic emancipation and civil rights for Jews, had known Evans since 1832, and placed 'very great confidence in him', adding that there was no question of his abilities or his integrity. Although he had a personal interest in Evans's success, he wrote, 'you will give me credit for not exceeding the truth . . . least of all when the interests of the Tower Hamlets are at stake'.

Although his position precluded his involvement, the Right Honourable the Lord Brougham and Vaux, former Lord High Chancellor of Great Britain, suggested to Evans that he communicate with Colonel Fox, Lushington's successor as Member for Tower Hamlets, using Brougham's name. 'I can conscientiously affirm that a better choice could not be made, and that the Court will gain exceedingly by so competent a person being named', he concluded.

Several others attested to Evans's zeal, energy, skill and knowledge, mostly singling out his integrity. Joshua Evans of the Bankruptcy Court, and other magistrates like Henry Selfe who had enjoyed a close friendship with Evans for fifteen years, vouched for his legal skills, his 'calm and even temper, most business-like habits, and a judgment cool, impartial, discriminating and prompt'.

Charles Buller, the rapidly rising MP, graciously protested that:

> . . . a Testimonial from so very humble a lawyer as myself to one of your far higher attainments in all legal knowledge would appear

> a presumption on my part. But I cannot forego the opportunity of expressing the high opinion which I entertain of those attainments, and the high reputation which you enjoy with those who are every way better qualified to speak to your professional character . . .

John Pye Smith, DD, LLD, FRS – the former leading committee member of Mill Hill School – amply atoned for its earlier treatment of Evans by attesting to his 'extraordinary talents, his eminent attainments in literature, and the remarkable energy of his character'. Of the 'eminent attainments in literature' we can only surmise that Evans had published pamphlets on various subjects pertaining to reform or colonisation as well as contributing significantly to the Company's publications. As a member of the Law Reform Society he may have written pamphlets on that subject as well.

Benjamin Hawes Junior, MP for Lambeth – a member of the Aborigines' Protection Society and currently Stanley's right-hand man – attested especially to Evans's 'most honourable character'; while Colonel Torrens,[42] one of the earliest promoters of Gibbon Wakefield's South Australian scheme, spoke of 'the zeal, ability, integrity and success with which [Evans] conducted the important and difficult business which I entrusted to [his] sole and exclusive guidance'.

Reverend Samuel Hinds, chaplain to the Archbishop of Dublin, spoke of the 'worldly care' Evans had endured while they had worked together for the 'religious and moral welfare of the Colony', but added, 'it was to my mind, one of the hopeful features of the scheme that a man of your attainments and character was embarked in it'.

William Hutt wrote that he had 'habitually' referred to Evans's 'vigorous and well-instructed mind and high moral character' when discussing him with others, and emphasised that although their work together had sometimes needed 'the exercise of all the highest attributes of the mind and disposition', at all times and under 'very arduous circumstances' Evans's conduct had been 'distinguished by . . . ability, patient labour, and steady benevolence'. And William Burge, who had recently been most impressed by Evans's 'information and qualification', added his recommendation.[43]

In spite of these impressive testimonies from illustrious contacts and friends, Evans soon learned that he had been unsuccessful in his application. Nothing could compensate for his lengthy absence from England: in fact, his legal experience in England was virtually non-existent. Instead, he was a returned colonist – a second-class citizen – and he was tainted by his association with the New Zealand

Company. Gibbon Wakefield later wrote of the plight of the returning colonist: being ignored, passed over when positions were at stake, and noticeably absent from the dining tables and salons.[44]

When the government's concessions were announced in the Company's nineteenth report on 16 October, Evans's usefulness to the directors was made effectively redundant.[45] But he had not severed his relations with them. November found him at New Zealand House in conference with Gibbon Wakefield, Aglionby, George Young and John Lance. Edmund 'Pukunui' Halswell was there, having recently returned from New Zealand.[46]

Having paid no principal or interest to Monro on the mortgage, Evans had been forced to make a painful decision. He wrote formally to the directors, offering the Company his property in Wellington, consisting of fifty town and country sections, a total of 5050 acres, with the proviso that he retain three town sections for his family.[47] For the directors, who were busily fielding questions about the Company's plans from all quarters while lobbying hard for a loan from the government, it was an opportune time to acquire lucrative land for their own estate, and they accepted his offer with alacrity. They interviewed him first on 18 December, so for Evans his first Christmas back in London with his family must have been bleak.

In the New Year a select committee of Raikes Currie, Gower and Lyall began their inquiry into Evans's offer, listening to his evidence and that of Edmund Halswell and John Knowles, former secretary to Colonel Wakefield.[48] Evans had simply asked for the purchase price with interest, reminding them to take into account the cost of improvements on his town sections, one of which was a beachfront property. The others would naturally increase in value with the town's progress. Of the country sections – at 100 acres per section – there were 'eight at or near Porirua Harbour, and 21 of 25 acres each', originally intended for 'cultivation allotments . . . on the line of road to Wairarapa'. It was this site that the committee provisionally earmarked for their intended Church of England settlement. They were impressed with the calibre of Evans's property, and when they met on 5 February decided on terms that were not generous: Evans was to be offered only 'not less than' the original price he had paid. And they refused to consider improvements, maintaining that wooden buildings could not be insured.[49]

Later, again in the absence of William Hutt, they appointed another committee to deal specifically with Evans and his mortgagees Robert Monro and the Chethams, as they were busily dealing separately with John Wright's assignees over Wright's thirty-three sections. Largesse was falling into their laps as several impoverished settlers were being forced to resell their land.

During a special committee meeting on 16 February, Lyall 'declined to act', probably lacking the stomach for the sort of deal the directors anticipated with Evans. Gower and Currie conferred with Evans, and with Company solicitor Few. Samuel Brees, the former chief surveyor of Wellington, confirmed the value of his sections, and scotched the committee's objections to wooden buildings, confirming that the buildings were of brick. Evans told them his Wellington agents had just confirmed that the ground rent was £315 for the beachfront property. The property was secured with leases that had 15–17 years to run, and the interest on the properties was 10 per cent.

After absorbing the details, the directors offered to purchase Evans's entire property – including the three town sections that he had wanted exempted – at the original purchase price with just a 5 per cent increase for the six years he had held them, regardless of the improvements on many of the sections. The payment would take effect from the date of the land orders to the date of the court's approval, and after their solicitors had approved the land titles.[50] Evans 'stoutly resisted' the offer on his improved sections, saying he had spent a great deal of money building on many of them, but agreed to accept the committee's price for the unimproved sections. Everyone knew he was desperate and three days later, while he attended his brother Alfred's wedding to twenty-two-year-old Emily Clark,[51] William Hutt, who was fully aware of Evans's plight, reluctantly seconded the motion accepting the committee's report on Evans's property.

With the whiff of a remarkable deal in the air, George Young, backed by Gibbon Wakefield, proposed that the Company refuse to pay any interest at all to Evans. But decency prevailed and the other directors rejected the mean-spirited move. It was not unusual for Wakefield to turn against his supporters, frequently treating his followers merely as tools for his own end. Lord Howick had warned a decade earlier that 'ultimately, anyone who disagreed [with Gibbon Wakefield] in the slightest' was regarded as an enemy 'with the worst possible spirit and an utter contempt for truth'.[52] Wakefield's cavalier treatment of Evans in fact mirrored his betrayal of others, such as Robert Gouger in the South Australian venture. Like Evans, Gouger had been an indefatigable worker, 'studying colonial conditions, writing to men of influence, distributing pamphlets, visiting MPs and officials at Downing Street, lecturing, preparing advertisements, articles and letters for the press'. He and Hanson had written much of the material attributed to Wakefield. He had also expended a great deal of his own money on the scheme. When Wakefield broke with the South Australian promoters in 1835, 'he declared in a fit of pique that Gouger was merely his delegate on the committee'. But all too frequently the 'mere delegate' was left to foot the bill. After discarding Gouger, who had made sacrifices and suffered personal tragedy to further the Company's goal, he had found just the right man for his next venture in Evans. In this latest betrayal, Wakefield was indeed 'sulky, petty and egocentric'.[53]

The directors wrote to Sir Edward Strode (Chetham's father) for details of the mortgage, and Strode purchased Monro's remaining interest in the property. Swallowing the last of his pride, Evans asked if his wife and stepdaughter could retain the rents they received on their dwellings before Harriet was informed of the sale, and be given time to find other accommodation.[54] The directors graciously complied, instructing Colonel Wakefield to offer Harriet 'all accommodation in his power'.[55] It would be another seventeen months before Evans received reimbursement for his land. Without the practical help offered by his brother James Cook, Evans might never have survived financially. He would never forget it, marking his gratitude much later in the best possible way.

CHAPTER SEVENTEEN. A COLONIAL IN LONDON

> The Victorians in their full vigour at the middle of the century were idealists. It was not until the dismal end of the century that the Victorians put their money-bags and power first and became imperialists . . . . The Victorians had great courage, great energy, and great kindness of heart.
>
> R. J. Cruikshank, *Charles Dickens and Early Victorian England*, Pitman & Sons, London, 1949, pp.117, 270

By the end of March 1846, Evans had found chambers in brand new rooms in Number 7, the newly built addition to the six stone buildings of Lincoln's Inn. From there he soon found employment on the western circuit and at the Bristol, Bath and Somerset sessions where he enjoyed 'a fair practice'.[1] He was fortunate, as the early years of any barrister's practice were lean; there was an over-supply of lawyers, and competition for work was fierce. A barrister needed only one or two early successes to establish his reputation, but the cost of travel, keeping a clerk and stopping overnight in inns was formidable, so Evans supplemented his income by his writing – mostly for *The Times* but also for *The Spectator* and probably the *Morning Chronicle*.[2]

Hanson had replied to his letter of the previous year. Well used to Evans's frequent fulminations, the pragmatist opened in exasperation:

> My Dear Doctor, What are you about now? This is the grand question whenever I chance to see Mrs. Evans . . . . the rule which I have discovered in order to preserve a 'Colonists' peace of mind is, never to conjecture . . . . Some time or other we shall know all that it is fitting we should know, and in the meantime, we must have patience. This is, I dare say, good philosophy, and tolerably easy for me, who are only sympathetically interested in your proceedings, and their result, but rather difficult for Mrs. Evans, to whom consequently I very seldom preach it.

Hanson said he had 'for a very long time' given up hoping for any 'good news' from England, either from the Company or from the government. He did not doubt the integrity of individual directors, but believed they would deny any claims that would affect the shareholders' interests, and any that could not be made legally available. The government would not help, because 'if we will identify our cause with that of the Company we can look for nothing but that hostility which the Company has provoked'. He added that if nothing was to be 'hoped' from England, then very little was to be hoped from the colony itself, 'except in the increase of our flocks and herds'.

Everything in New Zealand was 'languishing'. Nobody was profiting, cultivation was diminishing and things were as bad as they could be. Hanson predicted ultimate success, although many settlers would be ruined. The most likely prospect for export was hogs' tallow, he confided, as he detailed his own speculations and prospects.[3]

Untrammelled by marriage, family or debt, Hanson had sensibly spread his investments. Cool and imperturbable, he was a model colonist, taking advantage of each opportunity. He could criticise with impunity both the Company and the government, carrying no banner of responsibility for the settlers or the Wakefield scheme. But he did care about Maori, believing they were a 'reasoning' and 'tolerably reasonable' race.[4] He severely disapproved of Grey's solutions to the Wellington problems and of his arrest of Te Rauparaha in July for treason.[5] Not long after Evans received his letter, however, even Hanson finally eschewed his own maxim, admitted defeat and left New Zealand for good. After relinquishing his government appointments he sailed to Adelaide, where he published a pamphlet entitled *Extracts from a Letter to Captain FitzRoy R.N. from R. Davies Hanson Esq.*, and embarked on a distinguished career.

In June when the government fell, Lord Russell succeeded Peel with Earl Grey (Howick) as his Colonial Secretary, which delighted the Company. But the saga between Evans and the Company dragged on. Evans asked for an advance of £200 at the end of the month. The directors agreed to give him £50 – but only if he provided an 'Abstract of the Title'. When the directors met the next day, George Young had replaced the fair-minded William Hutt on the panel. In July, Hutt resigned, but the directors begged him to reconsider and attend when he could. Their differing interests and goals had been slowly creating fissures in the Company's structure, which became so apparent that in Wellington, after the twentieth report of the Company was published in December, Revans and Roots moved a vote of no confidence in the directors at a public meeting.[6]

The strain even took its toll on the Company's leader. On 18 August, Gibbon Wakefield suffered a massive attack of paralysis and retired to recuperate. In the same month Parliament passed the first New Zealand Constitution Act, sanctioning a loan to the Company of £100,000 against their lands at interest of 3 per cent.

A month after Wakefield's collapse, on Tuesday, 20 September, Evans's father was 'seized with an attack of paralysis' at the age of sixty-seven, 'whilst apparently in the enjoyment of his usual vigorous health, and calmly expired'. The pastor of his church at Mile End for thirty-eight years, he had 'preached at 567 [named] places of worship and many more [unnamed] . . . gratuitously visiting at different times 26 counties of England and Wales'.[7] He had retired to Thames Ditton, but not before he had witnessed the human tragedy of his earliest parishioners in Stepney, Mile End and Bethnal Green. The silk weavers had been virtually starved out of existence by the power looms that had replaced their hand looms, which grew in number from 2400 in 1813 to well over 200,000.[8]

Reverend Evans's life had indeed been one of enormous self-sacrifice. Evans mourned him all his life. His own lack of success and his having chosen a different path from the one his father had mapped out for him might have added a layer of guilt to his grief. In later years Evans caused much amusement amongst his colleagues with frequent references to his 'honoured parent'.[9]

The Reverend's clever sons had all elected to pursue more ambitious professional paths. James Cook's career mirrored that of his elder brother. A teacher and headmaster, he became a barrister at Lincoln's Inn, wrote for *The Times* and was also an accomplished watercolour artist. He later became Secretary for the South Western Railway. Alfred was a successful medical practitioner. Even William, the 'greatly afflicted' near-invalid who resided with his parents and two sisters Hannah and Mary in the parish of St Matthew, Bethnal Green, was recorded as a surgeon in the 1841 census. He did not appear in the census of 1851 so it is presumed he passed away in those years. The girls displayed similar enterprise. Claudia and Mary were principals of a girls' school in Kent, and Hannah was a part-owner of the property.

In early February 1847, Evans's wife Harriet arrived in London with Edward Chetham and Amelia. Harriet had leased their house on Golders Hill to James and Mrs Coutts Crawford.[10] Chetham believed Evans was attempting to dispose of the property he had 'gifted' him unfairly behind his back, and he had come to intervene or, as Evans put it, to 'interfere'. After lengthy negotiations he made a further arrangement with the Company, under which certain sections – ten in all – were to be excluded from the sale.[11] Chetham then purchased his father's interest in the mortgage. But Evans was uneasy at the switch and was proving difficult, resisting to the end. Exasperated, Few and Co. threatened Evans with litigation. So he and his wife 'reluctantly' entered into an arrangement with Chetham, when a Deed of Conveyance was drawn up on 29 May 1847.

As the sale to the Company would yield £4,253 4s 8d, a balance of £1,251 would remain after the mortgage was paid off, and be given to Chetham. Evans wanted £2,000 to be handed over to his wife's trustees to satisfy their claims on her estate, so Chetham agreed to 'take a charge of the exempted property as advance of the difference – that is, £749'. On this understanding alone, Evans had agreed to the transfer of the land from Sir Edward Strode to his son. Although Evans believed the land to be worth £5,000 at the time, he was not worried about the discrepancy, as he viewed the Deed as an informal family arrangement.[12]

At the time the Deed was signed, both Evans and Chetham owed the Union Bank of Australia considerable sums – Evans, who had resigned his directorship earlier, owing £3,000. He had given the bank a mortgage on his property, subject to Monro's mortgage. Chetham's name had been included in the debt 'by way of accommodation'. With reference to the pair's legal partnership, the Deed was to protect Chetham's interests (as well as those of Harriet Evans's trustees), securing him against his 'accommodation acceptances at the bank', and the repayment of £749 when advanced by him. Evans vowed later that the Deed was executed '*nominally* to pass Chetham's interest in the sections to Evans, but *actually* to make Chetham carry out certain family arrangements which protected the estate without benefit to himself'. Chetham 'thoroughly understood the object of the arrangement'.[13]

On 10 June, the directors wrote to Chetham, reminding him of his power of attorney from Evans, which he had used to deal with part of the land, and warning him to 'execute an indemnity against the claims of all parties arising out of his own acts'. After he complied a month later, the cheque for £4,253 4s 8d was made out to Evans, but only 'partially signed by two signatories'. On 6 August 1847, twenty months after Evans had first offered his property to the Company, Few sent Evans the cheque for the sale of 3436 acres of land and transferred the deeds.[14]

Evans's view of the actions of Amelia's husband had deteriorated markedly over the entire transaction. A few days after the deal with the Company was finalised, he wrote from Serjeants' Inn protesting against the 'inference that he had *voluntarily* joined with Sir Edward Strode in the Conveyance to the Company, or from any other motive than to avoid the litigation under a Bill in Chancery with which he [had] been threatened by the Company's solicitor'.[15]

He vented his spleen and frustration elsewhere. In July, when the New Zealand papers were considered by Parliament, *The Times* led with:

> The history of New Zealand is the history of a great design defeated by the incapacity of those who have been entrusted with its execution. It is a history of petty jealousies, of personal quarrels, of Colonial Office intrigue, of rapacious avarice under the garb of religious zeal, of malice pretending to humanity, of civilization triumphing by fraud over barbarian ignorance, of barbarian revenge wreaking itself in cruelty upon the weakness of its oppressors, of alternate neglect and meddling folly, of imbecile indifference and presumptuous misgovernment. The annals of European colonization do not, with perhaps one exception, furnish an example of so fair a beginning conducted to so foul a conclusion.

When Governor Grey arrived in the colony, he found Maori in 'open and successful rebellion, smarting under wrongs for the most part imaginary and emboldened by the vacillating indecision of a Government without justice or judgment':

> He found a company the head and origin of a more flourishing settlement, paralysed by acts of oppression. He found settlers expelled by pretence or sufferance of law from lands which they had bought and paid for . . . he found a bankrupt treasury, an unequal and suicidal taxation, a Legislature without confidence in itself, and a people without trust in their rulers.[16]

Evans made every effort to recoup his losses, but his financial anxieties led to bouts of illness. In November that year typhus fever broke out. In a city of over two million people where the average age of mortality was twenty-seven years and where refuse and waste flowed into the Thames – the water supply for many of its inhabitants – a quarter of the population succumbed and London was considered 'a doomed city'.[17] Cholera also struck that year and 'no Londoner was ever completely well'.[18]

The colonial debates dragged on. In late 1847 Evans moved his chambers to 5 Serjeants' Inn, Fleet Street. The proximity to *The Times* offices was the deciding factor, as he was contributing columns on the subject of New Zealand. The leader of 15 December 1847 might also have doubled for Evans's personal overview of the history of colonisation in New Zealand. It is stamped with his signature: the sometimes obscure or quirky literary reference, the 'sesquipedalian phraseology' containing anachronisms such as 'Brummagem', and the vivid similes. It is laborious by modern standards, but still has flashes of genius when it speaks of Earl Grey (Lord Howick) and Evans's friend Ben Hawes of the Colonial Office, whose Constitution for New Zealand had been rejected and returned by Governor Grey:

> New Zealand since the date of the Treaty of Waitangi has been the subject of a succession of the most cruel experiments. A rabbit in the hands of Dr. Majendie could scarcely have met with harsher treatment. From Captain Hobson to Captain FitzRoy, from Secretary Normanby to Secretary Stanley, and from him to Secretary Gladstone, these unfortunate islands have been tossed about like a shuttlecock to the entire and perfect ruin of every white settler who has had the misfortune to be connected with them. [There follows a subjective sketch of the various disasters caused by incompetence] . . . .
>
> *The civilization of Great Britain got spoiled and rusty in the sea voyage to the Antipodes* . . . . In a moment of blissful inspiration the happy thought occurred to some fortunate statesman, that . . . New Zealand had occasion for one thing, and one thing only – to be governed by a *man* . . . . Governor Grey was appointed, and as far as the conduct of a Governor at the Antipodes can be criticized with safety, he seems to have been eminently worthy of the trust . . . . The event has happened . . . when a man of real ability and force of character takes the place of a mere pretender to these qualities. A sort of spell has fallen on the islands. Hostile aborigines are conciliated, native chiefs checkmate each other . . . . The man for New Zealand had been found. It was too much to expect that he would be left to carry out his task without interference from home . . . there never was a secretary at the Colonial Office who has had the good of the colonies more earnestly at heart than Earl Grey. In Mr. Hawes, he has found a painstaking and enlightened coadjutor. Between them . . . they manufactured a spick and span constitution for the islands of New Zealand . . . . There were to be municipal bodies, and electoral bodies, and distinct Houses of Assembly, and a united House of Assembly . . . . All the nice and delicate machinery, in short, which revising barristers and the common Pleas, and Parliamentary Committees can scarcely maintain in its vicious perfection at home, was suddenly to be transplanted into New Zealand . . . . when their new Brummagem constitution arrived at the Antipodes, there was a man there of sufficient sense and sufficient determination to pack it up in a blue box and send it home again to Downing Street . . . .

> We unfeignedly admire Earl Grey for the sincerity of purpose . . . it is a bitter moment when you are compelled to gulp down the work of your own hands . . . . When Captain Grey tells him that the New Zealanders will refuse to submit to a taxation imposed by the votes of a small minority of whites, he assents . . . and asks Parliament . . . to suspend indefinitely his own favourite scheme.[19]

When he was not writing for *The Times* and also contributing to *The Spectator*, Evans toured Bristol and the western circuits regularly, out of Gibbon Wakefield's orbit.[20] Although Gibbon Wakefield had moved on after his recovery to prepare for the settlement of Canterbury, Evans no longer belonged to his inner circle of assistants and advisors. Evans's practical needs were of more importance. But the two never severed their ties. Wakefield would find use for Evans in the future, so it is possible he asked for his help occasionally during this time.[21]

In late November 1848, when Charles Buller died suddenly (of erysipelas complicated by typhus) at the age of forty-two, his loss shook everyone and boded ill for the Company. News arrived a month or so later of Colonel Wakefield's death in Wellington from apoplexy on 19 September 1848. William Fox as his trustee succeeded him as Principal Agent. Wakefield's funeral attracted 'about a third of the Wellington population, Maori and Pakeha' – an unprecedented number. Te Puni was one of the pallbearers.[22]

After his own recovery, Gibbon Wakefield turned on the directors, telling the Parliamentary Committee that they had 'sold the honour of the Company and the interests of the colony for money':

> My incapacity changed the whole character of the direction of the N.Z. Company's affairs, which then fell into the hands of those in whose minds sound principles of colonization and colonial Government were as nothing compared with pounds, shillings and pence.[23]

Wakefield complained the Company had 'ruined' his vision' – 'causing him to exclaim' that it was 'founded by great men with small pockets; it has since fallen into the hands of small men with deep pockets'.[24]

Just before Christmas 1849, Brees's Panorama of New Zealand was exhibited at 6 Leicester Square amidst advertising and publicity. The article in *The Times* that gave a detailed description of the panorama was preceded by a laudatory brief history of the Company's bold enterprise in founding the colony 13,000 miles away. Although Evans was not its author, he was given credit for having influenced the colony's progress. After a brief history of the Wairau affray and

Heke's exploits in cutting down the flagstaff and sacking Kororareka, the article continued:

> These events concurring with the arrival in England of Dr. Evans, one of the earliest and most influential of the settlers, the attention of the public was called to the state of New Zealand both in Parliament and by the press, and finally measures were taken which it is hoped have by this time re-established the fortunes of the settlers, and which are now leading to the renewal of emigration upon a large scale to that colony.[25]

The Company staggered on till July 1850, when 'without its able advocates and powerful friends', it surrendered its charters and all its claims to land in the country, 'without having granted a single legal title to a single person of a single piece of land'.[26] Afterward, Harington explained Evans's land sale to Ben Hawes in November: 'The sum paid for Dr. Evans's land was fixed by adding to its original price subsequent interest. I must mention also an adverse claim on this property by an incumbrancer, but the Company's counsel is of the opinion that the Company's title is good.'[27]

When William Fox arrived in England in February 1851 as Wellington's Honorary Political Agent, he met up with Evans and other colonial reformers. He worked closely with solicitor Henry Sewell, Gibbon Wakefield and others on the New Zealand Constitution Act, although much of the credit went to Governor Grey who contributed to it. Fox later paid tribute to Evans in his series of six articles in the *Herald* in 1890, which became the pamphlet, *How New Zealand Got its Constitution*: 'Those who really got New Zealand her constitution were the colonists themselves and their friends in London.' Among some 'of the leaders in the colony' of Wellington he included 'Featherston, Fitzherbert, Clifford, Weld, Dr. Evans, the brothers Dorset, [and others]'.[28]

Little is known of Evans's last years in London. His career seemed to be, if not stellar, at least steady and successful. In 1849 he felt optimistic enough to take out an eight-year lease on new chambers in 2 Elm Court, Temple.[29] Many of his fellow barristers noted his vast store of classical knowledge, and were more than a little intrigued by his great vocabulary and ponderous, Johnsonian phraseology, even in his everyday conversation. They called him 'the Doctor' after the great lexicographer, a compliment he enjoyed.[30] In Evans's spare time, he began to make notes for a sequel to Gibbon's *Rise and Fall of the Roman Empire*, a long-held ambition for a man who was never happier than in a library surrounded by his books.[31]

But ill health always dogged him. That winter, there was a cholera epidemic. Concerns for public health and the need for sanitation were publicised by Dickens and others.[32] When Evans was offered the appointment of Chief Justice of Newfoundland by Sir John Jervis, he turned it down, probably because of the harsh climate. Then he was promised 'the next vacancy as *puisne* Judge in India'.[33] In 1851 he became so ill that his doctor advised him to move to a warmer climate.[34]

This meant New Zealand, but family business had to be disposed of first. On New Year's day, 1852, Edward Chetham, who had not yet paid anything to Harriet's trustees, signed a memorandum to the Deed giving Evans £1,333 – the £749 plus interest. It was agreed Evans would repay the sum with interest the following year and release Chetham from all claims of the Union Bank of Australia. In return Chetham would allow Evans to repurchase the property within two years. Evans refused to examine the account, as 'the Deed and the Conveyance were "*all bosh*"' – an informal family agreement. But the 'family agreement' was to culminate much later in one of the most sensational court cases witnessed in Wellington.[35]

When Evans and his wife finally turned their backs on the country of their birth and boarded the *Stag* for New Zealand, they had witnessed great progress. They had visited the Great Exhibition, seen people waving from balloons in the sky above London, and watched as the quaint old eighteenth-century buildings that had nurtured generations of great poets and thinkers were beginning to be torn down and replaced by a city better ordered, but less familiar. London was a city grooming itself for the modern age.[36]

CHAPTER EIGHTEEN. BACK TO WELLINGTON

Horace: Vir bonus est quis? *Quinctius*: Qui consulta patrum, qui leges juraque servat; Quo multae magnaeque secantur judice lites; Quo res sponsore, et quo causae teste tenentur. *Horace*: Sed videt hunc omnis domus et vicinia tota Introrsum turpem, speciosum pelle decora.	*Horace*: Who then is the good man? *Quinctius*: He who keeps the decrees of the senators, the laws and the constitution; by whom, as a judge, many and great causes are decided; by whom, as surety, property is retained, and by whom, as a witness, causes are won. *Horace*: But yet his whole family, and the entire neighbourhood sees that this man is inwardly and thoroughly base, though covered with a cloak of hypocrisy.
Horace, *Epistles*, B. 1. 16, 39 ff.	Trans. G. S. Evans, *Independent*, 22 December 1852

En route to Wellington, the *Stag* stopped at Victoria, where Evans saw for himself the growing legal and political prospects in the colony following the discovery of gold. He disembarked at Port Nicholson on 19 June 1852, and the *Independent* was 'most happy to find him in the enjoyment of good health, and to behold him receive from his old acquaintances the hearty welcome he so well deserves'.[1]

When he climbed Golders Hill to his house, Evans gazed out on a landscape little different from the one he had left eight years earlier, but the practical assistance he had given the merchants in the early 1840s had paid off. They were beginning to thrive. Pastoralism was gaining in prominence, especially in the Wairarapa, and was quickly becoming the mainstay of Wellington's economy. Now part of New Munster, the South Island and the lower part of the North Island had their own parliament and a governor, explorer Edward Eyre. But the concerns of Maori had been steadily subsumed by government and settler self-interest, and the population in Wellington was in steady decline.[2] Of the 436 capitalists of the early days, fewer than 85 had stayed.[3] At Pipitea, Wairarapa's only son, the last of his line, had died in late 1842,[4] and other chiefs like Moturoa were old or had passed on.

Evans was amongst friends and felt optimistic about his future in the colony. His old comrades Featherston and Fitzherbert were co-editing the *Wellington Independent*, which supported speedy self-government,[5] and he was able to congratulate the achievement of twenty-five-year-old Thomas McKenzie, the paper's part-owner and co-editor.[6] He also met Richard Wakelin, a senior journalist.

Within a week he had found work in court, helping solicitors Hugh Ross and Robert Hart argue for a ruling absolute in the case *Charles Enderby v Dundas and Preston*. While outlining his arguments in chambers, he came up against John King, an able man who was also working hard for the town's progress. Soon afterwards, the two men collaborated on a case that caused a sensation throughout the country.[7]

When Henry Chapman had resigned his position of *puisne* judge to take up the post of Colonial Secretary in Tasmania, his place had been taken by Sidney Stephen, a cousin of Sir James Stephen and fellow of Lincoln's Inn. Two years earlier, Stephen had moved from Australia to Otago, then to Lyttelton, where he had spent a short time as Supreme Court Justice. It was rumoured, apparently falsely, that in Otago he had dispensed his own brand of justice in a case concerning two brawling women, about which it was said he had been unwilling to wait for 'the slow and tardy process of the law'.[8] He was otherwise reputed to be 'clever and sharp'.[9]

About a fortnight after Evans's arrival, two men were summoned to sit on a jury of the Supreme Court, but failed to do so, incurring fines of £5 each. Charles Clifford, a wealthy farmer, excused himself on the grounds that he had been up the Wairarapa coast on business and was forgiven the fine. But Samuel Robinson, owner of the largest drapery on Lambton Quay, who could not leave his shop because he lacked staff, was ordered to pay. Robinson was so aggrieved at the inequitable treatment accorded 'the shopkeeper and the squatter' that he wrote a letter of complaint to the *Independent*, in which he obliquely referred to the incident involving Stephen in Otago. He disregarded Richard Wakelin's advice and signed the letter that was published on 17 July, which was preceded by an editorial written by Evans on the subject of Grey's despotism and the necessity for immediate self-government. Stephen promptly summoned Thomas McKenzie, as the paper's part-owner, for contempt of court, and McKenzie retained Evans as counsel for his defence.

The colony was in a fever of excitement. Meetings were held, the defiant settlers loudly advocating the freedom of the press and trial by jury. Solicitor John King was given a few days to prepare the case for Robinson, but Evans had barely a day to prepare his for McKenzie. What took place in court occupied Evans's energies for several months afterward. He took over the leading columns of the *Independent* to wage a war of words against the *New Zealand Spectator*, the judge and his 'illegal proceedings', and, said Wakelin, 'did not relinquish his hold' over the columns until some time later the following year.[10]

When Evans had left in 1844 he had been appalled at FitzRoy's bizarre behaviour, believing the arbitrary actions of those in power lacked foresight and judgement. The judiciary was another matter entirely. He thought it was unfair to fine the humbler man but not the landowner, writing caustically:

> We want a sliding scale, of the probability of guilt in any given case, which will be in the inverse ratio of the prisoner's wealth; the presumption of criminality being at the maximum in the case of total indigence, and diminishing gradually, in proportion to the amount of riches.[11]

Evans believed the case was also important as it threatened the very freedom of the press in publishing a signed letter critical of a decision of a member of the judiciary.

On Saturday 24 July, when King appeared for Robinson, Stephen demanded Robinson's presence in court. King objected that the proceedings were highly irregular as his client had not been served with an affidavit. Stephen retorted that an affidavit was unnecessary and again demanded Robinson's appearance. King refused, citing various precedents, Stephen lost his temper and King, 'evidently under strong emotion', left the court to confer with his client. He returned saying he had nothing more to say, at which Stephen called loudly in vain for Robinson and finally adjourned court.

During this exchange, Evans had risen to announce that he was appearing for McKenzie and asked for leave as he had had only one day's notice to prepare his case. Stephen had to check with the court's clerk Robert Strang – who affirmed that two days' notice were necessary – before he granted Evans's application, extending the recess until Tuesday. Robinson meanwhile was remanded in custody for six days.[12]

On Tuesday the wrangling continued between King and Stephen, King demanding Robinson's release. On King's advice Robinson refused to answer the affidavits and was ordered to prison for one month. Evans rose for McKenzie, and after the affidavits were read, objected to the order's validity, citing *Regina v. Woolmer.* Stephen replied that the case did not limit the power of the court. Evans objected: 'I must say, your honour that I am placed in a most awkward position. I am maintaining a most unequal contest; I am contending against the Court [rather than against Counsel].'

He told Stephen he had looked through every single similar case and found none where there could be a 'contempt of Court in a matter *coram non judice*'. The irregularity lay in the order having been issued by a judge in chambers where it ought to have been made in full court. The order, he said, was 'the foundation of the proceedings, and if the order is wrong, it is a fatal error to the proceedings, "*ab initio*" (from the beginning)'.

Stephen argued that a recent Act of Parliament had granted a judge in chambers 'in such cases, full power of the Court'.

> Evans: Will your Honor oblige me with the name of the Statute? I have practiced in the Bail court for the past seven years, and I have never heard of such a Statute or such a practice.
> Justice Stephen: I am surprised, Dr. Evans, that you cannot see the cases you have adduced do not bear in any way upon the present one.

Evans protested that as the proceedings were informal, McKenzie should be granted an immediate and unconditional discharge. The cases he had looked into were 'very numerous indeed, for I have a cart-load of volumes here and not in any one of them can I find a precedent, nor any analogous case'. After more argument, Stephen referred Evans to Blackstone as the pre-eminent reference. Evans disagreed, saying:

> Not long ago, I received a very sharp rap over the knuckles from a learned Judge, for quoting Blackstone as an authority equal to that of the decisions of the judges. Blackstone is all very well as a text-book, or for the law student, but it would never do in these days to quote Blackstone in opposition to the recognized reports of the Courts at Westminster.

The two men debated point by point until Evans recorded his objection and Stephen his reply. McKenzie was called, appeared and stated he was in the hands of his counsel. Evans said that McKenzie 'honestly and conscientiously believed he was not responsible for the letter's publication as the writer's name was attached to it', but Stephen objected that no affidavit had been filed to that effect. King broke in, saying there had been none as they believed the proceedings were wrong. The court was adjourned again for the affidavit to be drawn up and presented at midday the next day. The mood in the crowded court was overwhelmingly sympathetic toward the defendants.

Evans, who believed the case should have been decided by a trial by jury, penned a lengthy editorial inveighing against the 'arbitrary proceedings in the Supreme Court of Wellington', saying, 'For a man to be at the same time prosecutor and Judge, is a violation of the first principle of natural justice, and repugnant to the spirit and practice of the British laws.' He quoted more than one sage on the topic of freedom of speech, including John Milton, who said, 'To count a man not fit to print his mind is the greatest indignity to a free and knowing spirit that can be put upon him.'[13] The *Independent* sparred with the *New Zealand Spectator and Cook's Straits Guardian* on the subject of contempt of court. McKenzie and his 'coadjutors' were first attacked by the *Spectator*, to be swiftly countered by the *Independent*:

> Dr. Evans and Mr. King, will however, know how to take care of themselves; and if they are forced into a conflict, to defend themselves or their professional character, they . . . will probably carry the war much farther than will be agreeable to our contemporary or his 'co-adjutors' . . . .
>
> *Imperia legume potentiora quam hominem*, – 'the empire of laws more powerful than that of individuals' – is the definition which a great historian gives of a state of liberty, as distinguished from one of slavery.[14]

In late August, Stephen delivered his report and judgment. He condemned the editorials in the *Wellington Independent* and, using several legal references, found in his own favour.[15] Robinson was ordered to pay 'a fine of £20 and find bail himself in £100 and two sureties of £50 each, to be of good behaviour for twelve calendar months, and to be imprisoned until such bail be given and such fines paid. In the case of Mr. McKenzie, that he should find bail himself, in £100, and two sureties of £50 each, to be of good behavior for twelve months, and to be imprisoned until such bail has been tendered and accepted.' Both men were sent to jail. The court was in such uproar at one point that Stephen ordered the sheriff to arrest everyone.[16]

Wakelin felt it 'worthy of remark that all [this] time the leading members of the Constitutional Association maintained an ominous silence: though there is reason to believe that more than one of them were aware that Judge Stephen was insane at the time, though the fact never leaked out until after his death . . .'.[17]

At a protest meeting the following night, Saturday, 28 August, a committee was appointed to raise subscriptions to cover the cost of the fines. Evans was asked to write a memorial to the Secretary of State, protesting at the injustice of the sentence, but illness and 'pressing engagements' forced him to drop the undertaking. The committee sent their report with copies of the affidavits to Grey, who ordered the immediate release of the two men. McKenzie had been imprisoned for three weeks.[18]

By December when the settlers had had no reply to their memorial requesting justice, they sent another. Evans continued taking swipes at Stephen. He abhorred the fact that Judge Stephen had excused the wealthy Charles Clifford on his 'veracity', and had cited 'our old friend Horace' to illustrate the 'just and upright citizen'. In fact, said Evans, Horace had been illustrating exactly the opposite. Evans took his readers line by line to the true meaning of the passage – that the man may be seen as upright, but is in reality 'covered with a cloak of hypocrisy. So dangerous is it [for Stephen] to play with edge tools', Evans observed, 'but notwithstanding this, we can more readily excuse a learned judge for taking his classical quotations from the Eton Grammar, than we can for deriving his law from such an authority as Blackstone's Commentaries.'[19]

At a meeting of the McKenzie-Robinson Committee in late December, a letter from Robinson with a cheque enclosed was read and tabled. It 'would be impossible' for the committee to accept the cheque, observed Evans, adding, with more than a hint of sarcasm, that the committee first seek Robinson's permission before publishing his letter.[20]

It was not until early January that the settlers who had twice petitioned Grey – in September, and at the end of December – received his reply. The Colonial Secretary, Alfred Domett, explained by letter that Grey had consulted the Crown's law officers, only to find that he had no power or authority to 'enquire into the judicial acts of the Judge', as he would then effectively become a Court of Appeal. Undaunted, the committee drew up a petition to be sent to the Secretary of State through the Governor. Daniel Riddiford proposed the vote of thanks to the committee, and thanks were also carried by acclamation to the counsels, Evans and King.[21] Thus, the case was temporarily put to rest.

In the meantime, Evans had turned to other matters.

Throughout July, Evans had written on the necessity for local self-government in his usual inimitable style. He was concerned that Grey's manipulation of power centred 'all the powers and functions of a Legislative body in his own person' and, in doing so, harmed the future of the settlers:

> Not that he has wilfully and with malice aforethought, injured us – but because the debarring us from the exercise of local powers of Self-Government has been of itself an injury to us of such magnitude, that but few persons can form an adequate conception of it; while the evils of which it has been the direct cause, have doubtlessly been very great – though as those were patent to all, they have been more insisted on than the gigantic curse of which they are but the fruits.

Although the Act for self-governance had been passed by the British Parliament in August 1846, Grey had argued that its comprehensive systems of government were premature for the immature country and that its measures would alienate Maori. The Constitution Act was suspended for five years. Evans believed Grey had done 'his best to deprive' them of the 'institutions, rights and privileges of our fathers':

> . . . and has likewise done his best to unfit us for the due enjoyment and proper exercise of them. For to pretend that the forced stagnation to which our political life's blood has been subjected, will turn out to be highly conducive to the health of the body politic; is as absurd as to maintain that a mechanic could more skillfully and ably use his right arm after having kept it confined five years in a sling.[22]

Later that month Evans gave his opinion on Grey's Provisional Councils Ordinance, saying that in its present form it would not be passed, but that he personally wanted to have the Governor appoint one-third of its legislators, rather than the election of the entire council being left in the hands of 'a privileged few' who, with their wealth and influence, had less need of a vote than any other class:

> We believe with Montesquieu, that in a free state every man who is supposed a free agent ought to be his own governor, and that therefore the legislative power should reside in the whole body of the people. And, as Bentham has well observed, in order that the universal interest may be advanced, all particular interests must be comprehended and advanced, except where it can be shewn that the advancement of any particular interest would injure the advancement of the universal interest . . . . We hold that every man ought to have a voice in the making of the laws by which he is to be governed . . . we want the privilege of doing something for ourselves. Had we possessed the powers of Local Self-Government

> at the outset, our progress would have been much more rapid, and our prosperity a reality and not a shadow . . . . If free local action in each of the settlements be secured in their freely chosen Councils, it will not matter much where the seat of the General or Imperial Government is placed. We are too young and too loyal to desire absolute independence, and this would, perhaps never be desirable if we had guaranteed to us full powers of Local Self-Government.[23]

At the end of the month, in announcing that the New Zealand Bill had passed its second reading, his tone was more than a little mocking at the future state of the colony under the new Bill:

> Having passed that, *pons asinorum,* it remains now to be mauled and hacked, and dovetailed and tinkered in Committee; and it will be marvellous indeed, if it is neither mutilated or botched, to say nothing of the danger of destruction, in its ulterior progress through the two houses . . . . The House of Commons will, very likely, at the eleventh hour, pass the Bill, with little discussion, when compared with the jabber and rhodomontade that would have been elicited by it, at any former period, within the last four or five years . . . . by the time everyone is gone to the [Melbourne] diggings, New Zealand will enjoy the possibility . . . of working its six subordinate and two supreme legislative assemblies, at the same moment. What a nation of politicians and statesmen we shall become, in a few years if we avail ourselves of our privileges! *The Times* . . . insinuates that . . . in future in New Zealand, that every man you meet is a legislator, and the onus will lie upon himself to repudiate the calumny. What is to be done, when the bulk of our male population shall have gone to the diggings, we are at a loss to conjecture; unless we do justice, and let in the women to the enjoyment of the franchise and eligibility to sit in Parliament.[24]

That last vision was probably the first time the suggestion was ever put in New Zealand's press, no matter how ironic or flippant the tone.

Fox's letter to *The Times* stating it would be 'morally unfair' to saddle the settlers with a debt due from the home government to the Company became highly relevant.[25] The Company would last until 1858, settling its outstanding financial arrangements. The directors reimbursed themselves, blaming the Company's failure on the 'withholding of representative institutions', but the debt of £268,370 (with interest of 3.5 per cent) to its shareholders was secured by law against income from projected land sales. This huge injustice was finally extinguished by New Zealand's legislature years later when, as Rusden said, 'Many of the great men who initiated the Company had passed away, but their lesser comrades received a return of their money with joy, and were profuse in self-laudation.'[26]

Evans was not slow to unleash his bile on the Company's directors. Goaded by the *New Zealander*, which accused the *Independent* of not having registered any protest, Evans turned his fury on them, declaring that no resident would accept their claim as a debt:

> The shareholders and jobbing managers of the Company may rest assured that we will resist it to the last extremity, and rather permit those lands to be squatted upon to the end of time, than suffer one shilling to be extorted from the purchasers, under the pretence of any legal or moral obligation on our part, to indemnify the company for any losses they may have incurred.

It was 'the height of injustice' and 'the most shameless effrontery' for it to throw the burden on 'those whom they have impoverished and exhausted by their own misconduct, or even through their quarrels with the Colonial Office'. The Company had:

> . . . with its unconscionable and flagitious claim, fastened onto the scheme, like a cancer, to devour its vitals . . . a piece of rascality, which is meditated by the gang of disappointed speculators in Broad Street. They may rest assured, however, that the colony will never pay their debts, or indemnify them for their losses, until, at least, the account is expurgated of all those items which have been created by fraud, and peculation, and jobbery, and the most stupendous ignorance and self-sufficiency that ever characterized the proceedings of a Joint Stock Company.

Agents and consignees had given champagne breakfasts and entertained everybody imaginable 'on a scale of magnificence avowedly copied from the east India Company'.

A sum of £7,000 had been set aside for 'native purposes', Evans noted, but in the Governor's hands it might be used to influence elections, as soon as Maori were 'admitted to the franchise'. On the suggestion of separating the provinces and making the upper North Island – New Ulster – an independent colony, he protested it was a retrograde step. 'Would it not be better', he suggested, 'to fall back on the institution of native tribes, to get ourselves naturalized in them and give up all idea of forming a great nation, in New Zealand, with an individual will and a unity and identity of character?' They should connect the settlements by roads and steam navigation rather than 'plead the barbarous condition of the country as a reason for taking refuge in a kind of savage isolation'. Municipal institutions were, he maintained, the 'foundation of all constitutional government'.

There were two other pressing concerns: preparing the country for steam navigation and for the masses of people who might be attracted from the gold diggings in Australia. If these issues were not addressed by the public and the government, he despaired of New Zealand's prosperity – 'at least during the present generation: But these things are to be accomplished, if there be only a will; and New Zealand may yet attain to its position, and fulfil its destiny, as the Great Britain of the South.'[27]

He wrote a lengthy editorial championing Gladstone's views on colonisation, and giving a wistful sketch of the government's colonial history up to that point. Evans praised Charles Buller and Sir William Molesworth, adding:

> But none of them ever came up to Mr. Gladstone, in the bold and unqualified manner in which he has expressed himself, on several vital questions affecting the government of the Colonies. Not that others wanted either the knowledge or the courage requisite. But the time was not ripe, for a full disclosure and manifestation of the truth; and Parliament itself was so stiff-necked, and incorrigible in its prejudices, that we have seen its members almost ready to stone those assertors of Colonial rights. Events themselves have now forced the perception and acknowledgement of principles upon the minds of men; and Mr. Gladstone is fortunate in occupying a position which enables him to become the last champion in Parliament of the most advanced doctrine, on the subject of the true relation between colonies and the mother-country . . .

In an age when personal attacks in the press were all too common, many of Evans's good, practical ideas and much of his wisdom were obscured by his use of intemperate language:

> It must have done some of the shareholders and directors good to hear [the last paragraph of Gladstone's speech] – if they were susceptible of shame and remorse; and one of them at least, who rejoices in the appellation of the '*fat boy*' of the concern, must have required all the comfort that could be derived from the *thousands of guineas* which he has received as chairman of committees, to save him from absolute despair, when he heard the damnatory sentences pronounced, in which Mr. Gladstone uttered the final doom of the New Zealand Company. After this, its threatened resuscitation is impossible; but we have still to guard against it, as a vampire or a ghoul, which threatens to visit us from its grave, and to prey upon our vitals, as those monsters are fabled to do upon the victims of their obscene rapacity, – under the pretext of a parliamentary charge upon the land revenue of this country.[28]

He was no friend of the Company, no friend of government, no friend to the 'social pretensions of the red-tape nobility, picked out of the refuse of our local politicians'.[29] In the spirit of the *Independent* he wanted only self-government. But it was a sad farewell to the Company that he had helped bring into being fourteen years earlier.

Later in the year news arrived that the second New Zealand Constitution Act had been passed by Sir John Pakington on 30 June. Six provinces were established, each presided over by a superintendent and Provincial Council. There would be a General Assembly, a House of Representatives and other safeguards. The Act was supposed to take effect as soon as possible, but would languish for another eighteen months, until the General Assembly met in May 1854.

Evans still maintained his lively interest in the success of local commerce. At a meeting of principal merchants in November, he was appointed to a committee to form a company to work the coal mines in the Massacre Bay District.[30] He worried about the stagnant economy caused largely by the labourers having 'gone to the diggings' in Australia. New Zealand's 'labour and its circulating medium', he said, had undergone an 'almost fatal depletion'. Taxation was heavy – 'for the relief of the Australian markets'. Although merchants had 'made a legitimate profit . . . a good deal of suffering and demoralization' had resulted. He could not resist a jibe at the missionaries:

> Without labour, New Zealand must speedily go to destruction, or fall back into that quiescent, unprogressive state, which always commended itself, as the golden age, to the missionary intellect – a state in which the colony would consist principally of barbarians, slowly advancing towards civilization, with a few white people on the coast, tolerated for the purpose of importing blankets, tobacco, and gunpowder; just as it was before any real colonization began in 1840.[31]

Sales of land had been poor for two years, largely because of difficult, bush-clad terrain; absentee landlords not employing labour to cultivate it; the 'sufficient price'; and the complexity of Maori tribal relationships and Maori reluctance to sell.

After a series of meetings in New Munster, Grey purchased large tracts of land from Maori, issuing a proclamation for its disposal on 4 March. He established sales by auction, reducing the price of land from £1 to a fixed price of 10 shillings an acre, or an auction reserve of 5 shillings.[32]

His announcement coincided almost exactly with the arrival in Canterbury of Gibbon Wakefield and solicitor Henry Sewell, agent for the Canterbury Association. The Association had fixed its price of land in the new settlement at £3 per acre, so with Grey's popularity being assured throughout the country – including some quarters of Wellington – Wakefield and Sewell were furious. In addition, Wakefield was determined to assert his importance over Grey. Early on 7 March, exactly thirteen years to the day after Evans's first dramatic landing in New Zealand, Sewell and Wakefield arrived in Wellington, accompanied by a violent southerly storm.[33]

Many of the settlers sent a letter of welcome to Wakefield as the 'founder' of the colony. Wakefield graciously replied, protesting that Wellington had many founders, while 'My own share was that of a helper; constant indeed and indefatigable whilst health lasted, but whose efforts could have had no result unless in aid of the efforts of others.'[34]

He and Sewell had decided to seek an injunction against the Governor's Land Proclamation to forestall the Commissioner for Crown Lands, Dillon Bell. While they debated the move, Sewell was meeting Wellington's residents, many of whom were either in favour of the proclamation, or of two minds. He guessed correctly that this was because of the prospects for jobbery – the acquisition of cheap land and possibilities of large profits to be made. Although Featherston privately backed Sewell's legal case, like the other constitutionalists he disapproved of the high price policy of the Association.[35]

Wakefield approached Evans to present their case. Although he had never acknowledged Evans's contribution to the Company or the founding of the settlement of Wellington, Wakefield viewed Evans as a friend and ally for this particular power play. While Sewell drew up his Bill of Protest, Evans prepared his arguments, and Dorset filed the affidavit using a land order given him by Gibbon Wakefield.

On Tuesday, 22 March 1853, Sewell and Evans personally served notice of their application for an injunction on Dillon Bell at the Land Office. Dillon Bell was unsure what to do. He tried apologising on behalf of Governor Grey for not taking the matter to the General Assembly first, but added lamely that cheap land was popular.[36]

From there Sewell and Evans called on Evans's nemesis, Judge Stephen. Stephen struck Sewell as being odd and evasive when pressed for a date for the hearing. But 30 March was finally decided on, and Evans and Sewell informed Dillon Bell and his representative, Attorney General Daniel Wakefield. At first Daniel Wakefield was 'very surly', but after reading a copy of Sewell's Bill and consulting the Governor's Legislative Council, he returned in the evening, 'mightily cheerful and amiable', according to Sewell. He assured them he would not activate the Land Proclamation while the case was under examination.

The next morning he reneged on his promise, telling Evans and Sewell 'the Government would give no undertaking'. When they called on Stephen with Wakefield and told him of this, an angry Stephen retorted, 'Mr. Bell would proceed at his peril.' In the ensuing conversation, Sewell and Evans became more confident their injunction might succeed. When Stephen suggested they file another affidavit with material evidence, they reminded themselves of his reputation. In Sewell's view, Stephen was not of the highest 'Calibre'.

On Tuesday, 29 March, when Evans and Sewell walked to the Land Office to witness the first day's 'Applications for Land' under Grey's Proclamation – 'probably 100,000 acres' – they were shocked at the lack of preparation. They were told the maps of the land open for selection 'would be ready in about ten minutes . . . . In short the whole proceedings were the strangest and most irregular I ever witnessed. No Maps or Surveys of the Districts opened were ready; or even in preparation, except some partial Surveys of a small portion made up from the company's old Surveys . . .'. Grey's secretary, Alfred Domett, suggested they leave, so they proceeded to the commissioner's room where they watched people paying for hundreds of acres of land with scrip rather than money.[37] Evans and Sewell agreed that opportunities for jobbery and favouritism under such a system were abundant.

The next day Evans accompanied Sewell to court to witness his admittance to the Bar. Then the case opened, with Evans detailing his arguments. On first meeting Evans, Sewell was unsure about his ability,[38] but having observed him in action he was impressed, saying Evans handled it 'remarkably well, mainly confining himself to reading the Bill [Sewell's work], but told the story a good deal better than loose slipshod speaking':

> Now and then he enforced the argumentation with a telling comment, particularly as to the Governor's utter neglect of the instructions received by him from [England], as to proceeding only with the consent of the settlers, etc . . . . Nobody appeared for [Dillon Bell] or the Crown, and we had it all our own way . . .[39]

To their delight, Stephen granted the injunction, saying it did not appear that the Governor had sufficient authority to issue his proclamation.[40] The official camp, said Sewell, was 'intensely angry', not knowing what to do. And the settlers were amazed. The majority had been sold on the idea of cheap land – they were 'all corrupted', even 'the most intelligent', said Sewell. Evans and he were in a minority with Dorset, Wakefield and a few others.

That night when they all dined at Alsdorf's Hotel, Evans was 'infinitely amusing, but rather loud', said Sewell, confirming that Evans was 'a stout upholder of Wakefieldism'.[41] Of Wakefield's theory and work, Evans was a champion to his dying day, but on the man personally he remained silent.[42]

But their celebration was short-lived. On Friday, 1 April, when Sewell went to the Registrar's Office of the Supreme Court, he found John King applying to set aside the proceedings on a technicality regarding the service of a writ. Domett and Daniel Wakefield attacked Sewell for a breach of confidence, and Sewell contacted Evans who met him at Alsdorf's Hotel. In the midst of their discussions King arrived to suggest they give up their injunction. The pair spurned his offer, challenging him to have his case heard any time he wished, providing nothing was done under Grey's proclamation. King refused. That evening, they were notified that a hearing for Tuesday, 5 April, had been granted 'to set aside the proceedings on the ground that no particulars of demand were served with the Writ, that the motion was made without special leave of the Court and that the Defendant had no sufficient notice'. The council also believed the Attorney General should have been made a party to the suit, and objected to the *Independent* having aroused public attention to the case in publishing Sewell's Bill and arguing points of law. But when Daniel Wakefield later resigned, it was the first step towards responsible government, the *Independent* defiantly said.[43] The hearing was adjourned for two days as Stephen was suffering from the influenza that was felling many in the town. Evans may have been afflicted as well, for his involvement in the case seemed to be over.

At the last minute, King withdrew his motion at the request of the Executive Council. Sewell applied for costs and, after meeting both King and Stephen, was dissatisfied with both, believing the latter to be frightened of opposing the Governor. The government asked to have the writ altered, hoping to find a loophole that would allow the injunction to be quashed without the case being aired. Stephen complained bitterly about the proclamation's illegality.

The injunction was 'automatically dissolved' on 21 May, when no one appeared in court to reply to the government's defence. Wakefield instead wrote to Secretary of State Newcastle, enclosing the memorandum on the case drawn up by Evans, a copy of Stephen's judgment and a lengthy complaint about the arbitrary proceedings of the government ever since.[44] But the repercussions of Wakefield's challenge to Grey's authority were considerable. The Governor retaliated by pointing out instances of Wakefield's deep involvement with the much-loathed Company, even though Wakefield protested that he had 'been dead to the Company from 1846'. Meanwhile others who had mistrusted Wakefield, including Fitzherbert and Featherston, became increasingly vocal in their opposition.

In England, although the Colonial Office criticised Grey's edict, believing its legality was in doubt and his unilateral move meant the scrip would depreciate, it also dismissed Sewell's arguments on the ground that the contract between Dorset and the New Zealand Company did not preclude the Governor from lowering land prices as he had authority from the Crown to do so.[45] But the actions of Wakefield and Sewell, backed by Featherston and Evans, were a landmark of sorts. They had opened up the possibility 'for the exercise of local control in certain places'.[46]

Sewell was shocked at the lack of opportunity for a solicitor in the colony, observing that 'the whole practice of the Bar would not feed an Attorney's Clerk at colonial rates of living'. Evans agreed, and his thoughts were turning more and more to Victoria where prospects appeared to be decidedly better. Gold had lured an influx of talented men, and opportunities in the press and at the Bar looked healthy. Besides, at the age of sixty, Evans's wife did not relish the idea of more years of struggle and hardship in a small colony full of petty social and political intrigue. During their absence, the St Hills, Cliffords and other landowners and merchants had secured themselves as the leading lights, and with the younger generation now reaching adulthood, a new order had sprung up. Family was no longer enough to keep Harriet there, as Daniel, Harriot and their children lived at Orongorongo, an isolated farm that was difficult to reach. In fact, the stoical and admirable Harriot was visited only once by a European woman – possibly Harriet Evans – during the decade she lived there, from 1845 to 1855. She was rowed to Wellington only to give birth to her numerous children, and in that time her family grew from three to twelve children. They enjoyed the special experience of growing up alongside children from the neighbouring pa, learning to converse fluently with Maori and sharing in their culture.

Sewell had also remarked on the petty political atmosphere. How much more can it have disheartened a man residing in a town whose population was stagnant at 3000 and included at least seven solicitors and a large number of hostile government servants?[47] For Evans, the political environment was unattractive, prospects in legal practice too limited and the odds too uneven to tempt him to stay.

Gibbon Wakefield was, as ever, looking for an angle to further his ambitions for power in the new legislature. From April through July he addressed meetings in both the Hutt and Wellington, vowing to address ways of getting rid of absentee landholders. At the fourth public meeting, after Wakefield had called for prospective candidates to declare their interest, Evans was invited to speak, to his evident surprise. He was quite ill but used the opportunity to remind them of their collective history in Wellington and of the key part he had played. He spoke to them, he said, as a disinterested party, as 'circumstances might again compel him to leave them (*no, no!*)'.

As ever, he gave credit to Wakefield for his tireless work on their behalf, saying:

> Ever since the spring of 1839, Mr. Wakefield's labours in the cause of New Zealand had been unremitting and really gigantic; and it was through his great influence with the press, with leading public men and with the public in general that the Colonization of New Zealand had been launched on so grand a scale (loud cheering) . . .[48]

But Evans implored them to 'avoid the dictation of either a government or an association (hear)', urging them 'to meet often . . . and anxiously to deliberate as to whom they should choose for members . . . [so they could] present a model to all the colonies in the southern hemisphere (loud cheering)'.

On 27 May Wakefield delivered a speech at the Hutt that lasted several hours, and was punctuated by occasional opposition from Revans. Wakefield took full credit for the colonising of New Zealand, saying he was proud of 'having done more than any other man has done or attempted, in the work of giving effect' to its success. He was 'the conscience of the Company'. Evans watched incredulously as he 'threw himself, body and soul into the arms of the party that were agitating for compensation', and put such a spin on the question of 'sufficient price' that he stupefied everyone. In a speech that Fitzherbert called 'the most sophistical' he had ever heard, Wakefield adroitly focused the question of 'sufficient price' by speaking of acquiring enough revenue to raise overseas loans. He wooed the labourers, who were leasing subdivided land, by convincing them they were as entitled to compensation as the resident land purchasers. A government commissioner should give them a hundred acres of land free of charge, he declared.

Although weak from illness, Evans could not remain silent. He addressed the meeting as a 'disappointed claimant, the committee of landowners having declined to adjudicate on his case'. He held in reserve only 'a few sections in the Hutt as a refuge for [his] old age'. His town acres were held under dispute by Chetham. Personally he felt aggrieved and sore, but was convinced –

> . . . that the arrangement itself was founded on justice and public policy. It was notorious however that one class only, the land-purchasers – the capitalists had benefited by it. They provided for themselves and of course got the lion's share (hear); and the industrious working classes . . . had been quite left out. (cheers)

He went on, asking rhetorically, 'Did Mr. Wakefield really mean' that a commission should 'inquire into the claims of all the working men in the colony, and award those who proved their case a free grant of one hundred acres of land each?' He answered his own question: 'Impossible!' 'He could only say, as the member for Midhurst did when the Reform Bill was first introduced into the House of Commons, that 'It was too much for him; that it took away his breath; that he must have time allowed to consider it (hear).'

The question of 'sufficient price' was a 'problem the conditions of which were infinitely variable; that what was a fair price here and now, might be a very unfair one, whether too high or too low – there and then'. Evans deplored the tactics of opposing factions who disputed the 'fair price' of land, comparing such proceedings to 'a Dutch auction, where the whole territory of New Zealand was offered for sale at 10s an acre':

> Five shillings! Five shillings! Half a crown is now bid by a gentleman on the platform. Thank you, sir. But if I were inclined to start as a political mountebank I should outbid everybody, by offering to give the land for nothing and a pot of beer into the bargain; and I am afraid I should carry my election. (Shouts of laughter) . . . . it is a serious business. It relates to forty millions of acres of valuable land, your property – mind that (hear); your property and no longer that of the Crown, to be administered by irresponsible officers – your property, which you now hold in common, as the shareholders in a joint stock company might do (cheers); and the question is, how you can dispose of it most advantageously – by which I mean the most conducively to the general and lasting prosperity of the colony . . . not of yourselves merely – the 26,000 men, women and children now scattered over it – but of the unborn millions who will succeed you in future times (loud cheers).

Evans was an advocate for cheap land only in the Wakefield sense – land sold without profit to the state, at a price that would only repay the outlay and the expenditure on surveys, bridges, ferries and other public amenities. He cautioned the colonists against giving themselves up 'to any party, or to any individuals who were trying to catch their votes by the art of popularity (cheers)':

> . . . this was probably the last opportunity he should have of addressing them for some time to come . . . [but] the question was one which ought to be reserved for their House of Representatives, and could not be determined satisfactorily at a public meeting (much cheering).[49]

The favourable reception of his speech was the most remarkable incident of the meeting, observed the *Independent*, which noted that Wakefield's 'breathtaking' scheme would require 50,000 acres at £1 per acre. It was a huge amount to take from revenue.[50] Noting how well Evans's words were received by the colonists, Wakefield suggested to him privately that he stand for office there or in another electorate, but Evans declined.

Wakefield was true to his word and the next day put his own property on the market for 'working settlers'. Although Evans and his peers at the *Independent* fell short of directly attacking him for his part in the Company's failure, there were many questions raised about Wakefield's veracity by the constitutionalists, who were mostly Evans's friends, and by Grey himself. Isaac Featherston attacked Wakefield's assertion he had been 'dead to the Company in the years 1846–50', and fought bitterly with him throughout July. Governor Grey proved that Wakefield had attended Company meetings during those years. It was one thing for Wakefield to take full credit for having founded the colony, but another entirely to claim full credit for the purchase of the *Tory*. Fitzherbert and Captain Daniell went further, taking issue with him directly.[51]

In July, Fitzherbert made a sustained attack on him, using the issue of the *Tory* purchase to support his argument against Wakefield's veracity. Fitzherbert informed the adjourned meeting for the Compensation of Working Classes that after Wakefield's return from Quebec, Evans had told him that he and others had already bought and paid for the *Tory*. There were other matters – a question of directors' fees that had been voted at a Company meeting but which Wakefield denied ever having received. Later, Daniell also rose and declared that Wakefield was by no means the first to found New Zealand. He said again that Wakefield had been in Quebec when the ship was bought, and asserted Evans's role in the founding of the colony. In fact, he claimed, 'They had much to learn respecting the foundation of this settlement: It was to Dr. Evans that all the credit was due for saving this country from the grasp of France. If Dr. Evans's opinions had been acted upon, this country would never have been burdened with its debt.'

He called on Evans to reply. Evans was clearly struggling to control his emotions as he addressed them 'in a low tone but with remarkable precision and deliberation'. The *Tory*, he said, was not purchased until September 1838. Before that, after Baring's New Zealand Bill was thrown out, the last meeting of the Association had been held on 9 June 1838. He, Evans, had then drawn up the scheme of a company with a capital of £40,000 in shares of £500. He again sketched the background of the purchase of the *Tory*, describing Wakefield's late entry.

He had already described his and others' parts in the early transition when every other sentence had been greeted with lusty cheering. Of his establishment of the New Zealand Land Company, he had recalled:

> Well! The thing was done! 26,000 Englishmen were here, in defiance of the Colonial Office (loud cheers). But those early efforts were long and often in danger of being overwhelmed. He remembered meeting Captain Daniell in the rooms at the Adelphi, when the whole colony of New Zealand was carried to Hans Place in a hackney coach (great laughter). Now there was indeed something greater and vaster to be seen, – land of the free, thy kingdom is yet to come – (cheers).

Wakefield rose and agreed with each detail of Evans's description, adding his inflated version of his own role in the purchase. He conceded he might have been 'hasty' in crediting himself, 'but what he meant was that he had been the prime mover in the transactions by which the ship had been at length bought'.

Evans was gracious in reply, calling Wakefield 'the prime mover of the colonization of New Zealand (cheers)'. But, he added, the 'credit which he and his associates claimed' centred on the actions they took in Wakefield's absence. 'They kept the project alive (hear hear) and collected some of the materials with which [Wakefield's] great ability formed the powerful New Zealand Company (cheers).' For himself, Evans 'only claimed to be one of the oldest New Zealanders':

> . . . he had been a very unfortunate one, and although he had been enabled in some degree to retrieve his misfortune, he was about to try his fortune elsewhere . . . . if he thought Mr. Wakefield would

> rob him or Captain Daniell of any part of the credit due to them for their exertions in the summer of 1838, he should think such injustice was unpardonable (hear, hear). But Mr. Wakefield had assured him such was not the case . . .

Evans tried to reconcile his two old friends, 'who both deserved his gratitude and confidence'. He could not have done without Captain Daniell's 'hearty co-operation' in 'keeping the project alive. The colony was much indebted to Captain Daniell's zeal and public spirit (hear, hear, hear).' Wakefield's labours too had been 'unremitting and really gigantic . . . . It was the duty of every lover of the colony to see if these feelings of animosity could not be put an end to by a manly, cordial, and generous reconciliation (cheers).' Wakefield was smooth in reply, declaring that in his long association with Evans he 'had never had occasion to differ from him'. Whenever the occasion arose, he, Wakefield, had always stated that 'the colony would never have existed without' the 'exertions and sacrifices' of Evans '(hear, hear)'. He had lately had occasion to repeat that statement 'to persons who were unwilling to give Dr. Evans the credit due to him'. In fact, the Wellington settlers 'had never yet given Dr. Evans the credit which he deserved'. He had tried to persuade Evans to stand in some constituency, possibly the Hutt, urging him 'not to leave the colony just when free institutions were about to be enjoyed, when he might therefore attain the high place which his talents deserved (cheers)'.

Wakefield 'cordially' accepted Evans's offer of mediation, twice offering his hand to Daniell, but Daniell publicly snubbed him by saying that he had been 'branded as a liar and would not accept the offer unless an apology was made. Mr. Wakefield asked when? where? – no such word had ever passed his lips.' Daniell said that it was implied by Mr Wakefield's assertion that he had bought the *Tory*. Mr Wakefield thought the captain was mistaken and again offered his hand, but Daniell refused his offer and rose and left the room.[52]

Wakefield's words rang hollow. He had always guarded his fame jealously, rarely giving credit to others in public, and then only reluctantly. Evans was unmoved by his flattery. It was too little, too late, and he had not the stomach to betray his oldest supporter and ally Edward Daniell or his other friends by nailing his flag to Wakefield's mast. Evans knew Wakefield's overtures were just a show for his own promotion. He also knew Wakefield would expect his loyalty at all times and use him for his own ends. He would be a useful ally for Wakefield, but would be irrevocably yoked to him, a mere lackey for a man whose political sleights of hand indicated his ambition for power at any cost.[53] Evans would lose the independence he prized.

It was time for him to move on. The settlement was divided in its opinion, personal rancour was intense and he was torn between two opposing sides. As so often happened when he was under intense emotional strain, he became ill, but it was Wakefield's opportunism that was the last straw. It not only took Evans's breath away. It also sent him away from the colony he loved, to Melbourne and a new career.[54]

After farewelling his friends, Evans stopped in Sydney en route to Melbourne long enough to renew his acquaintance with a few of his influential contacts. William Bland (1789–1868) was a medical practitioner who had become famous for his operations on cataracts and bladder stones. Evans's meeting with Bland might have been primarily a medical consultation, but their connection also embraced political activity, Bland's network including many of Evans's old colleagues. As a noted agitator for representative government, Bland had been voted in as Sydney's representative at the first election in New South Wales in 1843; and as chairman of the Committee of the Australian Patriotic Association he had corresponded regularly with its parliamentary agents in London, Bulwer-Lytton and Charles Buller.[55]

Evans also met Henry Parkes (1815–1896), who had switched his allegiance from republicanism to the liberal movement and launched the *Empire*, 'the chief organ of mid-century liberalism, [serving as] the rallying point for the sharpest radical and liberal minds of the day'.[56] These influential men might have offered him openings in Sydney, but his sights were set on Melbourne where there was a journalistic opening, and legal and political careers were distinct possibilities as well. Besides, Melbourne was preferable because it had barely been tainted by convict settlement.[57]

PART FOUR:
MELBOURNE AND WELLINGTON
1853–1868

CHAPTER NINETEEN. EDITOR AND POLITICIAN

> 'Now, are the circumstances of the country such, that a man of Mr. Micawber's abilities would have a fair chance of rising in the social scale? I will not say, at present, might he aspire to be Governor, or anything of that sort; but would there be a reasonable opening for his talents to develop themselves – that would be amply sufficient – and find their own expansion?'
>
> 'No better opening anywhere,' said my aunt, 'for a man who conducts himself well, and is industrious.'
>
> 'For a man who conducts himself well,' repeated Mrs. Micawber, with her clearest business manner, 'and is industrious. Precisely. It is evident to me that Australia is the legitimate sphere of action for Mr. Micawber!'
>
> Charles Dickens, *David Copperfield*, Chapter 53

His timing could not have been better. Earlier that year, Victoria had gained its independence from New South Wales and was making plans for self-government. Melbourne's population had ballooned. Thousands of opportunists lured by the discovery of gold two years earlier meant the fields swarmed with diggers, and in town, merchants and bankers flung open their doors, English cadets lounged around looking for openings, and lawyers descended to jostle for jobs. The streets may have been little more than muddy tracks and the services were still primitive, but progress was in the air. S. W. McGowan's construction of eleven miles of electric telegraph line between Melbourne and Williamstown augured well for faster and better communication.[1]

Having found lodgings with his wife in Flinders Lane, Evans was entered at the Victorian Bar in November. He may have found some legal work, but he also made valuable connections. Barrister and journalist Archibald Michie quickly enlisted Evans to write for the *Melbourne Morning Herald*, which he and his friend Thomas Turner à Beckett had bought from editor Fred Sinnett's parents. They hoped to turn the paper's ailing fortunes around by acquiring a central office and new press and type, but their chief rival the *Argus* maintained its lead, as its co-editors Edward Wilson and Lauchlan Mackinnon – who were noted for their 'bold spirit, enterprise and popular democratic tone' – attracted more advertising revenue. With less time being spent at the *Herald* and more time at the Bar, Michie and his business partners lost their 'momentum and business savvy', as well as thousands of pounds, and a steady stream of staff was lured to the more lucrative goldfields.[2]

In the months following the storming of the Eureka Stockade at the Ballarat diggings in December 1854, Michie and other prominent lawyers devoted their time to defending the prisoners.[3] This raised their profiles, and Michie became the 'popular idol' of the diggers and their supporters.[4] Sinnett left to write for the *Argus* and co-founded *Melbourne Punch*, and Evans was persuaded by Michie to take up the *Herald*'s editorship on 1 March 1855. While the educated and politically minded reader may have taken notice, Evans's generally ponderous style,[5] strewn with literary allusions and preaching the glories of the British constitution, gained little sympathy amongst the semi-literate diggers and adventurers who were eager to escape the fetters of Britain and make their fortune.

But Evans was also capable of addressing lighter topics. One of his first editorials was a whimsical tilt at the government for its refusal to make Melbourne race day a national holiday:

> A party of Englishmen playing at cricket within the walls of the Colisseum, or regaling themselves with the product of their breweries on the summit of the great pyramid, have been pointed out by foreigners as fair samples of the obstinate nationality and invincible prejudices of our race. What would they say if they witnessed the population of Melbourne, under a burning sun, with the thermometer standing at 120 degrees in the shade, forcing their way through clouds of sand that would have driven the tiger to his jungle, and the alligator to his swamp, and flocking with as much gravity as they do to a funeral or execution, to the solemn duty of attending the Melbourne races? It is, in fact, a national duty, in the estimation of most Englishmen, to attend these races. They are among our most venerable and time-honoured institutions, and we wonder that they have not been treated with greater respect by our legislators, who might have secured themselves and the reporters a holiday, by following the example of the British Parliament, which always adjourns over the Derby . . .[6]

When the colony's new constitution arrived in October that year, Michie feared losing government advertising, so he instructed Evans to take a neutral stance towards the unpopular Haines government of 'Downing Street despotism'. The other owners disagreed with Michie and the worst fears of the *Herald*'s stalwarts were realised. With even heavier financial loss, Michie sold out, despite – or perhaps because of – having earned £8,000 in the courts that year.[7] At that point Michie might have partially blamed Evans for the loss, but in fact he had lost interest in the enterprise. Evans was left to soldier on alone, and would later simmer with resentment at his misplaced loyalty and the opportunities he had lost at the Bar.

Left to his own devices in his office in Bourke Street East, Evans had a Herculean task writing 'nine out of ten editorials' and trying to resurrect the paper's fortunes. After a year at the helm, the strain had taken its toll on his health. The respiratory illness that had dogged him all his life had now been compounded by bouts of kidney stones. These attacks were frequent, but he managed to hide his condition from all but his closest friends. There was the option of an operation – he may have tried that course already – but it was a gruesome resort, extremely painful and hazardous.

In June, Evans received a letter from Henry Parkes, the owner of the *Empire* newspaper in Sydney. Parkes asked him to publicise a case in which he had been sued for libel by a member of the New South Wales Legislature. Evans immediately complied. The freedom of the press was a subject dear to his heart, and it was the theme of an article he wrote entitled 'The Journalist and the Jobber', in which he compared the court proceedings with the plot in *Don Quixote*. Parkes (the lion) had been sued by Arthur Holroyd ('the knight of the rueful countenance'), who received £2,000 as Bathurst's representative, yet had also agreed to act as Brisbane's temporary Crown Prosecutor for another £80. The *Empire* had dared to criticise his opportunism. In his article Evans wrote:

> [Holroyd] took the eighty pounds, nevertheless, and absented himself from a town where representatives were scarce and nominees abundant, where a single vote may have turned the scale against an oligarchy whose doings during a long and dreary dispensation of corruption, might have provoked, and would have justified, revolution in a larger and more powerful community . . . [and] went off . . . – leaving the Legislature, his constituents at Bathurst, and the public at large to take care of their political interests, as best they could, during his patriotic absence.

Holroyd's defence lawyer, Edward Broadhurst, was 'a bit of a wag in his way, [and] must have felt the humour of it':

> . . . we find him going through his part as gingerly, and with as much apparent dread of exploding his own case, as if he had been compelled to walk, with hob-nails in his shoes and a pipe in his mouth, through a powder magazine . . . . the only one who seemed to laugh in his sleeve was the learned judge . . . . The cream of the jest was the verdict . . . whilst the plaintiff who, no doubt, calculated on something much more pleasant but far less profitable in a moral sense, gained nothing by his action but liability to costs, and went home, let us hope, 'a sadder and wiser man'.[8]

Evans told Parkes:

> I [have written] a leader in this morning's paper, but I regret that the bad state of my health has prevented me from saying all that I could have wished. I am glad to renew your acquaintance . . . . I sometimes think I shall return to Sydney and practise at the bar. Your climate is better than this. If I should come, I hope to be useful . . .

He confided that his responsibilities were 'too much for one man'. He was ashamed at not having written to his 'old friend Dr. Bland . . . but the continual torment of what the doctors here tell me is calculous disease must be my excuse'.[9]

He had been studying the political situation, especially the property qualification for representatives in Victoria under the new constitution. To qualify for election to the Council (or Upper House) of thirty members, a candidate had to be at least thirty years old, and own freehold property to the value of £5,000. Those voting for Council members had to fulfil the same conditions. The sixty elected members of the Legislative Assembly – twenty-one years and over – would have to own land worth £2,000. To be eligible to vote for the assembly, a man had to earn £100 per annum, own freehold property to the value of £50 or occupy leasehold land worth £10 per annum. As Evans complained, the property qualification worked 'horribly':

> It shuts out nearly all the new blood. Our elective upper house will be a perfect oligarchy, and we are all puzzled what to do. We watch your experiment [in seeking a new constitution] with great interest; but my own suggestion, (which I make, I hope, not arrogantly) is to do away with these upper houses, – establish a federation, and have a senate for the whole, simply as a house of revision and appeal – except in international matters, where it should have the power to originate, – and let it be composed of a small (but equal) number of men from each colony, chosen by universal suffrage, – to meet in a neutral territory, like Washington – say Twofold Bay – Corner Inlet – Launceston – or any where else – to preclude jealousy. Pray excuse

> my running on in this way; but I cannot help thinking that a little communication of this kind, 'without prejudice', may be sometimes useful . . . [10]

He had first mooted the idea of federation at least a year earlier in the paper's columns. At the time there had been no real effort made to link the colonies, although the draft of Victoria's constitution recommended setting up a General Assembly of the Australian Colonies. But competition and jealousy in the areas of trade and steam postal services prevailed, and in spite of interchanges in population, the colonies remained isolated from one another. After the efforts of William Denison and Hugh Childers in 1855 resulted in free trade across the Murray River, the issue had begun to be taken more seriously.[11] Evans continued to promote federation frequently in his leaders, pointing out the anomalies in the existing system. In one article he spoke of Albury in the district of Murrumbidgee, Sydney, on which the Sydney government had spent a total of £1,400, while it had received more than £25,000 since 1816 from the sale of Albury land:

> Does not Sydney then deserve to lose Albury, as she has already lost Port Phillip, and is on the point of losing Moreton Bay? . . . . the existence of several sovereign states [would be] a constant source of annoyance – of inconvenience to commerce, and derangement of all the social relations . . . . we have already a multiplicity of commercial codes . . . . a set of hostile tariffs, and extensive smuggling on the frontier of three colonies has only been obviated by an arrangement that inflicts serious injury on the trade of the Southern Capital.

Each colony had separate currencies, so that legal tender in Sydney, for example, was rejected in Melbourne. Evans imagined the impact of diverse marriage and criminal codes whereby 'villainy hunted out of one colony may find a sanctuary in the next':

> Every new colony erected hastens the day for federation. A federal council is as practicable now as it will probably be ten years hence, if the subject were to be taken up in earnest . . . . such a parliament . . . [would leave] intact the power of each [colony] to deal unreservedly with the management of its local affairs, [and] would afford to all a uniform tariff, and a uniform code of civil and criminal law . . . it would prepare us to glide easily at length into the waters of that new and untried sea above which will some day float the free standard of Australia . . . and the existence of such a theatre of action would infallibly call forth all that we have amongst us of true statesmanship and civic worth.[12]

His 'idea' in detail was too early to bear fruit by several decades, but as a general principle it very quickly caught on. It may have been mooted by others in New South Wales and elsewhere at the time, but Evans's letter might have been useful for Parkes, who preserved it in his collection of correspondence.[13] In 1901, five years after Parkes's death when federation was established, Parkes was proclaimed its 'Father'.

In Victoria, responsible government under its new constitution was to be a 'new experiment in parliamentary democracy'. Its efforts to produce a satisfactory party system would involve a long and bitter struggle. The colony's society was 'in flux', and any parliament would have faced problems in struggling to satisfy its demands.

By the time elections were called for the Legislative Assembly, Evans had moved to George Street in Richmond and decided to contest the metropolitan seat. He was prepared to judge each issue on its own merits, but he was not ignorant of his electorate's interests. As a radical, he professed strong democratic opinions, 'stating that he considered such principles, if properly pursued, would . . . render the people worthy of that high destiny which Providence seemed to have in store for them'.[14]

In an article entitled 'Pledges Against Apostasy', he urged the voters to avoid personal antipathy – advice that fell on deaf ears in a colony full of ambitious young men who guarded their honour as zealously as they harboured their prejudices. He also suggested extending the number of members of the House:

> . . . not merely by one or two to each electoral district, but conceding manhood suffrage, remodeling constituencies on a democratic basis, and then providing for representation of the Colony by at least 100 members, not more than eight or ten of whom should be permitted to hold office in the Government. Should these measures all fail, in preserving us from [the kind of factious and disreputable scenes seen in New South Wales] there is still federation to look forward to . . .[15]

He wrote on division and factions in an article entitled 'The Fox Without a Tail', condemning the *Argus* – the 'Old Fox of Collins Street' – for recommending dispensing with political principle – in fact, 'cutting off our tail'. He urged voters to put a candidate's capacity and character ahead of his political opinions:

> The great disruption of parties in England, which began in 1829, has destroyed the ancient standard of Whig and Tory, and even that of Radical has no meaning, and has lost its distinctive and exhilarating power . . . . It seems perfectly plausible that men should go in for perfect independence and conscientiousness – never inquiring how others are going to vote . . . but . . . whilst it leaves the control of legislation and government almost exclusively in the hands of a Ministry practically irresponsible, it leaves a boundless opportunity and license to the jobbing and intriguing propensities . . . . Faction is founded on persons, but party on principles; and whilst the one is the weakness and the abuse, the other is the mainstay and the glory of the common wealth. Without strongly marked and inflexible principles there can be neither attraction nor repulsion among statesmen, no gravitation, no polarization – in a word, no parties – without parties, no real and effective antagonism and discussion – and, without these, no real and practical responsibility.[16]

His speech outside St Stephen's church in Richmond reinforcing this stand was a triumph, and he won Richmond easily.[17] But in the euphoria that arose before the opening of Victoria's first Parliament he reminded his readers:

> New Zealand preceded us, in extorting this right from the Colonial Office and the British Parliament; and the truth is that the illustrious nonentities in this colony, who would fain take credit to themselves . . . had about as much to do with it as the fly upon the wheel had with raising the dust, with the struggle or the victory at the Olympic Games. Honour to whom honour is due. The battle was fought, not here but in England, and by men the Chiefs of whom are now laid silent in the grave. Buller and Molesworth were among the earliest and most zealous champions of colonial reform. Wakefield, their acknowledged master and teacher – and who has contributed more to the same object, during the last quarter of a century, than any man in Europe – is not dead, but lies hopelessly incapacitated, somewhere in the forests of New Zealand. Barkly, our new Governor lent his timely aid . . . Rintoul lent the columns of the *Spectator* to the cause, to which Lord Durham had bequeathed the legacy of his great name. Humbler men co-operated. The colonies were roused to a sense of their own degradation . . .[18]

With the formalities over on 21 November, on the first day of the first session of Parliament, the members' entry into the unfinished Parliament House in Spring Street was rather ignominious. Skirting around the hazards and workmen while protecting their top hats against low obstacles; 'sinking up to the knees in deep beds of shavings, clambering over ladders and planks, – scrambling up the wrong staircases and entering at wrong doors . . .'.[19]

With two others, Evans arrived in the House late, taking his seat on the Opposition benches with Michie, David Blair (then writing for the *Age*) and nearly twenty others, the 'wavering centre' of 'liberals, opportunists, and eccentrics of various kinds, the key group [being] made up of liberal Presbyterians and non-conformists who were often merchants'. Another twenty formed the conservative side.[20] The elected government was an all-Anglican conservative Legislative Council or Upper House of thirty members led by Dr William Haines, 'a man of no brilliant talents, but of immense weight of character – [an] honest, jovial, undisguised old English Tory'.[21] The *Herald* carefully produced a table of each member's occupation, country of origin and religion. Evans was one of nine religious 'Independents' in an assembly of thirty-six Anglican, six Catholic and seven Presbyterian members.[22] In Melbourne – as in England – one's religious affiliation was important. Prejudice against Catholics especially was lively.

The Opposition's leader and member for Melbourne and Kilmore was John O'Shanassy, a forty-six-year-old Irish Catholic who had been a member of the first Legislative Council since 1851, and a member of the commission of inquiry into the goldfields. O'Shanassy 'stood out' as working for the common good rather than his own interests. He was a leader of the mercantile group in politics and an independent man of principle.[23] Although he was clever and able, his Catholicism was viewed with great suspicion by the establishment men.

Another formidable Catholic with experience and ability was Charles Gavan Duffy, the Irishman who had tried to unify Catholic and Protestant factions and who had been elected to the House of Commons in 1852. Duffy's English contacts were impressive – he was on close terms with John Stuart Mill and Carlyle – but, like Evans, he would never fulfil his 'great promise': 'there was nobility in the man and great charm, but also pettiness, petulance and egotism'. One acquaintance believed 'his temper' had been 'soured by adversity'. He was not popular with his peers, and his religion was regarded as a great handicap.[24] Throughout the following decades, the 'Protestant–Catholic polarity remained to complicate and poison political life'.[25]

Having entered Parliament, Evans soon found himself embroiled in the cauldron of faction and division he had feared – which would produce seven ministries in as many years. But the intellectual quality of the first assembly was of such a high order it has rarely been rivalled since, believed the late Melbourne historian Geoffrey Serle.

'By comparison with any period in Australian history, except perhaps about 1900, the all-round quality of the leading politicians was high.'[26] Besides William Stawell and Duffy, Evans was one of the five lawyers who 'stood out', with T. H. Fellows, Butler Cole Aspinall, Travers Adamson and Archibald Michie. Michie based his campaign on the 'people's programme', which 'he was not to be allowed to forget'.[27]

Not long after the assembly first met, the new Governor Sir Henry Barkly arrived with his wife. The forty-year-old Scottish intellectual brought vast experience in politics and constitutional law to the office. Evans was delighted with the choice: he had met Barkly during the historic debate on New Zealand in the House in 1845, when Barkly had supported Buller. The two men renewed their acquaintance, and no doubt Evans ensured that his colleagues knew of the friendship.[28]

Evans's age and colonial experience marked him out. Most of the men in the assembly were significantly younger than the fifty-four-year-old, some by as much as a generation, including Butler Cole Aspinall, Thomas Howard Fellows, Travers Adamson and John Henry Brooke. Michie was more than a decade younger, while Duffy was his junior by fourteen years, and O'Shanassy by eight. Evans eventually made a friend of one of the young men, John Dennistoun Wood, aged twenty-seven, 'a clever honest spiteful Tasmanian' and graduate of Edinburgh University.[29] The relative youth of most members made Evans aware of his age and dwindling opportunities, but it also gave him the chance to grandstand and regale them with his experiences in England and New Zealand. He became quickly noted for his wealth of knowledge, especially in constitutional law.[30] He also made much of having made extensive notes for a sequel to Gibbon's great work *The History of the Decline and Fall of the Roman Empire*. But he had not lost the schoolmaster's temptation to lecture his audience. Many referred to him as an 'old man',[31] and thought of him as 'a learned and ponderous bore';[32] he became known as 'Old Evans' – the pompous, scholarly eccentric whose inconsistency and volatile temperament would garner more political enemies than friends in the years ahead.

His primary interest was the continuation of parliamentary reform. In a landmark decision, the secret ballot had been forced through early that year against the Council's wishes. While Duffy moved for the abolition of the property qualification for members, Evans spoke out in December against the law denying naturalised foreigners the vote for another three years. He was 'in favour' of:

> . . . opening the doors of the Constitution to the natives of every country under Heaven, and especially to America and those

> countries of Europe who enjoyed the same constitution, professed the same religion [Christianity], and in many instances, spoke the same language as themselves.[33]

In the New Year he presented two petitions for the Naturalization of Foreigners and for a 'more speedy right to exercise political privileges', the first signed by 800 Germans in Melbourne, the second by between 800 and 900 Germans from Ballarat. And the following day he presented a petition from the voters of Richmond to strike out the fourth clause and every other clause giving votes to non-residents for the districts in which they possessed property.[34] His suggestions caught the attention of *Melbourne Punch*, which immediately depicted him as a vote-catcher.[35]

On 16 January 1857, Duffy appointed Evans to his select committee of twelve to consider federation, the resulting report becoming one of the basic documents of the federal movement. But the debates that followed eight months later drew a mainly sceptical response. Haines invited delegates from other colonies to an inter-colonial conference, but only South Australia and Tasmania responded, while Parkes's territory – New South Wales – put the question aside. In spite of Duffy's committee's continuing efforts in the following three years, the topic eventually lapsed.[36]

The government's revenue for assisted immigration was partly financed from the income it received from farmers' annual pastoral licences. When it tried to alter the conditions of assisted immigration from Britain, Evans took the opportunity to praise Wakefield's scheme in the *Herald,* pointing out that it was more than just an idea of colonisation to 'be applied according to time and space and circumstances. [Wakefield's] principles have never yet been applied, in their integrity, to any colony whatever.' He begged parliamentarians to:

> . . . read, mark, learn and inwardly digest, before criticizing and still more so before they assume the falsehood of what Mill and Gladstone and Molesworth and Buller and other men of the same calibre, have received as scientific truth . . . . [Wakefield] thought he had discovered a self-acting regulator in the price of land. And so he had, for a country that was purely agricultural. But the discovery of gold is an instance of disturbing causes not contemplated by any of us . . . we must . . . give some fresh development to the emigration principle.[37]

Twenty-five thousand builders were out of work in Britain while Australia had four colonies of fertile land and a population of less than one million. Evans conceded the difficulty in giving 25,000 men free passage, but he reiterated that he had 'long been of [the] opinion that some application of the joint-stock or co-operative principle is necessary, and it would solve many of the problems connected with land and emigration'.[38]

In March, O'Shanassy – with Michie seconding his motion – successfully carried a vote of censure on the government, forcing Haines to resign after only three and a half months as premier. O'Shanassy immediately asked Evans and Michie to help him form a cabinet, but both refused. Evans's refusal possibly meant he was reluctant to risk his political future by allying himself with Catholics. Also, unlike O'Shanassy, he believed that state aid should be abolished, later reciting statistics showing the great results achieved by the non-establishment bodies in England compared with the established church between the years 1801 and 1851.[39]

O'Shanassy then enlisted another Catholic, Henry Chapman – Revans's old friend and correspondent from the time of the voyage of the *Adelaide* – and John Dennistoun Wood as law officers.[40] But his attempt to position himself in the centre was a failure, and in the campaign that followed Evans played a major part in a relentless political attack on O'Shanassy in his leading columns.[41] Three by-elections were lost, and when Parliament re-assembled in April, a group of state aid abolitionists, led by James McCulloch and Michie, rejoined Haines. Michie helped Haines form a new ministry and was rewarded with the coveted position of Attorney-General.[42]

But Evans missed out entirely. In July, *Melbourne Punch* reported that Evans had asked Michie to appoint him Solicitor General. Evans disputed this in Parliament, saying Haines had met him in the Collins Street Club and asked for his help on one of the Boards of Lands and Works. McCulloch had repeated the offer in Michie's office, but each time Evans had replied that he would only consider taking office in the law. (Haines did not recall asking for Evans's assistance, but remembered Evans saying he would take no appointment but a legal one.) To confirm his story, Evans read out the note he had dashed off to Michie: 'If Fellows will not take the Solicitor Generalship I will, provided the Government will go on with Parliamentary reform.'

There had been clearly been double-dealing. When Fellows – 'the cold, subtle, venomous, old-Etonian arch-Tory' – had asked Evans to take the office after telling him he had turned it down, Evans refused, remarking 'the Government must get Sitwell'. Fellows had then accepted the appointment.[43] Michie did not refute Evans's story, merely retorting that he might publish the letter 'to the world if he liked'.[44] Evans had been elbowed out. *Punch* compared it with the quarrel scene in *Julius Caesar* – Evans as Brutus, Michie as Cassius. Evans never forgave Michie the snub, nor the leak to *Punch*.[45]

Within six hours of Michie's appointment of Fellows, Evans joined O'Shanassy's Opposition of non-conformists and Catholics. In doing so he laid himself open to taunts of having married into the very party he had so vehemently opposed in the press. In spite of Michie also being on morally shaky ground, he could not forgive Evans's 'defection' and the battle between the two men commenced in earnest. It was a battle marked by Michie's cold spite and fury, and his religious bigotry, colliding with Evans's hot anger and moral outrage.

In fact, Evans was most comfortable among a group of outsiders. He preferred passionate beliefs to the cold clinical approach. But at first O'Shanassy's group was 'vague on the land question' – one of the two principal issues, the other being railways – and divided on state aid to religious schools. Initially, John Dennistoun Wood dismissed Evans as 'the gentleman of sesquipedalian words, who acted as a sort of Boswell' to O'Shanassy. He quickly revised his view as Evans proved to be most powerful in debate.[46]

The day before the second Haines ministry replaced O'Shanassy's, Evans gave notice of a motion for parliamentary reform of electoral districts, thus tabling the first resolution leading to the adoption of universal suffrage. He moved for an increase in the number of representatives on the basis of population and industry, the shortening of the duration of Parliament, the simplification of taking the ballot and the registration of voters.[47] A month later when his resolution was defeated he accused the Haines government of 'ruses' against him, and complained he 'had been led to believe they would adopt [it]'.[48]

Although Haines was 'not enamoured of political reform', it was expedient for him to support manhood suffrage, especially as it would give him the advantage over O'Shanassy, Duffy and Evans. But first there were problems to be addressed. The registration of itinerant workers and hundreds of thousands of unrepresented diggers was a difficult issue. Plural voting and strict residential qualifications were others. In spite of the arguments of Evans, O'Shanassy and others against the finer points being more robust, and their protest against 'clogging' of the principle, it would take several months for the Bill first tabled by Evans to be passed as Haines's Bill.[49]

Communication was another vital issue in the sprawling continent. During a debate on postage for newspapers, Evans recalled the impact of Lord Ashburton's remark in the House of Lords: 'The Post Office ought to be regarded not as a source of revenue, but as an agent of civilization', adding:

> From that time the restrictive impost was abolished, and he thought [Victoria] would do well to follow the example . . . the difficulties of communication in Australia were far greater than in England. . . . this very fact afforded another reason why newspapers should have as widely and extended a circulation as possible, for the dissemination of information, and the communication of knowledge – more especially in a new country like this – political knowledge.[50]

The dissemination of information was one thing, but one of the most difficult and immediate problems facing the first ministries of Victoria was the land question. After the discovery of gold, the population had exploded from a mere 77,000 to about 410,800 by March 1857. 'The land in Victoria totalled 56,245,760 acres, of which 30,000,000 acres in Melbourne, Geelong, Portland and other coastal areas were in the hands of squatters.' By 1856 only 115,000 acres were being cultivated for agriculture and were occupied by annual licence rather than by legal possession. The occupants' rights prevailed. Now, as goldmining decreased and the diggers' demand for land to grow their vegetables and fruit grew, land values increased. 'The cry went up, "Unlock the land!".'[51]

Moses Wilson Gray, who had arrived with Duffy a year earlier, had seen the same problem in Ireland. He launched a Land Convention in July, suggesting solutions that appealed instantly to the well-informed men who flocked to join: abolition of the existing pastoral occupation and removal of squatters; free selection for the real settler at a uniform price without auction; the allocation of all unsold Crown Land to form open pasturage free to the people, or 'free commonage'; the conferring of no new pastoral tenancies when such lands were 'resumed' by the Crown; selection before survey of blocks of a certain size at a fixed price; a down-payment requirement of only 10 per cent; and reserves to be granted to the goldfields and other valuable land such as water frontages exclusively.[52]

But the squatters had powerful allies among the merchants in the assembly and the Council members, so that, although sympathetic to many of the Land Convention's demands, O'Shanassy's group generally drew the line at the removal of squatters and free commonage, and refused to ally themselves with the body that might have given them real political clout. David Syme, the editor of the *Age*, was a member of the convention, and his loathing of O'Shanassy and Duffy probably influenced O'Shanassy's decision. But Duffy, who believed in the poor man's right to land, objected to O'Shanassy's stance, and as events unfolded Evans appeared to agree with Duffy. Meanwhile, although they were against Haines's Land Bill, and cool towards the convention, they attempted to woo the squatters with suggestions of an alliance.[53]

When some of the government members began making amendments generous to squatters, Evans accused the government of collusion. Michie retorted that Evans 'was unfortunately, always smelling out a plot', a taunt Michie would fling more than once. But Evans was no fool. His suspicions would be confirmed several times in the years ahead.

The government was determined to push the Land Bill through, refusing time to discuss the many amendments. Five weeks after the second reading, Evans complained that they still had no idea what the government wanted: the Bill had changed substantially; it was too fragmentary. His opposition reached a climax on a night in July when he threatened to retire from the committee.

Michie was furious, declaring he had no confidence in Evans, who 'had put himself forward as an *Anacharsis Clootz* – an Attorney General for the whole human race – as though he were a guardian angel, with a flaming sword, appointed to watch lest there should be an invasion of any of the rights of the country'. He continued in this vein for some time until Evans rose to the bait:

> His character was of some importance . . . since he had been in the House he had endeavoured so to act as not to wound the feelings or susceptibilities of any gentleman in the House; and if he had done so he was now, as always ready to apologise . . . . if he were to give way to a malignant imagination, he might compare [Michie] to *Sqanarelle* or the *Scapin* of the French comedy, but he would refrain from doing that . . .[54]

Everyone was riveted by the battle of words that followed, but many were mystified by the clever literary comparisons. *Punch* later enlightened those who had missed the allusions, in a rhyme entitled *A Chimney Sweep*:

> There's Sqanarelle, as beat his wife
> And practised on Valére
> A charlatan and churlish cur,
> For which see Molière
> Likewise Scapin – a low poltroon
> A cheat and sharper too –

> Who gave Geronte the sack, and beat
> The old man black and blue . . .[55]

The *Herald* reported that the 'debate was of an irregular but singularly exciting character':

> In the course of it there were evoked some of the finest bursts of oratory which have yet echoed in the walls of the Victorian Parliament. Perhaps there never was witnessed, out of St Stephen's itself, a grander oratorical 'passage of arms' . . . . To bystanders it recalled some of the finest passages in the Parliamentary contests of Fox and Pitt. It fairly electrified the listening throng within the walls of the Assembly . . .[56]

Over ten years later, reporters were still recalling the evening. From the time of his entrance into the assembly, Evans's 'well-selected phrases and sonorous tones never failed to gain the ear of the House and rivet the attention of strangers', commented the *Australasian Gazette*:

> By far the finest oratorical displays which our local St Stephen's has witnessed took place when Dr. Evans sat in Opposition and lost no opportunity of fastening upon [Attorney General] Mr. Michie. One evening, when these two doughty champions encountered each other, will long linger in the memory of those who were present. The struggle of parties, which was at its height, seemed for the moment to concentrate itself in a single combat. Both men fought the intellectual tournament with all their might. The biting sarcasm, irritating innuendoes and lively sallies of Mr. Michie were well-matched by the polished satire, fierce denunciations, and admirable invective of his more ponderous antagonist. It was an encounter almost worthy of what we know of the most trenchant days of English Parliamentary warfare, and there has been nothing to compare with it since . . .[57]

After the debate there was an unprecedented walk-out by Evans and most of the members of the Opposition. They protested at what they termed 'the obnoxious Bill in committee, in order to send to their electorates their collective message of disapproval, in the light of the National Convention's disapproval – a body of men fighting the measure – and the petition of 60,000–70,000 people'.

CHAPTER TWENTY.
A MOST UNCOMMON MAN

> George Samuel Evans, Doctor of Laws, barrister of Lincoln's Inn, journalist, legislator and scholar, was an uncommon man – certainly one rarely encountered in the colonies.
>
> J. L. Forde, *The Story of the Bar of Victoria*, Whitcombe & Tombs, Melbourne, 1913, p.160

Evans's entry into the Legislative Assembly provided *Melbourne Punch* with a rich vein of material, which it mined for many years. He was a gift to cartoonists and satirists alike. *Punch* played on Evans's idiosyncrasies, his faults, his every mannerism, and his stream of classical and historical allusions. It dismembered his cherished memories and re-assembled them for the amusement of its readers. Over several years, Evans was to be the subject of numerous full-page cartoons and articles; poems, one entitled *Childe Evans' Pilgrimage*; and a few plays in three acts. He was depicted in various roles, mostly Shakespearean tragic heroes such as Brutus, Lear, Coriolanus and the Antique Roman, as well as Diogenes. He was for the satirists that quintessential enigma, 'The Original Sphynx', a noble sage and countless other characters. *Punch* created a series of *Parliamentary Biographies* satirising the background of each prominent member of the Legislative Assembly. Evans's was the fifth biography, and the only member allowed a three-part analysis:

> To show our conviction that thou art no common man, (and it would be difficult we think to pay thee higher compliment) thy Biography extending over three chapters, will for three weeks occupy the pages of Punch, to the exclusion of notices already *in limine* on our easel of other eminent legislators . . .[1]

The first part was accompanied by a full-page cartoon of Evans as 'The Original Sphynx' where:

> Apostrophising his cranium, we may say with the elder Napoleon, 'from yonder summit forty centuries look down upon us'; or with

> the author of *Eothen* we may reflect that those stony sphynx-like eyes have looked upon ancient dynasties of Ethiopian and Egyptian kings, upon Greek and Roman, upon Arab and Ottoman conquerors . . . [2]

Evans's New Zealand background and his relationship with Maori were drawn on heavily. Amused by the pride he took in his relationship with the indigenous inhabitants of New Zealand, he was dubbed 'King of the Maories'. Referring to a strange scar on his lower back – which suggests he may have undergone an operation for kidney stones – *Punch* imagined Evans being tattooed by Maori,[3] destined to become Macaulay's '*New Zealander* [Maori] *on London Bridge*'. (In his *History of England*, Thomas Macaulay had predicted that London – the centre of the western world – would be consumed by fire and superseded by the new order, in the shape of a member of the indigenous race of Britain's newest colony.)

ᏫᏒ

When not in the House, Evans could be found at his chambers at 22 Temple Court, Little Collins Street West. Otherwise, he was usually at his office at the *Herald* in Bourke Street. He was generally liked by his staff. He was approachable and had a keen sense of humour. At about this time, David Blair, a young Irishman and former independent clergyman and intellectual who had co-founded the *Empire* with Parkes, joined the *Herald*.[4] He came to know Evans well and recorded his impressions thirty years later in an article entitled 'Three Melbourne Barristers'. Blair proclaimed that Evans was:

> . . . beyond all comparison, the greatest scholar (in the now almost obsolete sense of the word) I have ever known. He was exactly the model of an old Templar of Dr. Johnson's days . . . . he had acquired the rather ponderous manner and sesquipedalian phraseology which the great lexicographer had brought into fashion in his time. [Evans] had a manner of delivering his full-rounded sentences with a species of snort (there really is no other word for it) which was very comical. His was a style that lent itself very readily to caricature, and the witty fellows of the comic press made him their prey accordingly. But all this was only the scarf-skin of the frame . . . beneath it lay as solid a body of learning as ever Englishman carried about with him. It was difficult, indeed, to find where the limits of his scholarship ran.[5]

The staff called Evans 'Bozzy', as his 'style and manner, even his resemblance to portraits' of Boswell reminded them of Johnson's devoted disciple. But when Evans heard of it he was shocked, exclaiming, 'Blair, you fellows call me Bozzy. When I had chambers in the Temple in London, I was commonly known as "the Doctor", in allusion to "Bozzy's" master.'

His erudition seemed boundless. In the summer of 1857–58, Blair and Evans were discussing the Indian mutiny of May 1857, when the 'Himalaya mountains' were mentioned. The doctor spoke:

> 'Did it ever strike you, Blair, that the first syllable of that word is connected with the Latin word *Hiems*, winter?'
> 'It never did, but what is the connection, Doctor?'
> 'Why, *Himalaya* is Sanscrit, coming direct from the original Aryan, and *Hiems* is derived from it.'
> 'Is the Latin language only a branch of the Sanscrit?'
> 'It is a branch of the Aryan, which is the mother tongue of all the Western languages.'
> 'Where, may I ask, did you learn all this, Doctor?'
> 'I studied Sanscrit for two years under George Long with a view to going out to India to practise at the bar there.'

On another occasion, Blair told Evans he had just read a translation of Aristophanes' *The Parliament of Women*:

> 'Ah', said Evans, 'You mean the *Ecclesiazusæ*. You should read it in the original Greek. No English translation can do justice to it. And if you are bent on reading of that kind get the Greek romancers, "The *Scriptores Erotici Grœci*," and you will find them a treat.'
> 'Doctor, you are amazingly well-versed in Greek literature.'
> 'My dear boy, I spent years in reading and making notes for a great history in continuation of Gibbon, and I read the forty volumes of the "Byzantine Historians" in the original Greek, from cover to cover.'[6]

Punch may have been humorous and Blair respectful, but in the House the gloves were off for deadly combat, with the target being the most precious treasure of each member – his honour. Debates in the House were riddled with rancour and irrelevancies, and no two men could ever entirely trust each other. The Speaker, Francis Murphy, struggled to keep order as 'debates frequently degenerated into violent squabbles'.[7] Michie continued to harry Evans. Irritated by Evans's questions on details of the proposed Land Bill, he referred to him as 'Dr. Syntax'. Evans's reply was deliberately elaborate:

> . . . notwithstanding the sarcasms of the hon. and learned attorney-general, I hold to my point; and notwithstanding that it is the second time he has attached to me the sobriquet he has now used, and though I could retaliate, did I not feel it too great a shame within the walls of this House, yet I have too deep and kindly a remembrance of the friendship I once felt for that gentleman, and I have too keen a recollection of the sincere and honest devotion which I gave to him in periods of difficulty, and of the sincerity with which I gave it, to render it possible for me – under even the provocation offered to me – to follow so bad, so injurious, and so dangerous an example, and to retaliate upon him the sobriquet with which it has pleased him to distinguish me.[8]

Michie merely apologised for his 'inadvertence'. Later, when Evans asked Michie to enlighten him on the wording of a clause relating to squatters' tenure, saying it appeared no different from that which Michie 'had so eloquently opposed last December', Michie's reply was ungracious and unsatisfactory. When Evans persisted, outlining his objections to the clause, Michie ignored him. Some time later it was left to J. M. Grant to point out that Evans's remarks 'had not been duly weighed by the House'.[9] A political historian combing through the Hansard of those years would find many such examples of suggestions being ignored or simply rebutted for the satisfaction of point-scoring.

Members were not paid, so that while Evans threw himself heart and soul into debate, he still shouldered the *Herald*'s editorial responsibilities. Others had businesses or – like Michie – lucrative legal practices to attend to during the day. Parliament assembled at 4 p.m. and the long hours of sitting through the night took their toll, forcing many members to resign for practical reasons.

There was the question of raising the taxation of Chinese immigrants. In an article two and a half years earlier, Evans had expressed concern at the massive influx arriving for the goldfields, although he was fascinated by their appearance:

> John Chinaman has for some time past sent his fans, and teapots, and lanterns, and basketwork, and screens and caddies to Melbourne, accompanied by figures which seem to have stepped off from their natural flat confines, to have become round and animate, and who have then sauntered about our streets buying rice and strong shoes, and finally picks and shovels, with which they have gone away to their diggings . . . . troops of forty or fifty and upwards, have been common among various incursions of Chinese upon our shores . . . they have done nothing for the good of trade, and in four and

> twenty hours, or less, they have been seen perched or piled upon one another in drays, like so many dusky birds upon so many basket bags . . .[10]

In Melbourne, as in South Australia, the population generally recoiled against the habits and practices of the Chinese who came to the diggings.[11] Evans spoke for them all when he appealed to the assembly's pride as Englishmen – and to their xenophobia – in his speech on the taxation question. The Chinese were 'rice-eating and opium-chewing Mongolians (laughter)'. He believed 'If there were to be 400,000 Chinese in the colony', he –

> . . . looked beyond the commercial advantage of disposing of a certain quantity of rice and sugar, to the question affecting the moral, social and religious welfare of the future of [Victoria]. He anticipated the arrival of the day when this continent would be peopled by millions of pure Caucasian blood, speaking the English language, and maintaining the laws and institutions on which they prided themselves, and which had placed them in their present position as a wealthy, an influential and a moral nation. It was in [their power] to determine whether this country should thus perpetuate the greatness of the English nation, or become merely an outlet for the teeming millions of China . . . . If he were to tell them of the practices of the Chinese in this city it would make their ears tingle . . . they were demoralizing to a frightful extent our youth, of both sexes and of the most tender years, in a manner that he dare not mention in a Christian Assembly. (Hear, hear).[12]

Evans had been most vocal in opposing Haines's Land Act, which scraped through the Legislative Assembly by a small majority. Next, he turned his guns on the government's proposed railway schedule. Several times in his columns Evans had pointed out the logic of creating two rail lines: firstly, the 'Grand Central Trunk Line' from Melbourne to Ballarat, then later a line from Geelong to Castlemaine crossing at right angles. The population of almost half a million, he argued, was scattered as far as Ballarat, sixty miles from Melbourne. Evans accused the government of being unduly influenced, presumably by its powerful supporters, and of being extravagant in selecting two railway lines to be constructed together – from Castlemaine to Melbourne and Geelong to Ballarat.[13] For once, the *Argus* agreed with him.

On 30 September, Evans repeated his objections in the House, calculating that the lines would incur a loan of £8 million – £5 million more than the government's revenue. He compared the cost unfavourably with Britain's railway networks, but Michie attacked his statistics, again accusing him of 'always smelling out a plot'.[14]

The property qualification for members of the assembly had been abolished in August – the first step in electoral reform – and in November universal manhood suffrage for electors of the assembly was approved. But the second Haines administration was under threat, and Michie knew it. Haines's Land Bill was a most unsatisfactory piece of legislation that did not resolve the squatting question. The Council, which proved to be in bitter opposition to so many of the assembly's Bills, overwhelmingly dismissed it late in September, the convention rejoiced and nine months of acrimonious sittings in the assembly had produced very little.[15]

In October, a young English doctor and ambitious new arrival, George Wakefield, wrote to his father in England:

> I told you that my old schoolmaster Dr. Evans is here or at least in Melbourne. He is editor of the Herald, a member of the Legislative Assembly. And altogether a highly influential personage, at least he will be for at present he is one of the leaders of the opposition, and when his party gets into power which I trust will happen before long, I intend to make myself known to him and endeavour to get some appointments through his interests . . . . I intend to try it on – for I mean to make my pile somehow.[16]

When Parliament reassembled after a short break on 13 October 1857, Evans was again a member with O'Shanassy, Richard Ireland, George Harker and eighteen others. In December, when Henry Samuel Chapman joined them, they could sense victory. The hostile Council obstructed Michie's Bill for State-Aid Abolition, which Evans had supported, and in mid-December, when Michie's actions as Attorney General came under scrutiny in the press, O'Shanassy's Opposition renewed its attack.[17]

By this time, Evans had penned about a thousand articles over his three years as editor. He decided to terminate his contract with the *Herald* in January, partly for health reasons and perhaps because he predicted a change of government. He had also been appointed to several committees. Duffy reappointed him to the select committee on Federal Union of the Australian Colonies, and in January, he was appointed to a select committee to consider Bills for increasing the franchise, for Electoral Registrations and for the Duration of Assembly. In due course, Parliament's length was reduced from five to three years, and the assembly was increased from sixty members to seventy-eight. But distribution of the vote was a sticking point.

When the representation of minorities came under debate,

O'Shanassy and his Opposition were vigorously opposed by the conservatives who were determined to exclude Catholics and diggers from electoral registration. Like O'Shanassy, Chapman and Ireland, Evans advocated the minorities clause. In February he spoke in its favour, ridiculing an article in a paper that he read to the assembly, who reacted with laughter:

> He thought it was absurd if there were 2,000 persons of one way of thinking in a locality, and 1,000 people of another way of thinking, that the 2,000 should have their representatives, and the 1,000 not be represented at all. In the progress of society they might expect to see great changes. In spite of all that had been said about America or the continent, there was a great mistrust with regard to that sort of representation. He believed that in the Assembly of France, if there had been even a small minority to urge the delay of any important question, instead of having an heterogeneous mass of people who bowed to the will of a usurper, France might have been preserved from infamy. He would rather see a powerful minority of gentlemen, if they represented the interests of the country in the House, than that they should be fretting out of doors because they had been shut out from the legislation of their country.[18]

He gave the examples of England's rotten borough system that had held sway before Parliament had made 'provisions' for the representation of minorities. But then he added a rider: 'Nations', he said, 'were subject to periodical fits of madness, and he wished to secure the country against such events.' But he was torn. He spoke out, warning against diving helter-skelter into new freedoms. He wanted, he said, to 'put a drag on the wheels of democracy', a remark that alerted the electorate, particularly as it appeared to conflict with his vows of liberalism.[19]

Ebenezer Syme, owner of the *Age*, agreed with Evans, saying:

> The drag upon the democratic machine had been again alluded to, and the necessity for preventing the machine from going too rapidly down the incline. For his [Symes's] part he was opposed to the drag and he was opposed to the incline. He was opposed to going down the incline at all . . . . If universal suffrage was so dangerous it ought not to be adopted. He himself had not voted for universal suffrage absolutely, but had voted for the education test; and he was prepared to take such measures as would be necessary, in order to do away with the incline and consequently with the drag.[20]

Many other members drew back at the speed of social change and the advance of democracy represented by the convention and other groups in and out of the House.[21] The principle was also unpopular outside the House. George Higinbotham, an Irish barrister editing the *Argus*, argued with his co-editor Wilson on the matter.[22]

On 23 February, the change to the schedule took members by surprise. The original plan to debate the division of the colony into eighty districts with three members for each had been replaced by another. The new proposal was based – as Evans believed – on 'classes and interests', but he voted for it – including the contentious minorities clause – believing that 'when such reforms came into law, a future government with wider representation' could then eliminate its objectionable elements.[23]

But Haines had made the land issue one of confidence, and his provisions for minorities were inadequate. The goldfields, for example, were given fewer seats than their fair share. The protesters dug their toes in, the squatters withdrew their support, and in late February and early March the Haines ministry collapsed.[24]

On 10 March, Barkly asked Chapman to form a ministry. The events around the fall of the Haines ministry and the construction of Chapman's and O'Shanassy's are mired in controversy. As Serle explains:

> Accounts of these negotiations are very inconsistent. The situation was complicated by uncertainty about what the precise issue was on which the government fell (*Vic. Hansard*, iii pp322–5, 332–4), and by dissension within the government and unwillingness of some members to continue. The most amusing and credible version is the excellent rhymed account of 'How Henry Samuel Formed a Ministry' in *Punch*, 11 Mar, 1858.[25]

Evans had no problem in being returned by the Richmond electorate early in April. There was a story, perhaps apocryphal, that one night while addressing a meeting of his electors he was as usual 'thundering on about the glories of the British Constitution, when a thirsty voice from the audience interjected, "Oh, damn the British constitution! What are you going to shout?"'[26]

When the roars of laughter had subsided, Evans replied: 'let me tell that gentleman that it would be highly illegal and unconstitutional, not to say most imprudent, for me to comply with the request which he has just made. But he may be interested to know that *there* is a gentleman (pointing to the chairman of his election committee) who may not have the same respect for the law and the constitution that I have, and who, if the same suggestion were made to him, might not repel it with the scorn and indignation with which I at once reject it![27]

Chapman – who had juggled the minorities clause with Evans

– formed the ministry on the understanding that its Reform Bill would not include provision for minorities. O'Shanassy selected the premiership, Chapman was Attorney General, Ireland became Solicitor General, and Duffy took up Crown Lands and Land and Works. Henry Miller and George Harker climbed aboard, the latter accepting the role of Treasurer, while Evans was rewarded with the role of Postmaster General.[28]

As he approached his fifty-sixth birthday, Evans was at last, and for the moment, financially secure. On a salary of £1,200 per year he felt, as *Punch* was quick to depict, '*Something Like Comfort at Last*'.[29]

Debate in the House shattered any complacency he may have felt. Only a few days after Evans took office, Michie began his attack, much to the disgust and wonderment of the press and Parliament. They were again discussing the minorities clause, Evans declaring he would not obstruct their Electoral Reform Bill but would vote for the second reading of the Bill, 'and reserve for himself an unfettered judgment and expression of opinion on the Minorities Clause'. Wood accused Evans of inconsistency and of lacking the courage to face opposition to the Bill. Michie agreed, observing pointedly that the character of public men was important.

Hansard reported that here Evans 'leaned forward and looked the speaker in the face, and as the observation was repeated, he raised his hand and pointed at' Michie. Unfazed, Michie continued, remarking that Evans might 'go on face-making, but it would have less effect on him than even the paper pellets of the brain so often launched at him'. He quoted from the *Herald* – insinuating that Evans was its author – which 'branded with infamy those who voted in the minority, and would yet take office under the new government'. His attack continued until Evans, who displayed 'great excitement', appealed to the 'Assembly and . . . public at large' for his vindication. He had terminated his contract with the *Herald* three months earlier, and declared it was 'the unhappiest day' of his life when he 'became connected with him (pointing to Mr. Michie) or his miserable journal'. Cries of 'Oh, oh' and 'Order' were recorded.

The House was in uproar, but there was great discomfort and clearly sympathy for Evans. When three members tried to speak up for him, he foolishly protested that Michie had not been interrupted in his 'long train of calumnious remarks'. Speaker Francis Murphy said he could not censure Michie, who had shown 'extreme skill in keeping within the bounds of order', while O'Shanassy begged them to stop, and expressed his support for Evans. But Evans persisted, demanding to be heard. Murphy intervened, agreeing that while 'every excuse should be made for' Evans, he would ask him 'as a personal favour to desist'. He added kindly, seeing Evans was close to breaking down, that he was sure the members were 'now quite sensible that the hon. gentleman is really deserving of their sympathy.'

But Evans seemed unhinged. He rose again amid loud cries of 'Chair!':

> Sir, I should not deserve to live till tomorrow morning if I permitted this occasion to pass over without saying that which I think it necessary to say in vindication of my honour against the observations which have been made by the hon. member Mr. Michie. Sir, I was proceeding to say that it was a most unhappy, a most unfortunate day for me when I became connected with the journal which –
>
> Dr. Greeves rose and was interrupted by Dr. Evans who said: Sir, you may rise five hundred times, but I will defend myself from this foul – (Loud cries of 'Chair!' and great confusion).

Murphy forbade Evans to speak any further ('Cries of "Question"'). When the vote was taken on the Bill's second reading, Evans voted with the majority.[30]

Punch's poem on the 'preposterous fight' blamed mostly Michie who 'screamed' abuse, 'swollen with rage'. It observed, 'each loses character and neither wins':

> Reporters o'er their notes disgusted leant –
> Michie's museum of abuse was spent –
> Sated with slander each retired at last,
> And none knew what the conflict really meant –
> While sorrowing patriots asked – and stood aghast –
> Have we indeed to such disgraceful courses passed.[31]

Evans's conduct had been 'outrageous', decided the *Argus*, which also condemned Michie's 'acerbity' and 'ill-nature'.[32] Its editor George Higinbotham slated the whole assembly as 'a mere rabble of political desperadoes'.

But a month later, Higinbotham – whose journal had endured harsh criticism from Evans when the latter was editor of the *Herald* – had a rare moment of praise for the Postmaster General. Evans's first act, he declared, had been 'an eminently practical one'. He had been the first to detect and stop the fraudulent use of postage stamps by a Mr Calvert:

> . . . he stuck to Calvert . . . with an adhesiveness only to be equaled by that of the stamps in question; and, if a law point was reserved, it was the Attorney-General's business to look after it, not the

> Postmaster's. So far Dr. Evans performed the new broom excellently; he detected and put a stop to a style of robbery that might have long continued but for his interference . . . . A really useful measure [will be] the money-order system . . . . We understand Dr. Evans means to inaugurate this very shortly . . . . We can think only of one other great piece of administrative reform done, or being done under his auspices . . . . he and the President of Land and Works . . . have hit upon the pattern of iron receiving boxes to be put up for the convenience of the public in various quarters of the city.[33]

Thus, Melbourne received its first public post-boxes. Late in May, Evans brought in a Bill to enable himself as Postmaster General to issue money orders in Victoria. A few days later the second reading of his Money Orders Bill – the clauses of which 'were taken verbatim from the English Act' – was agreed to in committee, and the next night his Bill was passed. Several members wanted to keep the telegraph lines open all night for mail news and in Melbourne for sending messages till 10 p.m. Evans agreed to keep the line open as long as was practicable but demurred at nightly communication, unless the government was prepared to justify the expense.[34]

Chapman's modified Electoral Reform Bill passed quickly in April, but the Council vetoed it by two votes. The Land Convention's supporters were furious. O'Shanassy asked for Parliament to be adjourned until after the Council's elections in August. The Bill would be reintroduced but, if it were rejected again, his government would demand constitutional reform of the Council.

Some time earlier, Harriet had visited Amelia in London. She had also extended an invitation to Evans's sister Mary to join them in Melbourne. There was no future for Evans's sisters in England, all unmarried. Hannah was resigned to caring for her mother. Evans wrote to Mary 'to confirm' the invitation, but suggested that if Claudia were willing to give up her position as governess they had 'a home for her also'. He added optimistically, 'pack up and come down to Egypt where there is gold, if not corn. Give my love to all the rest and say I will help them in turn.'[35]

His optimism was premature, as for the next sixteen months he and his colleagues struggled to hold their own. Besides, his earlier remark about putting a brake on democracy had 'caused general distrust in him as a legislator'. His political enemies would never allow him to forget it.[36] And without unified agreement on policy, without power, and – in the case of both Ireland and Evans – always under suspicion of promoting their personal interests, they battled an Opposition that had 'no better policy than to fan the flames of religious hatred'.[37]

CHAPTER TWENTY-ONE.
FIRE, STEAM AND ICE

O Evans, you are yoked with a lamb
That carries anger as the flint bears fire
Who, much enforced, shows a hasty spark
And straight is cold again.

Melbourne Punch, Vol. IV, 9 July 1857, p.186

When Evans's friend Dr Isaac Featherston was elected Superintendent of the Province of Wellington for the third time late in June, it augured well for the two men. For since his election to office, and over the break, Evans had been working toward establishing steam communication between the two colonies. He had met with H. W. Farrar of the Melbourne Chamber of Commerce, and organised a petition to be drawn up for the Governor. A few days after Parliament reassembled, O'Shanassy, Evans and Chapman presented it to Barkly, who received it 'most favourably'.[1]

Evans took that as approval, so that when he decided to visit Wellington in August, the *Wellington Independent* was cock-a-hoop, announcing that Farrar had informed his Wellington counterpart John Johnston that the Victorian government had agreed to 'place £6000 on the estimates' for 'immediate action' in steam communication between Wellington and Melbourne. Featherston had already set aside a sum of £2,000 per annum for steam, and the Wellington Chamber of Commerce was prepared to increase the amount if necessary. The editors had learned from private letters that 'the success of the enterprise . . . is entirely owing to . . . our old and well known fellow-Colonist, Dr. Evans':

> To this gentleman it is that Wellington is indebted for the position which the accomplishment of this desirable measure will secure to her; and his long residence in and intimate acquaintance with New Zealand, is a sufficient guarantee that if we are but true to ourselves, the proposed steam communication with this port will not want for efficient support from the Melbourne Government.[2]

When the *Queen* arrived in Port Nicholson on the morning of 21 August, Evans and Harriet were greeted with 'quite an ovation' from a large crowd.[3] A few days later, Evans was guest of honour at a special general meeting of the Wellington Chamber of Commerce. Many of his friends were there – Johnston and George Hunter, Kenneth Bethune, Levin and, of course, Evans's oldest acquaintance, James Taine – who all added to the 'unusually large' attendance.

In his address, Evans outlined the advantages of steam communication with Melbourne, stressing the acceleration of commerce. He had 'always felt and taken a very warm and lively interest in everything connected with [Wellington's] social and commercial progress, and from what he knew of his fellow Wellington colonists he confidently anticipated' they would reciprocate Melbourne's gesture.

Melbourne was the central point of the Australian colonies and Wellington the central point of New Zealand. Melbourne's Chamber of Commerce had assessed the cost of the establishment of the service to be £12,000, of which half should come from Wellington and the southern settlements. Evans thought it reasonable that as the principal settlement, Wellington should provide £3,000, and the southern settlements – Nelson, Canterbury and Otago – the other half.

Captain William Rhodes, a successful businessman and landowner who had built Wellington's first wharf in 1841, was pleased with the 'extremely liberal' terms and recommended that the commercial community should seize the opportunity. If they adopted 'a little more of the Yankee go-ahead principle', the colony might make more rapid strides in wealth and prosperity. If the provincial government could not meet the cost, he pledged he would personally 'do his share in the matter'. The approval was unanimous.[4]

The project rapidly gained momentum. A deputation visited Featherston and Evans to ask Evans to purchase a steamer in Melbourne, to be paid for by the provincial government. Evans was in his element as he proposed an even bolder vision for Wellington. Before leaving Melbourne, he had asked for a report from the general superintendent of Victoria's Telegraph Department on the feasibility of connecting the two colonies by electric telegraph.

On 15 September, the *Independent* announced the publication of 'one of the most remarkable documents in connection with New Zealand that has, perhaps, ever been laid before the public'. This proposal to lay down a submarine cable was 'visionary in the extreme'. When the Panama lines opened, the news from New Zealand could be 'flashed into Australia a week earlier than the steamer arrives there, and flashed out again, a week later than the steamer leaves there'. This innovation – the laying down of 1350 miles of telegraph wire – would be 'comparatively nothing, and the cost – (£180,000) a mere trifle', taking into account Melbourne's annual gold exports of 'upwards of £12,000,000'. McGowan's detailed report added the cost of a preliminary survey – thought to be about £1,800 – and suggested that all colonial governments interested 'in establishing closer relations with our distant sister colony' should bear the cost.[5]

Evans's idea was a coup. The night before his return to Melbourne, Wellington's merchants hosted 'the most elegant entertainment yet given in Wellington' in his honour at the Commercial Hotel. Forty of Wellington's leading gentlemen attended, with the Hon. Charles Clifford in the chair. The manager of the Union Bank, Alexander McDonald, had died unexpectedly the previous day, so Featherston, unable to attend, sent his apologies in a letter dated 21 September:

> . . . nothing would have afforded me greater pleasure than to have joined my fellow settlers in paying such a compliment to one who may justly be regarded as the founder of this colony, who bore a prominent part in all its early struggles, and who has paid his present visit chiefly for the purpose of conferring upon us the great boon of direct steam communication with Melbourne.

Apologies also came from Gibbon Wakefield, who had a prior engagement to attend a Maori feast at Petone; Colonel Charles Gold, ill at home; and Henry St Hill, a close friend of the late Mr McDonald. Postponement of the celebration was out of the question, as the *Queen* was due to leave the following morning for Melbourne.

In toasting Evans, Clifford thanked him for the part he had played in drawing Victoria's attention to the geographical and commercial importance of Wellington. The difficulties of communication between the two colonies had been so great that the mercantile community of Wellington had thought they were insurmountable. But Evans, he declared, 'like Columbus, had broken their egg, and at once solved their difficult problem'. The chairman quickly reviewed the many services Dr Evans had rendered the colonists in former days, when his 'powerful voice, sage counsel and able pen were constantly in requisition':

> The days of trouble had now gone by; but while they rejoiced in the prosperity of New Zealand they equally rejoiced in meeting one who though he had largely shared in and greatly suffered from the disasters that attended the early colonization of Wellington, had so far recovered as to meet them that night in the honorable and responsible capacity of the accredited minister of the most powerful of the Southern Colonies.

Evans rose amidst loud applause. In a speech peppered with his 'well-known humour', and 'heartily applauded throughout', he praised the perseverance that had turned the early dark days into the bright days of Wellington's future. Wellington was the 'fruit of the indomitable courage with which every obstacle had been met and overcome'. Taking into account the drawbacks Wellington had suffered, 'which none of the other provinces had encountered in anything like the same degree – he was surprised at the progress that had been made'.

Wellington was the obvious choice for the centre of communication, in its trading port, and in its future as an attraction for Australians with its 'salubrious climate'. Although he did not directly refer to it, he had held an unwavering belief in its becoming the capital of New Zealand, saying instead that he 'hoped he would yet see the Province of Wellington take that position to which the spirit and energy of her people entitled her'. And responding to Rhodes's toast to 'the Progress of the Colony of Victoria', Evans told them that the advantages of the electric telegraph could not be over-estimated. It was not an illusion – in fact, he hoped to see it in a very short space of time. He concluded to 'tumultuous applause': 'With this girdle round the world, and the assistant aid of steam, he hoped to see Victoria and Wellington become twin sisters.'[6]

The next day, 25 September, accompanied by Featherston, Evans's party boarded the *Queen* to a farewell by numerous dignitaries and a crowd of well-wishers. But a northerly gale forced the steamer to return and wait for more favourable conditions to put to sea.[7] This unexpected delay meant that when the ship berthed in Melbourne early in October, Parliament had reassembled two days earlier.

The Opposition had wasted no time, with James Service querying the nature of Evans's trip to New Zealand.[8] O'Shanassy replied that the visit had been partly on private business, and partly to discuss a 'system of steam postal communication between Melbourne and that country'.[9] A fortnight later, Evans was asked to give a postal return – the number of letters posted in Victoria for New Zealand – to explain the benefit Victoria would gain from steam communication with New Zealand. Evans promised to furnish the House with the returns as soon as possible, but reminded those present that it was the discretionary privilege of the Governor 'to make arrangements for the transmission of mails in this colony'. But he knew Parliament first had to agree to the expenditure.[10]

In mid-November, when the *Wellington Independent* announced that the Melbourne ministry had agreed to grant a subsidy of £6,000 or two-thirds of the cost of a steamer between the two ports 'without waiting for the vote of the legislature', the omens were not favourable for Evans. Advertisements for tenders for a steamer to carry mail from Melbourne on the 10th and Wellington for Melbourne on the 25th of each month were signed by Evans. And eleven days later, the *Independent* announced with delight that Dr Featherston had obtained a contract for the *Wonga Wonga*, the sister ship to the *City of Sydney*.[11] This event, it declared, was second in importance only to the passing of the Constitution Act.

When, two days later, Featherston returned to Wellington in the *Wonga Wonga*, 'after a splendid run of only six days', and flourished European news that was only two months old, he was greeted at Plimmer's Wharf with loud cheers, a salute of guns from shore and a display of 'sky rockets, blue lights, etc.' With this 'leap in time', Wellington hoped it was closer to being the seat of government and becoming New Zealand's capital city.

☙

Evans knew his opponents were primed to challenge his initiative on steam communication, but first they attacked him about his inconsistency on the minority clause. He responded during the debate on constituency boundaries, expressing his astonishment at the Opposition's having revised its plan for the subdivision of the district of Melbourne, which would raise its status above others. They had:

> . . . taken [the schedule] from their own Bill, brought in by the late President of Land and Works himself, who now sat on the other side of the House [David Moore], and actually took part in the destruction of his own measure. (Loud cheers.) He did not wish to speak offensively, but when sometimes the taunt of inconsistency was raised in that House, he could not help thinking that hon. members opposite, in now turning round upon their own Bill, had made out a very excellent demonstration of it.

Evans again promised to explain his stance on the minorities clause, hoping to have the opportunity to refute the 'malicious calumnies, slanders and insinuations which had been heaped upon him before the House and the country with respect to his conduct'.[12]

He was forced to justify his separate office of Postmaster General by pointing out that he had increased the number of post offices, given Melbourne and its suburbs three deliveries of letters per day at a postal rate of 2d instead of 4d each letter, and saved £8,000 on the estimates. His department could not merely be a branch of another: having fewer ministers would make it impossible for them to perform their departmental duties and their duties as Cabinet councillors, as well as finding the time to participate in the debates of the House.[13]

Three months later, in February 1859, when an additional £15,000 for the mail service was proposed, Evans's colleague, Mr Harker, moved that the amount promised for establishing steam postal communication with New Zealand be put aside for that purpose. Dr Thomas Embling objected, saying he would like further discussion on the issue, as it had been 'strongly censured out of doors'.

Evans gave the background to his actions, beginning with a Treasury Minute of 27 November 1856, and again in April of the following year, when the 'Home Government' recommended arrangements should be made for branch steamers to be 'provided to ply between New Zealand, South Australia and Tasmania, the cost to be added to the cost of the main service, and divided among the respective governments'. He had not approached the Treasury for the amount as he felt it would save time, he said, being sure 'the Home Government would not oppose the contract'. He had provided for any setback by ensuring the contract could be discontinued at six months' notice, otherwise he would be personally liable for the amount.[14]

He won that round, but during the debate the next day in committee, when Harker moved to solicit the Governor's approval for Evans's initiative, some objected that the exports to New Zealand and the postal traffic did not warrant two-thirds of the cost being borne by Melbourne.

Evans pointed out again that he had brought the schedule down in a despatch from the Governor. Another objection centred round the contract having been entered into with Wellington, instead of with New Zealand's central government. Evans cited statistics proving Auckland was 'commercially speaking, a mere dependency of New South Wales'. He thought it strange that Melbourne 'had no direct steam communication with a place comparatively near them, as large as England, and containing 60,000 white people, and 100,000 native population, [who were] as civilized as the average of white people. (Laughter).'

Evans was anxious to deny any hidden agenda, assuring the members that he had entered into the contract 'with no indirect or sinister motives whatever'. Michie was sceptical about the arrangement, telling Evans that he –

> . . . had become rather a laughing stock in New Zealand on the return of Mr. Featherston . . . . He knew that one gentleman from that colony had met a member of the House in the street and had –
> Dr. Evans: What is his name?
> Mr. Michie: The name of the member of the House?
> Dr. Evans: No; the name of the gentleman.
> Mr. Michie: I must leave the Hon. member to whom I allude to tell that if he think proper.
> Dr. Evans: I insist upon knowing it. ('Oh, oh' laughter, and cries of 'six o'clock', 'We are not at the Old Bailey!')

Michie continued, alleging that the 'gentleman had said that Dr. Featherston got the best of [Evans] in making these arrangements'. He understood Dr Featherston had 'received quite an ovation on his return to New Zealand for the victory he had obtained over the simple-minded Postmaster General of Victoria'. This personal barb was greeted with laughter. Michie believed that Evans was being disingenuous, suggesting Evans had simply pre-empted any hostile attempts to block the contract.

But D. S. Campbell was able to clarify the situation, pointing out that as a member of the Chamber of Commerce he knew that the question had first arisen on 12 July the previous year, when a 'distinct sum was asked for by the Chamber'. Dr Evans was 'in New Zealand at the time'. Campbell believed 'no interested motives should be attributed to that Hon. Member – such motives as had been insinuated by certain hon. members'. Campbell mentioned that after Dr Evans had negotiated with Dr Featherston, the latter had promised that Wellington's contribution to steam communication between the colonies would be £3,000. Campbell supported the original motion for Victoria's parliament granting the full amount first proposed of £6,000, as 'by opposing it he should be doing great injustice to the mercantile interests of the colony'.[15]

In support of Evans, Chapman also objected to Michie's arguments, reminding the House that they should be debating whether the contract was advantageous to the colony or not. Arguing in detail, he and O'Shanassy objected that 'the House had wasted a great deal too much time' quibbling over paltry amounts when the mercantile community would clearly benefit from the move. Nevertheless, Michie pressed for an early annulment of the contract, and when William Nicholson moved an amendment reducing the government's contribution to £3,500 – less than one-half of the total amount required – and annulling the contract after six months, it was carried, seventeen votes to thirteen.[16]

In Wellington the news was greeted at first with disbelief. The *Independent* believed the Opposition was motivated by unnecessary jealousy: 'the secret influences that have been at work have temporarily triumphed; Wellington is used to having obstacles thrown in her path, and equally used . . . to overcome them manfully'. Dr Featherston had negotiated successfully with steamship owners in Sydney and Melbourne to reduce the cost for both. 'The credit in all other respects was due, and heartily awarded by Dr. Featherston himself, to Dr. Evans. A credit alike acknowledged to be his by all parties in Wellington.'[17]

A month later the *Argus* carried an extract from the *Wellington Independent* which detailed the advantages of advancing steam communication between Wellington and the Australian colonies. It would make New Zealand 'the nearest of the Southern colonies to Great Britain instead of the farthest', and would raise New Zealand 'from comparative insignificance into importance'.[18]

But Melbourne thought differently. Although Featherston finally clinched the deal after Barkly intervened, the Opposition fought on against renewing the contract until the following year, when the mutual agreement guaranteeing a subsidy of £9,000 to the Australian Steam Navigation Company for two years to run monthly steamers between the two colonies was rejected.[19] Personal spite and petty politics had prevailed.

In January 1859, at the opening of the Melbourne and Murray River Railway, the members of the ministry and other dignitaries assembled to lay the foundation stone of a viaduct across Jackson's Creek. Halfway down the eighty-foot-high stone, coins and papers of the day, together with a scroll with inscriptions of the names of O'Shanassy's ministry, were laid in a cavity. There was a grand fête at Sunbury, and at the lunch Evans sat on the left of the Chair with O'Shanassy and Speaker Francis Murphy, the Chief Justice and the Bishop of Melbourne. The Speaker of New Zealand's governing assembly also attended.[20]

In late February, an Act was passed by the assembly providing for a new set of electoral rolls to be drawn up. But the divisive Council had amended the Bill. When the Opposition fastened on the government over a suspected malpractice, Governor Barkly was left to cool his heels while the House 'brawled' for hours before he could dismiss his first Parliament on 24 February 1859.[21]

Meanwhile, O'Shanassy's Cabinet courted the members of the Land Convention and the goldfields on the land issue, promoting their ministry as 'a popular radical government'. But where the *Argus* thought O'Shanassy's land scheme was 'an honest and liberal attempt at settlement', the Convention deemed it to be 'crude, vague and delusive', thereby incurring O'Shanassy's enmity.[22] On 22 March, Duffy resigned after a dispute with O'Shanassy over the distribution of agricultural land – land that Duffy believed ought to be reserved for selectors.[23]

Evans was allotted Duffy's portfolios, becoming president of the Board of Land and Works, and Commissioner of Crown Lands and Survey. These were crucial roles, as on the land question much manouevring had been going on behind the scenes, of which Evans was fully aware. Michie and his cohorts on the Opposition benches had formed an alliance with the Conventionists to put forward Dr G. Mackay, lawyer and early Conventionist. Mackay was 'well-intentioned' but 'not very wise', observed the *Argus*, knowing that the odds were stacked against him in Richmond.

When Evans went to Richmond to seek re-election, he was greeted with suspicion. Earlier he had expressed his unease at the effects the speedy application of democracy might have on the electorate, suggesting that they could 'put a drag on the wheels of democracy'. This was rich coming from the man who had advocated universal suffrage, but he was alarmed at seeing uneducated men being 'treated' or bribed by smooth-talking agents for parliamentary candidates or factions, amongst other things.

At one election meeting Evans made an admission which had nothing to do with the issues. Having been misreported as once spending some time in Canada, he explained, 'I referred to the part I had taken in framing some land resolutions with reference to that country, and also assisting the Earl of Durham in drawing up his report . . .'.[24] An intriguing aside – but the prime issue of the day was arguably the land question. At the meeting on Thursday, 31 March, Evans's views were unable to be heard over the din, so late on Sunday evening two members of the Land Convention, G. H. Batten and Christopher Cutter, called on Evans at his home to clarify his views. At first he thought they came as individuals, as the Convention was never referred to during the meeting. But the next day they gave him a memorandum summarising his views:

> . . . he interprets the programme to mean that . . . all exclusive occupancy [of unsold lands] should cease, and that, *personally*, he

> believes there should be no re-letting of these unsold lands to any new tenants. That he desires, however to use this limitation, that the geodetic survey should precede the selections; which survey should, if the country will grant the money for it, be accomplished within the two and a half years. Further that his opinion is that free selection should be the universal rule, and the auction system, as applied to town and suburban lands, generally admitted to be of exceptional value, should be the exception to the rule, and that Dr. Evans seeks the suffrages of the electors of Richmond on these principles.

Evans signed it, adding in a brief note, 'Without presuming to speak on behalf of my colleagues, this is the meaning I attach to the Ministerial Programme'. When the memorandum was read at the Convention's meeting the following evening, it caused uproar. Mackay appealed to his supporters, threatening to withdraw. His allies lost no time in denigrating Evans's character, one member reminding them it had been 'only a very short time ago that [Evans] said it was necessary that there should be a drag put upon the wheels of democracy'.[25]

Evans was well received at two meetings that evening, but the following night he declared he had never regarded the Convention as a threat. He did not agree with some of its views on the disposal of public lands, nor did he believe in deferred payments – which meant the public and the government were left in the position of debtor and creditor. He also preferred selection after survey to free selection. But he believed the Convention had been 'of eminent service to the country' when the Land Bill was under debate in Parliament. The combined efforts of 'delegates from the goldfields and other populous districts' had produced a 'salutary effect . . . upon public opinion and upon the Legislature'. His speech was welcomed with enthusiastic applause.

At the same time, at the conclusion of the Land Convention's meeting, it was resolved to withdraw support from Mackay and to back Evans, as he was obviously in a more powerful position to help them. It was, as Serle later wrote, a 'prime tactical blunder' for the Convention, as O'Shanassy's ministry was only playing out time.[26] Mackay took his supporters into a newly formed Democratic Society.

Evans's colleagues in the ministry immediately distanced themselves from his views. And the *Argus* – which came under fire in the House for its *ad hominem* attacks, 'not on the mosquitoes but the larger animals' – unleashed a furious attack the next day on the entire assembly.[27] The Opposition was deplored for its dishonourable motives in harassing the ministry by 'fraternising with an ultra-conventionist [Mackay]'. The Land Convention had abandoned its 'dupe', and Evans was attacked for the vagueness of his address – it was still unclear if he 'supported the [Land Convention's] doctrine of free pasturage'. Higinbotham complained that Evans should have been unequivocal about the issue being the method of settlement, not the method of occupation. Instead of Evans explaining the ministry's policy, he had presented its views 'as a local bribe'. Higinbotham added:

> What is most vexatious in Dr. Evans's misconduct is, that he seems to take pains to disgrace himself . . . . he has made a clumsy and ineffectual attempt to recant his written statement after it had served the immediate political purpose with which it appears to have been made . . . . Whatever may be Mr. Duffy's faults, no person will believe that he would, even for any consideration, have acted like the disreputable old man that has succeeded him.[28]

That sobriquet, 'disreputable old man', would be picked up and used more than once, haunting Evans for years to come. Even the *Herald* put the ministry on the spot by challenging it to adopt Evans's views or reject him as a member of Cabinet. Had the Opposition laid a trap? Or had Evans been used as a dupe by O'Shanassy – who loathed the Land Convention – to 'play out time'? [29]

If it had been a ploy it could not have had a better result. Richmond returned him to power with a large majority, but then Evans's colleagues forced him to repudiate the agreement he had made with Batten and Cutter. It was a bitter blow. Trust in Evans as a legislator was now at a crisis point. He was full of chagrin, but his maverick conduct and curious political naivety was to become a liability more than once, even if the concept of political parties barely existed at the time.

Some outside his circle spoke up for Evans. During the campaigns, Mr Barton, the successful candidate for North Melbourne, had conceded that most politicians had agreed with Evans's statement on free selection. Evans had said it would become the basis of all future legislation on land, and he was likely to be right, said Barton. In fact, it was not politically expedient for any faction to ally itself overtly with the democratic Land Convention.[30] But Justice Redmond Barry, the first Chancellor of Melbourne University, wrote to Vice-Chancellor Hugh Childers in London, exalting:

> You know Duffy has left our ministry sadly disappointed. I believe there has not been a revolution. Thereupon old Evans succeeds him and has eaten much dirt at his election for Richmond. But are not all of these things written in the *Argus* . . . [31]

While Evans was experiencing this political anguish, in March 1859, Daniel and Harriot Riddiford's eldest son, seventeen-year-old Edward Joshua, had arrived to stay with his grandparents in George Square, Fitzroy. He spent the year at Scotch College, then worked for six months as a drover, moving cattle from Queensland to Victoria, during which he gained valuable farming experience.[32] He would go on to become one of the most successful farmers of his day in the Wairarapa, amassing large blocks of land and great wealth. He also forged very strong links with the Maori of the lower North Island, who addressed him as King. His upbringing in Orongorongo had isolated him, his siblings and his heroic mother Harriot from Pakeha; but by growing up, playing with and living alongside Maori he learned to speak their language fluently. Thus began the lifelong mutual respect that still exists between the family and iwi.

At the end of June, James Service, 'that combative and intensely sincere Scot', led a deputation of protest to Barkly.[33] The size of the deputation surprised Barkly, but he was even more astonished at their purpose. The background was not complicated. It centred on the St Vincent de Paul Orphanage in Emerald Hill, to which Evans had granted an additional area – so the girls could be housed separately and gardens could be cultivated – without first consulting the Municipal Council. The council had been negotiating with Duffy before his departure, as it objected to more reserves being granted that decreased the value of private land in the area. Service assured Barkly that there were no sectarian motives to their objections but condemned Evans's conduct as 'discreditable', adding that the council asked for Evans's impeachment.

Barkly was astounded. He rebuked the deputation for having exceeded its privilege, and pointed out that Evans had acted within the realms of his power. Service imputed no dishonourable motives to Evans, but objected to the manner in which he had granted the additional land without the prior notice he had promised, and after only a cursory examination with the surveyor.

Barkly felt sure that Service was labouring under a misapprehension and hoped some compromise could be reached, but he also admitted the matter was 'involved in considerable difficulty'.[34] Evans's energy and drive had clearly dwindled with age and ill health.[35] His unpredictable behaviour may have frustrated his colleagues, but it served to fuel the fire of his political enemies. Yet in this instance he may well have been shrewd: being aware of the anti-Catholic faction, he may have decided to agree to the orphanage's request before objections could be raised.[36]

His unpopularity aside, Evans seemed always to be teetering on the brink of financial ruin. There were suggestions he was drinking – possibly quite heavily. *Punch* made one or two oblique hints in its *Biography*. He dined at the Club, entertained at home and made short trips back to Wellington. He received many invitations from the Governor, but attended few official soirées in Melbourne. At the end of one grand affair, when he discovered his hat was missing, he roared for it several times before stomping off bareheaded into the night sheltering under an umbrella. He declared he disliked the Melbourne social milieu, preferring the solace of the new Parliamentary Library, and 'a quiet life'.[37]

C. W. Dilke might have been referring to a personal encounter with Evans when he wrote that in Victoria:

> . . . class animosity runs much higher and drives its roots far deeper into private life . . . than in any other English-speaking country I have seen. Political men of distinction are shunned by their opponents in the streets and clubs; and . . . I have seen men in Victoria refuse to sit down with a statesman from whose views on land questions they happen to dissent. A man once warned me solemnly against dining with a quiet grave old gentleman, on the ground that he was 'a most dangerous radical – a perfect firebrand'.[38]

In July the Opposition led by Michie launched the Constitutional Association, whose manifesto was nothing more than bigotry – a barrage of criticism aimed at O'Shanassy and other members of the ministry, which was so highly offensive and personal that it backfired. As Serle points out, the Association 'let loose a spate of propaganda which was remarkable both for sustained virulence and the absence of positive policy'.[39] The *Argus* denounced Michie's personal brand of malice and spite. Two years earlier, Duffy had observed that Michie's parliamentary skills could be compared with those of Disraeli. Evans agreed, but added – presumably without a trace of irony – 'Would to God his judgment and consistency were equal to his genius!'[40]

In August, they faced the first election under manhood suffrage. For Evans it was too soon after the Batten and Cutter debacle. But he knew what his electors wanted to hear and he gave it to them. At the White Star Hotel in Swan Street, he was largely well received, although there were a few vocal opponents. He boasted of a record clear of favouritism and corruption. Protectionism was the popular cause of the moment, supported by the merchants and diggers, and backed by the powerful Protectionist League. When asked for his views, Evans replied that if protectionism were embraced it would return them all 'to Druidism' and he would retire to take up his profession. A voice interjected 'New Zealand', followed by much laughter. Evans's response was defiant, but the first word of his reply suggests a defensive and uncharacteristic hesitation:

> Evans: Well, he was not ashamed – (A Voice, 'You ought to be'; and renewed laughter) – of the part he had taken many years ago in founding that colony, and he felt that it was a proud thing for him to believe that when dead and gone, nothing could erase that portion of his career from the book of history. (Cheers).

To counter the charge that the government was delaying the reassembling of Parliament in order to eke out the two years' service required for its members to receive a pension, he declared that no Cabinet member needed a government pension. Three months later he had changed his mind, but at the time his speech was received with 'three vociferous cheers'.[41]

When he arrived at the Star and Garter in Bridge Road, the scene was unlike anything he had experienced. It was obvious the voting demographic had changed. The building was crammed with 'boys and greasy unwashed rogues', and the yells, groans, hooting and laughter drowned out his attempts at reasoned argument. He finally left the room after a heckler insisted on interrogating him.

The next day at the meeting for the nomination of candidates, in proposing Evans, his old friend Dr Wilson reminded them of 'the lowest devices' to which the Opposition had resorted. This swayed the audience so that the vote favouring both Evans and Mr Francis was carried by a large majority the next day.[42] Three days later, Evans spoke at the Yarra Yarra Hotel for two hours, reminding them of all he had done for the district – the markets, the mechanics' institutes, the new and extended roads. He had every reason to feel confident, but after the votes were counted, Evans found he had lost.

He was furious to hear that bribery had taken place. Voting had been held in several pubs where men under the influence of drink 'had been persuaded' to vote other than they would have. The two successful candidates, James Francis and Alfred Woolley, had not sanctioned the bribery, but their friends and supporters had used the system of 'shouting'. In addition, the names on the voting papers had been confusing, and several votes had been discounted as a result.[43]

Having lost at Richmond, Evans wasted no time in entering the race for the Avoca district, a goldmining area west of Maryborough. With six candidates in the running, the campaign was hectic as Evans rode from venue to venue, making lengthy speeches, justifying his record and explaining his policies.

On 13 September, at the Bull and Mouth Hotel in Dunolly, he faced a large crowd and excused himself and his colleagues from the charges made against them. He then distanced himself from them, saying he was eager to leave the ministry, but had been persuaded by Barkly to keep it united until the next Parliament met. It was the declaration of an opportunist deserting a doomed ministry, but ideologically there were deep rifts within the Cabinet. The vote of confidence was carried easily, and nine days later Evans won the election resoundingly, by almost 200 votes. His victory speech was full of bombast and flattery:

> A great campaign was before them, and he was prepared to fight their battles hand in hand with his honourable friend, Mr. Grant, without flinching from the fight. When he reflected on the honour that had been conferred on him, he was delighted that he was not then member for Richmond – a metropolitan suburb – but had been promoted to be representative of a large district – one he might call an extensive county. They would have assembled shortly 27 representatives from the gold-fields, and, if they did their duty, he foresaw that they must rule the Government . . . [44]

It was a 'characteristic speech', the *Argus* commented drily.

Later, *Melbourne Punch* spelled out this difficult period for Evans in its own inimitable way:

> Your innocent coquetries with the Convention on the 'free grass' question, which, dullard as I am in such modern trickery, seems to me to have been a mere puerile flirtation to keep a falling ministry in power, is turned to your detriment; your ardent devotion to your constituents in local jobs, and your subsequent abandonment of the poor devils in their pettifoggery when they basely stood out for their rights in 'free selection', and sent you forth rejected to seek for 'free grass' and pastures new in the West Riding of Victoria, are made the vehicle of the contemptuous sneers of your enemies, while your learning, science, and traditions, expose you to the ridicule of the illiterate crew who coolly boast 'they know nothing about nobody', unless they have 'lagged' behind the world in Australia.[45]

Just before rejoining his colleagues, Evans was elected by the University of Melbourne to its council. When he arrived to take his seat for the opening of the Second Parliament on 13 October, the first under manhood suffrage, no fewer than forty-four Opposition members faced the government members. O'Shanassy and his ministers put on a collective brave face, but the 'great gaps behind them' said it all. Evans, it was noted, 'kept his dignity' and 'looking like a last relic of the *Parcae* cabinet of the classical ages, smiled on space with a broad and sinister benignity'.[46]

CHAPTER TWENTY-TWO. OPPOSITION

> Reputation is an idle and most false imposition;
> Oft got without merit, and lost without deserving.
>
> William Shakespeare, *Othello*, 11, iii, lines 368–70

A week after Parliament re-assembled, Evans was 'physically incapacitated'. He was subjected to a sustained attack by the Opposition for three long days and nights over his agreement with Batten and Cutter. With defeat staring them in the face, Evans made a last defiant stand. Members were not allowed to use notes, making Evans's orations more remarkable for their faultless grammar, autobiographical musings, colourful historical references and constitutional knowledge. Evans 'said good things', as Duffy put it, 'but they were witty and wise rather than humorous'.[1]

Now Evans felt compelled to record his own achievements. He exulted in their ministry having been the instrument of parliamentary reform. He felt 'something like those parents who perish at the moment of introducing into the world their offspring (Laughter)'. He also reminded the House that it was he who had placed the resolutions before the House for electoral reform in the Haines ministry.

During the nineteen months he had held office, he defied any member to show that he appointed 'a single individual to any office in my department on any ground, other than that of his qualification'. He had economised in the Post Office by merging two inspectorships into one. He had abolished the secretaryship of the department of Public Lands. ('Hear, hear.') He had, in spite of the denunciations of himself and his colleagues, left the Post Office department 'in a better and more efficient state than it was . . . (Hear, Hear)'. He had:

> . . . established 130 branch post offices throughout the country districts (hear) by means of the branch lines of railway communication . . . established a system of money orders in the principal towns in the interior (hear, hear), and . . . been enabled to say to the treasurer of this country, 'I have saved a sum of £8,900 out of the sums placed

> for the estimates for my department.' (Hear, hear.) Well, Sir, it is a pitiful thing to allude to one's own conduct, but on such an occasion as the present, what would at other times appear an unpardonable liberty, may be excused by an indulgent auditory. (Hear, hear.)

Evans explained that he had agreed with his colleagues on a Land Bill, and while he remained a member of that administration he was 'bound in honour to support the principles of the details of that Bill'. They had all agreed that the Bill they presented to the House was never 'a complete, final and unalterable measure, but one suited to the present exigencies of the country'. The very point made out to be its fault was, he believed, its 'chief excellency which . . . will do all for the complete development of the resources of this country'. It was a Bill 'favourable to the squatters and equally favourable to the Convention'.

On his own behalf and that of his 'colleague who is not a member of this House', he referred to his experience in New Zealand:

> . . . we have not come here to learn the circumstances of a new country, or the advantages of free selection, as it is more than twenty years since we took part in forming the land systems of neighbouring colonies, the first principle of which is free selection before surveys.

If their Bill had fallen short of that, it was because they 'considered the circumstances of this new country made it too bold an experiment'. (This was greeted with loud cries of 'Hear, Hear'.) He believed changes should be gradual, 'proceeding smoothly, so that no great interest in the community should feel a shock'.

He had travelled over 500 miles from Melbourne to Geelong, to Ballarat, Creswick, Clunes and almost to the River Murray. He had 'looked with amazement on the thousands and millions of acres of fertile land unoccupied except by sheep and cattle'. He found it 'monstrous to see such vast spaces of land occupied or pretended to be occupied, not by farmers, not by producers, but by men running cattle merely to keep a supply of cattle for the neighbouring diggings which might with ease be made to occupy only one-tenth part of it'. He outlined his theory of land settlement:

> . . . namely, a previous survey of the land, and the establishment of agricultural municipalities or councils . . . . the whole land of this colony should be as rapidly as possible brought under survey by a geodetic method, that these lands should be thrown open to selection without auction, except such lands as were particularly

> and specially valuable, and which, I suppose, no reasonable man would leave open to mere scramble. . . . agricultural areas should be open to free selection, so that auction should be the exception, and free selection the rule of the colony. I would also have a law that, as soon as possible after a given number of inhabitants settled on a district, they should have the right to call upon the Government to form them into district councils, and that, once formed, they should exercise every power which they could possibly exercise away from the central Government. (Hear.) We were extending the same principle to the gold-fields, leaving it to those who are the best judges of their own interests to regulate their own affairs. I say that the large body of the men engaged in mining, in consulting their own interests, consult those of the public . . . . Because I conceived that the [Land Convention's] programme framed the basis of such improvement, I consented to it as part of the project to be submitted to this country, and I defy the people to say we were ever so narrow-minded as to say that this Bill would confine, in the four corners of it, all that was necessary to the agricultural interests of this country, but that it would contain all the sound principles of legislation, and that from it we could go on improving.

He accused the Opposition's Constitutional Association of having bribed men in the House to 'use influence in the election of gentlemen opposed to the Government'. When challenged by Nicholson to provide names, Evans said Mr M. Prendergast had been offered what appeared to be the going rate of £200.

At that revelation the House threatened to erupt, but Evans persisted, congratulating Nicholson 'upon the means by which his success had been gained, and upon the agents which have assisted him'. Nicholson rose to order, but was denied, and Evans continued. He said as a member of the Cabinet, he was ready to answer for his colleagues 'in a corporate capacity'. He had lost his election at Richmond by five votes according to the returning officer, and there was a controversy over 53 votes, tendered on his behalf but refused. He was successful at the Avoca by more than 600 votes, placed '200 ahead of one of the best representatives that ever sat in this house. (Hear Hear).'

He concluded one of the best speeches of his career by warning the incoming ministry of his vigilant attention to their 'policy and conduct': 'We shall make no compromises with them, they have shown no magnanimity to us, and it will be our duty to the public that we show no weak indulgence to them.'

When Prendergast rose amidst loud cries of 'Divide, divide' to defend himself – rather weakly – half the members rose to leave the

House. Evans's speech moved J. T. Smith to declare his confidence in their ministry, believing 'they had defended themselves from the charges brought against them'.[2]

Evans 'passed an uneasy night, and deep and hollow groans were heard to issue from his cell', wrote the *Argus*' reporter. The very next day, that week's issue of *Punch* hit the newsstands. Before this, *Punch* had tempered its criticisms of Evans with levity, but now it attacked him on an entirely different matter.[3] Some months earlier, Evans had alleged that John Brooke – a former reporter on the *Herald* and self-taught nonconformist and democrat – had approached him, 'tearfully supplicating a certain office' in the O'Shanassy government.[4] It was the sort of throwaway remark many members might have made in the heat of the moment, but at best it was exaggeration, at worst, a lie.

Brooke challenged Evans to repeat the statement or deny it. Correspondence was published in the *Herald*, and for nearly a month Evans foolishly kept the public in suspense. Finally he wrote what *Punch* called 'a creeping crawling cringing' reply, which explained nothing, but merely broadened the allegation to cover 'several distinguished patriots whom [he] had seen with tears in their eyes because they could not obtain office'.

Punch accused Evans of having 'prostituted great abilities to vilest uses', and asked whether he had ever really held a 'deep conviction' of any kind. The reporter protested 'against the awful deterioration' of Evans's character. Here was –

> . . . a man of the Crown, a man of education, a journalist well stricken in years, a politician of illimitable experience and indefinite erudition, one of the forensic ornaments of Westminster Hall, and our infallible authority upon all questions of constitutional history . . . . You have been degraded and disgraced in the eyes of the community, and in those of *Melbourne Punch*.[5]

Evans's political flaws were there for all to see. He had not yet learned to temper his language of absolutes. He had laid himself open to charges of inconsistency.[6] He had tried to deflect criticism by creating diversions. And his debating prowess was weakened time and again by his suspicion of other members' motives. By the end of October, the O'Shanassy government had been replaced by the Nicholson ministry and Evans was back in the Opposition.[7]

Evans was always ready to help family and old friends. Captain Daniell's eldest son Edward was a clever but restless young man whose ambition to join the army in England had been thwarted by his father. He had tried farming, surveying and bank work in New

Zealand but disliked each one. He had become engaged to one of the Misses Riddiford – who later broke the engagement off. When Evans heard of this he suggested he might find him a good position in Melbourne. Edward arrived there just before Evans lost office, but nevertheless Evans found a job for him helping to lay the telegraph from Melbourne to Ballarat.[8]

Land was still the topic of the day. Hours were spent wrangling over various clauses in the Land Bill, and debates on land dragged out over weeks because of personal rancour. Evans warned the Legislative Assembly against risking 'their public credit and public faith with European governments' over the sale of Crown Lands, and against allowing 'landsharking' and 'speculation' to predominate. He suggested that a 'portion [of land] ought to be reserved by the government . . . on each side of the line' for working men to purchase.[9]

As representative for Avoca, Evans accused the government of having reduced the sum put aside for Avoca 'as a punishment'. This accusation caused much mirth.[10] But a fortnight later, when he gave notice of a motion for a grant of £4,000 to repair and extend the main roads in the Avoca district, Evans again found the sum laid down had been altered, while others had been left intact. He complained that the district, which needed '60 or 70 miles of road, had been left to its primeval barbarism'. James Service challenged Evans's motion, saying that if Evans had not got the required £4,000, he had at least got a 'magnificent grievance'. The two quibbled for a while over sums and areas, until, at a loss, Service asked to see O'Shanassy's copy of the estimates. O'Shanassy refused 'in a sneering tone'. Later, in spite of Service recommending they throw out Evans's resolution, it was carried 20 to 18.[11] The petty politics that had motivated Service to oppose Evans was but one example of the mire that members fell into again and again.

In May, Evans faltered badly. Speaking of the Law of Evidence, he remembered hearing the former Chief Justice of England, Lord Denman, speak 'of the torrent of perjury which had been let in upon the courts of law', after changes in the law of evidence allowed plaintiffs and defendants to be examined as witnesses. Dr Augustus Greeves challenged Evans's memory, pointing out that the law allowing parties to give evidence in their own cases had been passed in 1851 – after Lord Denman had quit the bench. ('Hear, hear' and great laughter.)

Evans insisted that the Act had been passed earlier. He had heard Denman use those words himself 'in the Court of Queen's Bench', and he was able to prove it. But J. R. Bailey joined Greeves, quoting from a copy of the *Edinburgh Review* that confirmed the Act was passed in 1851. When James Service rejoined the fray, he was interrupted 'very energetically' by Evans, who dared anyone to dispute his statement. He challenged the House, asking: 'Does any hon. member dispute the literal accuracy of what I said in my place here?'

> Michie: That is not the question.
> Evans: I say that is the question. (Hear) The question is a question of personal honour and veracity, and I will not permit any . . . (Cries of 'Hear, hear' and 'chair').

Service protested it 'never entered [his] mind to impute want of veracity to the hon. and learned gentleman (hear, hear)'. But he asked for documents of proof.

> Evans: I don't rely on documents. ('Hear, hear,' and cries of 'Chair, chair') I have made a statement in this House on my personal honour and veracity, and beyond that, I will not go. (Hear, hear).

Service explained that he was 'endeavouring to show – not that the hon. gentleman has made a mis-statement, for I frankly say I do not believe he is capable of standing up there and making a mis-statement, chronologically or otherwise (hear, hear)' – but that Evans was labouring under a misapprehension.

Evans lost the round, but in recess he consulted his books. His extraordinary sensitivity had suffered a blow. He did not return to the House. Instead, at the end of the session, Wood spoke for his friend: Evans wished to state that Denman's observation had referred to the County Court Act, which authorised persons to give evidence on their own behalf, and which Lord Denman said 'let loose a flood of perjury over the land'. When O'Shanassy took the opportunity to accuse 'a combination on the part of four or five persons on the other side of the House to doubt [Evans's] veracity', Greeves, Michie and others protested against the 'insinuation'.[12]

On 4 July Evans delivered a speech that became famous overnight. Their group had been strenuously attacked for blocking Nicholson's proposed Land Act.[13] But Evans mused on the fact that the Bill proposed by the government had undergone so many amendments, it bore little resemblance to the original proposal:

> Where is the Bill introduced by this liberal and patriotic Government? *Echo* answers, Where? I should like to see the bill submitted to this House by the Government compared with what has been provided for us in the new bill sent down by the Legislative Council. Sir, I, in my youth, read much on what is called the peculiarities of personal idiosyncrasy. (Laughter) I should like to know on what point resides the personal idiosyncrasy of this bill which has been submitted to us by this wise and patriotic Government. I recollect, Sir, a philosopher who lived in the reign of Queen Anne. (Loud laughter, especially from the Opposition benches, together with various cries of, 'Did you know her?', and 'What was she like?')
>
> Evans: Sir, the scholar is contemporary with all time. (Cheers.) I may say, Sir that in the retirement of my study, I have conversed with men of all ages through their works. (Hear, Hear) And I remember that a philosopher in the reign of Queen Anne – Mr. Martinus Scriblerius – propounded a question which engaged the serious attention of the philosophers of the time – as to the identity of Sir John Cutler's silk stocking. (Great laughter.) That silk stocking had first got a new foot and then a new leg, and the question was propounded to the philosophers whether this was the identical original stocking or a new stocking. (Hear, Hear.) Again, the ship *Argo* had been held up in ordinary for so long a period and had undergone so many repairs, that it was admitted that not a single portion of the original vessel remained. Then the question arose whether this was or was not the ship *Argo*. (Laughter). Hon. Members may at home amuse themselves by endeavouring to find out wherein resides the metaphysical identity of the bill contained in the amendments I hold in my hand with that originally brought down by the Government. If I have not mistaken the principles of this bill and that originally brought before this House by the Government, this is fundamentally a new bill which has been sent down to us by the other House for our acceptance, and even with the amendments it does not appear to me a very wise measure. I have gone through it, Sir, very carefully, clause by clause. The Hon. Member for Kilmore [Michie] said there were 250 amendments proposed, I find the precise number to be 252 – not merely a series of grammatical blunders. Sir, I do not wish to be severe upon the hon. Gentlemen sitting on the Treasury benches, who, I presume, are not familiar with the literature of the reign of Queen Anne. (laughter.) – and I really believe they are not much better acquainted with that of the reign of Queen Victoria. (Laughter)[14]

The topic of land was especially hot at the time and a large riot on land laws broke out on the evening of 28 August. Two days later, still smarting from Evans's speech, Michie launched an extraordinary attack upon Evans who, he declared, had 'considerably improved upon the character of Judas':

> The original Judas was content to go and hang himself, whereas the ex-Minister seemed to have so far improved upon the original as to be able to hang himself, and cut himself down in succession, in an extraordinary manner (a laugh), coming before the House, when everyone expected him out, and announcing, like the clown in the pantomime, 'Here we are again' (laughter), and apparently ready to supply the information to be found in the play-bills – 'This entertainment to be repeated until further notice'.[15]

The next day Evans dismissed Michie's interjections while making an authoritative speech on the subject.

> . . . the fact was the whole territory of this colony was now occupied by a class of tenants – gentlemen who called themselves, and were entitled to do so, tenants of the Crown – who were in the present occupation of the whole of those lands under the authority of the other orders in Council, which were of equal validity and force with the one now peculiarly and specially relied upon. (Hear, hear). This, therefore, was a mere *brutum fulmen* (hear) – it was an imaginary power, entirely useless in the hands of a Minister, for the simple reason that before he could use it he must begin by dispossessing those who were in the possession of the soil under the authority of another Order in Council of a prior date and of equal authority. (Hear, hear). It would not be necessary with a member of the legal profession to argue the question that a person in possession of the legal estate under a promise of a lease was in equity, considered in the same position as if he had the lease. (Mr. Michie,— 'With all the conditions of the 9th clause.') That subject had been worn threadbare, not merely in this colony and in New South Wales, but even in Westminster, that all the reservations under the 9th clause were tied up, and limited by the old principle of legal interpretation – the *ejusdem generis* principle. (Hear.)[16]

The *Argus* decided Mr Michie was –

> . . . the great comet of our constitutional system. His motions are as eccentric as his appearances are startling . . . . [he] belongs to no fixed order of stars and altogether defies either observation or calculation . . . he careers wildly though space . . . . Nor is his light less uncertain than his motion. Sometimes a bright, clear, honest irradiance, it is sometimes only what most comets are said to be – a nebulous fire, a mist, empty, intangible, harmless . . .[17]

Punch brought Michie to heel years later, observing that, 'although quick, he was rather shallow'. He was cruel, and not above plagiarism:

> Archy thought he was a great wit, and when he got the worst of an ar-gu-ment, he would try to make the boys laugh at his op-po-nent. He preferred to mimick [*sic*] his voice, or the way he walked, or something of that sort. Some thought it was funny and clever – others said it was rather low . . . his jokes were often not his own . . .[18]

After a bitter and drawn-out battle, the assembly finally accepted Nicholson's Land Bill, but the Council savaged it, so that it became, as Evans had observed, and the *Age* had echoed, 'a misshapen, emasculated thing . . . a sham which offers no facility to industrious men of small means to settle on the land'.[19] And in spite of all the criticism of Evans's attempts to amend it, the Bill which passed led to 75,000 acres of fertile land being snapped up in two months by squatters and speculators by the system of dummying.

In early September, Evans became ill and was confined to bed for five days. He was noticeably more frail and in severe pain when he finally struggled into the House and spoke, as he said, 'under considerable difficulty'. He was still unwell the following day, only giving a brief reply when Wood asked him to clarify a legal point.[20] Just two days later, when there was a vote of lack of confidence in the Nicholson ministry, Michie was absent, having already abandoned his party. The *Argus* blamed him for the defeat of several members of his own party: Service, Richard Heales, Aspinall and Nicholson.[21] It had been, as the *Argus* observed, a long, barren session (397 days) whose performance was by far the worst in the short history of responsible government. Apart from the disastrous Land Bill, more than half of the nearly seventy Bills introduced had collapsed 'before they had passed the first House'.[22]

Evans should have been optimistic but he had a fresh concern. The Constitution Act included a pension list of £4,000 for ministers who had served at least two years, each being entitled to a pension of about £800 from the total sum. The subject was a contentious one, the House generally believing that only those who were embarrassed or reduced in circumstances should be entitled to a pension. Heales's Bill to abolish the pension had been passed through its first stages that year.

In spite of assuring his electorate that he had no need of a pension, Evans's finances were far from healthy. He had supplemented his earnings with the occasional article, and he still had rooms in chambers at Temple Court. But with the cost of keeping his sisters and grandson and travelling to Wellington adding to his everyday expenses, the bailiffs were hovering.

Yet Evans was still able to wield considerable influence by calling on his important contacts in England. During the parliamentary recess in October, he wrote to Lord Merivale, the Under Secretary to Lord Newcastle who was Secretary of State for the Colonies. Evans reminded Merivale of their acquaintance on the western circuit, and mentioned that he enjoyed the personal respect and confidence of Governor Barkly. He drew Merivale's attention to the Bill for the abolition of pensions to retiring ministers, which needed only the Queen's approval. Evans had sacrificed his position at the Bar and his 'valuable appointment as Editor of the oldest daily paper here' to accept office. He had held office for only one year and seven months until 'a violent democratic reaction expelled me and my colleagues from the Government'. The Opposition had then passed the Bill as an act of 'revenge'.

He observed that the Upper House was useless 'against violent legislation'. The government was guilty of the 'undisguised repudiation of a contract'. The people could now only rely on the honour and independence of Her Majesty's advisors. He begged Merivale to pass his letter to Newcastle for his consideration.[23] This letter had some effect. The Colonial Office reserved its decision and Newcastle returned the Bill to Barkly for reconsideration in January the following year.[24]

When the Nicholson ministry finally fell on 21 November, Evans accompanied the Opposition, the Speaker and others to Barkly's residence with the record.[25] After both O'Shanassy and Charles Ebden declined to form an administration, Brooke was approached and accepted. But in forming his ministry, Brooke made several tactical errors. Most of the members wanted Ebden as premier, but Brooke chose Heales. He also brought together 'a curious combination' of men from all sides of the House. Then his members found that Brooke had abolished the position of Solicitor General. And, after approaching several members – but not Evans – he had given Attorney General to Ireland.

On 8 December, Evans gave his thirty-eight-year-old sister Claudia in marriage to Frenchman Zephyrin Pierre Edouard Permezel, who was just one year younger. But the lavish reception probably added to his debt, and he took a brief trip away in January. On his return, *Punch* published a song to the tune of 'Willie We Have Missed You', supposedly devised by a Supreme Court bailiff:

I've seen you in the street,
And it made my heart rejoice,
For I knew that stately footstep,
And that loud commanding voice –
Was like music in my ear,
In my lonely bailiff's room,
Oh! Samuel we have missed you,
Welcome out from home.[26]

When Parliament reassembled on 3 January 1861, Evans was in the Speaker's gallery 'meditating for some considerable time where he should dispose of himself', before defecting to the Opposition and taking his seat in what was known as 'The Corner', leaving thirty-three on the government side.[27] Brooke was stung by Evans's 'indecency' in defecting, and Evans had isolated himself again, having twice defected when spurned for office.

Brooke accused Evans of having asked for the position of Solicitor General. Evans replied that he had opposed Brooke's abolition of the position merely 'as a member of the Bar'. Johnston supported Brooke's story, saying that on the evening of selection, Evans had spent the time hanging around outside like a desperate outcast anxious for admission:

> During the whole of that night's discussion, lasting up to 11 o'clock, the Hon. Member for Avoca was waiting, sometimes in one room and sometimes in another, keeping up a constant series of irritating communications with [O'Shanassy] as to what was going on inside.

He reminded Evans that even after being 'fully aware that neither O'Shanassy nor the member for Brighton would join the Ministry, he had publicly asserted that if seven doorkeepers of this House were appointed a Ministry, he would sit behind them, rather than allow Mr. Nicholson to return to power'. Evans tried to make light of the allegation, quipping in reply:

> It is true Sir, that I said, rather than the attempt to form an administration should be abandoned, and the late Ministry be allowed to come back again, I would send for seven porters or messengers of Parliament to take their places in the Ministry; but if I were allowed to go on I should now think it necessary to apologise to the porters and messengers for having proposed to place them in such a position. (Laughter)[28]

Early in January, when the introduction of the Torrens Bill of South Australia came under discussion, Evans spoke of the finer legal points. As a member of the Law Reform Society in London, he had paid close attention to the stages by which Sir Hugh Cairns's superior Bill had been passed in England. But, he complained, this one was the draft of the Bill submitted by the Amendment Society to the Commons' Committee. It had arrived 'piecemeal' in the colonies, which meant the Torrens Bill 'undoubtedly contained numerous defects'. To cheers, Evans suggested they study the successful Cairns Bill, 'not to prevent law reform, but to accomplish it in a solid and efficacious manner'.[29]

Having been appointed to the select committee for the payment of members, Evans ensured he could not be accused of inconsistency by referring to his views on the subject over the previous year. On 25 January, his motion for a petition to Barkly for payment of £300 to members was successful.[30] Five days later the Bill was read a first time and ordered to be given a second reading in a week. But the Council ultimately rejected the Bill and it would not be until 1870 that members of the assembly would receive pay. This extra pressure, and the fact that the Council threw out more Bills than it passed, placed a heavy burden on men like Evans who were forced to look for income elsewhere.

The Bill to reduce the salary of public servants provoked a huge outcry. The salaries of police were to be slashed by 20 per cent, and the new taxes were to produce revenue of £500,000 – in a colony whose income was £3,000,000.[31] Evans spoke against the Bill, protesting that in the Telegraph Office men of education and ability worked for sixteen hours a day for worse than a journeyman mason's pay. The motion was finally withdrawn, although (as Serle points out) the revenue for the previous year had left a deficit and both Heales and George Verdon – the treasurer – knew new taxes of £500,000 would have to be imposed. As a member of the Committees of Supply and Ways and Means, Evans summed up the efforts to slash expenditure in disgust, saying 'practically – whatever it might have been formerly – they seemed at that moment to be without a responsible Parliamentary Government. (Hear, hear.)'[32] He reluctantly seconded the amendment to reduce expenditure to meet the revenue of £3,000,000, but:

> . . . wished it to be understood that he by no means desired to disturb the existing administration (derisive cheers from the right). If he understood right the feeling of the House, it was . . . that the Government should not be kicked out at once, because there was a great deal of disagreeable work which they intended the Government to do. (Laughter, and 'Hear, hear'.)[33]

When a clause for the abolition of capital punishment was proposed in committee, Evans suggested that such an important subject should be introduced as a separate measure. He spoke of a friend of his in London who had written a pamphlet in 1846 suggesting abolition. It had 'produced considerable sensation'. (This might have been Ben Hawes, as he advocated it later.) Evans generally believed in abolition, and also favoured his London friend's plan of separate prisons for murderers.[34]

Shortly afterward, Heales resigned his Cabinet, saying he had made allowances for the Committee of Supply to operate for the next two months on a budget of £300,000, but had been unable to get a majority vote for imposing duties. Barkly begged him to continue. Heales refused, so Barkly sent first for Ebden, then Michie to reconcile the O'Shanassy and Nicholson factions.

Finally, on 6 February, he sent for Evans.

CHAPTER TWENTY-THREE. TROJAN SOUL

He reads much,
He is a great observer and he looks
Quite through the deeds of men.
Seldom he smiles and smiles in such a sort,
As if he mock'd himself and scorn'd his spirit
That could be moved to smile at anything.

William Shakespeare, *Julius Caesar* [on Cassius],
II, i, lines 209 ff.

In July 1860, *Melbourne Punch* had used this reference to Cassius in Julius Caesar to describe Evans, cleverly hitting the mark.[1] Now, after Evans's summons by Barkly, the *Herald* exulted. Ever Evans's champion in the face of criticism from the press, especially the *Argus*, it had only recently sniffed, 'When we find a man of Dr. Evans's calibre ridiculed, we feel the force of Mr. Prendergast's remark the other day in the House, that we are in a colony of speculators, overlying a colony of convicts.'

On the other hand, the *Argus*, usually critical of Evans, was, naturally, surprised at Evans having been summonsed, citing the *Mount Alexander Mail* of 8 February: '[Evans] stands alone in the Assembly, distrusted by all – a man of remarkable ability and attainments, but with no force of character and no fixity of principle.'[2]

But after the fall of Nicholson's government, there had been such 'shameless intrigue by . . . groups and combinations' that Evans's efforts 'to reconcile such bitterly opposing factions' proved hopeless. Barkly's next choice Haines also failed, so Heales was eventually persuaded to return to office.[3] The major players' explanations in Parliament disappointed the *Argus*, which expected rancour and scandal, but heard only a 'very proper and sober explanation' of events.[4]

The last vote on the motion for the Land Bill on 19 June was defeated 42 votes to 26, and three days later the ministry resigned.

But as there had already been six ministries, all 'characterized by political instability, faction and intrigue', and as 'no group could command a secure majority', Barkly decided to dissolve Parliament, which provoked a spirited debate on the constitutional legality of his act. Evans was at his best, citing a speech made by Brougham on 6 August 1839, referring also to 'the great contest between Pitt and Fox in 1784', and recommending May's *Constitutional History of England* to Attorney-General Ireland, who had been mistaken in his interpretation of the law. When Evans concluded his speech by mourning the absence of a Pitt on the Treasury benches, Ireland – sharp, witty and 'the terror of judges in Court' – quipped, 'I see a "Fox"', which was met with 'great laughter'.

In his memoir of 1889, David Blair said that Evans then 'instantaneously collapsed and was silent for the rest of the evening'.[5] Blair's memory was faulty: after Ireland's sally, Evans continued unperturbed, saying he was suffering with a heavy cold that made him hard of hearing –

> . . . and could only gather from the expression on the countenance of his hon. friend that he was modestly offering himself as the illustrious type of that great man, in order to console the House for the absence of a Pitt on those benches . . .
>
> His speech continued for a few minutes, concluding with his support for the motion to protest Barkly's move.[6]

The second Parliament was finally dissolved on 11 July to prepare for new elections on 5 August. Evans objected to the length of recess – Parliament was to resume in September but Evans believed the end of August gave ample time for elections.[7] Michie resigned in protest at the Governor's action, and Ireland, who had been refused his pension although he had served two years as a minister, also resigned.

Evans must have been close to despair, as his age and ill health took their toll and his opportunities dwindled. He continued to hope for a pension for his retirement. But the first two Parliaments had been blighted by an intransigent and deeply conservative Council or Upper House that had rejected thirty-two Bills – including Evans's Payment of Members Bill. Any attempt at reform had been largely futile, as the Council had been hostile to O'Shanassy, had humiliated Nicholson's ministry and had 'violently opposed Heales to the limits of its capacity'.[8]

One of the major issues for the Melbourne electors was the question of protection – 'relief and encouragement . . . to our industrial pursuits', as Heales put it.[9] When Evans returned to the Richmond hustings, the 'rowdiest meeting' took place at the White Horse Hotel on 29 July, where 'continual uproar prevailed – Dr. Evans was heard with the greatest difficulty'. The meeting moved from the room to the street, Evans speaking from the balcony, but it was impossible for reporters to hear much of what he said. When Evans's champion Dr Wilson proposed the vote of confidence in Evans it 'was negatived by a large majority'. Meetings for the other candidates – Francis, Thomas Lambert and Cutter – were just as noisy. Evans demanded a poll for 10 August. After several more meetings, he gained ground but came in third at the poll. Then a rumour circulated that Evans was 'safe', and 'plumpers' were given for another candidate, which meant the votes were split and Evans lost.[10] He was disappointed but realised that as the electorate's demographic had changed, he had not given himself the time to 'make himself known to the class who had not resided in the district when he had formerly represented them'. But he had the last word:

> He would rather be the rejected representative of Richmond having maintained his principles – he would rather be drawn out as the champion of Free Trade – he would rather suffer any loss, or ignominy of any description, than have resting on his conscience the responsibility of having let loose on the colony the flood of controversial debate and malice, which had divided man from man, and had struck a blow at their prosperity which would not be healed for many years . . . (Cheers).[11]

Many barristers were dumped in favour of the working man – including Wood, Higinbotham and Hibbert Newton. Of the forty-four Opposition members, twenty-three lost their seats and only twenty-one were returned. At a public banquet at Collingwood, Heales lambasted the *Argus*, saying it 'contained attacks on men whose characters would at least bear favourable comparison with the man from whose pen issued those leading articles'. Aspinall expressed similar sentiments. The *Hansard* records of the day are littered with countless protests from members at articles in the papers. The *Argus* was the worst offender, but in those days before libel suits, only the papers' owners faced being hauled before the parliamentary bar. Ireland had been accused of dishonesty, Evans had been vilified or misreported, Duffy was mocked as Heales's jester, and other reputations similarly suffered. Of the attacks on himself Evans had said a few months earlier:

> He had been abused, calumniated, and ridiculed in turn with equal and impartial malice, by all the journals of the colony. ('Hear, hear',

> and laughter.) But with the high-minded consciousness of integrity, and of having done his duty fairly and honestly, he might say that he was able to treat all such attacks with profound indifference. He was able to stand up and bare his breast against malice and unjust attack from whatever quarter they came. ('Hear, hear', and great laughter.)[12]

When Parliament reassembled on 3 September, thirty-seven government members outnumbered the Opposition by four. But Evans found another lifeline. Ireland had won two seats and relinquished Maryborough. Evans's name went forward on 15 October, when polling was scheduled for just a week later. Others contesting the seat were D. W. Virtue, George Higinbotham and Richard Pitt.

Evans was looked on with favour from the start. Maryborough was a large goldfield and farming district north-west of Melbourne. Here the Chinese diggers – who numbered over 42,000 – were rumoured to spend a proportion of their income on opium; four out of five were said to be gamblers; and it was also believed they had child prostitutes. Evans had cited each one of these allegations in the House years before.[13] Land occupation and cultivation licences were important issues for the electors, who welcomed Evans's liberal views on these matters. Brookes's record as president of the Board of Land and Works in the Heales ministry had been woeful in the eyes of many voters. The *Maryborough Advertiser* believed that Mr Brooke's cultivation licence scheme was 'a wretched sham by comparison with the Nicholson Land Bill before it was mutilated by Mr. Heales and his friends'. In another article it attacked Brooke as an 'unscrupulous adventurer', concluding:

> Well may a constitutional lawyer, like Dr. Evans, inveigh against the 'slavery and ignominy of being governed by proclamations'. If Parliamentary rule is to be superseded by a despotism in Victoria, let us have for our despot a man of commanding character and ability, and not a shallow trickster. A Cromwell might be tolerable, but a Lord Protector Brooke is simply ridiculous.

The *Advertiser* backed Evans all the way, promoting his election as the most beneficial for the district and colony.[14] During the campaign, Barkly and his entourage visited the towns of Dunolly and Maryborough – a visit which can only have helped Evans, who enjoyed a close relationship with the Governor.

But the campaign was a gruelling challenge for a man nearing sixty. After the first show of hands favoured Virtue, Evans demanded a poll. On Monday, 14 October, he spoke at length at Mark Brewin's

Store, Newtown, and Watkins' Store, White Hills. At each he was favourably received, and the usual vote of confidence carried unanimously. In the evening he met a large gathering at the Town Hall in Carisbrook, where he spoke again at considerable length. The vote in his favour was almost unanimous, only five hands being held up against him in a room of 150 people. Two days later he addressed a large meeting at Gunst's Hotel, Adelaide Lead, and another at Samuel Taylor's Store at the Alma. On both occasions, votes in his favour were unanimous. Higinbotham pulled out of the race the next day.[15]

After ten days at this pace, Evans was hoarse and exhausted, having rushed from place to place by coach or horse, attended twenty-two public meetings in ten days, and spoken at each for an hour and a half or two hours. He had covered a variety of issues, especially debating the gold duty with the leading miners in Chinaman's Flat, Golden Point and other places. The miners wanted the duty to be reduced to a nominal sum, rather than have a reduction in the export duty, and he promised it would be reduced by 6d by July 1862, and another 6d by the following January.[16]

He won the seat easily, and returned to his home at 31 George Street East, Melbourne, for a brief rest. News of his success came as an unpleasant surprise for his enemies, but *Punch* was thrilled, portraying him as Coriolanus seated on a grand chair consenting to pleas from the meek supplicant Volumnia (Maryborough).[17]

Politics was momentarily overwhelmed by the tragic deaths of the explorers Burke, Wills and Gray at Coopers Creek. Their expedition to the Gulf of Carpentaria had been sent with such high hopes and much celebration. The formal state funeral in Melbourne attracted a huge turnout, temporarily uniting the members of Parliament who attended.[18]

Twelve days after Parliament reopened on 17 December to O'Shanassy's third ministry, Evans took his seat as Postmaster General.[19] Duffy had resumed his old role as president of the Board of Land and Works, and Ireland, Attorney-General in the Heales administration, had jumped back again to take up the same post for O'Shanassy. John Dennistoun Wood was Minister of Justice, and the prominent Anglican, Legislative Council member William Clark Haines, Treasurer. As there was no ministry for mines, Evans was given the extra duty of granting mining leases, an arrangement criticised by the Opposition.

But the *Argus* believed that the government 'was the strongest in character and talent that has ever held office in this country'.[20] The rapid shift in social change over the previous decade was reflected in the composition of the Legislative Assembly. Evans was frustrated by the different composition of the third Parliament, with the significant addition of the less-educated men from the goldfields. And few of the English-style conservatives of 1856 remained. Replacing them were most of the 'traditional liberals' like Evans, who, finding themselves 'outflanked on the left and appalled by the heresy of protection', were now on the 'conservative' side. Erstwhile popular leaders like Wilson, O'Shanassy, Michie, Evans and now Duffy were some of the many who had become 'pillars of society'.[21]

With conservatives and liberals on one side and democrats on the other, and with full Cabinet support, Duffy now proposed a Land Act more ambitious than any before. The system of annual squatting licences on Crown land brought in by Heales was continued, but ten million of the thirty-five million acres held under licence were reserved for the 'absolute settler'. Sale by lot replaced auction, and land was offered for purchase at £1 an acre on deferred payment for up to eight years. The strong opposition to the Bill's provision for the squatters became an issue that would later divide O'Shanassy's party.

A little after Parliament reassembled after the New Year, Evans received a letter from Charles Izard, who had recently taken over Dudley Ward's role as official solicitor for the Union Bank of Australia. Izard urged Evans to return to Wellington to resolve the matter of the agreement over the land with Chetham. He told Evans:

> I at present retain your papers with Dr. Featherston and Mr. Riddiford's full assent, as the interests of the bank are in no respect antagonistic to yours. They claim no interest in the property and are only anxious to avoid litigation . . . I am now addressing you privately and not as the solicitor of the Bank.[22]

Evans knew he must respond, which increased the strain and financial uncertainty already dogging him.

Added to that, his old friend Dr William Bland had been treated very shabbily by the Legislative Council in New South Wales. Bland had contributed a great deal to various committees, and worked for universal suffrage and 'for the right of a man to be judged by his peers', amongst other humanitarian issues. He had helped the sick, performing cataract operations and removing bladder stones. He had written various medical tracts and presided at the banquet to celebrate the new Constitution in 1856. Yet in 1861, when he resigned with other members from the Legislative Council, he was refused an annuity, and later that year he was declared bankrupt. Evans was so moved by his plight he wrote an article in the *Empire*:

> . . . there is a class of men among the old colonists, to whom those locks, whiter than the driven snow, are a crown of glory: and who, when they shall follow him to his grave, will feel that, whoever may come after him, none can ever assume his place, as one of the earliest founders and patriarchs of liberty on this continent. For more than forty or perhaps fifty years, has this brave, consistent and accomplished man been struggling, sometimes against imperial, and at other times against local tyranny, on behalf of a people who at one moment appreciated his motives, and at another joined with their own oppressors in disparaging, if not in vilifying their greatest benefactor. An elegant scholar, a man of science, and a gentleman of that antique school of urbanity and refinement, which modern barbarism and ruffianism have almost trampled into oblivion – William Bland.[23]

Evans must have identified with his old friend, realising his own political future was dimming.

This affected his performance in the House, making him more irascible. He broke his own rule of never attacking a member personally, during a debate on the gold export duty in February, when he and others were charged by George Verdon – who reminded them of having advocated the abolition of the gold duty when in Opposition – with inconsistency. Evans retorted that when they had retired from office in October 1859, O'Shanassy's ministry 'had left in the Treasury a sum of not less than £440,000 in credit'. But after what he called Verdon's 'first juvenile experiment in the manipulation of the finances':

> . . . instead of a balance of £440,000 to the credit of the country there was a sum of £240,000 on the wrong side of the ledger. (Laughter). Now he presumed the Hon member, after his diligent attendance at the classes of the University, was sufficiently master of arithmetic to know that £440,000 added to £240,000 would make something like £680,000.

Verdon was surprised at the attack, observing that Evans was normally very polite, usually only attacking a member's weakness of argument rather than anything else. Evans, who had once pointed out that in debate 'he had never attacked anyone in such a manner as to prevent their meeting him on terms of private friendship', apologised for having wounded Verdon's 'sensibility, which he would be the last man in the world intentionally to wound'.

A little later in the debate he suggested that by proposing a total abolition of the gold duty, the Opposition was in fact setting the O'Shanassy government up for defeat. The Heales administration had not proposed it:

> Nothing could be more absurd and illusory than the attempt to secure the total abolition of the duty at the present time. If [Verdon] were not a man of high character and principle, but capable of political chicanery, the most ingenious thing he could do would be to secure a majority that evening in favour of the total abolition of the duty; for [Verdon] knew perfectly well that the inevitable result would be that the Upper House would secure the Treasurer against any reduction at all, by rejecting the abolition; and the duty would continue as at present for a long time to come. (Hear, hear).[24]

In April 1862, when the subject of the press's defamation and misreporting of members' speeches arose again, the *Argus* once more came under fire. This time the member for Collingwood, Mr Charles Jardine Don – a stonemason who had been the first working man elected to Parliament – complained that he was a victim of misreporting. 'The man who wrote such things was a scoundrel', he declared. Amidst cries of 'Order', Evans interjected gloomily, 'You are all finding it out now', which caused a ripple of laughter. Don continued:

> . . . they had seen an hon. member who had more brains in his skull and more learning inside his head than half the scoundrels who wrote leading articles in the public journals, called a 'disreputable old man', but as it happened at a time when [Evans] was seeking re-election as a Minister, and therefore did not belong to the House, the villains who wrote the abominable slander were allowed to escape free . . .[25]

Evans no doubt appreciated the support, but it did not help that the very next day the weekly journal the *Leader* produced a highly critical portrait of him on its front page. An uncanny echo of Hanson's criticism in the *Colonist* twenty years earlier, it referred to Evans as having 'repudiated' his contract with Batten and Cutter, and concluded:

> Dr. Evans's career in this colony, as a journalist, places him in the first rank of public writers. His varied and extensive acquirements – his singular resonant voice, sustained by a masculine delivery, and the amplitude of his eloquence – had he also practical vigor and unswerving principles – would not alone grapple with the exigencies of political life, but few could emulate or challenge his superiority.

> As it is, however, few men in the Assembly command less respect, in the House or out of it, than George Samuel Evans.[26]

The Opposition needled Evans about this at every opportunity. During a routine debate a month later, he convinced the majority to vote for a road to be built through Newstead in Maryborough. But a few days later when the subject came up again, a new member, John Orr – who admitted he knew nothing of the standing orders of the House – asked for clarification. Evans explained that the road was not included in the estimates and complained of 'certain officers of the Government' having 'repudiated the promises made to the people of Newstead, who had [purchased] land there ten years ago on the understanding that the main road to Maryborough was to be taken through Newstead'.

Orr – who had clearly been put up to it – rose again, appealing to the Chair 'whether [Evans] was right in using the word "repudiation" so often', thus underlining the word with which the *Leader* had condemned Evans a month earlier. Evans snapped that he was 'not going to study the meaning of an English word from a member who had risen for the first time'. Orr stood again and Evans exploded: 'Sit down, Sir! I will not be interrupted, or I will call upon the Chairman to support me!'[27]

The chairman told Orr that no point of order had been raised, and Orr subsided for the remainder of the session. Evans took the opportunity to deliver a diatribe against both the slanging matches in the House and the Conventionists whom he said had addressed him 'in seductive tones': 'He had not yet awakened from that dream which entered his mind years ago, when he believed it would be possible for them to rise ultimately to the respectable dignity of a Parliament. (Hear, Hear.)'[28] A few days later, George Higinbotham joined the assembly as member for Brighton, his presence serving as a constant reminder to Evans of his public criticisms.

Evans was still capable of acts of kindness. When asked if he had employed a man named Murray who had been found guilty of 'impersonating' in the Mornington election, Evans admitted he had, but the job was only temporary. Evans had edited the journal Murray once owned, and only employed him to save him and his family from starvation, as Murray had lost 'years of savings in an unfortunate speculation'.[29]

When debating the proposal to abolish the denominational school board and replace it with a board of education, a governor in council and seven commissioners, Evans observed that they 'were now approaching the difficulty of the question'. He compared it to something he had read in studying the history of the Long Parliament:

> He had found there the representation of 'a Jew going to h—l on the back of a Jesuit', and he might, in following up the illustration, say, they had now the opportunity of altering it to the case of a Presbyterian, followed by some other Christian, unattached. (laughter) . . . . if a proper system of education was to be carried out, they should follow some such example as had been set them in France, when Guizot was the Minister of Public Instruction. They should have a responsible Minister of Education, who should be a member of that House, where he could be subjected to the wholesome discipline of questioning and cross-questioning, which, in a great measure, kept ministers to the proper performance of their duties.[30]

He also suggested establishing mining schools where the science and practice of goldmining could be taught. Duffy, O'Shanassy and Haines wanted to retain state aid, but Richard Heales's Common Schools Act establishing the board of education was passed that year. By the time Parliament was prorogued until the end of July, twenty-four Bills had been passed – more than in any other session.[31] Yet O'Shanassy's government was still dogged by suspicion. During the break Evans took his wife to Wellington. His trip must have included discussions with his lawyers over Chetham's claims on his property, and meetings with Featherston and Crosbie Ward, New Zealand's Postmaster General, over steam communication via Panama.

As Acting Minister for Mines, Evans was still able to be of use to the Wellington settlers. Revans wrote to his nephew, Sam:

> Dr. Evans – an old Wellington settler but who has lived some years in Melbourne was in the province lately. Mr. Coutts Crawford gave him specimens of rocks and minerals collected by himself around Wellington. These have been submitted to the Melbourne Mining Board and they, I hear speak most highly of the mineral properties of our province . . . . their scientific and practical acquaintance if successful would cause an immense change in the value of property in this part of the island . . .[32]

☙

There was bad news for O'Shanassy's government. Duffy's Land Act had passed in September but was a disaster. Attorney-General Ireland had failed to close the obvious loopholes. The Council had also put up a weak show of resistance, which should have alerted them. When the Bill became law, 'evasion and corruption resulted immediately'.[33]

Of the one million acres sold, about two-thirds went to a hundred men. The dummy system was rife, and Evans's anathema, land-sharks and their hangers-on, benefited. Duffy had intended that land applications be personal, but it was not legally required, so that in nine days half a million acres were sold to the least deserving. 'False applications easily passed to the squatters the runs they occupied' – the runs 'that Duffy's Bill was to have returned to the Crown'.

By the following year, people realised that the Bill had failed to open up agricultural land and encourage small-holdings. With public pressure gathering ominously in the background, David Syme of the *Age* called the Bill 'wholesale confiscation', and declared that the Cabinet consisted of 'a band of insolent factionists and dilapidated place hunters'.[34] In spite of this, the government clung on grimly for nearly another year.

Like other MPs, Evans's views on democracy and liberalism had altered. During a debate on reducing the Governor's salary, Evans digressed to condemn the 'strange exhibition which gentlemen who professed to be the peculiar and especial advocates of liberalism and democracy now made of themselves'.

> His public life was rapidly drawing to a close, and when it did close, it would be with the bitter and sorrowful feeling of the inefficacy of those labours and toils in which he and others had been engaged in trying to establish the principles of liberty and constitutional government in this part of the world . . . . There was no more sorrowful spectacle than that of a liberal democracy as it termed itself, becoming the subservient slave of power . . .[35]

He grappled with an overworked Post Office, appealing for more resources, and had to postpone the introduction of the Postal Bill to find out if they could incur a loss of £35,000 a year by reducing postage to a uniform rate of 2d.[36] There were telegraph line extensions to be discussed, and he had already tabled plans for telegraph communication to Parliament and other public offices.

After the three weeks of adjournment in April, the government tried to amend Duffy's Land Act, but the motion was defeated in June over the estimates of revenue from pastoral runs. With forty-five members sitting in Opposition, Evans was not surprised. He was about to lose his £1,200 salary per year and now had nothing to hope for but his pension.

As well as its failures – most notably Duffy's Land Act – the O'Shanassy government had some successes. It had passed a Distillation Act and an Immigration Act to attract skilled labourers from

Europe to boost the wine industry.[37] Transport and local government had also been improved. The most important administrative reforms included the Civil Service Act, classifying salaries and setting out principles for promotion; the Local Government and Municipal Acts; and the Electoral Act Amendment Act, which abolished public nomination and charged £50 per candidate at assembly elections. The government had also introduced the 'principle of plurality of votes' and, by so doing, created an 'improvement in the political temper'. These Acts alone were 'destined to leave a permanent influence on the character of our Victorian Institutions', wrote the *Argus*. 'It was the first step recorded in history of a nation endowed with universal suffrage, deliberately setting itself at work to curb and keep within bounds the perilous gift.' The assembly had never been 'so active and zealous in the work of legislation as during the twenty months of Mr. O'Shanassy's reign', the paper added. It also noted that the government had 'endured with remarkable unanimity and with surprising vigour'.[38]

In his role as Postmaster General, Evans had overseen a fast-developing and increasingly important communication business. From his first term in the role in 1858, he had introduced the Post Office Money Order system, cast-iron letter boxes, mail communication by steamer with New Zealand, and an improved method of sorting and distributing letters. Ten years after the first telegraph wires were laid, there were 2500 miles of electric telegraph wire connecting Melbourne to Sydney, Adelaide, Launceston, Hobart and other towns in Victoria. The central Post Office in Elizabeth Street had taken longer to build than anticipated in 1859 and it would not be completed until 1867. However, a perfectly serviceable telegraph office was situated for years in Flinders Lane.[39]

A few weeks after the House had reassembled on 4 August, Evans asked if the government intended to assist New Zealand in its Land Wars by sending the *Victoria* or another such vessel. The assembly learned that there had been an inexplicable delay in the arrival of letters from Sir George Grey asking urgently for 400 men to assist in the Land Wars. It had been decided to send 121 men and the battery of Armstrong guns. The issues of liability of costs and local defence were debated until the Treasurer agreed to Evans's request to 'lay the papers on the table'.[40]

The pension for retiring ministers had not yet been abolished, so after his two terms as Postmaster General, Evans was one of a handful seeking a pension. Ireland was another, having already been refused by the Heales ministry. When the subject of Evans's pension arose

This photograph of G. S. Evans was probably taken in 1858 when Evans became Postmaster General in the second O' Shanassy ministry of Victoria's First Parliament. It is signed by Evans, 'Very faithfully yours'. Image by kind permission of Mrs E. A. Riddiford.

The scorching exchange between Evans and Archibald Michie, after Evans believed he had been betrayed by his former ally. 'Brutus and Cassius', *Melbourne Punch*, Vol. IV, 9 July 1857, p.189.

Michie enjoyed goading many members, but none more so than Evans. Here he is jeering at Evans's negotiations on behalf of the Victorian government, on steam communication with Wellington. 'Bear Baiting', *Melbourne Punch*, Vol. VIII, 24 February 1859, p.37.

THE INDIA RUBBER BROTHERS.

"The elasticity of these Acrobats and the manner in which they cling together and balance themselves is truly remarkable."—*Daily Paper.*

The Minorities Clause of the push for electoral reform was a thorny subject for many members. Here Evans and Attorney-General Henry Samuel Chapman wrestle with the issue. Chapman returned to New Zealand early in 1864 to take up his position as Judge of the Supreme Court. 'The India Rubber Brothers', *Melbourne Punch*, Vol. VI, 1 April 1858, p.85.

THE TRAVELLED MINISTER.

(Probable appearance of the Postmaster-General on his return from New Zealand.)

Evans had left Melbourne to further the negotiations for steam communication with Dr Isaac Featherston, Superintendent of Wellington. 'The Travelled Minister', *Melbourne Punch*, Vol. VII, 12 August 1858, p.19.

The eldest son of Harriot and Daniel Riddiford, Edward Joshua Riddiford stayed under the auspices of the Evanses in Melbourne for a year. He gained some experience droving cattle in Australia. Later, at the urging of his mother, he returned from the goldfields in Otago to forge a formidable career as a runholder. With kind permission of Mrs E. A. Riddiford.

The final chapter of Evans's Biography in three parts mocked his close association with Maori, predicting he was destined to be the subject of Macaulay's prophecy. 'Macaulay's New Zealander on London Bridge', *Melbourne Punch*, Vol. IX, 15 December 1859, p.167.

This cartoon accompanied the first of three articles satirising Evans's life and predilection for classical and historical references in his speeches and writing. 'The Original Sphynx', *Melbourne Punch*, Vol. IX, 1 December 1859, p.153.

THE OLD ROMAN:

After a severe struggle with his desire to retire into private life, consents once more to sacrifice himself for the good of his country

Evans resorted to supporting the views of the Land Convention – which were also his own – in order to be re-elected. It was a major error. 'The Old Roman', *Melbourne Punch*, Vol. VIII, 7 April 1859, p.85.

CORIOLANUS RELENTS

AND IS WILLING TO RETURN FROM POLITICAL EXILE AT THE INSTANCE OF THE IMPORTUNATE VOLUMNIA.

Maryborough was as anxious to secure Evans as its representative as Evans was to gain the seat, having lost at Richmond. 'Coriolanus Relents', *Melbourne Punch*, Vol. XIII, 24 October 1861, p.261.

THE END OF THE COMEDY.

This belies the real achievements of O'Shanassy's third ministry. O'Shanassy (later knighted for his political achievements) dances an Irish jig, former Attorney General Ireland retreats with his pension, a member (possibly Minister of Justice Dennistoun Wood) thumbs his nose at a bailiff, and Evans leaves the stage for his beloved New Zealand. 'The End of the Comedy', *Melbourne Punch*, Vol. XVIII, 26 May 1864, p.173.

This engraving of G. S. Evans was made probably in 1864–65. It clearly shows the effects of illness and disappointment on Evans after such an active, exhausting career. Wood engraving by C. H. H. accompanying article by David Blair, 'Three Melbourne Barristers', *Centennial Magazine*, Vol. 2, No. 9, April 1890, p.692. Courtesy of the State Library of Victoria.

in committee, he scrupulously rose and left the chamber – in spite of protest from his allies. Thomas Howard moved for Evans to receive his pension, commenting that there was a 'general feeling of something like sympathy for the late hon. and learned Postmaster General'. Evans had a moral claim to be placed on an equal footing with Duffy and Ireland. McCulloch agreed, although he was opposed to pensions, as did Heales. The last to speak was, surprisingly, Higinbotham, who had found that being a member of the assembly was a good deal more difficult than being merely an observer. He had also reassessed the importance of Evans's contributions to the House. Now he regretted that his colleague McCulloch had objected to the idea of pensions, because 'apart from its legal aspect, he thought [Evans's] claim . . . just and reasonable'. The motion was put and carried.[41]

But the old order was changing. In September, Evans's long-term ally Sir Henry Barkly resigned as Governor to be replaced by Sir Charles Darling, who prorogued Parliament until mid-October. And Evans's application was refused. Out of a limit of £4,000, Ireland and Duffy – the latter of whom summed up the first two Parliaments as having been 'a perpetual guerilla warfare of surprises, ambuscades, plots and single combats' – each received pensions of £1,000 per annum on the understanding that they remained in Australia for life. The new Governor who refused to sanction Evans's pension might have acted on the Council's advice or reasoned that Evans could live off the income of his land in New Zealand and would likely return there. But Evans's claims to that land were far from settled. The *Argus* dismissed the whole system of pensions as a 'huge scandal', and shortly after this allocation, the pension for retiring ministers was cancelled.[42]

Evans had deferred his land dispute with Edward Chetham Strode for several months, but he could delay it no longer. Strode was now suing him for his property in Wellington and the Hutt.

On the death of his father, Admiral Sir Edward Chetham Strode, the previous year, Edward had inherited the estate of Southill, in Cranmore, Somerset, and taken the family name Strode. In spite of having received a generous allowance from his father for some time, which had forced the retired Admiral to mortgage the estate, Edward took out further mortgages. He and his wife Amelia never lived there, staying instead in a small flat in London, close to the gambling dens and high life of the city. As financial ruin faced him, he had turned to the one document that might save him – the memorandum that Hanson had urged Evans to sign as a temporary measure when Chetham had taken the Monro mortgage to his father in London.[43] Chetham Strode had issued a writ against Evans and the trial, Strode vs Evans, was due to take place in Wellington's High Court after the New Year.

Evans left Melbourne, arriving in Wellington with Harriet on 24 November on the SS *Lord Ashley*. The family's Christmas celebrations must have been a subdued affair, clouded by the impending trial as Strode vs Evans promised to be the *cause célèbre*, the sensation of the year for Wellington society. As the *New Zealand Spectator and Cook's Straits Guardian* reported:

> Owing to its involving an historical survey of the earliest circumstances of the colony, it excited great public interest, several ladies being among the audience; while the importance of the legal principles involved in the investigation attracted the constant attendance of every gentleman of the legal profession in Wellington.[44]

An able advocate like Evans may not have been daunted at the prospect. But for his wife, in her seventy-second year and a stranger to such an arena, it must have been an ordeal. Her formidable strength had stood her in good stead over the many years of controversy and public humiliation, but Harriet was about to give evidence against her daughter's husband. The court was filled to capacity when the trial began on 4 January 1864. It lasted three days, concluding late on Wednesday evening.[45]

The case centred on the mortgage Evans had first taken out from Monro in 1839, but hinged mainly on the spirit in which the memorandum taken by Chetham to England in 1842 had been drawn up. Was the memorandum a temporary 'family agreement', or a legally binding document? The special jury took just forty-four minutes to find in Evans's favour on all but one of the seven counts. But in his summing up, even though the judge intimated he agreed with the verdict, he left an opening for Strode to appeal – an opening that Strode seized upon with alacrity.[46]

Back in Melbourne, the press wasted little time in turning its guns on the new administration. When George Higinbotham, now Attorney-General in the McCulloch government, complained about the press's attacks on members of the ministry, the *Argus* responded with 'That's rich!'[47] And *Punch* pounced, in a skit entitled 'The Good Boy and Master Evans'. Evans was 'the biggest and oldest boy and best scholar in the school', but when he had gone to Richmond and said something George Higinbotham 'didn't like', Higinbotham had called him 'a dis-re-pu-ta-ble old boy'. *Punch*'s advice to Higinbotham was 'not to be always thinking of his name of Good George, and to believe that he is not so very much better than other boys, because

. . . he may become what these boys call him – a regular hy-po-crite before he grows to be a man'.[48]

Two years later, J. Wilberforce Stephen published Higinbotham's election card promises alongside his votes in assembly, pointing out the u-turns he had made after entering Parliament. He had pledged to retain the gold duty, but in February 1865 voted for its abolition. He was opposed to payment of members, but in April 1865 he voted for the payment of £300 to each of them. He was against allowing the Governor the power to dissolve the Upper House, yet, by April he agreed to give him this power.[49]

Evans stayed in Opposition till June 1864. He contested Maryborough in August against John W. Mason and Nathaniel Levi, was defeated in October, and handed a letter of protest to the returning officer accusing Mason of 'bribery and corruption and treating'.[50] Characteristically, he threatened to pursue the case in the criminal courts and 'before a committee of the Legislative assembly'.[51] McCulloch's government was returned with fifty-three members, all supposedly pledged to a protection tariff. Of Evans's political peers, only thirty-eight were returned.[52] An indication of the mood change was highlighted by the *Argus*, which pointed out that, having first tried for the seats of Polwarth, South Grenville and Belfast, Michie was only returned for St Kilda in second place after an auctioneer.[53]

Ever scurrilous, the *Argus* lamented the city's electoral results:

> . . . the one notable result is the return of a crowd of members either altogether obscure or grossly and ludicrously unfit, under any theory of popular government, to be the representatives of the people, under the influence of the Government cry of 'Protection to native industry' . . . . The loss of men of Parliamentary experience and reputation has been great indeed . . . . Dr. Evans, Mr. Haines, Mr. Wood, [and five others] have been defeated . . . . [Dr. Evans's] undoubted ability and oratorical powers have been very much obscured by the unsavoury odour of his political career.
>
> The Ministry, it is believed is a protectionist ministry; . . . it is certain that Mr. McCullough is indebted to this belief for his present large majority –the shameless prostitution of personal honour and of individual opinion to the humour of the mob, or the exigencies of party, has thus been carried farther than at any previous election in Victoria . . . . the statesman of Australian renown – . . . – is beaten by the obscure charlatan, the professor of promises, the trader in vulgar ignorance . . .[54]

Evans had grappled with the most contentious issues of land and reform, as had his peers. But his need for financial stability – for 'place and pay' – had overwhelmed his valuable contributions in the assembly and in the press. The great error of his political career was his reneging on the Minority Clause of the Electoral Bill. It does not matter that others too drew back at its implications – he had been such a staunch promoter of universal suffrage. The Batten and Cutter agreement was the final nail in the coffin. Rusden summed up Evans's political career with the sweeping observation: 'If his honesty in adhering to a principle had been equal to his intelligence, he might have made his mark in any colony.'[55]

On another level Evans may have been correct in his views on land and other subjects. But being allied with O'Shanassy was a definite setback to his career – unfair as that was, for vitriol and bigotry reigned supreme in the House. Historians have credited O'Shanassy with many fine qualities, not least his broad outlook on working towards the future well-being of the colony. He was chairman of the board of the Colonial Bank for fourteen years. From his first foray into politics as a member of the Legislative Council in 1851, he was a tower of strength until his third premiership ended in 1863. Although re-elected for Kilmore in 1864, he had left by 1866. O'Shanassy would continue his career out of politics as an 'unflinching upholder of the claims of Roman Catholics'. He was 'one of the most broad-minded advocates of conservative or Constitutional politics . . . . The only impediment to complete success as a statesman was his primary devotion to Roman Catholicism.'[56]

The face of politics changed after Evans left. H. G. Brewer wrote to Henry Chapman on 17 December 1864:

> [Politics in Victoria] seem to be degenerating into old style notions very rapidly . . . protection duties . . . and a new fangled land Bill . . . . O'Shanassy is almost alone on the Opposition benches – but will soon gather a trail. Judge Molesworth has at last come to the court and come off rather damaged, so did Ireland but people are beginning to think them injured individuals . . . . Quite a third rate sort of man seem to be coming to the surface . . .[57]

After the McCulloch government of June 1863–May 1868, political warring degenerated even further.[58] A wave of nostalgia for those first few brilliant members of the debating chamber lasted – for some – into the twentieth century.

After his exit from politics, Evans retired to his house in South Yarra, eschewing company and nursing his chronic illness.[59] He was an old man at sixty-two – a spent force. Bitterness scorched his mind – he felt betrayed by the Victorian government in denying him a pension, betrayed by his stepson-in-law and betrayed by his political enemies.[60] Later he would tell Wellington's correspondent for *The Times* of London that he resented bitterly his tabling of the resolution that had led to the adoption of universal suffrage by Victoria. It was 'an Act for which he hoped to atone, if health permitted him, by writing the history of democracy in Australia'.[61] With the ownership of the Wellington properties still unresolved, Chetham Strode having taken the case to the Privy Council, Evans picked up his pen once more for the *Herald*, and possibly *Punch*, writing as many articles as his health would allow, and continuing his futile fight for the pension.[62]

By October 1865, Evans was in dire straits. His mother had recently died, leaving Hannah in the family home in London, but Claudia and Mary were not far away, having founded the Melbourne Ladies' College. When Mary wrote asking her brother for money, he turned her request down, pleading poverty. He was appalled at her suggestion they sell their mother's house, reminding her it was charged with an annuity for Hannah's lifetime. As selling it would throw Hannah out, he was prepared to renounce his claim if they agreed not to sell it until after 'poor forlorn' Hannah's death. He refused any 'personal interviews', saying, 'I am not at present in health of mind or body.'[63]

A few months later he was informed that the Privy Council had found in his favour, turning the remaining seven prime acres he had 'purchased' in 1839 over to his estate. For perhaps the first time in his life Evans was free from financial worries, but it was a pyrrhic victory. At the age of seventy-three, Harriet was frail and Evans had finally accepted he would get no pension from Victoria.

He and his wife returned to their home on Golders Hill. It was too late to turn back the years, but no one could deny he had been steadfastly committed to the successful colonisation and prosperity of Wellington.

And that year Wellington was finally declared the capital of New Zealand.

CHAPTER TWENTY-FOUR.
'THE SCARF-SKIN OF THE FRAME'

> Well, some may hate, and some may scorn,
> And some may quite forget thy name;
> But my sad heart must ever mourn
> Thy ruined hopes, thy blighted fame!
>
> Emily Brontë, xvii [105], *Stanzas to ---*,[1] 1846

Not long after their return, Harriet Strother Evans died on 31 March 1866, aged seventy-four. Her funeral may have been one of the last conducted in the first St Paul's church, then situated behind today's Parliament, as the new church, now known as Old St Paul's, was consecrated and opened for services in June.

Just four weeks before her death, Harriet had made her will, leaving generous bequests to members of her family. She bequeathed £250 to both the London RSPCA and the Wellington Hospital, £100 to a school in Melbourne, and £500 towards the formation of an orphanage in Wellington for 'both sexes and of any denomination without any exception or preference'. The rest of her estate, which she believed to be worth at least £4,200, was left to her 'dear husband'.

Yet not much more than a month later, the two executors, Isaac Featherston and Nathaniel Levin, filed a disclaimer before the Supreme Court, refusing to act in proving the will, renouncing 'all the personal estate and effects whatsoever given and bequeathed' by Harriet, and resigning their offices. Two days later, Evans filed an affidavit in the Supreme Court testifying that Harriet's estate amounted to just under £2,100. He undertook to administer her estate 'as far as the property will extend and the law binds', and to supply an inventory of her effects within a year.[2]

Harriet had been Evans's rock, his confidante, his partner. He was broken by her death, yet he continued taking an interest in the colony's affairs. In May he was appointed one of the twelve members of the provisional committee for the New Zealand Patriotic Fund, whose patron was Sir George Grey, and attended the opening of the first session of the fourth Parliament of New Zealand a couple of months later as an honoured guest.

The following year when the seat for Wanganui became vacant in the House of Representatives, his name was put forward as a possible candidate. But, seriously dogged by ill health, for him it was out of the question.[3] He attended a levee or two and struggled along in April to a ceremony of presentation to the outgoing priest, the very Reverend Father J. J. P. O'Reilly, to commemorate his twenty-four years of ministering to the wider community of Wellington. Evans proposed Featherston as chair, which may have been the last public duty he performed.[4] In March 1868 he was one of the distinguished guests presented to the new Governor, Sir George Bowen.[5]

He then spent his last days in his home on Golders Hill.[6] What thoughts crowded into his mind as he gazed out from his window to the bustling little city below? What memories drifted into his consciousness as he grappled with the insidious pain of his fatal illness, oedema? Did he recall those heady, exciting days of preparing his family for the great adventure of colonising a new land? Of the rambles he had taken with friends over Primrose and Golders Hills and across the Heath in London? Did he hear the roar of the crowds at meetings, the hum of polite conversation at his clubs, recall the swelling sounds of approbation as he fought for the settlers so long ago in Wellington, the jeers and applause that greeted his colourful speeches in Victoria?

Evans had given his adopted family a chance that would have been denied them in the 'mother country'. Now it was their turn to comfort him. His two favourite step-granddaughters Thomasina and Eliza visited, and Daniel Riddiford made frequent pilgrimages to his side. Friends drifted in and out offering comfort, while he told them stories about his amazing and adventurous life. He recalled his family, the famous literary and political people he had known, but mostly, the person who had been the greatest influence in his life, his father.

His confident stride was reduced to a shuffle, then sitting for long hours, and ultimately he was confined to his bed. The pain, discomfort and nausea increased as his kidneys and lungs, already weakened by years of malfunction, surrendered together with his other organs. The fire and passion faded from the old doctor's eyes, and his heart. And as the world outside diminished and narrowed, even his town, Wellington, the capital of New Zealand, slipped away from his consciousness.

He died in the early hours of 23 September, at the age of sixty-six. Two days later Premier Hon. Edward Stafford moved the adjournment of Parliament, to enable Members to attend Evans's funeral, commenting:

> There were not many of the original founders of British settlement now left to them, and he felt sure that it would be strictly in accordance with [their] feelings to give this last testimony they could bestow to the acts of one of the most active members of the Colony, and that not merely as an act of settlement, but as a series of acts which assured this beautiful country to the British Crown.

Meanwhile Dr Daniel Pollen adjourned the Legislative Council, reminding his members that Evans was 'a gentleman whose name was well known in connection with the early history of public affairs, not of Wellington alone but of the whole country'.[7]

Following a short funeral service, Evans's coffin was carried from St Paul's church in Mulgrave Street to the Church of England cemetery where Evans was to be interred with Harriet. A 'large number' of mourners followed, 'including the Premier and other members of the Ministry, members of both Houses, and some of the principal merchants of Wellington. The pall-bearers were his Honour Judge Ward, the Hon. John Johnston, N. Levin, C. J. Pharazyn, W. M. Bannatyne and W. Fox, Esquires. The chief mourners were Daniel Riddiford and G. S. Cooper', husband of Ellen Chaffers Riddiford.[8] A notable absence was Isaac Featherston, who was suffering from severe illness.[9] Coincidentally, on the same day, Donald McLean successfully forced a vote which resulted in a tie on a motion denouncing the government's native policy, thereby helping to turn the tide against the worst abuses of that system.[10]

Evans's death was widely noted. In London, a short obituary penned by Wellington's correspondent appeared in *The Times* on 27 November. Closer to home the *Wellington Independent* reminded its readers that Evans was:

> . . . one of the founders, if not the real founder of the colony, having taken a leading part in the organisation of the New Zealand Land Company when Mr. Gibbon Wakefield, owing to his connection with Lord Durham's mission to Canada, might be said to have abandoned the undertaking. There is scarcely an official document of the period in which his name is not conspicuous . . .[11]

In New Zealand, other notable men like Featherston and Fox agreed.

In Melbourne there was no question. Over forty years later J. L. Forde wrote that Evans 'was the founder of Wellington, just as Fawkner is the originator of Melbourne'.[12] And with reference to the part Evans played in the transfer of the town from Petone to Wellington, biographer Philip Mennell went further, calling him 'in a sense, the father of Wellington'.[13]

Evans's closest friends knew he had 'suffered from an illness of a most painful and almost incurable character' for some time, yet the news of his death was greeted with shock in Melbourne.[14]

The *Australasian Gazette* reminisced:

> By far the finest oratorical displays took place when Dr Evans sat in opposition . . . . [Michie, Attorney-General in the Haines administration] was well matched by the polished satire, fierce denunciations and admirable invective of [Evans] . . . there has been nothing to compare with it since . . . . he unhappily suffered from the plague of 'want of pence' . . . and was apt to lay more store by the wants of office than was consistent with a high order of political usefulness . . . . Yet among the few – the very few names which shed lustre on the early constitutional history of Victoria – the name of the eloquent old man . . . will be placed in a prominent position.[15]

A personal tribute came from another source:

A something darts along the wire
And flashes past one as 'tis read,
And tells me of a grand old man
Now slumbering among the dead.

No petty wars of politics
Again may wake that Trojan soul;
Divided shrinks the silver cord,
And shattered lies the golden bowl.

Calmly he sleeps at peace with all,
Where even Demos comes no more;
Cold tenant of that newest grave
Upon the troubled Maori shore.

And there I lay my little flower,
Sorry so few with it to see,
For he had kindly thought for all,
And more than kindly will to me.

S. James, Melbourne, October 1868[16]

Samuel Johnson once wrote, 'More knowledge may be gained of a man's real character by a short conversation with one of his servants, than from a formal and studied narrative.'[17] Evans's colleagues and staff of the *Melbourne Herald* were loyal to the point of fierceness.

Their heartfelt tribute was published in journals in both Wellington and Melbourne:

> . . . especially in Eastern languages and literature he was one of the finest scholars of the present century . . . we can scarcely trust ourselves to write about one with whom only so recently we were intimately associated. An affectionate and valued friend has left us. The world has lost an eloquent speaker, a brilliant writer, and one of its ripest scholars. Dr. Evans did much to elevate the standard of our Public men; he did more to raise the tone of the Press of Victoria. By both politicians and journalists his death will be severely felt; for, although it is long since the walls of the Legislative Assembly have echoed with his sonorous tones, its *habitués* had not forgotten 'the old man eloquent'. Some of the best speeches ever made in it were delivered by Dr. Evans; and even his political enemies bore full testimony to his powers as a speaker. May he rest in peace.[18]

In Victoria, after many years of poor representation, nostalgia for the public men of Evans's era grew.[19] They had been true pillars of the state, leaving nobody capable of replacing them. The 'Golden Age' of Victoria, in which Evans had played a prominent part, had been not only the era of the enormous wealth that gold brought to the colony, but also the era of glorious oratory and debate in the House; of superb writing in the press of the day; of the arts, which grew and flourished; and of bold exploration – the days of Burke and Wills.

Years after his death, Evans was still being remembered. In 1888 after working on the Judicial Committee of the Privy Council in London, Victoria's former Solicitor-General John Dennistoun Wood had returned to Melbourne. His impressions of the immense changes he saw in Victoria were published in a collection of poems in 1903. 'Melbourne Revisited' mourns the lack of political talent:

> Where are the skilful masters of debate
> Who once were deemed the pillars of our state?
> Evans, the learned, once my genial host,
> Has long slumbered on New Zealand's coast;
> Where a tall sculptured cross its shadow throws . . . [20]

Two decades earlier, David Blair had contributed an essay for the *Centennial Magazine* recalling 'Three Melbourne Barristers' of the scores he had known.[21] Evans was the third who stood out. And for years after his death, Evans's sisters Mary and Claudia were invited to every important social event on the Governor General's calendar in Melbourne, a compliment understood to be in honour of their late brother.

ɷ

In Evans's Last Will and Testament he bequeathed the bulk of his property to James Cook Evans's son, James Samuel Evans, if he came to live in New Zealand.[22] But if he left the country for longer than three years, the legacy would pass on to another young man, George Samuel Evans Dale, 'now or lately of the Grammar School at Emerald Hill in Melbourne, whereof Robert McGregor is Master'. George Dale was in any case bequeathed '£100 per annum' until he reached '25 years or die'.

If this was a surprise, there was another: if James Samuel failed to fulfil the conditions, or leave descendants, the entire estate would devolve on George Samuel Evans Dale 'for his maintenance and education during his infancy or otherwise'.

One hundred and fifty years later, we can believe one of two things. Evans was the father of the boy who bore his name. Or the child may have been an orphan from one of the ragged schools, adopted by Dr and Mrs Dale, and educated at Evans's expense. It was not uncommon for an orphan to adopt the names of his benefactors, and Harriet Evans had always maintained an active interest in the education of all children, particularly those from orphanages and ragged schools. The fact that the boy is not mentioned in Harriet's will might also suggest that, as Evans was still alive, he would provide for his future.

Born in New South Wales in 1854, George Dale's choice of career and ambitions appear to have mirrored those of his benefactor. He was educated in Melbourne, and 'articled' to D. M. Myers, solicitor of Bombala, at the age of twenty. In 1880 he was admitted as Attorney of the Supreme Court of New South Wales. He practised for some time, marrying Louise Harriet Hogarth in October 1877, and moving to Narrabri about 1882. He took an active interest in local affairs and was appointed the first Captain of the Corps of the Voluntary Reserve Company. He had liberal views on the land question, so was defeated by the squatting community when he stood for Parliament in the Namoi electorate. A gifted orator and debater, he received a majority at the poll in Narrabri, and was given a public reception on his success. In 1884 he was elected to the Borough Council, and again in 1888 when his colleagues voted him Mayor.[23] He stood unsuccessfully for Parliament in 1887, and died in March 1920 at the age of sixty-six, of acute nephritis and uraemia, illnesses similar to those of Evans. The evidence does seem to suggest he may have been Evans's son.

In his will, Evans also fulfilled Harriet's wish to bequeath £1,000 each to both Amelia and Daniel Riddiford, and Daniel received an additional £500 'in full satisfaction of the £1,000 payable to him' under Evans's marriage settlement. Evans left £500 each to three of his step-grandchildren – Edward Joshua Riddiford, Eliza and Thomasina; and £100 to each of his sisters – Mary Pantin Evans and Claudia Permezel in Melbourne, and Hannah Evans in London. He fulfilled Harriet's legacy to her servant Ann Croly (Gleeson) of £50, at £10 per year from the date of his wife's death. Two codicils bequeathed an additional £500 to Thomasina, and £100 to his niece Linnaea Lamb Evans, for life.[24] The money was intended solely for the women's own use – 'to the exclusion of any husband they may have or marry later'. This, during a time when the husband enjoyed the right to administer his wife's wealth, reflected Evans's empathy toward women. The second codicil had been signed by his own shaky hand, and his two faithful servants Ann Gleeson and Denis Cashen. The will's probate was granted to Charles B. Izard of Izard and Pharazyn on 9 January 1869.[25]

But the conditions of Evans's will were never fully honoured. His nephew James Samuel never settled in New Zealand for any period. Less than three months after Evans's death, the *Independent* noted James's arrival on the *Tararua* from Melbourne,[26] and while he stayed until at least March the following year, advertising Evans's treasured three sections on Golders Hill for sale,[27] he appears to have left soon afterward. In spite of transgressing the will's requirements, he somehow enjoyed the income from his uncle's estate from 1869 until his death in 1933. In turn, his widow, Amy Burgess Farren Evans,[28] received all remaining monies until her own death in 1942. In July 1953 the Certificates of Title of her Government Stock were surrendered to the Reserve Bank. It has been estimated that the revenue from Evans's city sections on Lambton Quay alone was considerable.[29]

Perhaps as a token gesture of compliance with Evans's will, James Samuel and his wife sent his half-sister, Linnaea Lamb Evans, a middle-aged spinster, to Wellington to teach. She supplemented her salary with Evans's annuity of £100 per annum for her life, purchased a house in Hobson Street, Thorndon, and seemed to thrive. Late in 1875, her half-brother and her uncle's namesake, George Samuel, then aged twenty-eight, travelled from London to visit her, stopping en route to visit his aunts, Claudia and Mary, in Melbourne.[30] Linnaea later moved to Dunedin, where she died on 20 September 1898, almost thirty years to the day after her uncle's death. The public trustee recorded her estate at £66 14s 4d.

Amelia Riddiford, whose marriage to Edward Chetham Strode had been promoted by her mother and stepfather, cannot be said to have lived a happy life. Her husband's financial woes had escalated over the years, fuelled by his gambling and fast life in London. The couple lived in a small flat in the City, never taking possession of the grand house and estate he had inherited, as over the years it became fatally mortgaged. There were no children, and when he died in 1896, leaving an estate of £1,500, Amelia had predeceased him by several years.

Ironically, Amelia's jilted suitor Richard Davies Hanson enjoyed an illustrious career. After being premier and Attorney-General of South Australia from 1857 to 1860, he was appointed Chief Justice. He was knighted in England in 1869 and was premier again for six months in 1872–73. He was the first chancellor of the University of Adelaide from 1874 until his death in March 1876. He passed many major Acts designed to create responsible government, but was most famous for introducing the Act abolishing the public execution of criminals, legislation later adopted by England.[31] In 1851 he married Ann Hopgood, the twenty-four-year-old widow of Captain Scanlon of New Zealand. They had five children, a son and four daughters. He was accorded a state funeral in 1876.

EPILOGUE

At the first dinner to celebrate the establishment of the Early Colonists' Association nearly five years after Evans's death, George Hunter Jnr, who had arrived in Wellington in 1840 at the age of nineteen with his parents and nine siblings aboard the *Duke of Roxburgh*, offered a toast. He spoke at length about the men who had forged their path to eventual personal success and had brought the small colony into being. He gave credit to Colonel Wakefield and other members of that family, and: 'After these, other names crowded upon him. Dr. Evans, Mr. Molesworth, Mr. Dorset, Mr. Swainson of the Hutt, Mr. Barton and hundreds of others.'[1]

Wellington had indeed attracted 'men of energy and enterprise, many persons of high intelligence and the best education, fellows and members of the English, Scotch [*sic*] or foreign universities' – even Hobson had attested as much.[2] As a later historian wrote:

> New Zealand owes much to its *intelligentzia* of those early days. They edited its newspapers, voiced the complaints of its colonists in powerful and choicely-worded petitions, served its Governors, especially the wisest and best of them all . . . and represented its settlements . . . . Were it not for them and their ceaseless petitioning (the inhabitants of Auckland were comparatively silent on the point of self-government), New Zealand would never have obtained the boon of free political institutions as early as 1852.[3]

It is strange that George Samuel Evans, who felt himself tied so indelibly to Wellington and who was recognised by his contemporaries for his pivotal role in its creation, is now so little associated with the city's history, and so little known. There are several reasons for the eclipse of Evans's reputation. They involve his personality and education, his family and the times in which he lived, as well as the revisionism of history.

Although socially genial and hospitable, Evans was not a popular man. He was brilliant, difficult and volatile, a man whose superior abilities were neutralised by a disturbing lack of judgement and consistency, and by a mercurial temperament. Evans was often described as 'uncommon' or 'singular', and was ever the schoolmaster, ever a person apart. For many, his knowledge made him seem pompous, even boastful. Had his conduct been more acceptable to the majority of his fellow colonists, his popularity might have been high, for the appearance of conformity and collegiality were necessities in a small colony.

Eccentric he might have been – a man of baffling contrasts – but if there was one area in which he never wavered, it was his work for the successful colonisation of Wellington. While others pursued their business interests and created a strong future for their families, much of the work Evans carried out for the settlement was gratuitous. He had wrestled with the practicalities of life in a struggling colony while maintaining his role of Crown adversary. If remembered at all, Evans is connected to the Wakefields as their trouble-shooter and right-hand man. But Evans also honoured his commitment to the settlers' interests in New Zealand, and again in England in his work for the country's self-governing constitution. He was always ready to help Wellington during his political career in Melbourne, and above all he was proud of his bond with Maori.

Yet his career in the colony, while often addressing fundamental political, legal and social issues surrounding the successful establishment of a new settlement, seemed merely to be a series of passionate efforts to achieve his goals, which were neutralised by his fiery temperament and erratic behavior. Had he remained in Wellington in 1853 and followed Wakefield's advice to 'attain the high place which his talents deserved', he might be remembered by historians still. But his lengthy absences from the colony meant that much of his work was forgotten, continued by others or merely dissipated. The small town that eventually became the capital city of New Zealand was really the 'child' Evans never had, as one biographer observed.[4]

Evans's wish for his nephew James to make Wellington his home was thwarted. He left no family in this country to foster his memory for generations to come. Evans's great sacrifice in forgoing his own career in England to give his adopted son a future in a new land is forgotten. Furthermore, the man and his work have faded almost entirely from the collective memory of his adopted family, the Riddifords, as they have forged their own distinctive identity.

By the time of his death many of his contemporaries had died or emigrated elsewhere; and 60 per cent of Wellington's population was under twenty-one years of age. There were still older men, though, who had the energy and will to promote their importance in establishing the city. As the *Independent* commented on Evans –

> . . . owing to age and failing health he did not take that active part in public questions which had distinguished his career on his first arrival here in 1840, and after his arrival in Melbourne in the year 1853. In consequence of this retirement, the decease of Dr Evans will not be so much felt as it would have been had he lately occupied that public position, which his great talents, learning, and colonial experience would have fully entitled him to hold . . . . In his day [he had] done this colony some service.[5]

Evans's motives for emigrating were indeed mixed: colonisation, and profit on his capital – all of which he had risked on this idealistic venture – but above all he believed –

> . . . the great feat of Christ's incarnation lies at the foundation of all civil and religious liberty, 'THE GOOD OLD CAUSE' – the cause which we bled for, in the persons of our ancestors, and which we have brought with us to the antipodes, as the *Palladium*, or rather as the most sacred deposit that could have been given to us from the ark of God . . . . this is the patrimonial gift and heir loom – CIVIL AND RELIGIOUS LIBERTY – which we trust they will prize above all things, and hand down to the latest of their posterity.[6]

When William Fox told Donald McLean that Evans was 'perhaps the most influential originator of New Zealand colonization we ever had', he did not say it lightly.[7] We might wonder what would have happened had Evans never become involved with Wakefield, never joined his Association. Would events have been different? In an age when the British government was a powerful force, would anyone else have dared to defy it? In the face of the Colonial Office's trenchant refusal to sanction the move, Evans forged ahead with his committee, and with the help of others bought and outfitted a ship and increased the momentum towards the goal of emigration to a new colony.[8] Edward Gibbon Wakefield was fortunate indeed in attracting talented men to help realise his ambitious vision. In George Samuel Evans he found prodigious gifts, huge energy and utmost loyalty.

How different would Wellington be today if the primary town had been built at Petone? How would trade and commerce have fared? The merchants were ever grateful for Evans's protection, particularly when he intervened by assisting Colonel Wakefield to ensure Hobson did not issue the edict that might have terminated the infant colony.

During those early tumultuous years of New Zealand's settlement, would the outcome have been very different if Colonel Wakefield had relied chiefly on another man for advice? And what advice did he actually take? He was notoriously secretive and often refused assistance. Would there have been quite the defiant and determined spirit that saw the early colonists struggle against almost insurmountable odds and survive?

Maori have a great legacy of oral history. One man whose forebears left positive impressions of Evans was Lionel Brown, the great-great grandson of James Brown, a weaver and publican who arrived from Paisley, Scotland, in 1841. James used to row Evans, his wife and stepson up the Hutt River. Lionel's mother was descended from the northern tribe of Whui Mutu Heteraka.[9] Lionel was told Evans was the 'lynch-pin' of Wellington, without whom the settlers would have drifted in a 'rudderless ship'. Evans was, he said, nui, 'great mind'; nui, 'great heart'; rangatira, 'great leader'.[10]

Over the last century, the outlook on our history has changed. For many decades after Evans's death the early founders and settlers of New Zealand were honoured and respected. Writers like William Gisborne were laying the blame for the Company's trials squarely on the Colonial Office and on the earliest governors of the colony. Gisborne believed Hobson's 'greatest fault was his treatment of the New Zealand Company' which he regarded 'with unmitigated aversion, and pursued . . . with unceasing enmity'. The Company 'had on the whole a just cause . . . . It stood out . . . from the mass of those harpies who greedily clutched at all land for selfish purposes [whose] aim was to make money *quo-cunque modo*, [while] the aim of the Company was colonization.'[11]

A. J. Harrop wrote in 1926 that New Zealand's first governors – Hobson, Shortland, FitzRoy – were weak, but its first colonists were strong:

> That it should have been proved possible to found a British Colony without exterminating the native race, and without tarnishing the British name, is perhaps the best justification not only for those who laboured in the cause of British colonization of New Zealand, but for those who insisted from the beginning on the necessity of protecting the interests of the natives. It is, in a word, the justification of Dandeson Coates and James Stephen, as well as the justification of Charles Buller and Edward Gibbon Wakefield.[12]

Evans featured high on the lists of the men who made a difference. He rated as one of Cox's *Men of Mark*, and was given due credit in Irma O'Connor's *Edward Gibbon Wakefield* of 1928.[13]

Then came the First World War. Gallipoli was a defining moment for New Zealand. After the Second World War, New Zealand continued forging her own identity, and a fresh wave of research began to take place. New documents came to light, and no longer was the daring enterprise of the Company seen as a romantic adventure. A cloak of shame and condemnation was thrown over both it and its servants, obliterating its goals and achievements and darkening the reputations of the Company men.

Evans's role was a poisoned chalice. His fame has been blighted essentially by his association with the Company. The whole enterprise of pre-selling land in a remote country peopled by a socially progressive and culturally intact indigenous race is now regarded as a presumptuous and foolhardy act, and in hindsight an arrogant usurpation of the rights of Maori. Evans's accusations of despotism in the government's use of power evoke little sympathy today when weighed alongside the Company's blunders in land acquisition and the protests of Maori. The events that provoked Evans's strongest objections are viewed as merely the birth pangs of a small but powerful European community in a new colony, and his acts of protest are dismissed as part of a disruptive phase of New Zealand's history.

But it was not the Company that ultimately betrayed Maori – it was, as Evans had warned, the Crown, the real robbery coming with its land confiscations after the New Zealand Wars.

History has been kinder to some than to others. The image of Samuel Revans, the hot-tempered fiery Republican who fell out with so many and argued with his peers as much as Evans ever did, has been softened, and he is chummily referred to as 'Sam' by historians, for whom he is something of a favourite. An acknowledged identity of early Wellington and the popular folk hero of early journalism, his first career in the country came about largely through the financial backing of the Company and its officials. But his association with the New Zealand Company snapped when he forcefully opposed the Wakefields from the mid-1840s, and his fame has not been blighted by it. Apart from a few forays overseas, Revans always engaged in the colony's affairs, while dabbling in a variety of ventures. He earned his status by living in Wellington and the Wairarapa, the quintessential bachelor pioneer suffering the vicissitudes and enjoying the rewards of early pastoral life.

After one hundred and fifty years, his image remains strong. Scholefield's 1940 biography and other historians described him as an unorthodox firebrand. He has an entry in the 2000 *Dictionary of New Zealand Biography*, yet Evans, who is given due credit by Scholefield, has no entry in that esteemed publication.[14]

If it were not for Evans's thousands of pieces of journalism, accounts of him in newspapers and the records of the Victorian Legislative Assembly, as well as the later testimony of Horace Fildes, son of Jessie Taine, and grandson of Liocadia and James Taine, we would never know the part Evans played in establishing the city of Wellington, and contributing to the constitutional development of the state of Victoria.

Meanwhile, one link with Evans's city was broken when in 1909 the *Dominion* reported the sale of his estate that 'extended along the greater part of the western side of Lambton Quay'. And another when in 1927 the City Council proposed to change the name of Golders Hill to the more prosaic Eccleston Hill after Premier Seddon's home town. In spite of vigorous resistance and an impassioned plea from Horace Fildes, who called Evans the Father of Wellington as well as of the judiciary, the change went ahead and another reminder slipped away.[15] Evans's name remains only in Evans Bay and in George Street, Thorndon, and his wife's in Harriett Street.[16] But the Wellington Club he founded in 1841 is the only survivor of the early clubs – and it thrives to this day.

The final indignity came when his remains, his wife's and those of other early settlers were disinterred in October 1969 and placed in a communal grassed plot in Bolton Street to make way for the urban motorway built in 1973. The gravestones were removed to their present bleak, desolate site, separated from Wakefield and other notable settlers. The headstone is accompanied by another that recorded his legacy, but the words have been obliterated by time and harsh weather.

HE WAS INTIMATELY CONNECTED WITH THE
EARLY DAYS OF THIS COLONY
ARRIVING WITH HIS WIFE IN
WELLINGTON
IN THE YEAR 1840 HE ENCOUNTERED
WITH HER MANY OF THOSE PRIVATIONS TO WHICH THE
EARLY SETTLERS WERE SUBJECT
HE DEVOTED HIMSELF FOR SOME
TIME TO THE INTERESTS OF THIS PROVINCE
SUBSEQUENTLY HE WENT TO MELBOURNE

WHERE HE HELD THE HIGH POSITION OF
A MINISTER OF THE CROWN
HE AFTERWARDS RETURNED TO WELLINGTON
TO SETTLE WHERE HE DIED
HIGHLY HONOURED AND DEEPLY
LAMENTED[17]

Evans may be forgotten, yet some of his vibrant spirit lives on in the vision, resourcefulness and originality of Wellington's citizens. It is there in the heart of a beautiful and thriving capital city at the end of the world.

In all the lonely landscape round
I see no sight and hear no sound
Except the wind that far away
Comes sighing o'er the heathy sea.

Emily Brontë[18]

APPENDICES

APPENDIX ONE

Song of the Colonists Departing for New Zealand
Thomas Campbell

Steer, helmsman, till you steer our way
By stars beyond the line –
We go to found a realm – one day –
Like England's self to shine.

Chorus:
Cheer up! Cheer up! our course we'll keep
With dauntless heart and hand,
And when we've ploughed the stormy deep,
We'll plough a smiling land.
A land whose beauties importune –
The Briton to its bowers,
To sow but plenty's seeds and prune
Luxuriant fruits and flowers.

Chorus:
Cheer up! Cheer up!
A sunny land with varying sweets
Of healthy plains and hills,
With giant woods to build our fleets,
And floods to drive our mills.

Chorus:
Cheer up! Cheer up!
There tracts uncheered by human words.
Seclusion's wildest holds,
Shall hear the lowing of our herds,
The tinkling of our folds.

Chorus:
Cheer up! Cheer up!
Like rubies set in gold shall blush
Our vineyards, girt with corn,
And wine, and oil, and gladness gush
From Amalthoea's horn.

Chorus:
Cheer up! Cheer up!

Britannia's pride is in our hearts,
Her blood is in our veins;
We'll girdle earth with British arts,
Like Ariel's magic chains.

Chorus:
Cheer up! Cheer up!

From *New Zealand Gazette*, 21 August 1839

APPENDIX TWO

Regulations for the Emigrants of the New Zealand Company's First Colony

In September 1839 three emigrant ships of the New Zealand Company lay at Gravesend ready to sail with over five hundred passengers to establish the first colony of the Company in New Zealand. The preliminary survey ship, the *Tory*, had left hurriedly in May, followed in July by the *Cuba*, to make preparations for the reception of the settlers. One of the directors of the Company, Mr G. F. Young, armed with a copy of the regulations and agreement, addressed the emigrants from the poop deck of the *Adelaide* and, after explaining that it was necessary that some provision be made for the maintenance of good order in the settlement, asked them to sign the agreement. The document read as follows:

> We, the undersigned, intending to inhabit the New Zealand Land Company's first and principal settlement, with the view to provide for the peace and order thereof, do hereby agree among ourselves and pledge our honour to submit ourselves to the following provisional regulations and to enforce them on each other: that is to say, –
>
> **1st.** That all the persons, parties to this agreement, shall submit themselves to be mustered and drilled under the direction of persons to be appointed as hereinafter mentioned.
>
> **2nd.** That in case any of the persons, parties to this agreement, shall commit any offence against the law of England, he shall be liable to be punished in the same manner as if the offence had been committed in England.
>
> **3rd.** That in case any dispute shall arise between any of the persons, parties to this agreement, such disputes shall be decided in the manner hereinafter mentioned.
>
> **4th.** That a committee shall be formed of the following persons:
>
> Colonel William Wakefield, the Company's principal agent.
> Dr. George Samuel Evans, Barrister-at Law
> Hon. Henry William Petre
> Dudley Sinclair
> Francis Alexander Molesworth
> Capt. Edward Daniell
> Lieut. William Smith, the Company' Surveyor- General

Richard Davies Hanson
Edward Betts Hopper
George Duppa
George Hunter
Henry Moreing
Henry St. Hill
Thomas Mitchell Partridge
Major David Starke Durie

That Col. Wm. Wakefield shall be the first President thereof. That in all cases the Company's Principal Agent shall be the President. That the Company shall have power to appoint five additional members. That the committee shall have the power to appoint five additional members. That the number of members shall not exceed twenty five. That five members shall be a quorum for all purposes. That Samuel Revans Esq. shall be the first Secretary to the committee.

5th. That the Committee shall have the power to make rules for their meetings, and to appoint the necessary officers, and that a meeting of the Committee shall take place within three days after five members shall have arrived in the settlement.

6th. That the Committee shall have power to appoint a person who shall be called an umpire; and that George Samuel Evans Esq., Barrister-at-law shall be the first umpire. That the umpire shall preside in all criminal proceedings, and assisted by seven assessors shall decide on the guilt or innocence of the party accused.

7th. That if the party be declared guilty the Umpire shall state the punishment to be inflicted; provided that without the special approval of the committee no imprisonment to be stated by the Umpire shall exceed three months, and no fine to be so stated shall exceed £10.

8th. That in all civil proceedings the Umpire shall preside; that each party may choose an arbitrator who shall sit with the Umpire, and the award of the majority shall bind the parties; and the Umpire shall have all necessary powers of compelling the attendance of witnesses and the production of books and papers, and of examining the witnesses.

9th. That the Committee shall have power to appoint five of their members, who shall be called a Committee of Appeal, and to such Committee an appeal may be made in all cases civil and criminal, and the decision of such Committee shall be final.

10th. That the Committee and the Umpire shall be authorised to make such rules and orders for their government in the execution of their duties as they shall think fit.

11th. That the Committee may direct in what manner the assessors shall be chosen.

12th. That the Committee shall direct the calling out of the armed inhabitants, and shall make rules and regulations for the government of the same.

13th. That the Company's principal agent shall have the highest authority in directing the armed inhabitants when called out; and that the Committee shall have the power to appoint such other persons as they think fit to assist in such direction.

14th. That the Committee shall have power to make regulations for preserving the peace of the settlement and shall have power to levy such rates and duties as they shall think necessary to defray all expenses attending the management of the affairs of the colony and the administration of justice.[1]

1 Edward Jerningham Wakefield (ed. Sir Robert Stout), *Adventure in New Zealand, from 1839 to 1844, with Some Account of the Beginning of the British Colonization of the Islands*, Whitcombe & Tombs, Christchurch, 1908; and Arthur H. Carman, *The Birth of a City: Wellington 1840–1843*, self-published, Wellington, 1970, pp.2–4.

APPENDIX THREE

The New Zealand Company's Contract with Samuel Revans for Management and Editing of the *Gazette*

In the contract four trustees were appointed: John Ward, Evans, George Hunter and Richard Davies Hanson. Five hundred pounds was outlaid, £200 of which came from the Company, with Revans and the trustees investing the balance. The presses, type, machinery, paper and other equipment belonged to Evans, Hunter and Hanson, and at any time, any of the men could demand its return. Revans was to be sole managing editor, replaceable only by serious default or breach of his contract. The paper would rely on advertising and subscriptions for revenue. For the first year Revans would reap all the paper's profits, and in the second year the Company would receive 5 per cent on its investment. Evans, Hunter and Hanson were empowered to 'exercise a general control over the nature of the written articles and advertisements', and to ask Revans at any time to omit or not insert any material which 'may be injurious to the said newspaper or to the [Company's] ends for which the same was established'. Revans was to conduct his editorship 'under the general control' of the trustees 'for the time being', with the option eventually to buy out the shareholders. His salary was fixed at £150 per annum – half that of Evans – on 16 September 1839, with an advance of £50.[1]

In his memoir, *Adventure in New Zealand*, Jerningham Wakefield writes: 'The apparatus of the newspaper had been obtained by subscription among the principal colonists,[2] and the management of it undertaken by Mr. Samuel Revans . . .'.

1 NZC, Despatches from Secretary to Principal Agent, 9, 16 and 17 September 1839, pp.101–4, NZC 102/1/1, ANZ.

2 Edward Jerningham Wakefield (ed. Sir Robert Stout), *Adventure in New Zealand, from 1839 to 1844, with Some Account of the Beginning of the British Colonization of the Islands*, Whitcombe & Tombs, Christchurch, 1908, p.198.

APPENDIX FOUR

Ratification and Extension of the Provisional Constitution of the Settlers of the First Colony by the Sovereign Chiefs of Port Nicholson (drawn up by Dr. George Samuel Evans and Richard Davies Hanson, with the approval of Colonel William Wakefield)

We, the Sovereign Chiefs of the District of Port Nicholson, being moved thereto by the representations of Colonel Wakefield, President of the Council of the White People who have settled in the aforesaid district, and by a consideration of the interests of all the inhabitants of the said district, as well native as otherwise, do hereby ratify and confirm the within agreement, and do declare that the same shall have the force of law within our territories, and shall be binding upon all parties residing within the same, subject, nevertheless to the modifications and stipulations hereafter mentioned.

1. That the Council within named shall continue in office for the space of one year, from the first of January 1840; and that at the expiration of that period a fresh Council shall be elected for the space of one year, by the votes of the majority of the male inhabitants of the colony, not legally disqualified, and also have resided in the colony for the space of three months; and that on the first day of each succeeding year a similar election shall take place; the manner and time of holding the first and all subsequent elections to be determined by the said Council.

2. That the President of the said Council shall remain in office for the space of five years from the said first of January, 1840. That at the expiration of that period, a President shall be elected by an electoral body, equal in number to the Council for the time being, to be chosen on that principle by the majority of the votes of the male inhabitants of the Colony, not legally disqualified. That the President shall have a veto upon all resolutions of the council, but that any such resolution, if adopted by a succeeding Council, shall have the force of law.

3. That the Council within named, and all succeeding Councils to be elected as aforesaid, shall possess and exercise all such powers of legislation, and by means of their President, shall perform all acts, not being repugnant to the law of England, which we, as such sovereign chiefs, might exercise and perform, we hereby ratifying and confirming whatsoever they shall do, or cause to be done, in the lawful exercise of the powers so conferred upon them.

4. That we will not levy any taxes, nor impose any duties, nor do any other act which may affect the interests of the Colony, or the right conferred by the within agreement, or this our ratification thereof, without the advice and consent of the said Council.
5. That all the native inhabitants of the district aforesaid shall possess a perfect equality of rights with the colonists, except that they shall not, for the first five years, vote at the election of the Council, nor serve as assessors, except in cases in which the rights or interests of a native are concerned; and that in any such case, at least three of the assessors shall be natives.
6. That for the first five years, no law shall be made affecting the rights of the native population, without our consent specially obtained thereto.[1]

1 *New Zealand Journal*, Vol. 1, 1840, p.220, citing *New Zealand Gazette*, 18 April 1840.

APPENDIX FIVE

Extract from a Meeting of Burgesses held in Barrett's Hotel on 18 September 1842

Dr. Evans then enquired of the chairman whether any motion had been proposed by Mr. St. Hill, and on being answered in the negative, proceeded to address the meeting, who received him with a diversified melange of cheers, hisses, and groans, accompanied with various imitations of the canine and feline species. The chairman in vain endeavoured to obtain a hearing for the learned Doctor; who, making a footstool of the knee of one gentleman and the shoulder of another, mounted the table amidst roars of laughter. Mr. Wade and Mr. Annear followed his example, and the chairman, after another attempt to obtain a hearing for the learned Doctor, told him pointedly that he would now leave the chair, and that whatever breach of the peace might occur, or damage done to property, it would be at the Doctor's risk and peril.

Mr. Lyon then left the chair.

Dr. Evans, however, maintained his position on the table, amidst the most deafening uproar; cries of 'No burgess,' 'Off off,' 'Turn him out.' 'Hear the Doctor,' etc., etc. The learned Doctor continued to pace the table with great dignity, folding and extending his arms alternately, and going through every variety of gesticulation, though we were unable to distinguish a word he said. Mr. Wade, Mr. Roots, and Dr. Dorset, now mounted on the table. The Doctor paced the table, vainly attempting to be heard by the tumultuous meeting.

The uproar still continued unabated, when suddenly we saw the Doctor give way, as if seized by some one by the legs – for a second he tottered, and then fell back over the heads of those near, and was lost to sight amidst the sea of heads and arms. A scene now ensued which baffles all description. The Doctor struck out furiously around him on all sides – and presently he and the person with whom he was grappling were carried bodily out at the upper end of the room – the chair was shortly afterwards vacated, and Dr. Evans again appeared at the head of the table still determined to be heard – he at length gained the chair, and after many minutes of prolonged uproar, obtained something approaching to a hearing.

He had been told he was no burgess; he was a burgess as much as any one in that room. He had a large stake in the colony, as large perhaps, as any man there. He bought of the Company largely at the first, and owned many hundreds of acres in this Island, though he had not got them all yet. (Hear.) The money he had paid for land, had brought out 200 emigrants to the colony, and was it to be said he had no stake in this colony; that he had no right to have a voice in such a meeting as the present? He had tendered his One pound and the usual declaration to the Police Magistrate, and he was refused, he was informed he was too late, it was after the hour which Mr. Murphy had appointed to receive the names of burgesses. He had come there that night to show that he had a right, as much as any man, to be heard in this town; he had come to show the Police Magistrate how little he regarded the course he had thought proper to pursue, and to show this meeting that he was resolved to maintain his right, and he was determined to punish that government stipendiary, to pull up Mr. Murphy, so help him God, before the Supreme Court (cheers). Five and twenty years ago, gentlemen, I laboured heart and soul, in England, in the glorious cause of radical reform; I have always been a supporter of the rights of the people, I have always maintained their interest. I have never advocated this party or that party, but the only cause I have ever supported has been the substantial welfare of this colony, and the happiness and prosperity of the universal people. (Cheers.) Gentlemen, I had the honour to propose this very Corporation Bill to Sir George Gipps. During my visit to Sydney, I had the honour to suggest this very measure which is about to confer upon you one of the greatest political privileges: and now, Gentlemen, after having been instrumental in framing and bring about this Corporate Bill, having been the first to press upon you the expediency of adopting it, I did not expect that when I attempted to address the burgesses of the Borough of Wellington on this important subject, that I should have been dragged from the table by a ruffian from South Australia; a person who has only lately landed on our shores, and whose whole time here, I am informed, has been spent in traducing and abusing the state and prospects of our colony, while he puffs South Australia, a colony at this moment on the brink of insolvency and ruin. (Cries of shame, shame.) I had not at first intended to qualify myself for a burgess, but I was told that on first occasion of exercising our high municipal privileges, it might seem unmanly and cowardly to shrink from the task; I therefore went on the last day, at 12 o'clock, at night. But I maintain, that on that account, I am no less a burgess virtually. I have no less stake in this town and colony; I have therefore, an equal right to be heard on such a subject. Gentlemen, in the preamble to the Bill, we are told that this is to be but a step to a higher degree of political privilege. We are led to believe that if we approve ourselves as municipal electors, we may expect to receive the higher and more substantial privileges of a more extended self representation. But this is not the way to fit ourselves for those privileges; it is not by stifling discussion by noise and uproar – by party spirit, and animosity, and faction that we shall prepare ourselves for those higher functions of political franchise. Gentlemen, I would warn you against those lists that have hitherto been adopted; I would not advise you to pledge yourself to any man; promise not to vote for any list, until the day of election; let each man carry home with him, canvass, in his own breast, the names of those men who, in his own private, individual, and unbiassed opinion, are best calculated to represent the true interests of the colony; let each man, from his own knowledge and experience of those around him, give his vote, unpledged, on the day of election. But, Gentlemen, there are parties in this town against whom I would warn you; let me entreat you to return to the Council no agent of absentee landlords – no officer of the New Zealand Company – no stipendiary of Government! Yes, there are party ties of the local government, and who are employed to run down and oppose the best interests of this community. I am informed, from authentic sources which you unfortunately cannot obtain, there is a party – and a powerful party – in England, backed by the Government at home, and aided by the local government in the colony, whose object is to stir up the Native mind in opposition to the settlers – to keep them from their land, to retard their progress, and, in fact, stay the growth and success of the colony altogether! Gentlemen, I ask you, would you return a man of your Council in any way connected with such a party? Let me press upon you, to return no agent of absentee proprietors – no officer of the Company or the Government, to your Council! There are men here, in this room, against whom I would warn you – men whom, in their private capacity, I admire and respect, but who, from their connection with absentee landlords, or the local government, must ever prove the enemies of your true welfare. This is Mr. St. Hill! I respect him as a man; but, Gentlemen, from his connection with the absentees in England, who own thousands, and tens of thousands of acres, in the untrodden wilderness of this colony, which they have never seen, and for which they have done nothing – men who are connected with the colony as a profitable speculation – who have done nothing for you or for the colony; from his connection with such men, I say, Mr. St. Hill is unfit to represent you; his interests must always be inimical to your true prosperity! And, there is also another man, whom I respect and admire in his private capacity, and whom I have left a few minutes since in my own family circle, but who, from his connection with local government, whose every effort and wish is for your oppression and destruction, is unfit to represent you in Council. I mean Mr. Hanson! (Cries of oh! Oh – now, it's coming out!) Gentlemen, let me once more warn you against pledging yourselves to any man, or to any list; reserve your votes for the day of election, and act upon your own judgement – think for yourselves. Remember that this is but preparatory to more extended political privileges; I trust the day is not far distant, when the representatives of many cities shall meet in the town, then the centre of the colony, in our own representative assembly! Look upon this Corporation as merely the step to higher political privileges – to more extended powers of representation! Once more, I entreat you, pledge yourself to no man's lists – Mr. Sutton's list, or Mr. St. Hill's list, or the working-men's list or Mr. Anybody-else's list. Scatter your lists to the winds of heaven, and dare to think and act for yourselves! Again, I implore you to endeavour to approve yourselves in your present capacity of municipal electors, as soon to merit those more extended powers of election and representation which are promised in the preamble of the Bill – by giving to each man an open hearing – by temperate discussion, and by the display of no personal animosity or spirit of faction, to endeavour to conduct yourselves, that soon shall be said to you as to the steward in the parade 'Well done, faithful Borough! Thou hast been faithful over one town, thou shalt represent many cities!' (Mr. Roots then made some observations which we could not catch, when Dr. Evans said, We want no slaves to power here; we will not be dictated to by the baseborn slave of an arbitrary faction.)

Mr. Roots next addressed the Meeting: –

He said, Dr. Evans had talked a great deal about Governor Hobson, and abused the Government; but it turned out, after all, he only wanted to have a slap at Mr. Hanson. Dr. Evans had gone all the way to England for politics; what had that to do with Whig and Tory? What had that to do with our borough? He (Mr. Roots) was anxious that every man should have a fair hearing; that every man should speak his own opinion, and think and vote for himself; he begged them to pledge themselves to no man – to no list. He abhorred the Corporate Bill from his soul; he had always opposed its adoption; it could never benefit them: but now that it was inevitable he trusted they would think and act for themselves, and return those men who are most likely to support the working men's interest, in which are involved the best interests of the colony.

Mr. Roots left the Chair amidst cheers and groans, shouts and hisses, from all parts of the room. The uproar continued for many minutes, when at length Mr. Revans appeared, and endeavoured to be heard: –

He was surprised, he was disgusted, with what he had witnessed that evening; he had witnessed a display that evening of paltry animosity, and opposition of petty faction, which he had little expected from the intelligence of the Borough of Wellington. He had all his life mixed in political struggles; he was a democrat himself; he had always been a democrat: but the soul of political life was open and free discussion. Let each man be heard; let each man freely state his own opinion. He was sorry to see such petty feeling displayed in so small a community; he had always courted discussion; it was the only way to get at the truth; he was sorry to see so much animosity and personal ill-feeling as he had witnessed in that room; he was always willing to give his political opponents credit for as much honesty as himself; he thought it possible for there to be bad men on both sides, and good men on both sides; there might be honest Tories as well as honest Whigs; he thought the Tories had done much mischief by their line of policy; he had always opposed them; but he was willing to give them credit for as much honesty of purpose as himself; he had been prevented by circumstances from becoming a Burgess; and had he been in a situation to be elected into the Council, he should fear the onerous and responsible nature of duties such an office would impose upon him, while he should endeavour to serve their interests if they had elected him; he should by no means wish to fill so heavy and responsible a station; he begged the electors of the borough to beware of class representation; it had been the curse of England; the extent of the present franchise was as much as the greatest advocates for universal suffrage could desire; how many a man in England would hug such a privilege! He thought, with Dr. Evans, that they should tear up all lists and think for themselves; above all this, to approve themselves as municipal electors, and prepare themselves for future political regeneration. They should not strive thus to put down discussion, the proceedings of this night was [*sic*] a disgrace to the town. He hoped he might never see a repetition of similar uproar and noise.

Mr. Rowland Davis here begged to ask Mr. Revans a question. Whether he thought it right women should interfere on such occasions. He had heard of two ladies who had canvassed even on the Sabbath. (Cries of 'Shame! Shame!'). Did Mr. Revans approve of this?

Mr. Revans said he had thought and studied much on that point in political economy, but he had never been able to make up his mind decidedly. However, as the ladies in this instance were not electors, talking of aged spinsters, in such terms, was at least indelicate, at such a meeting . . . .

Mr. Fitzherbert next addressed the meeting.

He was sorry for the way in which Dr. Evans had been treated that evening. He had not the pleasure of an intimate acquaintance with the Doctor, but he respected his public spirit, and admired his talent, he thought there was no man in the room, he might say in the colony, better fitted to address them, or represent them. He thought the Doctor had not been fairly treated; every man had a right to be heard. He had lately found the benefit of the Doctor's benevolence, determination, and talent, when he (Mr. F.) had lately been dragged before a Police Court, and he felt assured the Doctor was in every way deserving of a fair hearing and of public confidence. He concluded by urging upon the electors to reserve their votes, to give no pledges, and to think for themselves.

Mr. Forster here moved for a vote of censure upon Dr. Evans, for his improper conduct in resisting the authority of the chair, and causing all the disturbance which had taken place, through his obstinacy. Dr. Evans ought to have left the table when he found the meeting was against him, he was no burgess by his own confession, and had no right therefore, to speak to a meeting of burgesses, against their inclination.

An amendment on Mr. Forster's resolution was then proposed, to the effect that those parties who were for censuring Dr. Evans should themselves be censured by the meeting.

The Chairman (Mr. Roots) said, in putting the resolution and amendment, that the meeting had ceased to be a meeting of burgesses when Mr. Lyon vacated the chair – it then became a public meeting, and he was inclined to be of the opinion that Dr. Evans had only been guilty of a breach of etiquette, which might be considered pardonable under all the circumstances.

Dr. Evans then appeared at the lower end of the room, and moved as an amendment to the resolution and the first amendment – that the most businesslike way of closing the meeting was by passing a resolution to the effect – that this meeting do not hold themselves pledged to vote for any particular man or any particular list, but for such men only as each individual considered worthy of confidence, and would conscientiously discharge the duties of a Councilman. It was objected by many voices, that a similar resolution had been put at a late meeting, and some pressed for the original amendment; the chairman asked Dr. Evans if he would consent, on that ground, to withdraw his amendment; Dr. Evans would not consent to do so; it was then seconded, and in being put from the chair was carried by acclamation.

A vote of thanks was passed to the chairman amid much confusion, and that functionary having thanked the meeting for the compliment, and the *attention* they had shown him during the evening, left the chair, and the meeting broke up.[1]

1 *New Zealand Colonist and Port Nicholson Advertiser*, 23 September 1842; and Arthur H. Carman, *The Birth of a City: Wellington 1840–1843*, self-published, Wellington, 1970, pp.85 ff.

APPENDIX SIX

Extract from the *Wellington Independent*, Saturday, 9 January 1864

SUPREME COURT
Adjourned Civil Sittings

STRODE v EVANS

(Before His Honor Mr. Justice Johnston, and a Special Jury)

The hearing of this case commenced on Monday last, and was not concluded until late on Wednesday evening. The great length to which the evidence extends altogether precludes our publishing the case *in extenso*, but we append a comprehensive summary of it.

The following special jury was empanelled, viz.: – W. W. Taylor, Esq., foreman; E. Miller, E. Battersbee, W. Hickson, G. Crawford, G. Hunter, C. J. Pharazyn, W. B. D. Mantell, J. Yule, W. Lyon, A. P. Stuart, and J. Kebbell, Esqrs.

Mr. Brandon and Mr. C. Allen appeared for the plaintiff and Mr. Hart for the defendant.

This case arose out of a claim preferred by the plaintiff, who was formerly a settler in Wellington, but now a resident in England, against the Union Bank of Australia, Wellington Branch, for an assignment of certain securities on landed property in Wellington, the money due thereon having been fully paid and satisfied. This the Bank declined to do, as the defendant in the present action – Dr. G. S. Evans, formerly a resident in Wellington, and recently Postmaster General of Victoria – also claimed to be entitled to them, and on an action being brought they inter-pleaded, the following issues being agreed upon between the plaintiff and defendant: –

1. Was the sum of £749 in the deed of the 29th day of May 1847, expressed to be paid by the plaintiff to the defendant, ever actually paid?
2. If not actually paid to the defendant, was it ever paid or advanced to any one for or on behalf of the defendant?
3. Was the sum of £1,251 or any part thereof; and if any part thereof, what was paid by the plaintiff to the defendant, or to Harriet Strother Evans, the wife of the defendant, or to her trustees?
4. Was the deed of the 29th day of May, 1847, executed to protect the interest of Mrs. Evans' trustees, and, incidentally to indemnify the plaintiff against any sums he might be compelled to pay by the Union Bank of Australia on account of bills by the defendant, bearing the plaintiff's indorsement, [*sic*] or for either of the said purposes?

5. Was the said deed of the 29th of May, 1847, understood by the plaintiff and the defendant to be a conveyance to the plaintiff in trust for the defendant and Mrs. Evans' trustees, but subject to the right of the plaintiff to hold the same as a security for the sum of £749 when advanced by him, and the costs of the said deed, and such sums as he might be compelled to pay to the Union Bank of Australia, on behalf of the defendant, or for any or either of the said purposes?
6. Has the plaintiff paid anything, and if anything, what, to the Union Bank of Australia on behalf of the defendant, except what he may claim to have paid by virtue of receipts by the Bank, of rent of the property, or the sale by the Bank of a portion of the property mentioned in the pleadings, the proceeds whereof have been appropriated by the Bank in satisfaction of its claims?
7. Was the deed of the 29th day of May, 1847 a family arrangement, and was it understood by all parties at the date of the execution thereof then to be for other purposes than appeared on the face of it?

The plaintiff relied upon a deed dated 29th May, 1847, whereby the property in question, then under mortgage, was assigned to the plaintiff thereto, and the incumbrances affecting it being got rid of, the plaintiff required a transfer of them to him. The defendant answered that the deed was a voluntary deed, intended to effect a different object than that which it expressed; that the plaintiff had not made any payment on his behalf; that the deed was intended to operate as a family transaction, and other pleas; and the real point in dispute was whether the deed was a *bona fide* conveyance as it purported to be, or whether there was a private understanding that it was intended to be used for other purposes, and not for the benefit of the plaintiff. Upon the questions raised upon the issues the affirmative was thrown upon the defendant.

Mr. Hart thereupon opened the case, stating that the object of the enquiry was to ascertain whether a certain deed of the 29th May, 1847, purporting to convey the defendant's (Evans's) property, in New Zealand, to the plaintiff, was intended to operate as an actual *bona fide* conveyance, or, as he contended, was merely a means employed to protect that property and not intended as an absolute sale, and in support of this conclusion he argued strongly that the inadequacy of price was sufficient to disprove the alleged contract. That the plaintiff was aware of the exact nature of the defendant's position, and of the real value of the land, and that he took the deed upon certain conditions to secure the defendant and his family and never had any real interest in the property, and had no lien or charge upon it.

The defendant, G.S. Evans, was called and examined. He entered into a detailed account of his antecedents, and described the manner in which he became connected with the N. Z. Company, having been a member of the old N. Z. Association, in which he lost some £500. A deed of amalgamation had been effected between it and a rival company, and the shares improved thereby; that he had invested £1,000 of his own, in the form of scrip, for 500 acres, and £1,000 of his wife's in the same, and the directors had awarded 500 other acres for his services under the old Company. That he borrowed through a Bank a sum of £1,750 of a Mr. Monro, before leaving England on the security of the land scrip, and agreed to execute a mortgage to Monro after selecting the land; that he arrived in New Zealand, and after selecting the land executed a mortgage in favour of Monro; that shortly after his arrival the plaintiff came out, and being qualified to act as a lawyer they entered into partnership together and were admitted, he thought, as solicitors of the Court here; he was a barrister in large practice in England, and a contributor to *The Times* and several other English newspapers; soon afterwards the plaintiff married Amelia, the daughter of Mrs. Evans, and defendant having built a house for himself in Hill-street, commenced another for the use of the daughter; after her marriage it was finished, and the plaintiff lived in it; Monro pressed for payment, and plaintiff offered to go home to make arrangements, stating that his father, Sir E. C. Chetham, had money to invest and could lend it on more reasonable terms, and defendant accepted the offer; before leaving, plaintiff presented an instrument to him for signature, binding him to convey certain property to plaintiff in lieu of settlement on the daughter, and that at the instigation of Mr. Hanson, his then solicitor, who stated that it might be some use to plaintiff in England, he signed the document; that he *gave* plaintiff £300 to go home with, considering that he was going partly on his account, and he got the money from the Union Bank on a bill accepted by the plaintiff, and upon which the defendant, who was a director or shareholder of the Bank, raised the money; plaintiff went home, effected a partial arrangement – induced his father to pay off the arrears of interest and a portion of the principal, and then returned to New Zealand.

Times had gone badly in New Zealand, and, defendant being unable to pay off Monro's mortgage, which was threatened to be foreclosed, went home to England to try to arrange matters himself; being unable otherwise to accomplish his object, he negociated [*sic*] with the New Zealand Company for the sale of the whole of his New Zealand property. He had become indebted to the Union Bank at Wellington a considerable amount, partly on his own private account, and partly on account of the partnership, and gave a mortgage to the Bank on the same property, subject to Monro's mortgage, and to the interest of Mrs. Evans in the £1,000 investment, the New Zealand Company offered the defendant to repurchase the shares at the original price of one pound per acre on town and country sections all round, and without regard to improvements, together with the interest thereon for six and a half years, making in the whole one pound six shillings and sixpence per acre; this proposal was stoutly resisted by the defendant on the ground that he had expended large sums of money in building on and improving many of the sections; though he agreed to take the price offered for the unimproved sections, he declined to take it on the improved land, and he tried hard to get the improved sections excluded from the transactions; the New Zealand Company, however, ascertained that the property was mortgaged, and applied to Sir E. Chetham Strode, who had altered his name, for particulars of his claim; Sir E. C. Strode, at the instance of the plaintiff, and to prevent Monro from selling under his mortgage at a sacrifice, purchased the remaining interest of Monro in the property, and took a transfer of the securities; the plaintiff, shortly after this arrived in England, ascertained that the defendant was, as he conceived, attempting to dispose of the property given to him, in an unfair manner, behind his back, and he interfered, and after a lengthened negociation he made a further arrangement with the Company, under which certain sections (those in gift to plaintiff) were to be excluded from the sale; the plaintiff then purchased up his father's interest in the mortgage, and the sale to the Company was carried out; out of the amount received from the Company the mortgage was paid off, and a balance of £1,251 remained in the plaintiff's hands; the defendant desired that £2,000 should be handed over to the trustees of his wife's settlement, and to raise that sum the plaintiff agreed to take a charge, or the exempted property for the advance of the deficiency, viz. £749; a deed of conveyance was accordingly executed *nominally* to pass plaintiff's interest in those lands to defendant; but as defendant asserted *actually* to make him carry out certain family arrangements, and to protect the estate, without the least intention of benefitting [*sic*] the plaintiff, and he thoroughly understood the object of the arrangement; to the deed of conveyance a memorandum was attached, signed by the plaintiff, under which he agreed to allow the defendant to repurchase the property within two years from that time on payment of £1,333 and interest, in which amount the £749 was included; defendant returned to New Zealand shortly afterwards, and plaintiff, as he was leaving, gave him an account, shewing [*sic*] how the £1,333 was made up; but defendant said he did not then examine it, and treated it and the original document and the conveyance as '*all bosh*.'

After his return to the colony he negociated with the Bank, who were in possession of the property; settled accounts with them on his own and the partnership behalf, and for disputed and other accounts, they allowed him a liberal and large deduction, and gradually by applying the improved income of the property towards the payment of this debt, were ultimately paid; that he acted under a power of attorney which plaintiff had sent after him because the Bank were aware that plaintiff claimed an interest in the property; that the plaintiff had not accounted for the £2,000 in his hands, and that he had been informed by Mr. Serrell, plaintiff's attorney in London, that he had speculated in the funds and had incurred losses; but having such implicit faith in the honor and integrity of the plaintiff he had not mentioned the matter to him; he swore stoutly to his belief that the accounts returned under the commission were fabricated and forgeries, and that the plaintiff had not paid the money to Sir E. C. Strode or any one on his behalf, and that he never advanced the £749 to make up the deficiency of the £2,000. He was cross-examined by Mr. Brandon, but adhered and added to his evidence in chief, admitting, however, that plaintiff had paid him a small sum of money as the balance of account due to his wife and the account shewed that plaintiff treated it as interest on £1,860 at 6 pounds [*sic*] percent.

Mrs. Evans was examined, and in some particulars corroborated the defendant's statement; she denied having received £153, debited to her in one of the accounts; but she admitted to have received interest at 6 per cent for ten years, from 1847 to 1857, from the plaintiff, and £100 in 1848, which was the last payment; she also admitted that, having full confidence in the plaintiff, she intrusted [*sic*] the £2,000 to him to invest according to his discretion.

Mr. J. H. Wallace was called to prove the value of the Wellington property in 1857; he considered it worth about £5,000.

Mr. George Hart was also called to confirm that valuation; and stated that when in England in 1848, he had bought adjoining property at £7 per foot frontage, knowing its value; but on cross-examination he stated that he bought a very large quantity of other land in Wellington about the same time at a very much lower rate.

The case was late in the evening adjourned to the following day.

On the re-opening of the Court Mr. Brandon stated the case for the plaintiff, relying strongly upon the written documents and deeds made by the defendant in favor of the plaintiff, and the letters which had passed between the parties, in which the plaintiff continually asserted, and the defendant never denied, his title. And he argued at considerable length on the absurdity of the defendant's contention, supported as it was only by his own verbal evidence, and contradicted by the formal deeds he had executed.

In support of his contention he called:

Mr. D. Lewis, who produced certain documents filed by the defendant relating to the property, which were read; he put in the so-called memorandum which turned out to be an agreement to give plaintiff five country sections, and the acre and house on Golder's Hill, on his foregoing his [plaintiff's] wife's claim to her reversionary interest in Mrs. Evans' settlement, also the deed of the 29th May 1847, whereby the defendant absolutely conveyed the lands excepted from the purchase by the N. Z. Company to the plaintiff, and the memorandum attached thereto, authorising the defendant to repurchase within two years for £1,333, and interest; also the power of attorney in which a similar recital occurred, and power was given to the defendant to sell certain property in Wellington (excepting however the town acre, 481), if necessary and to satisfying all the Bank claims in full, and he read a long correspondence between the parties in which the same state of facts were set up. On having finished his evidence the Court rose again and adjourned.

On the re-opening of the Court, Mr. Brandon summed up the plaintiff's case, and forcibly pointed out the difficulties the jury would encounter in taking the defendant's view as correct, and he went carefully through the evidence on both sides in detail; contrasting the different assertions of the two sides, and called upon the jury to find that the deed of the 29th May was an absolute and unimpeachable conveyance.

Mr. Hart in reply on the whole case also reviewed the various facts, and insisted upon an answer to the issues favorable to the defendant urging that there was no proof of any consideration existing between the parties to maintain the deed, and the plaintiff had made no payment on behalf of the defendant.

His Honor summed up the evidence at great length, elaborately reviewing and commenting upon the various conflicting statements, but evidently inclining towards the defendant's contention, and directed the jury to give a distinct answer upon each issue. The jury after retiring for half an hour returned, finding a verdict for the plaintiff on the second; and for the defendant on all the other issues.

NB. In his exhaustive summation and decree in March, Justice Johnson made two final points:

The first was that although Evans should be 'let in to redeem the land in question' on payment to Strode of the £749 plus interest, together with the money paid by Strode to the Bank of Australia on behalf of Evans; Evans's estate should be charged £2,000 payable to the trustees until the sum had been reimbursed by Strode 'or otherwise', as Evans had not 'exonerated himself' towards his wife's trustees. This matter, however, could not be dealt with by his Court.

The second point concerned the Memorandum of March, 1843 between Evans and Strode. It was not mentioned in the Deed of 1847, 'nor in the power of attorney given by Strode to Evans in January 1852'. As it had not been referred to in the pleadings or put as a separate issue to the jury, the Court had no power to make a decree on the matter. As the other issues had been dealt with, Strode 'must have recourse to further proceedings against [Evans] . . . and the decree in this case will be without prejudice to [Strode's] right to institute such proceedings. Decree accordingly'.[6]

Notes

1 Edward Jerningham Wakefield (ed. Sir Robert Stout), *Adventure in New Zealand, from 1839 to 1844, with Some Account of the Beginning of the British Colonization of the Islands*, Whitcombe & Tombs, Christchurch, 1908; and Arthur H. Carman, *The Birth of a City: Wellington 1840–1843*, self-published, Wellington, 1970, pp.2–4.

2 NZC, Despatches from Secretary to Principal Agent, 9, 16 and 17 September 1839, pp.101–4, NZC 102/1/1, ANZ.

3 E. J. Wakefield, *Adventure in New Zealand*, p.198.

4 *New Zealand Journal*, Vol. 1, 1840, p.220, citing *New Zealand Gazette*, 18 April 1840.

5 *New Zealand Colonist and Port Nicholson Advertiser*, 23 September 1842; and Carman, *The Birth of a City*, pp.85 ff.

6 *Wellington Independent*, 16 March 1864.

APPENDIX SEVEN

Sample Pages of G. S. Evans, The Grammar of the New Zealand Language, 1839

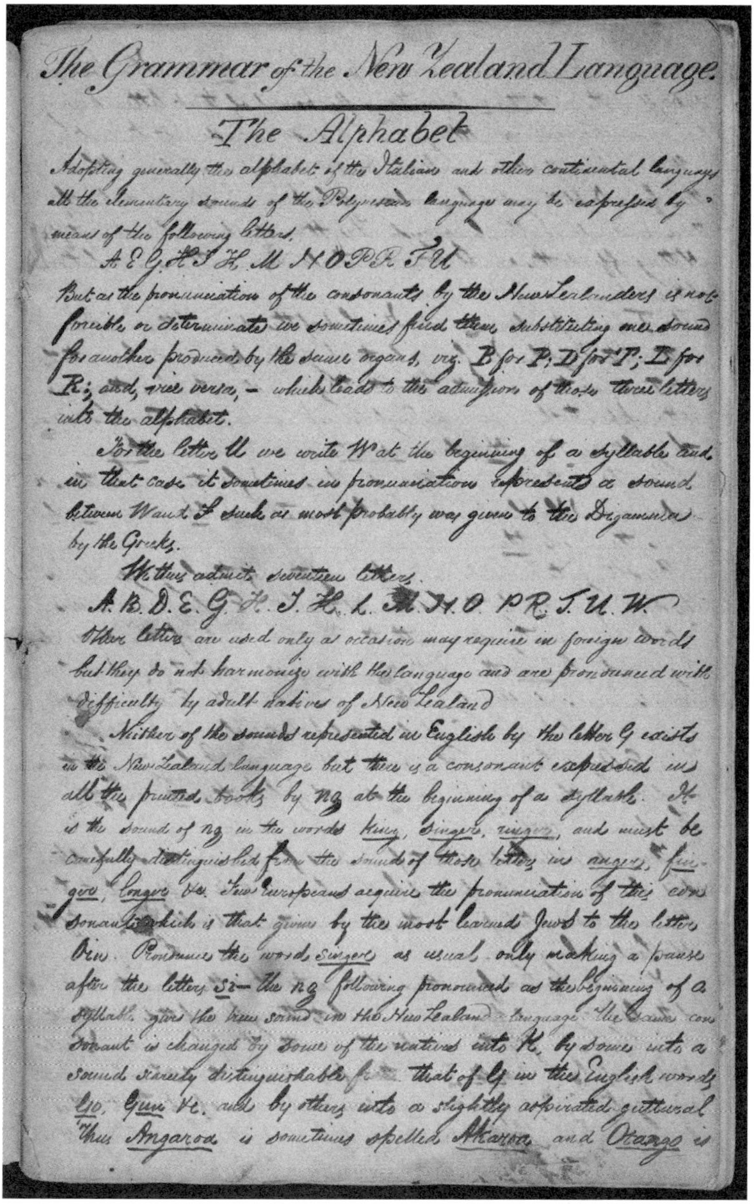
The Grammar of the New Zealand Language.

The Alphabet

Adopting generally the alphabet of the Italian and other continental languages all the elementary sounds of the Polynesian language may be expressed by means of the following letters.

A E G H I K M N O P R T U

But as the pronunciation of the consonants by the New Zealanders is not forcible or determinate we sometimes find them substituting one sound for another produced by the same organs, viz. B for P; D for T; L for R; and, vice versa, — which leads to the admission of those three letters into the alphabet.

For the letter U we write W at the beginning of a syllable and in that case it sometimes in pronunciation represents a sound between W and F such as most probably was given to the Digamma by the Greeks.

We thus admit seventeen letters.

A B D E G H I K L M N O P R T U W

Other letters are used only as occasion may require in foreign words but they do not harmonize with the language and are pronounced with difficulty by adult natives of New Zealand

Neither of the sounds represented in English by the letter G exists in the New Zealand language but there is a consonant expressed in all the printed books by ng at the beginning of a syllable. It is the sound of ng in the words king, singer, ringer, and must be carefully distinguished from the sounds of those letters in anger, finger, longer &c. Few Europeans acquire the pronunciation of this consonant which is that given by the most learned Jews to the letter Ain. Pronounce the word singer as usual only making a pause after the letters si — the ng following pronounced as the beginning of a syllable gives the true sound in the New Zealand language. The same consonant is changed by some of the natives into K, by some into a sound scarcely distinguishable from that of G in the English words Go, Gun &c. and by others into a slightly aspirated guttural. Thus Angaroa is sometimes spelled Akaroa, and Otango is

Evans compiled this dictionary, probably referring to the earlier work of Thomas Kendall, which was published in England in 1820, but also learning from his guest Hiakai, a young Maori from Banks Peninsula. Images courtesy of Alexander Turnbull Library (**qMS-0688**).

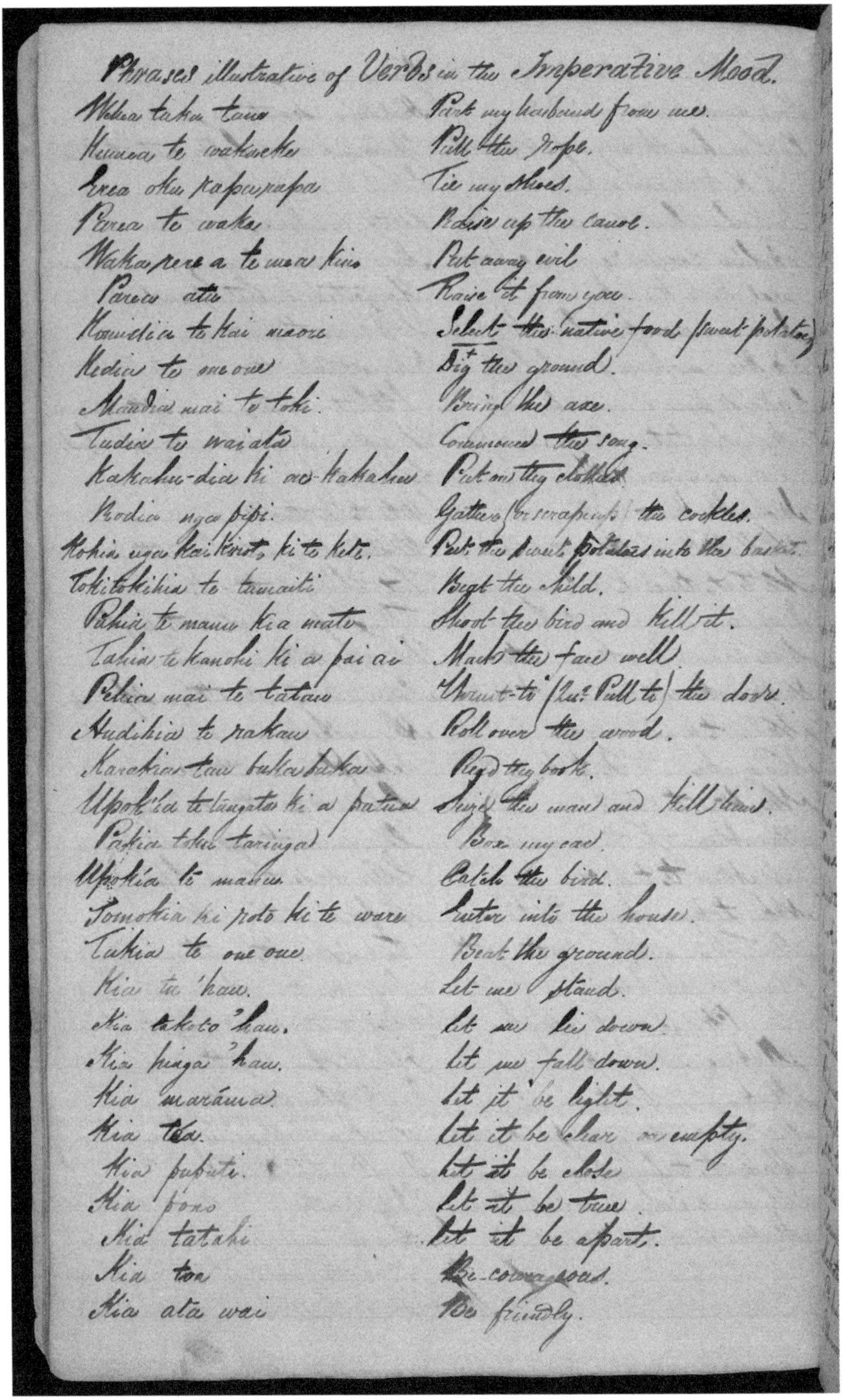

Phrases illustrative of Verbs in the Imperative Mood.

Wehea tahu tane	Part my husband from me.
Hunea te wakaweke	Pull the rope.
Erea oku kapurapa	Tie my shoes.
Perea te waka	Raise up the canoe.
Waka rere a te mea kino	Put away evil
Parea atu	Raise it from you.
Kowhiria te kai maori	Select the native food (sweet potatoes)
Keria te oneone	Dig the ground.
Mauria mai te toki.	Bring the axe.
Tuaia te waiata	Commence the song.
Kakahu-dia ki ou kakahu	Put on thy clothes
Kodia nga pipi.	Gather (or scrape up) the cockles.
Kohia nga Kaikiria ki te kete.	Put the sweet potatoes into the basket.
Tokitokihia te tamaiti	Beat the child.
Pakia te manu kia mate	Shoot the bird and kill it.
Tahia te kanohi ki a pai ai	Mark the face well
Pehia mai te tatau	Thrust-to (lit. Pull to) the door.
Hurihia te rakau	Roll over the wood.
Karakia tau bukabuka	Read thy book.
Upokia te tangata ki a patua	Seize the man and kill him.
Pakia toku taringa	Box my ear.
Upokia te manu	Catch the bird.
Tomokia ki roto ki te ware	Enter into the house.
Takia te one one.	Beat the ground.
Kia tu 'hau.	Let me stand.
Kia takoto 'hau.	Let me lie down.
Kia hinga 'hau.	Let me fall down.
Kia marama.	Let it be light.
Kia tea.	Let it be clear or empty.
Kia pubuti.	Let it be close
Kia pono	Let it be true.
Kia tatahi	Let it be apart.
Kia toa	Be courageous.
Kia ata wai	Be friendly.

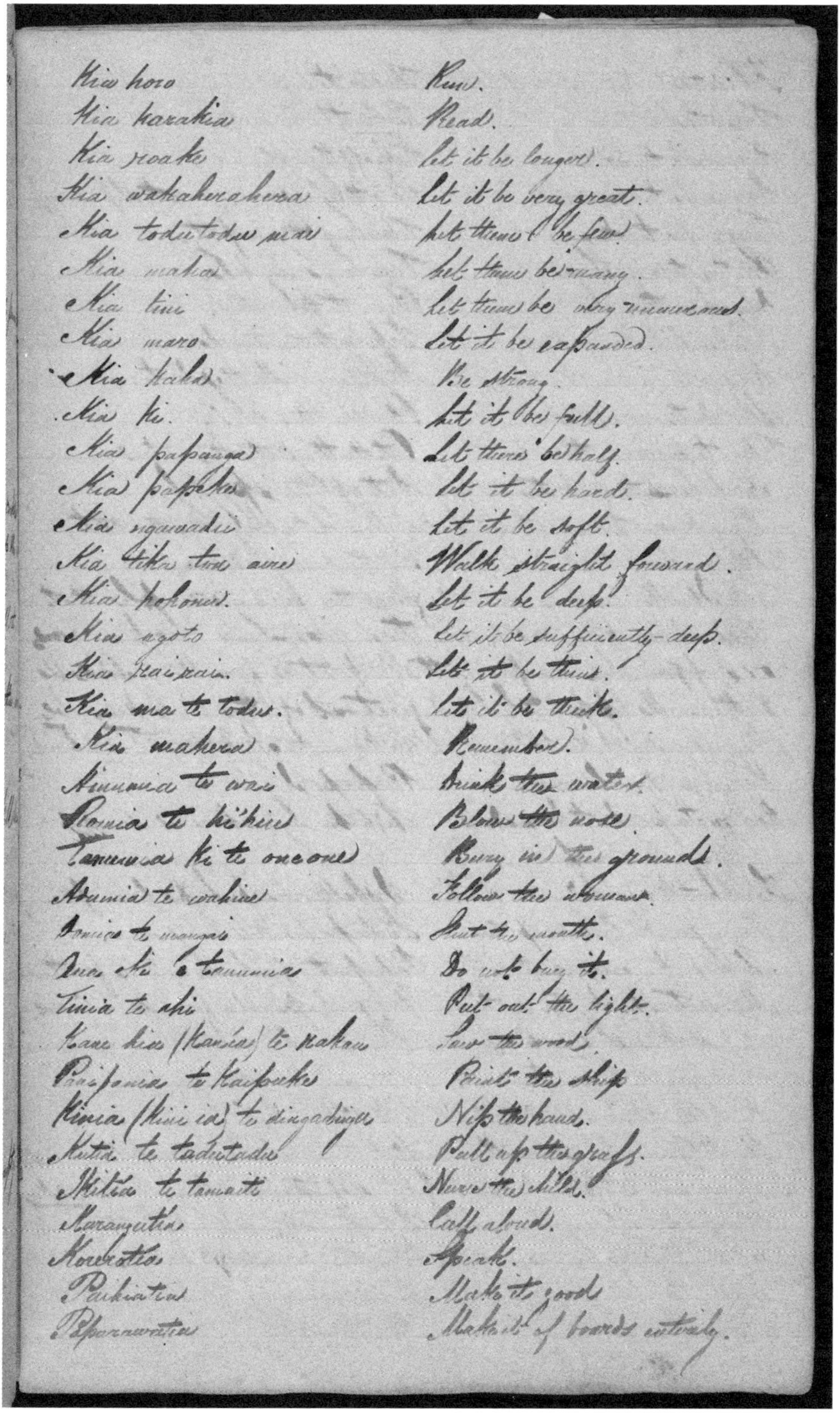

Kia horo	Run.
Kia karakia	Read.
Kia roa ake	let it be longer.
Kia wakahirahira	let it be very great.
Kia todutodu [illegible]	let there be few.
Kia maha	let there be many.
Kia tini	let there be very numerous.
Kia maro	let it be expanded.
Kia kaha	Be strong.
Kia ki.	let it be full.
Kia papanga	Let there be half.
Kia pakeke	let it be hard.
Kia ngawadi	let it be soft.
Kia tika tou aire	Walk straight forward.
Kia hohonu.	Let it be deep.
Kia ngoto	let it be sufficiently deep.
Kia rairai.	let it be thin.
Kia ma te todu.	let it be thick.
Kia mahara	Remember.
Ainumia te wai	Drink the water.
Hongia te ki'hu	Blow the nose.
Tanumia ki te oneone	Bury in the grounds.
Arumia te wahine	Follow the woman.
Kopia te mangai	Shut the mouth.
Aua e te tanumia	Do not bury it.
Tinia te ahi	Put out the light.
Kani kia (Kania) te rakau	Saw the wood.
Paipania te kaipuke	Paint the ship
Kinia (Kini ia) te ringaringa	Nip the hand.
Hutia te taditadi	Pull up the grass.
Hikitia te tamaiti	Nurse the child.
Karangatia	Call aloud.
Korerotia	Speak.
Paikiatia	Make it good
Paparawatia	Make it of boards entirely.

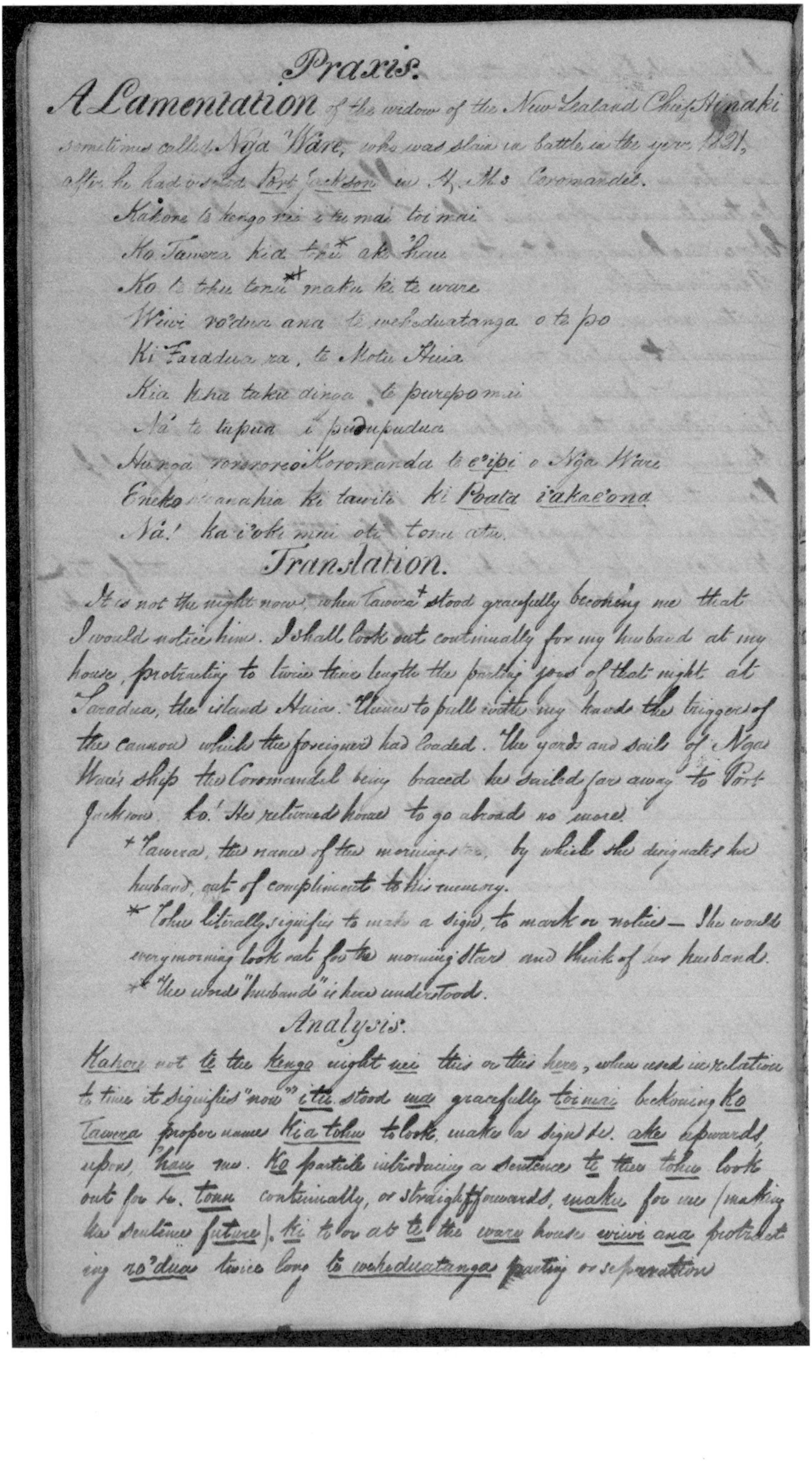

Praxis:

A Lamentation of the widow of the New Zealand Chief Hinaki sometimes called Nga Ware, who was slain in battle in the year 1821, after he had visited Port Jackson in H. M.s Coromandel.

Kahore te kengo nei i tu mai toi mai
Ko Tawera kia tohu* ake hau
Ko te tohu tonu*+ maku ki te ware
Wiwi ro'dua ana te wehedua tanga o te po
Ki Faradua ra, te Motu Huia
Kia kite taku dinga te purepo mai
Na te tupua i pudupudua
Hunga rorrore Koromanda te e'ipi o Nga Ware
Eneko wanahia ki tawite ki Poata i akaeona
Na! ka i'oki mai ote tonu atu.

Translation.

It is not the night now, when Tawera+ stood gracefully beckoning me that I would notice him. I shall look out continually for my husband at my house, protracting to twice time length the parting joys of that night at Faradua, the island Huia. Unwo to pull with my hands the triggers of the cannon which the foreigners had loaded. The yards and sails of Nga Ware's ship the Coromandel being braced he sailed far away to Port Jackson. Lo! He returned home to go abroad no more.

+ Tawera, the name of the morning star, by which she designates her husband, out of compliment to his memory.

* Tohu literally signifies to make a sign, to mark or notice — She would every morning look out for the morning star and think of her husband.

*+ The words "husband" is here understood.

Analysis.

Kahore not te the kengo night nei this or this here, when used in relation to time it signifies "now" i tu stood mai gracefully toi mai beckoning Ko Tawera proper name Kia tohu to look, make a sign &c. ake upwards, upon, hau me. Ko particle introducing a sentence te the tohu look out for &c. tonu continually, or straightforwards, maku for me (making the sentence future). Ki to or at te the ware house wiwi ana protracting ro'dua twice long te wehedua tanga parting or separation

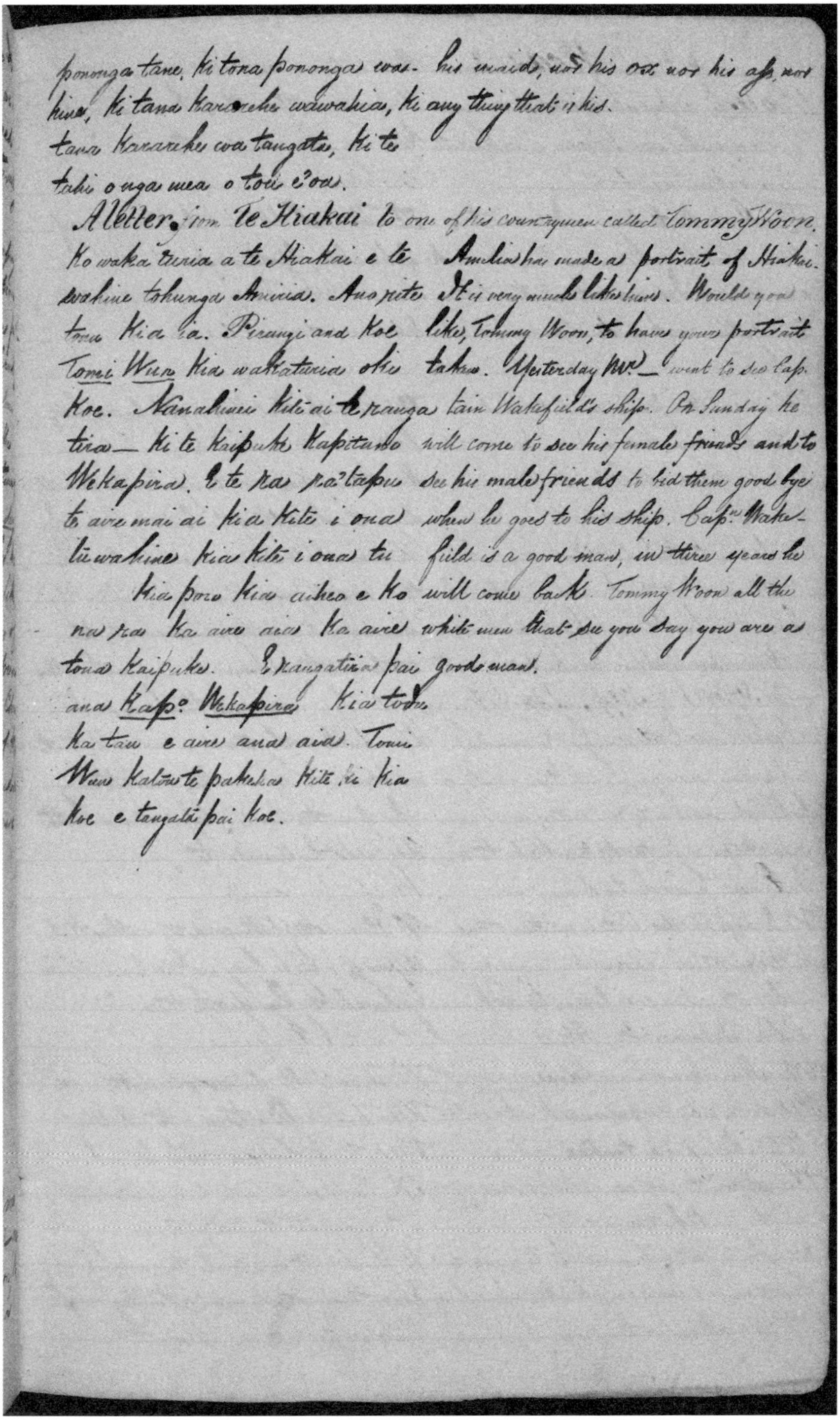

ponongo tane, ki tona pononga wa- his maids, nor his ox, nor his ass, nor
hine, ki tana kararehe wawahia, ki any thing that is his.
tana kararehe wa tangata, ki te
tahi o nga mea o tou e'oa.

A letter from Te Hiakai to one of his countrymen called Tommy Woon.
Ko waka tenia a te Hiakai e te Amelia has made a portrait of Hiakai.
wahine tohunga Amiria. Ano rite It is very much like him. Would you
tonu kia ia. Pirangi ana koe like, Tommy Woon, to have your portrait
Tomi Wun kia wakatuia oku taken. Yesterday Mr. — went to see Capt.
koe. Nanahinei kite ai te ranga tain Wakefield's ship. On Sunday he
tira — ki te kaipuke Kapitano will come to see his female friends and to
Wekapira. E te ra ra'tapu see his male friends to bid them good bye
te aire mai ai kia kite i ona when he goes to his ship. Captn. Wake-
te wahine kia kite i ona ta field is a good man, in three years he
kia poro kia aiheo e ko will come back. Tommy Woon all the
no ra ka aire aia ka aire white men that see you say you are a
tona kaipuke. E rangatira pai good man.
ana Kapo. Wekapira Kia toru
ka tau e aire ana aia. Tomi
Wun katoa te pakeha kite ki kia
koe e tangata pai koe.

NOTES

Preface

1 J. J. Taine (ed. H. W. Fildes), *Reminiscences*, Vol. 1, p.222, qMS-1974, ATL.
2 Paul Johnson, 'And Another Thing', *The Spectator*, 8 November 1997, p.28
3 Editorial by G. S. Evans, 'The Journalist and the Jobber', *Melbourne Morning Herald*, 30 June 1856.
4 Introductory remarks to Correspondence and Documents of the New Zealand Company, 1836–1887, C184, ML, also held as MS-Micro-460, ATL.
5 Ibid., C184, ML, and Micro-MS-460 ATL.

Prologue

1 Now spelt Petone.
2 Thomas Wilmor McKenzie, McKenzie Family Papers, Folder 1, p.26, MS-Papers-1357, ATL. This account is also based on J. J. Taine (ed. H. W. Fildes), *Reminiscences*, Vol. 1, pp.89–92, qMS-1974, ATL.
3 McKenzie Family Papers, ibid. The volunteers were 'captained' by William Luxford, a steerage passenger aged thirty-nine, a butcher, farmer and father of six. It took one mile of hard rowing, with the boat nearly capsizing more than once.
4 'Dr. Evans, one of the earliest members of the Association of 1837, burst into the tent, soaked through, but apparently wild with excitement etc.': Edward Jerningham Wakefield (ed. Sir Robert Stout), *Adventure in New Zealand, from 1839 to 1844, with Some Account of the Beginning of the British Colonization of the Islands*, Whitcombe & Tombs, Christchurch, 1908, p.157. Taine, *Reminiscences*, p.92, added, '. . . he was warmly greeted by all present'.
5 King George III was believed to have been suffering from porphyria, but lately another view leans towards a diagnosis of manic depression degenerating into Alzheimers.
6 G. S. Evans, Grammar of the New Zealand Language, 1839, qMS-0688, ATL.
7 E. J. Wakefield to his father, E. G. Wakefield, 8 March 1840, *New Zealand Journal*, Vol. 2, p.204; and Taine, *Reminiscences*, Vol. 1, p.122, ibid.
8 The colonising associations and companies formed between 1825 and 1839 are as follows:
1825 New Zealand Company: members were John George Lambton (Lord Durham), Colonel Torrens, Edward Ellice, J. W. Buckle, Stewart Marjoribanks and George Lyall (referred to as the 1825 Company);
1837 New Zealand Association, formed by E. G. Wakefield in May and later including some members of the 1825 Company (the Association);
1838 New Zealand Colonization Company, formed by Evans in August and with fourteen other members of the 1837 Association (the Colonization Company);
1839 New Zealand Land Company, later shortened to New Zealand Company, was formed in May after its board of directors, which included Wakefield, was elected (the Company).
9 *Evening Post*, 23 September 1868; *Wellington Independent*, 24 September 1868; and Isaac Featherston, by letter published in *Wellington Independent*, 25 September 1858. See also '[Evans] was the founder of Wellington, just as Fawkner was the originator of Melbourne': J. L. Forde, *The Story of the Bar of Victoria*, Whitcombe & Tombs, Melbourne, 1913, p.162.

10 Susan Butterworth, *Petone: A History*, Petone Borough Council, Petone, 1988, p.39.

11 'I enclose a letter from Mrs. Riddiford about Captain Humphrey, who is engaged to her daughter Mary. I can't conscientiously press his claims as I always thought we had too many Colonels and Adjutants, and if I were in this Government could not but concur in the reductions. Nevertheless if anything else should turn up, he might have your sympathy on the young lady's account, as the relative of old Dr. Evans, one of our earliest Colonists, and perhaps the most influential originator of New Zealand Colonization we ever had': William Fox to Donald McLean, 21 November 1872, Sir Donald McLean, Papers, 1839–1877, Vol. 39, p.265, MS-1349, ATL. Four-time premier Fox had surrendered his third premiership to Stafford that year.

Chapter One

1 '<u>George Samuel</u>, Son of George and Hannah Evans. Born June the 3, 1802, in the Parish of St. Mary, Glocester [*sic*] and baptized August 8, 1802 in the City of Bath at Lady Huntingtons [*sic*] Chapel – By me Geo. Evans'. Certificate written and signed by Rev. George Evans: Permezel Collection. Other sources give his birthplace as Streatley, Berkshire, and the year 1800 (*Melbourne Leader*, No. 327, 5 April 1862, is correct with St Mary, Gloucester.)

2 G. S. Evans wrote his family tree on the back of a paper napkin in Melbourne c. 1863. He wrote 'Furze (or Furst)'. The Cadbury Crop that was said to be 'good for man and horse' might have been a crop of oats or other grain: *Ilford: 175 Years of History*, Permezel Collection.

3 Mary Carpenter (1749–1833) was the daughter of Thomas Carpenter (1719–99). She married George Evans (1744–1821).

4 Selina, the Countess of Huntingdon of Walcott Vineyard, Bath (1707–91), was a deeply religious evangelist, mocked by her own class and spurned by serious-minded people of the 'Blue-Stocking' set. She spent £100,000 on works of charity and founded sixty-four chapels: John Timbs, *Curiosities of London*, Virtue, London, 1868, p.222. See also Muriel Jaeger, *Before Victoria: Changing Standards and Behaviour 1787–1837*, Chatto & Windus, London, 1956, p.5; and Roy Porter, *London: A Social History*, Penguin, London, 2000, p.201.

5 David Thomson, *England in the Nineteenth Century: 1815–1914*, Penguin, London, 1986, pp.59–60, citing Sydney Smith, *Letters of Peter Plymley*, 1807.

6 Douglas Pike, *Paradise of Dissent: South Australia 1829–1857*, Longmans Green, London, Melbourne and New York, 1957, p.13, citing S. R. Carpenter, *Church and People: 1789–1889*, London, 1933, pp.54–100. See ibid., pp.12–21 for a history of 'church reform'.

7 Pike, *Paradise of Dissent*, p.13; Paul Johnson, *The Offshore Islanders: A History of the English People*, Weidenfeld & Nicholson, London, 1972, pp.303–4. Bridgewater lived in Paris from 1780 to 1829.

8 For example, see Jenny Uglow, *The Lunar Men: The Friends Who Made the Future, 1730–1810*, Faber & Faber, London, 2003. Also note Wilberforce, and those who supported him in reform. Any British history of the eighteenth and nineteenth centuries is filled with such men.

9 Obituary of Reverend Evans, *Congregational Year Book*, Vol. 1, 1846, p.176, Permezel Collection. Reverend Evans at the time of his death held the record for delivering more sermons than any other minister in England. For more information on ministerial posts, see Surman's Index, Dr Williams' Library, *Survey of London*, Vol. XXVII, online, http://www.english.qmul.ac.uk/drwilliams/surman/intro.html.

10 Porter, *London: A Social History*, pp.158–9; Ben Weinreb and Christopher Hibbert (eds), *The London Encyclopaedia*, Macmillan, London, 1983, p.808.

11 Red Lion Street is now Commercial Road: Weinreb and Hibbert (eds), *London Encyclopaedia*, p.88. The Black Eagle was owned by Sampson Hanbury, who was joined

in partnership by the great reformer and evangelist Thomas Buxton in 1808.

12 'Filth and grime added to the stench of slaughterhouses in Aldgate, sugar-making in Shadwell, lime-turning in Limehouse, and the breweries of Spitalfields and Mile End': Andrew Davies, *The East End Nobody Knows*, Macmillan, London, 1990, p.4. These industries were famously known as 'the stink industries': see Peter Ackroyd, *London: The Biography*, Chatto & Windus, London, 2000, pp.676–7.

13 Timbs, *Curiosities of London*, p.716.

14 Porter, *London: A Social History*, pp.158–9. Petticoat Lane is the modern spelling. Spelled 'Peticote' in the early nineteenth century, it was renamed Middlesex Street in 1830: Weinreb and Hibbert (eds), *The London Encyclopaedia*, p.594.

15 'It took 600 movements to produce a single inch of velvet, including the full weight of the weaver's chest pushing on a heavy beam 60 times. The shuttle has to be thrown 180 times, 180 times the treadles have to be worked, 60 times the wire has to be inserted, 60 times to be withdrawn, 60 times the knife has to be guided along the whole breadth of the work, and 60 times the pressure of the chest has to be exerted on a heavy beam': Reverend Isaac Taylor (St Matthias), 1867, cited in Timbs, *Curiosities of London*, p.744.

16 Porter, *London: A Social History*, p.371, citing William Cotton's first-hand account. Cotton was a 'Limehouse rope and sail-maker and director (later Governor) of the Bank of England' who assisted Bishop Blomfield, the Bishop of London, by raising funds to build ten churches in Bethnal Green from 1839 to 1850: Jerry White, *London in the Nineteenth Century: 'A Human Awful Wonder of God'*, Jonathan Cape, London, 2007, p.428.

17 This may have been the chapel on the corner of Church (Fournier) Street and Brick Lane. 'The Wesleyans (Methodists) purchased the former Huguenot chapel in 1809', but by 1897 its congregation had 'dwindled away to nothing'; it was sold to a Jewish Immigration Society and became a synagogue in that year (and more recently a mosque): Alan Palmer, *The East End: Four Centuries of London Life*, John Murray, London, rev. edn, 2000, p.78.

18 Church Street around the corner from Red Lion Square culminated in Brick Lane, on the other side of which were several small fields; further east, Church Street began again. High Street was parallel with Brick Lane on the other side of the fields.

19 Palmer, *The East End*, p.24.

20 Reverend Evans wrote, with his characteristic mingling of affection and moral strictures (to Hannah, aged nine):

'I am sometimes annoyed by the noise which you and your romping sisters make . . . . I hope you get the Bible every morning and read a chapter and that your <u>dear Mother prays with you all</u> and that you don't forget to pray for yourself. You must also pray for me that I may be brought home safe again . . . . I don't know what I must bring you home. This is the toy shop of Europe. You will present my best love to Mother, my Duty to Grandmother and Grandfather – love to my dear Mary Claudia, to Uncle and Aunt Cook and Hannah and Jane and . . . and all our good friends. God bless you my dear daughter and give you Grace and make you a Blessing to your parents, and prepare us all for the Kingdom of Heaven You must give Claudia plenty of kisses for me.'

(and to Mary, aged seven):

'. . . you must take Hannah with you and visit the old ladies in the Alms Houses, remember me to them . . . and that they must all pray for me that I may be soon home safe. I went to see a Minister yesterday whose wife died and left him with eight little children. The oldest is Mother about fourteen years old. They are all such good sweet children, they behaved so well, made such nice bows, and curtsies, laid the cloth for a lunch, seemed so loving to one another when I came away said good morning Sir, and were so pleased with my little poney [*sic*]. I suppose you would have laughed to see me riding a poney, not much bigger than a donkey, but he carried me quite well. But those dear children have no mother to . . . pray with them. How thankful you ought to be my dear Mary that you have. You must tell [?] that your brothers are all such fine fellows with their Greek and Latin that they will be ashamed of their sisters if they don't mind and attend to their learning. You must get Mother to write an answer to these letters for you and you must write your name to it. You must give your dear Mother plenty of kisses till I come home then I will pray with you all. I think I have written you a long letter. God bless you my dear girl and make you a Good Girl. Your loving father Geo. Evans': Reverend G. Evans to his daughters Hannah and Mary, from Birmingham, 20 and 21 November 1824, Permezel Collection.

21 R. J. Cruikshank, *Charles Dickens and Early Victorian England*, Pitman & Sons, London, 1949, p.205.

22 G. S. Evans in Victorian Legislative Assembly, 24 November 1857, *Victorian Hansard*, Vol. 2, SLV. Evans was speaking on state aid to Catholic and other religious schools, and referring to the British civil wars of 1642–51.

23 See G. M. Trevelyan, *English Social History*, Longmans, London, rev. edn, 1986, p.508.

24 Porter, *London: A Social History*, p.200. In 1812 an Act 'designed to give relief to Nonconformity, virtually repealed the old repressive Conventicle and Five-Mile Acts': Paul Johnson, *The Birth of the Modern: World Society 1815–1830*, Phoenix, London, 1996, pp.383 ff.

25 G. S. Evans, Editorial, Christmas Day, *Melbourne Morning Herald*, 25 December 1857.

26 Timbs, *Curiosities of London*, p.722.

27 'The fee was £1–£2 p.a. and breaking up money at Easter, 12/-': F. W. M. Draper, *Four Centuries of Merchant Taylors' School*, Oxford University Press, London, 1962, p.116.

28 Millicent Rose, *The East End of London*, Cresset Press, London, 1951, p.37.

29 Draper, *Four Centuries of Merchant Taylors' School*, pp.133–4.

30 Mathews, the future great actor and comedian, described bitterly the harsh treatment he had endured from the headmaster: Charles Dickens Jnr (ed.), *The Life of Charles James Mathews, Chiefly Autobiographical with Selections from His Correspondence and Speeches*, 2 Vols, Macmillan, London, 1879.

31 The library contained 'a fair collection of Hebrew and other Oriental works of reference . . . nearly all the standard classical and other lexicons; and the best writers in English Theology': Timbs, *Curiosities of London*, p.522.

32 Draper, *Four Centuries*, pp.118, 121. Negus was a hot drink of port, sugar, lemon and spice. Young Charles Mathews wrote: 'I ate, viz. a bit of fowl, a pear, an apple, half a jelly, a roll, five glasses of negus, half a tumbler of ale, and three cups of coffee and a glass of water': Dickens, *Life of Charles James Mathews*, Vol. 1, p.17.

33 Porter, *London: A Social History*, p.208. He adds: 'It was the last [Frost Fair]. Once old London Bridge was demolished in 1831 the improved flow of the river prevented it freezing over.' See also Evans's reference to 'skating' in his Christmas Day editorial, *Melbourne Morning Herald*, 25 December 1857.

34 Ackroyd, *London: The Biography*, p.344.

35 *Victorian Hansard*, Vol. 2, 24 April 1857, SLV. For a description of the ceremony, see also *Parliamentary Biographies*, 'George Samuel Evans: Chapter Two', in *Melbourne Punch*, Vol. IX, 8 December 1859, p.158. In 1807 there were forty-five dissenters in one House of Parliament and sixteen in another: see Thomson, *England in the Nineteenth Century*, p.59.

36 Timbs, *Curiosities of London*, p.723. 'He [Evans] is shown as attending this school from 1813–1815, when the headmaster was Thomas Cherry . . . . Other details simply do not exist . . . there are discrepancies and gaps to explain': J. G. Brown, Merchant Taylors' School Archivist, by email, 17 February 2000.

37 *Melbourne Leader*, No. 327, 5 April 1862.

38 Jaeger, *Before Victoria*, pp.73 and 179. For this attack in the *Examiner*, 1812, Hunt was thrown into prison for two years for seditious libel, and became a national hero.

39 In Hoxton Square. The school had been originally supported by Coward's Trustees but had closed down in 1785. Thomas Wilson, a wealthy evangelical, acquired the school later. It lay at the eastern end of Old Street, north of Liverpool Street Station in Hackney, east of the city proper: Dr J. Thompson, Historian, Coward Trust, London, to author by letter, 10 January 2001.

40 In 1828, Wymondley moved to London and became Coward College.
41 Jaeger, *Before Victoria*, pp.177–80.
42 The Williams Dissenting Library contained, among other things, 'Manuscripts of the early history of the Reformation, and rare and illuminated books of religion, and royal ceremony; copies of details from rare Vatican paintings, the Baptismal font of the Princess, soon to be Queen Elizabeth, and portraits of Dissenting ministers': Timbs, *Curiosities of London*, p.526.
43 *Victorian Hansard*, Vol. 6, 4 July 1860, SLV. This revelation produced 'laughter', and led into his famous 'Queen Anne' speech.
44 Alexis de Tocqueville (ed. J. P. Mayer), *Journeys to England and Ireland*, G. Lawrence and K. P. Mayer (translators), Faber & Faber, London, 1958, pp.60 ff.
45 Glasgow College's famous alumni included James Watt and Adam Smith.
46 See Maurice Lindsay, *Portrait of Glasgow*, Robert Hale, London, 1972, p.51; J. Marwick, *The Water Supply of Glasgow*, 1910, cited in Andrew Gibb, *Glasgow: The Making of a City*, Croom Helm, London, 1983, p.104. Ten years after George had first attended Glasgow, a report into the situation revealed that of the thirty wells catering for the needs of a population of over 200,000, only fourteen were in good order.
47 Ref. no. F-81505-1/2-, ATL (see cover photograph).
48 Reverend G. Evans to his daughters, Hannah (aged nine) and Mary, 20 and 21 November 1824, Permezel Collection.
49 *Glasgow University Calendar for the Session, 1826–27.*
50 G. S. Evans, Testimonials, in Evans Papers, MS-Papers-10552, ATL.
51 *Glasgow University Calendar for the Session 1826–27.* See also W. Innes Addison, *Prize Lists of the University of Glasgow*, University of Glasgow, Glasgow, 1902, pp.260–2; W. Innes Addison, *Roll of Graduates of the University of Glasgow from 1727–1897*, University of Glasgow, Glasgow, 1898, p.181; and J. M. Reid, *Glasgow*, Batsford, London, 1956, pp.147–8.
52 Testimonials of Professor Sandford, 24 May 1827, 8 May 1828; and T. Campbell, 23 May 1827, Evans Papers, ibid.
53 L. Stephen and S. Lee (eds), *Dictionary of National Biography*, Oxford University Press, London, 1917, Vol. II, pp.1364.
54 Robert Stewart, *Henry Brougham: His Public Career 1778–1868*, Bodley Head, London, 1986, p.184. Brougham had already given an example by supporting the work of others in such organisations as the Mechanics' Institute and the Society for the Diffusion of Useful Knowledge.
55 Stephen and Lee (eds), *Dictionary of National Biography*, Vol. III, pp.844–8.
56 The other supporters were James Mill, Joseph Hume, the Radical MP Francis Horner, and the Dissenters' Provisional Committee. It is now known as University College London. The Lords' rejection meant that the university would be unable to grant degrees. But Somerset House was instituted on 28 November 1826 for 'rendering academical honours accessible, without distinction, to every class and every denomination'. See also Timbs, *Curiosities of London*, p.810.
57 Who noted his 'diligence, quickness of apprehension and enthusiastic ardour': Evans Papers, ibid.
58 The site was near the corner of Mile End Road and Cow Lane, according to John Permezel, G. S. Evans's great-great nephew: *Congregational Year Book*, Vol. 1, 15 September 1846, p.176, Permezel Collection. It was razed to the ground in the Blitz of the Second World War, but the almshouses survived.
59 'The notice of Evans's appointment to the church in White-row, Spitalfields' appeared in the *Evangelical Magazine and Missionary Chronicle*, April 1827, p.157. His duties were to begin 'on the first Sabbath in May', but his name does not appear in 'the *Survey of London*'s account of the chapel': Dr John Thompson, Historian, Coward Trust, London, letter to author, 10 January 2001.
60 Several of the testimonials were written in May 1827, and others, including that of Charles Mayo, were written in May 1828.

61 Henry Brougham to the House of Commons, 29 January 1828, Hansard, 2nd Series 28, pp.57–58, cited in Stewart, *Henry Brougham*, p.183.

Chapter Two

1 The committees covered printing, school or education, appointments, visiting and house. The problems lasted well into the next century. See Roderick Braithwaite, *Strikingly Alive: The History of the Mill Hill School Foundation 1807–2007*, Phillimore, London, 2006.

2 March arrived 12 January 1826 and catered for the parish as well as the school, as there was just one chapel for worship. Wilberforce built another that still stands. See N. G. Brett-James, *The History of Mill Hill School, 1807–1907*, Mill Hill School, London, 1909, pp.79 ff. This part of *The History* relies heavily on March's diary entries for this period.

3 March disapproved of Bedingfield, the third classical master, castigating his 'continual utterance of ungrammatical sentences'. He 'seemed to make a good beginning of [his] acquaintance with Mrs. Riddiford the Matron', but it was not long before he changed his mind about her: Brett-James, *The History of Mill Hill School*, Chapter V, 'The Chaplain's Diary', pp.78–99.

4 In fact Evans was twenty-five: ibid., pp.93–95.

5 G. S. Evans, Testimonials, in Evans Papers, MS-Papers-10552, ATL.

6 The monitorial system had been invented by Joseph Lancaster in the early years of the century. One schoolmaster could run a school of many hundred pupils by the relaying of information. First he taught the older children, and the brighter of these passed the lessons to the junior children in groups. The method was adopted for a time at schools such as Charterhouse, although it was more usual in schools run by the British and Foreign School Society – dissenting schools such as Mill Hill. Methods used were copying from charts, chanting and the invariably rough discipline associated with the practice.

7 David Thomson, *England in the Nineteenth Century: 1815–1914*, Penguin, London, 1986, p.60. Over 500 anti-Catholic petitions had been organised, and Wellington fought a duel with the arch-conservative Lord Winchilsea over the Bill. The Bill was supported by the dissenters' pressure group made up of Congregationalists, Baptists and Unitarians.

8 Asa Briggs, *The Age of Improvement*, Longmans Green & Co., London, 1969, p.230. 'It was only in conjunction with the Municipal Corporations Act of 1835 and the second Reform Bill of 1867, that the repeal of the Test Act effected the full political emancipation of non-conformists': G. M. Trevelyan, *History of England*, Longmans, London, 1926, reprinted 1960, p.631.

9 Frederick Helmore, *Memoir of the Rev. Thomas Helmore, M.A.*, Masters, London, 1891, pp.10 ff.

10 Evans was headmaster of and taught at Mill Hill School from 29 January 1828 until 24 June 1828, a period of only five months. There was no headmaster until January the following year when R. Cullen took up the reins. Mill Hill School historian Roderick Braithwaite, to author, 3 December 1999, by post. (My words.)

11 Brett-James, *History of Mill Hill School*, p.98; Helmore, Memoir, pp.10–11. March said Evans became intemperate, but Helmore's version had the class burst in before he could speak.

12 Evans Papers, ibid. The introductory note to the Testimonials reads: 'Mr. Evans has the authority of several Members of Council to state that, from a numerous list of candidates, the selection was finally determined between himself and the Professor who has been appointed.' But *Melbourne Leader*, Vol. 10, No. 327, 5 April 1862, says: 'the appointment . . . was placed at his command. He was however induced [by] his friends to decline, as it was determined he should pursue his legal studies at Lincoln's Inn.'

Long taught at London University until 1831, and from 1842 to 1846 he was Professor of Latin in the same university: L. Stephen and S. Lee (eds), *Dictionary of National Biography*, Oxford University Press, London, 1917–1938, Vol. XII, pp.102–3.

13 G. M. Young (ed.), *Early Victorian England*, Oxford University Press, London, 1934, Vol. 2, p.495.

14 *Morning Chronicle*, 23 July 1829; *The Times*, 24 July 1829.

15 Mary C. Borer, *London Walks and Legends*, Academy Publishers, Chicago, 1982, p.98.

16 Helmore, *Memoir*, pp.11 ff. Thomas Helmore was ordained and went on to become a Priest in Ordinary to the Queen, and a Master of the Children of Her Majesty's Chapel Royal, where he immediately abolished the practice of fagging: p.53. He was a distinguished teacher and a gifted musician, translating many ancient psalms and hymns, and setting them to music. He taught Arthur Sullivan of Gilbert and Sullivan fame. The Mill Hill School Helmore Music Bursary was named after him.

17 See Hugh Monro's review in *Literary Review*, January 1998, of Jeremy Potter, *Headmaster: The Life of John Percival, Radical Autocrat*, Constable, London, 1998.

18 'Prospectus of the Private Grammar School at North-end House, Hampstead conducted by George Samuel Evans LLD' (1831), Permezel Collection.

19 The fee for boarders was fifty guineas a year for boys under ten and seventy for those aged ten to sixteen. (By comparison, Merchant Taylors' had charged £40 per year for boarders sixteen years earlier.)

20 'Report of the First Half-Yearly Examination, conducted by Thomas Campbell, esq. Late Lord Rector of the University of Glasgow; extracted from the *New Monthly Magazine* for January 1830': in 'Prospectus of the Course of Education pursued under Mr. George Samuel Evans, A. M. at North-End House, Hampstead, MDCCCXXX', p.19: Permezel Collection.

21 The Literary Club was founded in 1764 by Dr Samuel Johnson and Sir Joshua Reynolds, with a restricted membership of forty. Other members included Lords Aberdeen, Carlisle and Glenelg, and William Wilberforce.

22 Stephen and Lee (eds), *Dictionary of National Biography*, Vol. II, p.569.

23 The friend was Mrs Dugald Stewart: W. Beattie (ed.), *Life and Letters of Thomas Campbell*, Hall Virtue & Co., London, 1850, Vol. 1, p.248.

24 Charles Buller, 1806–1848: Stephen and Lee (eds), *Dictionary of National Biography*, Vol. III, p.247.

25 Dickens also wrote for Black, beginning as a political reporter in 1834 and contributing articles later included in his *Sketches by Boz*. Evans might have met Dickens, who harboured a decided aversion to dissenters: see Peter Ackroyd, *Dickens*, Random House, London, Vintage edn, 1999, p.532.

26 '[Evans] was . . . a contributor to *The Times* and other English newspapers': Evans's evidence in Strode vs. Evans, Supreme Court Wellington: *Wellington Independent*, 9 January 1864, Appendix 8.

27 E. Halevy, *A History of the English People in the Nineteenth Century*, Vol. 1: *England in 1815*, Benn, London, 2nd edn, 1949–51, pp.422–3.

28 Briggs, *The Age of Improvement*, pp.241–3.

29 Dr G. S. Evans to Parliament, *Victorian Hansard*, Vol. 3, 11 February 1858, SLV.

30 Briggs, *The Age of Improvement*, p.178.

31 Dr Evans to Parliament, *Victorian Hansard*, Vol. 3, 9 February 1858, SLV.

32 Thomson, *England in the Nineteenth Century*, p.23.

33 Joseph Hamburger, *James Mill and the Art of Revolution*, Yale University Press, New Haven, 1963, p.33. Revolutions had taken place in Paris, Belgium, Germany, Switzerland and Warsaw. France had captured Algiers.

34 D. K. Sandford to Evans, 2 December 1830; and Reverend R. Buchanan to G. S. Evans, 21 December 1830: Permezel Collection. The letter clearly stated that the degree was conferred by the 'University', although the address was that of the College of Glasgow. The term 'College' was used at the time for all universities. Over the years Evans seems to have adopted the alternative abbreviation DCL occasionally, which was conferred

by Oxford; in England, Cambridge University bestowed the LLD: Claire Daniel, Duty Archivist, University of Glasgow, email to author, 18 July 2012. The point is important because it confused a few journalists of the time, and even led a couple of writers to question the validity or origin of Evans's LLD. See, for example, A. W. Beasley, *The Club on the Terrace: The Wellington Club 1841–1996*, The Club, Wellington, 1996, p.21; and Robin Cooke, QC, *Portrait of a Profession: The Centennial Book of the New Zealand Law Society*, A. H. & A. W. Reed, Wellington, 1969, p.27.

35 Hamburger, *James Mill and the Art of Revolution*, Chapter 3, 'The Language of Menace', pp.28 ff.

36 G. H. Scholefield (ed.), *Dictionary of New Zealand Biography*, Department of Internal Affairs, Wellington, 1940, Vol. 1, p.150.

37 J. A. Roebuck, *History of the Whig Ministry of 1830 to the Passing of the Reform Bill*, London, 1852, pp.343–4, cited in Hamburger, *James Mill and the Art of Revolution*, p.49.

38 Briggs, *The Age of Improvement*, p.241.

39 W. N. Molesworth, *The History of the Reform Bill of 1832*, Chapman & Hall, London, 1865, pp.194–5.

40 Evans to Legislative Assembly, *Victorian Hansard*, Vol. 2, 2 June 1857, SLV. Evans's reference to the Liberal party was a slip of the tongue. The Liberals equated to the Whigs at the time. He was debating state aid, illustrating his opposition to the move, saying its supporters would introduce 'the antidote along with the bane'. He illustrated this point also with facts and figures proving that non-state-funded churches in Britain had far more places of worship.

41 Hamburger, *James Mill and the Art of Revolution*, p.49.

42 In Spitalfields, the shopkeepers vowed to keep 'a political fast day' and close their shops, and in the next two months the peers were the targets of violence. 'The Duke of Newcastle was assaulted and his London home attacked by the mob; the Duke of Cumberland was dragged from his horse; and the Marquis of Londonderry, riding in a cabriolet, was stopped and struck so violently he might have been killed if his driver had not whipped the horse into a gallop': Molesworth, *The History of the Reform Bill*, pp.261 ff.

43 Permezel Collection.

44 Molesworth, *The History of the Reform Bill*, passim.

45 House of Lords Journal, Vol. 64, 13 July 1832. 'Petition for Abolition of Slavery, from Brunswick Chapel, Mile End Road, presented by Rev. G. Evans and Members of Congregation of Protestant Dissenters of Independent Denomination', Permezel Collection. 'Almost one half of the 5,000 petitions presented to the reformed parliament on this subject came from Methodist Societies': Douglas Pike, *Paradise of Dissent: South Australia 1829–1857*, Longmans Green, London, Melbourne and New York, 1957, p.17.

46 Evans to Parliament: 'there was a time in England when to be a reformer was to be an object of scorn and derision': *Victorian Hansard*, Vol. 3, 9 February 1858, SLV.

47 John Briggs and Ian Seller, *Victorian Nonconformity*, Edward Arnold, London, 1973, p.1, citing E. A. Payne, *The Free Church Tradition in the Life of England*, p.101.

48 Edward Betts Hopper, Diary: 1836–1838, MS-1034, ATL. Byron married Annabella Milbanke, Lady Melbourne's daughter, in 1815 and in the same year Ada was born. She became, like her mother, a clever mathematician and assisted Babbage in his development of the first computer. She was 'pretty, small, slight and dark, with her father's lovely speaking voice': Paul Johnson, *The Birth of the Modern: World Society 1815–1830*, Phoenix, London, 1996, pp.538, 566.

49 Robert Owen (1771–1858) was a self-made mill owner who believed in treating his workers well. 'Every aspect of modern welfare work was undertaken, ranging from public health, temperance, and education to provision of social security': Thomson, *England in the Nineteenth Century*, p.45.

50 Betts Hopper Diary, ibid.

51 He might have been nominated by Brougham as two members might nominate an

applicant. 'I am glad to find that James is going the right way to work in studying "pleading" – it is the foundation of everything in law': G. S. Evans to his father, 14 January 1843, Permezel Collection.

52 Halevy, *A History of the English People in the Nineteenth Century*, Vol. 1, pp.23 ff.

53 *Melbourne Leader*, 5 April 1862. At Campbell's funeral and burial in Westminster Abbey in June 1844, a Polish noble in the cortege scattered upon his coffin a handful of earth from the grave of the Polish martyr Kosciusco: Stephen and Lee (eds), *Dictionary of National Biography*, Vol. III, p.848. Other references to the Polish Society name Richard Graves Meredith as secretary. There were several branches of the society. Evans acted as honorary secretary for a period in London.

54 Alexis de Tocqueville (ed. K. P. Mayer), *Journeys to England and Ireland*, G. Lawrence and K. P. Mayer (translators), Faber & Faber, London, 1958, pp.47–48. The 'Duffey' mentioned in the extract could be Charles Gavan Duffy, who later went to Melbourne and was in Parliament there with Evans.

55 For further information on schooling in this era, see Young (ed.), *Early Victorian England*, Vol. 2, pp.463–4.

56 G. S. Evans, Testimonial for Richard Evans's application, Permezel Collection. James Cook Evans became a headmaster after marrying Linnaea Lamb, daughter of the former Medical-Surgeon at Waterloo. While she ran a school for girls, James ran a boys' school that may well have been North End Academy. Linnaea Lamb Evans and their two children, James and Linnaea, died some time before 1840, after which James Cook married Celia Shaw who had taught at his late wife Linnaea's School for Girls: Family History sent from John Permezel to author, 2000, updated, 14 November 2012, by email attachment.

57 Peter Ackroyd, *London: The Biography*, Chatto & Windus, London, 2000, p.404, citing Ford Madox Ford in *The Soul of London*, A. Rivers, London, 1905.

58 'In politics, London had long been more effective in fomenting ideas than in putting them into action. Its attractions for intellectuals, politicians and writers had encouraged the one while its inchoate class mix, its increasing separation between home and work, its absorption in "matters of business" and its unpredictable crowd behavior had all subverted the other': Jerry White, *London in the Nineteenth Century: 'A Human Awful Wonder of God'*, Jonathan Cape, London, 2007, p.364.

59 Muriel Jaeger, *Before Victoria: Changing Standards and Behaviour, 1787–1837*, Chatto & Windus, London, 1956, p.139, citing Thomas Macaulay writing in 1830. Carlyle wrote of the phenomenon, as did Bulwer-Lytton, Thackeray, Mill, Thomas Arnold and Ruskin. From the time of Waterloo, Britain had seemed to be in the grip of a powerful drama.

60 The Duke of Norfolk, Lord John Russell, the Earl of Durham, the Marquess of Queensbury and Baron Lionel de Rothschild were all members of the Reform Club. Two hundred and fifty of the members were Liberal MPs. Four hundred additional members were balloted. Exclusive of honorary, supernumerary or life members, there was a total membership of 1400. 'He [Evans] was a member of the Club from 1836 (the year of foundation) to 1865. He doesn't appear in our Ballot Book for 1836, which means he was a founder member': Simon Blundell, Reform Club Librarian to author, 6 and 9 August 1999.

61 Thomas Carlyle, *Works*, Chapman & Hall, London, 1843, Vol. XIII, Past and Present, Book III, Chapter II, 'Gospel of Mammonism', p.182.

62 David Blair, 'Three Melbourne Barristers: A Recollection', *Centennial Magazine*, Vol. 2, No. 9, April 1890, p.692; Obituary, *Melbourne Herald*, October 1868, cited in *Wellington Independent*, 31 October 1868.

63 Briggs, *The Age of Improvement*, pp.385–90.

64 Scholefield (ed.), *Dictionary of New Zealand Biography*, Vol. 1, p.412. Wakefield called Betts Hopper the South Australia scheme's 'projector'.

65 Alan Mulgan, *The City of the Strait: Wellington and its Province, a Centennial History*, A. H. & A. W. Reed, Wellington, 1939, pp.43, 44.

66 Evans 'soon became associated with Wakefield, Durham, Colonel Torrens, Sir George Sinclair and others in the Colonial movement, especially the negotiations which led to the formation of the South Australia Company': *Melbourne Herald*, cited in the *Wellington Independent*, 31 October 1868, and reproduced in G. H. Scholefield, MS-Papers-0212-C/02B, ATL. It is unlikely that Evans was involved in the earlier years of the South Australia Company, although Wakefield's lists of members are incomplete. For background to the South Australia scheme, refer to P. Bloomfield, *Edward Gibbon Wakefield: Builder of the British Commonwealth*, Longmans, London, 1961, pp.116–29 ff.; and Pike, *Paradise of Dissent*.

67 G. S. Evans giving Evidence on the State of the Islands of New Zealand, 18 May 1838, British Parliamentary Papers, *Colonies: New Zealand, 1837–1850*, Vol. 1, 1837–1838 (680), p.319, NL.

68 *Wellington Independent*, Meeting of the Hutt Electors, 13 July 1853. This was related in front of E. G. Wakefield who agreed with Evans's account.

69 Wakefield's grandparents were strong Quakers; his grandmother Priscilla was 'the pillar, the rock', in what was a 'properly dysfunctional family': Philip Temple, 'New Zealand: A Family Business', in Friends of the Turnbull Library, *Edward Gibbon Wakefield and the Colonial Dream: A Reconsideration*, GP Publications, Wellington, 1997, p.16. And see 'Wakefield's resolve to exclude the Church of England from obtaining in the new world its old-world privileges': Erik Olssen, 'Wakefield and the Scottish Enlightenment', in Friends of the Turnbull Library, *Edward Gibbon Wakefield and the Colonial Dream*, p.50.

70 Raewyn Dalziel, 'Men, Women and Wakefield', in Friends of the Turnbull Library, *Edward Gibbon Wakefield and the Colonial Dream*, p.77.

71 William Gisborne, *New Zealand Rulers and Statesmen, 1840–1885*, Sampson Low, Marston, Searle & Rivington, London, 1886, p.79. Gisborne also said Wakefield was 'untrustworthy and unscrupulous' and had 'no particle of generous chivalry in his nature'.

72 Keith Sinclair, *A History of New Zealand*, Penguin, Auckland, revised edn, 2000, p.63.

73 Bloomfield, *Edward Gibbon Wakefield*, pp.173, 198. Brougham despised Wakefield as a 'swindler'.

74 Thomas Wilmor McKenzie, McKenzie Family Papers, MS-Papers-1357, ATL.

Chapter Three

1 *Gazette*, 6 September 1839. Baring had been a member of a Commons' Committee that had examined 'The Disposal of Waste Lands in the British Colonies'. Note: The *New Zealand Gazette* was first published in London on 21 August 1839 and reissued on 6 September that year. The second edition was published in Port Nicholson on 18 April 1840. For a short period it became the *New Zealand Gazette and Britannia Spectator*. From 28 November 1840 to 25 September 1844 its title was the *New Zealand Gazette and Wellington Spectator*. It is referred to here as the *Gazette*. *The New Zealand Spectator and Cook's Straits Guardian* replaced the *Gazette* from 12 October 1844 to 1865.

2 See Douglas Pike, *Paradise of Dissent: South Australia 1829–1857*, Longman's Green, London, Melbourne and New York, 1957, pp.40 ff., esp. pp.76–77, where Pike credits Wakefield's father, the Liberals, the French, Wilmot Horton, the Swan River Colony, Torrens, Adam Smith and Bentham for having taught him such things as 'surveying . . . the folly of giving away waste lands . . . the wastefulness of dispersion, the idea of an emigration fund'. J. Stuart Mill and T. R. Edmonds claimed they first suggested the principles of systematic colonisation to him. Wakefield told the Committee on Colonial Waste Land in 1836 that he had 'acquired [his] opinions by degrees'.

3 Editorial on immigration, *Melbourne Herald*, 17 January 1857.

4 David Thomson, *England in the Nineteenth Century: 1815–1914*, Penguin, London, 1986, p.42.

5 Ian Wards, *The Shadow of the Land: A Study of British Policy and Racial Conflict in New Zealand 1832–1852*, A. R. Shearer, Government Printer, Wellington, 1968, p.5. For the French threat to the Association and its aims, see pp.15 ff. 'The Church Missionary Society and the Wesleyans organized [the 1837 petition] for British protection': Peter Adams, *Fatal Necessity: British Intervention in New Zealand 1830–1847*, Auckland University Press/Oxford University Press, Auckland, 1977, p.82.

6 Keith Sinclair, *A History of New Zealand*, Penguin, Auckland, rev. edn, 2000, pp.55, 56.

7 J. S. Marais, *The Colonisation of New Zealand*, Milford, London, 1927, p.3.

8 Patricia Burns (ed. Henry Richardson), *Fatal Success: A History of the New Zealand Company*, Heinemann Reed, Auckland, 1989, p.76, note (at bottom of page) citing R. C. Mills, *The Colonization of Australia*, London, 1915, p.54.

9 G. M. Young (ed.), *Early Victorian England: 1830–1865*, Oxford University Press, London, 1934, Vol. 2, p.356; G. M. Trevelyan, *British History in the 19th Century and After, 1782–1919*, Longmans, London, 1922, pp.256–7. In 1835 Glenelg's action in rescinding Governor D'Urban's annexation of a Kaffir tribe's territory, following a dangerous raid by the tribe on the Boer territory in the African colony, led to an outcry against the government for failing to protect the safety of its British and Dutch subjects. As a direct result, the Boers sold their farms and began the Great Trek across Africa into the settlements they called the Orange Free State and Transvaal. Glenelg had acted on the advice of some missionaries and members of the Clapham sect in 1835, which was one of the few sources of the Colonial Office's information. Unwittingly, viewing the Dutch and South Africa only from their perspectives, they 'sowed the seeds of future disaster'.

10 Pike, *Paradise of Dissent*, p.54, citing W. P. Morrell, *British Colonial Policy in the Age of Peel and Russell*, Oxford, 1930, p.41.

11 E. G. Wakefield to G. S. Evans, 16 May 1837, NZC, Correspondence and Documents of the New Zealand Company, 1836–1887, C184, p.12, ML, also held as MS-Micro-460, ATL. The pamphlet to which Wakefield referred was probably *Mr. Dandeson Coates and the New Zealand Association*, his response to Dandeson Coates's pamphlet *The Principles, Objects and Plan of the New Zealand Association Examined.*

12 Edward Gibbon Wakefield, *A Statement of the Objects of the New Zealand Association, with some particulars concerning the Position, Extent, Soil and Climate, Natural Productions, and Natives of New Zealand*, Black & Armstrong, London, 1837, pp.13–21. In the later book that appeared the same year (also attributed to Edward Gibbon Wakefield), *The British Colonization of New Zealand: Being an Account of the Principles, Objects, and Plans of the New Zealand Association*, John W. Parker, London, 1837, pages 271 to 288 correspond exactly with pp.13–21 in the pamphlet, with further examples and quotes.

13 E. G. Wakefield, *The British Colonization of New Zealand*, pp.27–30 ff.

14 E. G. Wakefield, *Statement of the Objects of the New Zealand*, pp.16 ff.

15 E. G. Wakefield, *The British Colonization of New Zealand*, pp.52–58.

16 Pike, *Paradise of Dissent*, p.77; Eric Richards, 'Wakefield and Australia', in Friends of the Turnbull Library, *Edward Gibbon Wakefield and the Colonial Dream: A Reconsideration*, GP Publications, Wellington, 1977, p.90. Some time later, John Ward (1805–90) was credited as co-author of the book, but it is unlikely. John Ward had written for the *Edinburgh Review* and other papers, and had been involved with the South Australia scheme and colonial reform generally. Ward may have contributed, as did many others, but his name as co-author may have been confused with Evans, as both men were consecutive secretaries for the New Zealand venture. Evans was secretary of the New Zealand Association from 1837 to 1839, and Ward was secretary of the New Zealand Land Company from May 1839. L. Stephen and S. Lee (eds), *Dictionary of National Biography*, 21 Vols, Oxford University Press, London, 1917–1938, credit Ward only with his *Information Relative to New Zealand for the Use of Colonists*, which was published by John W. Parker in 1839. There are several contributors to the book

published in November 1837: for example, pp.289–301 of the book contain Reverend W. White's exploration of the language and translation of biblical extracts. Reverend Montague Hawtrey also contributed, as did Dr Hinds.

17 Thomas Wilmor McKenzie, McKenzie Family Papers, Chapter 1, p.6, MS-Papers-1357-1B, ATL: McKenzie also wrote that Wakefield argued: 'It was now impossible to prevent occupation of the country; [New Zealand] was already being colonized in the most irregular manner, by the worst discription [*sic*] of settlers, viz: runaway convicts and sailors . . . . and that the Missionaries themselves had purchased large tracts of land from the Maories.'

18 Ben Weinreb and Christopher Hibbert (eds), *The London Encyclopaedia*, Macmillan, London, 1983, p.6.

19 Marais, *The Colonisation of New Zealand*, p.27. See Adams, *Fatal Necessity*, Appendices 3(a) and 3(b), pp.252 ff. for lists of directors from 1825 to 1839 of the New Zealand Company in its various guises, with biographical notes on each director. In 1833 J. G. Lambton was made first Earl of Durham.

20 Pike, *Paradise of Dissent*, p.85. See also Stephen and Lee (eds), *Dictionary of National Biography*, Vol. X, p.349.

21 H. Hussey, *New Zealand and How it Became a British Province*, p.24, fms-[114], ATL.

22 McKenzie Family Papers, p.10, ibid.

23 *Gazette*, 'Historical Sketch of the Colonization of New Zealand', 6 September 1839, p.5. Thought to have been written solely by Wakefield, it clearly also involved Evans. Italics in the original article.

24 'Dr. Coates's "dream of Southern theocracy" was shattered in 1840 when the New Zealand Company received a Government mandate': Keith Sinclair, 'The Aborigines Protection Society and New Zealand: A Study in Nineteenth Century Opinion', MA thesis, Auckland University College, 1946, p.2, ATL.

25 Marais, *The Colonisation of New Zealand*, p.31.

26 Adams, *Fatal Necessity*, p.133.

27 Ibid., pp.8–9. The work of the Aborigines' Protection Society commenced in June 1831.

28 Sir Benjamin Hawes (1797–1862), in Stephen and Lee (eds), *Dictionary of National Biography*, Vol. IX, p.187. He was a 'strenuous advocate for reform with a deep sense of public duty', like many of Evans's connections.

29 Sinclair, 'The Aborigines Protection Society and New Zealand', pp.9, 12–13.

30 *Gazette*, 6 September 1839, p.5.

31 The committee comprised Baring, Campbell, Ferguson, Hawes, Howard, Hutt, Molesworth, Lord Petre, Henry Ward, Sinclair and Wolryche Whitmore.

32 'Several of them therefore, abandoned professional engagements, sold property on the faith of the expectation virtually held out to them, and made preparations for emigrating': *Gazette*, 6 September 1839, p.5, re Howick's assurances.

33 Edward Betts Hopper, Diary: 1836–1838, pp.20–22, MS-1034, ATL. See the photograph of Betts Hopper in Louis E. Ward, *Early Wellington*, Southern Reprints, Papakura, 1928, p.442. Some of Betts Hopper's sketches are also contained in its pages.

34 Jerry White, *London in the Nineteenth Century: 'A Human Awful Wonder of God'*, Jonathan Cape, London, 2007, p.456.

35 Ngaiti's real name was probably Eriki Nono: J. J. Taine (ed. H. W. Fildes), *Reminiscences*, Vol. 1, p.237, qMS-1975, ATL. In the *Gazette* of 6 September 1839, Tiaki is named Hiakai, the name Evans knew him by.

36 G. H. Scholefield, *Captain William Hobson, RN, 1793–1842*, p.85, MS-1856, ATL; and Cecil and Celia Manson, *Curtain Raiser to a Colony*, Whitcombe & Tombs, Christchurch, 1962, pp.44–45.

37 E. G. Wakefield, *The British Colonization of New Zealand*, p.191.

38 *Gazette*, 6 September 1839, p.5.

39 Burns, *Fatal Success*, p.50.

40 G. S. Evans, 'Grammar of the New Zealand Language', 1839, qMS-0688, ATL. Here the young man is called Hiakai. In other references he is Tiaki or Te Kia Kai.

41 Horace Fildes Collection, Newspaper Clippings, *Evening Post*, 16 July 1927, Pq 993.1 FIL 1920, ATL.
42 Young (ed.), *Early Victorian England*, Vol. 2, p.354.
43 G. S. Evans to W. I. Beattie, 4 October 1837, p.33, NZC, Minutebook/Letterbook, 1837–1838, Micro 2811, ANZ. See also Correspondence and Documents of the New Zealand Company, 1836–1887, p.381, C184, ML, also held as MS-Micro-460, ATL.
44 NZC, Minutebook/Letterbook, Micro 2811, ANZ.
45 E. G. Wakefield to E. Betts Hopper, 24 November 1837, MS-Papers-3124, ATL.
46 Burns, *Fatal Success*, p.48, credits Evans with having broken the impasse. NZC, Minutebook/Letterbook, Micro 2811, ANZ, gives details of his solution. The compensation decided by Somes and his sub-committee was generous.
47 See Wards, *The Shadow of the Land*, p.4; and P. Bloomfield, *Edward Gibbon Wakefield: Builder of the British Commonwealth*, Longmans, London, 1961, p.166.
48 Colonel Torrens, MP, to G. S. Evans, 8 September 1845, G. S. Evans, Papers, MS-Papers-10552, ATL.
49 G. S. Evans and eight other signatories, including Wakefield, D. Riddiford, J. Campbell, Roy and Forbes, to John Wright, 11 December 1837, NZC, Minutebook/Letterbook, Micro 2811, ANZ.
50 'Autocratic and independent, courageous and with fitful gleams of political vision, [Durham] was also a theatrical unbalanced egotist whose infirmities of temper had been developed to the highest pitch by bad health, bad nerves and too much money': David Cecil, *Lord M. or the Later Life of Lord Melbourne*, Constable & Co., London, 1954, p.80.
51 Ibid., pp.92–93. Cecil adds, 'This was partly out of mischief. Earnest well-informed persons with liberal ideas and non-conformist consciences are always powerful stimulants to the comic spirit . . . [but] often [Melbourne] did not wish to commit the Government.'
52 The deputation consisted of Hon. Francis Baring, chairman; Dr Evans; E. G. Wakefield; Major Campbell; Messrs Enderby, Betts Hopper, Howard, Lyall, T. Mackenzie, Nicholas and Roy; Sir John Campbell; Sir William Molesworth, MP; Sir George Sinclair, MP; Reverend Dr Hinds; and Reverends Hawtry, White and Flatt: see NZC, Minutebook/Letterbook, 13 December 1837, Micro 2811, ANZ.
53 Adams, *Fatal Necessity*, p.133.
54 Wakefield's Evidence to Select Committee on New Zealand, 13 July 1840, *Minutes of Evidence*, British Parliamentary Papers, *Colonies: New Zealand*, Vol. 1, 1840 (582), pp.2–3, NL.
55 Ibid., pp.7–8, NL.
56 Betts Hopper Diary, 23 December 1837, ibid.
57 NZC, Minutebook/Letterbook, Micro 2811, ANZ.
58 Ibid.
59 Wakefield to Evans, 23 December 1837; Campbell to Evans, passed to Wakefield by 25 December 1837; Wakefield to Evans, sent on to Campbell (before the latter left town), Campbell to Evans: NZC, Minutebook/Letterbook, Micro 2811, ANZ.
60 Ibid.; and Burns, *Fatal Success*, pp.56–58. Philip Temple, *A Sort of Conscience, The Wakefields*, Auckland University Press, 2002, pp.201–3, gives a full account.
61 E. G. Wakefield to Select Committee, 16 July 1840, *Minutes of Evidence*, BPP, *Colonies: New Zealand*, Vol. 1, 1840 (582), p.29, NL.
62 *The Times*, 3 February 1838. Henry George Ward was a director of the Association.
63 McKenzie Family Papers, ibid.
64 For the background story of Wakefield's rescue of the two young men from the captain of the French whaler *Mississippi,* refer to Manson, *Curtain Raiser to a Colony*, p.43; and Bloomfield, *Edward Gibbon Wakefield*, p.165. Evans's testimony is to be found in the *Gazette*, 6 September 1839.
65 McKenzie Family Papers, p.5, ibid.
66 Betts Hopper Diary, ibid. For the first day or so, while each witness was closeted with the

panel, Betts Hopper hung around outside. As two Select Committee members returned, he overheard one say 'that he had told someone that the land ceded by the chiefs to the missionaries was never considered to be ceded to them in sovereignty but only in possession'. This should have provided food for thought for them all.

67 BPP, *Colonies: New Zealand*, Vol. 1, 1837–1838 (680), p.325, NL.

68 The chiefs of the tribes in the North Island declared themselves a nation under the title of the United Tribes on 28 October 1835.

69 G. S. Evans LLD, *Evidence on the State of the Islands of New Zealand*, to Committee of House of Lords, 18 May 1838, BPP, *Colonies: New Zealand*, Vol. 1, 1837–1840 (680), p.328, NL. The name of Cook's Straits was used for some time but it is referred to as Cook's Strait in Captain Chaffer's 'Sailing Directions for Cook's Strait', published in the *New Zealand Journal* (London), 16 May 1840. The artist Chevalier painted 'Cook's Straits' c. 1884, although the artwork is sometimes referred to as Cook's Strait. Cook's Strait gradually evolved into Cook Strait, probably from about that time.

70 'Dr. Evans, versed in international law, easily showed that no respectable person could settle in the colony under such a system, unless he went with an armed party of squatters, without authority from the Crown': R. Garnett, *Builders of Greater Britain, Edward Gibbon Wakefield: The Colonization of South Australia and New Zealand*, T. Fisher Unwin, London, 1898, pp.138 ff.

71 G. S. Evans, *Evidence on the State of the Islands of New Zealand*, BPP, *Colonies: New Zealand*, Vol. 1, 1837–1840 (680), pp.317–33, NL.

72 Copy of letter from Lord Howick, War Office, 27 June 1837, *Remarks of Draft of Bill . . . sent to him by Major Campbell; to H. G. Ward esq. MP*, Edward Betts Hopper, Papers, MS-0535, ATL.

73 Dr Evans to Parliament, *Victorian Hansard*, Vol. 6, 18 January 1861, p.201, SLV. He added 'the Parliamentary practice [in Victoria was] so much more stringent than in the House of Commons . . . in the Imperial Parliament, it was a mere matter of form for an Honourable member of the Government to rise in his place and declare, on the part of the Crown, whether the necessary assent would be given'.

74 Adams, *Fatal Necessity*, p.121. The Bill's clauses are outlined in T. M. Hocken, *The Early History of New Zealand*, John MacKay, Wellington, 1914, pp.255–6.

75 G. W. Rusden, pp.183–4, probably his *History of New Zealand*, Vol. 1, Melbourne, 1895, cited in J. Beaglehole, *Captain Hobson and the New Zealand Company: A Study in Colonial Administration in Decline and Fall*, Smith College Studies in History, Vol. 13, Nos 1–3, Massachusetts, 1928, p.23.

76 Adams, *Fatal Necessity*, p.133.

77 Wards, *The Shadow of the Land*, p.18.

78 Evans to Lord Glenelg, 25 June 1838; Stephen minute, 30 June 1838; Grey to Evans, 7 July 1838, cited in Adams, *Fatal Necessity*, p.142.

79 Dr Evans to Parliament, *Victorian Hansard*, Vol. 4, 16 November 1858, SLV (speaking against Mr Service's maritime Bill). He was making the point that 'he never knew any substantial measure of law reform that was not proposed by a lawyer'. He might have been referring to the Law Amendment Society, of which Brougham was a leading light.

80 McKenzie Family Papers, ibid.

81 Ibid.; *Evening Post*, 16 July 1927; and Obituary, *Australian and New Zealand Gazette*, 1 December 1868.

82 NZC, Minutebook/Letterbook, Micro 2811, ANZ. Attendees were: Baring; Evans; Lord Petre; Sir George Sinclair; William Hutt; and Messrs Howard, Ferguson, Rintoul, Betts Hopper and Riddiford.

83 *Wellington Independent*, 13 July 1853. Note that he was more interested in colonising the country than in investing in property.

Chapter Four

1 Of the group's reluctance, see Thomas Wilmor McKenzie, McKenzie Family Papers, MS-Papers-1357-1B, ATL. Folder 1 is McKenzie's diary on board the *Adelaide*. Folder 1B contains his description of the formation of the New Zealand Association up to the departure of the *Adelaide*. A New Zealand historian observes: 'Wakefield's idea of a national enterprise with no individual investment was not possible . . . the support of city bankers and shipping magnates was vitally necessary': Peter Adams, *Fatal Necessity: British Intervention in New Zealand 1830–1847*, Auckland University Press/Oxford University Press, Auckland, 1977, p.99.

2 *Wellington Independent*, 13 July 1853. Was Enderby the 'whaling magnate' mentioned in James Belich, *Making Peoples: A History of the New Zealanders from Polynesian Settlement to the End of Nineteenth Century*, Penguin, Auckland, 2007, pp.183–4? 'He made the laconic reply', were Evans's actual words: 'Compensation of Working-Classes – Adjourned Public Meeting at the Hutt', *Wellington Independent*, 13 July 1853.

3 Jerningham Wakefield attested, 'Dr. Evans was the principal promoter of the Company . . . . Amongst the names of those who had agreed to advance the capital were Captain Daniell, Mr. Le Motte, Mr. Ramsay, and others': E. J. Wakefield, Obituary of Daniel Riddiford, *New Zealand Times*, 24 March 1875: the 'others' were Lord Petre, Sir William Hutt, Henry Young, John Wright, Betts Hopper, Edmund Halswell, Daniel Riddiford and Heath.

4 The draft, labelled 'Private and Confidential', listed the names of the provisional subscribers: Lord Petre, William Hutt, John Wright, Joseph Somes, — Boulcott esq., Sir Henry Webb, Henry Young, I. Heath, Standish Motte, Captain Daniell, Edmund Halswell, E. B. Hopper, David Ramsay, Dr Evans, Daniel Riddiford, I. B. Gordon, F. Boucher esq. and I. Dorset. Trustees were Petre, Wright, Somes, Webb and Young. Standing counsel was Motte, and Evans was honorary secretary. See Draft Prospectus for Colonization Company, CO 209/4, p.521, Micro 352, ANZ. Also transcribed in Lord Durham, *Colonization Correspondence*, 1837–1840, qMS-1124, ATL.

5 Patricia Burns (ed. Henry Richardson), *Fatal Success: A History of the New Zealand Company*, Heinemann Reed, Auckland, 1989, pp.12, 85, 103, 170.

6 Somes, Enderby, Boulcott, Waddell, Everingham, Rhodes and Lord Durham.

7 NZC, Committees, 1837–1840, CO 208/185, ANZ. The formation of the Company took place at this meeting and the committee comprised: Messrs Evans, Halswell, Ward, Motte and Waddell, with (lawyer) Mr Few.

8 *Wellington Independent*, 13 July 1853.

9 Prospectus of The New Zealand Colonization Company: to be incorporated by charter or Act of Parliament (sub-heading). Evans is listed as a subscriber and honorary secretary. A transcribed copy of this is in Lord Durham, *Colonization Correspondence*, ibid.

10 The meeting resolved to sell all McDonnell's territory, reserving eight square miles – four square miles at Hauraki, and another four at 'Kiapara'. The Colonization Company was to pay him 5 per cent on the gross amount of the proceeds of the sale of his land, the sum of £1,000 to be paid on the execution of the arrangement. McDonnell was also to be retained as Colonization Company agent, at £500 per annum, and to be made a shareholder: see NZC, Committees, 1837–1840, CO 208/185, ANZ.

11 E. G. Wakefield to G. S. Evans, 11 December 1838, *New Zealand Papers*, 1836–87, C184, pp.80–81, ML. Also available at Correspondence and Documents of the New Zealand Company 1836–1887, C184, ML, held as MS-Micro-460, ATL (see pp.12 ff., Frame 413). In his book *Adventure in New Zealand*, Jerningham observed, 'It only remained therefore to adopt the views of the Colonial Office by considering New Zealand as a foreign country, and by proceeding to acquire land and form settlements in the manner hitherto sanctioned by the Crown. The new Company were thus forced into the adoption of what has been termed land-sharking': Edward Jerningham Wakefield (ed. Sir Robert Stout), *Adventure in New Zealand, from 1839 to 1844, with Some*

Account of the Beginning of the British Colonization of the Islands, Whitcombe & Tombs, Christchurch, 1908, p.12.

12 Burns, *Fatal Success*, pp.139–40, citing M. G. Fawcett, *Life of the Right Hon. Sir William Molesworth, Bart. M.P., F.R.S.*, London, 1901, pp.169–77.

13 R. Garnett, *Builders of Greater Britain, Edward Gibbon Wakefield: The Colonization of South Australia and New Zealand*, T. Fisher Unwin, London, 1898, pp.138 ff.; Burns, *Fatal Success*, pp.80–81.

14 They gave a generous dowry that included 'a twelve-piece canteen of silver, articles of linen and furniture, and a large and well-stocked medicine chest'. When it became evident later in the year that Mrs Riddiford was pregnant, 'they employed a nurse to accompany her on the long voyage': Terence Hodgson, *The Riddifords: Towards a Social History*, unpub., Wellington, c. 1998.

15 Evans to Durham, 17 January 1839, and Durham to Evans, 19 January 1839, *Journal of the Early Settlers*, Vols 1 and 2, 1912–1923, Lambton Collection, MS-Papers-0140-03, Micro-0527, ATL.

16 Evans to Glenelg, 4 February 1839, *New Zealand Papers*, 1836–87, CO 309/53, pp.453–4, ML.

17 See Adams, *Fatal Necessity*, p.133; Ian Wards, *The Shadow of the Land: A Study of British Policy and Racial Conflict in New Zealand 1832–1852*, A. R. Shearer, Government Printer, Wellington, 1968, pp.18–19.

18 Burns, *Fatal Success*, p.76; J. S. Marais, *The Colonisation of New Zealand*, Milford, London, 1927, pp.37–39.

19 Adams, *Fatal Necessity*, p.129.

20 Glenelg to Cabinet, 12 February 1839, CO 209/4, cited in Marais, *The Colonisation of New Zealand*, p.38.

21 Draft Prospectus for New Zealand Bank and Colonization Company, dated February 1839. Transcribed copy in Lord Durham, *Colonization Correspondence*, ibid.

22 Burns, *Fatal Success*, p.94.

23 Marais, *The Colonisation of New Zealand*, p.39.

24 Ibid., p.39, citing the following: Motte to Normanby, 4 March 1839; Stephen's Minute to Normanby, 6 March, 1839; Labouchere to Motte, 11 March 1839. Lord Petre was a Catholic and the banker John Wright was probably also a Catholic as his clients were predominantly Catholic churchmen and parishes. On p.40, Marais believed that the government committed 'two grave blunders' in forcing the New Zealand Company's hand. The first was to insist that the Association become a joint stock company 'and inscribe gain on its banner instead of public service'. Worse, by estranging a body of men that had in fact fulfilled all the conditions of the government, it had created 'two antagonistic powers in New Zealand'. Burns, *Fatal Success*, p.77, treats the minute decrying the Catholic element in the Company as a 'red herring', and indeed Normanby had favoured Catholic emancipation and been criticised for his tolerance towards Catholic leaders in Ireland. Nevertheless, the timing of these communications is too coincidental to be dismissed. Normanby may have been 'sympathetic' to Catholics, but Stephen's minute added another objection to the list accumulating against the Company. See also G. H. Scholefield, *Captain William Hobson, First Governor of New Zealand*, Oxford University Press, London, 1934, p.72; Adams, *Fatal Necessity*, p.137 ff.; A. H. McLintock, *Crown Colony Government in New Zealand*, Government Printer, Wellington, 1958, pp.46, 51. '[T]here was a religious barrier of formidable proportions: not only was England aggressively Protestant, but the body in New Zealand able to exert the most political pressure in London was the Church Missionary Society whose anti-popery attitude was inflexible. This attitude was shared by both the Secretary for the Colonies, Lord Glenelg, and by his permanent under-secretary, James Stephen': Wards, *The Shadow of the Land*, p.16. See also Alan Ward, *A Show of Justice: Racial 'Amalgamation' in Nineteenth Century New Zealand*, Auckland University Press, Auckland, 1995, pp.28 ff.

25 *Wellington Independent*, 13 July 1853.

26 *Gazette*, 6 September 1839.
27 Burns, *Fatal Success*, p.85. See also NZC, Committees, 1837–1840, CO 208/185, ANZ.
28 *Wellington Independent*, 13 July 1853.
29 Adams, *Fatal Necessity*, pp.137–8.
30 Ward, *A Show of Justice*, p.35.
31 E. Betts Hopper, Diary: 1836–1838, pp.7 ff., MS-1034, ATL.
32 NZC, Committees, 1837–1840, CO 208/185, ANZ.
33 Ibid. And see meeting 1 April 1839, ibid. Evans had copied all of the Testimonials to Colonel Wakefield for the directors. This letter of appointment of Colonel Wakefield as Principal Agent was possibly a collaborative effort between Evans and Wakefield. Temple suggests E. G. Wakefield composed it and Evans only signed it: Philip Temple, *A Sort of Conscience: The Wakefields*, Auckland University Press, Auckland, 2002, p.229.
34 NZC, Directors' Minutes, May 1839–1840, pp.49–219, CO 208/180, ANZ. From July 1839 to the end of 1840 and beyond, Motte pursued the matter. See also NZC, Directors' Minutes, 1839–1844, pp.144–345 passim, NZC 31/1/1, ANZ. Standish Motte was a member of the Aborigines' Protection Society and in 1840 wrote a treatise: *A System of Legislation for Securing Protection to the Aboriginal Inhabitants of all Countries Colonized by Great Britain*, cited in Ward, *A Show of Justice*, p.35.
35 Evans to Dudley Sinclair, 13 April 1839, p.20, NZC, Directors' Minutes, 1839–1844, NZC 31/1/1, p.20, ANZ.
36 NZC, Committees, 1837–1840, CO 208/185, ANZ.
37 With the advent of free trade, the Spitalfield weavers had found themselves squeezed out of employment by the competitive prices. By the late 1830s the parish was in dire straits. Tens of thousands of weavers were unemployed and cramming the poorhouses. '[F]ive in a bed; 6,000 receive parochial relief', Charles Greville, the political diarist (1794–1865), reported in 1832. 'The parish is in debt; every day adds to the number of paupers . . . principally small shopkeepers, beggared by the rates. The district is in a complete state of insolvency and hopeless poverty . . . but what can Government do? We asked the man who came what could be done for them. He said "employment", and employment is impossible': Roy Porter, *London: A Social History*, Penguin, London, 2000, pp.195–6.
38 G. S. Evans to Reverend G. Evans, 23 April 1839, Permezel Collection.
39 J. J. Taine (ed. H.W. Fildes), *Reminiscences*, Vol. 1, p.63, qMS-1975, ATL. (Apparently the name should be spelled Liocadia, according to Adrienne Longuet, who is a descendant and has Liocadia as her middle name. It is spelled with an e in several other references.)
40 McKenzie Family Papers, ibid.
41 William Hutt to Normanby, 29 April 1839; Labouchere to Hutt, 1 May 1839; Hutt to Labouchere, 1 May 1839: Lambton Collection, 29 April 1839, Folder 6, MS-Papers-0140, ATL.
42 Burns, *Fatal Success*, pp.76 and 77.
43 *Gazette*, 6 September 1839. The unidentified author of the *Historical Sketch of the Colonization of New Zealand* contained in the newspaper stated that it was not until after the Land Company was launched on 2 May that Wakefield 'now resumed the part which had been sustained by others during his absence from England'.
44 Other original shareholders were Lord Petre and Hutt, each having subscribed £500. Wakefield opted for a hundred shares in the Land Company, 3 May 1839: see NZC, Committees, 1837–1840, CO 208/185, ANZ. See also Ward's instructions to Daniel Riddiford on his role as Emigration Agent, 12 September 1839, NZC, Despatches from Secretary to Principal Agent, NZC 102/1/1, ANZ.
45 The idea of the sale of land as a lottery was Wakefield's. See Burns, *Fatal Success*, pp.101–2. Evans bought fifty sections, paying a total of £5,050. Forty of Evans's sections were mortgaged to Robert Monro later. These details are to be found in Certificates of Transfer, Old Land Orders, NZC 33/48d, ANZ. Forty-three of the sections are attributed to Evans in Louis E. Ward, *Early Wellington*, Southern Reprints, Papakura, 1928, pp.191–206 passim.

46 Colonel Torrens, Sir Henry Webb, Geo. F. Young, J. Abel Smith, William Thompson, John Pirie, Lord Petre, J. W. Buckle, Ellice B. Gordon, R. Fenwick, William Hutt, Lyall, Marjoribanks and Palmer. The bankers were Messrs Smiths, Payne and Smiths; and Messrs Wright and Co.
47 Committee: G. S. Evans, D. C. L. [*sic*], Hon. H. Petre, Capt. Daniell, D. Sinclair, E. Betts Hopper, G. Duppa, W. Swainson and R. H. Wood.
48 NZC, Committees, 1837–1840, CO 208/185, ANZ.
49 *Gazette*, 6 September 1839.
50 Ward, *Early Wellington*, p.442, citing the *Gazette*, 6 September 1839.
51 William Wakefield, Diary 1839–1842, 5 May 1839, MS-2102-2103, ATL. See also David P. Millar, *Once Upon a Village: A History of Lower Hutt*, New Zealand University Press, Wellington, 1972, p.11.
52 Specifically he was found guilty of: 'divers subtle stratagems, forgery, flagrant lies and intimidation for the sake of lucre and gain': John Miller, *Early Victorian New Zealand: A Study of Racial Tension and Social Attitudes, 1839–1852*, Oxford University Press, London, 1958, p.22.
53 Address given: 1 Adam Street, Adelphi, 8 July 1839: Prospectus for Literary Scientific and Philanthropic Institutions of First Colony of New Zealand.
54 G. S. Evans to Secretary, Church Missionary Society, 22 May 1839, in Webster Collection, Correspondence and Documents of the New Zealand Company, 1826–1841, MS-Micro-0302, ATL.
55 G. S. Evans to Dr Hinds, 20 May 1839, p.223; and To Wesleyans, CMS and Missionary Society; and Circular to interested parties, 22 and 28 May 1839, pp.226, 233–4, in NZC, Committees, 1837–1840, CO 208/185, ANZ.
56 Evans to Betts Hopper, 28 May 1839, Folder 1, Edward Catchpool Collection, MS-0077, ATL.
57 NZC, Committees, 1837–1840, CO 208/185, ANZ; and NZC, Directors' Minutes, 1839–1849, CO 208/180-183, ANZ.
58 A. J. Harrop, *England and New Zealand: From Tasman to the Taranaki War*, Methuen, London, 1926, p.69.
59 Cited in Burns, *Fatal Success*, p.105; and Wakefield's attendance, 4 July 1839, p.156, NZC, Committees, 1837–1840, CO 208/185, ANZ.
60 Meeting, 23 May 1839, NZC, CO 208/185, ANZ.
61 Dr Evans to Legislative Assembly, *Victorian Hansard*, Vol. 1, 27 January 1857, SLV.
62 Burns, *Fatal Success*, p.102.
63 G. S. Evans to Joseph Fogg, Jesse Fisher, Alexander Nicholson, H. Case, George Simson, Robert Park, Thomas Ward, John Hinton, William Barton, John Brooker, J. Jenkins, Charles Brooks, R. Liddell and Archibald Millar, Circular, 28 May 1839: NZC, Committees, CO 208/185, ANZ.
64 Marais, *The Colonisation of New Zealand*, p.97. Hobson did not receive his instructions until 14 August. See also Adams, *Fatal Necessity*, p.136, where it is related that by mid-June both Torrens and Lyall of the 1825 Committee had resigned. Both were reluctant to proceed without the government's sanction.
65 See Captain William Hobson to Dr G. S. Evans, 24 August 1840, Correspondence and Documents of the New Zealand Company, 1836–1887, C184, pp.479–81 [76–79], ML; *New Zealand Papers*, 1836–87, CO 309/53, ML; and Paul Moon, *Hobson: Governor of New Zealand 1840–1842*, David Ling, Auckland, 1998, pp.9, 306–7.

Chapter Five

1 G. H. Scholefield (ed.), *Dictionary of New Zealand Biography*, Department of Internal Affairs, Wellington, 1940, Vol. 2, p.224.
2 W. R. Lawrence, *'Huzza for New Zealand!': The Life and Work of Captain Mein Smith*, p.227, qMS-1139, ATL.

3 L. Stephen and S. Lee (eds), *Dictionary of National Biography*, Oxford University Press, Oxford, 1917–1938, Vol. IX, p.571.
4 Scholefield, *Dictionary of New Zealand Biography*, Vol. 2, p.224.
5 The *New Zealand Gazette* was first issued on 21 August 1839 and a revised edition published a fortnight later on 6 September. Both issues contained the article 'Historical Sketch of the Colonization of New Zealand', advertisements for the New Zealand Land Company, the Committee of the First Colony, the New Zealand Infant School and the Literary, Scientific and Philosophical Institutions, and advice for emigrants.
6 *Gazette*, 6 September 1839, pp.4–6.
7 NZC, Despatches from Secretary to Principal Agent, Vol. 1, pp.35a–35e, encl. 9, September 1839, NZC 102/1/1, ANZ.
8 Notice of Literary, Scientific, and Philanthropic Institutions, Permezel Collection. *Gazette*, 6 September, 1839; also cited in Louis E. Ward, *Early Wellington*, Southern Reprints, Papakura, 1928, p.442.
9 'Shares of Colonial land came on the market at a time when railway shares were temporarily out of favour, and during a curious and short-lived fashion for colonisation': M. Turnbull, *The New Zealand Bubble*, Price Milburn & Co., Wellington, 1959, p.59.
10 Labouchere to Reverend A. M. Campbell, 1 August 1839, Webster Collection, Correspondence and Documents of the New Zealand Company 1826–1841, Micro-MS-0302, ATL.
11 Patricia Burns (ed. Henry Richardson), *Fatal Success: A History of the New Zealand Company*, Heinemann Reed, Auckland, 1989, p.95.
12 Ian Wards, *The Shadow of the Land: A Study of British Policy and Racial Conflict in New Zealand 1832–1852*, A. R. Shearer, Government Printer, Wellington, 1968, p.17. Pages 15–17, 51 and 52 describe the progression of the French interest in the country.
13 *Gazette*, 5 January 1842, pp.4–6.
14 G. H. Scholefield, *Captain William Hobson, RN 1793–1842*, pp.81–87, MS-1856, ATL.
15 Burns, *Fatal Success*, pp.92–93. Lord Normanby was relieved of his duties on 30 August 1839 after serving as Secretary of State for the Colonies for only six months. Lord Glenelg, his predecessor, served for nearly four years; and Lord John Russell, his successor, held the position for two years.
16 G. S. Evans to his parents, 9 November 1840, Permezel Collection.
17 Regulations 6, 7 and 8 for intending emigrants to 'the New Zealand Land Company's first and principal Settlement': *New Zealand Papers*, 1836–1887, C184, pp.454–6, ML.
18 The Council of the New Zealand Company's First Colony was composed of: Colonel William Wakefield, Principal Agent; George Samuel Evans, Umpire; Hon. Henry William Petre; Dudley Sinclair; Francis Alexander Molesworth; Captain Edward Daniell; Lieut. William Mein Smith, Company Surveyor-General; Richard Davies Hanson; Edward Betts Hopper; George Duppa; George Hunter; Henry Moreing; Henry Saint Hill; Thomas Partridge; Major David Stark Durie. Samuel Revans was later selected as secretary to the council. There were fourteen rules set by the directors: see Enclosure in Despatch Number 30, *New Zealand Papers*, ibid.
19 Ibid.; and *Wellington Independent*, 9 January 1864.
20 Ward to Colonel Wakefield, 11 October 1839, Despatch no. 17, NZC, Despatches from Secretary to Principal Agent, NZC 102/1/1, ANZ. This despatch explains Evans's financial position: he was not to be paid until the first quarter of the second year as his first year's salary was held back to pay his mortgage on some sections.
21 Thomas Wilmor McKenzie, McKenzie Family Papers, MS-Papers-1357, ATL.
22 See Appendix One.
23 G. S. Evans to his parents, 9 November 1840, Permezel Collection.
24 *Gazette*, 18 April 1840.
25 Burns, *Fatal Success*, p.133.
26 F. L. Irvine-Smith, *The Streets of My City, Wellington, New Zealand*, A. H. & A. W. Reed, Wellington, 1948, p.183. In October 1841 the mill was ready for business.
27 NZC, Committees, 1837–40, pp.128, 157, 159, 161, CO 208/185, ANZ.

28 J. J. Taine (ed. H. W. Fildes), *Reminiscences*, Vol. 1, p.123, qMS-1975-1976, ATL.
29 *Gazette*, 18 April 1840, 6 June 1840.
30 W. Hutt to G. S. Evans from Gibside, 14 September 1839, *New Zealand Papers*, 1836–87, C184, pp.44 ff., ML. See also Douglas Pike, *Paradise of Dissent: South Australia 1829–1857*, Longmans Green, London, Melbourne and New York, 1957, pp.53–102 passim; A. J. Harrop, *The Amazing Career of Edward Gibbon Wakefield*, Allen & Unwin, London, 1928, p.52. Hutt may have had a premonition: in his association with Wakefield, Evans's path followed similar lines to the career of Robert Gouger, who had been for six years Honorary Secretary for Wakefield's South Australia plan
31 Under Dr Evans's patronage: James John Taine, 24, stores merchant; Francis Bradey, agriculturist, 45, wife, 38, daughter Emma, 20, servant to the Evans family; Robert Campbell, aged 17, servant; George Clarke, 25, agriculturalist; Thomas Guthrie, 26, and family, farmer; Mr and Mrs Edwin Ticehurst, 27, carpenter; William Turnbull, 24, engineer. Under Mrs Evans's sponsorship: James Buchanan, 55, schoolmaster; Mrs Margaret McKenzie, 35, and Thomas McKenzie, 13 (the same who became printer and editor); Ann Tilke, 20, schoolmistress; Eliza Williams, 35, cook and dairy-woman: Taine, *Reminiscences*, Vol. 1, ibid.
32 Taine, *Reminiscences*, Vol. 1, pp.79, 124, ibid. On p.61, though, he calls it Miss Matthews' School at Twickenham.
33 'The New Zealand Company', *Morning Chronicle*, 16 September 1839.
34 In order: Colonel William Wakefield, Dr George S. Evans, Hon. Henry William Petre, Dudley Sinclair, Francis A. Molesworth, Captain Daniell, Lieutenant William Mein Smith, Richard Davies Hanson, Edward Betts Hopper, George Duppa, George Hunter, Henry Moreing, Henry Saint Hill, Thomas Partridge and Major David Stark Durie.
35 *Morning Chronicle*, 16 September 1839.
36 Somes to Evans, 16 September 1839, Permezel Collection.
37 'Dr. Evans, who had come post haste from London, came off in a deal boat in a gale of wind; having succeeded in eluding the officers of the Government, who were endeavouring to prevent his departure for New Zealand, as the Chief Agent of the expedition': McKenzie Family Papers, ibid.
38 Taine, *Reminiscences*, Vol. 1, p.80, ibid.

Chapter Six

1 William Deans to John Deans senior, 8 March 1840, J. Deans, *Pioneers of Canterbury: Deans Letters 1840–1855*, A. H. & A. W. Reed, Dunedin, 1937, p.19. See W. R. Lawrence, *'Huzza for New Zealand!': The Life and Work of Captain Mein Smith*, pp.91–110, qMS-1139, ATL, for an account of Mein Smith's voyage of dramas, rows and arguments.
2 '[T]he events and circumstances are now unlikely to be unearthed': Philip Temple, *A Sort of Conscience: The Wakefields*, Auckland University Press, Auckland, 2002, p.161.
3 S. Revans to H. S. Chapman, 26 September 1839. S. Revans, Letters, qMS-1687, ATL.
4 Although only twelve or thirteen years old, his writing and observations are objective and mature. See Thomas Wilmor McKenzie, McKenzie Family Papers, MS-1357, ATL; and Hogg Scrapbook No. 6, p.87, 'Scrapbooks of newspaper cuttings, ca. 1880–1912', [microfilm] compiled by Alexander Wilson Hogg, ATL.
5 J. J. Taine (ed. H. W. Fildes), *Reminiscences*, Vol. 1, pp.80–89 ff., qMS-1974, ATL.
6 The *Adelaide*'s cabin passengers were: Dr G. S. Evans and Mrs Harriet Evans; Daniel Riddiford, Mrs Harriot Riddiford and infant; Miss Amelia Riddiford; Miss Liocadia Mary Oliveira; Captain Edward Daniell, Mrs Daniell and Master Daniell; Mrs Louisa Smith (wife of William Mein Smith, the chief surveyor) and two children; W. Johnston, MD, Ship's Surgeon; Charles Alsdorf; Samuel Revans; Henry Cole and George Cole; T. M. Partridge; Major David Durie; William Thomas and Joseph Thomas; Luke Nattrass and John Nattrass; James Taine; Henry St Hill and Mrs St Hill; Archibald Millar, Mrs

Millar and four or five children; J. H. Luscombe; H. and T. W. Cook; and F. Johnson. All accounts differ, but the best is that of Louis E. Ward, *Early Wellington*, Southern Reprints, Papakura, 1928, p.33: 'There were 37 cabin and 144 steerage passengers on board. Five births occurred during the voyage, totalling the number of passengers to 186.' See also British Parliamentary Papers, *Colonies: New Zealand, 1837–1840*, Vol. 1, NL. The adult cabin passengers each paid £75 for passage, for which they were allowed two tons of baggage per person. The adult steerage passengers paid, or had paid for them by a sponsor, £18 15s, and were allowed one-half of a ton baggage.

7 Taine, *Reminiscences*, Vol. 1, p.72, ibid.; David Hall, *The Golden Echo*, Collins, Auckland and London, 1971, p.59.

8 T. Partridge (1802–1847) was a literary gentleman working for *The Spectator*. He died in Sydney in 1847. He had been secretary to the Anti-Corn Law Society.

9 S. Revans to Eleanor, later Lady McGregor, 22 December 1839, Revans Letters, ibid.

10 F. T. Yates, Diary: 1839–1840, MS-2302, ATL. Yates is listed in the ATL reference as a cabin passenger. This was an error. He was not listed amongst the cabin passengers, and his diary entries indicate he was a steerage passenger. Yates was brought to New Zealand by Revans as a compositor. The diary is fragmented, as some has been torn away. He drowned in an accident in Wellington Harbour that claimed nine lives a year later.

11 Ibid.

12 Ibid.

13 S. Revans to H. S. Chapman, 21 December 1839, Revans Letters, ibid.

14 McKenzie Family Papers, Folder 1, ibid.

15 *Gazette*, 25 April 1840.

16 Ibid., for an account of the dinner.

17 McKenzie Family Papers, Folder 1, pp.10 ff., ibid.

18 Revans to Eleanor (later Lady McGregor), 22 December 1839, Revans Letters, ibid.

19 First published in London, February 1840.

20 Revans to Chapman, 21 December 1839, Revans Letters, ibid.

21 See Part Two for more details; and Lawrence, *'Huzza for New Zealand!'*, pp.27, 37, passim, ibid. Chapman told his father Mrs Smith was 'a woman of very equivocal reputation'. He also contended that Samuel Revans, who lived with the Smiths, 'carried out Smith's conjugal commitments'. Surveyor-General Smith was 'scholarly, retiring, religious', frequently absent for lengthy periods as he was 'devoted to his duties'. He was twelve years his wife's senior. Revans said Smith 'was as innocent as a child'.

22 Revans to Chapman, 21 December 1839, Revans Letters, ibid.

23 Yates Diary, 16 November 1839, ibid.

24 Taine, *Reminiscences*, Vol. 1, p.85, ibid.

25 Revans to Chapman, 4 November 1839, Revans Letters, ibid.

26 Taine, *Reminiscences*, Vol. 1, pp.84–85, ibid.

27 A. Marjoribanks, *Travels in New Zealand*, Smith Elder & Co., London 1847, reprinted Capper Press, Christchurch, 1973, p.24.

28 Captain Edmund Mein Chaffers had served as acting master under Captain FitzRoy on the famous voyage in the *Beagle* with naturalist Charles Darwin from 1830 to 1836, which visited New Zealand in 1835. He left the navy in 1839 to command the *Tory*. Accompanied by draftsman and artist Charles Heaphy, he mapped a very valuable chart with a detailed description for navigation of Cook's Strait (as he wrote it) and Queen Charlotte Sound, sending it to the Directors of the Company from Cloudy Bay on 18 October 1839. It was published in the *New Zealand Journal* in London on 16 May 1840. In early 1840 Chaffers was appointed Port Nicholson's harbour master but after a disagreement with the government, returned to England. See F. L. Irvine-Smith, *The Streets of My City, Wellington, New Zealand*, A. H. & A. W. Reed, Wellington, 1948, p.22.

29 T. M. Partridge to H. S. Chapman, 31 December 1839, H. S. Chapman, Letters and sundry, qMS-0417, ATL.

30 The account of the *Adelaide*'s trials and tribulations that follows is mostly dependent on the two letters sent by Revans: one to Chapman, dated 21 December, and the letter to his sister, Eleanor, which is longer and more detailed, dated 22 December 1839: Revans Letters, ibid. In all, Revans wrote three letters to Chapman and one to his sister.
31 Evans and other cabin passengers to Dr Johnston, 7 December 1839, Permezel Collection.
32 Captain Daniell was a farmer at Crofton (Ngaio) and afterwards a Rangitikei settler.
33 Lieutenant Josias Thomas was a merchant and settler; and later, chief surveyor to the Canterbury Association.
34 George Cole and Henry Cole were both constables.
35 Archibald Millar of Mickle Pinkerton by Dunbar, East Lothian, and his wife Mary had four children: Lucy-Ann, aged ten; Janet Godman, seven; Harry, four; and Roderick McKenzie, aged one. Their fifth, a son, was born on board, 11 November. Millar, it will be recalled, was one of the recipients of the circular Evans sent on 28 May 1839 outlining the Company's rules.
36 Yates Diary, 13 December 1839, ibid.
37 'Revans told the steerage passengers Dr. Evans had assumed an authority he was not entitled to': Taine, *Reminiscences*, Vol. 1, p.85, ibid.
38 William Deans to John Deans senior, 8 March 1840: Deans, *Pioneers of Canterbury*, pp.18–19. In fact there were going to be three duels. Millar and Evans were one, not two.
39 Baron Alsdorf's name was spelt Alzdorf and sometimes Von Alzdorf until some time after his arrival in Wellington. He is referred to here as Alsdorf.
40 Petition to Dr Evans written on board the ship *Adelaide*, 15 December 1839, Permezel Collection.
41 Louis E. Ward, *Early Wellington*, p.35; and cited in Cecil and Celia Manson, *Curtain Raiser to a Colony*, Whitcombe & Tombs, Christchurch, 1962, p.114.
42 Revans to his sister Eleanor, Sunday, 22 December 1839, Revans Letters, ibid..
43 Revans to Chapman, 21 December 1839, Revans Letters, ibid.
44 Partridge to Chapman, 31 December 1839, Chapman, Letters and sundry, ibid.
45 Taine, *Reminiscences*, Vol. 1, p.92, ibid.
46 See Taine, *Reminiscences*, Vols 1 and 2, ibid. Horace Fildes (1875–1937) was the fourth son of John Gifford Fildes' second marriage to Jessie Sophia Taine, J. J. Taine's daughter. There is no suggestion Liocadia was badly treated by the family at any time; in fact, quite the contrary. She was present with her 'friends Dr. Evans and his wife, Mr. and Mrs. Daniel Riddiford, and Miss Amelia Riddiford' at 1 Adam Street, Adelphi in London when Taine met her for the first time. See Article: Horace Fildes Collection, Newspaper Clippings, *Evening Post*, 16 July 1927, Pq 993.1 FIL 1920, ATL.
47 Revans to his sister Eleanor, 22 December 1839, Revans Letters, ibid. The remark 'much to do with boy' refers of course to Evans having been a schoolmaster.
48 *Colonial Gazette*, cited in the *New Zealand Journal*, Vol. 1, 1840, p.42.
49 Douglas Cresswell, 'Riddiford of Te Awaite', in *Early New Zealand Families, Second Series*, Whitcombe & Tombs, Christchurch, 1956, p.15; also memoir of E. Anthony Riddiford, Family Collection (unpublished).
50 G. S. Evans to John Wright, 19 April 1840, *New Zealand Journal*, 26 September 1840.
51 Lawrence, *'Huzza for New Zealand!'*, p.222, ibid.
52 Revans to Chapman, 25 October 1840, Revans Letters, ibid.
53 *Gazette*, 6 June 1840.
54 Taine, *Reminiscences*, Vol. 1, pp.88, 85, ibid.
55 McKenzie Family Papers, Folder 1, ibid. See the detailed account: pp.1–28.
56 Henry Moreing was a lawyer and member of the Aborigines' Protection Society in London. He believed in the Company's obligations to Maori. He spent four and a half years in Port Nicholson, and took up the Company's case with Evans when they returned to England at end of 1844: Taine, *Reminiscences*, Vol. 1, p.92, ibid.
57 Gavin McLean, *Wellington: The First Years of European Settlement, 1840–1850*, Penguin, Auckland, 2000, p.13.

58 Irvine-Smith, *The Streets of My City*, p.66. The name Evans's Bay is seen on the earliest maps of Wellington held in the ATL, and the *Gazette* of 25 April 1840 has an advertisement for an auction 'at Mr. Watts Cattle and Sheep Station, in Evans's Bay', directly under the account of the dinner held at Tenerife by the *Adelaide*'s cabin passengers for Mr Bartlett. Individual spelling varied between Evans' and Evans's, and by May 1842 the added 's' had been dropped. Eventually the apostrophe was dropped as well. An article in the *Evening Post* of 25 May 1937, which gave a brief outline of Evans's life, called it Evans Bay. But there must have been some controversy over the name behind the bay, as another *Evening Post* article of 4 October 1952 (Vol. 1, Pq993.1 PON, ATL) outlining his life under the heading 'Know Your Wellington' by Poneke, was prefaced thus: 'Evan's Bay or Evans Bay? Get it wrong and you slight the memory of the man who took the lead in ensuring that Wellington grew up where it did, instead of on Petone Beach.' The article itself began: 'George Samuel Evans is the name so there is no apostrophe.' Grammatically speaking, this is incorrect as there are two possessive forms of the name: Evans' and Evans's.

Chapter Seven

1 The purchase took place on 27 September 1839. 'E Puni even included Pipitea and Te Aro in his sale, although both he and Colonel Wakefield knew that these areas were not his to sell': Ian Wards, *The Shadow of the Land: A Study of British Policy and Racial Conflict in New Zealand 1832–1852*, A. R. Shearer, Government Printer, Wellington, 1968, p.219. See also David Hamer and Roberta Nicholls (eds), *The Making of Wellington, 1800–1914*, Victoria University Press, Wellington, 1990, pp.21–29.

2 E. J. Wakefield to E. G. Wakefield, 8 March 1840, *New Zealand Journal*, Vol. 1, p.204. This last observation is a mystery. Hiakai, Evans's Maori teacher, came from the South Island, not the North.

3 Edward Jerningham Wakefield (ed. Sir Robert Stout), *Adventure in New Zealand, from 1839 to 1844, with Some Account of the Beginning of the British Colonization of the Islands*, Whitcombe & Tombs, Christchurch, 1908, p.149.

4 J. J. Taine (ed. H. W. Fildes), *Reminiscences*, Vol. 1, p.94, qMS-1974, ATL.

5 Thomas Wilmor McKenzie, McKenzie Family Papers, Folder 1, p.28, MS-1357, ATL.

6 Gavin McLean, *Wellington: The First Years of European Settlement, 1840–1850*, Penguin, Auckland, 2000, p.13; E. J. Wakefield, *Adventure in New Zealand*, p.149.

7 The *Aurora*'s demurrage had taken eleven days as Evans's 25,000 bricks needed a specially built lighter to convey them to shore, and the *Oriental* had been similarly delayed: William Wakefield, Diary 1839–1842, 4 and 15 February 1840, MS-2102-2103, ATL. 'In bills of lading', an 'exception' was to be made for Dr Evans for 'peculiar reasons', and the directors made a special order allowing him 100 tons of freight – free of any charge – 'at the rate of 50/- measurement this allowance will amount to £250. The difference due from him is therefore so trifling that I have transmitted to him his Bills of lading separately, and he will account to you for the balance': J. Ward to Col. W. Wakefield, Despatch, 23 October 1839, p.149, NZC, Despatches from Secretary to Principal Agent, NZC 102/1/1, ANZ.

8 Basically this was a square with a river running through, with boulevards, etc. See W. R. Lawrence, *'Huzza for New Zealand!': The Life and Work of William Mein Smith*, qMS-1139, ATL, where the plan is described in detail, pp.96–97.

9 *Gazette*, 1 May 1844.

10 Wakefield to Directors, 27 February 1840, p.153, NZC, Drafts of Despatches from Secretary to Wakefield, NZC 13/1/1, ANZ; William Wakefield, Diary 1839–1842, MS-2102, ATL.

11 J. H. Wallace, *Historical Notes by Early Settlers*, pp.12 and 14, MS-Papers-0108, ATL.

12 Ibid. Also *Journal of the Early Settlers*, Vols 1 and 2, 1923, pp.13–14.

13 W. Deans to father, undated, *New Zealand Journal*, Vol. 1, p.220; *Gazette*, 6 June 1840.

14 E. Betts Hopper, Diary, 2 February 1840, MS-1034, ATL.
15 Horace Fildes Collection, Newspaper Clippings, *Evening Post*, 16 July 1927, p.31, Pq 993.1 FIL 1920, ATL.
16 Amelia Riddiford to Mrs Ramsay, Brompton, 10 March 1840, *New Zealand Journal*, Vol. 1, p.223.
17 E. J. Wakefield to E. G. Wakefield, *New Zealand Journal*, Vol. 1, p.204.
18 The account is described in Taine, *Reminiscences*, Vol. 1, pp.99 and 187, ibid.; and the description of Evans's address is in Lawrence, *'Huzza for New Zealand!'*, p.144, ibid.
19 E. J. Wakefield to E. G. Wakefield, *New Zealand Journal*, Vol. 1, p.204.
20 McLean, *Wellington: The First Years of European Settlement*, pp.17–18.
21 Alexander Mackay, *A Compendium of Official Documents Relative to Native Affairs in the South Island*, http://nzetc.victoria.ac.nz/tm/scholarly/tei-Mac01Comp.html, p.53.
22 *Gazette*, 1 May 1844. The quotation is from an article headed 'Surveys', written when Revans had picked up his duties as editor again. He was on the attack – attacking the Company in England, E. G. Wakefield and Colonel Wakefield.
23 Letters from Charles McGurk, 29 March 1840, *New Zealand Journal*, Vol. 1, p.210. See also David Millar, *Once Upon a Village: A History of Lower Hutt*, New Zealand University Press, Wellington, 1972, p.32.
24 Dr Dorset, *New Zealand Journal*, Vol. 1, p.205.
25 McGurk, *New Zealand Journal*, ibid.
26 Petition to Colonel Wakefield from Dr G. S. Evans and others, 15 March 1840, *New Zealand Papers* 1836–1887, C184, p.62, ML. The signatories were: G. S. Evans, E. Daniell, Daniel Riddiford, D. S. Durie, Henry Cole, J. J. Taine, Henry St Hill, Francis Bradey, John Nattrass, Frank Johnson, G. J. Cole, [?] Wingfield, R. Thomas and J. Thomas.
27 Wallace, *Historical Notes*, p.14, attested to the houses filled with three feet of water. See also Lawrence, *'Huzza for New Zealand!'*, p.142, ibid.
28 *Gazette*, 18 April 1840.
29 W. Wakefield, Draft of Plan for Administration of Justice before Government Representatives, NZC 131/8, ANZ. The District Magistrate was Major Richard Baker. There was a chief constable, and there were two district constables, Henry Cole and James Smith.
30 *Gazette*, 18 April 1840.
31 See Wards, *The Shadow of the Land*, p.50, for an outline of some of the measures the council took for protection of themselves and Maori against hostile tribes. He also validates the Company's concern about France's ambitions for colonising the country: 'every movement of the French in the Pacific aroused official interest', p.52.
32 T. M. Hocken, *The Early History of New Zealand*, John Mackay, Wellington, 1914, pp.256–7.
33 McGurk, *New Zealand Journal*, ibid.; Wallace, *Historical Notes*, pp.12–14.
34 Evans's whare was situated between what is now Molesworth Street and Old St Paul's near Pipitea pa. The whare for Evans was built on Wakefield's instructions before he travelled north.
35 See Taine, *Reminiscences*, Vol. 1, p.121, ibid., for a description of the whare. The *kerewati* he refers to is possibly *harakeke* (flax).
36 Several documents refer to Ruhia as the wife of Porutu, but in a display of Maori cloaks at Te Papa Tongarewa Museum of New Zealand 8 June–22 October 2012, she was referred to as his daughter-in-law. Awhina Tamarapa, the curator of the Maori collection, confirmed this on 30 September 2012.
37 McKenzie Family Papers, ibid. For other accounts, see Taine, *Reminiscences*, Vol. 1, p.121, ibid.; and Dinah Priestley, *Old Thorndon*, Anchorage Press, Wellington, 1988, p.12. McKenzie (1827–1911), Revans's apprentice, eventually branched out with Featherston and others to form the *Independent* newspaper in 1845, later becoming its co-owner. The paper eventually merged with the *New Zealand Times*. He died a few days before his eighty-fourth birthday on 3 March 1911. At his funeral, the same cloak

that had saved his life seventy-one years earlier was draped over his coffin and given to his family, who donated it to Te Papa Tongarewa Museum of New Zealand.

38 Lawrence, *'Huzza For New Zealand!'*, p.142, ibid.

39 Taine, *Reminiscences*, Vol. 1, pp.98–99, ibid. He adds: 'It will thus be seen that credit is due to Dr. George Samuel Evans and the pioneers who came out in the *Adelaide*, that the site of Wellington was definitely adopted', p.187. See also, '[Dr. Evans was] one of the loudest champions for removing from Pito-one to Thorndon': Lawrence, *'Huzza For New Zealand!'*, p.144, ibid.

40 J. Coutts Crawford, *Recollections of Travel in Australia and New Zealand*, Trubner & Co., London, 1880, p.45.

41 'Wm. Wakefield was a man of close reserve and of that peculiarly baffling secretiveness not synonymous with taciturnity': R. Garnett, *Builders of Greater Britain, Edward Gibbon Wakefield: The Colonization of South Australia and New Zealand*, T. Fisher Unwin, London, 1898, p.198.

42 William Gisborne, *New Zealand Rulers and Statesmen, 1840–1885*, Sampson Low, Marston, Searle & Rivington, London, 1886, p.19.

43 E. J. Wakefield, *Adventure in New Zealand*, pp.84, 91.

44 Lawrence, *'Huzzah for New Zealand!'*, p.263, ibid.

45 Hon. Henry W. Petre, *An Account of the Settlements of the New Zealand Company*, p.53, NL. See also J. Beaglehole, *Captain Hobson and the New Zealand Company: A Study in Colonial Administration in Decline and Fall*, Smith College Studies in History, Vol. 13, Nos 1–3, October 1927–April 1928, Massachusetts, 1928, p.51. The surveys were 'fatally held back by Smith'.

46 NZC, Wakefield to Secretary, Letterbook, NZC, 112/1, ANZ: reference to 'disunion', 22 March, Despatch 13; to ' importunities', 2 April, Despatch 14; to change of site, 6 April 1840, Despatch 15. This was published in the *New Zealand Journal*, Vol. 1, 29 August 1840. In the editorial of the *New Zealand Journal*, 18 July 1840, Chapman had already made up his mind, prompted by Revans. The *Adelaide*, he wrote, had been 'detained some weeks after her proper time, by injudiciously putting into the Cape . . .'.

47 Colonel W. Wakefield to Mrs Evans, Permezel Collection.

48 Taine, *Reminiscences*, Vol. 1, p.119, ibid.

49 Patricia Burns (ed. Henry Richardson), *Fatal Success: A History of the New Zealand Company*, Heinemann Reed, Auckland, 1989, p.71; Peter Adams, *Fatal Necessity: British Intervention in New Zealand 1830–1847*, Auckland University Press/Oxford University Press, Auckland, 1977, p.189.

50 Wi Tako, chief of Te Ati Awa, resided at Kumutoto pa, where the Wellington Club now stands on the Terrace. Sir George Gipps, and to some extent the Colonial Office, all believed, as did Gibbon Wakefield (and presumably Evans), in Dr Arnold's theory that 'the uncivilised inhabitants of any country have but a qualified dominion over it, or a right of occupancy only; and that until they establish amongst themselves a settled form of government . . . they cannot grant to individuals not of their own tribe any portion of it, for the simple reason, that they have not themselves any individual property in it': Wards, *The Shadow of the Land*, pp.55 and 56.

51 Evidence of J. W. Child, Report from Select Committee on New Zealand, 1844, p.229, cited in John Miller, *Early Victorian New Zealand: A Study of Racial Tension and Social Attitudes, 1839–1852*, Oxford University Press, London, 1958, p.48.

52 Evidence of Taringa Kuri to Court of Land Claims, 27–29 June 1842, Spain Commission of Inquiry into the Land Claims of the Settlers of Port Nicholson, New Zealand Company claimant, Case 374, OLC 1/906, Box 45, ANZ.

53 Spain Commission of Inquiry into the Land Claims of the Settlers of Port Nicholson, Robert Tod claimant, Case 229, and evidence of Moturoa, 1 June 1842, OLC 1/906, Box 22, ANZ.

54 Evans to Colonel Wakefield, 6 April 1840, Letter 33, NZC, Local and General Letters to Colonel Wakefield, 1840, NZC 108/1, ANZ. This letter and most others are missing from this file.

55 *Gazette*, 18 April 1840.

56 Reihana Reweti is Davis's signature on deed of transfer, 29 April 1840, Spain Commission of Inquiry into the Land Claims of the Settlers of Port Nicholson, OLC 1/906, Box 46, ANZ.

57 Testimony of Richard Davis at Spain's Land Court, 3 June 1842, Spain Commission of Inquiry into the Land Claims of the Settlers of Port Nicholson, OLC 1/906, Box 45, ANZ

58 OLC 1/ 906, Box 46, ANZ, contains the original Deed of Cession dated 29 April 1840 (Case 374). The deed was signed by Evans, Williams, Davis and Mein Smith. The box also includes the deed between Williams and Davis signed by Octavius Hadfield, Hemi, Wiremu and Reihana Tama. Evans to Wakefield, 30 April 1840, Letter 38, NZC, Local and General Letters to Colonel Wakefield, 1840, NZC 108/1, ANZ.

59 G. W. Rusden, *History of New Zealand*, 3 Vols, Melville, Mullen & Slade, Melbourne, 1895. Rusden adds: 'The Government later (1848) sold the native reserves, on the grounds that they were "not legally secured, and that having done so much for the [Maori], it was reasonable that it should be reimbursed from the lands originally set apart for reserves for the benefit of the [Maori]"', Vol. 1, pp.228–9. See also Wakefield to Secretary Ward, Despatch 29, 25 May 1840, pp.372–80, NZC, Despatches from Principal Agent, NZC 3/1/1, ANZ.

60 Dudley Sinclair to Hon. Algernon Tollemache, 23 May 1840, *New Zealand Journal*, Vol. 1, p.232. He added that Hobson had told him he planned to change the name of Thorndon to Durham.

61 'Sovereignty' had another meaning entirely in the Maori version, where the word 'kawanatanga' was used. See article 'Historical Sketch of the Colonization of New Zealand', *Gazette*, 6 September 1839, p.5, where Evans/Wakefield speaks of the missionaries as having invented a word for 'sovereignty'.

62 Miller, *Early Victorian New Zealand*, p.46.

63 F. L. Irvine-Smith, *The Streets of My City, Wellington, New Zealand*, A. H. & A. W. Reed, Wellington, 1948, p.66. See also W. H. Oliver, *The Story of New Zealand*, Faber, London, 1960, pp.48–50.

64 *Colonial Gazette*, 31 May 1845, p.343.

Chapter Eight

1 E. J. Wakefield, Diary, 27 March 1840–1843, 29 April 1840, MS-2208, ATL.

2 G. S. Evans to Mr Wright, Belsize Park, Hampstead, 19 April 1840, *New Zealand Journal*, Vol. 1, p.232.

3 G. S. Evans to Mr Wright, 9 July 1840, *New Zealand Journal*, Vol. 1, pp.292–3.

4 J. J. Taine (ed. H. W. Fildes), *Reminiscences*, Vol. 1, p.122, qMS-1975, ATL.

5 Ibid., p.123, ATL.

6 Ibid., p.101, ATL.

7 Evans to Court of Land Claims, 23 May 1842, Spain Commission of Inquiry into the Land Claims of the Settlers of Port Nicholson, OLC 1/906, Box 45, ANZ.

8 Court of Land Claims, 3 June 1842, Spain Commission of Inquiry into the Land Claims of the Settlers of Port Nicholson, OLC 1/906, Box 45, ANZ.

9 'About 8 am Wednesday 20 May 1840 he walked with Mr. Wade from his house . . . to Mr. Tod's. When they arrived they saw Captain Smith, Dr. Evans, Messrs Carrington and Stokes, besides several other persons collected, with the intention of pulling down Mr. Tod's house . . .': Copy of Certificate of Mr Farrar, 20 May 1840, Robert Tod claimant, Case 229, pp.465–8, Spain Commission of Inquiry into the Land Claims of the Settlers of Port Nicholson, OLC 1/906, Box 22, ANZ. Tod's claim was upheld by Commissioner Spain in 1845.

10 Ibid.

11 *Gazette*, 6 June 1840.

12 Hanson and Alsdorf to a Gentleman at Halifax, 14 April 1840, *New Zealand Journal*, Vol. 1, pp.293–4.
13 Gavin McLean, *Wellington: The First Years of European Settlement, 1840–1850*, Penguin, Auckland, 2000, p.42. See also Taine, *Reminiscences*, Vol. 1, p.71, ibid.
14 S. McD. Martin, *New Zealand in a Series of Letters*, Simmonds & Ward, London, 1845, pp.95, 96; G. H. Scholefield (ed.), *Dictionary of New Zealand Biography*, Department of Internal Affairs, Wellington, 1940, Vol. 2, pp.60–61.
15 Hobson to Normanby, 25 May 1840, referred to in J. Beaglehole, *Captain Hobson and the New Zealand Company: A Study in Colonial Administration in Decline and Fall*, Smith College Studies in History, Vol. 13, Nos 1–3, October 1927–April 1928, Massachusetts, 1928, p.59.
16 Ian Wards, *The Shadow of the Land: A Study of British Policy and Racial Conflict in New Zealand 1832–1852*, A. R. Shearer, Government Printer, Wellington, 1968, p.43. Hobson told Bunbury that 52 Maori had signed the Treaty. Wards adds: 'The single irrevocable step taken matched the single definite intention: notice was sent to the world at large and France in particular, that New Zealand had become British', p.48.
17 Paul Moon, *Hobson: Governor of New Zealand 1840–1842*, David Ling, Auckland, 1998, pp.148–9. This view coincides with that of Company director Somes, who remarked after reading the Treaty that it was merely 'a praiseworthy device to pacify and amuse savages for a time'. It is important to note that at least one contemporary historian agrees with Somes. Before this, any reference to Somes's comment has been treated as proof that the Company had a hostile view toward Maori – which is not borne out by research.
18 Hobson to Normanby, 25 May 1840, British Parliamentary Papers, *Colonies: New Zealand, 1837–1850*, Vol. 3, 1841 (311), pp.15–16, NL.
19 Moon, *Hobson*, argues that Gipps's appointment of Shortland was made deliberately to 'undermine Hobson's ability to effectively govern New Zealand, and thus increase Hobson's dependency on Gipps': p.66. Quoting Martin, he adds that the officials were selected for their 'known incompetency', that Hobson had 'no use for their services' in Sydney, 'and was 'consequently anxious to get rid of them': Martin, *New Zealand in a Series of Letters*, p.81. Robert Hughes, *The Fatal Shore: A History of the Transportation of Convicts to Australia, 1787–1868*, Collins Harvill, London, 1987, shows how busy the capable and humane Gipps was. It seems likely his appointments for New Zealand were injudicious but relieved him of many hangers-on.
20 Beaglehole, *Captain Hobson*, p.56, citing Martin, *New Zealand in a Series of Letters*, pp.95–98. For further insight into Shortland's supposed vanity, pomposity, and lack of literacy and social graces, see Beaglehole, *Captain Hobson*, pp.62 ff.
21 Ensign Edward Best (ed. N. M. Taylor), *Journal of Ensign Best*, Government Printer, Wellington, 1966, p.43.
22 Ibid., pp.224–5.
23 E. J. Wakefield, Diary, 12 June 1840, ibid.
24 Ibid., p.19, See also Evans's speech before Hobson's arrival: *Gazette*, 31 July 1841.
25 J. S. Marais, *The Colonisation of New Zealand*, Milford, London, 1927, p.226. 'Shortland, Cooper, Clarke and Mathew were all chastised by the Secretary of State for "irregular" land dealings, and were compelled to disgorge their acquisitions': Moon, *Hobson*, pp.67–68.
26 Revans to Chapman, 15 May 1840, 16 August 1840, S. Revans, Letters, qMS-1687, ATL.
27 Wakefield to Ward, 27 June 1840, Despatch 20, NZC, Despatches from Principal Agent, NZC 3/1/1, ANZ.
28 Ward to Wakefield, 15 November 1839, Despatch 29, pp.171–206, NZC, Despatches from Secretary to Principal Agent, NZC 102/1/1. Later, he was warned that the validity of the council's proceedings between 5 February, when the Queen had asserted her sovereignty, and 21 May, when Hobson had declared sovereignty over the whole of New Zealand, probably meant that 'the imprisonment of Captain Pearson

of the *Integrity* will be one day brought under the notice of a legal tribunal': NZC 102/1/2, pp.191–4, cited in A. J. Harrop, *England and New Zealand: From Tasman to the Taranaki War*, Methuen, London, 1926, p.74. See also Arthur H. Carman, *The Birth of a City: Wellington 1840–1843*, self-published, Wellington, 1970, citing Alfred Saunders, *The History of New Zealand 1642–1861*, Whitcombe & Tombs, Wellington, 1899, p.9.

29 NZC, Directors' Minutes, 28 November 1840, CO 208/180, ANZ.

30 *Gazette*, 4 July 1840.

31 Evans to Wakefield, 13 July 1840, NZC, Local and General Letters to Colonel Wakefield, NZC 108/1 (all letters now missing from ANZ), quoted in Cecil and Celia Manson, *Curtain Raiser to a Colony*, Whitcombe & Tombs, Christchurch, 1962, p.162.

32 Revans to Chapman, 31 January 1841, Revans Letters, ibid.

33 Taine, *Reminiscences*, Vol. 1, p.117, ibid.

34 Ibid., p.140.

35 This account differs markedly from that of Philip Temple, *A Sort of Conscience: The Wakefields*, Auckland University Press, Auckland, 2002, pp.262–3, 544, who accuses Evans and family of having treated Liocadia shamefully and cruelly, giving no authority other than Revans's letters. In fact, Taine's *Reminiscences*, edited by his grandson, evince the highest respect for and appreciation of the family's many kindnesses – hardly the sort of reaction one would expect from a man whose wife had been the subject of their abuse. See also Taine's letters to his wife, where he admonishes her for her moods: J. J. Taine, Outward Correspondence, MS-Papers-0587-01, ATL.

36 Wakefield to Ward, 25 May 1840, Despatch 19, NZC, Despatches from Principal Agent, NZC 3/1/1, ANZ. The whare Maori had built for Evans was used as the schoolhouse the following year.

37 G. S. Evans to J. Wright, 9 July 1840, *New Zealand Journal*, Vol. 1, pp.292–3.

38 *New Zealand Journal*, Vol. 2, p.65.

39 Hanson to Revans (as editor of *Gazette*), *New Zealand Colonist*, 2 December 1842. Evans's section ran from Woodward Street along Lambton Quay to just short of Stewart Dawson's corner, backing onto Kelburn Avenue, now known as The Terrace.

40 *New Zealand Colonist*, 2 December 1842.

41 Wakefield to Ward, 4 August 1840, Despatch 22, NZC, Despatches from Principal Agent, NZC 3/1/1, ANZ.

42 Capt. Wm. Hobson to Dr George S. Evans, 24 August 1840, *New Zealand Papers*, 1836–1887, C184, pp.76–79, ML.

43 Martin, *New Zealand in a Series of Letters*, p.119. Martin also said Hobson had imported 'useless stores . . . and a body of mounted police' who found the steep terrain of the Bay of Islands not good for exercising their horses.

44 Nine settlers died in a drowning incident: J. Pierce, W. Elsdon, R. Hight, Lancaster, Josiah Tucker, Martin, Griffin, Rogers and 'Colonial Bill'. Four were members of Revans's Pickwick Club. The tragedy 'cast a gloom over the community and the Council meetings were postponed until October': Louis E Ward, *Early Wellington*, Southern Reprints, Papakura, 1928, p.63.

45 *Gazette*, 22 August 1840.

46 Captain Fred. Geo. Moore Collection, 1815–1892, MS-1661-1664, ATL; News Clippings, Early Pioneer Days of New Zealand, in *Wellington Independent*, 10 December 1887, ATL. And see also comment, 'No man ever injured a place more than Shortland did New Zealand', in Martin, *New Zealand in a Series of Letters*, p.187.

47 Moore Collection, ibid.; News Clippings, Early Pioneer Days of New Zealand, in *Wellington Independent*, 10 December 1887, ATL.

48 'Dr. Evans, on several occasions at public meetings, pointed out very forcibly the offensive error of which Captain Hobson's Government had been guilty, in declaring the Sydney convict law in force in New Zealand; when by a different degree we might have been placed under the Laws of England': *Gazette*, 29 August 1841.

Chapter Nine

1 '[Hobson] thought that a clerk from the Police Office was the properest [*sic*] person he could get to make Chief Police Magistrate of the Principal settlement in New Zealand': *Gazette*, 15 and 22 July 1843.

2 Robert Hughes, *The Fatal Shore: A History of the Transportation of Convicts to Australia, 1787–1868*, Collins Harvill, London, 1987, pp.497, 515.

3 G. S. Evans to E. Betts Hopper, 26 September 1840, Edward Betts Hopper, Papers, MS-0535, ATL.

4 On 13 September, Betts Hopper, Henry Petre and some workmen were going down river in a boat laden with timber when it hit a snag. Betts Hopper, standing in the bow, was thrown out and did not resurface, in spite of every effort made to rescue him. It was believed he had been knocked unconscious. His body was recovered after fifteen minutes: Louis Ward, *Early Wellington*, Southern Reprints, Papakura, 1928, pp.63–64.

5 Supplement to the *Gazette*, 10 December 1840.

6 Ibid., which includes Papers and Letters to Sir George Gipps from: Dr Evans, R. D. Hanson Esq., and Henry Moreing Esq.: 24 September, 2 October, 23 October 1840; from E. Deas Thomson, Colonial Secretary, Sydney, 1 October, 20 October, 28 October 1840.

7 *Gazette*, 31 October 1840.

8 *Gazette*, 12 December 1840.

9 NZC, Wakefield to Secretary, Letterbook, pp.206–8, NZC 112/1, ANZ. The case cost £406 19s 1d: Despatches from Principal Agent, 1 January 1843, NZC 3/3/3, ANZ.

10 G. S. Evans to his parents, 9 November 1840, Permezel Collection.

11 *Gazette*, 31 July 1841; and see also Edward Jerningham Wakefield (ed. Sir Robert Stout), *Adventure in New Zealand, from 1839 to 1844, with Some Account of the Beginning of the British Colonization of the Islands*, Whitcombe & Tombs, Christchurch, 1908, p.299.

12 As 'the Duke of Wellington had supported Gibbon Wakefield's South Australia scheme of colonisation, the directors agreed' to change the town's name from Britannia to Wellington at their meeting on 5 May 1840: A. J. Harrop, *The Amazing Career of Edward Gibbon Wakefield*, Allen & Unwin, London, 1928, p.124.

13 George MacMorran, *Some Schools and Schoolmasters of Early Wellington*, Mackay, Wellington, 1900, p.72. The meeting was on 1 December.

14 W. R. Lawrence, '*Huzza for New Zealand!': The Life and Work of Captain Mein Smith*, qMS-1139, ATL, p.209.

15 *Gazette*, 10 December 1840, 19 December 1840; Arthur H. Carman, *The Birth of a City: Wellington 1840–1843*, self-published, Wellington, 1970, pp.14–15.

16 Colonel W. Wakefield to Dr G. S. Evans, 8 January 1841, p.95, *New Zealand Papers*, 1836–87, C184, ML.

17 Ward to Wakefield, 2 July 1840, Despatch 60, Revocation of memo to G. S. Evans, pp.40–45, NZC, Despatches from Secretary to Principal Agent, NZC 102/1/2, ANZ.

18 Ward to Wakefield, 6 August 1840, Despatch 66, pp.66–68, NZC, Despatches from Secretary to Principal Agent, NZC 102/1/2, ANZ.

19 Ward to Wakefield, 18 August 1840, Despatch 74, pp.114–16, NZC, Despatches from Secretary to Principal Agent, NZC 102/1/2, ANZ. Hanson lost 30 shares, Daniell 40, Daniel Riddiford 40, Dudley Sinclair 40, Betts Hopper 20 and John Dorset 20. The shares were secured 'by paid up share certificates calculated at par with a reservation of an Equity of Redemption of such shares on payment of the amount at which they were so calculated at any time before 15 January, 1840'.

20 Patricia Burns (ed. Henry Richardson), *Fatal Success: A History of the New Zealand Company*, Heinemann Reed, Auckland, 1989, pp.174–5, 178.

21 Revans to Chapman, 31 January 1841, S. Revans, Letters, qMS-1687, ATL.

22 Lawrence, '*Huzza for New Zealand!*', pp.196–7, ibid.; J. J. Taine (ed. H. W. Fildes), *Reminiscences*, Vol. 1, p.192, qMS-1975, ATL. After living for a time with Thomas

Partridge, Revans stayed with the Smiths in all their homes – in Petone, in Tinakori Road and later in the Wairarapa. See also A. H. McLintock, *Crown Colony Government in New Zealand*, Government Printer, Wellington, 1958, on Revans's diatribes in the press: 'many . . . were repelled by the extravagances of Revans': pp.271–2.

23 Revans to Chapman, 31 January 1841, p.56, Revans Letters, ibid.

24 Ibid. Revans wrote 'in a manner consistent with what Dr. McLintock calls [his] "turbulent and rather coarse character"'; 'Revans habitually hovered on the boundary of defamation, if he did not cross it': Robin Cooke, QC, *Portrait of a Profession: The Centennial Book of the New Zealand Law Society*, A. H. & A. W. Reed, Wellington, 1969, pp.23, 24.

25 Revans to Chapman 18 April 1841, Revans Letters, ibid.

26 Partridge to Chapman, 30 April 1841, H. S. Chapman Collection, qMS-0417, ATL.

27 Burns, *Fatal Success*, p.163.

28 Meeting held on 4 January 1841. Investors were: Evans, Colonel Wakefield, Hon. Henry Petre, Crawford, St Hill, Partridge, Revans and others. See Hon. H. W. Petre, *An Account of the Settlements of the New Zealand Company*, Smith Elder, London, 1842, pp.62–73. The committee comprised Evans, Captain Daniell, Crawford, J. Watt, W. B. Rhodes, David Scott, George Hunter, Wm. Brewer, Henry Moreing and R. D. Hanson. Brewer was secretary and Hunter treasurer.

29 *Gazette*, 13 March 1841.

30 *New Zealand Colonist*, 15 November 1842. In September 1843 it was announced that 'the machine recently invented by Messrs Reid and Harvey is now complete and ready for preparing [flax]': *Gazette*, 11 September 1843.

31 Dr G. S. Evans and others, to Colonel W. Wakefield, 18 January 1841, with reply from Colonel Wakefield, 3 February 1841, published in *Gazette*, 6 February 1841. See also Letter No. 22, 24 March 1841, NZC, Local and General Letters to Colonel Wakefield, NZC 108/1/2, ANZ.

32 Taine, *Reminiscences*, Vol. 1, p.207, ibid.

33 *Gazette*, 6 March 1841: letter signed 'One of the Billingsgates in response to Mercurator'. Although Hobson was rebuked by the Colonial Office for poaching Company labour, the petition failed largely because of its wording and because it had not been sent through the correct channels: Alfred Saunders, *The History of New Zealand 1642–1861*, Whitcombe & Tombs, Wellington, 1899, p.142.

34 M. Murphy to Hobson, 27 February 1841, pp.259–65, *NSW Governor's Despatches and Enclosures 1841–1843*, A-1267-20, ML.

35 Evans's evidence to Court of Land Claims, 23 May 1842, Spain Commission of Inquiry into the Land Claims of the Settlers of Port Nicholson, OLC 1/906, Box 45, ANZ.

36 Murphy to Hobson, 27 February 1841, ibid.

37 Evans to Major David Stark Durie, 3 March 1841, Robert R. Strang, Business Papers, 1840–1843, MS-0726, ATL.

38 Walter Brodie, *Remarks of the Past and Present State of New Zealand, its Government, Capabilities and Prospects*, Whittaker, London, 1845, pp.84–86, 111–12.

39 G. S. Evans to Colonel Wakefield, 24 March 1841, NZC, Local and General Letters, NZC 108/1/2, ANZ.

40 *Gazette*, 27 March 1841. The signatories to the petition were G. B. Earp, W. B. Rhodes, John Wade, Robert Waitt and Thomas Machattie.

Chapter Ten

1 *Gazette*, 3 April 1841.

2 *New Zealand Journal*, Vol. 2, 13 April 1841, p.224.

3 'The houses erected in Wellington have cost at least £18,000. In every direction, large stores and private dwellings are springing up': Hon. Henry W. Petre, *An Account of the Settlements of the New Zealand Company*, Smith, Elder & Co., London, 1842, p.29.

'There are about 25 houses under construction costing between £300–£900 each and about the same number costing £150–£300 . . . five times the number of native clay houses': Partridge to Chapman, 24 February 1841, H. S. Chapman, Letters and sundry, qMS-0417, ATL.

4 Michael King, *The Penguin History of New Zealand*, Penguin, New Zealand, 2003, p.172.

5 Golders Hill is now known as Eccleston Hill: George Macmorran, *Some Schools and Schoolmasters of Early Wellington*, Mackay, Wellington, 1900, pp.19, 20, 36. Miss Tilke had been teaching for a little over a year when she married Mr Lawrence, a farmer, surveyor and fellow passenger on the *Adelaide*. The couple moved (appropriately) to Adelaide and the school temporarily closed, but was soon taken over by Mrs Buxton who ran it until it was moved to Tinakori Road in 1850. George Grace was the first male teacher, arriving a week after the *Adelaide* on the *Lady Lilford*. He opened his school 5 October 1840 on Thorndon Flat.

6 G. S. Evans to J. Wright, 9 July 1840, *New Zealand Journal*, Vol. 1, pp.292–3. Brees' Panorama of Wellington (1847) was taken from the 'terrace in Dr. Evans's garden': S. C. Brees, *Pictorial Illustrations of New Zealand*, London, 1848, p.35, NL.

7 Charles Heaphy, *Narrative of a Residence in Various Parts of New Zealand: Together with a Description of the Present State of the Company's Settlements*, Capper Press, Christchurch, 1972 (facsimile edn), p.71. See also Bradey to prospective settlers, *New Zealand Journal*, Vol. 2, p.224.

8 *New Zealand Journal*, 6 August 1842. Also see W. R. Lawrence, *'Huzza for New Zealand!': The Life and Work of Captain Mein Smith*, p.168, qMS-1139, ATL. Curling Young drowned later that year while wading across a stream in Nelson.

9 *Gazette*, 17 April 1841.

10 Ibid. Petition of Magistrates to Governor Hobson, signed by Col. Wakefield, R. D. Hanson, G. S. Evans, H. St Hill, G. Hunter, E. Daniell. Also Governor Hobson to Lord Stanley, 24 May 1841 (encl.), British Parliamentary Papers, *Colonies: New Zealand*, Vol. 3, 1842 (569), pp.108–9, NL.

11 *Gazette*, Supplement, 17 April 1841, reproduced in *New Zealand Journal*, Vol. 2, pp.194–6.

12 Ibid., 8 May 1841. Other committee members were White, Strang, Wicksteed, Hunter and Earp.

13 Ibid., 10 April 1841; J. Beaglehole, *Captain Hobson and the New Zealand Company: A Study in Colonial Administration in Decline and Fall*, Smith College Studies in History, Vol. 13, Nos 1–3, October 1927–April 1928, Massachusetts, 1928, pp.84–85. There were six members of Hobson's Legislative Council: the Colonial Secretary (Shortland), Attorney General (Swainson), Colonial Treasurer (Cooper), and three Justices of the Peace. Hobson was president. The first session lasted six weeks.

14 S. McD. Martin, *New Zealand in a Series of Letters*, Simmonds & Ward, London, pp.131–4. He adds: 'the Government officials were choosing the best lands – far more than Gipps had allowed them. There were complaints, Hobson then reduced them – Shortland, Cooper [treasurer] and Felton Mathew [Surveyor-General] purchased more than eight acres over and above their other land – making in all about 14 acres for Government officers out of 38. Shortly after the sale, Shortland "the chief land jobber in the colony", sold his selection for which he paid £315 to Mr. Porter for about £1500. Immediately after the purchase, Porter, a newly arrived old ship's captain, was elected a member of the Legislative Council': pp.126 ff. '[George Sisson] Cooper the Treasurer and Collector of Customs was convicted of misuse of Customs monies and his career came to a sudden end': Alan Mulgan, *The City of the Strait: Wellington and its Province, a Centennial History*, A. H. & A. W. Reed, Wellington, 1939, pp.104–5.

15 T. M. Hocken, *Early History of New Zealand*, John Mackay, Wellington, 1914, pp.236, 252.

16 Hobson to Colonial Secretary, 24 May 1841, Encl., BPP, *Colonies: New Zealand*, Vol. 3, 1842 (569), pp.108–9, NL.

17 Arthur H. Carman, *The Birth of a City: Wellington 1840–1843*, self-published, Wellington, 1970, p.19. The council first met on 24 May that year.

18 Revans to Chapman, Partridge to Chapman, 27 June 1841, Chapman Letters, ibid.

19 Robin Cooke, QC (ed.), *Portrait of a Profession: The Centennial Book of the New Zealand Law Society*, A. H. & A. W. Reed, Wellington, 1969, p.29. Brandon became a qualified solicitor in February 1844, and enjoyed a distinguished career in Wellington.

20 F. A. Molesworth, William Swainson, G. S. Evans and others to Colonel Wakefield, 26 October 1841, letter 80, NZC, Local and General Letters to Colonel Wakefield, NZC 108/1/2, ANZ. Apart from Evans, the signatories to the petition were Francis Molesworth, William Swainson, George Hunter, F. M. Partridge, and Messrs Child, White, Barton, Stokes, St Hill, Moreing and Wicksteed. The directors told Wakefield it would pay only after the district became a municipal body. Wakefield sent the directors' reply to Evans, which was published in the *Gazette*, 29 January 1842.

21 Wakefield to Ward, Despatch with encl. Edmund Halswell to W. Wakefield, 9 February 1842, pp.148–9, NZC, Despatches from Principal Agent, NZC 3/2/2, ANZ. Davis's acre was at the northern junction of Davis Street and Thorndon Quay

22 Carman, *The Birth of a City*, pp.17–18.

23 J. H. Wallace and R. A. A. Sherrin (ed. Thomson S. Leys), *The Early History of New Zealand, from Earliest Times to 1840*, Brett's Historical Series, Auckland, 1890, p.564. Copies of the *Government Gazette* are stored in the NZPL.

24 This is similar to the speech recalled by Moore. Moore was correct in the timing, but not in the content, although the sentiments were the same.

25 *Gazette*, 31 July 1841.

26 *Gazette*, 7 August 1841.

27 Edward Jerningham Wakefield (ed. Sir Robert Stout), *Adventure in New Zealand, from 1839 to 1844, with Some Account of the Beginning of the British Colonization of the Islands*, Whitcombe & Tombs, Christchurch, 1908, p.196.

28 Hanson took the major role in drawing up the Corporation Bill. 'Nobody – not even Evans – had equalled the effort Hanson had put into the Corporation Act': *Colonist*, 23 September 1842.

29 *Gazette*, 21 August 1841.

30 Ibid. Given the men deputed to carry this out, two of whom 'defected' to the government within the week, it is not known if the resolution was seen through.

31 Petition to Governor Hobson on behalf of the Settlers of Wellington, BPP, *Colonies: New Zealand*, Vol. 3, 1842 (569), pp.108–10, NL. Wakefield, Henry St Hill, Hanson, Hunter, Evans and Daniell presented and signed the memorial. Also see pp.161–2 for Evans's relations with Governor Hobson.

32 '[T]hree gentlemen had not been restored to the Commission of Peace by Hobson, because of their objection to his seduction of labourers from Port Nicholson to Auckland': Wakefield to Secretary, 13 September 1841, Despatch 69, NZC, Despatches from Principal Agent, NZC 3/1/1, ANZ. 'The idea of the governor moving to Wellington appeared in many strange contexts, from the congratulations to Hobson of the six magistrates on . . . New Zealand becoming a separate colony, to a loyal address to the Queen on the birth of the Princess Royal': Patricia Burns (ed. Henry Richardson), *Fatal Success: A History of the New Zealand Company*, Heinemann Reid, Auckland, 1989, p.176.

33 *New Zealand Journal*, Vol. 4, 1845, p.458: comment following letter from S. Stephens, Nelson Magistrate, dated 11 May 1844. The editor added: 'It is only such men as Shortland, who governed Hobson, that are capable of doing things of this nature.' From 1843, when Chapman was appointed Chief Justice, William Bridges was editor of the *New Zealand Journal* and secretary of the New Zealand Society.

34 *Gazette*, 4 September 1841.

35 Bagehot on 'The Character of Sir Robert Peel', *Works*, cited in Walter E. Houghton, *The Victorian Frame of Mind, 1830–1870*, Oxford University Press, London, 1957, pp.397–9.

36 Hobson to Secretary of State for Colonies, Lord Stanley, with Encl. Hobson to Colonel Wakefield, 5 September 1841, BPP, *Colonies: New Zealand*, Vol. 3, 1842 (569), p.175, NL. Also see Peter Adams, *Fatal Necessity: British Intervention in New Zealand 1830–1847*, Auckland University Press/Oxford University Press, Auckland, 1977, p.191.

37 Petition to Governor Hobson from Residents of Wellington, BPP, *Colonies: New Zealand*, Vol. 3, 1842 (569), pp.108–10, NL; Comment on 'influential' settlers, and 'disaffected' settlers pressing for 'exclusive privileges', see pp.161–2.

38 *Gazette*, 3 July 1841. In fact the price Hobson paid was '£15,000, when its real value was less than one hundredth of that sum': A. J. Harrop, *England and New Zealand: From Tasman to the Taranaki War*, Methuen, London, 1926, p.150.

39 J. J. Taine (ed. H. W. Fildes), *Reminiscences*, 19 April 1841, Vol. 2, p.215, qMS-1975, ATL.

40 See Paul Moon, *Hobson: Governor of New Zealand, 1840–1842*, David Ling, Auckland, 1998, pp.182–213. Clendon's sale is discussed on p.171. The rebuke from Stanley appears in Stanley to Hobson, 10 May 1842, BPP, *Colonies: New Zealand*, Vol. 3 (569), pp.148–9, NL.

41 Captain Hobson to Secretary of State for the Colonies, 20 October 1841, ibid., p.161; on Hanson and Earp being 'warmest and most zealous supporters', ibid.

42 The deal was later annulled by the Colonial Office.

43 Douglas Pike (gen. ed.), *Australian Dictionary of Biography*, Melbourne University Press, Carlton, Victoria, 1972, Vol. 4, pp.336–40. Hanson had also differed from Wakefield's attitude towards Maori reserves and appropriation of land: see Burns, *Fatal Success*, pp.208–9, 213.

44 *Gazette*, 27 August 1841.

45 E. J. Wakefield, *Adventure in New Zealand*, pp.201–2. 'As a result [of Hobson's removal of the three magistrates] he was snubbed by all the influential landowners and some merchants': Wakefield to Secretary, 13 September 1841, Despatch 69, NZC, Despatches from Principal Agent, NZC 3/1/1, ANZ.

46 *Gazette*, 29 August 1841. Among the residents who did attend were Baron Alsdorf, Captain Campbell, Pharazyn, Chetham and Featherston.

47 Wakefield to Hobson, 24 August 1841, Appendix to Report from Select Committee, App. no. 26, Encls. no. 4, 6, BPP, *Colonies: New Zealand*, Vol. 2, 1844, pp.543 ff., NL; NZC, Wakefield to Secretary, Letterbook, pp.169–71, NZC 112/1, ANZ.

48 Ibid. NZC, Wakefield to Secretary, Letterbook, p.171, NZC 112/1, ANZ. Hobson to Residents of Port Nicholson, BPP, *Colonies: New Zealand*, Vol. 2, 1844, p.545, NL. Hobson to Secretary of State for the Colonies Lord Stanley, 13 November 1841, re validity of title to land and proclamation withdrawn, BPP, *Colonies: New Zealand*, Vol. 3, 1842 (569), pp.173–4, NL.

49 NZC, Wakefield to Secretary, Letterbook, 11 September 1841, pp.169–71, NZC 112/1, ANZ.

50 Hobson to Colonial Secretary, 14 December 1841, Despatch 72, Encl., BPP, *Colonies: New Zealand*, Vol. 3, 1842 (569), p.199, NL. Also see Mulgan, *The City of the Strait*, p.117.

51 E. J. Wakefield, *Adventure in New Zealand*, p.204.

52 *Gazette*, 25 September 1841. The siege of St Joan of Arc took place in the late fifteenth century, so this reference is puzzling. Perhaps Evans was referring to Liardet's forebears. Liardet was a naval captain. See obituary, *Lyttelton Times*, 17 June 1863. Also Jerningham's observation about the snub of Hobson during the toasts is not confirmed by the *Gazette*, which noted: '"The Governor of New Zealand" was then toasted, and out of courtesy responded to without opposition.'

Chapter Eleven

1 *Gazette*, 9 October 1841; Edward Jerningham Wakefield (ed. Sir Robert Stout), *Adventure in New Zealand, from 1839 to 1844, with Some Account of the Beginning of the British Colonization of the Islands*, Whitcombe & Tombs, Christchurch, 1908, pp.450–3. The Pakeha was given a sentence of three months.

2 A Maori cloak of Ati Awa origin, circa 1840 and now at Te Papa, was donated by William Lindsay of Scotland, a descendant of the Riddifords; see also the *Melbourne Punch* cartoon in which Evans is depicted wearing another cloak.

3 *Gazette*, 10 November 1841.

4 The Chamber of Commerce was officially established in 1856. James Kelham was the first president until 1858, then Hon. John Johnston, George Hunter, W. M. Bannatyne, W. Waring Taylor, Chas. J. Pharazyn, E. Pearce and Nathaniel Levin.

5 *Gazette*, 24 November 1841, published the new Commission of Peace.

6 Arthur H. Carman, *The Birth of a City: Wellington 1840–1843*, self-published, Wellington, 1970, pp.43–48; T. M. Hocken, *Early History of New Zealand*, John Mackay, Wellington, 1914, p.259.

7 *Gazette*, 27 November 1841.

8 *Gazette*, 15 and 18 December 1841. Chaffers was a 'very good Harbour Master' who had drawn up a 'very good chart of the harbour'. He had been employed by the government though not paid by them. After he signed the petition for the recall of Hobson, his two-year contract was terminated by Wakefield: see Despatch 44, 24 April 1841, NZC, Wakefield to Secretary, Letterbook, NZC 112/1, ANZ.

9 Gavin McLean, *Wellington: The First Years of European Settlement, 1840–1850*, Penguin, Auckland, 2000, p.55 asserts: 'The Wakefield Club, later renamed the Wellington Club . . . dominated by George Evans and . . . Molesworth, Partridge, Levin, Chetham etc'. Others also allege the Wakefield Club was renamed, but it is clear the two clubs were separate entities. See A. W. Beasley, *The Club on the Terrace: The Wellington Club 1841–1996*, The Club, Wellington, 1996, p.16, which does not include Evans's name in the list of the original members of the Wakefield Club, which was advertised as being open for joining on 1 October 1840, when Evans, Moreing and Hanson were in Sydney; and J. H. Wallace and R. A. A. Sherrin (ed. Thomson S. Leys), *The Early History of New Zealand*, Brett's Historical Series, Auckland, 1890, p.557, which lists the names of the Wakefield Club's members. Hunter Family Papers, MS-Papers-0049-137, ATL, lists them as: Messrs. Brewer, St Hill, Guyton, G. Hunter Sen., Major Baker, Alsdorf, Halswell, Hunt, Partridge, Dudley Sinclair, E. J. Wakefield and J. Wicksteed. Committee: Col. Wakefield, Messrs Daniell, Watt, Murphy, Crawford, Dorset, Molesworth.

10 *Gazette*, advertisement, 18 December 1841. The first committee of the Wellington Club comprised Evans, Hanson, Chetham, Durie and Waitt; note that Partridge was amongst the original members. His partnership with Revans had split up. Members: Messrs. Taylor, Levin, Hanson, Johnson, Moore, Mantell, Mocatta, Partridge, Hine, Alsdorf, Fitzherbert, Stokes, Bethune, Penny, Watt, Molesworth and Hogg. See also *Early Settlers' Journal*, Vol. 1, pp.14–15.

11 *Gazette*, 5 January 1842.

12 Reverend G. Evans to Dr G. S. Evans, 8 September 1841, Permezel Collection.

13 NZC, Certificates of Transfer, 30 January 1841, 15 March 1842, Old Land Orders, NZC 33/48d, ANZ.

14 W. Brewer to Chapman, 4 April 1842, H. S. Chapman, Letters, qMS-0417, ATL. In 1840 either Charles or William Brewer was involved in a duel on the beach at Kororareka with John Kelly. The reason for the dispute is unclear; one report (J. S. Gully) says it was over a woman, another (Eric Ramsden) over an unsettled debt. 'Part of Kelly's wig was blown away, and the opposing ball passed through Brewer's left whisker': Robin Cooke, QC (ed.), *Portrait of a Profession: The Centennial Book of the New Zealand Law Society*, A. H. & A. W. Reed, Wellington, 1969, p.28.

15 Brewer to Chapman, 12 April 1842, Chapman Letters, ibid.
16 W. R. Lawrence, *'Huzza for New Zealand!': The Life and Work of Captain Mein Smith*, pp.189–90, qMS-1139, ATL.
17 G. B. Earp (pp.110–15) and J. C. Crawford (pp.158–9), Evidence to Committee on New Zealand, 13 June 1844, British Parliamentary Papers, *Colonies: New Zealand*, Vol. 2, NL. Crawford added that Maori believed by denying the sale of land they might get more payment for it. 'They are . . . an exceedingly greedy race, . . . in several instances when a white man tried to settle upon land, they insisted on a fresh payment.'
18 *Gazette*, 2 April 1842.
19 David McGill, *Pioneers of Port Nicholson*, Reed, Wellington, 1984, p.32.
20 *Gazette*, 28 April 1842.
21 Despatch 15, 1 February 1843, pp.203–49 with encl., R. D. Hanson to Secretary of Aborigines' Protection Society, 24 May 1842, NZC, Despatches from Secretary to Principal Agent, NZC 102/5/11, ANZ.
22 George Clarke Jnr, *Notes on Early Life in New Zealand*, Walch & Sons, Hobart, 1903, p.47.
23 For Clarke, Spain was 'a man of solid intelligence but with a good deal of legal pedantry about him. Somewhat slow in thinking, very wooden in his . . . handling with new emergencies, steady and plodding . . . honest in intentions, utterly immovable to threats, though he might have been softened by flattery': ibid., p.47.
24 From 1824 until 1830 George Clarke Jnr had lived in New Zealand with his father. He spent seven years in Australia with Marsden, four of which he spent on his education in Hobart. From 1837 to 1839 he studied the classics under Reverend William Williams in New Zealand. From 1839 he made many missionary journeys in the East Cape. In December 1840 he had joined his father at the Bay of Islands, and acted as a clerk in the Native Department: see G. H. Scholefield (ed.), *Dictionary of New Zealand Biography*, Department of Internal Affairs, Wellington, 1940, Vol. 1, pp.159–60.
25 Clarke, *Notes on Early Life in New Zealand*, p.50.
26 Ibid., p.35.
27 Spain's court sat in a building in Manners Street: J. J. Taine (ed. H. W. Fildes), *Reminiscences*, Vol. 2, p.240, qMS-1975, ATL. Taine gives the date as 16 May.
28 William Shakespeare, *The Taming of the Shrew*, I, ii, lines 276–7.
29 Despatch 109, pp.377–93, NZC, Despatches from Principal Agent, NZC 3/2/2, ANZ.
30 *Gazette*, 28 April 1842. See also E. J. Wakefield, *Adventure in New Zealand*, pp.487–97 ff.
31 Wakefield told the Company's secretary that he expected the inquiry to be 'little more than a matter of form, except in those instances where compensation in land elsewhere was to be awarded to individuals making good their claims to small patches within the boundaries of that part of the Colony to which the Company is restricted': see Despatch, 30 May 1842, p.323, NZC, Despatches from Principal Agent, NZC 3/2/2, ANZ.
32 Wakefield may well have been correct. Thirty years later Wi Tako retracted his statement and said he believed Te Puni and Wharepouri were entitled to sell all of Port Nicholson to the Company. See Waitangi Tribunal, *Te Whanganui a Tara me ona Takiwa: Report on the Wellington District* (Wai 145), Legislation Direct, Wellington, 2003, available at the Ministry of Justice website: www.justice.govt.nz.
33 Robert Tod to Evans, 26 and 27 May 1842, Spain Commission of Inquiry into the Land Claims of the Settlers of Port Nicholson, Robert Tod claimant, Case 229, OLC 1/906, Box 22, pp.465–8, ANZ. Robert Park testified on 1 August that he believed the land to be worth £1,067 10s, as it involved 610 feet of frontage. He thought at the time of Tod's purchase it was worth only £20. Moturoa testified on 20 June he shared £20 with Mangatuku. Davis got some payment for one side of the land that he had cultivated, although he had given no payment for it. On 18 July, Mangatuku said he received £5 and Moturoa £15 for it. Mangatuku gave another £7 to Davis, and Moturoa another £2 to Davis.
34 Rendell McIntosh, Chairman, Parnell Heritage, Letter to Editor, *New Zealand Herald*, 19 December 2006.

35 George Clarke Jnr, letters to his father, 15 August 1842, 6 October 1842, 25 November 1842, Letters and Journals, Vol. 7, pp.257–77, qMS-0469, ATL.
36 Commissioner Spain's Report on Land Claims of New Zealand Company to Governor Fitzroy, 31 March 1845, Spain Commission of Inquiry into the Land Claims of the New Zealand Company, OLC 1/906, Box 45, ANZ.
37 *Gazette*, 4 June 1842.
38 Robert Tod claimant, 1 June 1842, Spain Commission of Inquiry into the Land Claims of the New Zealand Company, Case 229, OLC 1/906, Box 22, ANZ. Tod gave evidence on 26 and 27 May, 1 and 2 (or 7 – obscured) June, and 18 July 1842.
39 As expressed in his letter to parents, June 1843.
40 *Gazette*, 11 June 1842.
41 *Gazette*, report of meeting on 7 June 1842, published in *New Zealand Journal*, Vol. 4, pp.55–57.
42 *Gazette*, 4, 8, 18 June 1842.

Chapter Twelve

1 Spain to Wakefield, 20 June 1842, Letter 28, NZC, Land Claims Correspondence of William Spain and George Clarke, NZC 131/1/1, ANZ.
2 Letter 118, 22 July 1842, p.324, NZC, Wakefield to Secretary, Letterbook, NZC 112/1, ANZ.
3 Davis and Moturoa to Court (Mr Halswell), 18 July 1842, Moturoa to Court, 31 May 1842, Copy of Certificate of Mr Farrar, 20 May 1840, Spain Commission of Inquiry into the Land Claims of the Settlers of Port Nicholson, Robert Tod claimant, Case 229, OLC 1/906, Box 22, ANZ.
4 Ibid.; see also, Thomas Barker claimant, Case 287, 2 September 1842, OLC 1/906, Box 22, which is referred to in Spain's final report in New Zealand Company claimant, Case 374, OLC 1/906, Box 45, ANZ.
5 George Clarke Jnr to his father, 20 January 1843, George Clarke Jnr., Letters and Journals, Vol. 7, pp.281–2, qMS-0469, ATL. Clarke was also co-referee for the final claims adjustments with Wakefield and the Company's agents in the other settlements: Wanganui, Nelson and New Plymouth.
6 Clarke Jnr to father, 1, 8, 15, 17 March 1843, pp.299–372, Clarke Letters, ibid.
7 George Jnr Clarke, *Notes on Early Life in New Zealand*, Walch & Sons, Hobart, 1903, pp.53–54.
8 *Gazette*, 29 June, 1842.
9 *Gazette*, 4 February 1843.
10 J. J. Taine (ed. H. W. Fildes), *Reminiscences*, p.241, 25 June 1842, Vol. 2, qMS-1975, ATL. Edward Charles Chetham's family originally came from Derbyshire, but later adopted the additional surname of Strode, when his father, Admiral Sir Edward Chetham, succeeded to the estate of the Strode family of Southhill, Somerset, in 1845. Edward (1815–1896) arrived in New Zealand in 1841. His brother, Alfred Chetham Strode, who migrated with him, was appointed a Dunedin magistrate. He bought the Earnscleugh run with William Fraser in 1860: 'Pacific Island Travel', Permezel Collection.
11 *Wellington Independent*, 9 January 1864.
12 Henry Ware, Moses Ngaponga to Evans, 6 July 1842, Spain Commission of Inquiry into the Land Claims of the Settlers of Port Nicholson, OLC 1/906, Box 45, ANZ.
13 *Gazette*, 28 May 1842.
14 Te Puni to Evans, 7–8 July 1842, Spain Commission of Inquiry into the Land Claims of the New Zealand Company, OLC 1/906, Box 45, ANZ. Wairarapa had alleged the goods were for Korokoro, Tahataharoa and Parororangi.
15 Wakefield to Secretary, New Zealand Company, 22 August 1842, Encls. 27, 28, pp.554–65, NZC, Despatches from Principal Agent, NZC 3/2/2, ANZ. See also Despatch 11, pp.64 ff., NZC, Despatches from Principal Agent, NZC 3/4/4, ANZ, being an 'Account of Meeting with Mr. FitzRoy and others to discuss compensation to Maori'. FitzRoy

'strongly recommended Mr. Clarke not to be led away by the exaggerated notions of natives to make exorbitant demands for them and to Mr. Spain to award the most reasonable and moderate sum sufficient to meet the justice of each case'.

16 Fitzherbert had arrived in his 109-ton schooner, the *Lady Leigh*, almost a year earlier with a medical degree but wanting to set up in trade. Eight years Evans's junior, he was a fellow alumnus of Merchant Taylors' School.

17 Patricia Burns (ed. Henry Richardson), *Fatal Success: A History of the New Zealand Company*, Heinemann Reed, Auckland, 1989, p.213.

18 Rowland Davis to editor: refers to 'a learned doctor having written a leading article some weeks hence', *Gazette*, 19 October 1842. Davis was a strong working-man's advocate. Evans wrote several leading articles for the newspaper during this period.

19 Perhaps Evans was non-threatening politically at this time as this was a social event they were discussing.

20 The deputation consisted of Murphy, Halswell, Spain and St Hill.

21 Kelham to Wakefield, 3 August 1842, Evans to Wakefield, 8 August, Wakefield to Directors, 11 August 1842, pp.526–34, NZC, Despatches from Principal Agent, NZC 3/2/2, ANZ. Also Letter 132, p.332, NZC, Wakefield to Secretary, Letterbook, NZC 112/1, ATL.

22 Ward to Wakefield, 26 January 1843, pp.180 ff., NZC, Despatches from Secretary to Principal Agent, NZC 102/2/2, ANZ.

23 J. Beaglehole, *Captain Hobson and the New Zealand Company: A Study in Colonial Administration in Decline and Fall*, Smith College Studies in History, Vol. 13, Nos 1–3, October 1927–April 1928, Massachusetts, 1928, p.103. See also Spain's report on his Commission of Inquiry into the Land Claims of the New Zealand Company, 31 March 1845, Box 45, p.51, OLC 1/906, where he criticises Clarke's conduct at length.

24 William Gisborne, *New Zealand Rulers and Statesmen 1840–1885*, Sampson Low, Marston, Searle & Rivington, London, 1886, p.10.

25 A. J. Harrop, *England and New Zealand: From Tasman to the Taranaki War*, Methuen, London, 1926, p.145.

26 Ibid., p.150.

27 Kathleen Coleridge, 'Thriving on Impressions: The Pioneer Years of Wellington Printing', in David Hamer and Roberta Nicholls (eds), *The Making of Wellington 1800–1914*, Victoria University Press, Wellington, 1990, pp.89–106. *Government Gazette*, Appendix to minutes of Tuesday, 8 April 1845, NZPL, gives the details of the taxes etc.

28 *Gazette*, 29 May 1844.

Chapter Thirteen

1 In fact, the ordinance rules dictated that the elections were to be held in December, not October.

2 Gavin McLean, *Wellington: The First Years of European Settlement, 1840–1850*, Penguin, Auckland, 2000, p.47. The tenure of the council and its first mayor George Hunter was short. It was nullified by the government because 'its powers conflicted with the Crown's preemptive monopoly'. The Crown objected to two clauses: the right to erect beacons and lighthouses, and the power to deal with the waste lands within its territory, which was viewed as an attempt to seize its property.

3 *Gazette*, 17 August 1842, cited in Arthur H. Carman, *The Birth of a City: Wellington 1840–1843*, self-published, Wellington, 1970, p.67.

4 In favour, 43 votes; against, 33; with several men abstaining.

5 *Colonist*, 6 September 1842.

6 W. Cargill, E. S. Halswell, H. Moreing and E. J. Wakefield to B. Hawes, Under-Secretary of State for Colonies, 5 October 1846, in Edward Gibbon Wakefield, *A View of the Art of Colonization 1837*, J. W. Parker, London, 1849, p.503.

7 *New Zealand Colonist and Port Nicholson Advertiser*, 23 September 1842.

8 The extract tells of Neptune calming the seas after Aeneas' fleet had been nearly destroyed. Virgil wrote it to mirror the rise of Augustus between 44 and 31 BC when he had brought to a close Rome's civil war, a war that had raged for a hundred years.
9 For a full report of the proceedings from this point, see Appendix Five.
10 Virgil, *The Aeneid*, Book 1, Lines 148–53, C. Day Lewis, translator, *The Eclogues, Georgics and Aeneid of Virgil*, Oxford University Press, London, 1966, p.136.
11 *Colonist*, 27 September 1842. Rumsay Forster swiftly pointed out to the *Colonist* that he had not moved a vote of censure on Evans. He had merely 'made observations' in reply to Mr Revans, who had expressed deep regret at the conduct of the meeting in refusing Dr Evans a hearing. The motion of censure had been made by J. H. Greenwood. The *Colonist* apologised for its error.
12 *Colonist*, 23, 27 September 1842.
13 *Colonist*, 23 September 1842.
14 Henry Cockburn, Brougham's friend of forty years' standing, cited in Robert Stewart, *Henry Brougham: His Public Career 1778–1868*, Bodley Head, London, 1986, p.319.
15 William Hazlitt, cited in Stewart, *Henry Brougham*, p.182.
16 John Wade to Dr G. S. Evans, 26 September 1842, John Wade, Letters, 1842–1846, qMS-2085-2086, ATL.
17 Dr G. S. Evans to Colonel Wakefield, 1 October 1842, Letter 18, NZC, Local and General Letters to Colonel Wakefield, NZC 108/1/3, ANZ.
18 The remark 'we will not be dictated to by the base-born slave of an arbitrary faction' may have referred to Wade.
19 John Wade to R. D. Hanson, 1 October 1842, Wade Letters, ibid.
20 *Gazette*, 5 October 1842. The successful candidates for the town's council were: George Hunter with 273 votes, and, in descending order: Messrs Lyon, Fitzherbert, Wade, Scott, Molesworth, Dorset, Waitt, Guyton, Hort, Johnson, Jenkins, Wallace, Hanson, Cooper, Daniell, Machattie and Taylor.
21 The Fox case was reported in the *New Zealand Colonist*, 23 September 1842; the Healy case in the *Gazette*, 15 October 1842.
22 *Colonist*, 14 October 1842.
23 After an indictment had been preferred against Rangihaeata, Hanson had 'found a true bill against him', but the magistrates had declined to issue the warrant because only a Supreme Court Judge could issue it.
24 William Gisborne, *New Zealand Rulers and Statesmen, 1840–1885*, Sampson Low, Marston, Searle & Rivington, London, 1886, p.13.
25 *Gazette*, Court Case, 19 October 1842. Judgment and editorial comment from Fox, 8 March 1843: G. H. Scholefield, *Dictionary of New Zealand Biography*, Department of Internal Affairs, Wellington, 1940, Vol. 2, pp.61 ff.
26 Monro and Domett, editors of the *Nelson Examiner*, believed with Thompson at the time that the refusal of the warrant 'was calculated to weaken the influence of British Law upon the Native mind, and to lead to the belief of impunity in the commission of still further outrages': *Government Gazette*, 1843, p.203.
27 NZC, Despatches from Principal Agent, 10 November 1842, p.712, NZC 3/2/2, ANZ.
28 *Gazette*, 15 July 1843.
29 *Gazette*, 22 July 1843.
30 *Gazette*, 15 July 1843.
31 George Clarke Jnr to his father, 25 November 1842, George Clarke Jnr, Letters and Journals, Vol. 7, pp.279–80, qMS-0469, ATL.
32 Despatch 17, Enclosure 2, 28 January 1843, p.120, NZC, Despatches from Principal Agent, NZC 3/3/3, ANZ.
33 G. S. Evans to his parents, 14 January 1843, Permezel Collection.
34 *Gazette*, 21 January, 1843. Others in the deputation were: Messrs Molesworth, Clifford Guyton, Hanson, St Hill, Partridge and Hunter. Address published in *Gazette*, 4 February 1843.

35 Edward Jerningham Wakefield (ed. Sir Robert Stout), *Adventure in New Zealand, from 1839 to 1844, with Some Account of the Beginning of the British Colonization of the Islands*, Whitcombe & Tombs, Christchurch, 1908, pp.576–7.
36 *Gazette*, 29 May 1844.
37 New Zealand Company claimant, Spain Commission of Inquiry into the Land Claims of the Settlers of Port Nicholson, Case 347B, 8 February 1843, OLC 1/906, Box 45, ANZ.
38 A. G. Bagnell, *Transcripts of Evidence by R. D. Barrett before Land Claims Commission*, Case 374B, 8 February 1843–11 February 1843, ACC 88-103, Box 2, ATL. See also Philip Temple, *A Sort of Conscience: The Wakefields*, Auckland University Press, Auckland, 2002, p.310.
39 As expressed in his last letter to Betts Hopper from Sydney in 1840.
40 G. S. Evans to George Clarke Jnr, 13 February 1843, British Parliamentary Papers, *Colonies: New Zealand, 1837–1850*, Vol. 2, Appendix to Report of Select Committee on New Zealand, pp.308–9, NL.
41 Spain to Colonel Wakefield, 14 February 1843, NZC, Land Claims Correspondence of William Spain and George Clarke, 1842–45, NZC 131/1/1, ANZ.
42 *Gazette*, 30 August 1843.
43 Clarke to Wakefield, Wakefield to Clarke, 27 February, 28 February, 2 March 1843, NZC, Land Claims Correspondence of William Spain and George Clarke, 1842–45, NZC 131/3, ANZ.
44 Wakefield to Secretary, Despatch 27, Encl. 2, 9 March 1843, NZC, Despatches from Principal Agent, NZC 3/3/3. See also *Gazette*, 4 October 1843, for detailed analysis and description of land offered to Maori for their reserves.
45 Spain to FitzRoy, 31 March 1845, Commissioner Spain's Report on Port Nicholson Land Claims to Governor FitzRoy, 1845, New Zealand Company claimant, Case 374, OLC 1/906, Box 45, ANZ. Report also published in *New Zealand Spectator and Cook's Straits Guardian*, 27 June 1846, and in its Supplement no. 96, 1 July 1846.
46 H. G. Brewer to H. S. Chapman, 4 April 1842, pp.4–5, H. S. Chapman, Letters and sundry, qMS-0417, ATL.
47 Dr I. E. Featherston to his brother Robert, 8 September 1843, Isaac Earl Featherston, Family Papers, Micro-MS-0931, Reel 1, ATL.
48 Wakefield to Secretary, Despatch 65, 10 October 1844, pp.502–3, NZC, Despatches from Principal Agent, NZC 3/4/4, ANZ. Wakefield wrote that he had asked for Evans's assistance, who had 'attempted to bring Mr. Clarke to a more moderate estimate of the native claims, but without effect'.
49 *Gazette*, 29 May 1844. This article is a sustained criticism of Colonel Wakefield in which Revans accuses him of having written to Spain in 'July or August 1842', admitting the Company's titles were imperfect and suggesting the appointment of arbitrators. Spain had forwarded the letter to Auckland, Hobson had just passed away, but Shortland had met with Wakefield in Auckland and 'all the terms sought by the Company's agent were granted'. Wakefield told no one of that on his return to Wellington.
50 *Gazette*, 29 May 1844. The editor was Revans at this time. Wakefield informed the directors of Revans's censure of him: see Wakefield to Secretary, Despatch 35, 10 April 1844, pp.262 ff., NZC, Despatches from Principal Agent, NZC 3/4/4, ANZ.
51 *New Zealand Journal*, letter dated 24 April 1843, Vol. 3, p.260, sent by a colonist and published in *The Times*, Vol. 4, p.260.
52 Mrs Lucy Colley, *Life of the Hon. Henry W. Petre and Eleanor Walmesley*, MS-0593, ATL.
53 Mary Ann Eleanor Petre, Diary, 1842–1844, MS-1772, ATL.
54 *Colonist*, 21 March 1843.
55 The petition was signed by William Wakefield, Petre, Clifford, Vavasour, Mayor George Hunter, G. S. Evans, W. Brewer and Samuel Revans, amongst others.
56 *Gazette*, 5, 8 April 1843. The reasons for Fox's stand are detailed in the issue of 5 April.
57 Alfred Saunders, *History of New Zealand*, Whitcombe & Tombs, Wellington, 1896, p.179. Fox took over editing the *Gazette* for some months after his arrival in the colony

in 1843 until he was sent in November that year as the Company's agent to Nelson after Wairau. He returned to Wellington from Nelson and took over Colonel Wakefield's role after his death in 1848. He left Wellington three years later for England to join Evans and others in the fight for self-government. Evans was mentioned in letters to the paper from 1841 as the author of various leaders. He and the 'three Fs' later contributed to the *Independent* at different times. Saunders might have been confusing their input with that of the latter period, though these men did write for the *Gazette* at this time.

58 *Colonist*, 27 January 1843. The *Colonist* closed, in August 1843, largely because of lack of sales and a fire in its offices.

59 *Gazette*, 26 April 1843.

60 *Gazette*, 20 May 1843.

61 Despatch 13, 1 February 1843, p.181 with encl., R. D. Hanson to Secretary of Aborigines' Protection Society, 24 May 1842, NZC, Despatches from Secretary to Principal Agent, NZC 102/5/11, ANZ.

62 Wakefield to Secretary, Despatch 48, 16 June 1843 (sent 24 July 1843), NZC, Despatches from Principal Agent, NZC 3/3/3, ANZ.

Chapter Fourteen

1 S. McD. Martin, *New Zealand in a Series of Letters*, Simmonds & Ward, London, 1845, p.169. Shortland had also appointed Thompson county judge and protector of aborigines.

2 *Gazette*, 1 July 1843. Of the twelve 'gentlemen' in the group, three officials were unarmed. The rest had 'nothing beyond two or three pistols, and one fowling-piece among them'.

3 The creek was 'a deep rivulet 30 feet wide called Tua Marino [*sic*], not fordable'. Police Magistrate Thompson asked for a canoe to be placed across the rivulet 'to form a bridge, which was done by the Natives': *Gazette*, 1 July 1843, 'Massacre at Wairau'.

4 This was the eventual conclusion reached by the official government inquiry. It gave the European the benefit of the doubt in this respect. It was generally agreed a European had fired the first shot. See also G. W. Rusden, *History of New Zealand*, Melville, Mullen & Slade, Melbourne, 1895, Vol. 1, pp.328 ff. Puaha had been able to warn Te Rauparaha of the magistrate's intentions. He tried to act as peacemaker between the two parties and was held in high esteem by the government: Rusden, *History of New Zealand*, note 1, p.320.

5 *Gazette*, 21 June 1843. The meeting was attended by George Hunter, Colonel Wakefield, William Spain, Dr Evans, Hon. Henry Petre, Captain W. M. Smith, R. D. Hanson, Henry St Hill, William Fitzherbert, William Guyton, Charles Clifford and George White.

6 This was a major source of bitterness amongst the settlers. The only regular trips made by government representatives to Wellington, it seemed, were those made to extract taxes from the community to carry back to Auckland, the *Gazette* fumed.

7 There is some suggestion the men in the party helped Ironside in this task. The *Gazette*, 28 June, states that seventeen were buried the day the brig arrived, plus two bodies that were discovered by the party who landed from the brig. Sixteen had been sent home in whale boats and overland to Nelson, eight brought home by the brig, and four were still unaccounted for, making, with two others who came with Tuckett in the first brig, forty-nine.

8 George Clarke to his father, 6 August 1843, George Clarke Jnr, Letters and Journals, Vol. 7, p.340, qMS-0469, ATL.

9 John Miller, *Early Victorian New Zealand: A Study of Racial Tension and Social Attitudes, 1839–1852*, Oxford University Press, Oxford, 1958, pp.70 ff.; Rusden, *History of New Zealand*, pp.330–3. Te Ronga was the widow of Te Rauparaha's nephew Te Whaiti when Rangihaeata married her: G. H. Scholefield (ed.), *Dictionary of New*

Zealand Biography, Department of Internal Affairs, Wellington, 1940, Vol. 2. Both Te Rauparaha and Rangihaeata had refused to be 'Christianised'.

10 This account was printed in the *Gazette*, 1 July 1843, so presumably is the extent of the evidence the magistrates heard. Amongst the dead were several magistrates, a captain in the navy, a captain in the army, a county judge, and Richardson, the Nelson Crown Prosecutor. The incident was described in detail, together with a letter written by Fox in a supplement to the *Gazette* on 2 September 1843. See also NZC, Papers dealing with the affray at Wairau, NZC 131/3/12, ANZ.

11 George Clarke Jnr, *Notes on Early Life in New Zealand*, Walch & Sons, Hobart, 1903, p.57.

12 Moved G. White acting Police Senior Magistrate, seconded G. Hunter: *Gazette*, 1 July 1843. This issue also contains the earliest account of the massacre. Also see McDonough to Secretary of State for Colonies (via Acting Governor W. Shortland), 27 June 1843, pp.322–37, Wairau Correspondence, pp.289–382, NZC, Wakefield to Secretary, Letterbook, NZC 112/2, ANZ; and NZC, Papers dealing with the affray at Wairau, NZC 131/3/12, ANZ.

13 Mary Ann Eleanor Petre, Diary 1842–1844, MS-1772, ATL.

14 Clarke, letter to his father, No. 68, pp.350–1, Clarke Letters, ibid.

15 *Gazette*, 29 July 1843.

16 *Gazette*, 15 July 1843.

17 A. J. Harrop, *England and New Zealand: From Tasman to the Taranaki War*, Methuen, London, 1926, pp.150 and 152.

18 From Nelson, Dr Monro and Mr Alfred Domett were sent on the same errand.

19 Hobson had acquired from Ngati Whatua 1214 hectares of prime land for himself for the equivalent of the goods the Company had exchanged for land in Port Nicholson. He bought land for the price of '50 blankets, £50, 20 trousers, 20 shirts, 10 waistcoats, 10 caps, four casks of tobacco, one box of pipes, 91 metres of gown material, 10 iron pots, one bag of sugar, a bag of flour and 20 hatchets': *New Zealand Herald*, 11 May 2007, p.2.

20 Evans was presumably using the word in a pejorative and deeply ironic sense. See also note 23 below.

21 See also Ian Wards, *The Shadow of the Land: A Study of British Policy and Racial Conflict in New Zealand 1832–1852*, A. R. Shearer, Government Printer, Wellington, 1968, p.55, for a brief outline of the Maori view of land.

22 See, for example, Paul Moon, *FitzRoy: Governor in Crisis 1843–1845*, David Ling, Auckland, 2000, p.95. It is worth reading Moon's analysis of the Wairau affray and its aftermath to pinpoint such judgements as the Wellington settlers being 'poorly educated riff-raff', 'failures in Britain' and 'indulging in an opportunistic gamble'; Moon refers to 'hatred towards Maori' already being high among the New Zealand Company settlements, and that there 'were also sinister economic motives behind the New Zealand Company's propensity for war with the Maori'. He claims that the Company leaders harboured 'ingrained suspicion and contempt for Maori'; and he describes the Company's paper, the *Gazette*, as a 'distasteful propaganda sheet' (pp.91–96). The Company men are thus forever sealed in history as two-dimensional criminals, with no regard for anything or anyone but themselves and their extortion of land from Maori.

23 G. S. Evans to his parents, written on board the brig *Victoria*, off Cape Palliser, 2 July 1843, Permezel Collection. In two places, the writing has been worn away at the creases. The word 'philanthropists' did not bear the completely benign meaning then as it does today. See, for example, the poem, 'The Philanthropists', from *Blackwood's Magazine*, in *New Zealand Spectator and Cook's Straits Guardian*, 4 October 1845. People who called themselves 'philanthropists' were hypocritical in that they preached philanthropy, but did little to alleviate the sufferings of others, let alone their own families and neighbours.

24 Alfred Saunders, *The History of New Zealand 1642–1861*, Whitcombe & Tombs, Wellington, 1899, p.213. This has been contradicted by Philip Temple, *A Sort of*

Conscience: The Wakefields, Auckland University Press, Auckland, 2002, p.544, when he accuses Evans of having 'condemned Arthur with faint praise' in his report. Temple gives no reference for this assertion, and I could find no evidence to support it.

25 J. J. Taine (ed. H. W. Fildes), *Reminiscences*, Vol. 2, p.258, qMS-1975, ATL.

26 See also the *Gazette*, 15 July 1843, for an extract from the *Auckland Chronicle*; the 'comic' 'Jingle's Report' ridicules the event and the men involved. The *Colonial Gazette* of 16 December 1843 pp.788–9 cites the *Auckland Chronicle* article of 15 July. These supported Evans's view that they were being too dismissive of what was in fact a tragedy with great loss of life.

27 Rusden, *History of New Zealand*, p.343. Evans's comment was endorsed by the *Gazette*, 28 June, which complained bitterly that the Auckland papers were trivialising the tragedy, blaming the settlers and distorting the facts. Missionaries even denied that Te Rauparaha and Rangihaeata were present at the affray, then believed the story that Maori had personally taken ten of the wounded to seek medical assistance. Their information came from Maori who feared a backlash: *Colonist*, 27 June 1843.

28 Shortland to Rt Hon. Her Majesty's Principal Secretary of State for the Colonies, 13 July 1843, British Parliamentary Papers, *Colonies: New Zealand, 1837–1850*, Vol. 2, 1844 (556), App. 4, pp.132–4, 142 ff., NL.

29 *Southern Cross*, 15 July 1843.

30 I. E. Featherston to his brother Robert, 8 September 1843, and to his sister Eliza Milner, 18 May 1844, Isaac Earl Featherston, Family Papers, Micro-MS-0931, Reel 1, ATL; BPP, *Colonies: New Zealand, 1837–1850*, Vol. 2, 1844 (556), NL, which recounts W. Brodie, G. P. Earp and J. C. Crawford giving evidence to Commission of Inquiry into New Zealand, from 13 June 1844: Walter Brodie to Commission, pp.25–59; Earp to Commission, pp.93–158 passim; J. C. Crawford to Commission, pp.158–69.

31 *Southern Cross*, 22 July 1843; *Gazette*, 26 July 1843.

32 Martin, *New Zealand in a Series of Letters*, p.173. Martin wrote of Shortland: 'No man ever injured a place more than Shortland did New Zealand.' He himself was the victim of the government under Hobson and Shortland; as an opponent of the regime, he called for Hobson's recall. Three of the four directors of the paper he edited were government servants. Early in 1844 his paper closed down and the plant was sold to a new paper edited by the Attorney General, Swainson. FitzRoy made Martin a member of the Legislative Council in June 1844, but he resigned in March 1845, and returned to England to protest against the ill-treatment of the Maori: Scholefield, *Dictionary of New Zealand Biography*, Vol. 2, p.61.

33 *New Zealand Journal*, Vol. 4, pp.486–7. The *Southern Cross* condemned 'most government members [for] having purchased' the *Herald* 'with the money of the people' and accused it 'from the Governor downwards, with one or two exceptions, of forming a joint stock company for the purchase of the *Bay of Islands Observer* and the *Chronicle*, of which the Attorney General was the editor.'

34 Taine, *Reminiscences*, Vol. 2, p.226, ibid.

35 Ibid., Vol. 2, p.258, ibid.

36 Edward Jerningham Wakefield (ed. Sir Robert Stout), *Adventure in New Zealand, from 1839 to 1844, with Some Account of the Beginning of the British Colonization of the Islands*, Whitcombe & Tombs, Christchurch, 1908, pp.293–4.

37 *New Zealand Journal*, Vol. 4, p.331. It is worth reading Wakefield's descriptive despatch to the Secretary, for its detailed but clinical account. Even 160 years later, it leaves a deep impression on the reader.

38 Wakefield to Secretary, July–August 1843, pp.453 ff., NZC, Despatches from Principal Agent, NZC 3/3/3, ANZ.

39 E. J. Wakefield, *Adventure in New Zealand*, p.635.

40 Ward to Wakefield, Despatch 2, 28 January 1843, 8 March 1843, NZC, Despatches from Secretary to Principal Agent, NZC 102/5/11 ANZ. Halswell's post as Company Commissioner for the Management of the Native Reserves became obsolete – he was paid arrears and a further £300. Mr St Hill was appointed Manager of Native Reserves for

Port Nicholson, Wanganui and Taranaki, the directors informed Wakefield. Wakefield was instructed to reduce the number of officers working for the Company and save money. Riddiford and Dorset lost their posts. Labourers were to be paid 18 shillings a week without rations, and to work six-day, nine-hour-a-day weeks.

41 F. A. Carrington to Wakefield, 29 June 1841, Vol. 1, pp.32a, 44a ff., Vol. 2, pp.7 and 199, F. A. Carrington, Papers, MS-0471, ATL. Two years earlier Wakefield had treated Frederick Carrington shabbily; months of back-payments were never paid and his promised house never materialised. After Barrett confided in Carrington that he had agreed to build a boat with Wakefield so the two could profit from trade, Carrington accused Wakefield of having diverted funds intended for his house into his private scheme.

42 Wakefield to Secretary, Despatch 61, 24 July 1843, NZC, Despatches from Principal Agent, NZC 3/3/3, ANZ.

43 W. H. Oliver, *The Story of New Zealand*, Faber, London, 1960, pp.50–51.

44 Millar citing Hanson, *Extracts from a Letter to Captain FitzRoy*, p.6: David Millar, *Once Upon a Village: A History of Lower Hutt*, New Zealand University Press, Wellington, 1972, p.37.

45 *Gazette*, 6 September 1843 and 18 October 1843.

46 Secretary to Principal Agent, Despatch 10, 31 January 1843, pp.166–8, NZC, Despatches from Secretary to Principal Agent, NZC 102/5/11, ANZ.

47 Evans to Colonel Wakefield, 6 September 1843, encl. 2 in Wakefield to Secretary, Despatch 67, 18 September, NZC, Despatches from Principal Agent, NZC 3/3/3, ANZ.

48 R. A. A. Sherrin and J. H. Wallace (ed. Thomson S. Leys), *Early History of New Zealand*, Brett's Historical Series, Auckland, 1890, pp.672–3.

49 See Moon, *FitzRoy*, referring to the government organisation as being riddled with a 'contagion of corruption', p.117. See also pp.74–76 and pp.118–21 for further similar views of key Auckland officials.

50 *Gazette*, 18 October 1843.

51 David McGill, *Pioneers of Port Nicholson*, Reed, Wellington, 1984, p.37.

52 *Gazette*, 17 February 1844. See also Moon, *FitzRoy*, p.131.

53 G. Clarke to Colonial Secretary, 4 January 1844, BPP, *Colonies: New Zealand, 1837–1850*, Vol. 2, 1844, Appendix, p.122, NL.

54 Keith Sinclair, *A History of New Zealand*, Penguin, Auckland, revised edn, 2000, p.79. Elsewhere, others state that Maori appreciated displays of force, and respected and judged a government largely by this means.

55 Wards, *The Shadow of the Land*, p.176. Selwyn said, 'he believed that the Maori held a genuine belief in the superiority of European civilisation to their own, and that had the physical and moral weight of the government been sufficient to enforce its own jurisdiction, the more enlightened portion, perhaps even the majority of the Maoris, would have been thankful to be freed from their own barbarous usages', p.178, citing Bishop Selwyn to FitzRoy, November 1845, G/19/1, pp.128–9, ANZ. In late July a petition was drawn up by Featherston to be sent to both houses of Parliament, requesting an inquiry into Captain FitzRoy's decision in favour of the Maori 'perpetrators' of the bloodshed.

56 Michael King, *The Penguin History of New Zealand*, Penguin, Auckland, 2003, p.182.

57 Wakefield to Secretary, Despatch 85, December 1843, NZC, Despatches from Principal Agent, NZC 3/3/3, ANZ.

58 T. M. Hocken, *The Early History of New Zealand*, John Mackay, Wellington, 1914, p.60. The Act of Corporation was disallowed because the government had noted a clause that it believed interfered with the Royal Prerogative, and might be interpreted as an attempt to seize Crown land. The clause concerned the right to erect beacons and lighthouses, and to allow corporations waste land within Crown boundaries.

59 Wakefield to Secretary, Despatch 77, 15 November 1843, NZC, Despatches from Principal Agent, NZC 3/3/3, ANZ; Letters Nos 28, 52, NZC, Local and General Letters to Colonel Wakefield, NZC 108/1/4, ANZ.

60 *Gazette*, 13 December 1843.

61 This phrase is difficult to decipher. Or *Deus misereatur* – God be merciful (Psalm 67). For *dirtia misera* – 'miserable hospitality' – 'mean fare' or 'desperate circumstances' are the most likely translations.
62 W. C. Cotton, Journal 1841–1848, Vol. 6, pp.31–32, qMS-0566, ATL.
63 *Gazette*, 2, 30 December 1843; Cotton Journal, Vol. 6, pp.39–42.
64 Cotton to friend at Windsor, 18 August 1842, published in *Colonial Gazette*, 1 February 1843, pp.68–69, ATL.

Chapter Fifteen

1 *Gazette*, 6 January 1844. Featherston presided and Stoke read the memorial.
2 *Gazette*, 31 January 1844.
3 The official account of the meeting at Major Richmond's house is in OLC 1/906, Box 45, ANZ, signed and dated by FitzRoy, 1 February 1844. See also G. W. Rusden, *History of New Zealand*, Melville, Mullen & Slade, Melbourne, 1895, Vol. 1, p.349. Forsaith kept notes of the meeting; FitzRoy believed a pa was 'the ground that is fenced around their native houses, including the ground in cultivation or occupation around the adjoining houses without the fence'. Clarke said a pa would apply to any settlement by Maori. Spain believed it to be 'a native village': British Parliamentary Papers, *Colonies: New Zealand*, Vol. 5, 1846 (203), pp.18–20, Encl. 1, NL.
4 Wakefield to Secretary, 10 October 1844, p.507, NZC, Despatches from Principal Agent, NZC 3/4/4, ANZ.
5 Commissioner Spain's Report on Port Nicholson Land Claims to Governor FitzRoy, Spain Commission of Inquiry into the Land Claims of the Settlers of Port Nicholson, OLC 1/906, Box 45, ANZ. FitzRoy added in the margin, 'This opinion is in direct opposition to that given in a similar case in Taranaki. Signed: R. F.' Alfred Domett added to this note: 'Captain FitzRoy misses the point altogether . . . at Taranaki they HAD sufficient force, DID keep possession and would have done so to this day but for the Europeans.'
6 David P. Millar, *Once Upon a Village: A History of Lower Hutt*, New Zealand University Press, Wellington, 1972, pp.34–35.
7 Brad Patterson, 'A Queer Cantankerous Lot', in David Hamer and Roberta Nicholls (eds), *The Making of Wellington, 1800–1914*, Victoria University Press, Wellington, 1990, n. 19, p.65.
8 Wakefield to Secretary, 20 March 1844, Despatch 30 and Encl., pp.235–46, NZC, Despatches from Principal Agent, NZC 3/4/4, ANZ.
9 Ibid. Wakefield to Evans, 22 February 1844; Evans to Wakefield, 22 February 1844 (encls.), pp.244–6, ibid.
10 *Government Gazette*, 7 December 1844, p.161. See also W. R. Lawrence *'Huzza for New Zealand!': The Life and work of Captain Mein Smith*, qMS-1139, ATL, citing Chapman in letter to his father, pp.27 ff., 37, 228–33. When Chapman arrived in Wellington, he was surprised by the ill feeling between the settlers, but more dismayed by Revans's conduct. Revans was 'mixed up with half the squabbles on the beach' and 'involved in litigation not very creditable to him'. There was a rift between the two that healed only after a few years.
11 J. J. Taine (ed. H. W. Fildes), *Reminiscences*, Vol. 2, p.275, qMS-1974-1975, ATL.
12 *Gazette*, 31 July 1844.
13 *Gazette*, 17 April, 1, 8 May 1844.
14 Wakefield to Secretary, Despatch 35, 10 April 1844, pp.262 ff., NZC, Despatches from Principal Agent, NZC 3/4/4, ANZ.
15 Commissioner Spain's Report on Port Nicholson Land Claims to Governor FitzRoy, 31 March 1845, OLC 1/906, Box 45, ANZ. Published in *New Zealand Spectator and Cook's Straits Guardian*, 18 April 1846 (Supplement), 27 June 1846, and 1 July 1846 (Supplement).

16 George Clarke Jnr, *Notes on Early Life in New Zealand*, Walch & Sons, Hobart, 1903, pp.58, 59; William Fox, *The Six Colonies of New Zealand*, John W. Parker & Son, London, 1851, p.37.
17 'FitzRoy was totally lacking in the essential quality of cool judgment, resolution, and consistency of purpose': Keith Sinclair, A *History of New Zealand*, Penguin, Auckland, revised edn, 2000, citing W. P. Morrell, pp.79–81. Also see E. Hampden-Cook, 'A Headmaster's Eventful Career', *Mill Hill Magazine*, Vol. 46, No. 5, March 1919, pp.111–12: '[Evans] sided vehemently with Mr. Spain and against Governor FitzRoy, on the question of the land purchase at Waitara, Taranaki.'
18 Sinclair, A *History of New Zealand*, p.78.
19 Wakefield to Secretary, Despatch 61, 8 October 1844, pp.501–7, NZC, Despatches from Principal Agent, NZC 3/4/4, ANZ.
20 Taine, *Reminiscences*, Vol. 2, pp.274–5, ibid.
21 'Revans leased the equipment to his printers and let the *Gazette* close in September to be succeeded by the *New Zealand Spectator and Cook's Straits Guardian*. In August 1845 creditors called in a debt, forcing Revans to sell the printing equipment to the *Spectator* proprietors': Kathleen A. Coleridge, 'Samuel Revans', in W. H. Oliver (ed.), *Dictionary of New Zealand Biography*, Allen & Unwin/Department of Internal Affairs, Wellington, 1990, Vol. 1, p.360.
22 *New Zealand Spectator and Cook's Straits Guardian*, 12 October 1844.
23 Taine, *Reminiscences*, Vol. 2, p.276, ibid.
24 Gavin McLean, *Wellington: The First Years of European Settlement, 1840–1850*, Penguin, Auckland, 2000, p.75.
25 *New Zealand Spectator and Cook's Straits Guardian*, 14 December 1844; Robin Cooke, QC (ed.), *Portrait of a Profession: The Centennial Book of the New Zealand Law Society*, A. H. & A. W. Reed, Wellington, 1969, p.28.
26 Taine, *Reminiscences*, Vol. 2, p.276, ibid. However, his will included sections at Horokiwi.
27 Robert FitzRoy, *Remarks on New Zealand*, W. & H. White, London, 1846, pp.56, 62.
28 Taine, *Reminiscences*, Vol. 2, p.269, ibid.
29 *Gazette*, 30 September 1844.
30 *New Zealand Spectator and Cook's Straits Guardian*, 2 November 1844.
31 Patricia Burns (ed. Henry Richardson), *Fatal Success: A History of the New Zealand Company*, Heinemann Reed, Auckland, 1989, p.278.
32 Paul Moon, *FitzRoy: Governor in Crisis 1843–1845*, David Ling, Auckland, 2000, pp.76, 27.
33 Sinclair, A *History of New Zealand*, p.48.
34 Wakefield to Secretary, Despatch 69, 3 December 1844, NZC, Despatches from Principal Agent, NZC 3/4/4, ANZ.
35 Memorial to the Right Hon. Lord Stanley, *New Zealand Spectator and Cook's Straits Guardian*, 7 December 1844. Also BPP, *Colonies: New Zealand*, Vol. 4, 1845 (378), pp.13–22, 623–9, NL.
36 G. S. Evans to Lord Stanley on the subject of Governor FitzRoy, 6 May 1845, BPP, *Colonies: New Zealand*, Vol. 4, 1845 (378), pp.19–21, pp.629–31, NL.
37 Wakefield's secretary Kelham to Secretary NZC, Despatch 69/44, Encl., 5 December 1844, Evans to Kelham (encl.), 4 November 1844, NZC, Despatches from Principal Agent, NZC 3/4/4, ANZ.
38 The Deed 'was executed *nominally* to pass Chetham's interest in those lands to Evans, but as Evans [believed] *actually* to make him carry out certain family arrangements, and to protect the estate, without the least intention of benefitting [*sic*] [Chetham]': *Wellington Independent*, 9 January 1864.
39 Taine, *Reminiscences*, Vol. 2, p.276, ibid.
40 *New Zealand Spectator and Cook's Straits Guardian*; and *Independent*, 9 January 1864.
41 *New Zealand Spectator and Cook's Straits Guardian*, 14 December 1844. The other 'jewel' was a signed portrait of Queen Victoria. His funeral was attended by several

distinguished MPs including Sir Robert Peel, Lord Brougham, the Earl of Aberdeen and Lord Campbell. A Polish aristocrat in Campbell's cortege threw a handful of earth from the grave of Polish martyr Kosciusko on the coffin when it passed in procession to the Abbey: L. Stephen and S. Lee (eds), *Dictionary of National Biography*, Oxford University Press, London, 1917–1938, Vol. III, p.848.

42 Supplement to the *New Zealand Spectator and Cook's Straits Guardian*, 11 January 1845.

43 *New Zealand Spectator and Cook's Straits Guardian*, 14 December 1844. On the subject of the Land Claims, it gives the history of the Maori tribal settlement of the lower half of the North Island for the last thirty years, and castigates FitzRoy's mishandling of the entire issue.

44 *New Zealand Spectator and Cook's Straits Guardian*, 11 January 1845, which details the nineteen resolutions of the Commons Committee on New Zealand's affairs. The report was presented to the House on 29 January 1844. Lord John Russell told the Company's directors he did not 'suppose that any claim could be set up by the natives to the millions of acres of land, which are to be found in New Zealand, neither occupied nor cultivated, nor in any fair sense owned by any individual'. See BPP, *Colonies: New Zealand*, Vol. 2, 1844 (556), Report follows the Commission of Inquiry into the Affairs of New Zealand, pp.3–14, NL.

45 These tribes were: Te Aro, Kumutoto, Pipitea, Tiakiwai, Kaiwharawhara, Ngauranga and Waiwhetu.

46 Commissioner Spain's Report on Port Nicholson Land Claims to Governor FitzRoy, 31 March 1845, Spain Commission of Inquiry into the Land Claims of the Settlers of Port Nicholson, OLC 1/906, Box 45, ANZ. 'Spain's Court to determine the outcome of land sales lasted three years. The company laid claim to 20 million acres – they received only a portion of that': Sinclair, A *History of New Zealand*, p.78. It was not until 1847 that something approaching a resolution was made with regard to the Maori claims to land: Report published in *New Zealand Spectator and Cook's Straits Guardian*, 1 July 1846. 'So long and confused was the struggle over titles, that, though the Company was given authority to issue these to its settlers, when it moved to surrender its charter in 1850 it had not issued a single one': Alan Mulgan, *The City of the Strait: Wellington and its Province, a Centennial History*, A. H. & A. W. Reed, Wellington, 1939, p.115. See also BPP, *Colonies: New Zealand*, Vol. 5, 1846 (203), pp.3–18, Encl. 1, pp.18–20, NL, which details a meeting on 29 January 1844 at Major Richmond's house with Wakefield regarding compensation to natives. Also to be found in Spain Commission of Inquiry into the Land Claims of the Settlers of Port Nicholson, OLC 1/906, Box 45, ANZ.

47 Clarke Jnr to his father, 17 June 1844, George Clarke Jnr, Letters and Journals, Vol. 7, p.394, qMS-0469, ATL. Clarke (1823–1913) returned to Hobart in 1851, was appointed Congregational minister, and served for 52 years. Having helped found the University of Tasmania, he served as its Chancellor 1898–1907. He was 'eloquent, learned, zealous and broadminded': G. H. Scholefield (ed.), *Dictionary of New Zealand Biography*, Department of Internal Affairs, Wellington, 1940, Vol. 1, pp.159–60.

Chapter Sixteen

1 Gibbon Wakefield lived at 13 Hans Place in the period 1836–39. Hans Place (SW1) had been built by Henry Holland in 1777 after the style of the Place Vendôme. On the south side was the Pavilion, Holland's own house. Fields separated them from Westminster until mid-nineteenth century when Belgravia was developed. The 'plain brick terraces' were 'for people of moderate means': Ben Weinreb and Christopher Hibbert (eds), *The London Encyclopaedia*, Macmillan, London, 1983, p.363.

2 For details of the Company's secret committee, see *Colonial Gazette*, 31 May 1845, p.339; and see Edward Jerningham Wakefield (ed. Joan Stevens), *London Journal*, Alexander Turnbull Library/Victoria University of Wellington, Wellington, 1972, p.28.

3 See Philip Temple, *A Sort of Conscience: The Wakefields*, Auckland University Press, Auckland, 2002, p.544. It is unlikely Wakefield spared Liocadia much thought except in correspondence with her. He had willingly surrendered her to New Zealand, probably because her chances of a marriage were much better in the new colony. The talks more likely centred round Evans's disappointment, and his attacks on Wakefield's and the Company's lack of understanding of the ordeal and loss the settlers had endured. Evans's treatment of women was enlightened, if anything: see, for example, his Last Will and Testament, with Two Codicils, AAOM 6029/P300, ANZ.

4 See article, *Evening Post*, 16 July 1927. Horace Fildes was the fourth child of his father's (John Gifford Fildes') second marriage to Jessie Sophia Taine, the daughter of Liocadia and J. J. Taine.

5 G. S. Evans to Lord Stanley, 6 May 1845, British Parliamentary Papers, *Colonies: New Zealand, 1837–1850*, Vol. 4, 1845 (378), pp.19–22, NL.

6 E. J. Wakefield, *London Journal*, p.34.

7 *Colonial Gazette*, 31 May 1845, p.342.

8 Evans to Lord Stanley, 6, 22 May 1845; G. W. Hope to Evans, 26 May 1845: this correspondence was extensively published. See *New Zealand Spectator and Cook's Straits Guardian*, 8 November 1845.

9 *Colonial Gazette*, 31 May 1845, p.343; *New Zealand Spectator and Cook's Straits Guardian*, 8 November 1845.

10 Editorials from *The Times*, 29, 30 May 1845; published in the *New Zealand Spectator and Cook's Straits Guardian*, 1 November 1845. The second *Times* leader, 30 May 1845, directly cites Evans's speech.

11 J. S. Marais, *The Colonisation of New Zealand*, Milford, London, 1927, pp.187 ff. Editorial tone altered around September 1844: see *The Times*, 30 May 1845.

12 E. J. Wakefield, *London Journal*, p.3.

13 *Colonial Gazette*, 7 June 1845, p.361.

14 Well summarised in E. J. Wakefield's *London Journal*, pp.99–100.

15 Ibid., p.45, note 6.

16 The directors were Marjoribanks, Mangles, Currie and Sir John Pirie.

17 Gilbert Abbott à Beckett (1811–56), the poet, playwright and magistrate whose journalistic career had begun with the *Globe*, continued with *Punch* and led to his own famous journal, *Figaro*. See Evans's articles: *The Times*, 29, 30 May 1845; reproduced in *New Zealand Spectator*, 1 November 1845. For Beckett's obituary, see *Melbourne Herald*, 8 December 1856, when Evans was its editor. *The Times* of London was edited by John Delane from 1841 to 1877.

18 Jerningham's father, Edward Gibbon, described him as 'a wastrel and failure, talented and intelligent, but reckless, weak-willed, contentious, promiscuous and generally unstable': Gavin McLean, *Wellington: The First Years of European Settlement, 1840–1850*, Penguin, Auckland, 2000, p.39.

19 Black had been living in a cottage near Maidstone since his enforced resignation from the *Morning Chronicle* in 1843. His former staff, including Buller and Charles Dickens, had rallied round, raising enough money to give him a modest annuity of £150: L. Stephen and S. Lee (eds), *Dictionary of National Biography*, Oxford University Press, London, 1917–1938, Vol. II, p.571.

20 Debate on the affairs of New Zealand, 17 June 1845, *Colonial Gazette*, 21 June 1845, pp.386–8. See also G. S. Evans to his parents, 2 July 1843, Permezel Collection. For another aspect of the Company's reservations on the effects of the Treaty of Waitangi, see Irma O'Connor, *Edward Gibbon Wakefield: The Man Himself*, Selwyn & Blount, London, 1928, pp.182–6.

21 *Colonial Gazette*, 21 June 1845, p.388.

22 Article, and Leader and Parliamentary report, *The Times*, 18 and 19 June 1845.

23 Mr Henry Aglionby Aglionby, Whig MP and director, New Zealand Company, to House of Commons Debate on New Zealand, 18 June 1845, Hansard, Vol. 81, p.779; see hansard.millbanksystems.com/commons/1845/jun/18/new.zealand-adjourned-debate.

24 Chartists were a particularly vigorous – some said even seditious – group, demanding male suffrage, the secret ballot, equal constituencies and annual elections, among other things.
25 *Colonial Gazette*, Vol. 7, 14 June 1845, p.371; *New Zealand Spectator and Cook's Straits Guardian*, 28 December 1845.
26 A. Marjoribanks, *Travels in New Zealand*, Smith Elder & Co., London, 1847, reprinted Capper Press, Christchurch, 1973, pp.29–33.
27 W. M. Thackeray, 'Stiggins in New Zealand', *Punch*, Vol. X, 28 June 1845, p.3.
28 E. J. Wakefield, *London Journal*, p.103; letter published in *New Zealand Spectator*, 24 January 1846. The effect of the letter is recorded in *New Zealand Journal*, 4 July 1846.
29 *The Times*, Editorial, 15 July 1845.
30 Case brought up by Dr Evans, Book 41, p.81, NZC, Directors' Minutes, 16 January 1845–31 December 1846, NZC 31/4/4, ANZ. Also BPP, *Colonies: New Zealand, 1837–1850*, Vol. 7, 1851 (1398), p.76, NL, records that Evans's sale of land was finally completed in August 1847. For his 3436 acres, he was paid £4,565 12s 10d, with £200 4s for incidental expenses, totalling £4,765 16s 10d. And see encl. in letter from T. C. Harington to B. Hawes, 16 November 1850: 'the sum paid for Dr. Evans's land was fixed by adding to its original price subsequent interest. I must mention also an adverse claim on this property by an incumbrancer, but the Company's counsel is of opinion that the Company's title is good': Papers relating to Surrender of Charters by New Zealand Company, BPP, *Colonies: New Zealand*, p.78, ibid.
31 See *The Times*, 17 July 1845.
32 *Colonial Gazette*, 12 July 1845, pp.437 ff.
33 *The Times*, 17 July 1845.
34 *Colonial Gazette*, 12 July 1845.
35 G. W. Rusden, *History of New Zealand*, Melville, Mullen & Slade, Melbourne, 1895, Vol. 1, p. 383.
36 *The Times*, 23 July 1845, reproduced in the *New Zealand Spectator and Cook's Straits Guardian*, 20 December 1845. Evans's style was marked by contrasts and comparisons within sentences, Latin quotations, and lengthy, sesquipedalian sentence structure.
37 G. S. Evans to T. C. Harington, Secretary NZC, 7 August 1845; T. C. Harington to G. S. Evans, 8 August 1845, published in *New Zealand Spectator and Cook's Straits Guardian*, 10 January, 1846. Other directors present at the meeting were Messrs Pilcher, Boulcott, Mangles and Currie, and Captain Nairne. See also Letter 45/718, NZC, Directors' Minutes, 1839–1849, CO 208/180, ANZ.
38 Meeting of Resident Landholders of Wellington, *New Zealand Spectator and Cook's Straits Guardian*, 1 August 1846.
39 Rusden, *History of New Zealand*, pp.455–6. Extract from Letter to the Directors of the New Zealand Company from the Resident Purchasers of Land, Wellington, New Zealand; and Extracts from Memorial to Directors of New Zealand Company drawn up by Dr Isaac Featherston were published in the *New Zealand Spectator and Cook's Straits Guardian*, 14 and 21 November 1846. This followed several meetings of the shareholders to air their grievances against the Company and the directors' treatment of Dr Evans and themselves.
40 *The Times*, Feature, 'The State of New Zealand', 19 March 1846.
41 Geo. Fred. Young to Geo. Offor Esq., 2 September 1845, G. S. Evans, Testimonials, Papers, MS-Papers-10552, ATL. (My italics.)
42 And a member of the original New Zealand Company formed in 1825. Other members of the group that sent out two ships to form a trading settlement were Stewart Marjoribanks, Lord Lyttelton, J. G. Lambton (Lord Durham) and George Lyall. Torrens brought a land order from the later New Zealand Company. His town acre was within Te Aro pa: Ian Wards, *The Shadow of the Land: A Study of British Policy and Racial Conflict in New Zealand 1832–1852*, A. R. Shearer, Government Printer, Wellington, 1968, pp.4–5.

43 Testimonials, Evans Papers, ibid. It is worth noting that most of these testimonials came from men who have entries in Stephen and Lee (eds), *Dictionary of National Biography*: Sir Benjamin Hawes (1797–1862), Vol. IX, p.187; Stephen Lushington (1782–1878), Vol. XII, pp.291–3; Henry Peter Brougham, Baron Brougham and Vaux (1778–1868), Vol. II, pp.1356–66; Robert Torrens (1780–1864), Vol. XIX, pp.993–5; John Pye Smith (1774–1851), Vol. XVIII, pp.494–5; Sir William Hutt (1801–1882), Vol. X, pp.349 ff.; Charles Buller (1806–1848), Vol. III, pp.246 ff.; Samuel Hinds DD (1793–1872), Vol. IX, p.897.

44 See Edward Gibbon Wakefield, *A View of the Art of Colonization 1837*, J. W. Parker, London, 1849.

45 Marais, *The Colonisation of New Zealand*, pp.197–201; E. J. Wakefield, *London Journal*, pp.99–100; A. H. McLintock, *Crown Colony Government in New Zealand*, Government Printer, Wellington, 1958.

46 Halswell had acted as Commissioner for Native Reserves for the Company, and latterly been appointed a judge in Port Nicholson: E. J. Wakefield, *London Journal*, pp.67–68.

47 Evans owed the Union Bank in Wellington 'a considerable amount, partly on his own private account, and partly on account of the partnership [he shared with Chetham]'. He had given 'a mortgage to the bank on the same property, subject to Monro's mortgage, and to the interest of Mrs. Evans in the £1,000 investment': *Wellington Independent*, 9 January 1864.

48 See Louis E. Ward, *Early Wellington*, Southern Reprints, Papakura, 1928, p.130.

49 Minutes, pp.450 ff., NZC, Directors' Minutes, 1839–1849, CO 208/182. Also see Minutes, Book 41, pp.222–47, NZC, Directors' Minutes, 16 January 1845–31 December 1846, NZC 31/4/4/, ANZ.

50 Ibid. 'The Original price of one pound per acre, on town and country sections all round, without regard to the improvements, together with the interest thereon for six and a half years, making in the whole, one pound six shillings and sixpence': *Wellington Independent*, 9 January 1864.

51 The couple had 'at least one son, Alfred Fortes', who became a gifted musician: Permezel Collection.

52 June Philipp, *A Great View of Things: Edward Gibbon Wakefield*, Thomas Nelson, Melbourne, 1971, citing Lord Howick's *Journal*, 16 December 1833, p.6. 'Practically everyone who came into contact with Wakefield was eventually anathematised for disloyalty, heterodoxy or simply malicious refusal to obey': Ged Martin, 'Wakefield's Past and Futures', in Friends of the Turnbull Library, *Edward Gibbon Wakefield and the Colonial Dream: A Reconsideration*, GP Publications, Wellington, 1997, p.30.

53 Robert Gouger (1802–1846) had been Wakefield's honorary secretary in three associations from 1830 to 1836: the National Colonisation Society, the South Australia Land Company and the South Australia Association. Wakefield was accused of 'unblushing plagiarism', and described as being 'Machiavellian, satanic': Douglas Pike, *Paradise of Dissent: South Australia 1829–1857*, Longmans Green, London, Melbourne and New York, 1957, pp.99–101, 75, 77.

54 Evans to Directors, 27 February 1846, NZC, Directors' Minutes, 1839–1849, CO 208/182, ANZ.

55 Minutes, 5 March 1846, p.480, NZC, Directors' Minutes, ibid. See also Secretary Harington to Colonel Wakefield, Book 41, p.244, Directors' Minutes, 16 January 1845–31 December 1846, NZC 31/4/4, ANZ.

Chapter Seventeen

1 G. F. Holborn, Librarian, Lincoln's Inn Library, 28 July 2000, by letter to author.

2 See Horace Fildes, Collection, Newspaper Clippings, *Evening Post*, 16 July 1927, Pq 993.1 Fil 1920, ATL.

3 R. D. Hanson to G. S. Evans, 24 September 1845, pp.498–500, *New Zealand Papers, 1836–87*, C184, ML.

4 'From Adelaide in July 1846 [Hanson] published a 16-page pamphlet *Extracts From a Letter to Captain FitzRoy, R.N. from R. Davies Hanson, Esq.*': Patricia Burns (ed. Henry Richardson), *Fatal Success: A History of the New Zealand Company*, Heinemann Reed, Auckland, 1989, pp.290–1. In his Extracts (in the ATL) Hanson predicted the 'disastrous' results of Grey's 'violation of the principle' of Maori ownership of waste lands.

5 *New Zealand Spectator and Cook's Straits Guardian*, 25 July 1846.

6 Ibid., 12 December 1846.

7 Obituary of Reverend George Evans, *Congregational Magazine*, Permezel Collection. After his death, Hannah retired to Surbiton in Kingston upon Thames.

8 Paul Johnson, *The Offshore Islanders: A History of the English People*, Weidenfeld & Nicholson, London, 1972, p.278 (he says there were 224,000 in 1850).

9 *Melbourne Punch*, 'The Quarrel Scene in Julius Caesar', Vol. IV, 9 July 1857, p.185; 'The Return of the Prodigal', Vol. VII, 14 October 1858, p.96; 'The Deformed Transformed', Act Three, Vol. VIII, 7 April 1859, pp.81–83.

10 *New Zealand Spectator and Cook's Straits Guardian*, 14 February 1846.

11 The land orders transferred by the Deed comprised the town acres 38, 211, 216 and 693, with one section rented out for £270 per annum. The six country sections were 427, 607, 637, 642 and 643, with section 837 included but not yet selected.

12 *Wellington Independent*, 9 January 1864.

13 Ibid.

14 British Parliamentary Papers, *Colonies: New Zealand, 1837–1850*, Vol. 7, 1851 (1398), pp.76, 78 (the amount stated was £4,365 12s 10d); ibid., Vol. 9, 1852–53 (206), pp.93, 94, NL.

15 Minutes, 12 August 1847, p.164, NZC, Directors' Minutes, 1839–1849, CO 208/183, ANZ. Here, Evans is referring to the father. Sir Edward died in 1862.

16 *The Times*, 3 July 1847.

17 Peter Ackroyd, *London: The Biography*, Chatto & Windus, London, 2000, p.344.

18 Peter Ackroyd, *Dickens*, Random House, London, Vintage edn, 1999, p.405.

19 Leader, *The Times*, 15 December 1847. My italics. See also J. S. Marais, *The Colonisation of New Zealand*, Milford, London, 1927, pp.286–7, which agrees with this view of Earl Grey's constitution. In 1848, Earl Grey went back to Parliament and proposed a Suspending Act, which put a temporary stop to the constitutional provisions of the 1846 Act for five years and authorised Governor Grey to establish two provincial Legislative Councils.

20 'Dr. Evans [was] an able contributor to one of the London weekly papers during his residence in London': Richard Wakelin, *History and Politics, Containing the Political Recollections and Leaves from Writings of a New Zealand Journalist*, Lyon & Blair, Wellington, 1877, pp.22–23.

21 Horace Fildes wrote that in London, '[Evans] actively interested himself in furthering the colonization of the Wellington and adjacent settlements of the New Zealand Company': *Evening Post*, 16 July 1927 (see next chapter).

22 Philip Temple, *A Sort of Conscience: The Wakefields*, Auckland University Press, Auckland, 2002, p.408. 'Over four hundred Maori attended Colonel Wakefield's funeral, exhibiting great grief': J. J. Taine (ed. H. W. Fildes), *Reminiscences*, Vol. 2, p.369, qMS-1975, ATL.

23 Burns (ed. Richardson), *Fatal Success*, p.299; A. J. Harrop, *The Amazing Career of Edward Gibbon Wakefield*, Allen & Unwin, London, 1928, p.147.

24 Cited in David McGill, *Pioneers of Port Nicholson*, Reed, Wellington, 1984, p.28.

25 *The Times*, 26 December 1849.

26 Attn General Wm Swainson to Legislative Council of New Munster, cited in McGill, *Pioneers of Port Nicholson*, pp.40–41; G. W. Rusden, *History of New Zealand*, Melville, Mullen & Slade, Melbourne, 1895, Vol. 1, p.453.

27 Papers relating to Surrender of Charters by the New Zealand Company, encl. in letter from B. Hawes to T. C. Harington, BPP, *Colonies: New Zealand*, Vol. 7, 1851 (1398), pp.76, 78, NL.
28 Sir William Fox, *How New Zealand Got Its Constitution*, Pamphlet [342.029, 93], 1890, NL.
29 *Melbourne Herald*, 21 March 1857. Information on Evans's chambers and practice was supplied by Guy Holborn, Librarian, Lincoln's Inn Library, London, 28 July 2000, personal communication.
30 See David Blair, 'Three Melbourne Barristers: A Recollection', *Centennial Magazine*, Vol. 2, No. 9, April 1890, pp.689–92.
31 Janice Burns Woods, 'G. S. Evans', in Douglas Pike (gen. ed.), *Australian Dictionary of Biography 1851–1890*, Melbourne University Press, Carlton, Victoria, 1972, Vol. 4, p.143.
32 Ackroyd, *Dickens*, p.616.
33 *Melbourne Herald*, 21 March 1857.
34 'Ill health forced him to leave England': Woods, 'G. S. Evans', pp.142–3.
35 *New Zealand Spectator and Cook's Straits Guardian*, 9 January 1864; *Wellington Independent*, 9 January 1864: Strode v Evans. The original parchment of the Deed of Conveyance is framed and still hangs in the foyer of the legal firm Izard Weston and Co., in Wellington.
36 Ackroyd, *Dickens*, p.939.

Chapter Eighteen

1 *Wellington Independent*, 19 June 1852.
2 Gavin McLean, *Wellington: The First Years of European Settlement, 1840–1850*, Penguin, Auckland, 2000, pp.81–83.
3 James Belich, *Making Peoples: A History of the New Zealanders from Polynesian Settlement to the End of Nineteenth Century*, Penguin, Auckland, 2007, p.339.
4 He died of eating the 'toot' (tutu) berry: *Gazette*, 4 January 1843.
5 Alan Mulgan, *The City of the Strait: Wellington and its Province, a Centennial History*, A. H. & A. W. Reed, Wellington, 1939, p.200.
6 On 2 April 1845 the *Wellington Independent* was founded by the same Thomas McKenzie who, with his widowed mother, had been sponsored as a young boy by Evans and nearly lost his life in Dr Evans's whare. See also Mulgan, *The City of the Strait*, pp.200 ff.
7 John King (1810–62) arrived in Wellington in 1844, one of seven practising solicitors in the mid-1840s. See W David McIntyre (ed.), *The Journal of Henry Sewell, 1853–1857*, Whitcoulls, Christchurch, 1980, Vol. 1, p.199, note 1.
8 Richard Wakelin, *History and Politics, Containing the Political Recollections and Leaves from Writings of a New Zealand Journalist*, Lyon & Blair, Wellington, 1877, p.22.
9 '[Stephen] is an odd kind of person, and at present I am not in love with him though they say he is clever and sharp': McIntyre (ed.), *The Journal of Henry Sewell*, Vol. 1, p.214.
10 Wakelin, *History and Politics*, pp.22–23.
11 *Wellington Independent*, 22 December 1852.
12 *Wellington Independent*, 7 August 1852; extract from *Christchurch Guardian*, 26 August 1852, in *Wellington Independent*, 4 September 1852.
13 *Wellington Independent*, 28 July 1852.
14 *Wellington Independent*, 4 August 1852.
15 *New Zealand Spectator and Cook's Straits Guardian*, 1 September 1852.
16 *Wellington Independent*, 28 August 1852. See endnote 18.
17 Wakelin, *History and Politics*, p.23. Wakelin refers to Evans as having been 'an able contributor to one of the London weekly papers during his residence in London'. G. H.

Scholefield (ed.), *Dictionary of New Zealand Biography*, Vols 1 and 2, Department of Internal Affairs, Wellington, 1940, makes no mention of Stephen's insanity, and makes no reference to the case.

18 Thomas McKenzie wrote that he was imprisoned for three weeks and released on Governor Grey's orders: Thomas Wilmor McKenzie, McKenzie Family Papers, MS-Papers-1357, ATL.

19 *Wellington Independent*, 22 December 1852. Horace, *Epistles*, B. 1. 16

20 *Wellington Independent*, 29 December 1852.

21 *Wellington Independent*, 15 January 1853. The meeting was held on 12 January.

22 *Wellington Independent*, 17 July 1852.

23 *Wellington Independent*, 31 July 1852.

24 *Wellington Independent*, 29 September 1852.

25 William Fox to editor from Parthenon Club, *The Times*, 28 July 1851.

26 G. W. Rusden, *History of New Zealand*, Melville, Mullen & Slade, Melbourne, 1895, Vol. 1, pp.489–92.

27 *Wellington Independent*, 9 October 1852.

28 *Wellington Independent*, 20 October 1852.

29 *Wellington Independent*, 15 September 1852.

30 *Wellington Independent*, 20 November 1852. Other committee members were: Dr Featherston, Capt. Rhodes, and Messrs Bannatyne, Clifford, Bowler, Moore, Bethune, Waitt, Blyth and J. Smith Hickson.

31 *Wellington Independent*, 11 December 1852.

32 Peter Stuart, *Edward Gibbon Wakefield in New Zealand: His Political Career*, Victoria University Press, Wellington, 1971, pp.26–27. He adds that there was a leap in sales after his edict: in 1853, 150,681 acres were sold, and 290,437 acres in 1854.

33 McIntyre (ed.), *Journal of Henry Sewell*, Vol. 1, p.182.

34 Edward Gibbon Wakefield to Dr Featherston and others, *Wellington Independent*, 19 March 1853.

35 Stuart, *Edward Gibbon Wakefield*, pp.32 ff.

36 The Colonial Office also criticised Grey for not having done this: Stuart, *Edward Gibbon Wakefield*, pp.42, 43.

37 'Scrip' is explained in McIntyre (ed.), *Journal of Henry Sewell*, Vol. 1, p.184.

38 'Dr. Evans . . . I am doubtful about': ibid., pp.211–12.

39 Ibid.

40 For details of the Bill and judgment, see *Wellington Independent*, 2 April 1853.

41 McIntyre (ed.), *Journal of Henry Sewell*, Vol. 1, pp.213–22.

42 Ibid., p.384. He had little time for Brandon either, whom he called 'a sharp little man addicted to scrip and land jobbing': p.211.

43 Ibid. p.225; Stuart, *Edward Gibbon Wakefield*, p.40.

44 *Wellington Independent*, 13 April 1853.

45 Stuart, *Edward Gibbon Wakefield*, p.43.

46 Rusden, *History of New Zealand*, Vol. 1, p.530.

47 Ibid., pp.211–14, 222, 225, 227–8.

48 *Wellington Independent*, 14 May 1853.

49 *Wellington Independent*, 4 June 1853.

50 Ibid.; Wakelin, *History and Politics*, p.33; Philip Temple, *A Sort of Conscience: The Wakefields*, Auckland University Press, Auckland, 2002, pp.490 ff.

51 Stuart, *Edward Gibbon Wakefield*, pp.62 ff.

52 *Wellington Independent*, 13 July 1853. Stuart, *Edward Gibbon Wakefield*, p.66: Stuart separates the Company into two, saying two companies were interested in purchasing the *Tory* and that Evans's entity merged with Wakefield's. In fact, Wakefield joined Evans's venture after insisting on the committee of five, and later manoeuvred men like Motte out and promoted his own favourites. Evans's New Zealand Colonization Company, fully evolved, became the New Zealand Company. It was the 1825 Company that later in the year merged with the New Zealand Company. In due course, Wakefield

was elected in the Hutt for the Provincial Council and later for the General Assembly, but he lacked close friends.

53 Evans was right in choosing Melbourne before Wakefield. In the first Legislative Assembly, 18 June 1854, the government was headed by Weld, Fitzgerald and Sewell. Wakefield had persuaded Henry Sewell to join the government, on the assurance of his support. During the second reading of the Waste Lands Bill, 'without flinching, EGW denied Weld and worse, denied Sewell . . . . Fitzgerald wrote later Sewell said to him whilst Wakefield was still speaking, "I'm afraid, after all he is a very great scoundrel" . . . . In his unscrupulous bid for power, Wakefield had lost his one true ally': Temple, *A Sort of Conscience*, p.509, citing Fitzgerald to Godley, 23 April 1855.

54 Mrs Evans and three children (probably grandchildren) departed in late August in the schooner *Australiana*. Evans preceded or followed her, probably the latter. This suggests his contacts in Melbourne had arranged accommodation for them.

55 John Cobley, 'William Bland', in Douglas Pike (gen. ed.), *Australian Dictionary of Biography 1788–1850*, Melbourne University Press, Carlton, Victoria, 1966, Vol. 1, pp.112–15.

56 A. W. Martin, 'Henry Parkes', in Douglas Pike (gen. ed.), *Australian Dictionary of Biography 1851–1890*, Melbourne University Press, Carlton, Victoria, 1974, Vol. 5, p.400.

57 Interestingly, another George Evans was believed to have 'discovered' Melbourne: *Wellington Independent*, 27 June 1862, citing the *Daily Times* correspondent, 11 June 1862. An accident prevented Fawkner coming over in his first ship. Instead, George Evans and four other men came on the voyage, and discovered the Yarra. Mr Fawkner 'speedily joined them, and they allotted the site of Melbourne amongst themselves'. Evans's namesake became landlord of the Royal Oak Hotel.

Chapter Nineteen

1 Harold Balfe (ed. E. A. Doyle), *The Story of the Century 1851–1951*, Victorian Government, Melbourne, 1951, p.128.

2 James Bonwick, *Early Struggles of the Australian Press*, Gordon & Gotch, London, 1890, pp.67 ff.

3 See Geoffrey Serle, *The Golden Age: A History of the Colony of Victoria 1851–1861*, Melbourne University Press, Carlton, Victoria, 1963, pp.155–88, for a detailed description and analysis of the Eureka Stockade.

4 Ibid., p.262.

5 'The high quality of journalism is worthy of special mention . . . the intellectual and polemical quality of men like Wilson, Higinbotham, Blair, the Symes and Evans was high': ibid., p.360. See also *Australasian Gazette*, 17 October 1868: 'As a speaker and a writer, Dr. Evans would have attracted attention in any part of the world.'

6 *Melbourne Morning Herald*, 15 March 1855.

7 H. L. Hall, 'Sir Archibald Michie', in Douglas Pike (gen. ed.), *Australian Dictionary of Biography*, Melbourne University Press, Carlton, Victoria, 1974, Vol. 5, p.248.

8 'The Journalist and the Jobber', *Melbourne Herald*, 30 June 1856.

9 Evans is referring here to the condition of kidney stones.

10 G. S. Evans to H. Parkes, 30 June 1856, Henry Parkes Collection, *Autographed Letters of Notable Australians*, pp.154–6, A69, ML.

11 *Argus*, 31 March 1856, cited in Serle, *The Golden Age*, see pp.206–8.

12 *Melbourne Herald*, 18 November 1856.

13 G. S. Evans to H. Parkes, ibid.

14 *Leader*, Vol. 10, 5 April 1862, p.327.

15 *Melbourne Herald*, 13 November 1856.

16 *Melbourne Herald*, 7 November 1856.

17 *Argus*, 6 August–18 September 1856, on a series of meetings at Richmond.

18 *Melbourne Herald*, 19 November 1856.
19 *Argus*, 22 November 1856.
20 Serle, *The Golden Age*, p.259. There were sixty members in all. 'Childers estimated that the government had about twenty supporters . . . he divided the rest into about twenty "extreme Opposition", five "moderate Opposition", and fifteen waverers . . . . Nine of the eleven mining members, five of the six Catholics, and most of the members for Melbourne and Geelong were in opposition': ibid., p.258. Evans belonged to this last group.
21 Dr William Clark Haines (1810–66): born Hampstead, educated at Charterhouse and Caius College, Cambridge, he was friend of Thackeray, and migrated in 1841. He was a physician and farmer, and rose through the ranks of colonial government: Betty Malone, 'William Clark Haines', in Pike (ed.), *Australian Dictionary of Biography*, Vol. 4, pp.315–17. See also Serle, *The Golden Age*, p.189.
22 *Melbourne Herald*, 21 November 1856.
23 Serle, *The Golden Age*, p.122.
24 Ibid., pp.249–50.
25 Ibid., p.346.
26 Ibid., pp.255, 316.
27 Ibid., p.255. Remark on Michie, p.254.
28 Ibid., p.258; Debate in the House of Lords on the subject of New Zealand, *Colonial Gazette*, Vol. 7, 21 June 1845, pp.388–9.
29 See Serle, *The Golden Age*, p.255.
30 For an example of his erudition on constitutional matters, see G. S. Evans to Assembly on Procedure for Election of Magistrates, *Victorian Hansard*, Vol. 4, 1 December 1858, SLV.
31 See Charles Gavan Duffy, *My Life in Two Hemispheres*, T. Fisher Unwin, London, 1898, Vol. 2, p.207; David Blair, 'Three Melbourne Barristers: A Recollection', *Centennial Magazine*, Vol. 2, No. 9, April 1890, pp.691–2; George Higinbotham, *Argus*, 6 April 1859.
32 Serle, *The Golden Age*, p.255.
33 *Victorian Hansard*, Vol. 1, 18 December 1856, SLV.
34 *Victorian Hansard*, Vol. 1, 6–7 January 1857, SLV.
35 *Melbourne Punch*, Vol. III, 8 January 1857, p.181.
36 Duffy, *My Life in Two Hemispheres*, Vol. 2, p.163. See also Serle, *The Golden Age*, pp.313–14.
37 Editorial, *Melbourne Herald*, 17 January 1857.
38 *Melbourne Herald*, 21 March 1857.
39 *Victorian Hansard*, Vol. 2, 2 June 1857, SLV.
40 See Serle, *The Golden Age*, p.255.
41 The nine who voted to overthrow both the Haines and O'Shanassy governments were Beaver, Evans, Harker, McCulloch, McDougall, Michie, Moore, Palmer and Sargood. Eight of the ten Independents in religion voted against O'Shanassy: Serle, *The Golden* Age, p.262 (note).
42 As Serle says: 'Michie was a man with no very strong political convictions, and . . . not difficult to sway. A brilliant histrionic debater and popular speaker . . . he did not run very deep': ibid., p.262.
43 Ibid., p.255.
44 *Victorian Hansard*, Vol. 2, 2 July 1857, SLV.
45 *Melbourne Punch*, Vol. IV, 9 July 1857, poem entitled 'The Quarrel Scene in "Julius Caesar" (Improved)', pp.185–6; and cartoon of Brutus and Cassius, p.189.
46 *Victorian Hansard*, Vol. 2, 22 April 1857, SLV.
47 *Victorian Hansard*, Vol. 2, 28 April 1857, SLV.
48 *Victorian Hansard*, Vol. 2, 25 May 1857, SLV.
49 See Serle, *The Golden Age*, pp.264–6.
50 *Victorian Hansard*, Vol. 2, 5 June 1857, SLV.

51 Balfe, *The Story of the Century*, pp.68–70 ff.
52 Serle, *The Golden Age*, pp.270–1. The former Land League was dissolved to reconstitute the convention.
53 For an analysis of Haines's Bill and the land question, see Serle, *The Golden Age*, pp.266–73 ff. The Opposition's attitude towards the convention was strange, according to Serle, 'for if O'Shanassy and Duffy and the goldfields members had joined the Convention, they might have been irresistible': p.272.
54 *Victorian Hansard*, Vol. 2, 16 July 1857, SLV.
55 *Melbourne Punch*, Vol. IV, 23 June 1857, p.202.
56 *Melbourne Herald*, 17 July 1857.
57 *Australasian Gazette*, 17 October 1868.

Chapter Twenty

1 *Melbourne Punch*, Vol. IX, 1, 8, 15 December 1859, pp.155, 158, 166–7. The first 'chapter' is preceded by the full-page cartoon of Evans as 'The Original Sphynx', p.153. Even though the articles are very humorous, combined with Evans's editorials and ready confidences with colleagues, they have been a valuable source of biographical material.
2 Ibid.
3 '. . . the whole of the lower point of his back was covered with meaningless hieroglyphics . . . the pain from the wounds was excruciating. For some days he could not even bear the weight of the bedclothes upon him but was obliged to lie on the coverlid with his face downward . . . . As to the nature of the hieroglyphics on his person, it is a point on which the Doctor is exceedingly sensitive, and his most intimate friends have never been able to elicit any information concerning them. An impenetrable veil, in the shape of his "Corazza Shirt" (six for 42s.) hangs over this mystery. It is a secret never to be revealed': 'Biography of Dr. Evans: Chapter Three: Australian History', *Melbourne Punch*, Vol. IX, 15 December 1859, pp.166–7.
4 *Old Colonists Number of the Tatler: Containing One Hundred Portraits of Pioneers of Victoria*, Vol. 1, No. 40, George Robertson, Melbourne, 21 May 1898.
5 David Blair, 'Three Melbourne Barristers: A Recollection', *Centennial Magazine*, Vol. 2, No. 9, April 1890, p.692.
6 Ibid., p.692.
7 'Ireland, Fellows, Michie, Wood, Evans and others displayed their various brands of rowdyism, violence and spite, and nearly every man had his ring of personal enemies. Sensitive to their own honour, contemptuous of others' feelings, these men of the mid-nineteenth century allowed free rein still to their tempers and passions': Geoffrey Serle, *The Golden Age: A History of the Colony of Victoria 1851–1861*, Melbourne University Press, Carlton, Victoria, 1963, p.316.
8 *Victorian Hansard*, Vol. 2, 22 July 1857, SLV.
9 *Victorian Hansard*, Vol. 2, 5 August 1857, SLV.
10 *Melbourne Morning Herald*, 14 March 1855.
11 Bill Murray (ed.), *Crisis, Conflict and Consensus: Selected Documents Illustrating 200 Years in the Making of Australia*, Rigby, Adelaide, 1984, pp.97–101, citing P. Just, *Australia: Notes Taken During a Residence in the Colonies from the Gold Discovery in 1851 till 1857*, Durham & Thomson, Dundee, 1859, pp.206–7. See also *Sydney Morning Herald*, 2 July 1861.
12 *Victorian Hansard*, Vol. 2, 25 September 1857, SLV.
13 *Melbourne Morning Herald*, 14 September 1857.
14 *Victorian Hansard*, Vol. 2, 30 September 1857, SLV.
15 *Argus*, 24 February 1859. During the course of the first Parliament, of the fifty-one Bills the assembly introduced, only twenty-six passed both Houses.
16 George Wakefield, Letters to his Father, 10 October 1857, MS-6331-301/6, SLV.
17 *Argus*, 3 December 1857, rapped Michie and Moore for the change they had undergone

in power. On the hustings they had been most anxious for the land to pass to the yeoman farmer 'for the greatest happiness for the greatest number', but were now 'much less eager to bring [it] about': *Victorian Hansard*, Vol. 2, 14 and 17 December 1857, SLV.

18 *Victorian Hansard*, Vol. 3, 9 February 1858, SLV.

19 'Parliamentary Portraits', *Leader*, Vol. 10, No. 327, 5 April 1862. This is the title of the article on the front page accompanied by a large illustration of Evans.

20 *Victorian Hansard*, Vol. 3, 9 February 1858, SLV.

21 'Many liberals were wary of moving too quickly to "ultra democracy" and preferred to watch experiments before going further . . . . Support of manhood suffrage did not logically imply support of the full democratic programme': Serle, *The Golden Age*, pp.275 ff.

22 The Liberal non-conformists were Dr Embling, and Messrs Harker, Heales, Langlands and Sargood. Although referred to as radical by Serle (ibid., p.254), Evans is labelled as Liberal Opportunist along with Ireland and Wood; Michie is Liberal with Chapman and Clark. The democrats were Aspinall, Blair, Brooke, Grant, Cameron, Fyfe, Humffray, Owens, Pyke, Read and Syme. See ibid., p.259.

23 *Victorian Hansard*, Vol. 3, 24 February 1858, SLV.

24 Mr Haines 'gave a Ministerial Explanation' alluding to 'events which have taken place during the past week': *Victorian Hansard*, Vol. 3, 3 March 1858, SLV.

25 Serle, *The Golden Age*, p.278 (footnote).

26 The term 'shouting' is slang for buying beer or other alcoholic beverages for another, usually in a public house or inn. Here it was a form of persuasion for prospective voters.

27 J. L. Forde, *The Story of the Bar of Victoria*, Whitcombe & Tombs, Melbourne, 1913, p.161.

28 See cartoon of Evans and Chapman juggling the minority clause: *Melbourne Punch*, Vol. IV, March–April 1858, p.85.

29 *Melbourne Punch*, Vol. VI, 18 March 1858, p.69.

30 See Chapman's explanation: *Victorian Hansard*, Vol. 3, 14 April 1858, SLV. Both Michie and Wood also voted with the majority. Wood stated he had not attacked Evans. The quarrel was caused by Michie, about whom Evans complained that he had been 'traduced and calumniated by that disappointed man'.

31 *Melbourne Punch*, Vol. VI, 22 April 1858, p.107: 'A Fragment From a New Poem Entitled: The Revolt of Evans'.

32 *Argus*, 16 April 1858.

33 *Argus*, 17 May 1858.

34 *Victorian Hansard*, Vol. 3, 1 June 1858, SLV.

35 G. S. Evans to Mary Pantin Evans, 15 May 1858, Permezel Collection.

36 Front page, *Leader*, Vol. 10, No. 327, 5 April 1862.

37 Serle, *The Golden Age*, pp.283 ff. See also 'From the beginning the Government were [*sic*] assailed by persistent abuse of which Mr. Ireland and Dr. Evans were the chief objects': C. Gavan Duffy, *My Life in Two Hemispheres*, T. Fisher Unwin, London, 1898, Vol. 2, p.197.

Chapter Twenty-One

1 Letter from President of Chamber of Commerce, Melbourne, *Wellington Independent*, 18 August 1858.

2 Ibid.

3 'The Death of Dr. Evans', *Wellington Independent*, 8 October 1868.

4 *Wellington Independent*, 28 August 1858.

5 *Wellington Independent*, 15 September 1858.

6 'Farewell Dinner to Dr. Evans', *Wellington Independent*, 25 September 1858.

7 Ibid.

8 Geoffrey Serle, *The Golden Age: A History of the Colony of Victoria 1851–1861*, Melbourne University Press, Carlton, Victoria, 1963, p.296.
9 *Argus*, 8 October 1858, cited in *Wellington Independent*, 20 October 1858.
10 *Victorian Hansard*, Vol. 4, 28 October 1858, SLV.
11 *Wellington Independent*, 24 November 1858.
12 *Victorian Hansard*, Vol. 4, 28 October 1858, SLV. David Moore was president of the Board of Land and Works in the Haines ministry, from 29 April 1857 to 10 March 1858.
13 *Victorian Hansard*, Speaking to a Clause in the Officials in Parliament Bill, Vol. 4, 18 November 1858, SLV.
14 *Victorian Hansard*, Vol. 4, 17 February 1859, SLV; and *Argus*, 19 February 1859.
15 'The Boomerang Contract', *Wellington Independent*, 15 March 1859.
16 *Victorian Hansard*, Vol. 4, 18 February 1859, SLV.
17 *Wellington Independent*, 15 March 1859.
18 *Argus*, 11 April 1859, quoting the *Wellington Independent*, 29 March 1859.
19 *Wellington Independent*, 15 November 1859.
20 *Argus*, 14 January 1859.
21 See cartoon, 'Guying a Governor', *Melbourne Punch*, Vol. VIII, 3 March 1859. Serle, *The Golden Age*, p.286, describes 'the Opposition brawling with the government over a suspected malpractice in which the rights of the Assembly against the Council were involved, while the Governor waited several hours within the precincts of the House, before he could dismiss his unruly legislators'.
22 Serle, *The Golden Age*, pp.284–5.
23 C. Gavan Duffy, *My Life in Two Hemispheres*, T. Fisher Unwin, London, 1898, Vol. 2, p.197.
24 *Argus*, 4 April 1859.
25 *Argus*, 5 April 1859.
26 Serle, *The Golden Age*, p.288.
27 Editorial, *Argus*, 6 April 1859.
28 Ibid.
29 Serle, *The Golden Age*, pp.282–8. See pp.270–88 passim for the developing story of government and Opposition views towards land and the Land Convention.
30 *Argus*, 30 August 1859.
31 Redmond Barry to Hugh C. E. Childers, 15 April 1859, Correspondence 1859–1864, qMS-2079, ATL.
32 Scotch College historian Dick Briggs confirmed Edward Joshua Riddiford attended the college from 21 March 1859, but not the following year: John Permezel to author by email. See also Douglas Cresswell, 'Riddiford of Te Awaite', in *Early New Zealand Families, Second Series*, Whitcombe & Tombs, Christchurch, 1956, p.16. Back in Victoria he sought adventure in the goldfields for a while before returning to his family. Then the Otago goldrush lured him down south. It was there that he received a letter from his mother begging him to return to manage the family's station at Te Awaite, as 'your father is not very good at looking into things'.
33 Serle, *The Golden Age*, p.296.
34 *Argus*, 28 June 1859.
35 *Argus*, 16 April 1859, which accused Evans of having acquired a 'reputation for a predilection for an indolent leisure'.
36 'Ministerial characters were torn to shreds, minor administrative decisions – a grant to a Catholic orphanage in South Melbourne, commutation of the death sentence . . . – were presented as crucial to the future of the colony': Serle, *The Golden Age*, speaking of the Constitutional Association, p.290.
37 *Victorian Hansard*, Vol. 7, 1 March 1861, SLV.
38 James Grant and Geoffrey Serle, *The Melbourne Scene, 1803–1956*, Melbourne University Press, Carlton, Victoria, 1957, p.121, citing C. W. Dilke, *Greater Britain: A Record of Travel in English-Speaking Countries During 1866 and 1867*, Macmillan, London, 1868, p.325.
39 Serle, *The Golden Age*, pp.290–3.

40 H. L. Hall, 'Sir Archibald Michie', in Douglas Pike (gen. ed.), *Australian Dictionary of Biography*, Melbourne University Press, Carlton, Victoria, 1974, Vol. 5, p.248.
41 *Argus*, 17 August 1859. Also see Serle, *The Golden Age*, on the subject of how protectionism influenced the outcome of the election, pp.305–8.
42 *Argus*, 22 August 1859.
43 The name Francis prefixed to Woolley had been scratched out and Alfred substituted. A number of voters for the Evans–Batten coalition had not struck out the name Woolley, thinking it superfluous, and thereby negated their votes by leaving three names undeleted, instead of two: *Argus*, 29 August 1859.
44 *Argus*, 24 September 1859. Evans, 883 votes; Grant, 698 votes; Thompson, 549 votes.
45 *Melbourne Punch*, Vol. X, 12 July 1860, p.200.
46 *Argus*, 14 October 1859.

Chapter Twenty-Two

1 C. Gavan Duffy, *My Life in Two Hemispheres*, T. Fisher Unwin, London, 1898, Vol. 2, p.207.
2 *Victorian Hansard*, Vol. 5, 22 October 1859, SLV.
3 *Melbourne Punch*, Vol. XI, 16 August 1860, pp.28–29. In the 'Geographical Map of Members' Evans was depicted as a Bluff that 'looms large at a distance but approachable without any risk'. O'Shanassy was compared with the 'malodorous skunk and the unhandsome sloth'.
4 *Melbourne Punch*, Vol. IX, 20 October 1859, p.103.
5 Ibid.
6 On 24 July 1860, the government recited a litany of his inconsistencies: *Victorian Hansard*, Vol. 6, 24 July 1860, SLV.
7 Michie was part of Nicholson's government but with no Cabinet appointment. John Dennistoun Wood was Attorney General. He was a friend of Evans, but in the House this time his political foe. It was not until November 1861 that the two were together in O'Shanassy's third ministry.
8 Juliette Deane, *Reminiscences*, Daniell Family Papers, p.13, MS-2379, ATL.
9 *Victorian Hansard*, Vol. 5, 17 February 1860, SLV. In this speech, which was well-received, Evans illustrated his point with a reference to a meeting he and others had with 'some of the great capitalists of London, with a view of arranging a loan for a sister colony'. Evans was 'greatly struck' by the fact the first questions Mr Baring and the other capitalists asked concerned 'the sale of the public lands of the colony seeking the loan'.
10 *Victorian Hansard*, Vol. 5, 15 February 1860, SLV.
11 *Victorian Hansard*, Vol. 5, 15 February, 28 February, 8 March 1860, SLV.
12 *Victorian Hansard*, Vol. 6, 2 May 1860, SLV. Dr Greeves is classified as a 'conservative-opportunist': see Geoffrey Serle, *The Golden Age: A History of the Colony of Victoria 1851–1861*, Melbourne University Press, Carlton, Victoria 1963, p.259 note.
13 Various attempts at land Bills took place over these years: Service's Bill failed in 1860; the next year, in the Heales government, Brooke's Bill was declared illegal by the Supreme Court; and in 1862, Duffy's Bill in the O'Shanassy government was foiled by dummies and deputies: Harold Balfe (ed. E. A. Doyle), *The Story of the Century 1851–1951*, Victorian Government, Melbourne, 1951, p.70.
14 G. S. Evans to Victorian Legislative Assembly, *Victorian Hansard*, Vol. 6, 4 July 1860, SLV. See also Duffy, *My Life in Two Hemispheres*, Vol. 2, p.207.
15 *Victorian Hansard*, Vol. 6, 30 August 1860, SLV.
16 *Victorian Hansard*, Vol. 6, 31 August 1860, SLV; and *Argus*, 1 September 1860.
17 *Argus*, 3 September 1860.
18 *Melbourne Punch*, Vol. XVIII, 31 March 1864, p.105. Wood had accused Michie of cribbing his work, and Michie retaliated 'in his usual manner but made no attempt to prove himself to be the author'.
19 C. E. Sayers, *David Syme: A Life*, Cheshire, Melbourne, 1965, p.53.

20 *Victorian Hansard*, Vol. 6, 12 September 1860, SLV.
21 Of the 51 members present, 32 voted against the government.
22 *Argus*, 19 September 1860.
23 G. S. Evans to H. Merivale, Under-Secretary for the Colonies, 25 October 1860, *New Zealand Papers*, 1836–87, pp.451–2, C184, and CO 309/53, ML.
24 Serle, *The Golden Age*, p.307 note, citing Newcastle to Barkly, 26 January 1861.
25 Sayers, *David Syme*, p.53. Syme was editor of the *Age*. He loathed both Duffy and 'his long-time colleague' John O'Shanassy: p.51. For a description of the history of the distribution of land in Victoria, see pp.50 ff.
26 *Melbourne Punch*, Vol. XII, 31 January 1861, p. 4.
27 *Argus*, 4 January 1861.
28 *Victorian Hansard*, Vol. 7, 3 January 1861, SLV
29 *Victorian Hansard*, Vol. 7, 4 January 1861, SLV.
30 *Victorian Hansard*, Vol. 7, 11 January, 25 January 1861, SLV.
31 *Argus*, 21 January 1861.
32 *Victorian Hansard*, Vol. 7, 16 January 1861, SLV.
33 *Victorian Hansard*, Vol. 7, 29 January 1861, SLV; *Argus*, 30 January 1861.
34 *Victorian Hansard*, Vol. 7, 9 January 1861, SLV.

Chapter Twenty-Three

1 *Melbourne Punch*, Vol. X, 12 July 1860, p.200. *Melbourne Punch* had decided that this quotation from Shakespeare's *Julius Caesar* best summed up Evans.
2 *Argus*, 9 February 1861.
3 Geoffrey Serle, *The Golden Age: A History of the Colony of Victoria 1851–1861*, Melbourne University Press, Carlton, Victoria, 1963, p.303. Evans approached O'Shanassy, Ebden, Haines and others, using Ireland as negotiator.
4 *Argus*, 11 February 1861.
5 David Blair, 'Three Melbourne Barristers: A Recollection', *Centennial Magazine*, Vol. 2, No. 9, April 1890, pp.690–1.
6 *Victorian Hansard*, Vol. 7, 19 June 1861, SLV.
7 *Victorian Hansard*, Vol. 7, 26 June 1861, SLV.
8 Serle, *The Golden Age*, p.318.
9 Ibid., p.305.
10 *Argus*, 12 August 1861.
11 *Argus*, 13 August 1861.
12 *Victorian Hansard*, Vol. 7, 30 April 1861, SLV. (This occurred during a debate on granting a subsidy to the *Argus* for its publication of Hansard.)
13 *Victorian Hansard*, Vol. 2, 25 September 1857, SLV.
14 *Argus*, 20 October 1861, citing extract from the *Maryborough Advertiser*, 18 October. Julius Vogel had been editor of this paper but had just left. He may have influenced the positive attitude towards Evans there.
15 *Maryborough and Dunolly Advertiser*, extracts in *Argus*, 18 October, 21 October 1861.
16 *Victorian Hansard*, Vol. 8, 21 February 1862, SLV.
17 *Melbourne Punch*, Vol. XIII, 24 October 1861, p.261.
18 The men departed in August 1860 and died in June 1861. The *Argus* reported the tragedy on 4 November 1861.
19 See C. E. Sayers et al. (ed.), *One Hundred Years of Responsible Government in Victoria, 1856–1957*, Government Printer, Melbourne, 1956, p.207.
20 *Argus*, 14 November 1861.
21 Serle, *The Golden* Age, p.318.
22 Izard to Evans, 9 January 1862, cited in Julia Millen, *The Story of Bell Gully Buddle Weir 1840–1990*, Bell Gully Buddle Weir, Wellington, 1990, p.19.
23 John Cobley, 'William Bland', in Douglas Pike (gen. ed.), *Australian Dictionary of*

Biography 1851–1890, Melbourne University Press, Carlton, Victoria, 1966, Vol. 1, pp.112–15; citing article by Evans in the *Empire*, 21 January 1862. Bland died in July 1868, aged seventy-nine, and was honoured with a state funeral. His portrait hangs in the Mitchell Library, Sydney, New South Wales.

24 *Victorian Hansard*, Vol. 8, 21 February 1862, SLV.

25 *Victorian Hansard*, Vol. 8, 4 April 1862, p.927, SLV.

26 *Leader*, Vol. 10, No. 327, 5 April 1862.

27 *Victorian Hansard*, Vol. 8, 9 and 12 May 1862, SLV.

28 *Victorian Hansard*, Vol. 8, 13 May 1862, SLV.

29 *Argus*, 28 May 1862.

30 *Victorian Hansard*, Vol. 8, 29 May 1862, p.1229, SLV.

31 The *Argus* listed the Bills passed: 19 June 1862.

32 Samuel Revans to his nephew, 4 February 1863. Unfortunately, the stamp of the letter has been cut out, meaning that two or three lines are broken up: Revans' Family Collection, MS-2007, ATL. Evans was true to his word. James Coutts Crawford's lengthy report, together with the analysis of Mr R. Brough Smyth, 'Notes on Specimens of Rocks Collected in the Province of Wellington by Hon. J. Coutts Crawford' dated Melbourne, 13 January 1863, were published in the *New Zealand Government Gazette* of 2 March 1863, and in the *Wellington Independent*, 10 March 1863.

33 C. E. Sayers, *David Syme: A Life*, Cheshire, Melbourne, 1965, p.55.

34 Ibid., p.54.

35 *Victorian Hansard*, Vol. 9, 11 February 1863, SLV.

36 *Victorian Hansard*, Vol. 9, 3 March and 8 May 1863, SLV.

37 S. M. Ingham, 'Sir John O'Shanassy', in Douglas Pike (gen. ed.), *Australian Dictionary of Biography 1851–1890*, Melbourne University Press, Carlton, Victoria, 1975, Vol. 5, p.380.

38 *Argus*, 3 June 1864. Also see *Argus*, 1 January 1864.

39 Harold Balfe (ed. E. A. Doyle), *The Story of the Century 1851–1951*, Victorian Government, Melbourne, 1951, pp.128 ff.

40 *Victorian Hansard*, Vol. 9, 25 August 1863, SLV.

41 *Victorian Hansard*, Vol. 9, 21 August 1863, SLV.

42 C. Gavan Duffy, *My Life in Two Hemispheres*,T. Fisher Unwin, London, 1898, Vol. 2, p.205; *Argus*, 29 December 1863.

43 Admiral Sir Edward Chetham Strode died in April 1862. Edward and Amelia inherited the entailed estate, which ultimately was mortgaged 'fatally'. They never lived there but lived in London. Amelia and Edward had no children. When he died in June 1894, his wife having predeceased him, Edward Chetham Strode left an estate of less than £1,500. David Small to author, 2002.

44 *New Zealand Spectator and Cook's Straits Guardian*, 9 January 1864.

45 For a summary of the case, see Appendix Six; for a detailed report, see *Wellington Independent*, 9 January 1864.

46 *Wellington Independent*, 12 March 1864.

47 *Argus*, 27 October 1864.

48 'The Masters and Boys of the Bourke Street School', Skit three: *Melbourne Punch*, Vol. XVIII, 25 February 1864, p.72.

49 G. W. Rusden, *The History of Australia*, Chapman & Hall, London, 1883, Vol. 3, p.322.

50 *Argus*, 17 and 22 October 1864. See also C. Gavan Duffy, *My Life in Two Hemispheres*, T. Fisher Unwin, London, 1898, Vol. 2, p.205.

51 *Argus*, 26 October 1864. Letter signed and dated 22 October 1864. It is not known whether he pursued either course.

52 *Argus*, 5 November 1864.

53 A successful barrister, and staunch Protestant, Michie gained a St Kilda seat in November and was Minister of Justice in the McCulloch ministry from August 1863 to July 1866, 'although not a member after December 1865'. He successfully modified his

views on free trade, and became Attorney-General in the third McCulloch ministry. He lost his seat but stayed in office. From 1873 to 1879 he was Agent-General in London for Victoria, and he was knighted in 1878. 'His political convictions were not very strong': Hall, 'Sir Archibald Michie', in Pike (gen. ed.), *Australian Dictionary of Biography*.

54 Undated extract from the *Ballarat Star*, in the *Argus*, 5 November 1864. Michie was the 'spoilt child of Victorian politics – a sort of "chartered libertine" in the House, who comes and goes in obedience to some law peculiar to himself': *Argus*, 15 October 1864.

55 G. W. Rusden, *History of New Zealand*, Melville, Mullen & Slade, Melbourne, 1895, Vol. 1, p.235. See also G. H. Scholefield, *Dictionary of New Zealand Biography*, Department of Internal Affairs, Wellington, 1940, Vol. 2, p.263.

56 Philip Mennell (ed.), *Dictionary of Australasian Biography, 1855–1892*, Hutchinson & Co., London 1892, pp.358–9.

57 H. G. Brewer to H. S. Chapman, Dunedin, 17 December 1864, pp.1–2, H. S. Chapman, Letters and sundry, qMS-0417, ATL.

58 Between November 1856 and October 1875, a total of sixteen governments looked after the affairs of the colony. The longest was that of McCulloch, 1863–68.

59 'For many years it was known to his friends that [Evans] suffered from an illness of a most painful and almost incurable character': *Australian Journal 1850–1868*, Vol. 4, October 1868, p.153.

60 'George was very bitter at the end': John Permezel, personal communication.

61 *The Times*, 27 November 1868.

62 'A new era, then, is about to commence . . . . A learned scribe is already found. From the Treasury Benches there has just come one who will now gladly sit at PUNCH's feet . . . . Need it be said that we allude to our great ex-Minister of Letters, the sonorous gold-field senator who . . . will smoke his pipe and chat his Greek in the groves of PUNCH's Academe in philosophic peace': *Melbourne Punch*, Vol. XVII, 30 July 1863, p.39.

63 G. S. Evans to Mary Pantin Evans, 24 October 1865, Permezel Collection.

Chapter Twenty-Four

1 Emily Jane Brontë (ed. Janet Gezari), *The Complete Poems*, Penguin, London, 1992. Bramwell Brontë seems to be the most likely subject of the verse.

2 The will of Harriet Strother Evans, AAOM, 6029/P232, ANZ. To her son and daughter she left £1,000 each. Her grandchildren Edward Joshua and Eliza Riddiford were to receive £500 apiece. Amelia Willis, wife of William J. Willis of Rangitikei, inherited her pianoforte and music Canterbury. (A music Canterbury is a piece of wooden furniture which turns on a base and has several vertical partitions for sheet music. It can also be oblong and stand on legs.) Her granddaughter Thomasina was left her dressing case, and another granddaughter, Mary Riddiford, her new side-saddle. All the rest of her estate she bequeathed to 'my dear husband, George Samuel Evans, for his own use and profit'.

3 *Wellington Independent*, 3 May 1866 (Advertisement), 14 July 1866, 16 March 1867.

4 *Wellington Independent*, 23 April 1867

5 *Wellington Independent*, 7 March 1868.

6 'The death of his wife was a severe blow to him and hastened his own end': Horace Fildes Collection, Newspaper Clippings, *Evening Post*, 16 July 1927, Pq 993.1 FIL 1920, ATL.

7 Hansard, *New Zealand Parliamentary Debates*, 25 September 1868, Vol. 1V, pp.4, 6. The funeral took place at 3.30 p.m.

8 *Wellington Independent*, 26 September 1868.

9 Thus, Fox explained Featherston's absence to the Assembly earlier that day: *New Zealand Parliamentary Debates*, Vol. 4, 1868, p.26, NL.

10 G. H. Scholefield (ed.), *Dictionary of Biography*, Department of Internal Affairs, Wellington, 1940, Vol. 1, p.277. From that action the government's position deteriorated rapidly until the session of 1869 when William Fox moved a resolution of no confidence, carried 40 votes to 20, thus terminating Stafford's five-year term of office. By June, Fox was in office supported by McLean and Isaac Featherston, together with Bell, Vogel and Gisborne. The following year the last expedition was withdrawn from the field of war.
11 *Australian and New Zealand Gazette*, 1 December 1868; *Wellington Independent*, 24 September and 8 October 1868.
12 J. L. Forde, *The Story of the Bar of Victoria*, Whitcombe & Tombes, Melbourne, 1913, pp.160 ff.
13 Philip Mennell (ed.), *A Dictionary of Australasian Biography, 1855–1892*, Hutchinson & Co., London, 1892.
14 *Australian Journal 1850–1868*, Vol. IV, p.153.
15 *Australasian Gazette*, 17 October 1868.
16 Permezel Collection, Melbourne.
17 Samuel Johnson, 'The Art of Biography', from *The Rambler*, no. 50, 1750. Cited by Kate Chisholm, Book Review, *Spectator*, 8 April 2006, p.42.
18 *Melbourne Herald*, 12 October 1868, cited in the *Wellington Independent*, 31 October 1868, and the *Daylesford Mercury and Express*, 14 October 1868.
19 Geoffrey Serle, *The Golden Age: A History of the Colony of Victoria 1851–1861*, Melbourne University Press, Carlton, Victoria, 1963, p.255: 'The intellectual quality of [the first] assembly was of a high order . . . the government set a standard which subsequent administrations have rarely rivalled.' And p.316, referring to the period 1851–1861: 'By comparison with any period in Australian history, except perhaps about 1900, the all-round quality of the leading politicians was high.' Also see p.318.
20 John Dennistoun Wood, 'Melbourne Revisited', *Poems in Rhyme and Blank Verse*, Melville and Mullen, London, 1903, Permezel Collection.
21 David Blair, 'Three Melbourne Barristers: A Recollection', *Centennial Magazine*, Vol. 2, No. 9, April 1890, pp.691–2.
22 Evans's brother, James Cook Evans, who had latterly worked for the new railway industry, had died of a seizure 'following a disappointment in office': Permezel Collection.
23 W. Frederic Morrison, *The Aldine Centennial History of New South Wales*, Aldine, Sydney, 1888, Vol. 2, pp.622–3. Narrabri lies north-west of Sydney, and in 1888 was the terminus of the North Western Railway line. It had then a population of about 2000, and was rapidly growing in importance. The town was largely agricultural, and attracted a 'class of people, [who were] intelligent and thrifty, appreciated school facilities, and [who] have done much towards establishing educational institutions of a high order'. The Public Library was worthy of note, as were the School of Arts and the well-supported churches. It was seen as one of the prosperous towns of the interior.
24 Evans appointed Joseph Schroder Moore (Judge of the Supreme Court) and Charles Beard Izard as executors of his will and two codicils.
25 George Samuel Evans, Last Will and Testament, with Two Codicils, AAOM 6029/P300, ANZ.
26 *Wellington Independent*, 10 December 1868.
27 *Wellington Independent*, March 1869. Charles Heaphy bought Evans's house.
28 Amy Burgess Farren of Cambridge married James Samuel Evans on 19 October 1907 at St Luke's, Westminster: *The Times*. At the time of his marriage, James Samuel Evans' address was given as 31 Hildrop Road, Hoolway: Permezel Collection.
29 *Dominion*, 19 March 1909.
30 Letter from G. Evans to his mother, Celia: Permezel Collection.
31 Mennell (ed.), *Dictionary of Australasian Biography*, p.214; Douglas Pike (gen. ed.), *Australian Dictionary of Biography*, Vol. 4, Melbourne University Press, Carlton, Victoria, 1972.

Epilogue

1 *Wellington Independent*, 24 January 1873. George Hunter junior was the eldest son of George Hunter who became first Mayor of Wellington in 1842. Hunter senior was a successful businessman and was also involved closely with setting up the Exchange, the branch of the Australian Bank and promoting the flax industry. He was closely allied with Evans in these undertakings. He died in 1843.

2 William Fox, *The Six Colonies of New Zealand*, John W. Parker & Son, London, 1851, p.152.

3 J. S. Marais, *The Colonisation of New Zealand*, Milford, London, 1927, p.173.

4 'In 1845 Dr Evans led the way to obtain a charter for his child, the city of Wellington': J. L. Forde, *The Story of the Bar of Victoria*, Whitcombe & Tombs, Melbourne, 1913, p.164.

5 *Wellington Independent*, 24 September 1868.

6 G. S. Evans, Editorial, *Melbourne Morning Herald*, 25 December 1857.

7 Premier William Fox to Donald McLean, 21 November 1872, Sir Donald McLean, Papers, 1839–1877, Vol. 39, MS-1349, ATL.

8 In fact, on 6 May 1839, Britain was forced to suspend Jamaica's constitution after riots due to the emancipation of slaves. She had her hands full with problems like these.

9 Nga Puke is the iwi or sub-tribe. His mother was Roma whose parents were Peter Hohria Pirika Haimona (Simons) and Winika Marguerite Waatapapa.

10 Lionel Brown to author in conversation: Lionel's forebear James Brown had also said 'Mrs Evans was very difficult on board the *Adelaide* . . . full of complaints, and her husband spent a lot of his time trying to remedy them.' Sadly Lionel died in 2011.

11 William Gisborne, *New Zealand Rulers and Statesmen, 1840–1885*, Sampson Low, Marston, Searle, & Rivington, London, 1886, p.10.

12 A. J. Harrop, *England and New Zealand: From Tasman to the Taranaki War*, Methuen, London, 1926, p.811.

13 Alfred Cox, *Men of Mark of New Zealand*, Whitcombe & Tombs, Christchurch, 1886, pp.60–61; Irma O'Connor, *Edward Gibbon Wakefield: The Man Himself*, Selwyn & Blount, London, 1928, p.170. Evans is credited after Petre, Molesworth, Brown and Domett; well before Hanson, Martin, Fox and Featherston.

14 G. H. Scholefield (ed.), *Dictionary of New Zealand Biography*, Department of Internal Affairs, Wellington, 1940, Vol. 1, pp.232–3.

15 Horace Fildes Collection, Newspaper Clippings, *Evening Post*, 16 July 1927, Pq 993.1 FIL 1920, ATL.

16 F. L. Irvine-Smith, *The Streets of My City, Wellington, New Zealand*, A. H. & A. W. Reed, Wellington, 1948.

17 M. Alington, Bolton St Cemetery Inscriptions, Folder 25, MS-Papers-2260, ATL.

18 Emily Jane Brontë (ed. Janet Gezari), *The Complete Poems*, Penguin, London, 1992.

BIBLIOGRAPHY

Abbreviations

ANZ: Archives New Zealand
ATL: Alexander Turnbull Library, Wellington
AWMML: Auckland War Memorial Museum Library
BPP: British Parliamentary Papers: Colonies
CO: Colonial Office
La Trobe: La Trobe Reading Room, State Library of Victoria, Melbourne
ML: Mitchell Library, Library of New South Wales
NL: National Library of New Zealand
NZC: New Zealand Company
NZPL: New Zealand Parliamentary Library
OLC: Old Land Claims
PRO: Public Records Office, London
SLNSW: State Library of New South Wales
SLV: State Library of Victoria, Melbourne

Primary Sources

Papers, Letters and Manuscripts

Alington, M., *Bolton Street Cemetery Inscriptions*, Folder 25, MS-Papers-2260, ATL.

Bagnall, A. G., *Transcripts of Evidence by R. D. Barrett before Land Claims Commission*, Case 374B, 8 February 1843–11 February 1843, ACC 88-103, Box 2, ATL.

Barry, Redmond to Hugh C. E. Childers, 15 April 1859, Correspondence 1859–1864, qMS-2079, ATL.

Betts Hopper, Edward, Diary: 1836–1838, MS-1034, ATL. (Betts Hopper Diary)

Betts Hopper, Edward, Papers-MS-0535, ATL. (Betts Hopper Papers)

Bonwick, James, *Early Struggles of the Australian Press*, London, 1890, in *New Zealand Pamphlets*, Vol. 3, ATL.

British Parliamentary Papers (BPP), *Colonies: Australia*, Vol. 24, NL.

British Parliamentary Papers (BPP), *Colonies: New Zealand, 1837–1850*, Vols 1, 2, 3, 4, 5, 7, 9.

Vol. 1: *Reports from Select Committees on New Zealand with Minutes of Evidence, Appendix, and Indices, 1837–1840.*

Vol. 2: *Report from the 1844 Select Committee on New Zealand, Together with the Minutes of Evidence, Appendices, and Index.*

Vol. 3: *Correspondence and Other Papers Relating to New Zealand 1835–1842.*

Vol. 4: *Correspondence and Other Papers Relating to New Zealand 1843–1845.*

Vol. 5: *Correspondence and Papers Relating to the Native Population, the Distribution of Land and Other Affairs in New Zealand 1846–1847.*

Vol. 7: 1851.
Vol. 9: 1852–1853.
Index to *British Parliamentary Papers, Colonies: Australia and New Zealand*, Irish University Press, 1974, NL.
Carrington, F. A., Papers-MS-0471, ATL.
Catchpool, Edward, Papers-MS-0077, ATL.
Chapman, H. S., Letters and sundry, qMS-0417, ATL. (Chapman Letters)
Chapman, H. S., Papers (including letters), MS-Papers-0053, ATL. (Chapman Papers)
Clarke, George Jnr, Letters and Journals, Vols 6, 7, qMS-0468-0469, ATL. (Clark Letters)
Colley, Mrs Lucy, *Life of the Hon. Henry W. Petre and Eleanor Walmesley*, MS-0593, ATL.
Colonial Office 309, Secretary of State Victoria, Original Correspondence Offices and Individuals, 1860, CO 309/53, ML.
Correspondence and Documents of the New Zealand Company, New Zealand Papers, 1836–1887, C184, Reel 154, ML.
Cotton, W. C., Journal 1841–1848, Vol. 6, qMS-0566, ATL.
Daniell Family Papers, MS-2379, ATL.
Durham Lord (George Lambton), *Colonization Correspondence, 1837–1840*, qMS-1124, ATL.
Evans, G. S., Grammar of the New Zealand Language, 1839, qMS-0688, ATL.
Evans, G. S., Papers, MS-Papers-10552, ATL. (Evans Papers)
Evans, G. S., Last Will and Testament, with Two Codicils, AAOM 6029/P300, ANZ.
Evans, Harriet Strother, Last Will and Testament, AAOM, 6029/P232, ANZ.
Extracts From a Letter to Captain FitzRoy, R.N. from R. Davies Hanson, Esq., Adelaide, Australia, July 1846, ATL.
Featherston, Isaac Earl, Family Papers, Micro-MS-0931, Reel 1, ATL.
Felton Mathew, Sarah, Diary Extracts, qMS-1350, ATL.
Fildes, Horace, Collection, Newspaper Clippings, *Evening Post*, 16 July 1927, Pq 993.1 FIL 1920, ATL.
Fox, Sir William, *How New Zealand Got its Constitution*, Pamphlet [342.029, 93], NL.
Hanson, Richard, *see Extracts From a Letter*, ATL.
Hart, E. P. (ed.), *Merchant Taylors' School Register 1561–1934*, 2 Vols, Eastern Press, London, 1936, NL.
Hogg Scrapbooks, Micro Nos 6, 16, Scrapbooks of newspaper cuttings ca. 1880–1912 [microform] compiled by Alexander Wilson Hogg, ATL. (Hogg Scrapbooks)
Hunter Family Papers, MS-Papers-0049-137, ATL.
Hussey, H., *New Zealand and How it Became a British Province*, fms-[114], ATL.
Lambton Collection, MS-Papers-0140, ATL.
Lawrence, W. R., *'Huzza for New Zealand!': The Life and Work of Captain Mein Smith*, qMS-1139, ATL.
Mantell Collection, *Abstract of Diary, 1843*, qMS-46606, ATL.
McKenzie, Thomas Wilmor, McKenzie Family Papers, MS-Papers-1357, ATL. (McKenzie Family Papers)
McLean, Sir Donald, Papers, 1839–1877, Vol. 39, MS-1349, ATL.
Mitchell, David Scott, Papers: Miscellaneous Documents about New Zealand 1820–1890, ML.

Moore, Captain Fred. Geo., Collection, 1815–1892, MS-1661-1664, ATL.

New Zealand Company (NZC) (in its various forms):

Committees, 1837–1840, CO 208/185, ANZ.

Committees' Minutes, 6 January–21 December 1848, NZC 31/9/10, ANZ.

Correspondence and Documents of the New Zealand Company, 1836–1887, C184, ML, also held as MS-Micro-460, ATL.

Despatches from Principal Agent: 17 August 1839–6 December 1841, NZC 3/1/1; 5 February–21 December 1842, NZC 3/2/2; 1 January–23 December 1843, NZC 3/3/3; 1 January–5 December 1844, NZC 3/4/4, ANZ.

Despatches from Secretary to Principal Agent: 1 August 1839–29 May 1840, NZC 102/1/1; 29 May–1 December 1840, NZC 102/1/2; 1 December 1840–19 March 1841, NZC 102/2/3; 12 May–23 September 1841, NZC 102/3/5; 23 September–1 October 1841, NZC 102/3/6; 1 October–13 December 1841, 102/3/7; 1 January–15 June 1842, NZC 102/4/8; 18 June–29 August 1842, NZC 102/4/9; 29 August–8 December 1842, 102/5/10; 2 January–22 June 1843, 102/5/11; 12 June–14 October 1843, 102/6/12; 14 October–6 December 1843, 102/7/13; 11 January–14 November 1844, 102/8/14, ANZ.

Directors' Minutes: 1839–1844, NZC 31/1/1; 16 January 1845–31 December 1846, NZC 31/4/4; 7 January 1847–21 December 1849, NZC 31/5/5, ANZ.

Directors' Minutes, 1839–1849, CO 208/180–188, ANZ.

Draft letters outwards, 2 June–28 December 1847, Strode to Secretary, NZC 18/5, ANZ.

Drafts of Despatches from Secretary to Wakefield: 14 November 1839–14 November 1842, NZC 13/1/1; 26 January–8 December 1843, NZC 13/2/2; 11 January 1844–9 December 1845, NZC 13/2/3, ANZ.

Draft of scheme for administering justice at Port Nicholson before arrival of Government Representatives 1839–40, NZC 131/2/8, ANZ.

Draft Prospectus for Colonization Company, CO 209/4, p.521, Micro 352, ANZ.

Entry books of despatches to Secretary, 10 October 1842–10 September 1843 (Wairau Correspondence), pp.289–382, NZC 112/2, ANZ.

Land Claims Correspondence of William Spain and George Clarke, 1842–45, NZC 131/1/1, ANZ.

Local and General Letters to Colonel Wakefield: 1839–40, NZC 108/1 [all these letters are missing]; received 1 January–29 December 1841, NZC 108/1/2; received 15 February–22 November 1842, NZC 108/1/3; received 3 January–2 December 1843, NZC 108/1/4; received 6 January–21 December 1844, NZC 108/1/5, ANZ.

Minutebook/Letterbook, 1837–1838, Micro 2811, ANZ.

Old Land Orders (originals of transfer of Evans's Land Orders [forty sections] to Robert Monro, 15 March 1842, and related matter), NZC 33/48d, ANZ.

Papers dealing with affray at Wairau, NZC 131/3/12.

Wakefield to Secretary, Letterbook: 31 December 1839 –22 September 1842, NZC 112/1; 10 October 1842–10 September 1843, NZC 112/2; 12 September 1843–5 February 1848, NZC 112/3, ANZ.

New Zealand Company Papers, *see* Webster Collection, ATL.

New Zealand Papers, 1836–87, C184, and CO 309/53, ML.

NSW Governor's Despatches and Enclosures 1841–1843, A-1267-20, ML.

Offices and Individuals 1860, PRO 834-835, CO 309 VIC, VSL.

Parkes, Henry, Collection, *Autographed Letters of Notable Australians*, A69, ML.

Petre, Hon. Henry W., *An Account of the Settlements of the New Zealand Company*, NL.
Petre, Mary Ann Eleanor, Diary, 1842–1844, MS-1772, ATL.
Poneke: Know Your Wellington, Vol. 1, Pq 993.1 PON, ATL.
Revans, S., Letters, qMS-1687, ATL. (Revans Letters)
Revans' Family Collection, MS-2007, ATL.
Scholefield, G. H., *Captain William Hobson, RN, 1793–1842*, MS-1856, ATL.
Scholefield, G. H., MS-Papers-0212-C/02B, ATL.
Spain Commission of Inquiry into the Land Claims of the Settlers of Port Nicholson:
New Zealand Company claimant, Case 374, OLC 1/906, Box 45, and OLC 1/906, Box 46, ANZ.
Commissioner Spain's Report on Port Nicholson Land Claims to Governor FitzRoy, 1845, New Zealand Company claimant, Case 374, OLC 1/906, Box 45, ANZ.
Deed of Gift of Land from Rev. Henry Williams to Colonel William Wakefield for New Zealand Company, OLC 1/906, Box 46, ANZ.
Land Claims Correspondence, *see* NZC.
Robert Tod claimant, Case 229, OLC 1/906, Box 22, ANZ.
Thomas Barker claimant, Case 287, OLC 1/906, Box 22, ANZ.
Strang, Robert R., Business Papers, 1840–1843, MS-0726, ATL.
Taine, J. J. (ed. H. W. Fildes), *Reminiscences*, Vols 1 & 2, qMS-1974-1975, ATL. (Taine, *Reminiscences*)
Taine J. J., Outward Correspondence, MS-Papers-0587-01, ATL.
Taine, Mrs J. J. (Leocadia [*sic*] d'Oliviera), Outward Correspondence, MS-Papers-0587-05, ATL.
Victorian Hansard of the Legislative Council and Assembly of the Colony of Victoria, Wm. Fairfax and Co., Melbourne.
Volume 1, 21 November 1856–11 March 1857; Volume 2, 25 March 1857–24 November 1857; Volume 3, 3 December 1857–4 June 1858; Volume 4, 7 October 1858–24 February 1859; Volume 5, 13 October 1859–30 March 1860; Volume 6, 27 April 1860–18 September 1860; Volume 7, 20 November 1860–19 June 1861; Volume 8, 30 August 1861–18 June 1862; Volume 9, 7 November 1862–11 September 1863; Volume 10, 26 January 1864–2 June 1864; Volume 11, pt 1, 28 November 1864–19 May 1865; Volume 11, pt 2, 23 May 1865–28 November 1865. SLV.
Editions also held in New Zealand Parliamentary Library, NZPL.
Victorian Legislative Assembly, *Parliamentary Debates*, 1856–1864, Vols 1–10, 328.92/v, SLV.
Wade, John, Letters, 1842–1846, qMS-2085-2086, ATL. (Wade Letters)
Wakefield, E. G. to E. Betts Hopper, 24 November 1837, MS-Papers-3124, ATL.
Wakefield, E. J., Diary, 27 March 1840–1843, MS-2208, ATL.
Wakefield, George, Letters to his Father, MS-6331-301/6, SLV.
Wakefield, William, Diary 1839–1842, MS-2102-2103, ATL.
Wakefield, W., *Draft of Plan for Administration of Justice before Government Representatives*, NZC 131/8, ANZ.
Wakefield, W., Instructions for Deputation to Governor Hobson, NZC 131/10, ANZ.
Wallace, J. H., *Historical Notes by Early Settlers*, MS-Papers-0108, ATL.
Ward, J., New Zealand Colonial Secretary, MS-Papers-0704, ATL.
Webster Collection, Correspondence and Documents of the New Zealand Company 1826–1841, Micro-MS-0302, ATL.
Yates, F. T., Diary, 1839–1840, MS-2302, ATL. (Yates Diary)

Newspapers, Journals and Magazines

Argus, 1855–1868, Melbourne. ATL.
Auckland Chronicle, 1843, NL.
Australian Journal, Vol. 4, SLV.
Australia New Zealand Gazette.
Australasian, 17 October 1868.
Centennial Magazine, Melbourne, 1889–90, Vols 1 and 2, Q 059/ C, ML.
Colonial Gazette, 1839–1846, ATL.
Cornhill Magazine, January–June 1862, ATL.
Government Gazette, Appendix to Minutes of 8 April 1845, NZPL.
Illustrated London News, Vol. LV, July–December 1869, NL.
Journal of the Early Settlers, Vols 1, 2, September 1922, ATL.
Melbourne Morning Herald/Melbourne Herald, 1855–1868, SLV. [Note: *Melbourne Morning Herald* became *Melbourne Herald* on 8 September 1855]
Melbourne Punch, 1856–1868, Vols III–XVIII, SLNSW and ATL.
Melbourne Review, Vol. 1, 1879, SLV.
Men of Victoria, Part 1V, F A920.092/M, SLV.
Mill Hill Magazine, March 1919, Vol. 46, No. 5.
Morning Chronicle, 16 September 1839, SLV.
New Zealand Colonist and Port Nicholson Advertiser, Wellington, August 1842–August 1843, ATL. (*Colonist*)
New Zealand Gazette/New Zealand Gazette and Britannia Spectator/New Zealand Gazette and Wellington Spectator/New Zealand Spectator and Cook's Straits Guardian, 1839–48, ATL. (*Gazette*)
New Zealand Journal, London, Vols 1–4, 1840–1845, ATL.
New Zealand Law Journal, Vol. 24, No. 16, MS-Papers-0212-C/02B, ATL.
New Zealand Spectator and Cook's Straits Guardian, ATL.
Southern Cross, July 1843, AWMML.
Wellington Independent, Wellington, 1845–31 October 1868, ATL.

Online Sources

Aglionby, Mr Henry Aglionby, Whig MP and director, New Zealand Company, to House of Commons Debate on New Zealand, 18 June 1845, Hansard, Vol. 81, p.779; see hansard.millbanksystems.com/commons/1845/jun/18/new-zealand-adjourned-debate
Mackay, Alexander, *A Compendium of Official Documents Relative to Native Affairs in the South Island*, http://nzetc.victoria.ac.nz/tm/scholarly/tci-Mac01Comp.html
Surman's Index, Dr Williams' Library, *Survey of London*, Vol. xxvii, online, http://www.english.qmul.ac.uk/drwilliams/surman/intro.html
Waitangi Tribunal, *Te Whanganui a Tara me ona Takiwa: Report on the Wellington District* (Wai 145), Legislation Direct, Wellington, 2003, available at www.justice.govt.nz

Unpublished Manuscripts

Hodgson, Terence, *The Riddifords: Towards a Social History*, Wellington, c. 1998.
Permezel, J. H. W., *Family Papers*, Private Collection, Melbourne. (Permezel Collection)
Riddiford, E. Anthony, Memoir, Family Collection.

Secondary Sources

Books and Theses

Ackroyd, Peter, *Dickens*, Random House, London, Vintage edn, 1999.

Ackroyd, Peter, *London: The Biography*, Chatto & Windus, London, 2000.

Adams, Peter, *Fatal Necessity: British Intervention in New Zealand 1830–1847*, Auckland University Press/Oxford University Press, Auckland, 1977.

Alington, Margaret H., *Unquiet Earth*, Wellington City Council/Ministry of Works and Development, Wellington, 1978.

Anderson, Hugh, *Victoria: From Discovery to Federation*, Rigby, Melbourne, 1974.

Balfe, Harold (ed. E. A. Doyle), *The Story of the Century 1851–1951*, Victorian Government, Melbourne, 1951.

Beaglehole, J., *Captain Hobson and the New Zealand Company: A Study in Colonial Administration in Decline and Fall*, Smith College Studies in History, Vol. 13, Nos 1–3, October 1927–April 1928, Massachusetts, 1928.

Beasley, A. W., *The Club on the Terrace: The Wellington Club 1841–1996*, The Club, Wellington, 1996.

Beattie, W. (ed.), *Life and Letters of Thomas Campbell*, Vol. 1, Hall Virtue & Co., London, 1850.

Belich, James, *Making Peoples: A History of the New Zealanders from Polynesian Settlement to the End of Nineteenth Century*, Penguin, Auckland, 2007.

Best, Ensign Edward (ed. N. M. Taylor), *Journal of Ensign Best*, Government Printer, Wellington, 1966.

Blair, David, 'Three Melbourne Barristers: A Recollection', *Centennial Magazine*, Vol. 2, No. 9, April 1890, pp.689–92.

Bloomfield, P., *Edward Gibbon Wakefield: Builder of the British Commonwealth*, Longmans, London, 1961.

Boase, F., *Modern English Biography*, 6 Vols, Frank Cass, London, 1965.

Bonwick, James, *Early Struggles of the Australian Press*, Gordon & Gotch, London, 1890.

Borer, Mary C., *London Walks and Legends*, Academy Publishers, Chicago, 1982.

Braithwaite, Roderick, *Strikingly Alive: The History of the Mill Hill School Foundation 1807–2007*, Phillimore, London, 2006.

Brees, Samuel Charles, *Pictorial Illustrations of New Zealand*, John Williams & Co., London 1847.

Brett-James, N. G., *The History of Mill Hill School, 1807–1907*, Mill Hill School, London, 1909.

Briggs, Asa, *Victorian People, Reassessments of People, Institutions, Ideas and Events, 1851–1867*, Odhams Press, London, 1954.

Briggs, Asa, *The Age of Improvement*, Longmans Green & Co., London, 1969.

Briggs, John and Ian Seller, *Victorian Nonconformity*, Edward Arnold, London, 1973.

Brodie, Walter, *Remarks on the Past and Present State of New Zealand, its Government, Capabilities and Prospects*, Whittaker, London, 1845.

Brontë, Emily Jane (ed. Janet Gezari), *The Complete Poems*, Penguin, London, 1992.

Buick, T. Lindsay, *The Treaty of Waitangi; or How New Zealand Became a British Colony*, Mackay, Wellington, 1914.

Burns, Patricia (ed. Henry Richardson), *Fatal Success: A History of the New Zealand Company*, Heinemann Reed, Auckland, 1989.

Butterworth, Susan, *Petone: A History*, Petone Borough Council, Petone, 1988.
Carleton, Hugh, *The Life of Henry Williams, Archdeacon of Waimate*, Wilson & Horton, Auckland, 1874.
Carlyle, Thomas, *Works*, Vols XIII, XIV, Chapman & Hall, London, 1843.
Carman, Arthur H., *The Birth of a City: Wellington 1840–1843*, self-published, Wellington, 1970.
Cecil, David, *Lord M. or the Later Life of Lord Melbourne*, Constable & Co., London, 1954.
Churchill, Winston S., *A History of the English-Speaking Peoples*, Vol. 1V, Cassell & Co., London, 1958.
Clark, C. M. H., *A History of Australia*, Vol. IV, *The Earth Abideth For Ever, 1851–1888*, Melbourne University Press, Carlton, Victoria, 1978.
Clarke, George Jnr, *Notes on Early Life in New Zealand*, Walch & Sons, Hobart, 1903.
Clunn, H. P., *The Face of London: The Record of a Century's Changes and Development*, Simpkin Marshall, London, 1933.
Cobley, John, 'William Bland', in Douglas Pike (gen. ed.), *Australian Dictionary of Biography 1851–1890*, Melbourne University Press, Carlton, Victoria, 1966, Vol. 1, pp.112–15.
Cocks, Raymond, *Foundations of the Modern Bar*, Sweet & Maxwell, London, 1983.
Coleridge, Kathleen, 'Samuel Revans', in W. H. Oliver (ed.), *Dictionary of New Zealand Biography*, Vol. 1, Allen & Unwin/Department of Internal Affairs, Wellington, 1990.
Coleridge, Kathleen, 'Thriving on Impressions: The Pioneer Years of Wellington Printing', in David Hamer and Roberta Nicholls (eds), *The Making of Wellington 1800–1914*, Victoria University Press, Wellington, 1990, pp.89–106.
Cooke, Robin, QC (ed.), *Portrait of a Profession: The Centennial Book of the New Zealand Law Society*, A. H. & A. W. Reed, Wellington, 1969.
Cox, Alfred, *Men of Mark of New Zealand*, Whitcombe & Tombs, Christchurch, 1886.
Crawford, J. Coutts, *Recollections of Travel in Australia and New Zealand*, Trubner & Co., London, 1880.
Cresswell, Douglas,'Riddiford of Te Awaite', in *Early New Zealand Families*, Second Series, Whitcombe & Tombs, Christchurch, 1956, pp.13–22.
Cruikshank, R. J., *Charles Dickens and Early Victorian England*, Pitman & Sons, London, 1949.
Currey, C. H., *A Brief History of the British Commonwealth since Waterloo*, Angus & Robertson, London, 1954.
Dalziel, Raewyn, 'Men, Women and Wakefield', in Friends of the Turnbull Library, *Edward Gibbon Wakefield and the Colonial Dream: A Reconsideration*, GP Publications, Wellington, 1997, pp.77–86.
Davies, Andrew, *The East End Nobody Knows*, Macmillan, London, 1990.
Davison, G., J. W. McCarty and A. McLeary (eds), *Australians: A Historical Library: Australians 1888*, Fairfax Syme & Weldon Associates, NSW, 1987.
de Tocqueville, Alexis (ed. J. P. Mayer), *Journeys to England and Ireland*, G. Lawrence and K. P. Mayer (translators), Faber & Faber, London, 1958.
Deans, J., *Pioneers of Canterbury: Deans Letters 1840–1855*, A. H. & A. W. Reed, Dunedin, 1937.
Dickens, Charles, *Sketches by Boz*, Macrone, London, 1836.

Dickens, Charles Jnr (ed.), *The Life of Charles James Mathews, Chiefly Autobiographical with Selections from His Correspondence and Speeches*, 2 Vols, Macmillan, London, 1879.

Draper, F. W. M., *Four Centuries of Merchant Taylors' School*, Oxford University Press, London, 1962.

Duffy, C. Gavan, *My Life in Two Hemispheres*, 2 Vols, T. Fisher Unwin, London, 1898.

Fagan, Louis, *The Reform Club: Its Founders and Architect, 1836–1886*, B. Quaritch, London, 1887.

Fawcett, Dame Millicent Garrett, *The Life of the Rt. Hon. Sir William Molesworth*, Macmillan, London, 1901.

FitzRoy, Robert, *Remarks on New Zealand*, W. & H. White, London, 1846.

Forde, J. L., *The Story of the Bar of Victoria*, Whitcombe & Tombs, Melbourne, 1913.

Fox, William, *The Six Colonies of New Zealand*, John W. Parker & Son, London, 1851.

Fox, William, *How New Zealand Got its Constitution* (Pamphlet), Wilson & Horton, Wellington, 1890.

Friends of the Turnbull Library, *Edward Gibbon Wakefield and the Colonial Dream*, Government Printer, Wellington, 1977.

Friends of the Turnbull Library, *Edward Gibbon Wakefield and the Colonial Dream: A Reconsideration*, GP Publications, Wellington, 1997.

Garnett, R., *Builders of Greater Britain, Edward Gibbon Wakefield: The Colonization of South Australia and New Zealand*, T. Fisher Unwin, London, 1898.

Gibb, Andrew, *Glasgow: The Making of a City*, Croom Helm, London, 1983.

Gisborne, William, *New Zealand Rulers and Statesmen, 1840–1885*, Sampson Low, Marston, Searle & Rivington, London, 1886.

Grant, James and Geoffrey Serle, *The Melbourne Scene, 1803–1956*, Melbourne University Press, Carlton, Victoria, 1957.

Greenwood, James, *The Seven Curses of London*, Basil Blackwell, Oxford, reprinted 1981.

Greville Lord Charles (ed. Christopher Hibbert), *Greville's England: Selections From the Diaries of Charles Greville 1818–1860*, Folio Society, London, 1987.

Halevy, E., *A History of the English People in the Nineteenth Century*, Vols 1–3, Benn, London, 2nd edn, 1949–51 (Vol. 1: *England in 1815*; Vol. 2: *The Liberal Awakening*; Vol. 3: *The Triumph of Reform*)

Hall, David, *The Golden Echo*, Collins, Auckland and London, 1971.

Hall, H. L., 'Sir Archibald Michie', in Douglas Pike (gen. ed.), *Australian Dictionary of Biography*, Melbourne University Press, Carlton, Victoria, 1974, Vol. 5, pp.246–8.

Hamburger, Joseph, *James Mill and the Art of Revolution*, Yale University Press, New Haven, 1963.

Hamer, David and Roberta Nicholls (eds), *The Making of Wellington, 1800–1914*, Victoria University Press, Wellington, 1990.

Hampden-Cook, E., 'A Headmaster's Eventful Career', *Mill Hill Magazine*, March 1919, Vol. 46, No. 5.

Harrison, J. F. C., *The Early Victorians 1832–1851*, Weidenfeld & Nicholson, London, 1971.

Harrop, A. J., *The Amazing Career of Edward Gibbon Wakefield*, Allen & Unwin, London, 1928.

Harrop, A. J., *England and New Zealand: From Tasman to the Taranaki War*, Methuen, London, 1926.

Heaphy, Charles, *Narrative of a Residence in Various Parts of New Zealand: Together With a Description of the Present State of the Company's Settlements*, Capper Press, Christchurch, 1972 (facsimile edn).

Helmore, Frederick, *Memoir of the Rev. Thomas Helmore, M.A.*, Masters, London, 1891.

Hill, George Kirkbeck (ed.), *Boswell's Life of Johnson*, Clarendon Press, Oxford, 1971.

Hill, Rev. W. Alfred (ed.) *The Poetical Works of Thomas Campbell: With A Sketch of His Life by William Allingham*, George Bell & Sons, London, 1875.

Hocken, T. M., *The Early History of New Zealand*, John Mackay, Wellington, 1914.

Houghton, Walter E., *The Victorian Frame of Mind, 1830–1870*, Oxford University Press, London, 1957.

Hughes, Robert, *The Fatal Shore: A History of the Transportation of Convicts to Australia, 1787–1868*, Collins Harvill, London, 1987.

Ingham, S. M., 'Sir John O'Shanassy', in Douglas Pike (gen. ed.), *Australian Dictionary of Biography 1851–1890*, Melbourne University Press, Carlton, Victoria, 1975, Vol. 5, pp.378–82.

Innes Addison, W., *Prize Lists of the University of Glasgow*, University of Glasgow, Glasgow, 1902.

Innes Addison, W., *Roll of Graduates of the University of Glasgow from 1727–1897*, University of Glasgow, Glasgow, 1898.

Irvine-Smith, F. L., *The Streets of My City, Wellington, New Zealand*, A. H. & A. W. Reed, Wellington, 1948.

Jaeger, Muriel, *Before Victoria: Changing Standards and Behaviour, 1787–1837*, Chatto & Windus, London, 1956.

Johnson, Paul, *The Birth of the Modern: World Society 1815–1830*, Phoenix, London, 1996.

Johnson, Paul, *The Offshore Islanders: A History of the English People*, Weidenfeld & Nicholson, London, 1972.

King, Michael, *The Penguin History of New Zealand*, Penguin, Auckland, 2003

Lindsay, Maurice, *Portrait of Glasgow*, Robert Hale, London, 1972.

MacMorran, George, *Some Schools and Schoolmasters of Early Wellington*, Mackay, Wellington, 1900.

Malone, Betty, 'William Clark Haines', in Douglas Pike (gen. ed.), *Australian Dictionary of Biography 1851–1890*, Melbourne University Press, Carlton, Victoria, 1972, Vol. 4, pp.315–17.

Manson, Cecil and Celia, *Curtain Raiser to a Colony*, Whitcombe & Tombs, Christchurch, 1962.

Marais, J. S., *The Colonisation of New Zealand*, Milford, London, 1927.

Marjoribanks, A., *Travels in New Zealand*, Smith Elder & Co., London, 1847, reprinted Capper Press, Christchurch, 1973.

Martin, A. W., 'Henry Parkes', in Douglas Pike (gen. ed.), *Australian Dictionary of Biography 1851–1890*, Melbourne University Press, Carlton, Victoria, 1974, Vol. 5, pp.400–5.

Martin, Ged, 'Wakefield's Past and Futures', in Friends of the Turnbull Library, *Edward Gibbon Wakefield and the Colonial Dream: A Reconsideration*, GP Publications, Wellington, 1997, pp.20–44.

Martin, S. McD., *New Zealand in a Series of Letters*, Simmonds & Ward, London, 1845.

Mathews, Charles James (ed. Charles Dickens Jnr), *The Life of Charles James Mathews*, 2 Vols, Macmillan, London, 1879.

Mayne, Derek, *The Growth of London*, George G. Harrop & Co., London, 1952.

McGill, David, *Pioneers of Port Nicholson*, A. H. & A. W. Reed, Wellington, 1984.

McIntyre, W. David (ed.), *The Journal of Henry Sewell, 1853–1857*, Vol. 1, Whitcoulls, Christchurch, 1980.

McLean, Gavin, *Wellington: The First Years of European Settlement, 1840–1850*, Penguin, Auckland, 2000.

McLean, N. L. and B. H. Farland (eds), *Wellington Prospect*, Hicks Smith & Sons, Wellington, 1970.

McLintock, A. H., *Crown Colony Government in New Zealand*, Government Printer, Wellington, 1958.

Mennell, Philip (ed.), *A Dictionary of Australasian Biography, 1855–1892*, Hutchinson & Co., London, 1892.

Mill, John Stuart, *Autobiography of John Stuart Mill*, Columbia University Press, New York, 1924.

Millar, David P., *Once Upon a Village: A History of Lower Hutt*, New Zealand University Press, Wellington, 1972.

Millen, Julia, *The Story of Bell Gully Buddle Weir 1840–1990*, Bell Gully Buddle Weir, Wellington, 1990.

Miller, John, *Early Victorian New Zealand: A Study of Racial Tension and Social Attitudes, 1839–1852*, Oxford University Press, London, 1958.

Mills, R. C., *The Colonization of Australia, 1829–42: The Wakefield Experiment in Empire Building*, Sidgwick & Jackson, London, 1915.

Mills, R. C., 'The Composition of the Victorian Parliament 1856–1881', *Historical Studies*, Vol. 2, No. 5 (1942), pp.25–39.

Molesworth, W. N., *The History of the Reform Bill of 1832*, Chapman & Hall, London, 1865.

Monsarrat, A., *An Uneasy Victorian: Thackeray the Man*, Cassell, London, 1980.

Moon, Paul, *Fitzroy: Governor in Crisis 1843–1845*, David Ling, Auckland, 2000.

Moon, Paul, *Hobson: Governor of New Zealand 1840–1842*, David Ling, Auckland, 1998.

Morris, Edward E., *Memoir of George Higinbotham*, Macmillan, London, 1895.

Morrison, W. Frederic, *The Aldine Centennial History of New South Wales*, Aldine, Sydney, 1888.

Mulgan, Alan, *The City of the Strait: Wellington and its Province, a Centennial History*, A. H. & A. W. Reed, Wellington, 1939.

Murray, Bill (ed.), *Crisis, Conflict and Consensus: Selected Documents Illustrating 200 Years in the Making of Australia*, Rigby, Adelaide, 1984.

New, C. W., *Lord Durham: A Biography of John George Lambton, 1st Earl of Durham*, Oxford University Press, London, 1829.

Newnham, W. H., *Melbourne: Biography of a City*, F. W. Cheshire, Melbourne, 1956.

O'Connor, Irma, *Edward Gibbon Wakefield: The Man Himself*, Selwyn & Blount, London, 1928.

Old Colonists Number of the Tatler: Containing One Hundred Portraits of Pioneers of Victoria, Vol. 1, No. 40, George Robertson, Melbourne, 21 May 1898.

Oliver, W. H., *The Story of New Zealand*, Faber, London, 1960.
Oliver, W. H. (ed.), *Dictionary of New Zealand Biography*, Vol. 1, Allen & Unwin/Department of Internal Affairs, Wellington, 1990.
Olssen, Erik, 'Wakefield and the Scottish Enlightenment', in Friends of the Turnbull Library, *Edward Gibbon Wakefield and the Colonial Dream: A Reconsideration*, GP Publications, Wellington, 1997, pp.47–66.
Orange, Claudia, *The Treaty of Waitangi*, Allen & Unwin, Auckland, 1978.
Palmer, Alan, *The East End: Four Centuries of London Life*, John Murray, London, rev. edn, 2000.
Parliamentary Biographies, 'George Samuel Evans', three chapters in *Melbourne Punch*, 1, 8, and 15 December 1859, Vol. IX.
Patterson, Brad, 'A Queer Cantankerous Lot', in David Hâmer and Roberta Nicholls (eds), *The Making of Wellington, 1800–1914*, Victoria University Press, Wellington, 1990, pp.61–87.
Patterson, Brad, *Early Colonial Society Through a Prism: Reflections on Wellington's First Anniversary Day*, Wellington Historical and Early Settlers' Association, Wellington, 1994.
Petre, Hon. Henry W., *An Account of the Settlements of the New Zealand Company*, Smith, Elder & Co., London, 1842.
Philipp, June, *A Great View of Things: Edward Gibbon Wakefield*, Thomas Nelson, Melbourne, 1971.
Pike, Douglas (gen. ed.), *Australian Dictionary of Biography*, Vols 1–6, Melbourne University Press, Carlton, Victoria, 1966–74.
Pike, Douglas, *Paradise of Dissent: South Australia 1829–1857*, Longmans Green, London, Melbourne and New York, 1957.
Porter, Roy, *London: A Social History*, Penguin, London, 2000.
Potter, Jeremy, *Headmaster: The Life of John Percival, Radical Autocrat*, Constable, London, 1998.
Priestley, Dinah, *Old Thorndon*, Anchorage Press, Wellington, 1988.
Reid, J. M., *Glasgow*, Batsford, London, 1956.
Richards, Eric, 'Wakefield and Australia', in Friends of the Turnbull Library, *Edward Gibbon Wakefield and the Colonial Dream: A Reconsideration*, GP Publications, Wellington, 1977, pp.87–105.
Roach, John, *A History of Secondary Education in England, 1800–1870*, Longman, London, 1986.
Rose, Millicent, *The East End of London*, Cresset Press, London, 1951.
Royle, Edward and James Walvin, *English Radicals and Reformers: 1760–1848*, Harvester Press, London, 1982.
Rusden, G. W., *History of New Zealand*, 3 Vols, Melville, Mullen & Slade, Melbourne, 1895.
Rusden, G. W., *The History of Australia*, Vol. 3, Chapman & Hall, London, 1883.
Sanderson, Michael (ed.), *The Universities of the Nineteenth Century*, Routledge & Kegan Paul, London, 1975.
Saunders, Alfred, *The History of New Zealand 1642–1861*, Whitcombe & Tombs, Wellington, 1899.
Sayers, C. E., *David Syme: A Life*, Cheshire, Melbourne, 1965.
Sayers, C. E. (ed.), with Z. Cowen, J. A Robertson and V. H. Arnold, *One Hundred Years of Responsible Government in Victoria, 1856–1957*, Government Printer, Melbourne, 1956.

Scholefield, G. H., *New Zealand in Evolution: Industrial, Economic and Political*, T. F. Unwin, London, 1909.
Scholefield, G. H., *Captain William Hobson, First Governor of New Zealand*, Oxford University Press, London, 1934.
Scholefield, G. H. (ed.), *Dictionary of New Zealand Biography*, Vols 1 and 2, Department of Internal Affairs, Wellington, 1940.
Seaman, L. C. B., *Life in Victorian London*, Batsford, London, 1973.
Serle, Geoffrey, *The Golden Age: A History of the Colony of Victoria 1851–1861*, Melbourne University Press, Carlton, Victoria, 1963.
Sheppard, Francis, *History of London: London 1808–1870: The Infernal Wen*, Secker & Warburg, London, 1971.
Sherrin, R. A. A. and J. H. Wallace (ed. Thomson S. Leys), *Early History of New Zealand*, Brett's Historical Series, Auckland, 1890.
Sinclair, Keith, *A History of New Zealand*, Penguin, Auckland, revised edn, 2000.
Sinclair, Keith, 'The Aborigines Protection Society and New Zealand: A Study in Nineteenth Century Opinion', MA thesis, Auckland University College, 1946, ATL.
Stephen, L. and S. Lee (eds), *Dictionary of National Biography*, 21 Vols, Oxford University Press, London, 1917–1938.
Stewart, Robert, *Henry Brougham: His Public Career 1778–1868*, Bodley Head, London, 1986.
Stuart, Peter, *Edward Gibbon Wakefield in New Zealand: His Political Career*, Victoria University Press, Wellington, 1971.
Swainson, William, *New Zealand and its Colonization*, Smith, Elder & Co., London, 1859.
Temple, Philip, *A Sort of Conscience: The Wakefields*, Auckland University Press, Auckland, 2002.
Thomson, David, *England in the Nineteenth Century: 1815–1914*, Penguin, London, 1986.
Thompson, David M., *Nonconformity in the Nineteenth Century*, Routledge & Kegan Paul, London, 1972.
Thomson, Kathleen and Geoffrey Serle, *A Biographical Register of the Victorian Parliament 1851–1900*, Australian National University Press, Canberra, 1972.
Thorold, Peter, *The London Rich: The Creation of a Great City, From 1666 to the Present*, Viking, London, 1999.
Timbs, John, *Clubs and Club Life in London*, Chatto & Windus, London, 1872.
Timbs, John, *Curiosities of London*, Virtue, London, 1868.
Torless, Frances H., *Bygone Days*, Harrison & Sons, London, 1914.
Travers, Robert, *The Grand Old Man of Australian Politics: The Life and Times of Sir Henry Parkes*, Kangaroo Press, Sydney, 1992.
Trevelyan, G. M., *British History in the 19th Century and After, 1782–1919*, Longmans, London, 1922.
Trevelyan, G. M., *History of England*, Longmans, London, 1926, reprinted 1960.
Trevelyan, G. M., *English Social History*, Longmans, London, rev. edn, 1986.
Turnbull, Michael, *The New Zealand Bubble*, Price Milburn & Co., Wellington, 1959.
Uglow, Jenny, *The Lunar Men: The Friends Who Made the Future, 1730–1810*, Faber & Faber, London, 2003.
Wakefield, Edward Gibbon, *England and America: A Comparison of the Social and Political States of Both Nations*, R. Bentley, London, 1834.

Wakefield, Edward Gibbon, *A Statement of the Objects of the New Zealand Association, with some particulars concerning the Position, Extent, Soil and Climate, Natural Productions and Natives of New Zealand*, Black & Armstrong, London, 1837.

Wakefield, Edward Gibbon, *The British Colonization of New Zealand: Being an Account of the Principles, Objects, and Plans of the New Zealand Association*, John W. Parker, London, 1837.

Wakefield, Edward Gibbon, *A View of the Art of Colonization*, J. W. Parker, London, 1849.

Wakefield, Edward Gibbon (ed. M. F. Lloyd Prichard), *The Collected Works*, Collins, Glasgow, 1968.

Wakefield, Edward Jerningham (ed. Sir Robert Stout), *Adventure in New Zealand, from 1839 to 1844, with Some Account of the Beginning of the British Colonization of the Islands*, Whitcombe & Tombs, Christchurch, 1908.

Wakefield, Edward Jerningham (ed. Joan Stevens), *London Journal*, Alexander Turnbull Library/Victoria University of Wellington, Wellington, 1972.

Wakelin, Richard, *History and Politics, Containing the Political Recollections and Leaves from Writings of a New Zealand, Journalist*, Lyon & Blair, Wellington, 1877.

Ward, Alan, *A Show of Justice: Racial 'Amalgamation' in Nineteenth Century New Zealand*, Auckland University Press, Auckland, 1995.

Ward, Louis E., *Early Wellington*, Southern Reprints, Papakura, 1928.

Wards, Ian, *The Shadow of the Land: A Study of British Policy and Racial Conflict in New Zealand 1832–1852*, A. R. Shearer, Government Printer, Wellington, 1968.

Weinreb, Ben and Christopher Hibbert (eds), *The London Encyclopaedia*, Macmillan, London, 1983.

White, Jerry, *London in the Nineteenth Century: 'A Human Awful Wonder of God'*, Jonathan Cape, London, 2007.

Wilson, A. N., *The Victorians*, Hutchinson, London, 2002.

Wood, Anthony, *Nineteenth Century Britain: 1815–1914*, Longmans, London, 1960.

Woods, Janice Burns, 'G. S. Evans', in Douglas Pike (gen. ed.), *Australian Dictionary of Biography*, Melbourne University Press, Carlton, Victoria, 1972, Vol. 4, pp.142–3.

Wood, Lieutenant J., RN, *Twelve Months in Wellington, Port Nicholson*, London, 1843.

Woodbridge, George, *The Reform Club, 1836–1978: A History From the Club's Records* (in association with Reform Club Members), Clearwater Publishing Co., New York, 1978.

Woodward, Sir Llewellyn, *The Age of Reform: 1815–1870*, Oxford University Press, London, 1962.

Young, G. M. (ed.), *Early Victorian England: 1830–1865*, 2 Vols, Oxford University Press, London, 1934.

INDEX

Aborigines' Protection Society, xv, 38, 54–55, 67, 163, 230–1, 256
Adamson, Travers, 301
Adelaide (ship), xix, 72, 76, 77, 78, 79, 80–94, 100, 101, 102, 103, 105, 107, 108, 109, 118, 132, 193, 240, 303
Age (newspaper), 300, 305–6, 314, 344, 359
Aglionby, Henry, 243, 246–7, 255, 257
Alsdorf, Baron Charles, 89, 94, 116, 157
Alsdorf's Hotel, Wellington, 282
Anson, George, 245
Argus (newspaper), 294, 298, 312, 315, 317, 327–8, 329, 330, 332, 334, 339, 343, 344, 349, 351, 353, 356, 360, 361, 362, 363
Arnold, Thomas, 16, 20
Aspinall, Butler Cole, 301, 344, 351
Auckland, 117, 118, 119, 121, 162, 196, 201, 206, 207, 208–9, 211, 212, 213–14, 215, 216, 227, 230, 240, 242, 325, 375; as rival settlement to Wellington, 131, 134, 136–7, 144, 150, 151, 157, 163, 182–3, 210, 213–14, 216, 219, 226, 232, 254; land availability and purchases in, 119, 151, 152, 161, 168, 215, 230, 232; Legislative Council of, 144, 145, 150, 151–2, 153, 157, 225–7, 281
Auckland Chronicle (newspaper), 212, 213
Auckland Gazette (newspaper), 213
Aurora (barque), 76, 77, 78, 79, 89, 100
Australasian Gazette (newspaper), 307, 369
Australia, 164, 187, 270, 278, 297, 301, 305, 313, 321–3, 327, 334, 361, 363, 365; emigrants from, 30, 278–9; settlement of, 31, 32–33, 47, 49, 52, 302–3; *see also* Melbourne; New South Wales; South Australia; Sydney; Tasmania; Victoria; Western Australia
Bach, Adolphus, 27
Bagehot, Walter, 150
Bailey, J. R., 341
Baker, Major Richard, 79, 117, 130, 209
Bannatyne, W. M., 368
Baring, Francis, 31, 36, 42, 43, 47, 51, 52, 73, 158, 159, 287
Baring, Mabel, 65
Barkly, Henry, 247, 299, 301, 315, 320, 327, 331, 334, 345, 347, 348, 349–50, 352, 361
Barnabas, 110
Barnes, Thomas, 22
Barrett, Richard (Dicky), 102, 109, 114–15, 122, 131, 166, 169–70, 196–8
Barrett's Hotel, Wellington, 122, 123, 131, 141, 149, 152, 153, 159, 186, 203, 205
Barry, Redmond, 330
Barton, Richard, 375
Batten, G. H., 328–9, 330, 332, 336, 356, 364
Bay of Islands, 63, 111, 117, 125, 131, 150, 157, 229, 234–5
Bay of Islands Gazette (newspaper), 157
Beattie, W. I., 41
Beckett, Gilbert, 244
Beckett, Thomas Turner à, 293
Bell, Dillon, 280–1
Bengal Merchant (ship), 94, 100
Bentham, Jeremy, 21, 275
Berard, Commodore M., 203
Best, Ensign, 118–19
Bethune, Kenneth, 321
Betts Hopper, Edward, *see* Hopper, Edward Betts
Black, Dr John, 21, 70, 244, 245
Blair, David, xiv, 300, 309–10, 350, 370
Bland, William, 289, 296, 354–5
Boon, Robert, 101
Boulcott, John, 62
Boulcott's farm, 229
Bowen, Sir George, 367
Bradey, Francis, 141, 161, 195

Brandon, Alfred de Bathe, 132–3, 145
Brees, Samuel, 141, 258, 266
Brewer, H. G., 364
Brewer, William, xv, 145, 150, 158, 159, 161, 193, 200
Britomart (brig), 126
Broadhurst, Edward, 295–6
Brodie, Walter, 54
Brooke, John, 169, 206–7
Brooke, John Henry, 301, 339, 345, 346, 352
Brougham, Lord Henry, 12–14, 19, 21–22, 23, 25, 26, 29, 30, 53, 58, 190–1, 245, 255, 350
Brown, James, 378
Brown, Lionel, 378
Buchanan, James, 65
Buchanan, Professor Reverend R., 11
Buckle, J. W., 41
Buller, Charles, 21, 23, 33, 46, 62, 243–4, 245–7, 255–6, 266, 278, 289, 299, 301, 302, 378
Bulwer-Lytton, Edward George Earle, 27, 289
Bunbury, Major, 119
Burge, William, 250–1, 256
Burke, Robert, 353, 370
Burton, Reverend Henry, 122
Busby, James, 32, 44
Buxton, Thomas Fowell, 6
Byron, Lord, 26

Cairns, Sir Hugh, 347
Campbell, Captain William, 80, 81–86, 89, 90, 91, 92–93, 94, 110
Campbell, D. S., 326
Campbell, Major John, 44–45
Campbell, Reverend A. M., 72
Campbell, Thomas, 11, 12, 13, 21, 26, 27, 36, 75, 235
Canada, xx, 32, 46, 47, 52, 56, 57, 70, 328, 368; *see also* Wakefield, Edward Gibbon, and Canada
Canterbury Association, 280
Canterbury settlement, 266, 280, 321; *see also* Wakefield, Edward Gibbon, and settlement of Canterbury
Carlyle, Thomas, 28, 300
Carpenter, Mary [paternal grandmother], 1
Carrington, Frederick, 215
Carrington, William, 110, 116
Cashen, Denis, 372
Catchpool, Edward, 67, 76, 131
Chaffers, Captain Edmund, 59, 62, 86, 117, 118, 158
Chapman, Henry Samuel, 36, 70, 79, 83–85, 87, 88, 89, 90–91, 92, 121, 133, 134, 145, 160, 161, 200, 218, 227, 270, 303, 313–16, 318, 320, 326, 364
Chatham Islands, 114, 120, 121, 151, 169
Cherry, Thomas, 7, 8
Chetham, Amelia (née Riddiford), 176, 235, 257, 262–3, 318, 361–2, 372, 373
Chetham, Edward (later Edward Chetham Strode), 152, 159, 161, 175, 176, 200, 227, 232, 235, 257, 259, 262–4, 268, 285, 354, 358, 361–4, 373; *see also* Evans, George Samuel, RELATIONSHIPS AND FRIENDSHIPS: Other Relationships, and Edward Chetham
Chetham Strode, Admiral Sir Edward, 227, 235, 257, 259, 263–4, 361
Childers, Hugh, 297, 330
Church Missionary Society (CMS), xv, 33, 37–38, 44, 57–58, 66, 74; and land purchases of, 110, 232–3; *see also* missionaries
Church of England, 2, 6, 9, 36, 368; adherents and clerics of, 30, 36, 57, 66, 121, 220, 233, 247, 248, 300, 353; settlements of, 251–2, 257
Church of England Society, 25
Church of Scotland, 229; settlements of, 251–2
Churton, Reverend J. F., 121, 136
City of Sydney (steamer), 324
Clark, Emily, 258; *see also* Evans, Emily
Clarke, George Jnr, 164, 168–9, 171–2, 174–5, 182, 194, 196, 198–201, 206, 207, 208, 211, 212, 215, 217, 222, 223, 224, 225, 236; Evans, George Samuel, RELATIONSHIPS AND FRIENDSHIPS: Other Relationships, and George Clarke Jnr
Clarke, George Snr, 164, 168, 174, 175, 194, 200, 208, 211, 215, 217–18
Clendon, James, 151

Clifford, Charles, 206, 208, 227, 267, 283, 270, 274, 283, 322,
Cloudy Bay, 205, 206, 213, 214
Coates, Dandeson, 33, 36, 37–38, 56, 247, 378
Cobden, Richard, 70
Cobham, Samuel, 100
Cole, Constable [George *or* Henry], 118
Cole, Henry, 86, 87, 89, 192
Cole Catley, Christine, xvi
Coleridge, Samuel Taylor, 20
Colonial Gazette, 92, 250–1
Colonial Office, xvi, xxi, 29, 32–33, 36, 44, 47, 49, 57–58, 60, 67, 71, 73, 77–78, 230, 236, 251, 254, 264, 265, 277, 283, 299, 345, 377, 378; *see also* Evans, George Samuel, His Working Life: In England, and Colonial Office
Colonist and Port Nicholson Advertiser, 180, 184, 185, 186, 189–90, 203, 356
Commission of Peace, 144, 149, 157, 191
Committee on New Zealand, 212
Commons Committee on New Zealand Affairs, 235–6
Commons' debate on New Zealand, 243–4, 245–7, 251–2, 264, 301–2
Company of 1825, 41–42, 54, 55, 57, 60, 68
Congregational Church, 1, 13, 22, 236; *see also* dissenters
Cook Strait, *see* Cook's Straits
Cook, William, 36
Cook's Straits, 49, 51, 65, 68, 94, 102, 117, 126, 152, 206, 207, 236
Cooper, G. S., 368
Cooper, W. A., 150
Coromandel (ship), 30
Corrie, Dr, 16, 19
Cotterell, Hannah, *see* Evans, Hannah
Cotterell, Richard [maternal grandfather], 2
Cotton, William Charles, xiv, 220–2
Crawford, James Coutts, 107, 134–5, 162, 212, 235, 262, 358
Croly, Ann, 372
Crow, Eyre E., 244
Cruise, R., 34
Cuba (barque), 72, 79, 84, 132, 203
Currie, Raikes, 257, 258
Cutter, Christopher, 328–9, 330, 332, 336, 356, 364

Dale, George Samuel Evans, 371–2
Daniell family, 78, 82, 121
Daniell, Captain Edward, 53, 54, 55, 66, 67, 77, 78, 87, 88, 89, 93, 103, 108, 127, 133, 135, 136, 144, 181, 286–8, 339
Daniell, Edward [Captain Daniell's son], 339–40
Daniell, Mrs, 93, 121–2
Darling, Sir Charles, 361
Darwin, Charles, 28
Davis, Richard (Reihana Reweti), 110–11, 115, 116, 146, 170, 173, 177, 178, 184, 197
Davis, Rowland, 184, 185
Day, Mary, 19
de Tocqueville, Alexis, 10, 27
Deans, William, 79, 89
Denison, William, 297
Denman, Lord, 340–1
Dieffenbach, Ernst, 40
Dilke, C. W., 332
Disraeli, Benjamin, 245, 332
dissenters, xvi, 1–2, 4–6, 9–10, 13, 15, 16–17, 19, 23, 25, 30, 46, 181; *see also* Congregational Church; nonconformists
D'Oliviera, Liocadia, 63, 77, 84, 86, 91, 92, 93, 121–2; *see also* Taine, Liocadia; Wakefield, Edward Gibbon, and Liocadia D'Oliviera
Domett, Alfred, 274, 281, 282
Dominion (newspaper), 380
Don, Charles Jardine, 356
Dorset, Dr John, 66, 101, 103, 166, 187, 267, 280, 282, 283, 375
Doyle, Andrew, 244
Druid (iron sailing vessel), 73, 93
Duffy, Charles Gavan, 300–1, 302, 304, 305–6, 313, 316, 328, 330, 331, 332, 336, 351, 353–4, 358–9, 361
Duke of Norfolk, 122
Duke of Roxburgh (barque), 100, 375
Duke of Sussex, 63
Duke of Wellington, *see* Wellesley, Arthur
Duppa, George, 66, 100

Durham, Lady, 65
Durham, Lord (John George Lambton), xx, 32, 36, 41, 42, 44, 46, 52, 55, 56, 57, 59, 60, 63, 65, 95, 368
Durie, Major D. Stark, 77, 88, 90, 137, 159, 214

E Pokai, 175
E Puni, 221
E Wahu, 221
Earl, Percy, 239
Earp, George Butler, 149, 150, 151–2, 157, 162, 208, 212, 227
East India Company, 33, 41
Easthope, Sir John and Lady, 244
Ebden, Charles, 345, 348
Eccleston Hill, Wellington, ix, 122, 380; *see also* Golders Hill
Edinburgh, 67; *see also* University of Edinburgh
Edinburgh Review (journal), 12, 341
Egerton, Lord, 244
Eldon, Lord Chancellor, 17
Elizabeth (schooner), 183
Ellice, Edward, 28, 41
Embling, Dr Thomas, 325
Empire (newspaper), 289, 295, 309, 355
Enderby, Charles, 53, 54, 270
England, Captain Richard, 205
Eureka Stockade, 294
Evans Bay, 95, 121, 141, 380
Evans, Alfred [brother], 6, 75, 258, 262
Evans, Amy Burgess Farren [James Samuel's wife], 372
Evans, Claudia [sister], 10, 75, 262, 318, 345; *see also* Permezel, Claudia
Evans, George [father], 1–6, 8, 9, 10–11, 13, 20, 21, 24, 25, 62–63, 160, 194–5, 262
Evans, George Samuel
PERSONAL
Biographical Details
birth and childhood of, 1–7, 8; education of, 5–6, 7–13, 23; and training for ministry, 9–10; and legal studies, 26–27, 28, 36, 39; and departure for New Zealand, 75–76, 77–78; and journey to New Zealand, 75, 80, 81, 82–83, 87–90, 94; early years in Wellington, xix, 110–11, 116, 118–19, 180; his return to England, 231–2, 235, 236, 239–59; his return to Wellington, 268, 269–89; and Melbourne, xx–xxi, 269, 283, 289–365; final return to Wellington, 365, 366–73; health of, 177, 191, 227, 229, 231, 264, 268, 284, 285, 289, 295, 336, 344, 350, 365, 367, 372; houses of, ix, 122, 126, 141–2, 176, 235, 239, 269, 293, 353, 365, 367; characteristics and personality of, 19, 30, 67, 70, 121, 137, 185, 191, 216, 244–5, 330, 331–2, 339–40, 341, 355, 357, 375–6, 377–8; death, funeral and obituaries of, 367–73; *see also* Victoria, Australia, as possible home for Evans
Business and Finance
and business enterprises of, 137, 168; and land holdings of, 65, 74–75, 122–3, 135, 136, 137, 160–1, 195, 229, 230, 254, 257–9, 262–4, 267, 268, 285–6, 361, 380; and donations, 157, 194; finances of, x, 74–75, 130–1, 132–3, 135, 149, 176, 195, 218–19, 220–1, 232, 235, 254, 259, 262–4, 268, 316, 332, 344–5, 354, 358, 359, 360–1, 365; and Union Bank of Australia, 73, 263
Opinions and Views of
newspaper and journal accounts of him, xiv, 185, 186–7, 189–90, 203–4, 213–14, 267, 269, 306–7, 308–9, 317–18, 320, 332, 334, 335, 339, 345–6, 349, 351, 353, 356–7, 362–3, 368–70, 376–7; views and criticisms of, xiv, xvii, xxi, 76, 79, 84, 89–90, 91, 125, 136–7, 145, 161, 185, 189–91, 208, 216, 220, 231–2, 241, 244, 254–6, 267–8, 288, 301, 304, 309–10, 313, 317, 322, 329–30, 351–2, 355, 361, 367–71, 375–6, 378–9
IDEOLOGIES
Political Views
on Australian parliamentary reform, 301, 303, 304, 315, 316, 318, 336,

356; on British parliamentary reform, xvii, xx, 8–9, 22–27, 52, 163, 255; on colonial reform, xvii, 38, 267, 299; on democratic rights and liberalism, 27, 28, 191, 298–9, 314, 359; on freedom of the press, xiv, 143–4, 271–3, 295; on law reform, 52, 347, 364; on self-governance, xx, 149, 227, 270, 275–7, 279, 376; *see also* Great Reform Bill 1832; Law Reform Society (London); Reform Club (London)

Social Views

on civil and religious freedom, xvi, xvii, xix–xx, 6, 16–17, 25, 28, 36–37, 144, 149, 157, 195, 203, 255, 273, 275–6, 304, 348, 355, 359, 377; on education, xvi, 16, 20–21, 27, 72, 131, 194; on 'enlightened humanity' and human rights, 35–36, 37, 54, 78, 104–5, 149, 155, 187–8, 275, 306; on Maori, xiii, xx, 34, 35–36, 37, 38, 39–40, 46, 49, 54, 55, 74, 78, 104–5, 106, 109–10, 111, 113–16, 124, 126, 155–7, 164–5, 170–1, 175–6, 177–9, 193, 194, 196–200, 208, 210–11, 216–17, 219, 221–2, 223, 226, 228–9, 230–1, 242–3, 245–6, 247, 248, 275, 277, 376, 378; on universal suffrage, 22–23, 185, 296–7, 298, 304, 313, 314, 328–9, 332, 364, 365

HIS WORKING LIFE

In England

as educator and headmaster, 15–21, 27–28; and Church Missionary Society, 37, 66–67; and Colonial Office, 49, 241–3, 246, 287; and New Zealand Association, xiii, 33, 35–38, 40, 41–45, 46–52, 54, 64, 74–75, 377; and New Zealand Colonization Company, 53–58, 59, 60–62, 64; and New Zealand Company, xiii, xxi, 64–65, 66–69, 72, 75, 77, 119, 132–3, 138–9, 146, 149, 158, 162, 164–5, 181–2, 188, 191, 196, 198–9, 210–11, 214, 216–17, 226–7, 239–40, 249–50, 251–2, 256–8, 261, 262–3, 277–9, 280, 287, 379; and New Zealand Land Company, 63–64; law practice of, 26–27, 41, 256, 260, 264, 266, 267; *see also* Commission of Peace; Mill Hill Grammar School, London; New Zealand Company, and George Samuel Evans; North End Academy, London

In New Zealand

and missionaries, xiii, xx, 34, 35, 49, 115, 171, 210, 212, 232, 242, 249, 279; as Umpire, xix, 74, 104–5, 120; as Principal Agent, 78, 88, 132–3; and colonisation of New Zealand, xx, 30, 47–50, 53, 57, 73, 266–7, 282–3, 285–9, 368; and Maori language, xx, 39–40, 99, and settlement and establishment of Wellington, ix, xvii, xix, 101–2, 103–4, 106–8, 110–11, 112–13, 117, 120, 123–4, 131–3, 134–6, 138–9, 141, 142–3, 157, 159, 162–3, 180–1, 184, 186–9, 202–3, 253, 254, 284, 322–3, 365, 368–9, 375–8; as lawyer and legal adviser, 110–11, 116, 118, 119, 120–1, 133, 138–9, 140–1, 155–7, 159, 164–5, 166–71, 174, 192, 227, 255; as settlers' representative, 118–19, 135–7, 138–9, 140, 146–50, 158–9, 162–3, 188, 196, 202, 219–20, 223, 227, 231, 233–4, 241–2, 252–4; and deputation to Sydney, 127–30, 133; and Wairau incident, 205–13, 216–17, 240, 266; court cases of, 155–7, 159–60, 166–8, 168–72, 173–4, 175–6, 177–80, 192–3, 196–200, 270–4, 280–2; law practice of, 121, 136, 175, 183, 194, 218, 270–1, 283–4; *see also above* HIS WORKING LIFE: In England, and New Zealand Company; *see also* New Zealand Company, and George Samuel Evans

In Australia

political life in Melbourne, 289, 296–307, 310–19, 323, 324–34, 335, 336–9, 340–8, 349–64; as Postmaster General (Victoria), 316, 317–18, 324–5, 326, 336–7, 359, 360–1, 363; from Melbourne to

Wellington, 320–3; law practice and legal advice of, 295–6, 293, 298, 309, 344; *see also* Sydney, and Evans's deputation to
Speech-making and Writing
as speaker and orator, xiv, 87, 91, 102, 125, 143–4, 145, 153–4, 157–9, 163, 180–1, 186–8, 190, 203–4, 336, 339; political speeches of, xiv, 145, 149–50, 190, 231, 243–4, 285–6, 287–8, 299, 305, 306, 307, 311–12, 314, 315, 316–17, 318, 322–3, 329, 333, 334, 336–9, 341–2, 343, 347, 350, 351–2, 356, 357, 358, 359, 369–70; newspaper writings of, xiii–iv, 22, 71, 180, 244, 249, 260, 264–6, 271, 275–9, 293–4, 296–7, 298–9, 302, 309, 311, 313, 339, 344, 355, 362–3, 365, 369–70; political writings of, xiv, 34, 35–36, 71, 73, 252–3, 256, 298–9
RELATIONSHIPS AND FRIENDSHIPS
Friendships
21–22, 26–27, 28, 36, 46, 76, 84, 87–91, 126–7, 181, 202, 270, 288, 302, 321, 339–40, 354–5; with Edward Betts Hopper, 25–26, 126–7; with Richard Davies Hanson, 22, 121, 136, 164–6, 188–9, 190, 192, 216; *see also* Hanson, Richard Davies, and George Samuel Evans
Family Relationships
relationship with his family, 62–63, 75, 130–1, 160, 195, 318, 331, 345; relationship with his father, 13, 20, 62–63, 130, 160, 194–5, 210–11, 262; relationship with his wife, 17–19, 20, 29, 125, 126, 232, 321, 358, 362, 366
Other Relationships
159, 173, 281; and Archibald Michie, 294–5, 303–4, 306–7, 310–11, 312–13, 316–17, 325–6, 342–3; and Captain William Hobson, 144, 152–3, 226; and Colonel William Wakefield, xx, 103–4, 105, 119, 120–1, 149, 181–2, 183, 184, 190, 191, 201, 204, 215–16, 218–19, 224–7, 286, 376, 379; and Edward Chetham, 152, 159, 161, 175, 176, 200, 227, 232, 235, 257, 259, 262–4, 268, 285, 354, 358, 361–2, 373; and Edward Gibbon Wakefield, xiii, 30, 31–34, 38, 45, 46, 55–56, 59, 60, 74, 121, 196, 239–40, 241, 258, 282, 284, 285–9, 302, 376, 379; and George Clarke Jnr, 168, 171, 174; and Governor Robert FitzRoy, 219, 223–5, 240–1, 246, 271; and James Stephen, 274, 280; and Samuel Revans, 70–72, 82, 83–84, 87, 90–91, 143, 189; and Sir George Grey, 270, 275; *see also* Hanson, Richard Davies, and George Samuel Evans; Hiakai; Hobson, Captain William, and George Samuel Evans; Revans, Samuel, and George Samuel Evans; Wakefield, Colonel William, and George Samuel Evans; Wakefield, Edward Gibbon, and George Samuel Evans
Evans, George Samuel II [Linnaea Lamb Evans's half-brother], 372–3
Evans, Hannah (née Cotterell) [mother], 2, 5, 6, 62–63, 160, 194–5, 318, 365
Evans, Hannah Cotterell [sister], 9, 11, 262, 318, 365, 372
Evans, Harriet [wife], 20, 26, 29, 39, 56, 59, 63, 65, 69, 77, 108, 121, 124, 186, 195, 202, 208, 218, 220–1, 260, 268, 365, 372, 378; and her children, 56, 161, 176, 283, 318, 362; and journey to New Zealand, 76, 82–83, 84; and journeys with her husband, 29, 125, 126, 321, 358, 362; and land purchases and finances of, 65, 74, 122, 259, 272, 366; educational interests and philanthropy of, 65, 77, 141, 371; in Wellington, 114, 232, 235, 259, 260; others' views of her, 20, 133–4, 220–1; return to London, 262, 263; return to Wellington, 268, 283, 365, 366; death of, 366; *see also* Revans, Samuel, and Harriet Evans; Riddiford, Harriet
Evans, James Cook [brother], 4, 28, 75, 195, 244, 259, 262, 371
Evans, James Samuel [nephew], 371, 372, 376

Evans, Joshua, 241, 255
Evans, Linnaea Lamb [niece], 372–3
Evans, Linnaea Lamb [sister-in-law], 75
Evans, Mary [sister], 10, 75, 262, 318, 365, 371, 372, 373
Evans, Richard Cotterell [brother], 3, 9, 27–28
Evans, William [brother], 6, 62–63, 75, 262
Evans's Bay, *see* Evans Bay
Evening Courant (newspaper), 67
Evening Post (newspaper), xiv
Ewart, William, 244
Examiner (newspaper), 37
Exchange, Wellington, 131, 141, 157, 159, 166, 171, 180, 219
Eyre, Edward, 269

Falconer, Mr, 90
Farington, Joseph, 7
Farrar, A. S. (Alfred), 116, 167, 174
Farrar, H. W., 320
Featherston, Isaac, xv, 181, 200, 203, 212, 253, 267, 270, 280, 283, 286, 320, 321, 322, 323, 324, 326–7, 354, 358, 366, 367, 368
Fellows, T. H. (Thomas Howard), 301, 303–4
Few and Co., 249, 263
Few, Robert, 75, 258, 263
Fildes, Horace (H. W.), ix, xiv, 91, 240, 380
Fitzgerald, Dr John, 156, 189, 202, 222
Fitzherbert, William, 180, 189, 203, 267, 270, 283, 284, 286
FitzRoy, Governor Robert, 182, 217–18, 219, 220, 223–7, 228, 229–30, 232, 233, 234–4, 236, 240–42, 246, 248, 251, 261, 265, 271, 378; *see also* Evans, George Samuel, Relationships and Friendships: Other Relationships, and Governor Robert FitzRoy
Forde, J. L., 368
Forsaith, Thomas, 223, 224
Fox, Charles, 307, 350
Fox, Colonel Charles Richard, 255
Fox, Edward Thomas, 192
Fox, Reverend W. J., 5
Fox, William, ix, xiv, xxi, 202–3, 215, 266, 267, 276, 368, 377
France, and colonisation, 39, 49, 66, 73, 287
Francis, James, 333, 351

Gawler, Colonel George, 158–9
Gibbon, Edward, 9, 268, 301, 310
Gipps, Sir George, 69, 116, 124, 125, 126–9, 131–2, 133, 135, 138, 147, 152, 167, 188, 206, 253
Gisborne, William, xvi, 107, 182, 378
Gladstone, William, 265, 278, 302
Glasgow, 10–13; *see also* University of Glasgow
Glasgow Times (newspaper), 62
Gleeson, Ann, *see* Croly, Ann
Glenbervie (barque), 76, 94, 100
Glenelg, Lord, 33, 43–44, 46, 47, 51–52, 53, 56, 57–58, 64, 73–74
Globe (newspaper), 22, 24, 37
Godfrey, Colonel Edward, 220
Gold, Colonel Charles, 322
Golden Bay, 102
Golders Hill, Wellington, ix, 122, 141, 220, 262, 269, 365, 367, 372, 380; *see also* Eccleston Hill
Goldsmid, Sir Isaac, 13, 62, 239
Gordon, John, 54, 59
Gouger, Robert, 258–9
Government Gazette, 147, 213
Gowen, John R., 62, 257, 258
Gower, John R., *see* Gowen, John R
Grant, J. M., 311, 334
Grant, James, 207
Gray, Charles, 353
Gray, Moses Wilson, 305
Greenwood, J. H., 189
Greeves, Dr Augustus, 317, 340–1
Grey, Earl, *see* Howick, Lord
Grey, Lord, 23, 25
Grey, Sir George, 33, 37, 159, 248–9, 251, 261, 264, 265–6, 267, 270, 274, 275, 367; and Edward Gibbon Wakefield, 282–3; and land purchases, 279–80, 281–3, 286; and New Zealand Wars, 360; *see also* Evans, George Samuel, Relationships and Friendships: Other Relationships,

and Grey, Sir George; Wakefield, Edward Gibbon, and Sir George Grey
Guard, Mr, 192
Gurney, Joseph, 13
Guyton, William, 239, 244, 248

Hadfield, Bishop, 207–8, 218, 221–2, 248
Haines, William, 295, 300, 302, 303, 304, 306, 312, 313, 315, 336, 349, 353, 358, 363, 369
Halswell, Beauchamp, 248
Halswell, Edmund Storr, 53, 54, 55, 64, 146, 155, 163, 166, 171, 173, 176, 180, 181, 182, 185, 248, 257
Hamilton, J. W., 223
Hanson, Richard Davies, xiv, xvi, 22, 29, 37, 46, 72, 104, 116, 122–3, 124, 125, 157, 161, 258; and Colonel William Wakefield, 104, 151, 161, 165–6; and *Colonist*, 203, 356; and deputation to Sydney, 125, 127–29, 133, 159; and George Samuel Evans, 22, 121, 165, 186, 231, 260–1, 356, 361; and land purchases of, 122–3; and law practice in Wellington, 136, 145, 146, 151–2, 155–6, 165–6, 169, 171, 172, 175, 176, 181, 186, 192; and Maori, 163, 165–6, 231, 261; and New Zealand Company, 151; and settlement and establishment of Wellington, 106–7, 116, 119–21, 124–5, 130, 132, 133, 135, 136, 139, 143–4, 148–50, 151–2, 157, 158, 159, 163, 171, 180–1, 184–5, 186–90, 192, 206, 208, 223; and Wairau incident, 206; and Wellington Club, 159; as representative of settlers and advocate, 158, 180–1, 223, 231; business interests of, 227, 261; career of, 139, 149, 151, 227, 261, 373; personality and reputation of, 190, 191, 208; *see also* Evans, George Samuel, Relationships and Friendships: Friendships, and Richard Davies Hanson; Revans, Samuel, and Richard Davies Hanson; Wakefield, Colonel William, and Richard Davies Hanson
Harington, T. C., 249, 267
Harker, George, 313, 316, 325
Harrop, A. J., 378
Hart, Robert, 270
Hawes, Benjamin, 38, 256, 265, 267, 348
Hawke's Bay, Maori at, 231
Hazlitt, William, 190–1
Heales, Richard, 344, 345, 347, 348, 349, 350, 351, 352, 353, 354, 356, 358, 360–1
Healy, Dr Francis, 192
Healy, John, 192
Heaphy, Charles, 66, 141
Heath, John, 53
Helmore, Frederick, 17, 18
Helmore, Thomas, 17, 18, 19, 20
Hiakai, 39–40, 41, 46, 49
Higinbotham, George, 315, 317–18, 330, 351, 352, 353, 357, 361, 362–3
Hinds, Dr Samuel, 36, 53, 66, 256
Hobson, Captain William (later Governor), xvi, 44, 56, 69, 71, 226; and George Samuel Evans, 119, 120, 124, 150, 151, 152; and Maori, 151, 152; and New Zealand Company, 152, 182; as Governor, 73, 93, 94, 116, 117–18, 120–1, 123–4, 126, 128, 130, 131, 133, 134, 136–7, 142–5, 146–50, 151–3, 157, 158, 161, 164, 167, 171, 182, 184, 195, 232, 233, 265, 375, 377, 378; land purchases of, 151, 210; Evans, George Samuel, Relationships and Friendships: Other Relationships, and Hobson, Captain William
Holroyd, Arthur, 295–6
Hone Heke, 218, 229, 236, 248, 249, 267
Hope, George, 241, 245, 246
Hopper, Edward Betts, xiv, 25–26, 29, 38, 41, 44, 46, 47, 53, 66, 67, 73, 76, 100, 101, 105, 126–7, 133; *see also* Evans, George Samuel, Relationships and Friendships: Friendships, with Edward Betts Hopper
Howard, Thomas, 361
Howick, Lord, 36, 38, 52, 64, 71, 245, 248, 258, 261, 265–6
Hughes, Henry, 18
Hughes, Robert, 126

Hume, David, 9
Hume, Joseph, 23, 27, 28
Hunt, Leigh, 9
Hunter, George, 72, 73, 105, 124, 135, 144, 192, 203, 321
Hunter, George Jnr, 375
Hutt River, 100–1, 104, 105, 107, 127, 378
Hutt Valley, 100, 102, 103, 105, 112, 122, 132, 135–6, 141, 146, 180, 186, 202, 203, 212, 229, 230, 284, 285, 288, 361, 375; Maori from, 169, 212, 215, 225
Hutt, John, 37
Hutt, William, 36–37, 45, 46, 47, 53, 56, 58, 59, 60, 63–64, 65, 73, 76–77, 122, 252, 256, 257, 258, 261

India, 28, 30, 268
Ingestre, Viscount, 62
Integrity (barque), 117
Ireland and the Irish, 52, 300, 305, 309, 315
Ireland, Richard, 313, 314, 316, 319, 345, 350, 351–2, 353, 358, 360–1, 364
Ironside, Samuel, 206
Izard, Charles, 352, 372

Jervis, Sir John, 268
Jews, 2, 3, 9, 13, 255
Johnson, Paul, xv
Johnson, Samuel, 267, 309–10, 369
Johnston, John, 320, 321, 368
Johnston, John Stewart, 346
Johnston, Dr William, 87, 88

Kaipara, 68, 100
Kaiwharawhara, 101, 115, 137, 225; pa, 109, 148, 168, 177, 178, 179, 222, 225
Kaparatehau (chief), 229
Kapiti Maori, 39, 95, 227
Karori, 135, 202
Kelham, James, 181, 235
Kendall, Thomas, 40
Kerford, Professor G. B., 40
King Charles II, 16
King George III, xx, 2
King George IV, 12, 22
King William, 22, 23, 24, 25, 32, 38
King, John, 270–3, 274, 282
King, Michael, ix, xvi, xvii, 218
Kingi, Wiremu (chief), 248
Knowles, John, 257
Knox, Dr F. J., 131
Knox, Professor, 62
Koaka (chief), 166
Korokoro pa, 110
Kororareka, 147, 229, 236, 267
Kotiriki, 177
Kumutoto pa and environs, 108, 109, 110, 122, 141, 163, 178–9

Labouchere, Under-Secretary Henry, 58, 60, 63–64, 72–73
Lambert, Thomas, 351
Lambton Harbour, Wellington, 95, 100, 102, 104, 108, 113, 166, 201, 270
Lambton Quay, Wellington, 135, 141, 164, 191, 194, 270, 380
Lambton, John George, *see* Durham, Lord
Lance, John, 257
Law Reform Society (London), 256, 347
Le Breton, L. 34
Leader (journal), 356, 357
Leader, John Temple, 158, 159
Levi, Nathaniel, 363
Levin, Nathaniel, 185, 321, 366, 368
Lewis, William, 2
Liardet, Captain Francis, 153–4
Literary Club, London, 21, 26
Littleton, Edward, 41
Lloyd, John, 194
Locke, John, 9
London, conditions and life in, 2–4, 7, 8–9, 10, 13, 24, 32, 38–39, 62–63, 262, 264, 268
Long, George, 19, 28
Lord Ashley, SS, 362
Luscombe, J. H., 54, 78
Lushington, Charles, 38
Lushington, Stephen, 38, 255
Luxford, William, 94
Lyall, George, 41, 257, 258
Lyndhurst, Lord, 25
Lyon, William, 186–7

Lyttelton, 152, 270

Macaulay, Thomas, 28, 309
McCulloch, James, 303, 361, 362, 364
McDonald, Alexander, 322
McDonnell, Thomas, 54, 55, 62, 68, 72
McDonough, Police Magistrate, 175, 206, 207, 211
Macfarlan, Dr Duncan, 13
Macfarlane, Reverend J., 176, 229
McGowan, S. W., 293, 322
McGurk, Charles, 103, 104
McHugh, Thomas, 194, 196
Mackay, Dr G., 328, 329
McKenzie, Thomas Wilmor, xiv, 36, 52, 63, 75; and accounts of the journey of the *Adelaide*, 77, 78, 79–80, 81, 82–83, 85, 86, 89, 93–94; and early years in Thorndon, 99, 105–6; in court, 270–4
Mackinnon, Lauchlan, 294
McLean, Donald, 368, 377
Mahau, 169, 178–9
Mangatuku, 167
Mantell, Walter, 193
Maori: and colonisation, 38, 47, 48, 49, 52, 104–5, 116–17, 118, 127–9, 164, 210–11, 245–6, 248–9, 251; and land ownership, 109, 117, 153, 163–4, 171, 174, 177–9, 210–11; and land purchases and disputes, 62, 63, 65–66, 68, 74, 94–95, 102–3, 105, 109–11, 114–16, 117, 152–3, 164–71, 173–5, 176–80, 182, 196–201, 209, 217, 223–5, 228–9, 230–1, 233–4, 279–80; and rights of, 104–5, 117, 124, 128, 155–6, 164, 172, 193, 234, 245–6, 250, 275, 379; and sovereignty, 32, 37, 49–50, 58, 60, 69, 71, 111, 117–19, 234, 243; and traditional crafts, 63; and relationships with the settlers, 109, 110, 113–14, 119, 136, 143, 162, 175, 177–8, 182, 188, 196, 200–1, 209, 210, 212, 213, 215, 217–18, 229, 264; and settlers' descriptions of, 102, 106, 113, 114; and Treaty of Waitangi, 110, 111, 117; court cases involving, 155–7, 168–9, 175–8, 193, 196–200, 221–2; health of, 47, 200; trade and industry of, 134–5, 202; *see also* Evans, George Samuel, IDEOLOGIES: Social Views, on Maori; Hawke's Bay, Maori at; Hutt Valley, Maori from; Kaiwharawhara, pa; Kapiti, Maori at; Kumutoto pa and environs; Matehou tribe; New Zealand Wars; Ngapuhi; Ngati Awa; Ngati Kahungunu; Ngati Mutunga; Ngati Rangatahi; Ngati Raukawa; Ngati Tama; Ngati Toa; Otago, Maori in; Petone, Maori at; Pipitea, pa; Porirua, Maori in; Port Nicholson, Maori at; Hanson, Richard Davies, and Maori; Te Aro, Maori in; Te Ati Awa; Treaty of Waitangi; Waikanae, Maori at; Wairau incident; Waiwhetu pa; Wakefield, Colonel William, and Maori; Wakefield, Edward Gibbon, and Maori; 'waste land' policy
March, Reverend Henry, 15–16, 17, 84
Marjoribanks, Alexander, 86, 247
Marjoribanks, Stewart, 41, 52, 62
Marsden, Samuel, 164
Martin, Samuel, 117, 118, 124
Martin, Samuel McD., 213
Martin, William, 144, 145, 152, 164, 174–5, 193, 195–6, 202–3, 212
Maryborough Advertiser (newspaper), 352
Mason, John W., 363
Matehou tribe, 169, 178, 179
Matheson, James, 244
Mayo, Reverend Dr, 16
Mechanics' Institute and Library, 194
Mein Smith, William, *see* Smith, Captain William Mein
Melbourne, xiv, xvi, 276, 289, 293, 294, 297, 300, 301, 305, 309, 311–12, 313, 318, 320–2, 323–5, 327, 330, 332, 337, 340, 350–1, 353, 358, 360, 362, 365, 366, 368, 369, 370–1, 372, 373, 376, 377; *see also* University of Melbourne
Melbourne Chamber of Commerce, 320–1, 326
Melbourne Herald (newspaper), 295, 300, 302, 307, 309, 311, 313, 316, 317, 330, 339, 349, 365, 368, 369–70
Melbourne Morning Herald (newspaper), xiv, 293–4
Melbourne Punch, xiv, 294, 302,

303–4, 306–7, 308–9, 310, 315, 316, 317, 320, 332, 334, 339, 344, 345–6, 349, 353, 362–3, 365
Melbourne, Lord, 25, 38, 42, 43–44, 64, 73
Mennell, Philip, 369
Merchant Taylors' School, London, x, 7–9
Mercury (steamship), 77
Merivale, Lord, 345
Meurant, Edward, 206
Michie, Archibald, 293, 294–5, 300, 301, 303–4, 306–7, 310–11, 312–13, 316–17, 325–6, 328, 332, 341–4, 348, 350, 354, 363, 369; *see also* Evans, George Samuel, RELATIONSHIPS AND FRIENDSHIPS: Other Relationships, and Michie, Archibald
Mill Hill Grammar School, London, x, 13–14, 15–19, 84, 256
Mill, James, 21
Mill, John Stuart, 21, 23, 300, 302
Millar, Archibald, 87–88, 89, 90
Miller, Henry, 316
missionaries, 32, 33, 34, 38, 40, 49, 66, 71, 116, 161, 164, 206, 209, 217–18, 221, 222, 245; and New Zealand Company, xx, 38, 198; and land purchases of, 35, 110–11, 116–17, 171, 232–3, 245, 247–8; *see also* Church Missionary Society; Church of England; Evans, George Samuel, HIS WORKING LIFE: In New Zealand, and missionaries; Wesleyan missionaries and Church
Mississippi (ship), 39
Molesworth, Francis, 66, 100, 146, 159, 186, 220, 375
Molesworth, Judge Robert, 364
Molesworth, Lady, 65
Molesworth, Sir William, 36, 37, 46, 56, 65, 66, 278, 299, 302
Monro, Robert, 75, 161, 176, 227, 232, 254, 257, 259, 263, 361, 362
Montague, Lydia, 84
Montreal Advertiser (newspaper), 70
Moore, Captain George, 125
Moore, David, 324
Moore, Edward Duke, 27
More, Hannah, 2, 5
Moreing, Henry, xix, 61, 94, 124, 125, 126, 149, 159, 185, 244, 248
Mori, 110
Morning Chronicle (newspaper), 19, 21, 22, 24, 29, 37, 70, 75, 77, 78, 244, 260
Morning Post (newspaper), 24
Morpeth, Lord George, 27
Morrison, Mary [maternal grandmother], 2
Motte, Standish, 38, 54, 55, 58, 61–62
Moturoa (chief), 109, 110, 115–16, 166, 167, 169–71, 173–4, 177–8, 196–7, 270
Mount Alexander Mail (newspaper), 349
Municipal Corporation Ordinance, 157, 162, 218
Murphy, Francis, 310, 316–17, 327
Murphy, Michael, 126, 136–9, 140, 145–6, 148, 157, 159, 162–3, 180–1, 184, 186, 187, 188–9, 190, 194, 219

Nairn, Alexander, 62
Nelson, 152, 153, 186, 203, 205, 211–12, 213, 214, 215, 218, 226, 227, 236, 321
Nelson (brig), 235
New Plymouth, 153
New South Wales, 29, 32, 37, 47, 64, 69, 118, 123, 142, 143, 147, 151, 234, 289, 293, 298, 302, 325, 343, 371; Legislative Council of, 123, 295, 354–5
New Zealand Association, xiii, xvi, 31, 33, 34–39, 40–45, 46–52, 54, 57–58, 64, 71, 74, 127, 153, 166, 207, 216, 234, 287, 377; *see also* Evans, George Samuel, HIS WORKING LIFE: In England, and New Zealand Association; Wakefield, Edward Gibbon, and New Zealand Association
New Zealand Colonization Company, 53–59, 60–63, 64, 73–74; *see also* Evans, George Samuel, HIS WORKING LIFE: In England, and New Zealand Colonization Company; Wakefield, Edward Gibbon, and New Zealand Colonization Company

New Zealand Company, xiii, xv, xvi, xvii, xix, xx, 63, 71–72, 75, 77–78, 86, 87, 94, 107, 117, 118, 119–21, 147, 171, 172, 184, 213, 214, 231, 243–4, 248, 249, 261, 266–7; and colonisation of New Zealand, 150, 152–3, 215, 253–4; and George Samuel Evans, xxi, 90, 130, 132–3, 138–9, 196, 216, 242, 246, 252–3, 256–9, 261, 379; and land dealings of, 103–4, 105, 124, 152–3, 164–8, 169, 180, 196–200, 204, 218, 224–5, 228–9, 233, 235–6; and Maori, 103, 105, 116–17, 127–9, 146, 151, 162, 163–8, 171, 182, 194, 196, 198–200, 210–11, 225, 233, 245–6; and settlement of Wellington, 103–4, 119–20, 124, 127–30, 131, 135–6, 143, 146, 152, 158, 182–3, 199–200, 203–4, 215, 219, 236, 261; Charter of, 146, 181–2, 249–50; colonisation practices of, 126–7, 131, 138, 162, 165–8, 171, 172, 180, 182, 194, 198, 203–4, 230, 250–1; composition of, 42, 77, 83, 84, 87, 116–17, 121, 132, 208, 239, 242, 261–2, 267, 276–7, 286; finances of, 122, 126–7, 130, 132–3, 135–6, 158, 181–2, 196, 202–3, 215, 229, 262, 276–7; land purchases of, 102–3, 110–11, 116, 119–20, 127–9, 163–71, 209–10, 215, 223–4; later views of, xvii, 74, 378–9; reputation and criticisms of, 168, 171, 186, 188, 203, 208, 223, 225, 251, 276–9, 283; settlements of, 152, 212–13, 215, 225, 227–8, 236, 251–2; *see also* Company of 1825; Evans, George Samuel, His Working Life: In England, and New Zealand Company; Hanson, Richard Davies, and New Zealand Company; Hobson, Captain William, and New Zealand Company; New Zealand Association; New Zealand Colonization Company; New Zealand Land Company; Revans, Samuel, and New Zealand Company; Wakefield, Colonel William, and New Zealand Company; Wakefield, Edward Gibbon, and New Zealand Company
New Zealand Constitution Act, 262, 267, 275, 279
New Zealand Gazette, xiii, 71, 73, 80, 92, 119, 129, 131–2, 136, 140, 146, 149, 150, 152, 152, 158, 166, 169, 171–2, 185, 194, 203–4, 208–9, 212, 223, 227–8, 233, 235, 386
New Zealand Gazette and Wellington Spectator, 180
New Zealand Herald, 267
New Zealand Herald and Auckland Gazette, 213
New Zealand Land Bill, 123, 124, 125, 129
New Zealand Land Company, 63, 64–69, 70, 71–73, 74, 101, 105, 287, 368; *see also* New Zealand Company
New Zealand Patriotic Fund, 366
New Zealand Spectator and Cook's Straits Guardian, xv, 247, 248, 271, 273, 362
New Zealand Wars, 229, 236, 246; *see also* Grey, Sir George, and New Zealand Wars
New Zealand, colonisation and settlement of, xv, 30, 31–38, 59–62, 67–69, 72, 79–81, 91–92, 143–4, 148, 162, 265; *see also* Wakefield, Edward Gibbon, and colonisation of New Zealand
Newcastle, Lord, 345
Newton, Hibbert, 351
Ngaiti, 39, 46, 49, 66
Ngaki, 225, 174
Ngakurae, 169, 179
Ngaponga, Moses, 176
Ngapuhi, 110, 179, 229
Ngapuna (chief), 166, 177
Ngati Awa, 106, 169, 197, 225
Ngati Kahungunu, 168, 178, 179
Ngati Mutunga, 168
Ngati Rangatahi, 225, 229
Ngati Raukawa, 178
Ngati Tama, 109, 168, 225
Ngati Toa, 95, 135, 218, 229, 248
Ngauranga, 101, 136, 178
Nicholas, J. L., 34
Nicholson, William, 326, 338, 339, 341, 344, 345, 346, 348, 349, 350, 352
non-conformists, 7, 22, 121, 300, 304, 339; *see also* dissenters

Normanby, Lord, 58, 60, 63–64, 72–73, 75, 117, 265
North End Academy, London, 20, 27, 41, 75
Nugent, Lord, 27

O'Reilly, Father J. J. P., 367
Oriental (barque), 77, 78, 100
Orr, John, 357
O'Shanassy, John, 300, 301, 303–4, 305–6, 313–14, 315–18, 320, 323, 326, 327–8, 329, 330, 332, 334–5, 339, 340, 341, 345, 346, 348, 350, 353–4, 355–6, 358–60, 364
Otago, 270, 321; Maori in, 39
Owen, Robert, 26
Owhiro, 135, 202

Pakewa, 155–7, 159–60
Pakington, Sir John, 279
Pakuratahi, 230
Palmer, George, 41
Parau, 206
Paremata, 135
Park, R., 173
Parkes, Henry, 21, 289, 295, 296, 298, 302, 309
Partridge, Thomas, xiv, 77, 80, 84, 85, 86, 88, 91, 134, 145, 157, 159, 223
Patukawenga, 169
Pearson, Captain, 117, 130
Peel, Robert, 254, 261
Percival, John, 20
Permezel, Claudia (née Evans), 345, 365, 371, 372, 373
Permezel, John, ix, xiv
Permezel, Zephyrin Pierre Edouard, 345
Petone, xix, 94, 100–1, 102, 105, 106, 116, 120, 141, 146, 147, 167, 169, 171, 176, 178, 369; as alternative for Wellington, xxi, 100–1, 369, 377; Maori at, 114, 176, 178–9, 222, 225, 322
Petre, Eleanor, xiv, 202, 208, 209; *see also* Walmesley, Mary Ann Eleanor
Petre, Lady Emma, 65
Petre, Lord Henry, 36, 53, 58, 59, 63, 65, 66, 67, 72, 100, 107, 122, 136, 157, 202, 208, 209
Pharazyn, C. J., 368
Pickwick Club, 159
Pike, Douglas, 36
Pipitea, 111, 201; pa, 102, 105–6, 109–10, 114, 115–16, 126, 163, 168, 169–70, 171, 174, 175, 177–9, 221–2, 223, 270
Pirikawau, 248–9
Pitt, Richard, 352
Pitt, William, 11, 307, 350
Place, Francis, 28
Platina (barque), 120
Poki, 169
Pollen, Dr Daniel, 368
Pomare, 169
Pompallier, Bishop, 157
Ponga (chief), 169
Porirua, 135, 136, 138, 145–6, 148, 193, 208, 212, 224, 228, 257; Maori in, 162, 180, 193, 212, 215; *see also* Wakefield, Colonel William, and Porirua
Port Nicholson, xvi, 37, 92, 93, 94, 117, 118, 121, 123–4, 125, 126, 127, 131, 133, 142, 143, 144, 147, 149, 150, 151, 157, 163, 168, 188, 213–14, 218, 220, 230, 269, 321; Maori at, 102, 105, 110, 111, 143, 163, 168–9, 218, 225; sale and ownership of, 129, 169, 176, 177–80, 196–9, 203, 209–10, 215, 235–6
Porutu (chief), 106, 109, 166
Prendergast, Mr M., 338–9, 349
Presbyterians, 2, 300, 358
Pryce, Chief Officer, 82
Puaha (chief), 206–7
Punch (magazine), 247
Pye Smith, John, 15, 16, 256

Quakers, 3, 6, 13, 30
Queen (steamship), 321, 322
Queen Caroline, 12
Queen Charlotte's Sound, 166
Queen Victoria, 38, 42, 197, 233–4, 249, 342

Ramsay, D., 54
Rangihaeata, 135, 145, 146, 148, 193, 206–7, 211, 215, 217, 218, 222, 225, 228, 229, 248, 249

Raupo House ordinance, 162
Reform Bill 1832 (GB), xv, 23–27, 36, 164, 285
Reform Club (London), x, 28, 57, 75, 83, 90, 159, 244–5, 247, 252
Reid, Thomas, 9
Reihana Reweti, *see* Davis, Richard
Revans, Eleanor, 79, 81, 83, 87
Revans, Sam [Samuel Revans's nephew], 358
Revans, Samuel, xiv, 70–72, 119, 134, 157, 171, 303, 379–80; and business interests of, 131, 141, 159, 162, 201–2, 203, 227, 229, 379; and Colonel William Wakefield, 103, 134, 201, 228, 284; and Daniel Riddiford, 70–71, 79, 134; and Edward Gibbon Wakefield, 92, 227–8; and early years in Wellington, 103, 119–20, 121, 131, 143, 148, 157; and George Samuel Evans, 70–71, 83–85, 87–91, 92, 107, 121, 133–4, 145, 189, 192–3, 232, 240, 358; and Harriet Evans, 84, 133–4; and Louisa Smith, 84, 92, 133–4; and New Zealand Company, 70–72, 85, 92, 121, 158, 161, 171, 227, 261; and *New Zealand Gazette*, 71–72, 92–93, 172, 203, 227–8, 229; and political involvement, 136, 145, 148, 171, 186, 223, 284; and Richard Davies Hanson, 121, 123, 145, 171–2; and voyage to New Zealand, 77, 79, 80, 81, 82, 83–85, 86, 87–93; *see also* Evans, George Samuel, RELATIONSHIPS AND FRIENDSHIPS: Other Relationships, and Samuel Revans; *New Zealand Gazette*
Rhodes, Captain William, 321, 323
Ricardo, David Jr, 23
Richardson, G. R., 207, 218
Richmond, Major Matthew, 214, 217, 219, 220, 223, 233
Riddiford, Amelia [stepdaughter], 20, 29, 39, 40, 77, 84, 86, 101–2, 121, 161, 176; *see also* Chetham, Amelia
Riddiford, Anthony [great grandson of Daniel Riddiford, Evans's stepson], 92
Riddiford, Daniel [stepson], 20, 30, 37, 39, 56, 64, 66, 70–71, 79, 81, 133, 181, 220, 274, 283, 331, 352, 367, 372, 376, 378; *see also* Revans, Samuel, and Daniel Riddiford
Riddiford, Daniel [wife's late husband], 18–19, 20, 52
Riddiford, Daniel [great grandson of Daniel Riddiford, Evans's stepson], 92
Riddiford, Edward Joshua [step-grandson], 181, 331, 372
Riddiford, Eliza [step-granddaughter], 367, 372
Riddiford, Ellen Chaffers [step-granddaughter], 86, 368
Riddiford, Harriet, 15–16, 18–20; *see also* Evans, Harriet
Riddiford, Harriot (née Stone), x, 56, 84, 86, 283, 331
Riddiford, Thomasina [step-granddaughter], 367, 372
Rintoul, Robert Stephen, 36, 45, 46, 239, 243, 299
Robinson, Samuel, 270–4
Roebuck, J. A., 70
Roman Catholic Church, 58, 157, 255, 300, 331
Roman Catholics, 2, 9, 36, 37, 46, 58, 66, 122, 180, 247–8, 300, 303, 304, 314, 364
Roots, John, 187, 188–9, 231–2, 261
Ross, Hugh, xv, 270
Rous, Captain Henry, 245
Roy, Robert, 44, 45
Rugby Public School, England, 16, 20
Ruhia, 106
Rusden, G. W., xvi, 223, 276–7, 364
Russell, Lord John, 23, 24–25, 63, 75, 117, 145–6, 162, 174, 182, 245, 254, 261

Sandford, Professor Daniel, 11–12
Sandon, Lord, 244
Savage, John, 34
Scholefield, Guy H., xvi, 379–80
Scotland, settlers from, 67
Scott, David, 165, 171
Selfe, Henry, 255
Selwyn, Bishop, 180–1, 218, 220
Serle, Geoffrey, xvi, 301, 315, 329, 332, 347
Service, James, 323, 331, 340–1, 344
Sewell, Henry, 267, 280–2, 283–4

Shortland, Lieutenant Willoughby, 115, 117–19, 120, 125, 131, 144, 147–8, 149, 151, 167, 178; as Acting Governor, 182–3, 196, 197, 201, 207, 209, 211–12, 232, 378
Sinclair, Dudley, 62, 66, 111, 118–19
Sinclair, Sir George, 36, 62, 66
Singapore, 49
Sinnett, Fred, 293, 294
Smart, Lieutenant H. D., 118, 125
Smith, Adam, 9, 31
Smith, Captain William Mein, 72, 79, 84, 92, 100–2, 103, 105, 107, 109, 110, 111, 112–13, 115, 116, 118, 123, 132, 133, 134, 166, 167, 173, 201–2, 206, 223, 228, 229
Smith, Fanny, 84
Smith, George, 84
Smith, J. T., 339
Smith, John, 52, 105, 113
Smith, Louisa, 84, 88, 92, 94, 133–4; *see also* Revans, Samuel, and Louisa Smith
Smith, Reverend Sydney, 2
Smith, Wallace, 84
Somes Island, xix, 99, 109
Somes, Joseph, 52, 53–54, 55, 56, 59, 61, 64, 65, 78, 88, 122, 182, 239, 243, 249
South Africa, 32
South Australia Act 1834, 29, 37, 42
South Australia Association, 29
South Australia, colonisation and settlement of, 29, 37, 68, 70, 158–9, 256, 258–9, 302, 325, 347, 373; *see also* Wakefield, Edward Gibbon, and colonisation of South Australia
Southern Cross (newspaper), 213–14
Southern Cross Hotel, Wellington, 159
Spain, Commissioner William, 146, 163–6, 168, 170, 171, 172, 173, 175, 179, 180, 182, 183, 194, 196–7, 198–201, 205–7, 212, 223–4, 225, 229, 236; and his Land Commission, 115, 168–70, 173, 175, 176, 177, 180, 184, 196–7, 201, 204, 205, 207–8, 214, 215, 217–18, 223–4, 228
St Hill, Henry, 77, 84, 88, 93, 103, 111, 144, 180–1, 185, 186, 188, 206, 283, 322
Stafford, Hon. Edward, 367–8
Stag (barque), 268, 269
Standard (newspaper), 24
Stanley, Lord, 151, 223, 233–4, 240–1, 242, 243, 246, 249, 251, 253, 256, 265
Stawell, William, 301
Stephen, J. Wilberforce, 363
Stephen, James, 33, 37, 43, 51, 57–58, 63, 64, 69, 73–74, 78, 270, 378; *see also* Evans, George Samuel, RELATIONSHIPS AND FRIENDSHIPS: Other Relationships, and James Stephen
Stephen, Sidney, 270–3, 274, 280–3
Stokes, Robert, 116, 141, 162
Stone, Harriot, *see* Riddiford, Harriot
Strang, Robert, 145, 271
Sutton, Dr Manners, 2
Swainson, William, 66, 144, 145, 146, 164, 175, 195–6, 207, 211–13, 375
Sydney, 31, 115, 123, 124, 127, 130, 148, 159, 166, 202, 295, 297, 327, 360; and Evans's deputation to, 125, 126–30, 131–2, 133; as possible home for Evans, 130, 289, 296
Syme, David, 305–6, 359
Syme, Ebenezer, 314

Taine, James John, xiv, xv, 63, 77, 79, 80, 86, 89, 91, 93, 113, 114, 121, 151, 181, 227, 321, 380
Taine, Jessie, 380
Taine, Liocadia (née D'Oliviera), 240, 380; *see also* D'Oliviera, Liocadia; Wakefield, Edward Gibbon, and Liocadia D'Oliviera
Taranaki, 111, 135, 169, 225, 228–9
Tararua (steamer), 372
Taringa Kuri (chief), 109–10, 137, 168–9, 171, 180
Tasmania, 270, 301, 302, 325
Taylor, Sir Herbert, 25
Te Aro, 100, 131, 141, 178–9, 209; Maori in, 100, 102, 109–10, 114–15, 148, 155, 163–4, 166, 169–70, 178–9, 196–9
Te Ati Awa, 95
Te Kopo, 175–6
Te Puni, 95, 99, 102, 114–15, 116, 166, 169, 171, 176, 177–9, 266

Te Rauparaha, 39, 95, 102, 135, 146, 168, 169, 180, 205–8, 211, 214, 215, 217, 218, 225, 227, 228, 240, 248, 249, 261
Te Ringa Kura, 233
Te Rongo, 207, 217
Thackeray, William Makepeace, 247–8, 255
The Spectator, 36, 37, 144, 239, 260, 266, 299
The Times, 19, 22, 37, 46, 61, 133, 243, 244, 247, 249, 250, 251, 254, 260, 262, 264, 266, 276, 365, 368
Thom, Joseph, 138
Thomas Sparks (ship), 176
Thomas, Captain Josias (Joseph), 80, 87, 88, 90, 93
Thompson, Henry, 205–6, 207, 211, 212, 218, 223, 235
Thorndon, Wellington, 100, 101–2, 103, 105–6, 107, 108, 109–10, 112–13, 115, 116, 120, 131, 136, 141, 149, 169, 209, 372, 380
Tiaki, *see* Hiakai
Ticehurst, Edwin, 105–6
Tilke, Ann, 65, 141
Tite, Sir William, 15
Tod, Robert, 115–16, 118, 166–8, 169–71, 173
Tollemache, A. G., 62
Torlesse, Charles, 239
Torrens, Colonel Robert, 29, 41, 42, 60, 65, 256
Tory (barque), 56–57, 59, 61, 62, 63, 65, 86, 94, 109, 117, 132, 164, 169–70, 176, 177, 179; purchase of, 54–55, 56, 59, 61, 203, 286–8
trade and industry (Wellington): coal, 141; flax, 66, 134–5, 202; flour milling, 76, 131; timber, 100, 112, 146, 202
Treaty of Waitangi, 37, 94, 110, 111, 117, 152, 155–6, 166, 211, 233–4, 243, 245, 250–1, 265
Tuarau, 99
Tuckett, Frederick, 205–6
Tuhata, 116
Turnbull, William, 105
Tute (chief), 166
Tyne (barque), 136

Union Bank of Australia, 73, 105, 108, 176, 232, 252, 263, 268, 322, 352, 354
University of Cambridge, 9, 37
University of Edinburgh, 12, 62, 301
University of Glasgow, 10–13, 21, 23, 235
University of London, 13, 28, 53
University of Melbourne, 330, 334
University of Oxford, 9, 10, 16, 36, 202

Van Diemen's Land, 26, 64, 87, 160
Vavasour, William, 202
Verdon, George, 347, 355
Victoria (brig), 148–9, 205, 208, 209, 213, 214, 360
Victoria, Australia, xx, 269, 283, 293, 296, 297, 298, 305, 312, 318, 321, 322, 323, 326, 331, 360, 363–5, 370, 380; and land issues in, xvi, 305, 334; as possible home for Evans, 269, 283; Legislative Assembly of, xiv, 249, 296–307, 310–19, 320, 324–5, 326, 327–34, 335, 336–9, 340–8, 349–65, 367, 369, 380, 296–307, 323
Virtue, D. W., 352
Voltaire, 9

Waddell, James, 54
Wade, John, 117, 138–9, 146, 147, 148, 149–50, 163, 171, 185, 186–7, 191–2
Waikanae, Maori at, 207, 217, 248
Wairarapa (chief), 166, 169–70, 177–9, 270
Wairarapa (region), 203, 229, 257, 269, 270, 331
Wairau incident, xv, 205–14, 216–18, 223, 228, 232, 234, 239, 240, 245, 266
Waitt, Robert, 159
Waiwhetu pa, xix, 100, 178, 179, 225
Wakefield Club, 159, 194
Wakefield, Captain Arthur, 31, 34, 36, 37–38, 40, 153–4, 205–6, 207, 211, 212, 223, 240, 248
Wakefield, Colonel William, xv, xvi, xvii, xix, 59, 64, 66, 75, 78, 94–95, 99, 100, 102–3, 107, 110, 121, 141, 144, 157, 161, 198, 246, 257, 259, 380; as leader of expedition to New

Zealand and Principal Agent, 61, 64, 65, 74–75, 78, 91, 105–6, 117, 120–1, 132; and George Samuel Evans, xx, 108, 120, 132–3, 152, 181, 190, 215–16, 223, 225–7, 233, 280, 284; and land claims, 128–9, 214–15, 223; and land purchases, 65–66, 94–95, 102–3, 110–11, 113, 114–16, 119–20, 126, 135, 137, 151–3, 162–3, 164–7, 169–70, 173, 176, 177–80, 197–201, 210, 215, 218, 231, 233; and Maori, 99–100, 102, 104–5, 109, 109–11, 128–9, 163, 166, 178, 180, 197, 198–9, 200–1, 214, 215, 223–5, 228, 246; and New Zealand Company, 130, 165–6, 181–2, 183, 194, 202, 204, 214–15, 223–4, 226–7, 229, 235, 236, 259, 284, 286; and Porirua, 135–6, 138, 145–6, 162–3; and Richard Davies Hanson, 151, 161, 165–6; and settlement and establishment of Wellington, 99–100, 101–4, 105–6, 107–8, 109, 113, 117, 118, 120–1, 123–4, 127, 128–9, 130, 131, 132–3, 135–6, 144–5, 146, 148, 162, 183, 184, 190, 196, 202–3, 209–10, 236, 284, 375, 377; and Wairau incident, 206, 208; popularity and reputation of, 133, 168, 180, 215, 220, 225–6, 227–8, 380; death of, 266; *see also* Evans, George Samuel, RELATIONSHIPS AND FRIENDSHIPS: Other Relationships, and Colonel William Wakefield; Hanson, Richard Davies, and Colonel William Wakefield; Revans, Samuel, and Colonel William Wakefield

Wakefield, Daniel, 280–1, 282–3

Wakefield, Edward Gibbon, xvii, xx, 29–30, 55, 66, 71, 76, 83, 90, 91, 92, 131, 143, 144, 153, 166, 196, 216, 257, 322, 368, 377, 378; and Canada, 46, 52, 56, 286–7, 368; and Church Missionary Society, 44; and colonisation of South Australia, 29, 70, 256, 258–9; and colonisation of New Zealand, xiii, xvi, xx, 29, 30, 31, 32, 33–34, 35, 36, 37, 38, 41, 42, 43, 51, 52, 53, 56, 60–62, 64–65, 67–68, 73, 78, 124, 261, 284, 287–8, 378; and George Samuel Evans, 30, 39, 41, 55–56, 59, 64, 239–40, 257, 258–9, 266, 280, 288–9, 377; and Liocadia D'Oliviera, 63, 77, 121, 240; and Maori, 322; and New Zealand Association, 36, 41, 42, 43–45, 46, 47, 64; and New Zealand Colonization Company, 59, 60–62, 64; and New Zealand Company, 64–65, 67, 68, 78, 216, 258, 266, 286, 368; and New Zealand Constitution Act, 267; and Ngaiti, 39, 46; and principles of colonisation, xx, 29, 31–32, 33–34, 43, 74, 151, 227–8, 230, 282, 284–6, 299, 302; and settlement of Canterbury, 266, 280; and settlement of Wellington, 280, 284, 285–6; and Sir George Grey, 282–3; health of, 240, 262, 266; reputation and views of, 29, 30, 33, 37, 41, 44, 46, 258–9, 284–7, 288–9; writings of, 34, 35–36, 71, 73, 258; *see also see also* Evans, George Samuel, RELATIONSHIPS AND FRIENDSHIPS: Other Relationships, and Edward Gibbon Wakefield; Grey, Sir George, and Edward Gibbon Wakefield; Revans, Samuel, and Edward Gibbon Wakefield; *Tory* (barque), purchase of

Wakefield, Edward Jerningham, xiv, xvi, xvii, xix, 59, 66, 99, 102, 107, 112, 119, 135, 159, 166, 172, 185, 196, 201, 214, 239, 241, 244, 247–8, 255

Wakefield, George, 313

Wakelin, Richard, 270–1, 273

Wallace, John (J. H.), xvi, 100–1, 105, 184, 192

Wallace, William, 192

Walmesley, Mary Ann Eleanor (Eleanor), 202; *see also*, Petre, Eleanor

Wanganui, *see* Whanganui

Ward, Crosbie, 358

Ward, Henry George, 36, 46, 51

Ward, John, 37, 40, 65, 72, 132, 133, 136, 216

Ward, Judge Dudley, 354, 368

Ware, Henry, 176

'waste land' policy, 29, 32, 109, 143, 210, 216, 230, 233, 235–6, 241, 243

Watt, James, 12

Weld, Frederick, 267
Wellesley, Arthur (Duke of Wellington), 8–9, 23, 26, 245
Wellesley, Captain Hon. W., 37–38
Wellington: and founding and establishment of, xiii, xv, xvii, xxi, 100–5, 107–10, 120, 122, 123–5, 126–7, 131, 135–6, 140–1, 142–5, 151–2, 157–9, 161, 182–3, 184–7, 196, 202, 209, 213, 219–20, 226, 230, 232, 233–4, 236, 261, 280, 368–9, 380–1; and settlers' grievances and hopes, 253–4, 281–2; as capital city, 123–4, 254, 323, 324, 365, 375, 376, 377–8, 381; defence of, 206, 208, 209, 211, 212, 214, 215, 248; population and makeup of, 269–70, 283–4, 375–6; prosperity of, 261; *see also* Evans, George Samuel, His Working Life: In New Zealand, and settlement and establishment of Wellington; Hanson, Richard Davies, and settlement and establishment of Wellington; New Zealand Company, and settlement of Wellington; Petone, as alternative for Wellington; Port Nicholson; trade and industry (Wellington); Wakefield, Colonel William, and settlement and establishment of Wellington; Wakefield, Edward Gibbon, and settlement of Wellington
Wellington Almanac, 203
Wellington Chamber of Commerce, 320–1,
Wellington Club, 159, 380
Wellington Independent, xiii, xxi, 269, 270–1, 273, 277, 279, 282, 286, 321, 326, 376–7
Wellington Spectator, 180
Wellington–Victoria, communication between, 320–4, 325, 326–7
Wesleyan missionaries and Church, 247
West Indies, 32, 40
Western Australia, 33, 47
Whanganui, 135, 163, 169, 197, 201, 367; Maori from, 169, 215
Wharepouri, 95, 99, 100, 116, 148, 166, 169, 170, 171, 177, 178, 179
Wi Tako, 166, 169–70, 174, 176, 178–9, 197
Wicksteed, John 138, 148, 149, 150, 152, 153, 162, 163
Wilberforce, William, 16, 23
Wilde, Sir Thomas, 251
Williams, Archdeacon Herbert W., 40
Williams, Henry, 110–11, 115, 178, 247
Williams, William, 247
Wills, William, 353, 370
Wilson, Dr, 333, 351, 354
Wilson, Edward, 294, 315
Wonga Wonga (steamer), 324
Wood, John Dennistoun, 301, 303, 304, 316, 341, 344, 351, 353, 363, 370
Woolley, Alfred, 333
Wright, John, 37, 42, 54, 60, 61, 76, 92, 112–13, 122, 161, 257
Wright, Mr, 82
Wycherley, Captain, 120
Wyeth, Robert, 180
Wylde, John, 90
Wymondley College, Herefordshire, 9–10, 27

Yate, William, 34
Yates, Francis Thomas, xiv, 79, 81–82, 83, 85, 88, 93, 196
Young, George F., 77–78, 141, 254, 255, 257, 258, 261
Young, William Curling, 141–2, 194

Question. E aha te mea ki tou ding
hand? Answer. E matau kau and
wai oki i o mai nga matau kia ka
to thee? Answer. Na Taka ra oki
ra nei ia? Is he a good man — tha
Yes, indeed, a good man, a generous m
Where is his residence? Answer Ko Ka
Kua tai oti koe ki reira? Hast tho
oki kau. I have visited there. Qu
I te e'autoke ra oki; Katahi an
just now I have returned. Question
a wife? Answer E wahine ra oki
tamariki? How many children ha
tion E aire ana koe? Art thou go
Apopo, ka i oki mai kia wahi
tomorrow I do return that we